Of Many Times and Cultures

Fascinating Facts and Stories from World History

Marvin Scott

J. Weston Walch, Publisher
Portland, Maine

Gandhi cover photo courtesy of THE BETTMANN ARCHIVE

1 2 3 4 5 6 7 8 9 10

ISBN 0-8251-2071-3

J. Weston Walch, Publisher
P.O. Box 658 • Portland, Maine 04104-0658

Printed in the United States of America

— Contents —

— Introduction —

World history teachers and a woman named Scheherazade share a problem: the need to keep a tough audience interested. Scheherazade was in a bit more desperate situation than most of us. If she failed, she would be killed. She was about to be married to a sultan, which doesn't seem too bad, but this sultan always killed his bride the next morning! Scheherazade needed a way to motivate the sultan to let her live another day. She used an ancient device, telling him stories, carefully saving the end of each story for the next night. The sultan was fascinated and let her live for 1,001 nights. Her stories were written as *The Arabian Nights.*

We are not quite as desperate as Scheherazade. All we have to do is keep our world history classes alert, paying attention, and learning. On second thought, which looks easier? We can, of course, use stories to do this. In this collection, I have tried to include stories that not only interest or amuse but also make a point. There are not quite 1,001 stories here. The total on my tally sheet reads 567, enough for 3 a day for a 180-day school year.

The stories range around the globe and through many cultures. Several are about the status of women in China at various stages of history. One is on bicycles in the Vietnam War, and another is about guinea pigs in Peru. Others focus on Muhammad, Confucius, and Luther. They range in time from prehistory to the 1990's. Generally, the stories are designed to connect students somehow with an event, a person, or an idea important in world history. A familiar image like Clydesdale horses is linked with an unfamiliar subject like the Middle Ages. There are a few jokes. Generally, if material is common in textbooks, it gets a new twist, like my version of Moses and Buddha. Some of the stories go against the traditional version. Did you know Ethiopia had an air force in 1935? I selected stories I thought were interesting and memorable.

Since some topics are associated with more stories than others, that is reflected in the distribution. One chapter has 13 stories, and others run over 25. Most have about 20 stories and anecdotes. Each chapter has an overview with a few ideas for papers and bulletin boards. The paper topics can become discussion topics if you prefer.

Many of you will take these stories and use them as class openers, or as punch lines at the end of a presentation. They are written in colloquial language so you can simply read them aloud. Or you may just tell them in your own style. You will, of course, want to select some and reject others.

You may want to collect a few stories that are uniquely yours. When you can connect your school with a historic event, that is a powerful way of getting student interest. For example, when I tell my story about the NATO listening post in West Berlin, I can also point out that the soldier who told me about it was an ex-student of mine in Army Intelligence. If you can find a local connection, use it.

The same goes for a connection with current news. This collection features a lot of stories on Iran, largely because Iran was hot news as I wrote this. Later the Iraq-Kuwait border dispute became a major crisis, and I added material on that and other recent events. The current news has a way of giving you new material. You can often borrow a topical joke from comedians who do humor on current events.

Using this approach to teaching can be fun and interesting and get the job done.

Chapter I
Prehistory

— Overview —

This chapter contains stories illustrating two important ideas: our knowledge of prehistoric time is constantly being revised, and careful collection and analysis of evidence is central to supporting what we think we know. Subject matter includes how archaeologists work, some important discoveries, and the Stone Ages.

You may want to ask your students to update these stories by locating an article on recent discoveries using the *Readers' Guide to Periodical Literature* and writing a one-page summary. The really big discoveries are written up in newspapers and the weeklies like *Time, Newsweek,* and *U.S. News & World Report.* Some magazines routinely contain archaeology stories—*Scientific American, National Geographic,* and *Archaeology,* for example. Any student who can summarize a *Scientific American* article is very capable indeed, but if that journal is too advanced for your students, it is still an excellent teacher source.

You may be able to arrange for your class to see some Stone Age artifacts, perhaps Indian arrowheads, in a museum near you. You could bring in some flint and let your students chip a little, but flying fragments and smashed thumbs make this a little risky. Perhaps you could more easily take your students to the site of a demolished building. After inspecting the evidence, they could write up their conclusions about the site, stressing evidence and logic.

If you like imaginative papers, you could have students write about "How I Found the Missing Peking Bones," "A Day in the Life of an Archaeologist, " or even "A Day in the Life of Lucy" (or other example). One of the most interesting papers runs like this: "Assume all human life ended in this area with all the artifacts left just as they were when you left school today. What would an archaeologist uncovering it a thousand years later think about the people who lived here?" Students could even hold a conference to argue over which interpretation is more reasonable.

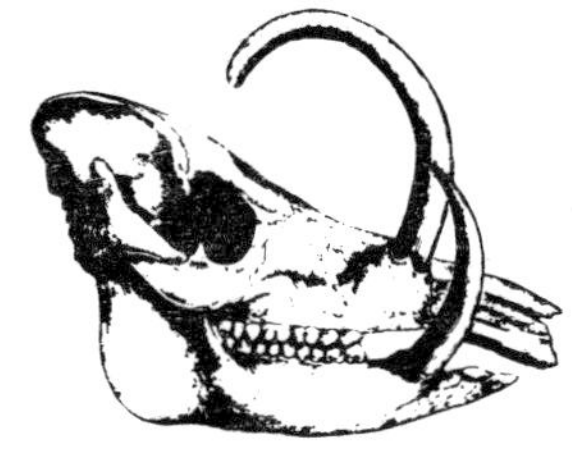

A. ARCHAEOLOGISTS

1. Archaeologists. You can always tell archaeologists are at work by their characteristic mark, neat square holes dug in the ground. They dig that way to keep records of every bone and pebble they find. It may seem picky to you, but this method lets them do some amazing things, like find—in solid dirt—where postholes used to be. Once you know the trick, it's easy. Postholes leave spots of dirt that are a different color. If you are alert, you can recognize these differences. The archaeologists even have a standard book that gives a number to each color of soil so they can record exactly what they have found. Finding postholes has helped archaeologists discover primitive villages built on stilts, ancient Greek boat houses, and 19th-century farm fence rows.

2. Dating. Establishing the date of a find is very important. Archaeologists use a variety of ways of doing this, including stratigraphy, tree rings, and radiocarbon. Stratigraphy is simple. The newer material is assumed to be on top: deeper means older. This works fine as long as no one has dug a basement through the layers. If they can find a piece of a tree on the site, archaeologists can look at the growth rings. Each year has a unique pattern, and archaeologists have them traced back about 6,000 years. Radiocarbon dating is based on the fact that radiocarbon—or carbon 14—is continually formed in nature. Once an organism dies, the amount of radiocarbon in its tissues decreases at a constant rate. As a general rule, the older an organic item is, the less radiocarbon will be present when the item is tested. There are some times, however, when newer material has less radiocarbon due to some fluctuation in radioactivity at the time. This was discovered in the 1970's. Before this, some buildings in northern Europe were assumed to be copies of similar buildings in the Mediterranean area. The new dates showed that the northern buildings were earlier. A whole set of assumptions about the cultures of the two areas was proven wrong by radiocarbon dating, a very powerful tool of archaeologists.

3. Dates. Archaeologists work with dates that have a substantial margin of error. It's important not to fall into the following fallacy.

The tour guide was leading a little group to a prehistoric site. "Here, 10,007 years ago these ancient peoples built their camp."

A woman in the back of the group was struck by the exactness of the date. "How do you know it was 10,007?" she asked.

"Well," replied the guide, "the archaeologist dug this site and dated it at 10,000 years old, and that was 7 years ago."

4. Experimental Archaeology. Archaeologists are not content just to dig up artifacts; they also try them out. One summer several years ago when an elephant died in a zoo, archaeologists asked for the body. Why did they want a dead elephant? They wanted to butcher the animal using stone tools. Then they could see the kinds of marks stone tools leave on bones. From this experiment the archaeologists hoped to learn how to recognize marks on ancient bones indicating that the animal had been butchered by prehistoric people.

If they needed stone tools, that would be no problem. Some archaeologists have become skilled at making stone tools using what they think are prehistoric methods.

B. Evolution of Humans

1. Lucy. The trend since 1945 has been for archaeologists to push farther back the record of human and humanlike creatures. One of the most dramatic discoveries came in Ethiopia in 1974 when archaeologists discovered Lucy. She was a female (the hipbones tell that), three feet tall, weighing about sixty pounds. Her fossilized bones were lying partly exposed in the side of a gully. At this writing she is the oldest, most complete skeleton of any erect walking human ancestor ever found, roughly three million years old. Why was she called Lucy? Technically she was AL288-1 of the Hadar collection, but the night after she was found, the archaeologists were playing a Beatles song, "Lucy in the Sky with Diamonds." They named her after the song.

2. Walking Erect. The fact that people walk erect and most apes walk on all fours has led to a lot of discussion and research. The critical questions have been: Which creatures walked erect, and how did walking erect relate to brain development and tool use? This has led to much analysis of fossil leg bones. Mary Leakey found the most dramatic evidence on this question in Laetoli, Tanzania. She actually found the footprints of three hominids walking upright. The tracks were in volcanic ash and seemed to be about 3.75 million years old.

3. Peking Bones Missing. Local people called the place Dragon Bone Hill because of the old bones on it. In 1929, archaeologists started digging on this site near Beijing (Peking) and found the remains of "Peking Man," a prehistoric human being who lived 250,000 to 500,000 years ago. The archaeologists were funded and directed by Americans, with Chinese labor and Chinese scientists working under them. By the time World War II began, the dig had yielded large boxes of bones and artifacts. Somehow during World War II all the material disappeared. It had been in the hands of Americans and may have been captured by the Japanese. But it has not yet surfaced, so the mystery remains unsolved. The Chinese resumed digging after 1949, and in 1972 they opened a display center for both Chinese and foreign visitors.

4. Neanderthals. Neanderthals are an example of how the image of early humans has changed. Early descriptions and reconstructed pictures showed Neanderthals as stooped, slow-moving, and ugly. Then analysis showed that the first specimens had arthritis. Newer pictures of Neanderthals show a quick, alert being. Analyses of Neanderthal gravesites have revealed pollen grains, a sign that these people buried their dead with flowers. This suggests that Neanderthals may have believed in an afterlife.

5. Accidental Discoveries: Cro-Magnon Paintings. Archaeology depends a bit on luck. In 1879, Don Marelino, a Spanish nobleman, was digging in a cave near Altamira, Spain. His 12-year-old daughter Maria wandered back into the cave and discovered a series of paintings on the wall. These paintings were done by Cro-Magnon artists.

In 1940, near Lascaux, France, a dog fell into a cave. It seems that a big tree was blown down by a storm and created a hole in the roof of the cave. Guided by the dog's barking, the boys who owned the dog found the hole and enlarged it to save their pet. Once in the cave, they noticed that the walls were covered with prehistoric paintings. This cave became so famous it was once the fourth biggest tourist attraction in France. Unfortunately, all those visitors breathing in the cave changed the temperature and humidity, damaging the paintings. So the cave had to be closed to tourists.

6. The Piltdown Fraud. The techniques used by early archaeologists were rather crude, creating a situation open to fraud. The most famous example was the so-called "Piltdown Man." In 1912, near Piltdown, England, a digger discovered a human-looking skull with an apelike jaw.

The scientific world accepted this as a legitimate specimen until 1953, when chemical tests and a careful examination revealed it as a fraud. The skull was human and the jaw was from an ape. Researchers are still not sure exactly who set up the fraud.

7. Behavior Studies. Not all studies of prehistoric people involve digging. Anthropologists also study the few surviving examples of Stone Age peoples to gain clues about early humans. Others have wondered if human behavior has its roots in animal behavior. Jane Goodall spent fifteen years living with chimpanzees at the

Gombe Stream Research Center in Tanzania. She observed some behavior that was so human it's embarrassing. Old friends hugged and kissed each other. The chimps also made tools. They would break off a piece of grass and stick it into an anthill, pull it out covered with ants, and then eat the ants. Goodall even observed male chimps fighting in groups, behavior similar to war among humans. This line of research may seem to be a bit extreme, but the chimps are not the limits. Other researchers are examining ants in the hope that their social behavior may hold clues to explain human actions.

C. The Stone Ages

1. Stone Tools Are Sharp. Stone tools can have a very sharp cutting edge. The Indians of Mexico used obsidian, a black volcanic glass, in knife blades. In modern Mexico, surgeons use obsidian blades in open-heart surgery. These blades are up to 500 times sharper than blades made of steel. Some researchers in the United States are experimenting with obsidian blades for surgery, claiming that they cause less bleeding and leave less scar tissue. They would be used in brain surgery, eye surgery, and plastic surgery if approved by the federal government. Not all stone tools are as sharp as obsidian tools, but even a flint knife can be quite sharp.

2. The New Stone Age. The Old Stone Age was clearly the longest stretch of time in human existence. The transition to the New Stone Age was gradual and took place a few settlements at a time. It did *not* happen as follows. Ogg and friend Ray were just getting up and looked out the opening of their cave to see the sun rising. Ogg turned to Ray and said, "Do you realize what day this is? This is the day! We are seeing the dawn of the New Stone Age."

Chapter II

The Ancient Near East

— Overview —

This chapter contains stories about Egypt, Mesopotamia, the Phoenicians, and the Hebrews. The study of Hebrew history is a sensitive area, since it touches on religion. Public schools cannot advocate a certain religion, but to be true to history we need to study religions. So you will notice that the stories in this chapter about the Hebrews are from a variety of viewpoints. Each of us is free to believe or disbelieve as our faith or lack of it guides us.

The material covered in this chapter is constantly being updated by archaeologists. You may want to ask your students to locate an article on recent discoveries and write a one-page summary. For helpful sources, see the Chapter I Overview. You could also have your students write a short paper on this topic: "Of the civilizations of the Middle East, which would you like to have lived in? Why?" You could grade papers on logic and use of facts. You could also have your students build models of ziggurats, pyramids, and Phoenician boats, grading them on the basis of accuracy and research.

You or your students could make a time line of the ancient Near East for your bulletin board. A time line uses space to represent time and lets people see which event happened earlier and relatively how much earlier. At the top of the bulletin board you put, "Time Line: Ancient Near East." Below that in slightly smaller letters, put four headings: "Egypt," "Mesopotamia," "Phoenicians," and "Hebrews." Under each heading, mark off a vertical column running to the bottom of the bulletin board. You can use strips of construction paper or colored yarn to make lines, perhaps with each column a different color. Then you establish the time scale by putting in some dates. You can put "3500 B.C." at the bottom; six inches up, put "3000 B.C."; "2000 B.C." would be a foot farther up. The scale in this example is one foot equals a thousand years. You may need a different scale to fit your bulletin boards. You can write the dates on paper with a felt-tipped pen. Be sure it is readable from some distance.

Next, you can locate events or people on the time line. Put the names and other information on pieces of colored paper with felt-tipped pen. "Hammurabi" would be placed in the "Mesopotamia" column about two inches above "2000 B.C." because Hammurabi lived in that area about 1792–1750 B.C. "Menes" would be placed in the "Egypt" column about an inch below 3000 B.C. because Menes lived about 3100 B.C.

You can even show major periods in history. "The New Kingdom" in Egypt can be represented by a strip of construction paper with "New Kingdom" on it running up the "Egypt" column from roughly 1580 B.C. to 1090 B.C. If you can get them, pictures add interest. You could then put another time line for Ancient Asia next to the Ancient Near East time line and compare. Time lines can be a lot of work, but they help people understand when events happened.

Perhaps your students could use an encyclopedia and make a bulletin board comparing ancient writing systems. For imaginative writing, students could do a paper on a court case decided by the Code of Hammurabi, the log of a Phoenician ship captain, or a day in the life of an Egyptian peasant under Akhenaton.

A. EGYPT

1. Pyramids. The pyramids are so huge and so old that they seem impossible. How could an ancient people build so precisely? The answer is that they used the same skills they used to develop an agricultural society on a flood plain. Each year after the Nile flooded, the Egyptians had to resurvey all the fields. They knew how to make right angles and measure distances. After that massive task, laying out the square base of a pyramid was simple. They did have to assemble and direct thousands of workers on the pyramids, but they also had to organize the whole country to irrigate and farm the land.

At first the stonework seems like a problem, but modern archaeologists have found that the stones in the quarry used for the pyramids break in straight lines and square corners. The quarry was across the river from the pyramids. The stone was simply floated on rafts that were made bouyant by inflated sheep's bladders. After the stones were floated to the site, it was a simple matter of a lot of people pulling on ropes as the blocks rolled on logs. They built ramps to raise the stones to the top. The ancient Egyptians were an amazing people. They managed to develop and thrive despite a difficult environment. After that, building the pyramids was comparatively easy.

2. Afterlife. Egyptians believed not only that people lived twice, but also that they could die twice. A person who died simply "went west" and, if properly supplied, lived a new life after death. This is the reason for mummies and the burial of servants with the dead. At first, Egyptians buried the bodies of servants with the pharaoh. Later, they used figurines and paintings in place of actual bodies. They also provided the mummy with food and other necessities for the new life. To kill a person in the next life, you took away these necessities. You also chiseled out the eyes of the pictures of the dead and destroyed the ability to get food so the person starved to death. This was done very rarely, and there is no clue as to who did it or why.

3. Tomb Paintings. The walls of Egyptian tombs are covered with paintings. Some of them are shaped by religious traditions. The pharaoh is always shown standing in a twisted position, feet sideways, shoulders facing front, and head in profile. Other paintings show daily activities and look more natural. From these we can learn much about Egyptian life. What did dancing girls wear at the royal court? They wore a necklace, earrings, and a narrow strip of cloth around their waists. What musical instruments did they have? They had a harp, a flute, and a lute. How did the pharaoh hunt ducks? He used a throwing stick a little like a boomerang.

4. Mummies. The Greek historian Herodotus traveled to Egypt and learned how mummies were made. Part of the process was to remove all the soft tissue. Otherwise, it would rot. No problem, really; the embalmers just cut open the body, removed the entrails, and filled the body cavity with spices. But that still left the brain. Again, no real problem; the embalmers just took an iron hook and put it up the nose, pulling out the brain in pieces. Then they covered the body with a preservative for 70 days, washed it, wrapped it in linen strips, and put it in a wooden case.

5. Champollion and the Rosetta Stone. The Rosetta Stone, which was eventually used to translate hieroglyphics, was discovered in 1799 by a work gang digging to build a fort for the French who had invaded the Nile Delta area in Egypt. It is a slab of black rock measuring 3 feet 9 inches high by 2 feet 4 inches wide and 11 inches thick. The stone itself came into the possession of the British in 1801. They had defeated the French in war, and the treaty specified that the British got the stone.

Around the same time, a young Frenchman, Jean François Champollion, began to devote his life to the study of hieroglyphics. At the age of 5, he taught himself to read. At 17, he was accepted as member of the faculty of Grenoble High School after he had read a paper on "Egypt Under the Pharaohs." He later studied ancient languages, including Sanskrit, Arabic, Persian, Hebrew, and Coptic.

In 1822, at the age of 36, Champollion succeeded in translating the Rosetta Stone. The stone carries one message in three systems of writing: Greek, demotic, and hieroglyphics. Tradition says that as Champollion completed his work, he declared, "I've got it!"

6. Boats. Ancient Egypt was very dry, and so had no trees. As a result, the Egyptians made their boats out of bundles of papyrus reeds. These boats moved up and down the Nile in a very active trade. Thor Heyerdahl, a modern adventurer, decided to see if a boat of papyrus could cross the Atlantic Ocean. He proceeded to build a reconstruction of a papyrus boat and sailed out. He had omitted a rope that ran from the high peak at the bow to the stern. In the middle of the Atlantic this ship fell apart. Heyerdahl tried again. This time he included the rope, just as the ancient Egyptians had. With his second, more authentic boat he succeeded in crossing the Atlantic. He concluded that the rope made the difference. This experiment does not show that Egyptians crossed the Atlantic, but it does show that their boats could have done so if built exactly as Heyerdahl's was.

7. Hatshepsut, Woman Pharaoh. Women played a vital role in ruling Egypt. Inheritance of the title was traced through the female line. Hatshepsut used this to gain power. She was the daughter of Thutmose I and married Thutmose II, her half brother. Her husband died, and at first she was regent for a boy who was the child of another wife of the pharaoh, but later she became pharaoh herself, complete with male dress and a false beard. The beard was a symbol of royal power.

During her reign Hatshepsut opened trade routes, built temples, and erected obelisks with inscriptions describing her achievements. She sent an expedition to the land of Punt. An inscription says the expedition brought back myrrh trees. Archaeologists have found the stumps of myrrh trees near Hatshepsut's temple. They would need to be watered to survive. Later, the boy that Hatshepsut was regent over, Thutmose III, asserted his authority. He became a great conquering pharaoh. One of his first actions was to destroy Hatshepsut's name on her temple and cover up the inscriptions on her obelisks. He was trying to destroy her memory. His efforts backfired. By covering up the inscriptions, he protected them from sun and sand. They survive in excellent condition.

8. Akhenaton: Religious Reform. There is a serious question about how much Akhenaton changed the religion of Egypt. It is clear that he made the cult of Aton the official religion. He seems to have intended that there be only one god, Aton, in Egypt. He changed his name from Amenhotep to Akhenaton in honor of the god and even started a new city to honor Aton. How much did all this affect the common people? Archaeologists give us one clue. In the houses of commoners in the pharaoh's new city, they have found idols of minor gods.

9. Amarna Letters Discovery. One of the major sources of information about Egypt and its empire is a collection of letters from allies and officials written to Akhenaton. These letters were buried in the rubble of the pharaoh's capital city, near present-day Tell el Amarna. They were uncovered in 1885 by a peasant woman digging out clay bricks to use as fertilizer. She found hundreds of baked clay tablets with cuneiform on them, put them in a sack, and loaded her donkey. She tried to sell them, but dealers thought they were fakes. Eventually they were recognized as genuine, but by that time many of the tablets had been broken and destroyed by the rough ride on the donkey.

10. The Ramses II Statue. Ramses II was a powerful New Kingdom pharaoh. He built huge monuments to himself, including a 67-foot-tall statue of himself carved out of solid rock. When the modern Egyptian government built the Aswan High Dam, the resulting lake would have covered the statue. But a major rescue effort saved it by cutting it apart and moving it to safe high ground.

B. Mesopotamia

1. Learning to Read Cuneiform. It's one thing to dig up and collect clay tablets with cuneiform writing on them and quite another to read them. The key to reading cuneiform came from Behistun in Iran. There on a cliff, Darius the Great, King of Persia, had a proclamation carved into the stone. The same message was written in three languages: Old Persian, Akkadian, and Elamite. Nineteenth-century scholars translated the Old Persian text first, then used it to translate the two older languages.

2. The Hanging Gardens of Babylon. When Babylon was the capital of the Chaldeans, King Nebuchadnezzar built the "hanging gardens." Tradition says his favorite wife came from the hills and was unhappy in the flat land of Mesopotamia. So Nebuchadnezzar built a tower with plants growing over it, the "hanging gardens." These were considered one of the seven wonders of the ancient world.

3. Code of Hammurabi: A Joke. I once asked one of my students, "What do you know about Hammurabi's code?" He replied, "It was used to send secret messages."

4. Persian Pony Express. The Persians built an empire stretching across the ancient Near East from Egypt through Persia. It was so large that just keeping in touch with it all became a big problem. In this age before electronic communication, messages moved slowly. The Persians developed one of the fastest ways of sending messages until the telegraph. They set up a system of men riding horses in relays. Each rider rode for a day and a night. This system sped messages 1,500 miles in 7 days. Herodotus, in describing the system, said, "Neither snow nor rain nor gloom of night stays these couriers from their appointed rounds." If this ancient statement seems familiar to you, that is because it is now the slogan of the United States Postal Service.

C. PHOENICIANS

1. Phoenician Sailors. The Phoenicians were the sailors of the ancient world. Ancient boats were wooden, and the Phoenicians lived in the area that is now Lebanon, one of the few places in the ancient Near East where trees grew. Modern Lebanon has a tree on its flag to commemorate this fact. Ancient ships were rowed or sailed and typically stayed close to land. The Phoenicians traveled all over the Mediterranean. One document says they went out of the Mediterranean and turned north, sailed to an island, and traded for tin. The only island north of the Mediterranean that has tin is Britain. The Greek historian Herodotus reports that the Lydians sailed around Africa. Ancient sailors could do this by simply traveling along the coast. All this was done about 2,000 years before Europeans explored the coast of Africa.

2. Purple Dye. The Phoenicians' purple dye was made from the secretions of a snail found in warm seawater. Technically the snails were *murex brandaris* and *murex trunculus.* To dye a cloth, you rubbed it against the underside of the snail. This produced a yellow spot that turned red if it was then wet with lemon juice. But each snail produced only a small spot of dye. It would take up to 10,000 snails to produce a fraction of an ounce of the dye material. The process of dyeing the cloth was a very smelly one. A Roman writer reported that the city of Tyre smelled. To the Phoenicians, traders that they were, it was the smell of money.

3. Phoenician Glass. The Egyptians made the first glass, but the Phoenicians improved it. The Egyptians learned to heat a mixture of sand, plant ash, saltpeter, and chalk to produce glass. They made beads and bottles, even learning to blow the glass into various shapes. But Egyptian glass was a milky white, and not transparent. It was the Phoenicians who, after learning the secret of the Egyptians, developed glass that was clear and transparent. They then mass-produced glass bottles and beads and marketed glass at such low prices that it replaced clay for use in drinking vessels.

4. The Assyrians and Lion Hunting. The Assyrians were a cruel warrior people whose kings were expected to be brave leaders and to protect them. Lion hunting was part of this tradition. The Assyrians at one time had a law that only the king could kill lions. One king, Ashurbanipal, liked to kill lions but did not enjoy hunting them. Soldiers went out and captured lions and brought them to the king. The lions were released from cages and the king killed them with his bow and arrows.

D. HEBREWS

1. Moses Raised by Egyptians. The Old Testament story of Moses' birth and youth tells this story. Hebrews were working as slaves of the Egyptian pharaoh, but the Hebrew population was growing. The pharaoh ordered every son born of a Hebrew to be killed. Moses' mother bore a baby boy in secret and hid him for three months; then she put him in a basket in the reeds near a river. The daughter of the pharaoh found the baby and named him Moses. She got a nurse for him from the Hebrews, who, as it turned out, was his real mother. After Moses had grown up, he saw an Egyptian beating a Hebrew. Moses killed the Egyptian and had to flee.

Moses' name tends to confirm the story. "Moses" is an Egyptian name meaning "son of." Notice that it is incomplete—"son of" whom? A typical Egyptian would put the name of a god next, but a Hebrew would show respect for the Hebrew god by not mentioning the holy name. The name Moses itself, then, seems to indicate a person named by Egyptians who worshipped the Hebrew god.

2. Moses: Rod into a Snake. The Book of Exodus says that when Moses was trying to free his people, the Lord told Moses to take his brother Aaron and go to Pharaoh, and when Pharaoh said, "Prove yourselves by working a miracle," Moses was to say to Aaron, "Take your rod and cast it down before Pharaoh that it may become a serpent." Moses and Aaron went to Pharaoh, and the staff did indeed turn into a serpent. When Pharaoh called in his wise men, sorcerers and magicians, they did the same thing. Each man threw down his staff, and they all turned into serpents. But Aaron's snake swallowed all the others. This display of magic did not, however, convince Pharaoh to release the Hebrews.

Modern science has a possible explanation of this event. It seems that certain snakes, when held with their heads up and bodies suspended, pass out. Their blood pressure is not high enough to get blood to their brains. It could be that Aaron and the Egyptian magicians knew this. Each man walked in before Pharaoh holding a snake by the head so it looked like a staff. Then, when thrown onto the ground, the snake revived and crawled around. Apparently Aaron's snake was larger than the Egyptians' snakes and ate them.

3. Passover in Egypt. According to the Old Testament, the Lord told Moses to ask Pharaoh to let the Hebrews go free. Pharaoh refused, so after nine other curses visited the Egyptians, the Lord invoked the tenth curse: He would kill the first-born child in each Egyptian family. The Hebrews were to mark their doors with blood so the Lord would pass over their doors and not kill their first-born children. The Hebrews were also to eat unleavened bread, roast lamb, and bitter herbs on that night. After this catastrophe struck the Egyptians, Pharaoh allowed the Hebrews to leave Egypt. This was the beginning of the observance of Passover, which continues to this day.

4. David and His Sling. David was the second king of the Hebrews, but he did not inherit the title. He started out as a simple shepherd boy. He was selected to play music for King Saul, who seemed to suffer from some kind of depression. Later David became a war hero and then king. Much of his fame rests on the fact that he killed a big Philistine in battle. The story says that he used a sling and killed Goliath. The awkward point is that another person, Elhanan (the son of Jaareoregim, the Bethlehemite), is also credited with killing Goliath in 2 Samuel 21:19. Some biblical scholars think that Elhanan killed Goliath and later Goliath's name was added into David's story.

David's weapon was a sling. This was not the modern slingshot with rubber bands. It was a weapon made of two thongs and a pocket. The user whirled the sling around and let go of one of the thongs. The stone then flew at high velocity. An expert could indeed kill a man with it. The weapon is still in use. In the 1988 Palestinian demonstrations, television news pictures showed Palestinians using slings to throw stones at Israeli soldiers.

5. The Wisdom of Solomon. Solomon, king of the Hebrews, had a great reputation for wisdom. His most famous case involved two women and a baby. Each of the two women claimed that the child was hers. Solomon ruled that the baby should be cut in half and divided between the women. One woman accepted the decision; the other rejected it and said that rather than see the baby harmed she would let the other woman have it. Solomon therefore awarded the baby to its real mother, the woman who had not wanted the baby harmed.

6. Solomon's Wives. Solomon is reported to have had a thousand wives. This is as much a reflection of his diplomatic life as his love life. In the Middle East, alliances were sealed by sending a daughter or sister to marry your ally. Solomon was king of the Hebrews at a time when there were several great powers, and even his relatively small country was a valued ally.

CHAPTER III

Early Asia

— Overview —

This chapter contains stories about India, China, and Japan. The main emphasis is on the beginnings of major Asian religions and philosophical systems: Hinduism, Buddhism, Taoism, and Confucianism. All of these start from a drastically different viewpoint from those of Western culture. They deserve careful study and respect. But this chapter also includes some items on milk, tea, writing, women, geography, and rulers. There is even a tale about one very early voyage.

You could have students write a paper to compare and contrast any two of the Eastern religions and philosophies. You could also have students contrast the life of Buddha with the life of Confucius or Moses. You could have your students prepare a time line of Asian civilization for your bulletin board. It would be an interesting comparison if they used the same time scale and put their Asian time line next to your time line of the Middle East. Your students could also prepare a bulletin board of "Asian Religions and Philosophical Systems." Each could be represented by a characteristic symbol.

Creative writing papers could be a story, "My trip through ________" (China, India, Japan).

A. INDIA

1. The Law of Karma. The Law of Karma says that the next birth of a person is determined by his or her actions in this life. The result often fits the cause. For stealing grain, a person is reborn as a rat. For stealing a horse, the person becomes a tiger. If the person steals fruits and roots, the next birth will be as a monkey. Stealing cattle leads to rebirth as a he-goat. Those who eat forbidden fruit become worms.

2. Hindu Gods. The Hindus believe in a tremendous variety of gods. At one point in the *Bhagavad-Gita,* Krishna says there are "three hundred thousand shapes that clothe my Mystery."

3. Hindu Meditations. Hindu religious exercises often involve meditations. These are designed to clear the mind and give the person a glimpse of nirvana. One such exercise has become known in the United States as transcendental meditation. In this exercise, the meditator simply sits in the lotus position, legs crossed, and repeats a mantra over and over for several moments. It is like the relaxation exercises sometimes used to relieve stress. In those exercises, the subject sits in a relaxed position and repeats the word *one* with each breath. Some meditators have been willing to let scientists examine them as they meditate. The scientists found that the meditators experienced lowered blood pressure and slowed heart rate.

Another Hindu meditation involves a rock. The meditator sits and moves the rock in a circle from hand to hand above his or her head. They try to concentrate on the rock and move into it. Westerners who have tried this report it is very difficult to keep concentrating on the rock. Hindus recognize this and have a saying, "The mind is a crazy monkey."

4. Sanskrit. The Indo-Aryans of India wrote a language called Sanskrit. It may seem like a very remote and exotic language, but its roots go back to the same ancient language that is the base for English. This is shown by looking at a few sample words. The Sanskrit word for father is *pitar.* This comes from the same root as the Latin *pater* or German *Vater* and the English *father.* The Sanskrit *matar* is much like the Latin *mater,* the German *Mutter,* and English *mother.* One feature of Sanskrit writing is very familiar. In Sanskrit, numbers—such as one, two, three—are written as numerals—1, 2, 3. The Europeans learned this way of writing numbers from the Arabs and inaccurately called them Arabic numerals.

5. *Yajur-Veda*—Prayer. The *Yajur-Veda,* an ancient Hindu book, contains prayers and formulas for a variety of purposes. One of the more interesting is a cure for baldness. The patient is to dig out a certain sacred root. During the process he is to chant or have chanted some incantations about "strengthen old hair, beget the new." A medicine man dressed in black, who has eaten black food, early before the crows rise anoints the patient's head with a black concoction made of the sacred root. This is an example of the variety of Hindu beliefs. It is quite a contrast with the ideas of the Hindu mystics.

6. Buddha's Life. This is the traditional story of Buddha. He was born to a powerful family in India in 560 B.C. His father believed that the son would either become a holy man or a great ruler. The father decided to conceal from his son the fact that people get old, get sick, and die. For many years the young prince grew up ignorant of these things. Then when he was out riding in his chariot he saw an old man. He asked his servants about this and was told that all grow old. Another day he saw a man who was sick. Again he asked about it and was told that all people become diseased. Later he saw a dead body and realized that all die. These sights caused the prince to be very sad. Then he saw a monk who seemed happy, and he decided to become a monk.

He gave up his home, son, and wife and went out to become a monk. He studied and fasted, starving down to nearly a skeleton. Then he decided to give up all the ways he had been trying to attain wisdom and just sit under a tree. Tradition says it was here that he became Buddha, the "Enlightened One." Here he experienced nirvana, the highest level a soul attains. He then went to a group of monks and taught them what he had learned. This started Buddhism—or, more accurately, started it this time. Buddhists believe that this Buddha was preceded long ago by others in earlier ages, and after this one is forgotten, there will be other reincarnations of Buddha.

7. Buddha the Teacher. One of Buddha's Four Noble Truths was that suffering exists. The following is a traditional story about how Buddha taught this idea in one case. Once there was a woman who had lost her child. The boy was playing nearby when a snake bit him and he died. The woman was so grief-stricken that she refused to bury the child. She wandered around visiting holy men. Finally she went to Buddha and asked him to restore the child to life. Buddha agreed, but specified, "You must bring me the seed of a black mustard, and you must get it by begging." He also specified that it must come from a household that had known no death in the family. So the woman set out to find a household that had never had a death in the family. Of course she found that every household had experienced death. Once she realized this, she became enlightened, and she buried her child.

8. Buddha Settles a Dispute. Once two rival families had a dispute over a dam. They brought the argument to Buddha to decide between them. He asked them, "What is the dam made of?"

"Sticks and stones," they told him.

"Which is more valuable, sticks and stones or your own blood?" he asked.

"Our own blood," they both agreed.

"Well, then . . ."

9. The Butter Buddha. Buddhism spread out of India to Tibet, China, Japan, and Southeast Asia. In the process, a number of forms of Buddhism developed. Tibet had its own distinctive version in which Buddhism became the official religion and government. The ruler of Tibet was the Dalai Lama, a man believed to be the reincarnation of the first Dalai Lama. When a reigning Dalai Lama died, the monks would search for a child born on that same day and proclaim him the new Dalai Lama. He would then be raised by the monks, who trained him for his important position.

One of the most unusual Tibetan ceremonies centered on a statue of Buddha made entirely of butter. It was roughly twenty feet high and took four months to build. People trekked through the mountains for days to attend the festival, coming from China, Mongolia, and Tibet. They arrived on camels, horses, and mules, then pitched their tents around the temple and filled the valley near the temple. On the day of the festival, the believers bowed to the idol and recited a prayer three times. Important religious leaders knelt on benches covered with red satin while the crowd of worshipers knelt on the ground. For a day the shrine was packed with worshipers and lit by lamps burning butter. Then the butter idol began to melt and people began a wild celebration, dancing and shouting.

The next day, priests shoveled out the melted lumps of butter and dumped them in a nearby ravine where wild animals ate them. The ceremony was already very old when Christian missionaries observed and reported it. They asked for an explanation and were given two. It was in honor of a Tibetan holy man, Tsong Kaba, or it was an illustration of how worthless a material body is. Whatever its explanation, the Butter Buddha of Tibet was a unique expression of Buddhism.

B. CHINA

1. Writing. Chinese writing is one of the oldest writing systems on earth. The oldest surviving examples, dated 2000 to 1500 B.C., are written on bones and shells. Chinese speakers who see these in museums report that they can read parts of them. This is because Chinese writing uses ideograms, symbols for ideas, rather than an alphabet designed to record sounds. This means the term *Middle Kingdom,* which is the name for China, is written as two characters, *middle* and *kingdom.* The word *middle* is a simple symbol, a rectangle with a line through the middle, like this: 中. Since each word has its own character or is made up of a combination of characters, each word must be memorized. This makes learning to read and write in Chinese an endless process of memorizing characters. The system does let people who speak different dialects understand each other. It doesn't matter how the word is pronounced; the symbol 中 means *middle.*

When Chinese is written in the Roman alphabet, it is usually written in the pinyin system. In 1979 the Chinese government directed that pinyin be used as the official transliteration system. Before then most American books and magazines used the Wade-Giles system. The two systems are noticeably different. For example, in pinyin the capital of China is Beijing. In Wade-Giles it is Peking.

2. Chinese Silk Legend. Legend says that the first silk was spun by Yilingshi, wife of Emperor Huang-Ti, in 2640 B.C. Silk is made from the cocoons of silkworms, which live on mulberry leaves. As early as 126 B.C. silk was traded over the 6,000-mile Silk Route to Persia and Arabia. The Chinese tried to keep a monopoly on silk production by making it a crime punishable by death to take silkworm eggs or cocoons out of China.

In spite of this, India began producing silk about 1000 B.C. Indians got the worms and mulberry trees from seeds and eggs smuggled out of China in the lining of the headdress of a Chinese princess.

3. China's First Emperor. Qin Shi Huangdi was the first emperor to rule a united China. His rule was marked by massive building and bizarre events. He built the Great Wall. It is roughly 1,500 miles long, 15 to 30 feet high, and 15 to 25 feet thick, with a top wide enough to drive a chariot on it. The wall was designed to keep out invading Huns and had forts along its length. It was built by forced labor, including criminals and scholars who were being punished. The bodies of over a million workers who died building it are enclosed in the wall.

Qin Shi Huangdi was such a tyrant that several attempts were made to assassinate him. He always kept a sword with him and constantly changed his sleeping quarters. He had several palaces, including 10,000 rooms, all equipped with food and servants. Anyone who revealed the emperor's location was put to death along with that person's whole family. Qin Shi Huangdi's own family was huge: 13,140 wives and 2,800 children!

He had a strong dislike for Confucius and tried to destroy the philosopher's books. He collected and burned copies of Confucian books, although he did allow the royal library to preserve some copies. Anyone caught with a copy of any book arguing that an emperor's power should be limited—as the Confucian writings did—was threatened with death. This was no idle threat. Qin Shi Huangdi did bury alive 460 Confucian scholars.

The emperor had a great interest in magic and eternal life, sending out expeditions to find the source of eternal life. He died while on an expedition seeking this magic. Only three people knew when he died: his younger son and two courtiers. They plotted to take power by concealing the emperor's death and removing the elder son, thereby allowing the younger son to inherit the throne. They returned home with the emperor. It was hot summer weather, so to conceal the fact that the emperor was a decaying corpse, they joined wagons of spoiled fish to their caravan.

Qin Shi Huangdi's tomb is now a tourist attraction. It is on a scale to fit the man. Archaeologists found a guard of 6,000 soldiers, all statues, standing in formation near the tomb. Each soldier is an individual, presumably modeled after the actual soldiers of the emperor's guard. The tomb is in Shensi Province and is a major attraction for Chinese and foreign visitors.

4. The Han Dynasty: Horses and Women. During the Han Dynasty, China had a shortage of horses, while Turkestan had a generous supply of them. The Chinese used two approaches to get horses: force and trade. One emperor sent 60,000 men to Turkestan to seize horses. He also married one of his female relatives to a barbarian. The price of the bride was 1,000 horses.

5. Tao Philosophy. Tao is a very difficult philosophy to talk about because it denies that words can explain the Tao. Lao-tzu reportedly said, "Those who know do not speak; those who speak do not know."

6. The Tao Legend of Tea. Taoism has the following legend about how the custom of serving tea to guests originated. When Lao-tzu, who founded Taoism, was old, he felt very sad and disappointed. His teachings were being ignored, and his homeland was near collapse. He got on a buffalo and headed out of China. Yin Hai was the guard at the Han pass on the border. He had been waiting for an immortal to go through the pass. He stopped Lao-tzu and served him a cup of tea. Then he talked him into writing down his ideas. The resulting book was the *Tao Te Ching,* the famous book of the Taoists.

7. Confucius on Bad Government. Confucius taught that good leaders make good government. He was traveling with his students and met a woman weeping beside a grove. As the wise man questioned her, she told how her father-in-law, husband, and son had all been killed by tigers. He asked why she did not move away. Her reply was that the government was good. He turned to his disciples and said, "Remember this. Bad government is worse than a tiger."

C. JAPAN

1. Earthquakes. The Japanese people have learned to live with earthquakes. Japan has an average of 20 a day. During one period of 4 days in 1909, the Izu Peninsula had 17,160 quakes. Only 380 of these were strong enough to be felt by residents. The Japanese say that they have learned that material things don't last. People are what matter.

2. Japanese Pottery in Ecuador. Archaeologists have uncovered a convincing indication of ancient sea travel involving the early Neolithic Jomon culture of Japan. They found pottery in Ecuador with a distinctive design. Then they located that design on pottery in earlier Jomon sites in Japan. They then carefully examined the ocean currents and winds. Their conclusion was that a fishing boat caught in storms could have been blown out to sea. The fishermen could live off the sea while winds and currents carried them to the coast of South America. Landing there, they then taught the people a design used at home. The fact that this is a decoration makes the argument convincing. Decoration serves no useful purpose and thus does not have to be any particular style. If the artifact were a useful tool, the similarity would not prove contact. Tools for a similar task have to be similar, or they won't work. Nearly identical tools for doing the same task have been independently developed in many locations.

3. Legend of the First Japanese Emperor. Japanese tradition says the emperor is a god. The sun goddess sent her grandson, Ninigi, to earth. He landed on the island of Kyushu carrying three symbols: a bronze mirror, a sword, and a necklace of curved beads. These symbols stood for purity, courage, and benevolence. Ninigi's grandson left Kyushu and conquered the rest of Japan, starting his rule in 660 B.C., when he became the first emperor of Japan, Jimmu. His descendants are still ruling Japan as emperors. This legend also helps explain the importance of the sun as a symbol of Japan.

Chapter IV

Ancient Greece

— Overview —

This chapter contains stories about early Greeks, the city-states, the Persian War, Greek literature, philosophy, mathematics, and Alexander the Great. The Greeks were the founders of many important ideas in the culture of Europe. They had ideas that seem surprisingly modern.

You could have your students write papers comparing and contrasting the Athenians with the Spartans. They could also write a compare-and-contrast paper on the Persians and the Greeks. You could have them look around your area for buildings made in imitation Greek style. They could make drawings or models of the Parthenon. They could make a bulletin board of "Great Greek Writers." They could make a bulletin board of "Greek Gods and Goddesses" or "The Olympic Games."

Creative writing papers could include, "I Visit ________" (Athens, Sparta, Troy), or "A Greek in America" (how an ancient Greek reacts to our culture).

A. EARLY GREEKS

1. Homer, Iron Age Poet. Tradition says that Homer was a blind poet who composed two epics, *The Iliad* and *The Odyssey.* Every educated Greek knew these stories. They were full of the adventures of Greek gods, goddesses, and heroes. The Greeks had a traditional date for the fall of Troy, which put in our usual terms is 1184 B.C.

Modern readers would like to know more about how the poems were written and when. They have come up with one conclusion. Homer lived long after the Trojan War. They point out that the heroes fighting at Troy were equipped with bronze weapons. Their armor was bronze and their spears had bronze tips. Clearly these were Bronze Age people. Yet Homer knew of iron, because he mentioned it in some places in his epics—for example, saying that a hero had strength like iron. Therefore, it seems reasonable to conclude that Homer wrote his poems in the Iron Age, looking back to earlier Bronze Age events.

2. Homer: The Gods at War. The Greeks thought of their gods as human, except that they had special powers and were immortal. In *The Iliad,* Homer describes one fight when the gods went down to the battlefield at Troy. Athena and Ares fought much as human sister and brother might. Ares, the god of war, had taken the Trojan side and was leading them against the Greeks. Athena came down to the battlefield and encouraged Diomed, a Greek hero, to fight Ares. She drove Diomed's chariot into the fight and even deflected Ares' spear, which was thrown at Diomed. She also guided Diomed's spear so it wounded Ares in the groin. Ares let out a cry so loud that both armies stopped fighting and looked around trembling. Wild with pain, he returned to Mount Olympus and complained to Zeus that Athena did not play fair. Zeus, like many a father dealing with his quarreling children, was angered and not very sympathetic.

3. Troy, a Real City. While the ancient Greeks apparently believed Homer's stories of the Trojan War, Europeans of the 19th century viewed them simply as myths. After all, who could take seriously a collection of tales about gods, goddesses, and superhuman heroes? But one man believed. Heinrich Schliemann was a grocer by trade, and his hobby, or rather his obsession, was Homer. He would recite Homer in the original Greek to his customers. In spite of this peculiarity, Schliemann made a fortune in the grocery business. Then he set out to find Troy. He dug on the traditional site of Troy and found not just one city, but a whole series of Troys one on top of the other! Then the problem became which of these, if any, was the Troy Homer wrote about? Since Schliemann's dig, historians and archaeologists have argued constantly about it.

4. Achilles' Heel. Achilles was the hero of *The Iliad.* The legend says that Achilles' mother, Thetis, feared that her son would be killed in battle, so she dipped him into the river Styx. Wherever the water touched, Achilles could not be harmed, but Thetis held him tightly by the heel as she dipped him in the river. Thus his heel became the one spot where he could be hurt. Toward the end of the Trojan War, Paris, a prince of Troy, shot an arrow at Achilles, and the god Apollo guided it to Achilles' heel. Achilles died of the wound.

The term *Achilles' heel* has become a part of our language. It means a point of weakness. Many an athlete has suffered an injury to the Achilles tendon, which connects the calf muscle to the heel. The story may also tell us something about warriors in the age of Troy. As archaeologists have uncovered bits of armor from that ancient time, they have made an interesting discovery. They have found specimens of bronze helmets protecting the head. The warriors clearly carried large shields that covered most of their bodies. They even wore bronze shin guards of a sort that covered the lower legs and feet. In fact, these Bronze Age warriors were well protected in most parts of their bodies—except their heels.

5. Ancient Greek Gods. The ancient Greeks believed that the gods were much like people, except that they had greater powers and never died. The family of Greek gods lived on Mount Olympus. Zeus was father of the gods, head of the family, and thunder god. Legend says that he once had a powerful headache. He ordered that his head be split open with an axe. When this was done, out stepped Athena, the goddess of wisdom, fully grown. Later she became the goddess of Athens and her bird, the owl, symbol of wisdom, appeared on Athenian coins.

6. The First Olympic Games. The Olympic Games were an important part of Greek culture. Tradition says that the first Olympic Games were held in 776 B.C. In that year a young cook named Cordebus of Elis won a 1-stade race. The stade is roughly 200 yards long. The event was held in Olympia, hence the Olympic Games. Later the Greeks added other events, so eventually they included the original 1-stade run, a 2-stade run, a 25-stade run, wrestling, boxing, chariot racing, races in armor, the pentathlon, and pankration, a fight combining boxing and wrestling. The Games were a religious event held in honor of the gods. The Greeks would stop their wars to hold the Games.

Only men could attend the Games. Women caught attending were to be thrown off a cliff. Women did have their own festival called the Heraea held once every five years. It featured a 100-foot race for girls.

The Olympic champion officially received an olive wreath and nothing more. In fact, an Olympic champion became a hero in his home city-state and often received a free house and free meals for life as well as money.

B. Greek City-States

1. Athenian Citizens. There must have been tremendous pressure on the citizens of Athens. They had to stay constantly in good physical condition because if war came, all male citizens were expected to serve. The rich owned armor and fought as heavy infantry, while the poor pulled the oars of the triremes in the navy. So for Athenian citizens it was important to make wise decisions in the assembly. A bad decision could get them killed in an unwise war. But the most serious threat came from the courts. Citizens sat on the juries deciding both the law and the facts of the case. Any citizen could be accused of a crime. Since there were no lawyers, the prosecutor was the citizen who had made the charge, and accused citizens were required to conduct their own defense. A citizen who was slow-thinking or a poor speaker could be in real trouble. Athenian courts could sentence people to death, so an Athenian citizen could not afford to be flabby in either body or mind.

2. Spartan Food. Spartan men ate in a sort of mess hall in which the food was notoriously bad. The Spartans said their food was seasoned by the two best spices: hunger and thirst. Visitors were not pleased. One diplomat who ate at Sparta said he now understood why the Spartans were so willing to die.

3. Spartan Women. Spartan women had more freedom than most Greek women. Spartan men were away in the military for much of their lives, so the women looked after family affairs. Even women in Sparta were expected to be in top physical shape so they would have strong, healthy babies. Spartan women worked out in the gymnasium. The word means roughly "place where people exercise naked." The other Greeks were somewhat scandalized by such behavior.

The Spartan mother played a role in inducting her son into the army. She presented him with his shield and instructed him to come back with his shield or on it. In ancient battles, losing armies would throw down their shields and run. The shield was also used as a stretcher to carry dead or wounded soldiers. So the mother was instructing the son never to retreat in battle, even in the face of death.

4. The Spartan Boy. A traditional Greek story illustrates the Spartan virtues. Spartan boys were taken from their families at about age 6 and began military training. They were not given enough food, so they would be forced to steal to get enough to eat. This was part of the training. An army had to live off the land—that is, steal food—when on the march. If caught stealing, the boy would be punished, not for dishonesty, but for being clumsy. One such boy stole a fox. Soon there was a search for the fox, so the boy hid it under his clothes. The fox bit the boy in the stomach; he began to bleed but did not cry out. Eventually he passed out from loss of blood and died. The Spartans buried him with full honors. He had lived up to the Spartan ideal.

5. Spartan Bravery. When Xerxes was invading Greece in the Persian War, an outsider tried to intimidate the Spartans. The Persian army was huge. Herodotus said it was over a million men. The stranger told the Spartans, "When the Persians shoot their arrows, they blot out the sun."

The Spartan reply was: "Good. We'll fight in the shade."

C. THE PERSIAN WAR

1. The First Marathon Run. A traditional story says that the first marathon happened as follows. After the Athenians defeated the Persians in the Battle of Marathon, they needed to send word of their victory quickly to Athens, 26 miles away. They feared that plotters inside Athens would start a rebellion to support the Persians. A report of the victory would stop this. A runner named Pheidippides was selected and sent on his way. He had run with other messages earlier, so he was very tired. But the urgency of the message gave him speed. He arrived at Athens just as Persian ships appeared off the coast. He gave his message, "Rejoice; we conquer," and died.

2. Thermopylae. The Battle at Thermopylae in 480 B.C. shows the Spartans living up to their ideals. The Persian King Xerxes was invading Greece with the biggest army anybody had ever seen. It was made up of units from every part of the Persian Empire. The elite unit was the force of 10,000 Immortals, the king's own bodyguard. Herodotus counted the army at over a million, but ancient sources are always unreliable about numbers. Modern estimates place the number around 100,000 to 150,000. Against this force, the Greeks were able to muster about 8,000 troops from several city-states. The elite unit was a force of 300 Spartans led by their king, Leonidas. The rest of the Spartan army had stayed home to observe a religious event.

The Greeks chose to make their stand at the pass at Thermopylae because it was narrow, and the numbers on the other side would not be in a position to surround them. On the first day, the Persians advanced. The Spartans advanced to meet them and cut down the attackers, even the Immortals. The next day's attack also failed. Xerxes was blocked.

But then Ephialtes, a Greek traitor, came to Xerxes and offered to show him a trail over the mountain. Xerxes sent his Immortals. The Phocians were guarding the trail, but the Immortals attacked them at dawn and the Phocians fled. They ran to the Greek camp and reported that they would soon be surrounded. All the other Greeks decided to leave. The Spartans, however, had been ordered to defend the pass, and a Spartan does not retreat. They stayed and fought to the last man. They are still there, in a mass grave. Over it is a monument saying, "Go, stranger, and tell the Spartans, here we lie, obedient to the law."

3. The Trireme. Triremes were the warships that won the Battle of Salamis against the Persians. They also were the backbone of the Athenian Navy when Athens dominated Greece through the Delian League. Yet the ship itself is something of a mystery. What did it look like? Did the oarsmen sit in fixed or sliding seats? How long were the oars? Were there 3 banks of oars or 2 banks of oars pulled by 3 banks of oarsmen? How could the trireme be so small and light yet stand the stress of ramming an enemy ship? Archaeologists are working at answering these and related questions.

There are some known facts about triremes, based on ancient sources. The people who pulled the oars were not slaves, but poorer citizens of Athens, who, as their contribution to defending the city, served in the navy. Each ship had 170 oarsmen and 30 soldiers. The ships were about 120 feet long. Recent underwater archaeology has recovered some ancient ships and shown how they were built.

In 1985, a team of archaeologists working with funding from the Greek navy built a reconstruction of a trireme. They recruited a crew of 140 men and 40 women and tested the ship. The *Olympias,* as she is called, has three banks of oars. Each oar is 13 feet 9 inches long and weighs 26 pounds. The crew's seats are fixed. The *Olympias* can reach a speed of roughly 7 miles per hour in 30 seconds. The crew is reported to be enthusiastic, and would like to find an old hulk so they can try ramming.

4. The Scythians. The Scythians were a tribe of warlike horsemen and archers who lived in what is now southern Russia and the Ukraine. They fought a series of wars against the Persians about the same time the Greeks did. If they killed an enemy, they would make a drinking cup of the skull. They were also probably drug users. Archaeology has turned up tents with hemp seeds in them, suggesting that the Scythians sat in tents filled with the smoke of burning hemp leaves or, as we now call it, marijuana.

D. Greek Literature and Mathematics

1. Aristophanes, Comic Playwright. The story has a modern feel to it because it deals with sex and war in a very direct way. Once in the early 20th century, a warrant was issued in Los Angeles to arrest the Greek who had written this obscene play. In the play, the women of a country at war band together with the women of the enemy country and decide to end the war. They simply agree not to go to bed with their husbands until the war is over. This creates a series of hilarious scenes as the frustrated husbands work out an end to the war. The play is not the product of a modern feminist or pacifist. The author is an Athenian named Aristophanes and the play is *Lysistrata,* written over 2,000 years ago. The war in question is the Peloponnesian War. Yet the play has made 20th-century audiences roar with laughter.

Aristophanes wrote other comedies about life in Athens. Often they read like cynical modern works. In *The Knights,* he takes on politicians. A sausage seller is chosen to rule Athens, but he is a simple man who objects that all he knows is how to chop things up and mix them together. This is how you make sausage, after all. This, the politicians insist, is exactly what a leader does. The sausage seller is from a bad family, he says, and the politicians tell him he is off to a good start for public life. Understandably, Aristophanes was not very popular with Athenian politicians.

He also wrote *The Clouds,* a play about Socrates and education. He has Socrates in a basket in the clouds because the ground is not the place for lofty speculations. In fact, Aristophanes wrote about a wide variety of topics, including war, city planning, and how to get rich. Two factors keep Aristophanes from being produced very often on modern stages. First, his work is too full of Athenian current events for most modern audiences. By now, of course, these are ancient history and it's hard to laugh at the joke if you have to read an explanation in the footnotes. Also, Aristophanes has his characters say and do things that cannot be said or done even on the modern American stage. Considering what we do allow, that says a lot about how open-minded the Greeks were.

The plays of Aristophanes and others were presented in festivals, and a prize was awarded for the best comedy. Each Aristophanes play has a chorus, as in all Greek plays. Aristophanes has his chorus talk about the action and even lecture the judges, telling them they had better give him the prize. If making people laugh and think was the goal of the contest, Aristophanes certainly deserved to win.

2. Sophocles, Greek Playwright. Sophocles is one of the three outstanding Greek tragedians, the others being Aeschylus and Euripides. While Sophocles' plays were originally written and produced for ancient Greek religious festivals, they are still produced in the modern world. *Oedipus Rex (Oedipus the King)* was made into a film in the 1960's, and *Antigone* was done on television in the 1950's. In fact, these plays are produced every year in some states and provinces. The production is often done by a college drama department.

Antigone is a very timely play. Antigone is the niece of King Cleon and faces a dilemma many modern people share. She must choose between her conscience and what the law requires. Her brother has been killed while leading a rebellion. The king has decreed that the body shall not be buried. Antigone must choose between her religious duty to bury her brother's body and her duty to obey the law. She chooses to cover the body with dust, thus burying it. This raises the question of how authority should deal with a crime committed for religious reasons. These issues are still debated in America today.

3. Socrates, Wisest of Greeks. Socrates was a stonemason by trade, but he had a love of wisdom. The Greek word for one who loves wisdom is *philosopher*. Socrates never wrote any books, so all we know of him is based on other Greeks' writings. Plato is the main source. Socrates started his philosophical career by visiting the oracle at Delphi. There he was rather surprised when the oracle called him wisest of the Greeks. He thought he knew nothing, so how could this be? He returned home and began to question his fellow Athenians. In the process he embarrassed many people who could not answer his sharp questions. He also developed a following of well-to-do young men like Plato, who enjoyed listening to Socrates.

Socrates questioned many traditional ideas and made many enemies. As a result, he was accused of the crime of corrupting youth and was put on trial before a jury of Athenian citizens. As was the custom, there were no lawyers. Socrates and his accuser presented their cases. The jury found Socrates guilty. Then each side got to propose a penalty. The accuser asked for the death penalty. Socrates offered to pay a tiny fine. The jury voted for the death penalty. At this point Socrates could have fled Athens and lived out his life in exile. Instead, he acted as a law-abiding citizen and stayed in jail. He drank the bowl of poison hemlock calmly. Then, while waiting for it to take effect, he discussed with his friends ideas of life after death.

4. Plato, Philosopher. Plato, a student of Socrates, wrote a number of books on philosophy. Plato's books were written as dialogues—that is, the record of conversations. Socrates was always the hero of the dialogues. He won the argument on the philosophical point.

Plato founded a school in Athens that lasted for centuries. He developed the concept that only ideas are real—that a chair is not real, but the idea of "chair" is real. Plato's books were not available in Europe during the Middle Ages, but were recovered and became very popular in the Renaissance. Plato's *Republic* is often on the required reading list for college freshmen.

5. Aristotle, Philosopher. Aristotle was the third of the big three of Greek philosophy: Socrates, Plato, and Aristotle. He was a student in Plato's Academy for 20 years. He was selected to be tutor to Alexander the Great. That's a little like having Einstein teach arithmetic to a prince.

Aristotle is credited as an author of books covering a wide range of topics. His book on *Politics* is still on the reading list for advanced students of political science. His *Rhetoric* and *Poetics* are of interest to advanced students of literature. His *Logic* spelled out the syllogism, a logical device used in reasoning. A sample is: All men are mortal. Socrates is a man. Therefore, Socrates is mortal. This system is still widely taught in college English and philosophy classes. In the Middle Ages Aristotle was viewed as simply "the philosopher."

Aristotle also wrote about physics and other natural sciences. He said that light objects fall more slowly than heavy objects. This idea has been discredited. Modern physicists observe that light and heavy objects fall at the same speed. He made a number of interesting observations on the natural world. Charles Darwin in his *On the Origin of Species* includes "An Historical Sketch . . ." reviewing people who had discussed the origins of species before Darwin. He cites Aristotle as having "shadowed forth" the principle of natural selection.

It may be that the books credited to Aristotle were not in fact written by him. Most historians believe that the books were produced in his school. They may be notes on his lectures or research projects done under his supervision.

6. Euclid, the Father of Geometry. Euclid was the Greek who invented a subject modern high school students still study. Euclid was the founder of the study of geometry—what is now called plane geometry. He was the leader of a sort of secret society. As members rose in the society, they learned the proof of more advanced theorems. Euclid developed the idea of proving a theorem in the step-by-step method still used in modern geometry books. In fact, most geometry books for centuries simply translated and reworded Euclid's original set of proofs. When Abraham Lincoln studied geometry, he read a translation of Euclid.

By now a bit of modern math has been added, but many problems are the same as those worked in Euclid's day. Euclid proved that triangles are congruent, given there are two equal sides and the angle between them is equal. Geometry, for the Greeks, was a study in clear and logical thinking. Plato had a sign over the entry to his academy, "Let no one ignorant of geometry enter here."

E. Alexander the Great

1. Alexander's Personality. Alexander the Great was larger than life in many ways. He had a huge ego and seemed to want to dominate everything. There is a story that toward the end of his campaign in Asia Alexander went up on a hill, and as far as he could see in every direction he ruled the land. He wept, because there was no more land to conquer.

He certainly wanted to be remembered. When he set out to conquer the Persian Empire, he took with him a number of scholars to study the area and report his exploits. He founded dozens of cities along his route. Most of them he modestly named Alexandria. These cities became islands of Greek culture. One of them, the Alexandria near the mouth of the Nile River in Egypt, became the greatest center of Greek scholarship. These cities, and the marriage of many of Alexander's officers to Asian women, may have been part of a plan to start a new culture based on a mixture of Greek and Asian ideas.

2. Alexander the Great and Bucephalus. Alexander the Great inspired a number of anecdotes. One of the most colorful tells how as a boy of 12 he tamed a war horse, Bucephalus. Philip of Macedon, king of Macedonia and Alexander's father, had paid a huge price for the horse, perhaps $15,000 in today's purchasing power. The horse turned out to be so wild that nobody could ride him. Alexander insisted that he could ride the horse and offered to pay the price of the horse if he could not. Finally his father gave in. Alexander calmly approached the horse and turned its head toward the sun. He had noticed that the horse was afraid of its shadow. He then mounted the steed and trotted him about and even took him off for a gallop.

Once Alexander returned, his father told him he needed to find a bigger kngdom. Macedonia was too small a place for him to rule. For many years, as Alexander led the Macedonians in conquering the Greeks and the Near East, he rode Bucephalus in battle. In Alexander's last victory out in Punjab in 327 B.C., Bucephalus was mortally wounded. He carried Alexander out of the battle to safety, then fell down and died. Alexander buried the horse with full military honors and founded the city of Bucephala in the animal's memory.

CHAPTER V

Ancient Rome

— Overview —

The Romans were a people who excelled at two things: war and politics. They built the largest empire to touch the ancient Mediterranean shores and made their subject peoples Romans. Their political history is full of violence and practical, effective solutions to problems. Culturally they were less elegant than the Greeks, but who isn't? Their art and literature were to be a treasured heritage for centuries.

You may want to use the first two stories as the basis for a paper on the Roman attitude toward women. Perhaps you could assign a paper comparing the struggle between patricians and plebeians and our civil rights movement. Students could even compare the republican Roman government with ours. The history of the Punic Wars can be the basis for a paper on the impact of new or unusual weapons—then, the corvus and elephants; and now, the Exocet missiles and Stealth bombers. It would be interesting to compare the Roman attitude toward Christians with our attitude toward people who burn the flag. You can have your students look about for imitation Roman buildings in the area.

Artistic students can do bulletin boards on "Roman Buildings," "Great Roman Rulers," or "The Roman Soldier." The imaginative student can do a paper on "My Day in Ancient Rome." Perhaps your students could do an interview with Hannibal, Cleopatra, or Constantine.

A. Early Rome

1. The Founding of Rome. The traditional founding date for Rome was 753 B.C. The Roman legend about the city's founding says that a vestal virgin was raped and became a mother, having twin boys. The mother was put into prison. The two boys were supposed to be drowned, but were left instead on the edge of the flood of the Tiber River. The two babies were found by a she-wolf, who raised them. When the two grew up, they were named Romulus and Remus. Romulus founded the city of Rome. While he was starting construction on his city wall, Remus jumped over it. Romulus killed him, saying, "This is the fate of those who attack my walls." The Romans, as you may notice, do not seem to believe in happy endings.

They probably didn't believe the wolf story literally either. Livy, a Roman historian in the age of Augustus, says it's likely that the boys were raised by a woman named Wolf. The Romans did, however, use pictures of twin infants and a female wolf on many of their coins.

2. The End of Kings. This is the traditional story of the last king of Rome, Tarquin the Proud, a cruel and harsh ruler. The incident that led to his downfall involved Lucretia, wife of a man named Brutus. Tarquin's son Sextus tricked Lucretia into letting him into her house while Brutus was away. Then at night he threatened her with death and disgrace and raped her. The next day he left, and Lucretia at once sent letters to her father and her husband. She told them of her disgrace, named Sextus, and then committed suicide. Death was the penalty for adultery in those days, and she insisted that she would pay the price. Her father and husband took her body into the public square and told the Romans what had happened. Brutus gave a fiery speech against the king and his family. There was an uprising, and the king was overthrown. After that, the word *king* would be hateful to all Romans, and Brutus was remembered as the liberator of Rome. Modern historians doubt that the story is literally true, but it does show Roman attitudes toward kings and adultery.

B. The Republic

1. Tribunes. Early republican Rome had within it two classes: the patricians, rich and powerful; and the plebeians, poor and powerless. The two classes were constantly quarreling. Since the patricians controlled the Senate and the consuls, they were in a position to take unfair advantage of the plebeians. At one point—tradition says around 494 B.C.—the dispute reached a crisis. The plebeians simply marched out of Rome to a hill a few miles away and refused to return, threatening to start a new city. Since they were the common soldiers of the army, they were leaving Rome defenseless. This threat brought a concession from the patricians. The plebeians would be allowed to select tribunes as their protectors. The tribunes would have the power to forbid the passage of laws harmful to the plebeians. If such a law came up, the tribunes could stop it by saying, "*Veto,*" which means "I forbid." There were five tribunes, all selected by plebeians. This arrangement satisfied the plebeians, and the army returned to Rome.

2. The Republican Tradition. Roman tradition says that the leaders of the early republic were sturdy, clean-living, and virtuous. Cincinnatus is one of their more famous examples. In times of emergency, the Senate would select a dictator, who would have absolute power for six months. In one such crisis they chose Cincinnatus. The delegation sent to call him to be dictator found him plowing his fields. He accepted the position and dealt with the crisis. Then he resigned and went back to plowing his fields.

3. The Roman Navy in the First Punic War. When Rome and Carthage began fighting, Rome was a land power but very weak at sea. To win, the Romans needed to build a navy. First, they found some Carthaginian ships that had washed ashore in Italy. They used these as a pattern. While building the ships, they trained crews by rowing on dry land. Ancient naval warfare required a lot of skill from the crew. Ships had to be rowed and steered with precision to ram the enemy, a skill that takes a long time to learn, but the Romans did not have time.

Instead, they developed the corvus, a sort of boarding bridge about 33 feet long by 3 feet wide rigged at a 45-degree angle from the mast of the ship. When a Roman ship got within range of a ship from Carthage, it would drop the corvus, which would stick to the enemy ship due to spikes on the end. Roman soldiers, the best in the ancient world, would then board the Carthaginian ship and take it. Using this device, the Romans won the sea battles that decided the First Punic War.

4. Hannibal's Name. The Carthaginian general Hannibal had a traditional name used by Phoenician people. Their god was Baal, and Hannibal means "beloved of Baal," "god love," or "god grace." The rest of the family also followed the tradition. Hannibal's brother was named Hasdrubal, which translates "Baal has aided," or "god help." Their father was named Hamilcar Barca. The name means "servant of Melgart." Melgart was another god worshipped at Carthage.

5. Hannibal and Elephants. Due to the general's famous attempt to use them to cross the Alps, elephants are almost a trademark of Hannibal. Somehow the image of these lumbering giants captures the imagination. Historians are puzzled about what kind of elephants Hannibal had. Carthage was in Africa, so he may have used African elephants. They are larger-eared and bigger but less docile than Asian elephants. Asian elephants are easier to train and were evidently the first war elephants. Alexander the Great had met armies using them during his Indian campaigns. Macedonian armies used Asian elephants. The opposing soldiers facing elephants for the first time must have been intimidated. Opposing cavalry had special problems. Horses were reported to panic when faced with these strange new monsters.

Impressive as elephants were, using them also had some drawbacks. Moving them over the Alps was a particular problem. Hannibal's force had to march through cold and snow while fighting off hostile tribes. The elephants were the least mobile part of the force. Roman sources refer to all of the force getting through a steep, narrow trail—"even the elephants." They were warm-weather animals, probably encountering snow for the first time. They also required massive amounts of food. All this might be worth it if they had been a sort of ancient tank. But they were animals, which means that they could stampede at any time in any direction, including right through their own army. Some armies took the precaution of equipping the person guiding the elephant with a spike that was to be used to kill the elephant if it got out of control.

The Battle of Zama in 202 B.C. illustrates the problem. Hannibal had 80 elephants in the front rank of his army. As the battle started, the Romans raised a cheer and blasted with horns and trumpets. Most of the elephants panicked and ran back through the Carthaginian army, causing considerable damage. Some elephants did stay steady and even charged, but the Romans ran out of the way and showered them with spears and javelins. These wounded animals soon turned back and ran through their own army. Zama is the battle in which Scipio Africanus defeated Hannibal to win the Second Punic War. It is worth noting that at the Battle of Cannae, Hannibal's greatest victory over the Romans, he had no elephants.

6. The Third Punic War and Figs. After its defeat in the Second Punic War, Carthage was no longer a match for Rome, but she was a rich prize, a source of grain, fruits, and vegetables as well as ivory, gold, and slaves. A Roman senator named Cato made a campaign of getting Rome to destroy Carthage. Every speech he made in the Senate ended with, "Carthage must be destroyed." Cato is reported to have held up a fine bunch of figs in the Senate and explained that they came from Carthage. Reviving agriculture and commerce meant that Carthage had recovered and was a threat to Rome, Cato argued. Shortly thereafter Rome declared war. This was the Third Punic War, which destroyed once-great Carthage.

7. Julius Caesar. The year was 44 B.C., and some friends were in Caesar's house eating and talking. Caesar, always busy, was sitting off to the side, writing. The discussion turned to a philosophical topic: What kind of death is most preferable? Caesar looked up and said, "A sudden one." A number of the guests must have been startled by the answer, for they were plotting a sudden death for Caesar. On March 15, 44 B.C., a group of senators including several of Caesar's friends attacked and killed the ruler.

8. Cleopatra. Cleopatra, queen of Egypt, was from a good Greek family. The Ptolemys were the descendants of one of the generals in Alexander the Great's army. She was the first in her family to learn to speak Egyptian. She had a way of getting along with powerful men. At the time of her rule, Egypt was a Roman protectorate. When Julius Caesar pursued his rival Pompey to Egypt, Cleopatra got a chance to meet the most powerful man in the Roman Republic. Tradition says she rolled herself nude in a carpet and arranged to have the carpet presented to Caesar. Evidently a meaningful personal relationship developed, because she later had a son she named after Caesar. She even visited Rome. This affair was viewed as a scandal and may have been a factor in the plot to kill Caesar, although Roman politics provided the main motives for the assassination. When Caesar was killed, Cleopatra returned to Egypt.

A few years later, she formed an alliance with Mark Antony against Octavian. Antony may have been attracted by the rich Egyptian treasury. Cleopatra may have seen another chance to be the most powerful woman in the world. It may even have been love. Cleopatra gave birth to twins. She and Antony were married. Then they lost the war. Cleopatra committed suicide by making a snake bite her. Even in death she played politics. In Egypt the snake was seen as the minister of the Egyptian sun god. So Cleopatra had made it clear to her subjects that she died like an Egyptian queen.

C. The Empire

1. Ships of Actium. After the assassination of Julius Caesar, his adopted son and grandnephew, Octavian, and his leading general, Mark Antony, formed an alliance. This lasted while they hunted down the plotters who had killed Caesar. But a few years later the two men fought a war over the control of the Roman Empire. The decisive battle was a naval action off the coast of Greece near Cape Actium.

There Octavian's smaller and more maneuverable ships defeated Antony's fleet. Antony and Cleopatra fled the battle, and later each committed suicide. Antony fell on his sword. Cleopatra held an asp (a poisonous snake) to her bosom. This left Octavian the uncontested ruler of Rome. He became Augustus Caesar, the first of the Roman emperors.

Octavian commemorated his victory at Actium by founding a city on a spot nearby. He called it Nikopolos, meaning "victory city," and built a monument there. It was a stone wall with the bronze rams of selected ships from Antony's fleet mounted on it. Ancient warships often sank the enemy by ramming them. For this purpose they had a cast bronze ram mounted on their bows. While the city and monument were famous in ancient times, later people simply took the rams and melted them down for their own use.

In 1983, archaeologist William M. Murray visited the site of the memorial. He had also studied an ancient bronze ram discovered on the floor of the sea near Athil, Israel. He discovered that the crumbling walll of the memorial had in it sockets that would fit a ram. He cleared away the high grass, cutting it with his Swiss army knife, and measured some of these sockets. The size of the sockets served as a clue to the size of the ships and the rams. The largest socket probably was made to fit a ram of two tons. Imagine—ancient craftsmen could cast two-ton rams of bronze! Murray also noticed that Octavian had carefully selected the largest of the captured rams to display, thus giving people the impression that his fleet had conquered a fleet made up entirely of huge ships, a nice little touch of propaganda.

2. Ovid and a Scandal. While the Roman ideal was a disciplined life of gravity and virtue, many did not live up to the ideal. Ovid lived and wrote poetry in the time of Augustus Caesar. The emperor was working hard at promoting the old Roman virtues of hard work and simple living. Ovid, on the other hand, seemed to enjoy a different approach to life. One of his books is called *The Art of Love.* In it he gives hints on how to pick up a girl at the circus and even how to get rid of a tiresome lover. Ovid is specific enough about lovemaking in this book that for years the U.S. Postal Service treated the volume as pornography.

Caesar exiled Ovid to a remote edge of the empire, a town called Tomis, in what is now Romania. Much learned speculation swirls around the idea that the exile was ordered because of Ovid's involvement with the emperor's daughter Julia. If this is true, the scandal was thoroughly hushed up. Ovid spent his exile polishing up his major book, *Metamorphoses.* It is a skillful poetic weaving of Greek and Roman myths all based on changes. It too is a spicy book containing some passages that look like sly pokes at the emperor.

3. Nero and the Olympic Games. The Olympic Games continued even under the Roman Empire, but were eventually desecrated, then ended. Nero, who was a notoriously bad man, desecrated the Games in A.D. 66. First he forced the Games to be rescheduled for that year, a serious violation of the religious tradition of the Olympics. Then he entered and won all the events, even a race in which he fell off his chariot. The other drivers kindly waited for the emperor to get back on and let him beat them. After this, the Olympics were a shattered institution, but they continued until roughly A.D. 388 when the emperor Theodosius, who was a Christian, abolished pagan festivals. That ban, of course, included the Olympic Games.

4. Roman Roads. To control their empire, the biggest in the ancient world, the Romans needed a way to move their army quickly. One of their solutions was to build a system of roads that has rarely been equaled. The road system ran through every major part of the empire. Roman roads were built by soldiers and ran in a straight line over hills, on raised causeways, through swamps, and across rivers. Once bridges were built, the nearest cities were required to maintain them. Roman roads were as wide as a marching legion column and paved with stone. They were built to last, often three feet thick, made of layers of stone. Historians have noted that Europe did not get a faster means of land travel until the railroads were built. Roman roads lasted for a long time. In fact, some are still in usable condition.

5. Stoic Philosophy. The Stoic philosophy was very popular in Rome. A good Stoic accepted what happened without complaint. Epictetus, one of the best Stoic writers, was a slave and had a bad leg. Tradition says that Epictetus's master got angry with the slave and began to twist his leg. "If you keep twisting my leg, you will break it," Epictetus told him. The angry master continued and broke the leg. Epictetus then said, "See, I told you it would break." Such was the Stoic attitude toward pain. Notice that Epictetus was a slave. Stoics thought that being slave or free didn't matter. They said, "No one is free who serves the body."

6. The Roman Army: Unity in the Empire. The Roman Army was not only a fighting force, but also a device to intermix peoples and spread Roman culture. For example, the Twentieth Legion, made up of troops from Syria, was stationed in Chester, England. Army camps tended to attract merchants and others to settle near them. Thus Roman camps became centers of cities. The Roman word for camp, *castrum,* became *caster* or *chester* in English. So cities like Manchester, Lancaster, and Chester began as Roman camps.

7. Slavery. Rome, like Greece, had slavery. In ancient times, slaves were debtors or prisoners of war. The First Punic War produced 75,000 slaves. The slaves were of the same race as the Romans. In fact, one visitor said Roman slaves were dressed like their masters and it was hard to tell the difference between them. But in the early days, slaves were treated harshly. They did the hard, dirty, dangerous work on the big cattle farms and were treated like the animals. They were bought and sold like horses. Sometimes they rebelled. Spartacus led a revolt from 73–71 B.C. that included an army of over 90,000 slaves. At the end of the revolt 6,000 slaves were crucified along the road between Capua and Rome. Slaves also became gladiators who fought in the Roman circuses, sometimes against beasts and other times against each other. Thousands of slaves died in such contests.

Not all slaves had such terrible jobs. Rich Romans often had slaves who read to them. Others were secretaries, teachers, philosophers, or architects. Some owners freed their slaves. There is even a record showing that one Roman family adopted a slave.

8. Christianity and Persecution. The pagan Romans had a hard time understanding Christians. The pagan world was very tolerant of variety in religion. The Romans had a whole series of gods and allowed conquered peoples to practice their own religions. They did require certain sacrifices to Roman gods, but to pagans this was not a problem. Pagans were open-minded about adding another god. The Romans even had an arrangement with the Jews. The Jews were unwilling to worship any god but their own, but they did offer prayers to their god for the emperor. All the original Christians had been Jews, but the faith spread to others, so the prayers-for-the-emperor arrangement did not cover them.

Furthermore, Christian ideas sounded weird to the Romans. Christians talked of being "washed in the blood of the Lamb"; they had a ceremony using wine; they talked about how they should "love one another." The Romans knew of some religions that actually did squirt blood from sacrificial animals onto the worshipers. They also knew of pagan faiths that included drunkenness as part of their festivals. Some cults also practiced orgies as worship. Add all those together, the Romans thought, and the Christians must be a very wild group indeed.

The Romans did consider Christians outlaws, but only persecuted them off and on. Eventually Constantine made it legal to be a Christian, and about a century later Christianity became the only religion permitted in the empire. Then it was the Christians' turn to persecute non-Christians.

As the Roman Empire was falling, the pagans complained it was the Christians' fault. The pagans argued that Christians were so meek, mild, and pacifist that they were unfit to lead an empire. Were the early Christians pacifists? Later Christians have certainly fought fierce and bloody wars. Have Christians changed, or did the Romans misunderstand the ancient Christians?

9. Constantine and the Christians. Constantine was the Roman emperor who made Christianity legal in the Roman Empire. He was a pagan until 312. He said that as he was preparing to fight the Battle of Milvian Bridge, he saw the sign of the cross on the sun. He had his soldiers put *chi rho,* a symbol for Christ, on their shields before the battle, which his army won. After that, Constantine issued the Edict of Milan, giving legal status to Christians. At that time, Christians were a minority in the empire. Pagans continued to be the majority and to worship the emperor as a god. Christians considered Constantine a ruler chosen by God.

Constantine directed the Church, choosing bishops and using them as advisors. When the Christians had disputes, he acted to settle them. He attended the Council of Nicaea, the first worldwide meeting of the Church, in 325 and was influential in developing the Nicene Creed. Constantine was not baptized until 337. Like many other Christians of the time, he waited until he was on his deathbed to be baptized.

10. Justinian and Silk. In the sixth century A.D., the emperor Justinian, ruler of the Byzantine Empire, arranged for two Persian monks to smuggle eggs of the silkworm and seeds of the mulberry tree out of Asia. The monks hid them in their hollow walking sticks. This was the beginning of the first silk industry in the West.

Chapter VI

Asia to the 17th Century

— Overview —

This was a period of conquests in Asia. Both India and China were taken over by outsiders from central Asia. While the Muslim rulers of India brought some new ideas to enrich the culture, the Mongol conquerers of China were pretty crude. The Japanese were able to resist being conquered, so their development was a bit different. Their emperors were dominated by shoguns, and they developed Zen Buddhism.

You may want to have your students write a paper comparing and contrasting the impacts of the invasions of India and China. They could also do a paper comparing Genghis Khan with Tamarlane or Akbar. Or they could do research on Zen's impact on art in Japan.

A number of imaginative papers are possible—"My Visit to the Taj Mahal," "I Traveled with Marco Polo to the Mongol Court," or "My Life As a Zen Monk," for example.

A. INDIA

1. Tamerlane (Timur the Lame). Tamerlane was a powerful leader in the Mongol conquest of India. He was a Muslim. In his youth his right leg was injured, leaving it shorter than the left. As a result, his left shoulder was higher than his right. The physical description is based on his skeleton, taken out of his tomb at Samarkand by Russian archaeologists in 1941.

Tamerlane had a brilliant mind. He always had scholars with him at court and loved to debate, particularly about history. He enjoyed playing chess. He learned to speak Turkic and Persian, but could not read or write them. He had a tremendous curiosity.

Like all Mongol conquerors, Tamerlane was a ruthless killer, destroying his enemies in war and killing any of his officers, great or small, who tried to cheat him.

2. Muslim Inventions. The Muslim conquerors of India brought inventions with them. They brought paper, gunpowder, the arch, and, from Persia, some advanced irrigation systems.

3. Akbar. Akbar was a very energetic Muslim ruler. Once, to put down a rebellion he rode 240 miles in 24 hours. He tolerated Hindus. In fact, his revenue minister was a Hindu. He even abolished the special tax on non-Muslims, then put down the rebellion of Muslims who objected. Although illiterate, Akbar encouraged art and collected a large library. He was an enthusiastic hunter.

4. Akbar and Fatehpur. Of the Mogul rulers of India, Akbar was the most colorful and the most unpredictable. In 1569, Akbar's wife gave birth to a son. Akbar believed it was because he had consulted a holy man named Salim Chishti. Akbar showed his gratitude by building a city on the spot where Salim Chishti lived. He personally designed buildings and even did some work cutting stones. The plan included separate palaces for Akbar's Turkish wife, his Hindu wives, and his Muslim wives. The town had a sewer system, something completely lacking in European towns in 1570. The town was called Fatehpur Sikri. It was a center for art; Akbar hired thousands of painters. It was here that the first portraits in India were painted. Fatehpur Sikri was a thriving city for 15 years—"greater than London," according to one European visitor. Then Akbar left it and never returned. Soon Fatehpur became a ghost town.

5. Shah Jahan. Shah Jahan is remembered as the Mogul ruler who built the Taj Mahal, a magnificent tomb for his favorite wife. The original plan called for a second building just like the Taj Mahal, except black, to be built facing it. For some reason the second structure never was built. Shah Jahan certainly had enough time—the Taj Mahal was finished years before he died. He lived an active life in his court. He said the five daily prayers required of Muslims, and the rest of the day was taken up hearing appeals and petitions from his subjects and meeting with officials of his empire. For entertainment he enjoyed elephant fights, a spectacle only the king was allowed to stage. A pair of elephants strained against each other until one was clearly dominant. Then they were separated. The elephants usually survived, but their riders often lost limbs or were killed. Shah Jahan also liked to relax with members of his harem at the end of the day. He was an active ruler until age 65.

After that he was sick and confined to bed. Over his bed was a mirror arranged to reflect the Taj Mahal. Shah Jahan died at age 74. Tradition says he was found dead with his face turned toward the mirror.

6. The Taj Mahal. Building the Taj Mahal was a huge project. The builders even changed the course of the Jumna River so the view from the tomb would be better. Twenty thousand workers labored for years to build the Taj Mahal. As they built it using materials imported from China, Tibet, Afghanistan, and Egypt, they also raised a scaffold made of brick. When the tomb was finally done, the experts estimated that tearing down the scaffold would take five years. But Shah Jahan got it down much faster than that. He announced that any peasants who helped tear down the scaffold could have all the bricks they took down. In a day the scaffold was gone.

7. Mogul Wealth. The Mogul rulers of India were incredibly rich. Shah Jahan, who is remembered for building the Taj Mahal, surrounded himself with expensive items. He owned seven thrones covered with jewels and a coat so heavy with gems that two servants had to hold him up under the garment's weight.

B. CHINA

1. The Mongol Tax Collectors. The Mongols dominated much of China and Russia from 1200 to 1400. The Russians called them Tatars or Tartars. The Mongol tax collectors seldom had trouble getting what they asked for. They would travel in small groups, a ragged little band of men who smelled bad and looked unimpressive. When they approached a settlement, they would ask for ten percent of everything: gold, silver, horses, women, and cattle. If the settlers gave them the tribute, all was well, but if the settlers refused, or harmed or killed the tax collectors, then real trouble broke out. Hordes of Mongols mounted on their ponies would swoop down on the settlement and destroy it. Storming the place, they would take everything, destroy the buildings, and kill all the people except one. The survivor was allowed to live and tell the people of nearby settlements what had happened. It is little wonder, therefore, that Mongol tax collectors were treated with great respect.

2. **The Golden Horde.** Apparently the Mongols named their headquarters on the steppes of Asia after an old Chinese system. The points of the compass were assigned different colors. North was black, south was red, east was blue, and west was white. The center was yellow, and that was the imperial color. The Mongol word for *camp* was *ordu,* which becomes *horde.* It's easy to see how "central camp" became "yellow camp" or "golden horde."

3. **The First Crossbow.** The first record of the crossbow dates from 1050 B.C., when "the Mongol Chou" people attacked "the Shang State" by advancing along the Yellow River armed with crossbows and riding in chariots. These early crossbows had bronze trigger mechanisms. Some of these have survived until today.

4. **Mongol Women.** Mongol women did a lot of the heavy work and were given more equality than women in the Muslim or Christian cultures of the time. They wore pants, rode astride, and were capable archers.

5. **Mongol Strategy.** The Mongols did not just use brute force in their conquests. Sometimes they used trickery. There are cases on record when the Mongols mounted dummies on horses to make their army look larger.

6. **Chinese Kites at War.** The people of China developed kites very early and even adapted them for a variety of uses. The Chinese used kites to carry musical instruments and even fishing lines. Once, in 1232, the Chinese used kites to carry a message. A city was under siege. The city dwellers put messages on kites and flew the kites over the besiegers' lines, to where the enemy held a number of prisoners from the city. When the kites were over the prisoners, the city dwellers cut the strings, and the kites fell among the captives. The messages on the kites encouraged the prisoners to rise up and escape.

7. **Chinese Women and Foot Binding.** During the tenth century, Chinese women became victims of a form of mutilation called foot binding. The goal was to produce tiny feet, a feature which supposedly made women more attractive. At age four, girls had their feet bound in a long bandage. Only the big toe stuck out. The

other toes were folded under so the foot looked like a lotus. The feet were kept bound for several years, so they were tiny. As a result, Chinese women could not walk normally. Instead, they minced along like dancers. Chinese women had to keep their feet covered at all times and not show them to anyone but their husbands.

8. The Mings Trade with Africa. The Ming Dynasty had a great tradition of shipbuilding and trade. One expedition started with a giraffe. In 1414, the city of Malindi on the Swahili coast of Africa sent a gift of a giraffe to the Ming emperor. A second giraffe arrived in 1417. The emperor then ordered a eunuch admiral named Zheng He to escort the ambassador from Malindi home. Zheng He sailed his ships to 36 countries that paid tribute to the Ming emperors. But then the emperor decided to forbid all ocean sailing. This policy left Africa open to the Europeans and isolated the Chinese.

C. Japan

1. Weak Emperors. Although the Japanese always thought of their emperor as the divine ruler, power was often in the hands of military dictators called *shōguns*. The wealth and power of the Japanese emperor reached its low point about 1500. When the current emperor died in 1500, he was not buried for six weeks, because there was not enough money in the treasury for his funeral. The next emperor was not crowned for twenty years because of lack of money for the ceremony. A later emperor raised some money by selling his autograph. He would write a quotation of ancient verse and sign his name. Clearly, the power of the emperor was at its low point.

2. The Divine Wind. The Japanese believed their islands were sacred and were protected by their gods. The following events reinforced this idea. During the 13th century, the Mongols were conquering much of Asia. They decided to attack Japan. In 1274, Kublai Khan sent a fleet to conquer the island nation, but the ships were forced to return to Korea because of storms. Again in 1281, the Mongols sailed with 150,000 men, but the fleet was destroyed by a typhoon. The Japanese called it *kamikaze*, "divine wind," a storm sent by their gods to protect them.

3. First Europeans in Japan. The first Europeans reached Japan in 1543, when Portuguese seamen were blown off course. St. Francis Xavier visited Japan from 1549 to 1551 and made converts. By 1582, there were about 150,000 Christians and 200 chapels in the country. But Japanese leaders had reservations about Christianity. Christians were supposed to serve their God before their earthly lords. Christians ate beef, which offended the Japanese. Christians also took some Japanese and sold them into slavery. The Christian idea of marriage to one woman was contrary to the Japanese practice of having concubines. In 1587, the ruler Hideyoshi issued a decree against Christians. It was not vigorously enforced until 1637, when Christian peasants revolted. After the rebellion was put down, Japan followed a strict policy of excluding all foreigners. Only the Dutch who stopped at an island in Nagasaki Bay and the Chinese could trade with Japan.

4. Japanese Falconry. Using hawks for hunting is a very old sport in Japan. The sport is also related to the social and political life of the people. About A.D. 355, the emperor Nintoku set up a special office for the care and training of hawks. The same office was also in charge of training dogs to hunt with the hawks. In 701, the office was given equal status with the army and navy. In one incident, hawking was considered more important than war. The Japanese military temporarily stopped a war against the Koreans in 1596 to trade food for hawks from Korea. After that, Japan continued to import Korean hawks.

Hawking was a noble activity, and rank had its privileges. Certain hawks were considered noble, while others were common. Among the common birds were hawk-eagles and sparrow hawks. Nobles used goshawks and put red leashes on their birds, while the emperor put purple leashes on his. Hunting parties were made up of large numbers of people. Beaters drove the game out before the hawks. Dogs flushed game birds, and porters carried the game after the kill. These parties would troop through the country for days at a time. Tokugawa Ieyasu, founder of the last shogunate of Japan, was an enthusiastic falconer. He once went on a hunting trip for 11 days. During that time his party took 25 cranes, 8 swans, and many ducks. We don't know how many hawks the party used, but 13 were injured.

Hawking parties were sometimes used to cover other activities. A lord would go hawking through the country and inspect his lands. He would sleep in farmhouses and see how the people lived and hear them talk. Sometimes secret political meetings were concealed behind the disguise of hunting parties. In one case a group of nobles pretended to be a hawking party and approached an enemy. When they got close, they threw off their disguises and attacked.

The Tokugawa period was the golden age of Japanese hawking. The Meiji restoration led to a decline in the imperial interest in hawks. For a time after 1866, the emperor had no hawks, but in 1882 the sport was revived, and the emperor still had hawks until at least 1962.

5. Zen Buddhism. Buddhism originated in India, spread to China, and from there came to Japan. The Japanese favored Zen Buddhism. In Zen the monks spend their days in meditation, trying to empty their minds. One of the most typical Zen meditations is simply to sit facing a blank wall. This sometimes causes a person to fall asleep, so one monk carries a stout stick and whacks any who doze off. While facing the wall, the monk ponders a *koan,* a sort of riddle or story intended to aid enlightenment. The *koan* might be a simple question such as "What is the sound of one hand clapping?" Or it may be a story. Zen is also expressed in the tea ceremony, the simple gardens made of rocks, and watercolor painting.

6. Zen and Swordplay. Zen Buddhism teaches that the way to nirvana is to forget self and just do. This idea was even applied to teaching swordplay. The following is a traditional Zen story.

A young man's father was killed by an evil man, and the young man burned for revenge. So he went to the greatest swordsman in Japan and said, "I want to take lessons and become a swordsman. I will practice hard."

The great man said that it would take a year to learn, but the youth was in a great hurry. "But I will practice day and night. I will try very hard." said the young man.

"In that case," replied the master, "it would take two years. No."

The young man was desperate and pleaded further. "I will do anything you say to become a great swordsman."

"In that case," the master said, "work in my kitchen," and set the youth to washing pots, pans, and dishes.

The young man was very puzzled, but he did as the master said. The next day as the youth was working in the kitchen, the master sneaked up behind him with a big stick and hit him. In fact, each day as the young man worked, the master would come upon him unexpectedly and give him a solid whack. Soon the young man lived in a state of constant alertness, always looking behind him and ready to jump aside at the slightest hint of danger. Then the master came to him and said, "Now you are ready for lessons." In six weeks he was the greatest swordsman in Japan.

The Zen point of this story is: Don't think; do.

7. A Legend of Zen and Tea. There are a number of legends about how tea was discovered. This is the Zen version. In A.D. 520, a Buddhist holy man named Bodhidharma or Daruma traveled from India to China. He was the founder of the Cha'an school of Buddhism, called Zen in Japan. When Daruma reached China, the emperor offered him a cave in the mountains near Nanking, the capital, as a temple. Here Daruma practiced the Zen meditation of sitting and staring at a wall. He did this for nine years. One day he fell asleep during the meditation. When he woke up, he was so upset at his lapse that he cut off his eyelids. Where his eyelids landed on the ground, a tea plant grew. The leaves of this holy plant were used to make a drink that would keep the drinker awake.

8. The Tea Ceremony in Zen. Zen Buddhism makes the tea ceremony a spiritual experience. The ceremony was developed around 1588 and is still practiced by the Japanese today. Zen stresses the experience of nature and of simple things. The object is to clear the mind of all thought and just be. The Zen tea ceremony is an art form expressing these ideals. The tea is served in a special tea house. The path from the residence to the tea house passes through a garden, which is really a carefully landscaped area, with the landscaping done so everything looks natural. The tea house itself is roughly ten feet by ten feet. The interior has a few very simple, but artistic, furnishings, usually including a flower arrangement and a painting. Red flowers are not used because they are too noisy. The door of the tea room is only three feet high, so guests have to crawl in, thus becoming more humble. Once inside, they contemplate the simple beauty of the room and drink tea.

A story from the 16th century tells of Riku, a master of the tea ceremony. Riku managed to cultivate a whole garden of morning glories at a time when these were rare and precious flowers. Word of this reached the emperor, who wanted to see the flowers. Riku invited him to tea. The emperor came and found himself walking through a garden of sand and rocks with not a flower in sight. He was growing angry when he approached the tea house. As he entered the door, he saw hanging in an antique vase one perfect blossom.

9. Zen and Archery. The ideas of Zen Buddhism influenced all aspects of life in Japan. This started in early times and continues today. In ancient times, the practice of swordplay and archery was heavily influenced by Zen, and some traditional teachers continue the art in the 20th century. Eugen Herrigel, a German philosopher, has written about his experience with such a teacher in a book called *Zen in the Art of Archery*. He explained that the whole point of the archery was to get the spirit right. The archer must become the bow, the arrow, and the target. Breathing correctly was very important. This reflected the idea that Zen was a way that tried to eliminate the self of the student as a way to nirvana.

At first Herrigel practiced with the target very close, then eventually with the target at longer range. His teacher kept telling him not to think about his shooting. This went on for six years. Finally Herrigel got in the right spirit and found the bow wonderfully easy to draw and shoot. He even got so he could practice archery without his bow.

This may be fine as a spiritual exercise, but how did this work in the days when archery was a life-and-death skill? Once the master gave a demonstration that showed Zen archery may have worked very well. He shot from a lighted practice hall toward a target in a dark room. His first arrow hit the center of the target. The second arrow split the first!

10. Buddhism and Martial Arts. The Buddhist religion and martial arts are intertwined in interesting ways. In the sixth century an Indian monk named Bodhidharma walked across the Himalayas to the Shaolin monastery. He found the monks there in bad condition both physically and spiritually. So he started a program of physical and spiritual exercises. It was this combination that produced kung fu, the fighting system, and Zen Buddhism.

11. Karate—Okinawan Hand. Like all the Asian martial arts, karate has its roots in Buddhism, but there is a unique political influence, too. When the Japanese invaded Okinawa in 1609, they quickly disarmed the residents. Some people of Okinawa turned to Chinese missionaries, who instructed them in the martial arts. The blend of these Buddhist Chinese styles with the native Okinawan fighting systems became known as Okinawan hand. In spite of the fact that Okinawans could attack an armored Japanese warrior, knock him off his horse, and kill him with a kick, they were not able to drive out the Japanese. The island became Japanese in culture. Later on, the Japanese learned of the Okinawan system, adopted it, and named it *Karate-do*, meaning "way of the empty hand."

Chapter VII
Islam

— Overview —

Islam is the newest of the world's major religions. It quickly spread over the Middle East and developed a culture centered on the religion. Muslim culture was a powerful influence on Europe, India, and other cultures it contacted. Islam remains a powerful influence in the 20th century. This chapter provides more detailed information on the basic beliefs of Islam and early Islamic civilization.

You may want to have your students clip and summarize articles about Islam in modern times. A world map with Islamic countries marked would be a good bulletin board. Perhaps you could have your students make a bulletin board of "Islamic Leaders Today." Individual leaders could be the subject of research papers.

This is the culture of *The Arabian Nights.* Perhaps you could have your students write an updated version of one of the stories: Aladdin, Ali Baba and the Forty Thieves, Sinbad the Sailor, or any story they choose.

A. Beliefs

1. The Flight. The flight of Muhammad from Mecca to Medina on June 20, A.D. 622, is the start of the Muslim calendar. It marks a move that led to the wider spread of Muhammad's teachings. The prophet had been teaching his family and friends for a few years and had branched out to teaching others as well. This was dangerous because Mecca was a city of 360 idols, and many people in Mecca were hostile to this new religion, which abolished idols.

Some people in Yathib, later called Medina, were impressed with the prophet's teaching, and 73 of them came to Muhammad and asked him to move to Medina. He waited for God's command. On the night when it came, he gave his cloak to Ali, his son-in-law, and had Ali lie in his—Muhammad's—bed so anyone looking in would think Muhammad was sleeping. Muslim tradition says Muhammad then went out, and the enemies who were watching his house and planning to kill him in the morning were blinded. He put dust on their heads as he went by without their knowing it. Muhammad then went to a cave outside the city. After some days, the search for him had slowed down, and he started at night for Medina. He traveled for days and arrived at Medina in the heat of the day. The Muslims of the city had been looking for him for many days, going out each morning and returning to the city as the heat became unbearable. The first person in Medina to see Muhammad was a Jew, who called out to the Muslims that their prophet had arrived.

2. The Creed. The Creed is one of the five pillars of Islam. "There is no god but the God and Muhammad is his Prophet." All Muslims must repeat the Creed once in their lives with full understanding. The word *God* in Arabic is *Allah.* Muslims have only one god. The Christian trinity looks like too many gods to them. A prophet is a messenger of God. Muslims recognize many prophets: Adam, Abraham, Moses, Jesus, and others, all of whom were mortal. Muhammad was the last prophet, according to Islam. Muslim tradition says that when Muhammad died, many Muslims tried to deny he was dead. Then Abu Bakr, an early convert and friend of Muhammad, said, ". . . For him who used to worship Muhammad, Muhammad is dead. But for him who used to worship Allah, Allah is alive and dieth not." Abu Bakr went on to recite from the Koran, ". . . And Muhammad is but a messenger, messengers the like of whom have passed away before him."

3. Ramadan. Fasting during the month of Ramadan is one of the five pillars of Islam. Ramadan is the ninth month of the Muslim calendar. The start and end of the month come when one trustworthy witness testifies that the new moon has been sighted. A cloudy night can therefore lengthen the month. Fasting takes place from sunrise to sunset, that is, from the time a black thread can be distinguished from a white thread until the threads cannot be distinguished. In other words, during daylight hours of Ramadan, Muslims fast: no food, no drink. After dark, they may eat and drink. Experienced travelers report that it is a bad idea to try to conduct much business during Ramadan because Muslims are often rather short-tempered during the day.

4. Almsgiving. Giving charity to the poor is one of the five pillars of Islam. Therefore, in Muslim countries some people make their living begging. These people are doing a religious service. It is understood that a person who gives alms to the poor receives a spiritual benefit. Therefore, the beggar, not the giver, is doing a favor.

5. The Pilgrimage—The Hajj. The pilgrimage to Mecca is one of the five pillars of Islam. Every believer is supposed to make it once in a lifetime. It is not a casual tourist visit, but a religious act done at a prescribed time and involving certain rituals. The pilgrimage ceremony takes place in Mecca on the seventh through tenth days in the month of Dhu Al Hijjah. As the pilgrims approach within six miles of Mecca they enter the state of *ihram:* they wash, pray, and remove their ordinary clothes, putting on seamless white cotton garmments. The pilgrims will be bareheaded under the desert sun, and they may not shave, cut their hair, or trim their nails. The first event is a visit to the sacred mosque. Before entering, the pilgrims wash hands, mouth, nostrils, and feet. The pilgrims enter barefoot and, chanting an Arabic prayer, circle seven times around the Kaaba, a small square building containing a sacred black stone. After that they walk seven times between two hills, Sofa and Marwa.

The next day, they go fourteen miles east of Mecca to hear a sermon at Mount Arafat and spend the night in the open. Then they go to the village of Mina and stone the three Devil's Pillars. Next they offer sacrifices of sheep or possibly cows or camels. The meat is given to the poor. Tradition says that when Muhammad made pilgrimages, he had his hair trimmed at this point, so pilgrims do the same. Some have their hair trimmed to a state of baldness; others have only a few symbolic locks cut off. Now the pilgrims change back to their regular clothes. They carefully save their seamless garments. They will wear the clothing once more when they go to the grave.

6. Prayer. Prayer is one of the five pillars of Islam. The faithful are required to pray five times a day—at dawn, noon, afternoon, sunset, and after nightfall. Before prayer, believers must wash. How can they do this in the desert? If there is no water available, they may use sand. At first, Muslims prayed facing Jerusalem, but they soon changed to facing Mecca. Every major Muslim city has towers called minarets, and five times a day the voice of the muezzin calls out, "There is no god but God" in Arabic to call the faithful to prayer.

7. The Koran. The Koran is the holy book of Islam. Muslims believe it contains revelations made to Muhammad by God through the angel Gabriel. At first these revelations were simply recited, but they were written down before Muhammad died. The Koran was written in Arabic, and it cannot be translated. According to believers, any attempt to translate produces a book in another language, which is not the Koran. Muslims have a tradition that the Koran cannot be bought. When a Muslim buys a copy of the Koran, the price paid is for the binding. The pages are always free. Many devout Muslims memorize the entire Koran.

8. The Koran and the Old Testament. Muslims believe their god is the same god who was revealed by Abraham and Moses. Therefore, it is not surprising that the Koran has a number of references to material from the Old Testament. A brief passage mentions Adam's sons and Cain killing Abel. A short description tells of the battle in which David killed Goliath. In Surah XII, the Koran devotes 111 verses to the story of Joseph. The story differs from the Old Testament in some significant details, but in broad outline it is very similar. In the Koran's version Jacob, Joseph's father, knows that Joseph has not been eaten by a wolf. In both versions Joseph becomes a slave in Egypt and later an important official. His brothers come seeking help and eventually find that the Egyptian official they are dealing with is their long-lost brother.

9. Shiites. Muslims will tell you, "Islam is one," meaning that Islam is not divided into Protestant, Catholic, and other denominations, as is Christianity. But to the outsider it looks as if Islam does in fact have a division: the Orthodox Sunnis and the Shiites. The Shiites will tell you: "We follow Ali." Most of Islam follows the caliphs, but the Shiites are different. Muhammad had no sons, but he did have a daughter, Fatima. Ali married her, becoming Muhammad's son-in-law. Shiites insist that only leaders who are descended from Ali have the right to be caliph. Shiites make up about 14 percent of the Islamic population, living mostly in Iran and Iraq. The Shiites believe in the leadership of an *imam,* who is an infallible spiritual authority. It is this belief that was the basis for the power of the Ayatollah Khomeini in Iran.

10. Sufism: Whirling Dervishes. Islam has contained a wide variety of practices. One of the more colorful is the whirling dervishes. Sufism was a mystical version of Islam. Believers tried to be unified with Allah by reciting prayers and by other spiritual exercises. Evidently one group of Sufis in Turkey moved as they recited, and this became a sort of dance. They became known as the dancing dervishes or whirling dervishes. This group now seems to have disappeared, except for some dervishes who perform for tourists.

B. ISLAMIC CIVILIZATION

1. Sinbad the Sailor. Sinbad was not merely a sailor. He was a merchant who went on seven voyages and in the process of fantastic adventures became rich. His story is a part of the *Arabian Nights* tales, but it is also an example of the life of a Muslim traveling merchant. The fantasy starts when Sinbad leaves his home in Baghdad to sail out into the world. The ship stops at what seems to be an island covered with plants, but it is really a whale that dives, leaving Sinbad to swim for his life. He survives and becomes a great favorite of the local king. He later finds his old ship and returns home enriched by generous gifts from the king.

On his second voyage, Sinbad meets a rok, a huge bird that carries him to a valley littered with diamonds. Sinbad manages to escape the valley with many diamonds and to return home. On Sinbad's third voyage, his ship is attacked by apes, and he and the crew are held captive by a man-eating giant. On his fourth voyage, Sinbad is captured by cannibals but escapes and becomes rich by teaching the native people how to make saddles and bridles. This leads to his marriage to a rich and beautiful woman. When she dies, he is horrified to learn that he is to be buried alive with her. He finds his grave full of treasure and again escapes, even richer than before.

In his fifth voyage, Sinbad is captured and ridden like a horse by an evil old man. On his sixth voyage, Sinbad is shipwrecked on an island of jewels and escapes by floating down an underground river. On Sinbad's seventh voyage, his ship is eaten by a sea monster, but Sinbad escapes and makes a raft. When he is washed ashore, he discovers his raft is made of precious sandalwood and once again he makes a handsome profit.

All these adventures reflect the fact that Muslim merchants traveled by sea over long distances. They engaged in an active trade with India, the east coast of Africa, and even islands in the East Indies. Scholars think that the Sinbad stories are exaggerations of actual experiences of these adventurous Muslim merchants.

2. Arabs and Coffee. The Arabs began to use coffee as a drink about A.D. 1000. At first this had religious values. A legend says that a dervish named Omar discovered coffee as a religious experience. While in exile in the desert, Omar had a vision of his dead mentor. Omar was shown the coffee tree; he picked the fruit and roasted the seeds. He used water to soften the seeds, but this failed, so he drank the resulting fluid. This gave him a feeling of energy and well-being, which he took as a sign from God.

Coffee spread rapidly through the Arab world as a religious drink. Then it became considered a medicine, prescribed by doctors.

Later, coffee lost its religious association and became a drink for social events. Coffee houses opened in Mecca and became centers of music, gambling, and discussion. The discussion ranged over religious, social, and political topics that sometimes encouraged revolt. The governments tried to shut down coffee houses three times in the 16th century but failed.

Coffee was the Arab beverage of choice. Muslims were forbidden wine, and no other drink was as satisfying as coffee. Eventually coffee became a part of social life at home. In Turkey it became so important that a woman could divorce a man who failed to supply her with coffee. Coffee remains an important part of Islamic culture today.

3. Algebra. As Islam spread, it was influenced by many cultural traditions. Muslim scholars studied the ideas of these cultures. For example, Muslims became experts on mathematics. They studied Greek works and solved new problems like cubic equations. Al Khwarizmi wrote a book called *The Rules of Restoration and*

Reduction. In it the unknown, today called *x,* was called *shai,* "the thing." Europeans learned about this book, and it became their main source of information on equations. They named such study after a part of the Arabic title, *al jabr,* or algebra.

4. Assassin. The word *assassin* comes from the name of a sect of Shiite Muslims centered in Persia and Iraq and lasting from roughly 1090 to 1273. Their most famous leader was called Old Man of the Mountains. He had agents and terrorists in the cities and camps of his enemies. Outsiders believed that the Old Man of the Mountains drugged selected followers and sent them off to kill his enemies. These followers were given hashish and then taken to a beautiful garden with pretty girls and other pleasures. When they returned, they were told that this was a preview of the paradise that awaited them if they died while trying to kill an enemy. These hashish-motivated killers were called *hashshashin,* "eaters of hashish." The sect became known as Assassins, and the word *assassin* became associated with any political murder. This story comes from sources outside the sect, so it may be a creation of the sect's enemies.

5. Women in Islam. Liberal Muslims argue that Islam resulted in an improvement in the status of women compared with the earlier Arab pagan societies. Polygamy was common before Muhammad. The Koran limited the number of wives to four and stressed that they should be treated equally. Women gained the right to inherit property and to own and dispose of property. A woman could even get a divorce if her husband did not perform his duties.

The life of Muhammad seems to set an example of respect for women. His first wife, Khadija, was running a business when she hired Muhammad; obviously she was not a secluded woman. She was also Muhammad's only wife as long as she lived. Later the prophet married several wives. These were political marriages or efforts to protect Muslim women from nonbelievers. Muhammad was a kind, considerate husband who treated his wives equally.

About two centuries after Muhammad, however, Islamic lands began to require women to wear a veil and to remain secluded in their homes.

6. Muhammad and Toleration. Muhammad himself started a tradition of toleration for Christians and Jews. He did not require them to convert. If they wished to keep their faith, they were charged a tax.

7. Turkey and Janissaries. Christians were tolerated by the sultans of Turkey, but at a price. Every three to five years the sultan would place a tax on the Christians, payable in children. He would take unmarried males between the ages of eight and twenty and make them his personal slaves. These boys would be trained in the Turkish language, Islam, and military skills. They would become Janissaries, the sultan's personal slaves and an elite fighting force. They were not permitted to marry or conduct business. Their job was to be ready to fight for the sultan. Often Janissaries became important officials. As a group they were feared and respected. They were the core of the Turkish army when it went to war.

8. Muhammad in Art. Muslim artists will not depict Muhammad's face in their pictures. When the Prophet is shown, his face is veiled or simply black.

9. One Hundred Names for God. Muslims say the Koran uses 99 names for God. A legend says the camel looks so smug because it knows a hundredth.

CHAPTER VIII

Africa and Latin America

— Overview —

Africa and Latin America have in common the fact that historians still are working on the basic outline of their histories. For years African history suffered from racist attitudes that said the story of Africa began when the Europeans arrived. Research in the last half of the 20th century has shown that idea was wrong, but we still have a way to go before the full story is uncovered. Latin America was discovered as a field for historic research a bit earlier than Africa, but historians are still working on completing the story. Some now report that they can read Mayan writing.

You may want to have your students search for recent breakthroughs in African and Latin American history. They could be the basis for papers or reports. The Benin masks are striking, and an artistic student could make a bulletin board about them. A map marked with the location of each culture would make a good bulletin board. Perhaps there is room to put a time line of these cultures next to the map. There are many possibilities for creative papers: "My Visit to Benin," "My Visit to the Swahili Coast," "A Sportswriter's Report on a Mayan Basketball Game," "Eating Aztec: A Restaurant Review," "My Journey Through the Inca Empire."

A. AFRICA

1. Africa's Size. In dealing with African history, it's important to remember the size of the continent. Africa is three times as big as the United States, including Alaska and Hawaii. In spite of this huge size, Africa's coastline is relatively very short and has few good harbors. While Africa's land mass is larger than Europe's, the African coastline is actually shorter than the European coastline.

2. The Sahara. The Sahara was not always a dry area. A group of 800 Stone Age paintings was found on the walls of a cave on Algeria's Tassili Plateau by a French explorer in 1956. They show giraffes, elephants, horses, and wild spotted oxen living on the Sahara. The people in the pictures are making a ritual sacrifice of a sheep. The people were cattle herders and gathered wild grain. Pictures show them playing musical instruments and dancing. Women are shown doing many tasks—tending cattle, raising children, and making baskets and pottery, as well as gathering and preparing food. The men hunted with bows and arrows and made stone tools. When the group traveled, the women rode oxen.

3. The Benin Bronzes. Tradition says the artists of Benin learned to make bronze masks from the artisans of the nearby city of Ife. The bronze casters of Benin developed the art further and left us an impressive collection of material. When Europeans discovered these works, they fascinated artists like Pablo Picasso, who copied their style in some of his paintings.

This is how the Benin artists did their lost-wax castings. The artist started with a piece of clay, shaping it into a head. This was smoothed with a stick shaped like a knife. After the head was smooth, melted wax was poured over it and smoothed with the same stick. Then pieces of wax were added and shaped like hair, ears, and nose. Once the face was done it was covered with mud, leaving one hole. The work was then left in the sun to dry.

After the mud had dried, probably several days after the head was made, it was time to prepare for pouring the metal. The artist built a charcoal fire and placed a pot of water over it with the figure over the pot. As the head got hot, the wax melted and dripped into the water. When all the wax was melted out, the mud mold was placed into the fire and heated until it was red hot. Using sticks or tongs, the mold was then taken off the fire and buried in a hole in the ground with the hole in the mold facing up.

Meanwhile, the artist had been melting copper, zinc, and lead in a pot buried in the charcoal fire. Now the hole in the mold was cleared, and the liquid metal was poured in until it filled the mold. The work was set aside to cool, and later the baked mud was broken away, leaving the finished work.

4. Iron Smelting. Africa has a tradition of smelting iron that goes back to the seventh century B.C. Recently anthropologists have reconstructed early iron-smelting technology, helped by the fact that some Africans continued to use these ancient techniques into the 20th century. One method used a tall furnace made of clay bricks and plaster. The builders put clay pipes at the base of the furnace to provide oxygen to the charcoal fire. Inside the furnace was a pile of iron ore, which was found in the area. The smelters raised the temperature in the furnace to 1150°F and melted out the unwanted minerals. They carefully kept the temperature below 1540°F so the iron would not melt. Such precise regulation of heat is very difficult. Once the process was done, the result was a sponge of iron with holes where the impurities in the ore had melted out. The iron smelters then took this "sponge" and worked it to further remove impurities.

5. Coffee. African people were the first to consume coffee. They took the berries from the wild coffee tree, mixed them with animal fat, and rolled the mix into a ball. The food was excellent for traveling war parties. Coffee berries have a high protein content and contain caffeine, which kept the warriors awake. The animal fat was a source of highly concentrated calories as well. Some modern research even shows that caffeine helps the body use fat for energy more easily.

6. Benin's Special Woman. The ruler of Benin was a powerful king. One of his older female relatives, usually his mother, also lived in special honor. Her position was unique. She lived in a special palace near the king and was the only person permitted to wear certain types of clothes. There was, for example, a sort of cone-shaped hat only she could wear.

7. The Talking Drums. One of the clichés of old movies is the African telegraph, the talking drums. The Ashanti and some other West African peoples actually did develop a way of sending messages with drums. The system was made possible by a feature of the people's language. They spoke a language that used tone and accented syllables to make words. In Congolese, for example, the words *fiancée* and *rubbish heap* are made up of the same letters. The tone and accent make the difference. African peoples developed drums that had a high and low tone and could be accented by the players' beat. The possibility still existed that short words would sound alike and be misunderstood, so the drummers worked out a way of clarifying. They added a second phrase to describe the item. People who spoke the language and knew the phrases understood. "Leopard" was not just sent as "leopard," but as "leopard, he tears off the roof." This was a reference to the hunting leopard tearing off the roof to get at animals put in sheds for the night.

The sound of the drums could carry for miles, and drummers passed on messages. So messages could be transmitted for great distances by the talking drums.

8. The Swahili Coast. The Africans were there first, but the Muslims named it. Before the Arabs came, there were African settlements along the east coast of Africa. When the Arab traders found this coast, they called it *Suahil,* Arabic for *coast.* We call it the Swahili coast. The Muslims converted many Africans and served to link the Swahili coast with a wider world. The trade reached out to Arabia, India, Ceylon, and China. The Africans carried the trade inland to get gold, ivory, and other goods. Their Bantu language with some Arabic vocabulary added became Swahili, still used by many people in East Africa as a common language.

Forty cities were engaged in the active trade of the Swahili coast. They would thrive until the Europeans came.

B. Mexico and Central America

1. Mayan Trade. The Mayan city-states traded some products; among them were salt, jade, cotton clothing, slaves, honey, and cocoa beans. Only the wealthy could afford to drink cocoa, but the poor used the beans as a sort of money. There is even some evidence of counterfeiting. The counterfeiters removed the beans' skins and glued them over stuffings of wax or avocado rind.

2. The Zapotecs: Monte Albán. Interpreting the archaeological remains of the early Indians is not always easy. There is, for example, the case of "the dancers" of Monte Albán. This is a site near the city of Oaxaca in southern Mexico. Monte Albán was the capital city of the Zapotec Indian empire. The dancers are a series of human figures cut into a stone wall. They are shown in a variety of postures— squatting, kneeling, and some with arms over their heads. At first the figures were thought to be a set of drawings of people dancing. Later interpreters noticed that the figures' eyes were closed and their mouths open. Perhaps they were people who had been killed by their enemies, probably captured rulers. More recently still, doctors have examined the drawings and noticed that many of the figures show recognizable symptoms. One report says a doctor recognized six well-known medical conditions in a twenty-minute tour of the dancers. Could it be that this is some kind of ancient Indian medical textbook? Was this the site of some kind of hospital or medical school? The mystery remains.

3. Central American Basketball. Both the Mayans and the Aztecs played a game that involved shoving a ball through a hoop. The game differed from basketball in several ways. Archaeologists believe it had religious significance. Skeptics say that archaeologists always think that when they can't explain something. The ball was solid rubber. The rubber tree is native to Latin America, and the Indians knew how to gather the sap and cure it into rubber. The hoops were stone disks with holes in the middle. They were mounted on a solid stone wall with the hole facing sideways. There were two of these hoops, one in the middle of the wall on each side of the court. The center of the court was level, but a sloping ramp as wide as the wall ran up almost to the hoops. Pictures show that the players wore protective pads. The Aztec rules said that players could not touch the ball with their hands. This would make the game a mix of soccer and basketball. The Mayan rules are not known.

4. The Aztecs: The Eagle and the Snake. A legend tells how the Aztecs chose the location of the capital, Tenochtitlán. In Aztec the name means "place of cactus in the rock." The Aztecs believed that they would settle where they found an eagle with a snake in its beak. The legend says they found the eagle and snake perched on an island in a lake. The Aztecs built their capital there. The city was where Mexico City is today, and together the eagle and snake are the national symbol of Mexico.

5. The Aztecs and *Xocoatl* (Chocolate). When the Spanish arrived in Mexico, they found that the top Aztec leaders drank a strange liquid concoction "all frothed up." This was *xocoatl* or, as we know it, chocolate. The Aztecs did not grow the plant chocolate was made from, but got cocoa beans from other tribes as tribute. The drink was made by mixing cocoa beans, vanilla, honey, and red pepper. When Montezuma, the Aztec ruler, dined, he drank this beverage from a cup of pure gold. One Spaniard reports seeing more than 2,000 large jugs of chocolate served at one meal.

This exotic new drink was taken to Spain in 1528, and later became known in France and England.

6. Aztec Women. Some Aztec women wore makeup, but these women were not respectable. There was a yellow cream for the skin and red dye for teeth. In one document a father advised his daughter not to wear makeup because those who did were shameless. It was better to dress well and have clean clothes and a clean body.

Women were married at age 16. In the wedding ceremony, they literally tied the knot; the bride's blouse was tied to the groom's cloak. While the wife had some rights to own property, she could be easily divorced for being sterile. The Aztecs, after all, needed children for their armies.

Once married, Aztec women spent much of their time processing corn into tortillas and tamales. They also wove cloth and did fieldwork.

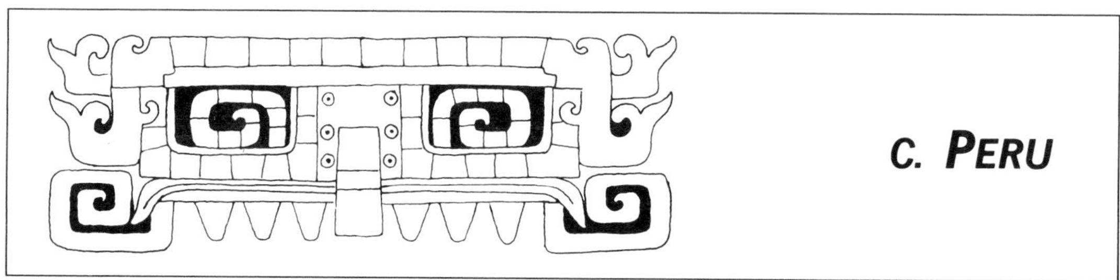

C. Peru

1. **Pre-Inca Canal.** The Chimu Indians farmed an area in Peru that was so dry they had to depend entirely on irrigation. They built a system of canals that carried water as far as 50 miles. In order to do this, they developed devices for surveying and designed canals with that same cross-sectional shape that modern engineers recognize as most efficient, a half hexagon. The Chimu were conquered by the Incas in about 1450. By this time they had kept their irrigation system operating for 500 years.

2. **Inca Runners.** The Incas had a system of runners to relay information. Since the Incas did not have a system of writing, the runners carried oral messages. They also carried *quipus*, the Inca way of keeping records. A quipu was a cord with knotted, colored strings attached. The quipus had to be interpreted by someone who knew the code of knots. The runners each ran a 2-mile part of the route, night or day. The message traveled at a rate of 150 miles a day.

3. **The Llama.** The llama was an important animal to the Incas. A llama could be a pack animal, carrying about 80 pounds 12 miles a day. Its fleece was a source of wool needed on cold mountains, and its manure was used as either fertilizer or fuel. Llama meat could be cooked fresh or dried and stored. The llama's milk was also consumed.

4. **Guinea Pigs.** The guinea pig was a native of Peru. These little furry rodents were raised by the Incas as a source of meat.

5. **Inca Stonecutters.** Inca buildings were often made of stones. Although the stones were irregular in shape, they were fitted together very closely. How could this be done? Archaeologists believe that Inca stonecutters used clay models to help get the shapes right. They cut the stones by drilling holes, and then wedged the stone to split it. They worked with stone tools, hammers, and axes. They also had bronze chisels. They used sand and water to grind and polish the stone.

6. **Bridges.** The Inca Empire spread across the Andes Mountains and was chopped up by river gorges. The Incas built suspension bridges over these rivers using ropes. They also directed that the villagers who lived near each bridge keep it

maintained. This was part of the Inca tax system. Some villages kept up the tradition after the Incas were conquered by the Spaniards.

7. Skull Surgery. Inca soldiers carried slings and a variety of crushing weapons. They had a mace shaped like a star that bashed nasty wounds in the skull. Inca surgeons treated these wounds by cutting away part of the skull with saws, drills, and chisels. Historians report that some patients survived the treatment.

8. Boats. The Incas were not sailors and had little interest in sailing. They did have rafts made of balsa logs lashed together. The logs came from modern Ecuador, which was outside the area of Inca rule. The sail was square, and the raft included a deckhouse with a palm-leaf roof. Food was cooked on a fireplace built behind the deckhouse.

The only other Inca boat was built of bundles of a reed that grows eight feet high and half an inch in diameter. These reeds were tied into bundles and the bundles tied together into small boats. These were used along the coast and in lakes in the Andes Mountains. The reed boats were usually very small, holding no more than three people. The Incas also used boats as pontoons to support some bridges.

9. *Kon-Tiki*. In 1947, an adventurer named Thor Heyerdahl built a raft of balsa logs and tried to float across the Pacific. He named the craft *Kon-Tiki* after an Inca god. He hoped to prove by his voyage that it was possible for the Indians of Peru to sail to the islands of the Pacific. At the time, many experts predicted the logs would become waterlogged and sink. Heyerdahl recruited a crew of five. They were at sea during May, June, and July, and kept in touch with their backup by radio. After 101 days of sailing, the raft washed up on a coral reef near an island in Polynesia. Heyerdahl had proved that a balsa raft could cross the Pacific. He wrote a book about the expedition called *Kon-Tiki,* which was very popular. Skeptical anthropologists point out that this only proves that such a trip was possible, not that it ever in fact happened.

10. Inca Food. The Incas had a number of foods that Europeans had never tasted. Corn was popular, but it only grew in the lower parts of the empire. Corn was eaten in religious ceremonies and made into a type of beer.

Potatoes grew farther up the mountains. The Incas made dehydrated potatoes by leaving small potatoes out at night to freeze. Next, the men and women smashed the water out by stepping on the potatoes, and then spread them to dry. Meal made by grinding the dried potatoes would keep a long time. The Incas added water before eating this.

The Incas also had other foods strange to Europeans: squash, sweet potatoes, manioc, peanuts, pineapple, papaya, and avocado.

CHAPTER IX

Medieval Europe

— Overview —

Even the name is a put-down: "The Middle Ages" or "The Age Between," suggesting that something great happened before and after, but in the middle, nothing. Certainly the Middle Ages produced no great, lasting empires and relatively few great books. People were scrambling to survive. In the process they became converts to Christianity and built the material base for European culture. The political history is a series of chaotic wars. Yet some legends like Robin Hood survive and charm us still. Some buildings survive too. Medieval cathedrals and castles are on the intinerary of most tourists in Europe. The people who produced these buildings deserve careful study.

You can send out your students to find buildings influenced by medieval designs. Hint: Many churches have a Gothic look derived from the Middle Ages.

Artistic students can do bulletin boards on "Coats of Arms," "Medieval Churches," "The Medieval Knight," or "The Vikings." The imaginative student can write up "My Visit to the Middle Ages." Mark Twain's *A Connecticut Yankee in King Arthur's Court* shows what can be done with this idea.

A. The Spread of Christianity

1. Saint Patrick. The Irish have adopted Saint Patrick as their patron saint and celebrate his day with parades. They tell the story of how Patrick converted the Irish to Christianity. Tradition says he was once arguing with an Irish chieftain. The chieftain challenged him to explain if the trinity was one or three gods. Saint Patrick picked a shamrock and asked the chieftain if it had one or three leaves. When the chieftain admitted he could not tell, the saint asked him why he should ask for an explanation of the trinity when he couldn't explain a simple leaf. Legend also says Saint Patrick drove all the snakes out of Ireland.

Historians view these stories as legends, not historical facts. There is evidence that there was a Saint Patrick. He wrote two documents that survive, a confession and a letter. But after that the evidence is confused. Some believe he went to Ireland in A.D. 432, but others dispute that date. Some even maintain that the stories are a mixing together of the lives of two or even three Saint Patricks. These scholarly disputes show the problems of researching the history of an age when there were few written records.

2. The Russians Become Christian. Some time between 986 and 989 Vladimir, a ruler of Kiev, made the decision that his kingdom would be converted to the Eastern Orthodox Christian faith. The traditional story of his conversion says that Vladimir considered a variety of faiths before he made his choice. First, he was approached by representatives of Judaism. But when he found that the Jews had been scattered from their homeland, he rejected that faith. Muslim missionaries told Vladimir that after death each man would have 70 women. As appealing as that idea was to the lusty Vladimir, he rejected Islam because Muslims must not drink alcoholic beverages. He did not believe Russians could live without drinking. The choice was now narrowed down to Christianity of either the Roman Catholic or Eastern Orthodox variety. Vladimir sent representatives to see what each religion was like. The people he sent to Germany reported that the Roman Catholic churches there had "no glory." The visitors to Hagia Sophia in Constantinople were at a loss to describe this church's splendor and beauty. Vladimir became an enthusiastic convert to Eastern Orthodox Christianity and forced his people to join him.

3. The Conversion of Clovis. Clovis was a warrior king of the Franks and a pagan. He worshipped the old Roman gods, Jupiter, Mars, and Mercury. Even after he married Clotilda, a Christian woman who insisted on baptizing their sons, he refused to believe in the Christian God. He argued that his wife's God could do nothing.

His wife continued to pray for him. Then in the middle of a battle against the Alamanni, Clovis found his troops being slaughtered, He called upon Jesus and pledged he would be baptized if he were saved from his enemies. Even while he was praying, the Alamanni began to run away. Their king had been killed, so they surrendered to Clovis. The queen quickly called in Remigius, bishop of Rheims and later a saint, to instruct Clovis in Christianity. Clovis became a convert and his people were all converted as well. Clovis and 3,000 of his men were baptized on the same day in the year 496.

B. CHARLEMAGNE

1. Crowned Emperor. The pope crowned Charlemagne Emperor of the Romans on December 25, A.D. 800. It was evidently something Charlemagne did not want to happen. Einhard, his friend and biographer, says Charlemagne declared that he would not have gone into the church on that day if he had known the pope's intentions.

2. Illiterate? Textbooks often call Charlemagne illiterate. This really doesn't do him justice, although it is technically correct. Charlemagne studied a number of foreign languages and could speak Latin like a native. He understood Greek, but could not speak it well. He studied astronomy and learned some arithmetic. He never learned to write, but kept writing materials under his pillow so he could practice. Perhaps he was too sound a sleeper, or more likely, as Einhard says, he started this study too late in life.

3. Einhard, Biographer. We are very lucky to have a reliable firsthand report of Charlemagne's life by one who knew him. This is the little book, about 50 pages, called *The Life of Charlemagne* by Einhard. Einhard served several years in Charlemagne's court, so he observed the great man directly.

C. VIKINGS

1. Raids. The first documented Viking raid was in 793 on a monastery on the island of Lindisfarne off the coast of England. The Vikings seemed to like raiding monasteries, probably because that was where the good loot was. Being pagans, they saw golden crosses as simply gold. They also captured the nuns and monks for sale into slavery.

The Viking raiders came by boat, but they reached far inland because they could row their boats upriver. One of their most famous raids was on Paris. They also entered the Mediterranean Sea and raided the southern coasts of Europe. They could carry horses on their ships, so they could also ride horses away from their beached ships to make attacks.

The Viking warriors wore a conical helmet with a nose guard. The helmet did not include horns, as often shown in cartoons. The Vikings carried swords, javelins, lances, and axes for attack. For protection they carried large wooden shields.

Sometimes Vikings would permit their victims to buy them off. In 991 Olaf Triggvason led 93 ships to England and was paid £10,000 not to attack. Later the tribute became more expensive. In 994 it cost £16,000, in 1002 it was £24,000, in 1007 it was £36,000, and by 1012 it was £48,000.

Teacher Note: The question of how much £10,000 in 991 would equal in today's money is very difficult. The pound is still the official currency in Britain. As of April 24, 1992, it listed as worth $1.7725, but that number varies with the foreign exchange market. Of course, a thousand years of inflation has shrunk the purchasing power of the pound. The dollar would not appear for many centuries after 991, and it too has suffered from inflation.

Usually the best way to compare values is to use purchasing power. What would $10,000 buy in 991? Clearly it couldn't buy a TV set, a tomato, or a chocolate bar, because all these were unknown in Europe in 991. Perhaps comparing the price of bread would help, but the Vikings didn't buy bread in stores as we do. In short, their way of life was so different from ours that comparisons are very hard to make.

It seems the one safe statement based on the tribute figures is that the tribute payments got bigger each time. This assumes that they grew faster than inflation.

2. Food and Drink Viking bread was made of unleavened, coarsely ground barley, although the rich ate white wheat bread. There was so much grit in the ordinary bread that it wore down the Vikings' teeth. Meat and fish were also a major part of the diet. The Vikings drank beer or mead from cattle horns. Once filled, a horn cannot be put down, so the horns must have been passed around until they were empty. As a result, Vikings probably got drunk very quickly at their feasts.

3. Travels. The Vikings traveled for long distances by ship. Although we are not able to establish how they navigated when out of sight of land with no compass, they did make such journeys. The most famous such trip was to "Vinland," a place now identified as the coast of North America. Vikings established a colony briefly in Vinland. They also settled on Greenland and Iceland. In those days the climate was warmer. These voyages are documented by sagas, oral traditions written down later. In 1965, a map of Vinland was discovered and dated roughly 1440. Later analysis showed that the map's ink contained a pigment first made in 1917. This clearly established that the map was a fraud. We do have physical evidence of other Viking travels. Archaeologists have found a bronze Buddha in Sweden. It could have come from northern India, Kashmir, or Afghanistan. Archaeologists have also found Arabic glass and a Persian glazed cup in Scandinavia.

4. Boat Reconstruction. Archaeologists have been able to dig up a number of Viking boats. Some were boats in which a person was buried with his or her possessions. A group of boats sunk in a harbor mouth to protect the town has been raised and studied. The boats are made of wood with relatively thin hulls, as little as an inch thick. The keel and outer shell were built first, then cross braces were added.

Viking boats used both sail power and oar power. Sails were square or rectangular, and the boats may have been able to sail into the wind. Dimensions vary, but in general merchant ships were four times as long as wide, and warships were slimmer, seven times as long as wide. A fering, a small boat carried by another ship, was 21 feet 4 inches long by 4 feet 7 inches wide. One has been reconstructed and can do ten knots per hour. The size of Viking long ships—that is, warships—varies. One of these is 59 feet 1 inch long and 8 feet 6 inches wide, while another is 92 feet long and 14 feet 9 inches wide. A trader measures 53 feet 6 inches long and 15 feet wide.

Great interest has developed in building and sailing modern reconstructions of Viking ships. In 1893, a ship named *Viking* crossed the Atlantic from Bergen, Norway, to Newfoundland in 28 days. It was exhibited at the Chicago World's Fair and is now on display in a park in Chicago.

5. Baths. Most medieval Europeans had little idea of cleanliness. The Vikings, however, had a tradition of bathing once a week. Hosts were expected to meet a guest with water and a towel.

D. Life on a Manor

1. Size of Fields. When working to determine the amount of land a medieval peasant farmed, historians have few records, and of course a typical field in one area could be much different from that in another. Some historians do offer rough numbers. In a European province called Brabant, the fields varied from 20 to 37½ acres. In France, the size varied from 12½ to 45 acres, with the average being about 32½ acres. In general, each family had to farm enough land to feed and clothe the family for a year and pay the feudal rents.

Teacher Note: For comparison, a typical Iowa farm in the 1990's is over 200 acres. An acre is 43,560 square feet. You may want to ask your students to name an area that measures an acre. A football field from goal line to goal line is 45,000 square feet, just a bit more than an acre. From the 5-yard line on one side to the goal at the other end is 43,500 square feet. Four typical city blocks total about a quarter of a mile. A square that measures one quarter of a mile on each side is 40 acres.

2. Farm Efficiency. Medieval farmers seem to have been more efficient than ancient farmers. The medieval farmer had a three-crop rotation system, letting a field lie fallow every third year. The ancient farmer let the field lie fallow every other year. Thus the medieval farmer had two thirds of the land in production, while the ancient farmer had half the land in production.

The ancient farmer used oxen or horses to plow the field. The medieval farmer got more out of the horse. First, the style of horse collar changed from the ancient ox yoke, which choked the horse, to a collar resting on the animal's shoulders. This made the horse up to five times as efficient. The horseshoe was also used, so the horse was less likely to split a hoof or otherwise be disabled. Besides this, medieval horses were bred to be larger to carry knights. Farm horses presumably also became larger and stronger.

The medieval plow was more efficient than the ancient plow. The ancient farmer had simply cut down a tree crotch and let it season through the winter. Plowing consisted of dragging this sharpened stick through the ground, making a groove, then plowing again going across the grooves. The medieval plow was a large, complicated device with wheels, a frame, and a moldboard blade that turned over the soil. With such a plow the farmer only needed to plow once. The plow was very hard to turn around, however. This seems to be the most convincing reason why medieval fields were made long and narrow.

E. Noble Life

1. Stirrups. The medieval knight was first of all a cavalryman. His code of life was *chivalry,* a word that stems from the French word for *horse.* His primary way of attacking was to ride toward the enemy and puncture him with a lance. But the ancient soldiers had mostly fought on foot or in chariots. Why did the medieval soldier find it so desirable to ride a horse?

One of the more convincing explanations is that medieval people had stirrups and ancient people did not. A person sitting on a horse without stirrups is not solidly on the horse. If such a rider takes a swing with a sword and gets a little off balance, the rider slides to the ground. Stirrups prevent this. Statues and pictures of ancient people on horseback do not show stirrups. Medieval pictures and statues done after 750 show stirrups.

This is also the time when armies seem to have been converting to cavalry. Charlemagne and his father Pepin, for example, encouraged their Frankish warriors to fight as cavalry. The tradition among the Franks was that every able-bodied male should report to the king if called to war. Charlemagne and Pepin urged them to come on horseback. Horses were very expensive items in those days, so Charlemagne and Pepin encouraged people to form groups, pooling their wealth and sending in one cavalryman. Why were Charlemagne and Pepin willing to have fewer men? Perhaps because they were more effective on horseback thanks to the new development, stirrups.

Archaeologists have tried to trace the development and spread of stirrups. It seems they developed in Asia and came to Europe in the early Middle Ages. Wherever they came from, they had a significant impact on the history of the world.

2. Easter Eggs. Medieval serfs paid for the privilege of working the lord's land by sharing the produce. They also were required to donate labor to the maintenance of the manor. If a serf went into the woods to gather firewood, half the wood was given to the manor house. When the crop was harvested, the lord got a share. In the spring when the chickens began laying, the lord was entitled to some eggs. This may be the origin of the tradition of Easter eggs.

3. Pages as Servants. The medieval custom of sending sons off to the houses of other noble families has left its mark on our language. These pages were expected to work about the house as servants and thus learn manners. Page boys were the waiters at the crude feasts held by medieval nobles. Even into the 20th century waiters were often called "boy." Many other serving jobs also used the word, such as "bellboy" and "busboy." French shows a similar pattern. For instance, the French word for "waiter" is *garçon,* which is also the word for "boy."

4. Blackbird Pie. A familiar nursery rhyme describes a medieval joke. The humor involved is not very subtle. The rhyme runs, "Four and twenty blackbirds baked in a pie. When the pie was opened, the birds began to sing. Wasn't that a dainty dish to set before the king?" Imagine the scene as the king is sitting at his banquet table and the pie is served. As it is cut open, not only do the birds sing, but also some fly out and flit around the room. Perhaps some dogs in the room become excited and begin barking. Servants may run around trying to catch the birds and shoo them outdoors.

5. The Clydesdale. The medieval knight was a deadly fighting machine. Heavily armored, carrying a long lance and sword, he was well protected and capable of cutting down his foes. He was also a terrible load for his horse. A coat of armor plus the lance and sword would add around 60 pounds to his weight. Such a load made the knight awkward. We have medieval drawings of knights being hoisted into the air by a block and tackle so the horses can be led under them. Once the knight was on the horse, the beast had better be sturdy enough to carry the man for a full day of battle.

In the Clyde Valley in Scotland, horse breeders developed a large, spirited animal to carry Scottish knights into battle. Later, some stallions were imported from Flanders. The result was the modern Clydesdale. In the 19th century, these large animals were used to pull heavy loads like brewery wagons, but their brisk gait and prancing feet recalled the days when their ancestors trotted forth with colorful armored warriors on their backs.

6. Medicine. In medieval Europe, medical treatment was hazardous to your health. One of the best treatments for a battlefield wound was called "weapon ointment." The doctor got the weapon that had inflicted the wound and put the ointment on the weapon rather than on the wound. This produced a better-than-average recovery rate, because putting the ointment on the wound would cause infection, while "weapon ointment" left the wound relatively clean.

7. Frederick II and Falcons. Frederick II ruled a complex collection of territories including the Holy Roman Empire and the Kingdom of Sicily. Yet for all his royal duties he still took time to study animals and falconry. Frederick collected a menagerie including elephants, dromedaries, camels, panthers, lions, leopards, gerfalcons, white falcons, bearded owls, and monkeys. He even had a giraffe, the first ever seen in Europe.

But Frederick's first love was the study and training of falcons, birds of prey trained to hunt. He was so devoted to falcons that once he lost a battle because he spent a day in sport with his birds when he should have been pressing the siege of a fortress. Many medieval nobles were devoted to hawking, but Frederick II also wrote a book about the sport. In this book, he draws on a vast knowledge of hawks to describe their care and training. He was educated enough to be familiar with the writing of Aristotle, and he knew enough about hawks to realize that Aristotle was not always accurate.

Some of his advice on birds dealt with how and when to catch them. He said that young birds should be taken from the nest as late as possible. They should be nearly full grown, because their parents know best how to feed the young birds. In capturing the young birds the greatest care should be taken not to harm them. They should then be kept in a place as much like the nest as possible, and fed food as nearly like what the parents would give them as possible. Frederick favored feeding young falcons the flesh of birds or fresh meat, about 9:00 A.M. He went into great detail on training falcons and discussed how they should be carried. He said it is best to carry them on either hand so they can face into the wind and not have their feathers ruffled. The handler must, of course, wear heavy leather gloves.

Scholars seem sure that Frederick either dictated his book or wrote it with his own hand. In an age when most people were illiterate, this was a major achievement. The book is over 400 pages long in English translation. Frederick probably wrote it between 1244 and 1250, a very busy time in his life.

8. The Crossbow in Europe. The crossbow, a bow mounted across a stock, was a weapon deadly against knights. We're not entirely sure when the crossbow came to Europe. It may have been used by the Romans. If they didn't use the hand-carried type, they certainly did use large versions as siege weapons. Evidence of Europeans using the crossbow came after the year A.D. 1000. In 1086 the Domesday Book listed a person known as Odo the Arbalester. *Arbalest* is another word for *crossbow*. Richard the Lion-Hearted, king of England, used crossbows in his armies during the Crusades. In fact, Richard was killed by a crossbow bolt. In 1139, the Second Lateran Council banned the use of crossbows except against infidels.

9. The Crossbow: Power and Range. The crossbow could kill a knight while the knight was some distance away. Around 1906, an interested sportsman did a few tests of a crossbow that had been made 400 years before in Genoa. He reported that the weapon had a range of 460 yards. That's four football fields, roughly a quarter of a mile. As for penetration, at 60 yards the crossbow sent a bolt right through a three-quarter-inch yellow pine plank. When the sportsman tested the weight needed to pull the bow, he found it took 1,200 pounds. That's over half a ton.

F. The Crusades

1. Crusader Burial. In England it was the custom to bury the noble dead in their local church with a brass engraving of their likeness over the spot. The graves of nobles who had gone on Crusade are easy to identify. Those knights are shown with their legs crossed.

2. Robin Hood. When King Richard the Lion-Hearted went off to the Crusades, he left his kingdom in the hands of his brother John. John, alas, became a tyrant. Among the people resisting John was an outlaw named Robin Hood, who lived in Sherwood Forest. Robin was deadly with a longbow, and killed the king's deer. There really was a Robin Hood, and the few facts above are the historical basis for all the stories, movies, and TV shows about Robin Hood. The rest of the story, as usually told, seems to be fiction. A pamphlet was issued in Nottingham saying that Robin's love, the maid Marian, and his friend, Friar Tuck, are mythical. This modern attempt to tell the story accurately has been opposed by today's sheriff of Nottingham, who wants to keep alive the medieval myth of Robin Hood.

G. Medieval Economics

1. A Just Price. In the Middle Ages, people believed there was a just price for a product. This price was fair, and trying to pay more or less was sinful. The following story about St. Gerald of Aurillac shows this attitude being carried to the extreme. St. Gerald was returning from a pilgrimage to Rome and met some Venetian merchants at Pavia. They tried to sell him some spices and other items from the East. He in turn showed them a fine cloak he had bought in Rome. When he mentioned the price he paid, they congratulated him, saying the cloak would cost much more in Constantinople. Gerald, feeling he had paid too little, sent more money to the merchant who had sold him the cloak. He felt that he had to do this or be guilty of the sin of avarice.

2. Coffee in Europe. As Europe began to trade with the East, coffee made its appearance in Europe. Some priests argued it was the work of the Devil. Satan had made coffee as a substitute for wine. Wine was a drink sanctified by Christ and used in the eucharist. Muslim infidels, on the other hand, drank coffee. Such arguments almost kept coffee out of Europe, but Pope Clement VIII sampled some coffee and approved its use by Christians.

3. Population of Medieval Cities. By modern standards, medieval cities were quite small. Nuremburg in 1450 had only 20,165 people. Frankfurt in 1440 had a mere 8,719. Basel about 1450 had approximately 8,000. Fribourg in Switzerland in 1444 had 5,200. Strassburg around 1475 had 26,198. In the mid-15th century, Louvain had 25,000 and Brussels 40,000. These were all trading towns in northern Europe.

4. The Journeyman. The medieval crafts had a regular system. A young person started as an apprentice, then became a journeyman, later a master. The word *journeyman* comes from the French word for day, *jour.* A journeyman was a man who worked and was paid by the day. Some textbooks tell it differently, but check it out in *Webster's Ninth New Collegiate Dictionary.*

5. A Medieval Airplane. Medieval people developed a number of inventions to use energy from sources other than human and animal muscle. They used water-wheels to do all kinds of work, like grinding, sawing, and hammering. In level areas like Holland and Denmark, windmills produced power. Medieval people were quite inventive about using wind.

One young monk in England conducted an experiment in 1095. He went up on the walls of the monastery wearing a pair of wings and jumped off. He flew very well. His wings carried him a distance equal to ten times the height of the wall. Ten feet horizontal for one foot down is a respectable glide ratio even today. The landing, however, did not go well. He broke both his legs! After noting that his invention needed a tail, he never tried to fly again. He lived to a ripe old age and left his records.

While the monk's experiment was a dead end, the practical applications of wind and water power were very important. They gave Europe the ability to do more work with less human effort. Historians studying the Middle Ages argue that this was the beginning of the economic advantage Europe developed over other cultures.

H. The Medieval Housewife

Since very few people in the Middle Ages could read and write, documents about certain groups are hard to find. Historian Eileen Power found a book written for a medieval housewife and describes it in her book *Medieval People.* It was written by a middle-class Parisian for his wife. She needed special instruction because she was so young, just 15. Her husband was 60. While some men actually required in their wills that their wives remain widows, this husband was training his young bride to be a good wife for her next husband.

He instructs her about proper conduct. It is suitable for her to grow violets and roses. She may sing and dance, but not go to lords' feasts and dances. Her attitude toward her husband should be loving, humble, and obedient. She should be able to keep his secrets and even to be patient if he takes up with other women. (Remember, this is the husband's idea of a good wife.)

Later on the husband comments on the relationship between men and women. As most medieval people would, he refers to religious stories. He points out that some people argue that if God had intended woman to be superior to man, she would have been made out of Adam's head. But the Bible story says she was made out of Adam's rib, so one expert argues she should be at man's side as a companion.

The husband offers a number of household tips. Supervise the servants closely. Always get workmen to quote a price before they do work or they will charge more. If servants fall ill, take good care of them. Medieval housekeeping was a constant battle against fleas. One way to get rid of them is to put a white spread on the bed. Then you can easily see the black fleas and kill them. The husband also recommends nets over the bed to combat mosquitoes. He offers a cookbook with recipes for jams made of turnips, carrots, and pumpkins. He also includes recipes for cooking frogs and snails—this is French cooking, remember. The medieval household had no electric timers, so the cook is told to time things such as stirring by reciting the Lord's Prayer a certain number of times.

The wife has a few proper forms of amusing herself. She can tell stories or listen to them. She and her lady friends can ask riddles or play games. If she goes out, she is to be in a group of respectable women of her own class.

This, according to one husband, was the ideal medieval wife.

CHAPTER X

Renaissance and Reformation

— Overview —

Historians still argue over the questions: Was there a Renaissance? The people who were rediscovering ancient literature and explaining new techniques in art simply asserted they were part of one. The opening stories in this chapter look at a few of the leading figures of the Renaissance. There is a short section on Renaissance economics. The wealth of the period may be related to all the rest somehow, although exactly how is still disputed. There also seems to be a relationship between the Renaissance and the religious reformers, so we close this chapter with stories about the Reformation. Luther gets the most attention because he was the first. We also briefly look at some of the religious persecutions of the day.

Students find "Was There a Renaissance?" a challenging topic for a paper. It also makes a stimulating discussion topic. Many Renaissance paintings are famous enough that students can easily find reproductions. If you display paintings with a religious topic, such as "The Last Supper," in a public school, you should take care to explain that the works are displayed as samples of art, not an endorsement of a particular religion. Interviewing pastors, priests, or ministers of various denominations is an interesting project that could produce papers or reports. For years after the Reformation the emphasis was on how different the various churches were. Now there is an ecumenical movement, that is, a movement to pull the churches together. In the 1980's the Catholics and Lutherans were talking about it. Depending on developments, it could be an interesting topic for further reading.

A. THE RENAISSANCE

1. Leonardo da Vinci. Historians know about a person from written records. In the case of Leonardo da Vinci, he left a fantastic source of information, his notebooks. He would be famous without them as the painter of the "Mona Lisa" and "The Last Supper," but with them we know much more. Da Vinci used his notebooks in at least three ways. As an artist he used them as sketchbooks to do studies and preliminary drawings for his paintings. As a scientist and inventor he used them as a sort of notebook to record observations from nature and ideas for inventions. As a businessman he kept copies of his letters.

Leonardo sketched a number of studies of human anatomy. At a time when artists were trying to show the body realistically, anatomy was an important study for an artist. Da Vinci also noted that there were fossil shells in the rocks on some mountains. His conclusion was that the mountains had once been at the bottom of the sea. He sketched a parachute, a tank propelled by people inside, a helicopter, and dozens of other inventions. His letters show that he worked as an engineer.

The notebooks are not easy to read. Leonardo was left-handed and wrote in a kind of backward mirror writing. The notebooks are not even easy to find. After da Vinci's death they were scattered through libraries in Spain, France, and elsewhere. There still may be some undiscovered notebooks hidden in archives somewhere.

2. Michelangelo's "David". The city fathers of Florence had a problem. They had bought a large piece of marble and hired a sculptor to do a statue. Unfortunately, he had botched the job and left a large gash in the stone. Most artists believed the material was ruined. Only Michelangelo was brave enough to even attempt to make something of it. The officials gave him the marble because they considered it useless. Michelangelo worked in secret, letting no one see his sculpture until it was finished. The result was a statue of David standing with his sling over his shoulder. This is one of the most admired statues in Europe. One Renaissance writer, Vasari, said it surpassed all other work, ancient and modern. Michelangelo had produced a masterpiece from a useless piece of marble.

3. The Medici Family. The Medici family is a good example of how people could rise from a low station in life during the Renaissance. The Medici were apparently unimportant when the first member of the family moved to Florence, perhaps around 1200. There is no record of the date, presumably because the family in question was too insignificant to notice. But the family got into banking and became part of an important guild and later a power in the politics of Florence. In 1434, Cosimo de Medici became the political boss of Florence. The Medici were the most powerful family in Florence for roughly the next hundred years and were important patrons of the arts, hiring people like Michelangelo and Raphael. They were thrown out briefly by a republic in 1494, but returned in 1512. Machiavelli's *Prince* is dedicated to Lorenzo de Medici, ruler of Florence from 1469 to 1492.

Not only did the Medici rise from insignificant peasants to bankers to local rulers. They also used their wealth and power to place family members in the Church and royal families. There were two Medici popes, Leo X and Clement VII. Leo X was an important patron of the arts. He hired Raphael to paint his portrait. He said, "God has given us the papacy; let us praise God and enjoy it." Two women in the family married French princes who became kings. Catherine de Medici was the wife of Henry II, king of France. For a time she was regent for her son Henry III. In effect that made her ruler of France. Later, Marie de Medici was the wife of Henry IV, king of France. The Medici did pretty well for a family that started out unknown.

4. Machiavelli. Niccolò Machiavelli (1469–1527) is such a famous author, his name has given rise to a word. He has also become a puzzle for historians. *Machiavellian* means that a person is dishonest, without morals, and power-hungry. The basis for this is found in Machiavelli's book, *The Prince.* In this little volume, Machiavelli did indeed write many things that seem immoral. *The Prince* is a book about how to be an effective ruler. Machiavelli made it clear he was not writing about moral improvement, but about what was really done, and what worked. The ruler should lie, cheat, kill if need be for power. If possible, the ruler should seem to be honest, virtuous, and moral, but these appearances should be used simply to make the manipulation more effective. *The Prince* certainly appears to be a book advocating an all-powerful ruler who cynically manipulates his subjects. But there is a problem.

Machiavelli's life seemed to contradict *The Prince.* He spent years working for the republic in Florence. The republic opposed the Medici family and their dictatorship. Machiavelli was a very trustworthy man. He was often chosen by the republic to go on diplomatic missions. In his other books about republics, a history of republican Rome and a history of Florence, Machiavelli's ideas seemed quite different from those expressed in *The Prince.* How can we explain this? Did Machiavelli simply sell out and become cynical in his later years? Or was he making a bitter commentary on the corruption of his day? Did he intend *The Prince* to be published? It wasn't published until after his death. Which do we believe—the ideals Machiavelli served in his life or the ideas he wrote about in *The Prince?*

5. Barbers. In the early days of medicine in Europe, barbers also performed surgery. As a symbol of this fact, barbers put a sign in front of their shop, a white pole with a bloody bandage wrapped around it. This was the beginning of the traditional sign for barber shops, a white pole with red stripes.

6. Erasmus and Kings.

Erasmus was often called the Prince of Humanists, but he was of humble birth. It was his ability to write Latin well that brought him the respect of kings. Henry VIII of England invited Erasmus to England in a letter written in the king's own hand. Francis I of France also asked Erasmus to visit. The young man who was to become Charles V, Holy Roman Emperor, also wrote to Erasmus. At the time, Charles was merely ruler of the Netherlands and Spain. Later he would give Erasmus a pension as imperial councillor. Two popes urged Erasmus to come and serve them in Rome. It seems that in those days, a good writer was admired as much as a sports hero is today.

7. Erasmus's *Praise of Folly*.

Erasmus illustrates several traits associated with the Renaissance. He clearly was a person who rose because of ability. He was the son of a priest. In spite of this, he was able to use his abillity to write elegant Latin to earn the chance to travel. He served as secretary to a number of officials and eventually became a popular author. His rise illustrates how highly prized elegant Latin was in the Renaissance. His popularity as an author was made possible by the printing press, an important invention of the time. Erasmus was born in Holland and traveled to Italy and then to England and other northern European countries. He was among the first of the humanists of northern Europe.

His *Praise of Folly* was a controversial book in its time. He said he thought of the title as a sort of pun on the name of Thomas More and *moriae,* the Greek word for *folly*. This is a typical humanist form of humor. He composed the book in his head while riding horseback across the Alps from Rome to England. When he arrived, he was so worn out by the trip, he became ill. Thomas More encouraged him to write the book while recovering. Erasmus said it was like teaching a camel to dance.

He put the book in the form of a speech by the Goddess of Folly delivered to the other gods on Mount Olympus, a classical setting stylish in the Renaissance. Folly claimed that most of the world's happiness depended on her. Some of her examples were harmless enough. She reported that husbands were often fooled by wives and that nobles had foolish traditions about hunting. Other examples had a sharper point. She complained that theologians were very hot-tempered, and charged that they shaped the Scriptures to suit themselves. She also noted that people foolishly credited saints with saving them from dangers. She even said that the idea that a sinner could pay money and be forgiven a sin was foolish. This was a reference to the practice of selling indulgences, which Martin Luther was later to attack. Erasmus's criticisms of current Church practices led to the saying, "Erasmus laid the eggs; Luther hatched the chicks."

8. Erasmus's Bible.

Late in his life, Erasmus became a serious student of the Bible. He learned Greek, the language of the New Testament, and used careful Renaissance scholarship to produce the most accurate translation up to that time. When Martin Luther did his studies of the Bible, he used Erasmus's Bible rather than the officially approved translation.

B. Renaissance Economics

1. A Robbery in Paris.

Life in the Renaissance was not as secure as it is in the 20th century. Robbers lurked on the roads and even in city streets. There was no police force.

Benvenuto Cellini was a Florentine goldsmith and adventurer. Today his most famous works are a statue of Perseus holding the head of Medusa, and a saltcellar decorated with golden figurines. The gold used in the saltcellar nearly cost Cellini his life.

Cellini contracted with the king to make the saltcellar and arranged to pick up the gold from the treasurer. He suspected that the treasurer was stalling him and that the servants were plotting. Nevertheless, he set out with the gold in a basket on his arm. He was wearing armor, a mail coat and gauntlets, and carrying a sword and dagger. Sure enough, in the darkest, loneliest part of the city, four men attacked him with swords. Celllini, who was a capable swordsman, coolly drew his own sword and began to defend himself. He also tried to convince the robbers that all he had to steal was his sword and cloak. The gold was hidden, held firmly against his left arm by the basket handles. The thieves were about half convinced they had the wrong man. Then Cellini ran yelling, "To arms!" and four young men with pikes came running from his house and chased off his attackers. As they did so, he loudly announced that the thousand gold crowns were breaking his arm and offered to meet his attackers later with a sword. Then he went off to supper.

2. *The Merchant of Venice.*

How did Renaissance businessmen reduce their risks? What were social prejudices toward Jews and women in the 1590's? Shakespeare's *The Merchant of Venice* gives a fictional description of attitudes.

Antonio, a merchant of Venice, protected himself against the sudden loss of all his goods by transporting his goods on several ships. He had ships going to Tripoli, India, Mexico, England, Lisbon, and the Barbary Coast. No one ship's loss could ruin him.

Feeling safe and prosperous, he took out a loan from Shylock the Jew. Jews in those days were a despised minority. They were often forbidden to own land, so it was common for them to become merchants or moneylenders. Shylock made the loan and Antonio offered as his bond a pound of his own flesh. Alas! All of Antonio's ships were wrecked, and he was unable to pay his debt. Venice, being a trading city, had courts for settling such disputes. Shylock was determined to collect his pound of flesh and took Antonio to court.

Since a woman could not be a lawyer, Portia, the rich and beautiful heiress in the story, disguised herself as a man and served as Antonio's defense attorney. After her brilliant emotional defense, the judge gave his verdict. Shylock was entitled to his pound of flesh and he could have it, but in the process of taking it he could not shed one drop of blood!

3. The Medici Bank.

The Italians developed some of the earliest banks in Europe. The Medici family owned and operated a large and powerful bank from 1397 to 1494. Headquarters was in Florence, but there were branches in major trading cities throughout Europe. Each branch was headed by a member of the Medici family, who was a partner. There were branches in Rome, Venice, Naples, Pisa, Milan, Geneva, Basel, Avignon, Bruges, and London. A traveler going to London from Florence could use the system to transfer money without the risk of actually carrying it. The traveler could buy a bill of exchange in Florence. The bank manager in Florence would write a note to the manager in London. "Dear Gerozzo [London partner and manager], The bearer of this note paid me ________ in florins [currency of Florence] on July 21, 1449. Please pay ________ pounds sterling on August 8, 1449. Signed Giovanni [the manager of the branch in Florence]." This was a bill of exchange. The bank did not use printed forms for these. The exchange rate changed with the market for currency then as it does now.

The Medici bank was also involved in a number of businesses besides banking. It owned two shops producing wool cloth and one silk shop. It ran the alum mines owned by the pope and, in general, acted as the pope's agent in all financial matters. It also imported cloth from Germany. This trade operated as a cover for a gold smuggling operation. Gold was hidden inside the bolts of cloth. This was kept secret until the 1960's, when historian Raymond de Roover discovered it while researching the history of the bank for his book *The Rise and Decline of the Medici Bank*.

The bank also made loans to businesspeople, church officials, and rulers. It seems loans to rulers were what destroyed the bank. Some rulers refused to pay back their loans, and that broke the bank in 1494.

C. THE REFORMATION

1. Indulgences Go on Sale.

How did it happen that an indulgence was on sale in Germany in 1517? The answer is complicated, and it shows high-level church authorities doing things that offended people who took religion seriously. Albert of

Brandenburg was already Bishop of Halberstadt and Bishop of Magdeburg. Now he wanted to be Archbishop of Mainz as well. He knew he would have to pay Pope Leo X for the title. This unholy business was conducted with cynical reference to some holy ideas. The pope's agents said the asking price was 12,000 ducats for the 12 apostles. The ducat was a gold coin widely used in those days. Albert made a counteroffer of 7,000 ducats for the 7 deadly sins. Eventually a compromise was reached at 10,000 ducats. Albert also got the right to sell indulgences. This would let him pay back the loan he took out to pay the pope. The pope would also share in half the income from the indulgence sale and use the money to pay for the new St. Peter's Cathedral in Rome.

2. Tetzel and Indulgences. In 1517, the Dominican monk Johann Tetzel sold indulgences freely. The church belief at the time was that a soul free of serious sins did not go directly to heaven. First it went to purgatory, where it was punished for its lesser sins before it moved on to heaven. Good deeds done on earth could shorten the time a soul spent in purgatory. When a person died, relatives could shorten the soul's time in purgatory by saying prayers, visiting holy places, or giving money in the dead person's name. Tetzel simplified all that. Pay cash and that's it. Tetzel's sales pitch assured the faithful, "As soon as the coin in the coffer rings, the soul from purgatory springs." Furthermore, Tetzel offered indulgences to the living for their past, present, and future sins. Many good Catholics thought this was too much.

3. Ninety-five Theses. What is a thesis? When Martin Luther posted his ninety-five theses on the church door at Wittenberg, he was doing a routine bit of university business. The door was the university bulletin board, and theses were part of the university routine. Theses were debate topics in Latin. A candidate for the master's degree was required to post a thesis and defend it in public debate. Professors routinely posted and debated theses. It was the medieval and Renaissance version of publishing a book or scholarly article. The public in those days paid about as much attention to the process as the public today pays to articles in journals on speech pathology. Most of the public couldn't follow the debates because they were conducted in Latin. Luther was simply seeking some scholarly debate in his field, theology. He was still a good Catholic.

Luther's theses were translated and printed because they touched on the issue of indulgences at a time when the issue was being discussed by many people.

4. Martin Luther and Marriage. As Martin Luther worked out the theology of his new church, he quickly rejected life in a monastery or convent. If sinners are saved by faith, good works such as the life of a monk or nun were not part of salvation. So Luther called on monks and nuns to leave their seclusion. It was fairly easy to find a way of making a living for the monks. They were placed as pastors in Lutheran churches. The nuns were another matter. There were few respectable positions for women at that time. Luther found himself acting as a sort of marriage broker for ex-nuns.

In 1523, he placed eight of nine women. One, Katherine von Bora, remained. She was getting pretty old for marriage by the standards of the time. She was 26. She rejected one possibility, but said she would marry Dr. Amsdorf of Magdeburg or Luther himself. Both were so old she may have been joking. Luther was 42, well past the usual marrying age. But Luther's father liked the idea, and Luther soon came around. On June 27, 1524, they were married. Luther walked to church with his bride. After the ceremony, there was a banquet and a dance followed by another banquet. The marriage was apparently a happy one. They had six children.

5. **John Calvin and Wine.** Even strict moral codes change. Calvin enforced a strict moral code in the city of Geneva. People were tried and punished for immorality such as adultery. Card-playing, dancing, plays, and other amusements were prohibited. Calvin's followers were required to attend three services a week: Sunday morning, Sunday evening, and Wednesday evening. They were to observe the Sabbath strictly and work hard the rest of the week. This tradition persisted in later churches based on Calvin's doctrines, notably the Puritans of England and America. Some American churches in the Calvinist tradition were quite active in the prohibition movement of the early 20th century. It is therefore interesting to note that Calvin drank wine. Of course in 16th century Europe, drinking water was dangerous. From time to time the Geneva town council would present Calvin with a "barrel of the best." The Puritans who came to America drank beer and made a point of bringing a barrelmaker with them.

D. The English Reformation

1. **Henry VIII and Annulment.** When Henry VIII decided to dissolve his marriage to Catherine of Aragon, he had a powerful political reason. He needed a son to be a strong ruler after him, and his long union with Catherine had produced only one living child, a daughter. Henry believed the marriage to be cursed. The Bible says that marriage to your brother's widow will be cursed and childless. Catherine was indeed the widow of Arthur, Henry's older brother. Now Henry wanted the pope to annul his marriage to Catherine so he, Henry, could marry someone who would bear him a male heir. Whatever the merits of his case, Henry's timing was terrible. When his petition reached Rome, the pope was in no position to decide the issue because Charles V, Holy Roman Emperor, and his army were nearby. Charles was Catherine's nephew and would not approve of an annulment. The pope delayed a decision by referring the case to experts for further study. Meanwhile Henry VIII, who felt he could not wait, separated the English Church from Rome. Ironically, the study probably would have supported granting the annulment, as one was given in a similar case.

2. The Death of Thomas More. In many ways Thomas More seems an ideal Renaissance man. He was the author of *Utopia,* a book about a perfect society, still studied today. He was a successful politician, serving as speaker of the House of Commons and chancellor to King Henry VIII. He was a close friend of the humanist Erasmus. He was also a man devoted to his religion. This was to cost him his life.

When Henry VIII put aside Catherine of Aragon and married Anne Boleyn, Catholics did not consider this second marriage valid. More refused to make a statement approving the marriage. The king had More imprisoned, tried, and executed. As he went to the beheading block, More is reported to have told the headsman, "Aim carefully, I have a short neck." As he placed his head on the block he adjusted his beard so it wouldn't be cut, remarking, "It has not committed high treason."

3. Edward VI, Child King. Edward VI was the son of Henry VIII and Jane Seymour. He was born October 12, 1537, and his mother died 12 days later. In those days, having a baby was dangerous even for a queen. Edward became king before he was 10 years old, on January 18, 1547, and died before his sixteenth birthday, on July 6, 1553. He didn't live to the age of today's typical high school sophomore. Religion in England became more Protestant under Edward bcause of his regent's policy.

E. INTOLERANCE

1. Michael Servetus, Heretic. The case of Michael Servetus shows us that leaders of the Reformation were not tolerant of differing religious views. Servetus was born in Spain about 1511. He became a doctor and studied the body, discovering that the blood moved from the heart to the lungs to pick up oxygen. He also studied theology and became a Unitarian—that is, he denied that Jesus was an equal part of the Trinity. This made him a heretic to both Protestants and Catholics. He managed to live for years in Catholic territory. At one time, the Calvinists sent information to the Catholics alerting them that the heretic Servetus was in their territory. Servetus faced a trial by the Inquisition at Lyons, but he managed to escape. Finally, he went to Geneva, where he was recognized while attending church service. He was promptly arrested. Calvin himself questioned Servetus and tried to persuade him to give up his heresy. When this failed, Servetus was burned at the stake on October 27, 1553. Not to be left out, the Catholic court at Vienna sentenced Servetus and burned him in effigy.

2. The Anabaptists. In 20th-century America, the Baptists are a large group, and Baptists are respectable citizens. During the Reformation, the Anabaptists were a small group of radicals persecuted by both Catholics and Protestants. These radicals insisted on baptizing believers only after they were old enough to understand religion. Since other churches baptized infants, the radicals were baptizing again. This led to their being called Anabaptists, meaning "baptizing again." The Anabaptists believed in reading the Bible and interpreting it for themselves. This led them to some radical ideas. A group of Anabaptists took over the town of Münster in 1534 and began practicing polygamy and communism. They argued that both practices were supported by the Bible. Lutherans and Catholics joined forces and wiped out the Münster Anabaptists.

Teacher Note: Denominations that started as Reformation-era Anabaptists include Mennonites, Hutterites, Amish, Quakers, and some, but not all, Baptists. Some English Baptists were in contact with the original Anabaptists. Baptists in the United States have no historical links to the Anabaptists.

Chapter XI

Europeans Explore and Conquer

— Overview —

The story of the European discovery that there were other peoples out there is a dramatic one. These explorers were ignorant of the Viking explorations when they set out to seek new trade routes. The Portuguese were first, but Americans tend to focus on Columbus. Once started, the process continued, and people like Cortez and Pizarro conquered huge areas with tiny forces. Often the culture and politics of the New World Indians helped make the conquest easier. After contact was established, neither Europe nor the New World was ever the same again.

Your students could write papers on "Columbus and Magellan Compared." Other good compare-and-contrast papers would be "Aztecs and Incas" or "Cortez and Pizarro." Notice that the stories on "La Malinche" and "Aztec Warfare" seem to be in conflict. One says the Aztecs planned a massacre, and the other says they didn't fight to kill. The two stories are from sources with conflicting biases, Spanish and Indian. Your students could do a paper on which version they believe and why.

A world map with yarn showing routes of various explorers would make a helpful bulletin board. Your students could write imaginative papers on "A Sailor's Diary of the First Columbus Voyage,'" "A Letter Home from One of Cortez's Soldiers," or "A Diary of a Soldier with Pizarro."

A. The Explorers

1. Bartholomeu Dias. When Bartholomeu Dias first rounded the Cape of Good Hope, he didn't see it. When he set out in 1487, he followed the African coast south. As he worked south he was blown away from the shore. When he returned, he found the shore was now angling northward. His sailors forced him to turn back, and on the way, in 1488, he first saw the Cape of Good Hope.

2. Hazards Faced by Coolumbus. Even if Columbus had been sailing into well-known waters, a trip of the length he took, more than seven months, had many dangers. He started out with three ships, the *Niña,* the *Pinta,* and the *Santa Maria;* he returned with two. On Christmas Day 1492, the *Santa Maria* ran onto a reef. The sharp coral cut into her hull and the ship had to be abandoned. Columbus sailed home in the *Niña.* It was a very rough trip. The sailors were so frightened that they vowed to go to church at the first opportunity. Eventually the *Niña* reached Europe, in March 1493, but was forced to land in Lisbon, Portugal. This was a risky decision. Portugal was a rival of Spain, but the *Niña* was badly damaged. While in the harbor at Lisbon, Columbus met Bartholomeu Dias, the Portuguese explorer who had discovered the Cape of Good Hope.

3. Columbus, Indians, and an Eclipse. On his fourth voyage, Columbus had several problems. There was a mutiny, and Columbus found himself on the island of Jamaica depending on the Indians to provide food for his crew. The Indians were at first willing to trade with the Europeans. But after a while the Indians had about all the European goods they needed and lost interest in trading. Columbus's crew desperately needed the food the Indians supplied. Columbus now tried to trick the natives.

He called the Indians together and told them that he and his crew were Christians. They worshiped a God who lived in the heavens. Their God was angry with the Indians for not providing food for the crew. Columbus then predicted that the moon would rise red that night. This would be a sign that God was angry with the Indians and would punish them if they didn't provide food.

Sure enough, as the moon appeared that night, it was red. It was slowly darkened by an eclipse. The Indians were terrified. They rushed to bring provisions. Columbus, with the timing of a dramatic actor, went into his cabin until the eclipse was total. Then he came out and announced that he had prayed to his God and assured God that the Indians would provide the crew with food. Therefore, God would uncover the moon. This happened, and the Indians were happy to provide food from then on. They were very impressed by the Christian God.

Columbus had predicted the eclipse using an almanac he had with him. His son, Ferdinand Columbus, told this story in a book on the life of his father. Ferdinand had traveled with his father on this voyage.

4. Columbus and Six Indians. Columbus brought back six Indians with him to Europe. Once they were in Spain they were baptized, with the king and queen serving as godparents. One of the Indians stayed at court and died a few years later. The remaining five learned Spanish and became interpreters. They returned to the New World when Columbus made his second voyage.

5. Scurvy, Scourge of the Sea. Trips grew longer as ships and navigation improved. Crews who spent more time on ships developed a disease called scurvy. The victim usually grew weaker and became depressed. Then the complexion grew pale, the legs swelled. Muscles ached, and the gums became tender and swollen. After a few weeks, the teeth might fall out. Many sufferers had skin eruptions and puffy yellow flesh. Finally, the victim became extremely weak with diarrhea and kidney or heart trouble. Even if the victims survived scurvy, they were so weakened that other diseases could easily finish them off.

Scurvy was deadly. When Vasco da Gama made his trip around the Cape of Good Hope about 1498, he lost 100 out of his 160 men. Scurvy killed over half of Magellan's crew. Cartier landed in Canada in 1534 with 100 out of 106 crew members sick with scurvy. Only the kindness of Indians saved the men.

The cure was simple: Give the sailors fresh fruit, especially lemons, oranges, or limes. Lemon juice was the best treatment. It could be carried in bottles, and a small dose prevented scurvy. The British Navy adopted limes as the official treatment. That is why British sailors became known as "limeys." The disease was caused by a deficiency in vitamin C, but this was not understood until 1912.

6. Magellan's Voyage. When Magellan set out from Spain, he had already seen much of the world. While serving the king of Portugal, he had sailed to India and fought battles there. He had a cousin living in the Spice Islands (Indonesia) who invited him to visit. When the king of Portugal refused to support such an expedition, Magellan turned to Spain. Its king, Charles V, readily accepted Magellan's services. The navigator proposed to sail toward the New World and then go south around it and directly on to the Spice Islands. Magellan believed this was possible because of two ideas of his, both wrong. He had been told there was a route through America to Asia. This was shown on a top-secret map. Also he believed, as did Columbus, that the earth was smaller than it is, about half as big. What could be simpler? He would sail through the secret channel and after a short trip arrive at the Spice Islands.

Magellan's crew was a mixture of nationalities. The Spaniards among them resented Magellan, who was Portuguese, and plotted mutiny. When the expedition reached South America, the channel shown on the map was not there. Magellan sailed south, and in a storm two of his ships were blown through a strait that opened on another ocean. He named the ocean the Pacific, hoping it would indeed be peaceful. It turned out to be huge, so big that the crew nearly starved before they landed on a lonely island.

Magellan was so disgusted with his charts (maps) that he threw them all away. The crew admired the flying fish and noticed that sharks were following them. Eventually they landed in the islands we now call the Philippines. Here Magellan was killed in a fight with islanders. The expedition continued around India and Africa and reached Spain in September of 1522. Five ships had started the voyage. Only one, the *Victoria,* returned. It had circled the earth.

7. Magellan's Death. Magellan's arrival in the Philippines was a triumph, just in time to save the crew. Late in the trip only one man had been strong enough to climb to the crow's nest to look for islands. In the Philippines, the Europeans traded successfully. The going rate was 10 pieces of gold for 14 pounds of iron. Magellan was also making willing converts to Christianity. But one chief, named Cilapulapu, refused to convert. Magellan led a force of 60 volunteers to punish him. The chief led 3,000 warriors. At first the Europeans attacked and drove the islanders back. Then Magellan's force began to fall back to the sea. As they reached the water's edge, discipline broke and the islanders rushed in and killed Magellan. Magellan's ships were just offshore and did nothing. The Spaniards in charge of the ships had hated Magellan and had mutinied against him before. Now they let him be killed. Only then did they move in and pick up five survivors.

8. Magellan and Black Henry. The European explorers had help from the people in the lands they were "discovering." Magellan owned a Malay slave, called Black Henry, who traveled with him and acted as interpreter during the voyage around the world. Black Henry fought by his master's side when Magellan was killed. He later helped trap the traitors who had let his master be killed. They foolishly let Black Henry act as interpreter when they dealt with Philippine rulers. Black Henry and a rajah who had been a friend to Magellan conspired together. The rajah invited the traitors to a banquet where, at a signal, they were killed.

B. The Conquest of Mexico

1. La Malinche, or Doña Marina. One of the gifts given Cortez by the Indians was a woman known as La Malinche. She was to be a valuable person indeed. She spoke both Maya, the language of the coast, and Nahuatl, the language of the Aztecs. She quickly learned Spanish and became very helpful to Cortez as a translater and general adviser on dealing with the Indians. She had been the daughter of an important chief when she was taken captive. Her captors passed her on to another tribe, who presented her to Cortez. As the Spaniards were moving inland from Vera Cruz toward Mexico City, they stopped at Cholulan. There an old woman warned La Malinche that she should leave the Spaniards because they would all be killed. La Malinche asked about more details and the old woman told her of a plan to ambush the Spaniards. Claiming she needed to go get her jewels, La Malinche went to Cortez and warned him. The following day the Spaniards turned the tables and killed 3,000 Indians. La Malinche took the Chrtistian name of Doña Marina, married a Spaniard, and became a person of great importance in New Spain.

2. Aztec Warfare. The fighting between the Aztecs and the Spaniards under Cortez was a war between two cultures. In two ways this worked against the Aztecs. It seems likely the Aztecs could have killed all the Spaniards on several occasions, but Aztecs did not fight to kill the enemy. They fought to capture prisoners, who would later be sacrificed to their gods. This handicapped them in fighting the Spaniards. The Indians also had an elaborate ritual before they went to war. Enemies were always given token shields, arrows, and cloaks before they were attacked. The Aztecs were thus shocked when the Spaniards, their guests, suddenly and without warning attacked them in their own city.

3. Cortez and Indian Allies. Cortez had a lot of help from other Indians as he conquered the Aztecs. They provided him with both supplies and warriors. For example, as Cortez prepared to capture Mexico City, he sent around patterns of copper arrowheads and arrows for crossbows. The Indians brought in 50,000 arrowheads and arrows they had made. When Cortez started his attack, he had 20,000 Indian warriors with him.

4. Indians and Religion. The struggle between Spanish culture and Indian culture took many forms. The Spaniards worked at converting the Indians to Christianity, but it was not easy. The record shows some of the Indians saying, "Our gods are dead. Let us die too." But the missionaries worked hard and replaced every Aztec temple or shrine with a church or statue of a saint. They even explained that communion, or the Eucharist, was the reenactment of a sacrifice. The Aztecs understood ceremonies of sacrifice. They had made human sacrifices. The Spanish even brought the Inquisition to Mexico, but it found few suspects.

But the early Indians had a secret way of keeping their old religion alive. Indians worked in the shops making crosses and saints' statues put up by the Spaniards. In about half the cases they put Aztec idols inside the Christian symbols. Thus an Indian could be praying before a cross and at the same time be worshiping an Aztec idol.

C. The Conquest of Peru

1. Pizarro's Character. Francisco Pizarro was born about 1475 in Spain. He grew up poor and uneducated and never even learned how to sign his name. He literally carved out a career with a sword. As early as 1510, he was part of an expedition of conquest. Next he became part of Balboa's expedition that discovered the Pacific. He settled for a time in Panama and was given lands and Indians, but he was restless. In 1523, he set out to explore south of Panama. At one time members of the expedition pressured Pizarro to return to Panama. They had fought fierce Indians who roasted human flesh in their camps. That and the hostile tropical forest and danger of starvation discouraged them. Pizarro drew a line in the sand and asked for volunteers who would go with him to cross the line. Either 13 or 16 men crossed the line (sources disagree). This tiny group went on to discover the coast of Peru. After this, Pizarro returned to Spain for permission to lead a major expedition. While there he recruited his four brothers. Armed with an agreement with the king, Charles V of Spain, they set out to organize an expedition to conquer Peru. By this time Pizarro was at an age when many modern Americans are considering retirement.

2. The Capture of the Inca. Pizarro marched on the Inca Empire with 180 men and 27 horses. He found it weak and divided by civil war. Two brothers had been fighting over the title of Inca, ruler of the empire. The Spaniards met the Inca, Atahualpa, at Cajamarca and had an audience with him. The next day they invited Atahualpa to come to supper with them. The Inca arrived, carried by nobles, sitting on a gleaming golden throne. He did not realize that the Spaniards were planning to seize him, so he and his escort came unarmed. The first Spaniard to meet him was a priest, who preached to him about the Trinity, the pope, and the Spanish king. Atahualpa was urged to convert and become a subject of the Spanish king. He argued back and asked for the book the priest carried, a Bible or breviary. He took the book and threw it down.

The priest returned to Pizarro, who was hiding nearby, and urged an attack. The Spaniards gave the cry, "Santiago and at them!" and rushed out of hiding to massacre the unarmed Indians. Between 2,000 and 10,000 Indians died that day. The only wound the Spaniards got was on Pizarro's hand. He put out his arm to protect the Inca, and one of his own men cut him.

3. The Inca's Ransom. After Pizarro's forces captured the Inca, he offered the Spaniards a generous ransom. At first the Inca offered to cover the floor with gold. Then he offered to fill the room with gold up to the highest point he could reach. According to William Prescott, a 19th-century historian, the room measured 17 feet by 22 feet, and Atahualpa's reach was 9 feet high. Pizarro had an agreement written up and notarized. The terms said that the gold did not have to be melted into bars, it could be brought in whatever shape it was in. Another smaller nearby room would be filled twice with silver. After all this was specified, the order went out from the Inca to bring in the gold. Much, if not all, of the ransom was paid, but the Inca was never released.

4. The Death of the Inca. The Spaniards gave Atahualpa a trial before they killed him. The charges show as much about the accusers as the accused. They charged the Inca with usurping the throne and killing his brother. He was accused of spending public money too freely. He was also charged with adultery (he had several wives) and idolatry, both crimes to the Catholic Spaniards. The most important charge was that he tried to start a rebellion against the Spaniards.

The trial went through the formality of questioning Indian witnesses, but the translation probably distorted their testimony. In the end, some objected that the evidence was not good enough, that the court had no jurisdiction, and that the trial should be held in Spain. They were outnumbered ten to one. The Inca was sentenced to be burned at the stake. As he was being dragged to the stake in chains, he converted to Christianity. As a result, he was spared being burned. The Spaniards strangled him instead.

5. Spanish Gold. It's hard to imagine the amount of gold that Spain took out of Mexico and Peru. One report gives us some idea. Remember, this is just the shipment for one year, 1583. On September 13, 1583, the Spanish fleet arrived from "Spanish India" (Latin America). The boats carried gold worth about $15 million in Spanish money. They left another million in Havana because the load was too heavy for the ships! Imagine so much gold it threatened to sink the ships!

CHAPTER XII
Rise of Monarchs in Europe

— Overview —

This chapter deals with the topic that gives history class a bad name: long lists of monarchs. There are two ways to make this sort of thing interesting to students. One way is to show that many rulers were interesting people; some were very odd and a few were really weird. The intellectual approach makes the point that these rulers were engaged in a serious task, building a strong country ruled by a single government. We take that sort of thing for granted today, but these people had to work to get it to happen. The English fumbled around and finally created a unified country with a representative government. The French kings were most successful, so Louis XIV became the ideal for all kings in Europe. The Spanish were successful at unification, but somehow slipped as a power. The Germans did not manage to unify, and suffered in weakness for a century. The Russians had a long way to go culturally and did not quite catch up with the rest.

Your students can write compare-and-contrast papers on many topics in this area: "Elizabeth I and Philip II," "Louis XIV and Peter the Great," "Frederick the Great of Prussia and Catherine the Great of Russia." The possible combinations seem limitless.

A. England

1. Elizabeth I. Queen Elizabeth I was one of England's greatest rulers. She knew exactly how to relate to her subjects. Just before the approach of the Spanish Armada she went to visit her army at Tilbury without a bodyguard. Some told her she should have a guard, but she refused. These were her "faithful and loving people." The soldiers of the army loved Elizabeth for it. They cheered and threw hats in the air. Monarchs were not elected, of course, but they needed popular support. Some later rulers would learn this lesson the hard way.

2. The Armada. The defeat of the Spanish Armada was caused by a variety of factors, but probably most important was the fact that the Spaniards were victims of a technical change in war at sea. In 1588, when the Armada sailed, Spain was a first-class power with a respected army and navy, but Spanish ships were equipped to fight in an outdated way. Sea battles up to then had been a lot like land battles. The ships would sail up to each other and grapple together. Boarding parties would try to storm aboard the enemy's ships, and the issue would be decided by close-quarter fighting. Consequently, Spanish ships were loaded with soldiers and built with tall castles on them. The taller ship could board the other more easily. Also, the Spanish ships carried short-range cannons designed to support boarding parties as they attacked the nearby ship.

The English, on the other hand, built ships to stand off from the enemy and sink them. The English ships were smaller and sailed faster. Their guns were designed to fire farther and aimed at the hull of the enemy. An English ship could sink a Spanish ship without coming in range of the Spanish guns.

At one critical point the English wanted to smoke the Spaniards out of the port of Calais, so they loaded some old ships full of fuel and set them to sail into the harbor spraying sparks. All ships were wooden in those days, so fire was a terror. The Spaniards rushed out in disorder and were easy prey for the waiting English. Later, off the coast of Ireland, the remains of the Armada ran into a fierce storm and were destroyed. The English called it "the Protestant Wind." The English victory was a turning point in the balance of European power. The English Navy would now rule the seas for centuries.

3. James I and Politics. James was one of the best educated kings. He wrote books ranging over a wide variety of subjects. His first book was about poetry, *The Essays of a Prentise in the Divine Art of Poetry* (1584). Later he wrote about the power of kings in two books, *The True Lawe of Free Monarchies* (1598) and *Basilikon*

Doron (1599). When he became king of England in 1603, James had an unfortunate tendency to lecture Parliament on his theories of monarchy. He also continued to write, producing *The Counterblast to Tobacco* in 1604. He had the evils of tobacco figured out, but not the ways of a British Parliament. The lawmakers did not believe his claim of divine right. James was set in his ways, however. He had been king of Scotland since 1567 and thought his 36 years of experience made him an expert.

The English were not impressed. James's physical appearance didn't help. He had a problem with uncontrolled drooling. He also had little ability to get along with people. The English Parliament had no intention of being ruled by an absolute divine-right monarch. They labeled him "the wisest fool in Christendom."

As might be expected, James and Parliament often differed. Money was a big problem. The most dramatic argument came over an attempt that James made to marry his son to a Spanish princess. This would have created an alliance with Spain. Parliament wanted James to become an ally with Protestants against Spain instead. James wrote a letter to the speaker of the House of Commons telling Parliament not to interfere with the king's diplomacy. The Commons made a protest and had it entered in their journal. James was so angry that he dissolved Parliament and tore the protest out of the journal—literally tore the page out of the book.

Within two years the Spanish backed out of the negotiations and James did in fact come around to a Protestant alliance. After that, his relations with Parliament were better.

4. James I and Religion. In an age when religion was very much a part of politics, James I had a complex religious background. His mother was Mary Queen of Scots, a Catholic. She was forced to abdicate by John Knox and other Protestants in Scotland. James was raised by tutors and regents, so his mother had little influence on him. As king of Scotland, he was the head of the Scottish "Kirk," which was Presbyterian. When he became king of England, he was also head of the Church of England. This church was different from Scotland's in organization and doctrine. So James was Presbyterian when in Scotland and Anglican when in England.

James was king during a time of religious wars between Protestants and Catholics. There were even fights between different Protestant groups. It was during the reign of James I that the Pilgrims left for North America on the *Mayflower.* The Pilgrims were separatists, people who wanted their church separated from the Church of England. Other separatists remained in England. James found himself ruling a people with religious differences almost as complex as his own religious background.

5. Charles I Tried and Executed. In 1649, the parliamentary leaders decided to execute King Charles I, whom they held as a prisoner. When Charles I went before the court that tried him, he refused to enter any plea. He said, "The king cannot be tried." His proud denial of rebel authority did not save him. He was sentenced to die. The execution took place in London on Tuesday, January 30, 1649.

It was a cold day. Charles was afraid that he would shiver from the cold and people would say that he shook with fear. He therefore wore heavy underwear as he stepped out to the platform for his execution.

6. Prince Rupert. Prince Rupert led the royalist cavalry during the English Civil War. He was a Protestant, but he was also King Charles I's nephew. Rupert was a dashing leader galloping over the battlefield with his white dog running beside him. At first Rupert's cavalry was the best on the battlefield. In the first battle of the English Civil War, Edgehill, Rupert's cavalry charged and scattered the parliamentary cavalry. The charge continued through the field and into the enemy camp. Rupert's troops spent the rest of the battle looting the camp. If Rupert's force had returned, they could have won the battle, but there were no walkie-talkies in those days to call them back. Unfortunately for the royal cause, the parliamentary foot soldiers and the royalists fought to a draw. The war continued until 1649, and by then Parliament had its own cavalry, Oliver Cromwell's Ironsides.

7. Puritans Change Names. Under the Puritans, people took good godly names. For girls, Faith, Prudence, Charity, and other biblical virtues became names. Some more enthusiastic believeers took names like Praise God and Put-thy-trust-in-Christ.

B. FRANCE

1. The Three Musketeers. Everyone has heard of the Three Musketeers. Several movie versions of their adventures have been made, full of flashing swords, dashing adventure, and romance. These exciting adventures are set in the reign of Louis XIII. The political history of France is lurking in the background. The villain of the story is the cardinal—Cardinal Richelieu, of course. Musketeers were soldiers in the king's forces, in this case King Louis XIII. Armies in those days had muskets and pikes, and soldiers were named for their weapons. Some Three Musketeers movies have included scenes at the siege of La Rochelle, a famous battle fought by the royal authorities against the Huguenots. The cardinal was trying to reduce the Huguenots' power to resist the king. Even the dueling that is so much a part of the movie stories has historical importance. Because dueling is a form of private war, the cardinal was dead against it. Nobles who fought duels or private battles might also be able to rebel against the king. Only the movies' romance seems unrelated to political reality.

If you haven't seen the movies, you may want to read the book. Alexander Dumas wrote it in French in 1844. It has since been widely translated. Enjoy!

Teacher Note: While Dumas used a period in history as his setting, he was willing to change history to make a good story, creating characters and incidents. Movie makers have taken further liberties with history.

2. Louis XIV and Personal Rule. Louis XIV probably never said, "I am the state," but historians find it such a neat summary of his rule that the saying survives. What Louis did say in 1661 when Cardinal Mazarin died was something a little different. He called his advisors together and announced, "I shall be my own prime minister." He was asked who should receive reports in the future. He said, "Bring them to me." Louis had tremendous power, but he had to work to keep it. He spent hours in meetings and more hours reading the rivers of reports that flowed into Versailles.

3. Manners at Versailles. While Louis XIV's Versailles was the height of fashion and elegance for its day, that day was the late 17th century, and life was sometimes rather crude. Elegant dining was still some time in the future. The knife and fork were new developments, and King Louis XIV refused to use them. Sometimes he would throw little balls of bread at ladies as a joke. One noblewoman was hit by some fruit thrown by the king and responded by throwing a salad at the king's head.

4. Versailles: The King's Food. In the morning, King Louis XIV rose about 8:00 A.M. and had a breakfast of bread, wine, and water. The king ate his dinner at 1:00 P.M. The kitchen was a distance away from the hall of the guards where Louis ate, so the king's meal was carried to him by a group of ten, including three armed soldiers. Any courtier who saw the meal passing was expected to remove his hat, bow, and say, "The king's meat." Before Louis ate, the food would be sampled by his servants as a precaution against poison. The king liked eggs, and figs were his favorite fruit. Louis XIV never ate potatoes. At that time the French did not grow them. He drank wine from Champagne.

Summer was the big meal of the day. It was served at 10:00 P.M. The king would have soup, perhaps a whole pheasant, ham, and a pastry, followed by fruits and sweets. The meal was followed by some form of entertainment.

C. Spain

1. Isabella. Isabella was not one to be subordinate to any man, and she showed this in many ways. Tradition in Spain said women rode mules. Isabella rode horses and was an excellent horsewoman. She was in her own right in line to be ruler of the Kingdom of Castile and León, so when Ferdinand's father began the courtship, Ferdinand was the inferior. As was the way in royal marriages, they negotiated a treaty. In it Ferdinand agreed to live in Castile and not leave unless Isabella gave her consent. He also agreed that all public acts and laws would be joint actions. Isabella had the exclusive right to appoint bishops and other church officials. They both agreed to fight the Moors. After the treaty, they met. He was an athletic, suntanned 18. She was a fair-skinned, blue-eyed beauty of 19. Her education was much better than his.

The mechanics of the wedding were a little sticky. They had to borrow money for the wedding. They were related, so a papal bull permitting the wedding was needed. Only years later did Isabella discover the bull they got was a fake, and then they secured a real one. These details taken care of, there was a week of nuptial celebration, at the end of which the newlyweds attended a public mass.

It was the marriage that made Spain. Isabella's kingdom of Castile and León, when joined with Ferdinand's kingdom of Aragon, made up nearly all the Christian territory in Spain, and most of the geographical area. The Moors, who were Muslims, had been in Spain for centuries. Now the royal couple set out to wipe out the last Moorish rulers, who held the kingdom of Granada. In 1492, they completed the task and all of Spain was Christian.

Isabella wanted a kingdom with one faith. There were a number of Jews in Spain. Now Isabella insisted they convert or leave. She used her authority to start the Spanish Inquisition.

Once the Moors were out of the way, Isabella also sponsored Christopher Columbus. As usual, she negotiated shrewdly. The agreement they signed stated that the crown would get one fifth of any gold coming out of new lands.

Isabella was an effective ruler. When she died, the crown was more tightly in control of Castile and León than ever before. Spain was unified under one ruler and one church. Ferdinand lived and ruled several years after Isabella's death.

2. Charles V. In royal families, marriages were political alliances, and the children of these marriages were the kings and queens of the future. Charles V shows just how well a policy of making the right marriage could pay off. By the time he was 15 he was Duke of Burgundy, a rich little duchy in the east of France. He was raised there and learned to speak French as his native language. Charles was the grandson of Ferdinand and Isabella of Spain, and when he was 16 he inherited the Spanish kingdom. He traveled to Spain, but never got along well there. The Spanish people resented the fact that Charles spoke poor Spanish and that he brought Burgundian advisors. They made fun of his looks. He had a Hapsburg family trait, a jutting jaw. In his case, he could hardly chew his food or fully close his mouth. Some insolent Spaniards suggested that flies might find their way into the monarch's mouth.

The Spanish people may not have liked Charles, but their country made him rich. During Charles's reign, Cortez conquered Mexico, and Pizarro conquered Peru. Both of these conquests resulted in shiploads of treasure for the mother country. They also made Charles the king of all known North and South America. But that isn't all.

The Holy Roman Empire elected its emperor by the vote of seven electors, who were easily bribed. In 1519, Charles outbribed the other candidates, Henry VIII of England and Francis I of France.

In 1520, Charles V was crowned Holy Roman Emperor. It was a busy time. One of his first duties was to try Martin Luther for heresy at the Imperial Diet held in Worms. For the rest of his reign Charles would have to deal with the problems resulting from the religious division between Protestants and Catholics. He also had to deal with Turks moving up to Austria, another of his inherited lands. Charles was a serious and conscientious ruler. One historian says he was never young. He ruled over a huge area including Spain, the Americas, the Low Countries, sections of Austria, and part of Italy. Each of those areas had its own problems. After years of hard work Charles retired to a monastery in 1556.

Charles left his titles to two relatives, thus starting two branches of the Hapsburg family. He left Spain to his son, Philip II, whose family ruled Spain until 1700. He left Austria to his brother Ferdinand, whose family ruled until the end of World War I in 1918. Charles spent two years in retirement before he died at age 59.

3. Philip II. Philip is a rather sad case. He was a serious, devout, hardworking king, but somehow he had a very difficult life, perhaps because of these very traits. He was married four times, but each seems to have been a political marriage. Most famous was Philip's marriage to Mary Tudor, queen of England and his first cousin once removed. The English people disliked Philip and resisted Mary's efforts to return the country to the Catholic religion. When Mary died, Philip returned to Spain. He was a very conscientious ruler, reading all the official reports. The Spanish called him the paperwork king.

Philip tried to advance his religion using the methods of the times. He strongly supported the Inquisition and was devoted to protecting the Catholic faith. He fought a futile war to subjugate the Low Countries and impose Catholicism on them. He sent out his Armada to conquer England. It met disaster. It's little wonder that all Philip's portraits show a gloomy expression. Philip built a royal palace, the Escorial, outside Madrid. It was not just a palace, however. It was a burial place for Spanish kings, a church, and a monastery, with a palace added. Philip lived in a simple apartment where he sometimes slept in his own coffin.

D. GERMANY

1. The Holy Roman Empire: States. Around 1790, the Holy Roman Empire was made up of about 2,000 separate territories. Some of them were less that 100 acres in area. The total included two important monarchies, Prussia and Austria. Then there were several hundred small principalities, each ruled by a local prince. In addition there were duchies, counties, ecclesiastical territories, free cities, and imperial knights. Each of these little bits had the right to self-rule. Voltaire summarized it all by saying of the Holy Roman Empire, "It was neither holy, nor Roman, nor an empire."

2. The Thirty Years' War: Defenestration in Prague. The Thirty Years' War (1618–1648) was fought over a variety of serious issues, but it started in an almost comic way. There was a dispute over who should be king of Bohemia. The Bohemians wanted a Protestant. The Holy Roman Emperor wanted a Catholic. The emperor sent two governors to Prague to settle the matter, but Bohemian leaders insisted on discussing the issue. Evidently the discussion did not go well, because both governors were defenestrated—that is, thrown out the window. Both men survived the 70-foot fall. Catholics claimed it was because the governors had called on Jesus and Mary. Protestants said it was because the men fell onto a dung heap. After this incident the emperor and the Bohemians went to war. The fighting eventually involved all of the Holy Roman Empire and troops from Sweden and France. The war lasted 30 years and was one of the bloodiest in European history.

3. Frederick William I of Prussia. Frederick William I, king of Prussia, weighed 275 pounds and had a waist five feet around. He was a miser who beat his children and government officials with a cane he always carried. Sometimes he was insane. But he was a good king. He made Prussia a respected power and governed it well.

Frederick William I lived simply in five rooms and made a point of saving money at all times. He sold off many jewels and horses he had inherited from his father. He realized that spending a lot does not make a king strong; having money in the treasury does. He made a point of rebuilding the towns of his kingdom. He was a simple, hardworking person and wanted his subjects to be the same. He hated French ways because he associated them with extravagance. He insisted that criminals be hung wearing French clothes so the people would reject extravagant French styles.

Frederick William was an absolute king and did not accept advice easily. The only time it was safe to advise him was during his "tobacco parliament," when each evening he and a few friends would get together, smoke pipes, drink, and play practical jokes.

Frederick William doubled the size of the Prussian Army. He trained its soldiers to march in step and built it into a first-class force. He was so fond of army-style discipline that he was called the Sergeant King. Frederick William liked the army so much that he was unwilling to use it in war. It was, however, valuable as a threat in diplomacy. Frederick William had his personal regiment, the Potsdam Guards, made up of very tall soldiers, some of them reaching seven feet. Diplomats who wanted to be on Frederick William's good side brought him a tall new soldier. Often these men were kidnapped.

The monarch had a disease called porphyria, which was hereditary. It inflicted all kinds of pain—migraine, piles, abscesses, boils, and stomach pain on Frederick William. At times the pain made him crazy.

Yet he was a capable and effective king. He made his kingdom prosperous and strong. He even managed to raise a capable heir. His son was Frederick II, more often called Frederick the Great.

4. Frederick "the Great" of Prussia. Frederick II never did learn to speak German very well. He preferred French. He was a dreamy boy who played the flute, wrote poems, and penned letters to Voltaire. His father, Frederick William I, worried about the boy and beat him. But the delicate prince became a king to be reckoned with.

As monarch, Frederick II kept his interest in the flute, and he had Voltaire as a guest at his court for a time. He also worked just as hard as his father had at ruling Prussia and building up the economy. It was as a soldier that he earned the title Frederick the Great.

In Frederick's most important war, the Seven Years' War (1756–1763) Prussia fought Austria, Russia, and France. The British were Frederick's ally, but they fought in India and North America, not on the European continent. In North America this war was called the French and Indian War. While the British were winning in India and Canada, Frederick II was battling three opponents in Europe, each of which was larger than Prussia. He had an outstanding army equipped with the new iron ramrods for their muskets, and he was the best general in Europe at the time. Prussia defeated each of its three opponents. By the end of the war, Frederick was respected throughout Europe, and his kingdom had grown. His subjects now called him *der alte Fritz,* meaning "Old Fritz." It was a name given in respect and affection.

In his later years, Frederick still enjoyed an evening of flute music or poetry. He died in 1786, but his memory was respected. Roughly 20 years later, the French under Napoleon conquered Prussia. Napoleon visited Frederick's tomb on October 24, 1806. As he stood there, he commanded his companions, "Hats off, gentlemen—if he were still alive we should not be here."

E. Russia

1. Early Moscow. Moscow began as a simple fort and grew into a city. The heart of the city was the Kremlin, the original fort. Next to appear was Red Square, used as a marketplace. *Red* is also the Russian word for "beautiful," so this name can also be understood as Beautiful Square. The next layer of growth was the White City, built of white stone. The outer ring of Moscow was the wooden city. Fire was a serious threat in Moscow. There were 17 major fires between 1330 and 1453. Some merchants set up a business selling precut logs to rebuild houses. Using these, a burned house could be replaced in a day or two.

2. The Russian Alphabet. Russian writing looks odd to Americans. Perhaps we are tempted to say, "It's Greek to us." And indeed it is Greek, or at least based on Greek. Russian is written in the Cyrillic alphabet, which was invented by a Greek missionary sent to the Slavs. About 860, Cyril and his brother Methodius became apostles to the Slavs—in other words, missionaries. Since the Slavs had no written language, Cyril developed an alphabet for them based on the Greek alphabet. If you read much about Russia, you will notice an oddity. Sometimes the ruler of Russia is called the czar and sometimes the tsar. This variety in spelling is the result of attempts to transliterate the Cyrillic alphabet into our Roman alphabet. No matter how you spell it, tsar or czar, the word is the Russian version of *caesar,* the Roman word for "emperor."

3. Russian and British Trade. During the reign of Ivan the Terrible, the Russians and the British carried on a lively trade. Russian ropes were considered the best in the world, and the British Navy used them on most of their ships. At one time Ivan considered a marriage to Queen Elizabeth I of England, but she was somehow able to resist the charms of a tsar already known as Ivan the Terrible.

4. **Ivan the Terrible.** Ivan the Terrible was tsar of Russia from 1547 to 1584. He did a number of things to build a stronger kingdom, but at times he was simply insane. He concentrated power in the tsar's hands and expanded his kingdom. He brought the first printing press into Russia and was a strong supporter of the Church. But he also killed thousands of Russians. After killing them, he would send lists of the names to the church so monks could pray for their souls. The surviving lists contain 4,000 names, and many more were lost. Ivan himself lost count, saying, "God knows their names." Among those he killed was his son and heir apparent, also named Ivan.

5. **The Education of Peter the Great.** Peter I had a very haphazard education. Mostly he simply ran wild in a village near Moscow. He organized a gang of boys, and they played at warfare, attacking a miniature fort. He found an old, neglected English sailboat and experimented with it on the river. He spent much time visiting foreigners, who taught him arithmetic and geometry. His later life would reflect these influences. Peter modernized the Russian Army. He started the first navy Russia ever had, and he had a lifelong fascination with Europe and its modern ways.

6. **Peter the Great.** Peter was a striking man. He was almost seven feet tall and so strong he could take a heavy silver plate and roll it up in his hand like paper.

In 1697, Peter made a 14-month tour of Europe disguised as Peter Mikhailov, commoner. During the trip he gathered knowledge about many topics. He studied artillery with a Prussian colonel. He observed the dissection of a cadaver in a medical school. In Holland he worked for a time as a carpenter. The English provided him a mansion and dropped all pretense that they didn't know who he was. Peter studied their shipbuilding, and the English even staged a mock sea battle for him. Peter left the mansion a ruin. The doors were torn off their hinges, and old portraits were shot full of bullet holes. It is reported he paid for the damages by handing over a dirty piece of paper wrapped around a huge rough diamond.

The purpose of Peter's trip was to modernize Russia so it could be a great power. Toward this goal Peter bought 35,000 muskets while abroad. He also hired 700 foreign experts to return with him to Russia. In his crude, direct way, he was determined to make Russia modern and strong.

7. **Peter the Great and Calendar Reform.** Peter changed the Russian calendar so it matched the European calendar. Russian religious tradition opposed this reform. The Russians traditionally started their calendar with the creation and began the year with September. They argued that the first year must have begun in September because that was when apples ripened. In January there were no apples on trees. If the year began with January, how could the apples have been on the tree when the serpent tempted Eve? Therefore, the old believers rejected calendar reform as the work of the Antichrist.

8. Peter the Great and Shaved Beards. Peter faced strong opposition to even his most superficial reforms. Shortly after returning from Europe, Peter himself shaved the beards of a number of nobles. Traditional Russians considered this a blasphemy. They argued that humans were made in God's image. Therefore, shaving off the beard was a sort of indirect mutilation of God.

9. Catherine the Great and Potemkin Villages. Catherine the Great worked very hard at modernizing Russia. Her efforts certainly changed the people in her court. The ordinary Russian peasant, however, continued to suffer. But through a trick of Potemkin, one of her lovers and a court official, Catherine was led to believe that the peasants were happy and prosperous. As she traveled down the Dnieper River to visit the Crimea, she would see neat peasant homes and peasants dressed in colorful embroidered costumes happily waving to her as they tended their flocks. In fact, the villages were simply fakes hastily built for the show. The peasants had been brought in from some distance. Many of them would die in the process of plodding back to their real homes.

CHAPTER XIII

Age of the French Revolution

— Overview —

France before the Revolution was full of people who had read enlightened books. These writings by people like Voltaire and Rousseau spread ideas about liberty and equality. Yet the French knew their regime was packed with abuses.

When the Revolution came, it cut through the whole fabric of society. Sometimes the cutting was literal, with the guillotine. The Revolution also changed the cut of a stylish person's clothes and brought many other changes in daily life.

Toward the end of the Revolution, a young general, Napoleon, took over. His rise is the story of a determined drive to power, over heaps of bodies if necessary. His fall was a losing struggle against the British Navy, the Spanish people, and the Russian winter, among other things.

You might try to get a recording of "La Marseillaise" and play it for your students. You might ask them to figure out what their birthday month would be on the revolutionary calendar. It's a little long, but the *1812 Overture* by Tchaikovsky is a stirring musical picture of the Russian campaign. An advanced class would probably enjoy it.

Your students could make a bulletin board showing the revolutionary flag and revolutionary slogans. They could write papers comparing the ideas of Voltaire or Rousseau with events in the Revolution. Was there a connection? They could write papers on why Napoleon rose so fast or what caused his eventual failure.

They could also do "I was there" accounts of "Storming the Bastille," "A Day at the Guillotine," "Trafalgar," "Moscow," or "Waterloo."

A. CAUSES

1. Voltaire's Writing Style. In his day Voltaire was admired for his wit. He had a way of saying things memorably. His words often had a bit of a sting to them. He is therefore a very quotable author. As a historian, he wrote of the Holy Roman Empire, "It is neither holy, nor Roman, nor an empire." When writing about a disagreement, he said, "I do not agree with a word you say, but I will defend to the death your right to say it."

Historians are always admiring old authors, so students are wise to be skeptical, but consider this. When *Playboy* magazine was just starting in the 1950's, it was a shaky financial venture. Money presumably went to the first Playmate, Marilyn Monroe, but there was little cash to pay for writers. Instead of hiring 20th-century authors, the magazine ran selections from older writers considered racy enough to appear next to an unclad Marilyn. One of the first selections was an excerpt from Voltaire's *Candide.*

2. *Voltaire and Religion.* Voltaire, like many Enlightenment writers, was skeptical about religion. He was always very critical of religious intolerance by Catholic or Protestant. His most famous statement about the Church was "Crush the infamous thing." He also built a church on his estate near Tourney in France near the Swiss border. Actually, he did an extensive rebuilding and had "Voltaire erected this to God" carved in Latin on its front. He even preached a sermon there on Easter 1762, speaking against stealing and drunkenness. The local bishop disapproved.

3. Jean-Jacques Rousseau. Like many an educational reformer after him, Rousseau was better at theory than practice. Rousseau wrote *Emile,* a novel that describes the education of a young man. The student was guided by his tutor through a series of experiences. Rousseau believed that the best education did not use books, but stressed experiencing nature. His books have been widely studied and were quite influential in some experimental schools of the 1960's. How did this educational expert educate his own five children? He sent them off to an orphanage. He says in the *Confessions* that the orphanage would be better than letting his wife's family bring them up. Considering the emotional instability he shows in the *Confessions,* he probably would have been a difficult person to live with.

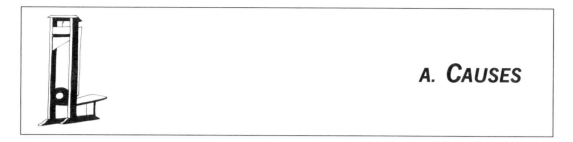

4. Talleyrand. The early life of Talleyrand illustrates some flaws of France before the Revolution. He was the oldest surviving son of an old noble family and should have made a career in the army, but he had a bad foot and walked with a cane. The family arranged for him to become a priest, even though he had little interest in religion and no interest in celibacy. By the time he was 15, he was having an affair with an actress. Family connections counted more than piety in those days, though. After Talleyrand completed his seminary studies, he was appointed abbot and later a bishop. He spent a good deal of his time in Paris enjoying the stylish, wicked life of the city.

When the Estates-General was called to meet, Talleyrand was elected to represent the clergy. He had read revolutionary ideas and supported changes. He suggested that the government seize Church lands, and later wrote the Civil Constitution of the Clergy, which took over the Church and made it part of the government. When the government needed new clergy because some of the old clergy refused to serve the new Church, Talleyrand ordained these new clergymen. He was, after all, a bishop. After this, he was excommunicated and took up a career in politics and diplomacy.

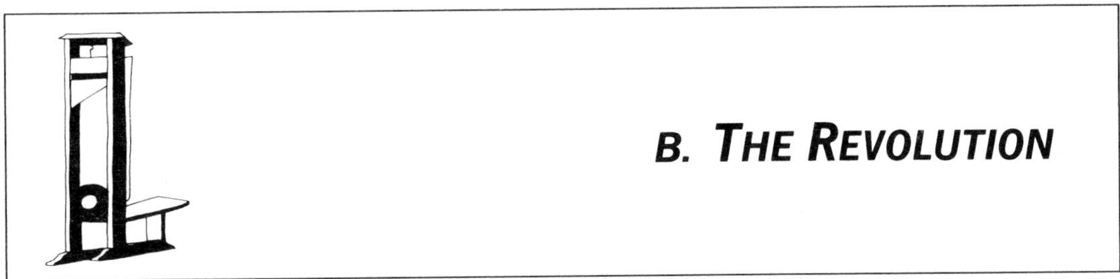

B. THE REVOLUTION

1. The Guillotine. Many, but not all, of the people executed during the Terror were killed by the guillotine. This device had a blade sliding in a frame. The victim placed his or her head in a notch, and at the pull of a lever the blade dropped and the victim was decapitated. The guillotine was actually a revolutionary reform suggested by doctor Joseph Ignace Guillotin, who was a member of the Constituent Assembly. In earlier times beheadings were done by executioners using an axe. If the executioner failed to remove the head with a single clean stroke, the victim suffered terribly and needlessly. With the guillotine, death was quick, painless, and certain. During the Terror, the humorists of the day remarked, "Everybody is losing their heads over Madame Guillotine."

2. The Revolutionary Calendar. The French revolutionaries rejected the traditional calendar and designed one of their own. In it they emphasized reason and nature. While it was adopted in October of 1793, it started with year I on September 22, 1792, the start of the Republic. There were twelve months with names matching the weather or season. Each month had three decades. A decade was a period of ten days which replaced the week. So each month was thirty days. There were five extra days at the end of the year, six in leap years. Such a system, of course, wiped out

Sunday and all the saints' days. It was more an official calendar than one used by the common people. It lasted until Napoleon restored the Gregorian calendar on January 1, 1806. He announced his decision on 22 Fructidor, year XIII.

Revolutionary Month Year II Start Date	*Translation*	*Gregorian Date for Start*
1 Vendémiaire	vintage	September 22, 1793
1 Brumaire	mist	October 22, 1793
1 Frimaire	frost	November 21, 1793
1 Nivôse	snow	December 21, 1793
1 Pluviôse	rain	January 20, 1794
1 Ventôse	wind	February 19, 1794
1 Germinal	seed-time	March 21, 1794
1 Floréal	blossom	April 20, 1794
1 Prairial	meadow	May 20, 1794
1 Messidor	harvest	June 19, 1794
1 Thermidor	heat	July 19, 1794
1 Fructidor	fruits	August 18, 1794

3. "La Marseillaise." The French national anthem was written during the Revolution. It was written in Strasbourg in 1792, but it became so identified with volunteers from Marseilles who sang the song as they marched to Paris and camped there that people called it "La Marseillaise." It was officially adopted on Bastille Day, July 14, 1795.

4. Clothing. The French Revolution changed nearly everything, even clothing styles. Before the Revolution, French aristocrats had worn knee breeches. Revolutionaries wore the full-length trousers of the working people. The red liberty cap was very popular. Women often dressed in the white robes of ancient republican Rome. Jewelry was frowned upon. Nearly everybody was expected to wear something in the colors of the revolution—red, white, and blue. Somebody even produced a deck of cards with the royalist kings, queens, and jacks replaced by liberties, equalities, and fraternities—the ideals of the Revolution.

5. The Terror and Name Changes. During the Revolution, the French language changed. People were no longer called *monsieur* or *madame,* but now became *citoyen,* "citizen." People changed their names. *Leroys* meaning "kings" now became *Laloys* meaning "laws." One enthusiastic Jacobin named his child Libre Constitution Letruc, or "Free Constitution Letruc." Street names changed in a similar way. Place Louis XV became Place de la Revolution. The Street of the Crown became the Street of the Nations. The word *king* was strictly forbidden. There was even an attempt to retitle the "queen bee" into the more revolutionary "laying bee."

6. Revolutionary Religion and the Supreme Being. The Catholic Church of Old Regime France was traditional and therefore rejected by the revolutionaries. Many of them were deists who believed in a sort of watchmaker God who had made the world and had given it natural laws to run by. It was this God, called simply "the Supreme Being," who was celebrated in a festival held June 8, 1794, in Paris. Robespierre was the chief speaker. The sermon was followed by singing and firing of cannons.

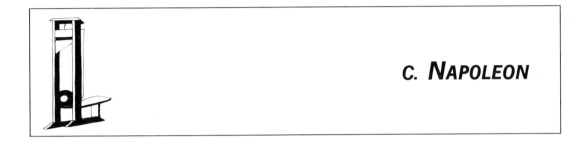

C. NAPOLEON

1. At School. Napoleon's background was at least as much Italian as French. He was born and raised on the island of Corsica just after it was made part of France. His father was part of the Italian resistance for a time before becoming a French official. Tradition has it that the students at military school teased Napoleon because he spoke French with an Italian accent. His political connections were poor. He chose to specialize in artillery because artillery demanded some technical ability. Artillery officers had to know some mathematics and physics to aim the guns. While cavalry and infantry officers had little skill except yelling "Fire!" or "Forward!" and were commissioned on the basis of politics, artillery was the only military branch that would let a poor boy with few political connections advance.

2. Napoleon's Rise. As a result of his important role in the siege of Toulon in 1794, Napoleon was made brigadier general at the age of 24. But his great chance came in Paris against civilians. In 1795, Napoleon was in Paris in charge of artillery guarding the Convention when a rebellion broke out, and attackers marched on the Convention. Napoleon coolly put them down with "a whiff of grape." That is, he packed his cannon with grapeshot—round balls about the size of grapes—and fired it at the rebels. Such fire quickly cleared the streets of all but dead bodies. Napoleon had saved the government. After that he was the most important general that the government, the Directory, had.

3. A Grave or a Title: Nelson at the Nile. In April of 1798, Napoleon Bonaparte was appointed to command a French army. His mission was to sail to Egypt and conquer the East, thus threatening British India. While Napoleon was able to win land battles, the British Navy under Admiral Horatio Nelson cut his supply line. Nelson found the French fleet at anchor in Abukir Bay near Alexandria. He remarked, "Before this time tomorrow I shall have gained a peerage or Westminster

Abbey." A peerage is a noble title. Westminster Abbey is the church in London where famous people are buried.

Nelson attacked. Even though the French fleet was anchored very close to the shore, Nelson's ships sailed between them and the shore and attacked from both sides. The French admiral had assumed that he was safe from the land side, so he had shifted all his guns so they pointed to sea. Nelson had two or more ships concentrated on a single French ship. Nearby French ships could only watch helplessly, knowing they were next. The battle started at sunset and ran through the night. The only light came from blazing guns and burning ships. By noon the next day, Nelson's force of 13 ships had destroyed or captured all but 3 French ships out of a fleet of 17.

Although Napoleon's army was still intact, it was now cut off from supplies and reinforcements. Defeat was only a matter of time.

4. A Blind Eye at Copenhagen. The British Navy was one force Napoleon could not overcome. The "Little Corporal" was matched by a short, slightly built English admiral, Horatio Nelson. Nelson saw some hard fighting. By 1801 he had lost an arm, and one eye was blind. The eye was to be very useful in the Battle of Copenhagen on April 2, 1801. The Danes were forming an alliance against the British, so the Royal Navy attacked the Danish fleet anchored in the harbor at Copenhagen. Nelson was technically second in command, but was in charge of leading the attack. As the battle was starting and smoke was billowing from guns, Admiral Hyde Parker, Nelson's superior, signaled by flags that Nelson should stop the attack.

Nelson was in the thick of the fight when he was told about the signal. He remarked, "You know I have only one eye. I have a right to be blind sometimes." Then he put his telescope up to his blind eye and remarked, "I really do not see the signal." In the next few hours, Nelson's fleet destroyed or captured 17 ships out of a fleet of 18. After that, Nelson went ashore and negotiated an armistice with the Danes.

5. Napoleon and the Pope. Ever since the Civil Constitution of the clergy, the French revolutionaries had been on bad terms with the pope. During the Consulate, Napoleon decided to end this dispute. He assigned his foreign minister, Talleyrand, to negotiate an agreement. Talleyrand was an expert on church-state relations. He was an ex-bishop and had written the Civil Constitution of the Clergy. He was also a skillful diplomat. In 1801, he worked out a concordat between Napoleon and Pope Pius VII. This included the delicate matter of married priests. The pope agreed that French priests who had married while under the Civil Constitution of the Clergy could stay married and still be priests. Some cynics called this the "Madame Grand" clause, because Talleyrand himself was married to Madame Grand.

After this agreement, the pope became a supporter of Napoleon. The pope was present when Napoleon was crowned emperor. He started to place the crown on Napoleon's head, but Napoleon took it from the pope's hands and crowned himself.

6. Trafalgar.

Napoleon had plans to invade England. He was massing troops as early as 1803. All he needed to do was somehow get the British Navy out of the way and the invasion would be on. The French admiral, Villeneuve, tried to do this by sailing to the West Indies. He hoped this would decoy the British fleet under Lord Nelson, and then while they hunted him in the West Indies, he would sail back to Europe and protect the invasion. It almost worked, but Nelson caught Villeneuve near Cape Trafalgar off the southwest coast of Spain on October 21, 1805. In this massive battle, the British fleet of 27 ships faced 33 ships of a combined French and Spanish fleet.

Nelson was eager for battle. Before the battle began, he sent a signal to his fleet using flags. The message was "England expects that every man will do his duty." Then he ran up another signal, "Engage the enemy more closely." Nelson's fleet closed with the enemy. The French and Spanish tried to stay in a single line, but the British broke through their line and concentrated their attack on the rear and center. Nelson on his flagship *Victory* was in the thick of the action. The British were much superior in sailing and gunnery, so the result was a lopsided victory. The British sank or destroyed 20 enemy ships, while the English forces did not lose a single ship of their own. There was, however, one tragic loss. Nelson was shot while pacing the deck of the *Victory*. He was taken below, where he died. His last recorded words were "Thank God I have done my duty."

After this defeat, Napoleon could no longer threaten Britain with invasion. The British still celebrate Trafalgar Day. Nelson's flagship is in a drydock in Portsmouth. She still flies an admiral's flag, and on October 21 each year, she displays Nelson's signal, "England expects that every man will do his duty."

7. Guerrilla Warfare.

When Napoleon put his brother Joseph on the throne of Spain, the Spanish people were determined to resist. They did not have a formal army, but they could and did form small groups of raiders to attack French stragglers and made life miserable for the French. Later, they would cooperate with the British Army as they pushed the French out of Spain. These small units fought small battles in a sort of "little war." In Spanish that becomes *guerrilla*. The word is used today in English to describe an irregular military force that uses harassing tactics against an enemy army.

8. Napoleon in Russia.

Napoleon's defeat in Russia was one of the great disasters of military history. It was caused by a combination of mistakes and made more horrible by Napoleon's attitude toward his soldiers.

Napoleon's "Grande Armée" was much too large to be supplied by the supply systems of the time. The army's numbers are estimated at various levels—530,000 or 600,000—but either number was too big. Even a friendly country couldn't supply that many soldiers. Poland did not have enough mills to grind their flour or enough ovens to bake their bread. The army's liquor supply was four million bottles of beer and brandy. The army started out with 200,000 animals, including 90,000 cattle and oxen that were to be butchered as needed. Convoys of wagons were to haul food to the army over the roads of Russia, which were narrow, rutted, and muddy. The convoys simply couldn't keep up.

While the Russians withdrew before the French advance, they did fight before Moscow. At Borodino the French lost 30,000 men and the Russians 45,000. Then the advance continued into Moscow. Ordinarily an army found quarters in a captured city. There was plenty of room. Moscow was normally a city of 250,000, and only about 15,000 remained as the army marched in. However, the governor of Moscow, Count Rostopchin, had ordered the city burned. On September 15, the city was on fire. The flames were so bright French soldiers four miles outside Moscow could read letters at midnight by the firelight. The 95,000 French soldiers in Moscow looted the place of furs, gold, jewelry, and church treasures. Three quarters of Moscow was burned before heavy rain stopped the fires. Napoleon waited for the tsar to surrender, but he never came. So far the weather was warm, but soon the Russians' best general, "General Winter," would come.

After a futile wait, the French Army moved out of Moscow for home on October 19. Many of the soldiers pushed wheelbarrows and handcarts full of treasures. They could have turned south and moved through rich farmland, but instead Napoleon decided to go back along a route nearly identical to that of the invasion. This decision would cost thousands of men their lives.

They marched past the site of their victory at Borodino and 30,000 rotting, unburied Frenchmen. Each river crossing became an exercise in terror as the Russians closed in on those left on the far side. Now the Russians could pluck jewels from the mud, thrown there by panicky French soldiers. On December 3, the temperature fell to -20°F. On that night 500 soldiers took shelter in a barn and slept huddled together around several fires. By the next morning three quarters of them had died of the cold. Discipline broke down and men stole clothes from the dead. One soldier started taking clothes from a dying officer who said, "Comrade, I am not dead yet." The soldier replied, "Very well, sir, I will wait a few minutes." By the time the French left Russia, only a fraction of the Grande Armée was still alive.

How had Napoleon survived this ordeal? He may have put on weight. He ate well, with linen on his table. He was served beef or mutton and his favorite vegetables. On December 7, he left the Grande Armée and dashed ahead to Paris. He had said, "An army marches on its stomach," but somehow hadn't provided for the stomach of his army. He had also said, "In war, men are nothing; one man is everything." He provided for the one man—himself.

9. The Return from Elba. After his disastrous Russian campaign and his resulting defeats, Napoleon was sent off to be emperor of Elba, a tiny island near Italy. It had a small army and a navy of ten boats. A British fleet patrolled the waters around Elba to see that Napoleon stayed put, but he did not. In February of 1815, Napoleon and 1,000 troops sailed from Elba and landed in France. This has to be one of the great gambles of history. The French Army was more than adequate to stop Napoleon if its soldiers stayed loyal. But Napoleon advanced. When he met some soldiers from the Grenoble garrison blocking the road with weapons ready, he stepped forward and opened his coat saying, "If one among you wishes to kill his emperor, I am here." The soldiers threw down their guns and followed him. Later another royal army under Marshal Ney, who had served under Napoleon in Russia, confronted the advancing ex-emperor. When they met, Ney embraced Napoleon and cried. Napoleon returned to Paris in a triumphant march followed by the soldiers sent out to capture him. Once again he was the emperor of France.This time he would rule for 100 days.

10. Waterloo. Napoleon was a gambler. Early in his career he had taken some gambles against long odds and won. At Waterloo he took a long shot and lost.

Once again Napoleon was facing two allied armies which, if combined, were larger than his own. In earlier days he had faced this threat and beaten it by defeating each army before they could unite. The Prussian Army under Marshal Blücher would be first; then the British under the Duke of Wellington could be destroyed.

The campaign went well at first. The French advanced against the Prussians and inflicted heavy losses on them in the battle of Ligny. Surely the 72-year-old Blücher and his tired, wounded army were out of the picture. Then the French turned on the British and forced them to retreat after an action at Quatre Bras. The British retreated to a piece of rising ground near the village of Waterloo.

It had rained the night before, and the morning of June 18, 1815, was cloudy. Napoleon waited until 11:30 A.M. so the mud would dry and give his cavalry better footing. Then the battle began. The French were attacking and the British grimly hanging on. Wellington rode among his troops encouraging them to stay steady. Napoleon commanded from a hill in the rear.

The French sent attack after attack against the British. "Hard pounding," observed Wellington as he watched the action. The French were trying to punch a hole in the British line and destroy Wellington's army. About 7:30 P.M. they almost made it. The French elite guard advanced and reached the crest of the ridge. They gave a cheer. They could see nothing before them. Then Wellington called out, "Now, Maitland! Now is your time!" A force of British soldiers who had been lying down in the field before the French stood up and opened a murderous fire. Soon the French broke and began to retreat, then to run. At this point Wellington ordered the British to charge.

Even by early afternoon Napoleon had realized that he was in trouble. He had seen troops wearing the blue uniforms of Prussia on his right rear as early as 1:00 P.M. The elderly Blücher was leading his battered force cross-country to the aid of his ally. By 7:30 they were closing in on the French from the flank and rear. Caught in the double attack from British and Prussians, the French Army crumbled.

Napoleon escaped from the battlefield, but he was soon captured and sent off to exile on the island of St. Helena. He had gambled at Waterloo and lost an empire.

CHAPTER XIV

Changes in Asia, Africa, and Latin America

— Overview —

During the 18th and early 19th centuries Asia, Africa, and Latin America saw some changes. India was ruled by the most unlikely government, the British East India Company. Japan went from strict isolation to energetic modernization. African cultures still flourished, but the continent was being bled weak by the slave trade. Latin America was a quiet colonial area.

Your students could do papers contrasting the proud tradition of African cultures with the treatment of slaves. They could do papers comparing and contrasting Japan in isolation with Japan modernizing. They could compare and contrast the Spanish colonial system in Latin America with the British system in India. Artistic students could make a bulletin board on the slave trade. They could use a map to show the trade routes, and they could draw ship-loading plans.

The imaginative student could write a paper on "A Japanese View of Commodore Perry," "A Visit to Benin" (or Timbuktu), or "A Log of a Slave Ship."

A. INDIA

1. The East India Company. The East India Company was a joint stock company, a device England used to encourage merchants to trade in certain places. Such a company was given the exclusive right to trade in a particular area. In return, the company paid a fee to the crown. Each company was made up of a group of stockholders. When the East India Company started, it had about 200 stockholders, including a grocer, a goldsmith, and a leather merchant. Once organized, the company hired people to conduct the business. In the case of the East India Company, the business would become ruling India.

Other similar companies were the Hudson Bay Company in Canada, the Muscovy Company trading in Russia, the Levant Company in the Middle East, and the Virginia Company, which started English colonization in North America.

The chief product of the East India Company was tea. It was East India Company tea that was dumped into Boston Harbor during the Boston Tea Party. The company, often called "John Company," had enough influence in Parliament to get special laws passed for its advantage.

B. JAPAN

1. Isolation. During the 17th, 18th, and 19th centuries, the Japanese insisted on keeping contact with foreigners to an absolute minimum. For example, in 1845, the American whaling ship *Manhattan* was off the Japanese coast and found seven Japanese marooned on a tiny island. Captain Cooper of the *Manhattan* took them aboard, searched the nearby seas, and found more Japanese on a wrecked ship. He decided to take them back to Japan. As he approached port, Cooper first landed some of the castaways on a point of land so they could tell Japanese officials about him. He sailed into the Bay of Yedo. When he reached the bay, his ship was surrounded by a thousand armed boats, and his crew was not allowed to leave the ship. The rescued Japanese were taken off the ship. The Japanese officials were not hostile; one even spoke some English. The Americans were given presents: tea, rice, wheat flour, vegetables, fifty chickens, a basketful of flatfish, and two octopuses. These would be a valued addition to the food supply on the long voyage. The Americans also were given a set of lacquered bowls and ten painted dishes. Then they were gently but firmly sent on their way.

For the Japanese authorities, the event had been cause for great concern. A report was filed. They noted that most of the crew looked like the Dutch, but that eight had black faces and bodies.

2. Opening Japan. Americans tend to think that Commodore Perry opened Japan alone, failing to realize that in 1854, Japan was under pressure from other countries as well as the United States. Even as Perry was making his second visit, the Russian Admiral Putyatin was also returning for a second time to Nagasaki. Within a few weeks Admiral Sterling of the British Navy entered Nagasaki and signed a treaty. A whirlpool caused by an earthquake later sank the Russian's ship. The Japanese welcomed the admiral ashore, and in February 1855 they negotiated a treaty with Russia. The Netherlands also got a treaty for more open trade in 1855. The Japanese had decided to open up to foreign contact and learn from the foreigners. The Dutch helped this process by giving the Japanese a steamboat, the first in the country.

3. Modernization. The Japanese learned modern ways quickly. They first saw a steamship in 1853. By 1860, a Japanese crew steamed a ship across the Pacific.

C. Africa

1. The Mosquito. The deadliest animal in Africa is the anopheles mosquito. It breeds in watery areas and carries malaria, even now a devastating disease. Early missionaries in Africa had a 50 percent fatality rate, mainly due to malaria. In spite of modern efforts to control the mosquito by draining and spraying, the insect still survives.

2. Benin and the Portuguese. The Portuguese made contact with Benin in 1486. Joao Afonso d'Aveiro established trading and diplomatic ties. Pepper from Benin sold for a high price. The king of Benin sent an ambassador to Portugal, and for over 100 years the two countries had diplomatic ties. In 1553, the king of Benin was reported to be able to speak Portuguese.

3. Benin Described. A Dutch visitor saw the center of Benin in 1602 and thought it was a very great town. Its main street was seven or eight times wider than the main street in Amsterdam and ran straight for four miles. The town was fortified by a ditch and a high, thick earthen wall. The town also had side streets and houses arranged in neat order close together, as in Holland.

Another Dutch traveler 60 years later reported that the king's palace was as big as Haarlem, a good-sized Dutch town. He also reported that the king's apartments were as big as those found in Amsterdam.

4. Timbuktu. Timbuktu at its peak was an impressive city. A Moor named Leo Africanus wrote a book around 1523 about his travels and described the city. Physically it was not showy. Houses had thatched roofs, and fire was a danger. Nearly half the town burned while Africanus was there. But Timbuktu did have a mosque and a palace. The people were cheerful and rich, including doctors, priests, and learned men. In fact, there was a brisk trade in books and manuscripts. The value of books sold was greater than the value of any other products traded, and there was a lively trade in many other items. European goods were available, and there were many linen and cotton weavers. The king had a royal scepter of solid gold. He also had an army of 3,000 cavalry and even more infantry. They were armed with bows and poison arrows.

5. The Kingdom of Mali. In 1352, a Berber named Ibn Battuta visited Mali. He hated the food. The ruler entertained him with a mixture of pounded millet, milk, and honey. Battuta noted that the people hated injustice, and that the ruler never pardoned someone guilty of it. He also noted that people were safe in this land, and even the traveler had no more reason to fear bandits than the person who stayed at home.

D. THE SLAVE TRADE

1. Sources of Slaves. One researcher interviewed some ex-slaves and found that they became slaves in the following ways. Kidnapping sent 30 percent into slavery, and 34 percent had been prisoners of war. But 7 percent were sold into slavery by relatives, and another 7 percent were sold because of debts. Courts sentenced 11 percent to slavery. Fully 11 percent could not give reasons for becoming slaves. These were all people from the 19th century. At other times the proportions of people made slaves for certain reasons would probably be different.

2. The Passage. Before they were put on the boat, all newly enslaved Africans had their heads shaved, were branded, and were given a generous meal. Then they were chained together; men and women were separated and packed tightly into the ships. They were brought up on deck twice a day to eat and exercise. The slaves often disliked the food, but if they refused to eat, they were force-fed. Rice was a common food. Slaves were given about a pint of water a day to drink and a chance to wash each day. The ship's crew was on constant alert against possible slave uprisings.

Figures on the death rate among slaves on the passage vary widely. Some records, from 1680 to 1688, indicate a 24 percent death rate. Later records in the 1790's show rates as low as 2.4 percent, but even then some ships had rates as high as 52 percent.

3. The Destination. Slaves from Africa were shipped to a number of destinations in North and South America. Of all African slaves shipped, Brazil received 37 percent. They were used in gold mining and had a life span of ten to twelve years in slavery. The British Caribbean received 17 percent; the French Caribbean, 17 percent; the Dutch, Danish, and Swedish Caribbean combined, 6 percent. These slaves were used mostly for growing sugar. Spanish America received 17 percent. Blacks came to Spanish America very early. Alfonso Pietro, who was pilot of the *Niña,* one of Columbus's ships, was black. The conquistadores imported slaves, and government officials were allowed slaves. Even priests were allowed to take three to eight slaves with them to the New World. Slaves often were helpful in conquering Indians. Some freed blacks became overseers and managers. Some freedmen even became slave-owners. When sugar became a major crop, slaves were needed for field labor. In 1518, Charles I of Spain granted permission to import 4,000 slaves a year to Spanish America. At that period, North America received only 6 percent of the slaves shipped from Africa.

4. African Culture in Latin America. The slaves who were shipped across the Atlantic Ocean often carried their culture with them. Sometimes cultural groups reunited in the new land. Yoruba, from what is now Nigeria, formed groups in Brazil and Cuba. In Spanish and Portuguese areas slaves were forced to be Catholic, but they often substituted African religious practices for official church events. Halloween became a time for ancestor worship and Easter a time for mourning dead ancestors. In Haiti, African gods were identified with Christian saints. There was a Saint Sun and a Saint Moon. In Cuba the Yoruba sky god became identified with Jesus. African practice shaped religion in a number of other ways. For example, Africans tell stories with a storyteller talking and the audience responding and calling out. This is the pattern in African-American churches even now.

Slaves also carried their traditional stories with them. The stories told by Uncle Remus about Br'er Rabbit, Br'er Fox, and other such creatures are transplanted tales originally told in Africa. The same stories are told in Brazil, brought there by slaves from their African homeland.

5. The Slave Trade Abolished. While churches did accept and even support slavery at times, they also were the major force pushing for abolition of the slave trade. In England, the Methodists and Quakers were most active. In the 1790's, there was great pressure on Parliament to abolish the slave trade. Abolitionists gave up sugar because it was so often the product of slave labor. A flurry of reports on the evils of the trade appeared, and finally, in 1807, England abolished slavery. This was a critical event, because the British Navy could now be used to shut the slave trade down. Denmark had abolished its overseas trade in 1802. The United States shut off slave imports in 1808. Later came Sweden in 1813, Holland in 1814, and France in 1815. Some other places were slower. Brazil took until 1852 and Cuba until 1888. Notice that it was the slave trade, not slavery itself, that was outlawed. In some places slavery continued within the country even though more slaves could not be imported. After 1815, however, the slave trade was banned in most of Europe. One result was that profits in the illegal trade doubled.

E. LATIN AMERICA

1. Mexico's First Printing Press. Mexico was settled by European colonists much earlier than the English settlement on North America. Mexico had a printing press in 1534, over 70 years before the first English were to settle at Jamestown in 1607.

2. Mexico's Independence. When Mexico became independent, the United States quickly sent an envoy to negotiate for trade privileges. The person chosen by President John Quincy Adams was Joel R. Poinsett. The mission was a failure. Poinsett returned without an agreement, but he did bring home a flower he found in Mexico. The flower is named after him, the poinsettia.

CHAPTER XV
The Industrial Revolution

— Overview —

Something dramatic started in Britain in the late 18th and early 19th centuries. The Industrial Revolution changed daily life so much that historians had to notice the common people a bit. The machines were wonders, making life easier, safer, and more pleasant, but they had a price, most of which was paid by the working people. Observers argued about how the new system worked. Some said it was perfect and couldn't be changed, while one named Karl Marx argued it was so evil it would inevitably be destroyed. Others took the middle ground, and argued for changes to fix obvious problems.

You could have your students do papers comparing and contrasting travel before and after railroads were built. You could have them compare and contrast the making of cloth before and after the Industrial Revolution. It takes research, but it's very revealing to compare the standard of living of an industrialized nation with the standard of living in one that is not industrialized: Britain and Bangladesh, perhaps. It is also interesting to compare the lives of working children in the Industrial Revolution with current American laws about child labor and child abuse. More able students could compare and contrast the observers' reactions to the Industrial Revolution: David Ricardo and Karl Marx or Karl Marx and George Bernard Shaw. Your dramatic students might even want to do a reading from a Shaw play that shows the playwright's ideas.

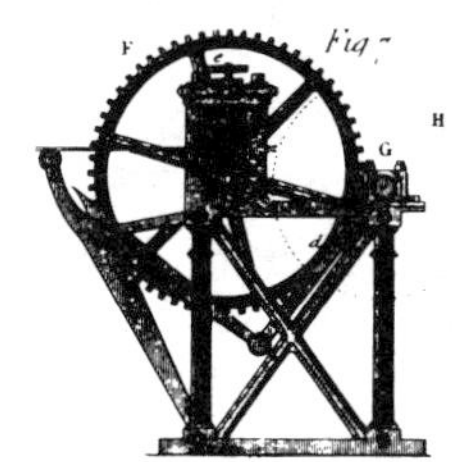

A. The Machines

1. Hand Spinning. The Industrial Revolution in England seems to have started in textiles. This is in part because England already had a brisk business in producing textiles by hand. Many of the workers were women. Our language reflects this. A "spinster" is an unmarried woman. In England before the Industrial Revolution, an unmarried woman would often have to make her living by spinning, thus becoming a "spinster."

2. The Spinning Jenny. About 1764, James Hargreaves, a poor spinner and weaver, invented the spinning jenny. His young daughter Jenny knocked over his spinning wheel, and he noticed that the spindle kept turning. It was in an upright position instead of horizontal on the wheel. Hargreaves figured out that several spindles could be put upright and turn out much more thread. His first "jennys," named for his daughter, were wooden and turned out eight times as much thread as the old spinning wheel. He and a partner built a mill and sold yarn to people who made stockings.

3. Railroads Develop. Railroads developed slowly from horse-drawn wagons to steam power. The rail is the key to the efficiency of railroads. There is much less friction resisting the rolling wagon wheel if the wheel is on a rail. This fact led some coal mines to build wooden railroads and have humans or horses pull the cars over the rails. Some systems even used gravity, simply letting loaded carts roll downhill, then pulling them back with horses. Coal was cheap in the mines, so the idea of using steam for power seemed attractive. A mining engineer named Richard Trevithick designed and built a steam locomotive, which on February 13, 1804, pulled 25 tons of iron 9½ miles at 5 miles per hour. Unfortunately, the machine was too heavy for the rails and was not used again. Several inventors now worked at the project, among them George Stephenson. He built the *Rocket,* which in October 1829 became the first practical locomotive. It could pull a 90-ton train of 38 carriages at a speed of 12–16 miles an hour.

The early railroad carriages were built much like the horse-drawn carriages of the day, and freight was hauled in wagons like those seen on the roads. The locomotives were simply flat platforms with wheels and steam engines mounted on them. The engineer and fireman stood out in the open behind or beside the engine. The first rails were strips of wood. Later they were topped by strips of iron, and eventually they were made entirely of cast iron.

4. Opposition to Railroads. The first steam railroads in England were opposed for a wide variety of reasons. People who owned land along the proposed routes feared all kinds of damage. They claimed that their cows would be frightened and stop giving milk. They feared that haystacks would be set on fire by sparks. They even argued that the railroad would frighten away foxes and ruin hunting. Of course, everybody who made a living serving horses or people traveling by horse or stagecoach objected that their business would be ruined. This group included innkeepers and blacksmiths as well as horse breeders and carriage-makers.

Then there were the medical objections. Doctors said travel through railway tunnels would produce colds, chills, or worse. Passengers with high blood pressure were warned that speedy travel produced apoplexy. One expert claimed that people didn't really sleep on trains; they were just unconscious from "concussion of the brain." Some people simply believed that speeds in the 20- to 30-miles-an-hour range were faster than nature permitted people to go and therefore blasphemous.

5. The *Orient Express*. In the later 19th century, passenger trains became a speedy and elegant way for the rich to travel. The *Orient Express* was one of the most famous of these luxurious trains. It took passengers from Paris to Constantinople in less than three days. The dining car featured snow-white linen, waiters in white knee stockings, and elegant food like champagne and oysters. Passengers rode in compartments with velvet-covered seats and damask-curtained windows. Paneling was of oak and mahogany. Over the years, the *Orient Express* developed a reputation for glamour and mystery. Famous mystery writer Agatha Christie drew on this in her *Murder on the Orient Express*. The train has even been a feature on television's *60 Minutes*.

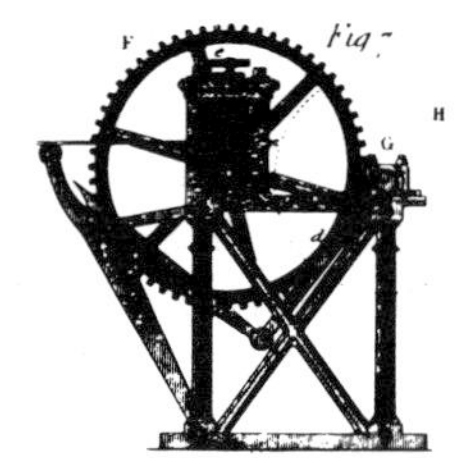

B. The Workers

1. Coal-Mining Hazards. The 1842 British Parliamentary Commission on the Employment of Children talked to owners of coal mines about conditions. One owner, David Musket, described how a boy was killed by some falling coal. The boy had asked an older boy if there was any danger. He was told there wasn't. So he went into that part of the mine, a crack developed, and the boy was buried in coal. Musket went on to say that he had seen no physical injuries to young people from their work. Then he said that the men usually developed asthma about age 50 or 55.

The person writing the commission's report spoke highly of Mr. Musket and blamed the boy who was killed for not being more careful. The writer failed to note the evidence of what we now call black lung disease.

2. Children's Deaths. The British Parliament was curious about child labor in the mines and factories. In 1842, it set up a commission to investigate. The report listed 50 deaths in a period of 3 years and 6 months in the coal mines of the Bradford and Halifax district. Of the 50 deaths, 34 were of children under 16. Here are some examples: Joseph Craven, age 7, fell down a mine shaft; Francis Taylor, age 11, died during an explosion in the mine (the owner had been negligent and did not go into the pit to check it); Joshua Stansfield, age 8, fell down a mine shaft; Enoch Hurst, age 10, was killed by a piece of coal falling on him. (There was a note that nobody was to blame because Enoch could have gotten out of the way.) The report also noted that the young workers often had injuries of the feet and legs caused by running over coal and stones without shoes. Their scalps were thickened and inflamed from friction on their heads caused by hitting the tops of the tunnel. They had lost their hair. The report noted that in general their health was good.

3. Children as "Hurriers." Many children had jobs as hurriers, pulling carts of coal as they crawled along through mine tunnels. The carts weighed from 200 to 500 pounds and rolled on cast-iron wheels. The hurriers wore a leather harness to pull the carts. They could not stand up because the roof of the tunnel was often very low, as little as 20, 18, or even 16 inches. The hours of work were not regular, but work started at 6:00 A.M. and could last until 7:00, 8:00, or 9:00 at night with no rest break. One boy reported that the boys stopped pulling after the horse quit working. The adult workers took days off, but the boys were expected to work every day. If they took off a day, they were expected to work extra the next day.

4. Children's Food. While children worked in the mines as hurriers, they needed to eat. They usually ate in the mine without washing up. Breakfast was usually oatmeal and hot milk or water; dinner, eaten at 9:00, 10:00, or 11:00 in the morning, was a six-ounce wheat pancake or a coarse, flat oaten pancake with a bit of butter or lard. Children went home after work for supper.

5. Parents Bring Children to the Mines. Children were often taken by their parents to start working in the mines. Joseph Gledhill sometimes took his child to the mine at age three. The child would hold a candle for him until tired, then sleep on a pile of coal. He took the child to work regularly at the age of four. He started two others in the mines at ages four and five. A sample of 30 children working the mines shows 17 between the ages of six and nine.

6. Working Families. The Commissioners on the Employment of Children received a report in 1842 on some visits to families. One was a family of a husband and wife with six children. The three boys aged 15, 13, and 11 all worked. The three girls were 7, 5, and 2 and did not have jobs. The father worked and the wife helped him. The father did his work in the upstairs room of their two-room house. Three children slept downstairs in a dirty bed with one ragged blanket. Upstairs there were two dirty beds and a wooden cradle. The father drank so much the family depended on the oldest son's earnings to buy food. Only one child could read, and none could write. In one family with six children, four could read but none could write. It was common that children could neither read nor write. One widower with seven children reported that work was irregular and that he and his children could not get enough to eat and drink.

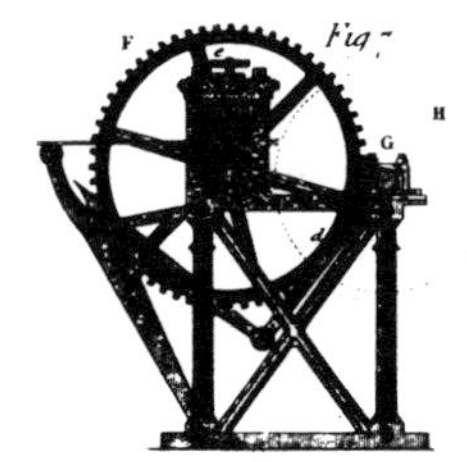

C. Some Results

1. London Fog. One of the trademarks of London in the 19th century was a dense fog, thick as pea soup. It was the product of the Industrial Revolution. All those coal-burning smokestacks were spewing out high-sulphur, high-carbon smoke. The smoke mingled with the moist air over London to produce the fog.

2. The Corn Laws. The repeal of the Corn Laws was a major change in British trade policy. No longer would Britain protect her farmers with tariffs. Britain would trade her manufactured products for food. How could a law about corn have such impact? Because the corn in question was not corn as most Americans think of it, in cornflakes or growing tall in Iowa. That grain is called *maize* in Britain. *Corn* in British English is wheat or other grains used to make breads. How could the British be so sure they could sell their manufactured goods? Because at the time, Britain was the only industrialized country on earth.

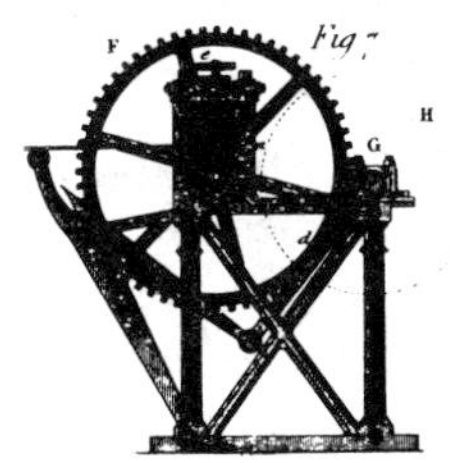

D. Reactions to the Industrial Revolution

1. Nonconformists. The political history of England makes frequent reference to "Nonconformists." Nonconformists were often active in reform efforts in 19th-century England. To Americans the word means an odd person, but in England it meant people who did not conform to the established church, the Church of England. These could be Quakers, for example.

2. David Ricardo. One of the most interesting responses to conditions in the Industrial Revolution came from David Ricardo, a businessman who lived from 1772 to 1823. Ricardo maintained that the working people were doomed to stay miserable forever, and nothing reformers could do would change it. He developed what he called the "iron law of wages." It said that wages would always stay at a level just barely above starvation. If workers were given wages that were higher than the starvation level, they would simply have more children. When these children went to work, the increased number of workers would again drive wages down to the starvation level.

This argument, of course, suggested that it was foolish for government to interfere in the operation of the economy, a position taken by the capitalist economists of the time. No wonder then that economics was called the dismal science.

3. Karl Marx. Karl Marx was an unlikely revolutionary, but he spoke out against the evils of the Industrial Revolution as he saw them. His father was a lawyer, his wife came from a prosperous family, and his best friend was the son of a factory owner. His family had been Jewish, but his father converted to Christianity to improve his law practice. Karl attended a good university and studied philosophy. After he completed his studies in 1841, Marx became editor of a newspaper, the *Rheinische Zeitung,* but the paper was suppressed for its radical views. Marx moved to Belgium and while there wrote his most famous book, *The Communist Manifesto.* It was published early in 1848. Marx's coauthor was Friedrich Engels, the son of a factory owner.

The *Manifesto* contained the ideas that were the core of later communism. It opened with: "A specter is haunting Europe—the specter of Communism." Then it outlined the history of Europe, stating, "All history is the record of class struggle." After explaining how a revolution would happen, the *Manifesto* proclaimed, "The workers have nothing to lose but their chains. They have a world to win. Workers of the world, unite!"

Although the *Manifesto* had no influence on the revolutions of 1848, Marx was run out of Belgium and, later, Germany, resettling in London. He spent the rest of his life researching his big book, *Das Kapital*. It is a huge, dull, three-volume work explaining the evils of capitalism.

Marx was so devoted to his work that his family was terribly poor. Only money from Engels kept them alive. At one time Marx had no stamps to mail articles to newspapers. One winter he had to stay inside because he had pawned his shoes and overcoat. His wife had to beg money to buy a coffin when one of their children died. Marx himself died in 1883. He had never led a revolution. He had a particular dislike for Russians and Russia. He had once said in exasperation, "I am not a Marxist."

The following story circulated in the 1950's. A bearded man approached the gates of workers' paradise and asked to be let in. The gatekeeper was skeptical. "What did you do for a living?" he asked.

"I was a scholar and philosopher," came the reply.

"What was your father's work?"

"He was a lawyer."

"Were you a part of the Russian Revolution?"

"No. I'm German and died years before it."

"You're not a worker; you never took part in a revolution. What makes you think you can get into the workers' paradise?"

"I thought my name would help. I'm Karl Marx."

4. Friedrich Engels. Friedrich Engels was the son of a prosperous business family. He became a radical and a friend of Karl Marx. In 1844, Engels published a study of how poor people lived. It was called *The Condition of the Working Class in England.* He based it on his visits to slums in Manchester, England. A story reports that once Engels was talking to a prosperous friend and remarked that Manchester was the worst-built city he had ever seen. The friend listened, then remarked that there was a lot of money made there and bid him good day.

5. Charles Dickens. Most of us have seen *A Christmas Carol* in one version or another. Charles Dickens wrote the story in the 19th century, and it is partly an attempt to make his readers more sympathetic to the poor. Scrooge is, of course, a hard-hearted businessman. At one point he says of Tiny Tim, "Let him die and reduce the surplus population." By the end of the story Scrooge has had a change of heart. The phrase "surplus population" is not one you hear anymore. It was the phrase used by economists of Dickens's day for people who did not work. By using lovable Tiny Tim as an example of the surplus population, Dickens was trying to soften the hearts of his prosperous readers toward the poor and unemployed.

Charles Dickens was a working author who made his living from his books. Many of them showed the poor people of England suffering. One of his other books, *Oliver Twist,* tells of the life of a poor orphan. Dickens was using his books to persuade his readers to support charities and reforms to help the workers of the Industrial Revolution.

6. George Bernard Shaw. Some of the funniest plays in English were written to promote socialism. *My Fair Lady,* the musical, is an adaptation of George Bernard Shaw's *Pygmalion,* intended as socialist propaganda. The message is simple: even a poor, scruffy flower girl can pass as a lady if taught to speak correctly. This suggested that the poor were not bad people, and that the differences between rich and poor were superficial. At the time, it was a radical thought.

George Bernard Shaw was indeed a radical. He was a member of the Fabian Society, a group of socialists who tried to bring changes in society by slow, peaceful means. Shaw wrote his plays to promote socialist ideas. Socialists saw war as a capitalist plot. In *Arms and the Man,* Shaw satirized war. His hero was a soldier who carried chocolate in his ammunition belt because he had needed food more often than bullets. Shaw's plays were popular in his day and are still produced. Many literary critics consider him one of the best British playwrights.

Chapter XVI
New Powers in Europe

— Overview —

The biggest story in late 19th-century politics in Europe was the unification of both Germany and Italy. Meanwhile, the old powers carried on. France had two revolutions, two monarchies, a republic, and an empire followed by another republic. Great Britain was an island of stability under Queen Victoria.

Perhaps your students could write a paper comparing and contrasting the German unification with the Italian. They could do a compare-and-contrast paper on French and British politics. Bulletin boards with maps showing German unification and Italian Risorgimento would be helpful.

A. German Unity

1. **Bismarck in 1848.** Bismarck was very conservative. When there was an uprising in Berlin in March 1848, he went to the king and offered to mobilize the peasants and put down the city mobs. King Frederick William rejected the idea.

2. **Schleswig and Holstein.** The political history of Schleswig and Holstein begins in the Middle Ages and is terribly complicated. Lord Palmerston, a British politican, once said there were only three people who had ever understood it; one had died, and one had gone mad. He was the third, and he had forgotten.

3. The Seven Weeks' War. The Prussians beat the Austrians very quickly in the Seven Weeks' War. Much of this was due to Bismarck's diplomacy. He had carefully isolated Austria. After that, the Prussian Army used some new technology. The Prussians had observed the American Civil War and learned from it. They had seen how the telegraph speeded messages compared with older ways of communicating. They had also seen the Union forces use the railroads to move troops. When the war came, Prussia had railroads already built to move troops to Austria quickly.

The Prussians also had the needle gun, a much improved rifle. Earlier rifles were muzzle loaders and much slower to load. A soldier had to go through a complex series of steps: bite open the paper cartridge, pour powder down the barrel, use a ramrod to ram bullet and powder securely into place, put the cap in place, aim, and fire. With the needle gun, the soldier opened a bolt, popped in a cartridge, closed the bolt, aimed, and fired. Prussian soldiers fired about five times as fast as Austrians.

The new Prussian rifle was called the needle gun because the firing pin was a long needle that penetrated the cartridge to set off the primer. Soon this arrangement was replaced by metal cartridges with primers in the rear.

B. Italy

1. Lack of Unity. In 1815, Italy was far from unified. At the Congress of Vienna, Metternich remarked that Italy was "merely a geographical expression."

2. Carbonari. One of the earliest nationalist movements in Italy was the Carbonari. It was a secret society and took its name from *carbone,* translated "charcoal," which was black in color but burned fiercely. The Carbonari had secret rituals and called each other "cousin." They plotted a number of unsuccessful revolutions.

3. Young Italy. The Young Italy society was started in Marseilles by Giuseppe Mazzini. Its mission was to make Italy a nation of free and equal citizens. The leaders were outside Italy but kept in touch with local branches in each part of Italy. Individual members, nearly always under age 40, had to pay dues and have a dagger, rifle, and 50 rounds of ammunition. By 1833, Young Italy had 60,000 members.

4. *Il Risorgimento.* In 1847, Count Camillo Cavour started a newspaper, *Il Risorgimento,* "The Resurrection," which became the most important of the newspapers leading a movement for a united Italy. The paper was so influential that the whole movement became known as *Il Risorgimento.*

5. War in 1859. The fighting between the French and Piedmontese on one side and the Austrians on the other produced tremendous casualties. The Battle of Solferino on June 24, 1859, had 40,000 casualties; typhus killed many of the survivors. A Swiss named Jean Henri Dunant served as a stretcher bearer and was horrified. He wrote a pamphlet about the experience, *A Memory of Solferino.* In the pamphlet, Dunant suggested that permanent societies of volunteers be organized to care for those wounded in war, regardless of nationality. This led to the organization of the International Red Cross. There are also reports that the French emperor, Napoleon III, was so disgusted by the slaughter at Solferino that he decided to negotiate a peace.

6. Garibaldi and Red Shirts. Garibaldi adopted the red shirt as his personal uniform while in Latin America. In 1843, in Uruguay he formed an Italian Legion made up of Italian immigrants. Their uniform was a red shirt. The shirts were mass-produced in Uruguay to be exported to packinghouse workers in Argentina. Being red, they didn't show blood. Garibaldi bought them because they were cheap, would hide the blood from wounds, and would make it easy to see a deserter. The red shirts became Garibaldi's trademark.

7. Garibaldi in Sicily. When Garibaldi set out with his 1,000 Red Shirts to liberate Siciliy, there was lots of confusion. The ships carrying ammunition did not meet the troop ships. Garibaldi solved the problem by putting on a general's uniform, landing in Tuscany, and talking a local commander out of a supply of weapons. When Garibaldi's forces tried to land at Marsala in Sicily, one of the ships ran aground. But the port's defenders put up a weak opposition partly because they thought the red shirts were red coats worn by British soldiers. The landing was made with no loss of life.

C. FRANCE

1. Talleyrand. Talleyrand represented the government of Louis XVIII of France at the Congress of Vienna. He was a somewhat slippery character who had served a number of French governments. His philosophy of life may have been the following statement attributed to him: "The gift of speech was given to man in order to conceal what he is thinking." There was a saying that Talleyrand would live a long time because the Devil wouldn't have him.

But Talleyrand was a skilled diplomat and represented France effectively at the Congress. Even getting to be a major voice in the Congress was difficult. After all, the Congress of Vienna was called to settle the situation created by Napoleon's wars. France was the losing power. Talleyrand argued that his master Louis XVIII was not responsible for Napoleon. He discreetly neglected to mention that he, Talleyrand, had also served Napoleon as foreign minister.

2. The French Nobles. One of the features of French politics in the period 1815–1870 was the group called the Ultras. They were ultra-royalists, more royalist than the king. This was literally true. They believed in unlimited divine-right monarchy, while King Louis XVIII had granted a constitution. It was said the Ultras learned nothing and forgot nothing. That is, they didn't get the message that the people would no longer tolerate powerful aristocrats. The French Revolution was not a strong enough hint for them. Yet they remembered everything they wanted back.

3. The Riots of June 1848. In June of 1848, the working people of Paris began a series of riots that became known simply as "the June Days." The series of events was complex, but the main cause of the revolt was the workers' resentment over losing their jobs in national workshops, a sort of work relief program.

By 1848, the French had plenty of experience with revolutions and had developed a certain etiquette. The workers barricaded the narrow, twisting streets of Paris by pulling up the flat stones used to pave them. The stones were then arranged in a sort of dry wall across the street. As each passerby approached the site of such a barricade under construction, the workers would call out, "A stone, if you please." The passerby was expected to pick up a stone from the street and place it on the barricade, thus showing solidarity with the workers.

Sometimes the workers used a faster method of construction. In 1848, a bus was a horse-drawn vehicle for carrying passengers. The workers would get a bus and turn it on its side. This would block the street, producing an instant barricade. When the work was completed, the workers would take a sign saying "full" from the bus and place it on the barricade. This word in French has another meaning, "complete," a little revolutionary pun.

This process of building barricades continued into the 20th century. Napoleon III reduced the possibilities somewhat by building broad, straight streets through the most radical areas. But even as late as the 1960's during student riots, the streets were torn up and the cry "To the barricades!" was raised. Shortly after that, the government paved the streets with asphalt, thus ending a French political tradition.

4. Napoleon III and Public Works. Napoleon III sponsored a wide-ranging program of public works including railroad construction, new streets in Paris, and sewers. All this construction work generated business for the middle class and jobs for the workers. The French economy grew and prospered. All the new buildings also served as propaganda for the emperor. The new street plan was full of parks and wide, straight streets. This helped modern traffic flow, but it also served political purposes. The wide streets often ran through neighborhoods that had been rebellious in 1848. Many houses were demolished and the people forced to move, thus breaking up the neighborhoods. The streets were too wide to be barricaded as the old streets had been in 1848. They also radiated from a circle at the center like spokes of a wheel, making it easy for a few cannons placed in the circle's center to fire down any street. Thus riot control was made easier.

The sewers were a major improvement. Paris had started as a medieval city, so it had no sewers in many places. The new sewers of Paris became a wonder to Europeans. They were so elegant they became a tourist attraction. They still are. A tourist's guidebook called *Europe Off the Wall* says the sewer tour includes a museum, a film, and a guided tour. For an hour, tourists walk beneath Paris in rubber-soled shoes admiring a project undertaken for the greater glory of the Second Empire.

D. BRITAIN

1. The British Attitude. A traditional story says that a British newspaper once ran a headline, "Fog in Channel, Continent Isolated." It nicely summarized the British attitude toward Europe and the rest of the world.

2. The Crimean War. The Crimean War came after a long period of peace. The British had a lot to learn about warfare in the 1850's. One unit, the 11th Hussar Regiment, prepared for war by having its members' swords sharpened, and the officers had patches of black leather sewn to the seat of their pants. Hussars are cavalry and they expected to be riding hard. The pants were a bright cherry red, a dashing color to wear to war.

3. Women's Rights. The women's rights movement in Britain took the form of dramatic protests. Women would break the law and invite arrest, then go on hunger strikes. Their jailers would force-feed them. Mrs. Emmeline Pankhurst was one of the most visible leaders. The story is told that she was comforting a young feminist in jail. The young woman told of the indignity of it all. "There, there, dear," Mrs. Pankhurst sympathized, "Pray to God. She will comfort you."

4. **Queen Victoria.** Victoria was queen of Britain for most of the 19th century. The usual image of the Victorian Age has it being very righteous. If a courtier told an off-color story, the queen would freeze the culprit by saying, "We are not amused." It is said that even the legs of Victorian pianos were covered with skirts lest they give gentlemen ideas. Victoria's husband, Prince Albert, was German. Tradition says he introduced the Christmas tree into England. When Albert died, Victoria went into mourning. The last years of her reign were conducted by a gloomy widow.

5. **Queen Victoria on Women's Rights.** Queen Victoria did not approve of women's rights. She called it "this mad folly."

Chapter XVII

Imperialism in Asia, Africa, and Latin America

— Overview —

In the 19th and early 20th centuries, people from European-based cultures conquered most of the world. Their motives varied widely. In Asia there were tense confrontations over imperial ambitions. Japan joined the Europeans in trying to get colonies. China was the victim of this and the presumed prize in the Russo-Japanese War. Somehow China survived and even began to build a modern government. Some countries like Iran and Ethiopia managed to resist the Europeans. In Africa the indigenous people often fought fiercely and lost. The British colonized much of Africa, but found that controlling the Dutch settlers in South Africa (the Boers) was more difficult than dealing with the Africans. In Latin America, the United States was the leading imperialist, taking a slice of Mexico, building the Panama Canal, and supporting dictators.

You could assign a student to do a bulletin board showing "Empires, 1914." You could have students write a paper ranking the empires. Britan was number 1 (probably), but who was number 2? Or 3? Why? Your students could also write a paper comparing and contrasting imperialism in China with imperialism in Africa or in Latin America. Students could compare Japan and China at this time. The creative student could write firsthand stories by a newspaper reporter on "An Interview with General Gordon in Khartoum," "An Interview with Sun Yat-sen on the Future of China," "Porfirio Díaz Speaks on Mexico."

A. THE MOTIVES

1. Coaling Stations. One of the factors pushing European nations to establish colonies was the need for coaling stations. This was a relatively new need created by the development of steamships. In the days of sailing vessels, a ship could sail great distances without ever needing fuel. The limits of endurance were set by the food and water sailing ships carried. In the last half of the 19th century, steam-powered ships began to appear. At first the steam engines were very inefficient and were only mounted on sailing vessels as auxiliary power. If a sailing ship was becalmed, unable to move for lack of wind, the crew fired up the steam engine. As steam engines got more efficient, the emphasis changed. The steam engine became the main power source, and sails were used only in emergencies.

Early steam engines burned coal, and steam-powered ships needed to be refueled roughly once a week. Navies developed colliers, ships to carry coal, but recoaling at sea was dangerous, so now a navy needed friendly harbors where its ships could coal up. This meant that once-obscure islands became strategically important, and ports along the coast of Africa, Asia, and Latin America became valuable as coaling stations. The seagoing powers of the world were now in conflict over these newly important places.

2. Rudyard Kipling. Kipling was born in India and as a young man spent years absorbing impressions there. Much of his writing is set in India. Two of his children's stories have become well-known films, *Kim* and *The Jungle Book.* He wrote a series of short stories and poems that spell out the attitude that upholds imperialism. He wrote one poem that has become a part of our language, "The White Man's Burden," to persuade President McKinley of the United States to make the Philippine islands a colony. In the poem, Kipling argues that it is the duty of white, Christian, civilized people to rule over the other races, lift them up and civilize them. He says it won't be easy because the backward people will fight against it and resent the colonizers, but it is the duty of the superior whites.

Kipling was a very popular writer in England and America around 1900. That says a lot about attitudes in those days.

B. ASIA

1. The British in Afghanistan. In 1839, the British sent an army and a puppet king into Afghanistan. When a British official commented on how easy it had been to get into Kabul, a wise old leader asked, "How will you get out?" It was a very good question. The people of Afghanistan rose in rebellion. The British lost 20,000 soldiers in their effort to put down the rebellion.

2. Germans at Manila Bay. In the summer of 1898, an American fleet faced the threat of battle with a German fleet. The dispute started with Commodore Dewey's blockade of the Philippine islands. He had defeated the Spanish in the Battle of Manila Bay, but he did not control the islands, only the waters of the bay. The Germans disputed Dewey's right to blockade and began to maneuver into position for a fight. They had four cruisers to Dewey's one, but the American firmly upheld his rights. He carefully quoted experts on international law supporting his position. In addition, the British fleet at Manila Bay moved into position to help the Americans. Faced with strong arguments and the combined guns of the American and British forces, the Germans backed down, but it had been a very tense situation. This incident in the Philippines was an example of competing imperialist powers getting into disputes over potential colonies.

3. Extraterritoriality in China. During the 19th century the Chinese government was forced to sign a number of unequal treaties with imperialist powers. In most cases, these treaties granted the citizens of the foreign power in question the right of extraterritoriality. That is, while these people were in China they would be governed by the laws of their home country, not the laws of China. This was humiliating and infuriating to the Chinese. Usually the foreigners were granted an enclave along the coast to live in. Since foreigners lived there, Chinese law did not apply to those areas. But even if a foreigner traveled in China, he or she was still immune from Chinese law.

While serious crimes like murder by foreigners were relatively rare, minor issues were a constant irritant. For example, local officials often collected tolls for using bridges. Foreigners could cross without paying because of their extraterritoriality, while Chinese had to pay. No wonder many ordinary Chinese learned to despise foreigners.

4. Sun Yat-sen, Revolutionary. Sun Yat-sen is the person most commonly named as the leader of the Nationalist revolution in China. He did in fact lead one attempt at revolution, and it failed. After that, he traveled around the world drumming up support for the Chinese revolution. While he was outside China, there were seven attempted revolutions, all failures, which Sun Yat-sen encouraged. After these, in 1911, came the uprising that did overthrow the Manchu Dynasty. In the city of Wuhan, a group of army officers was plotting. They were discovered and decided to go ahead with their rebellion. They started on October 10; "double ten," a lucky number in China. Nobody in the group was a member of Dr. Sun's Alliance Party.

Dr. Sun knew nothing of their activities. He was in Denver, Colorado, when he read about the uprising in his morning newspaper over breakfast. He quickly returned to China and led the Chinese Nationalist movement.

5. The Russo-Japanese War. In 1904, Russia and Japan collided as each tried to carve out a piece of China. The Japanese had Korea and were moving toward Manchuria. The Russians were moving from Siberia into the same area. It was clearly a clash of imperialist powers. The war began with the Japanese making a surprise torpedo attack on the Russian fleet at Port Arthur. The Russians looked like the favorite in the conflict, a big country fighting a smaller one.

But the naval war went badly for the Russians. They quickly lost their Asian fleet. They then decided to gather their Baltic fleet and put it under their best admiral, Rozhestvenski, and steam to Asia. The trip itself was difficult. The Russians had great problems arranging for coal along the way. The sailors were so panicky that they attacked a British fishing fleet thinking it was Japanese torpedo boats lurking off the coast of Britain! They somehow made it to Madagascar and took a brief rest, then steamed on to French Indochina for another pause. Finally they steamed toward Japan. As they passed between Korea and Japan, off the island of Tsushima, the Japanese fleet under Admiral Togo met them and destroyed them. Japanese torpedo boats moved in at night to finish them off. Rozhestvenski was captured.

The land war was also a disaster for the Russians. The Japanese beseiged and eventually took Port Arthur and fought the Russians to a standstill in Manchuria. The American president, Theodore Roosevelt, offered to mediate, and the peace conference was held in Portsmouth, New Hampshire. In it the Japanese received control of Korea, and Russia was pushed back. Japan was now the dominant imperial power in Manchuria.

6. The Nobel Peace Prize. Theodore Roosevelt received the Nobel Peace Prize for his efforts as mediator in the Russo-Japanese War. The Japanese emperor gave him a sword as a token of gratitude. Some time later, Admiral Togo, the hero of the war, visited Roosevelt's home on Long Island, New York. He asked to see the sword, and was horrified to see that the blade was rusty. He gave Roosevelt a lecture explaining that the blade of the sword was the honor of the owner and it must be kept spotlessly clean. Then Admiral Togo scrubbed the blade clean and polished it. The sword is still on display in Theodore Roosevelt's Long Island home.

7. Women in Iran. During the period 1906–1911, Iran was under pressure from both Russia and Britain. The women of Iran were an important part of the struggle for independence. Iranian women donated their jewelry so Iran could start a national bank without borrowing money from foreigners. Armed women played an active role in fighting against a prince supported by the Russians and British. One photograph shows 60 veiled women armed and guarding a barricade. After one street battle, it was found that 20 of the dead revolutionary soldiers were women dressed as men.

C. AFRICA

1. The Tsetse Fly. Have you ever wondered why African explorers didn't ride horses, or why they used human porters instead of pack mules, or why there were so few cattle ranches on African grasslands? The reason is a little brown fly with yellow stripes or spots underneath. It is named for the sound it makes when flying, the tsetse fly. It lives on the blood of mammals. It pierces the skin and sucks the blood, leaving a bite like a mosquito. Because the tsetse fly needs shade, it lives in areas where there is a mix of trees and grassland. The area includes most of Tanzania, part of Uganda, and some of Kenya. Few people live in the area because the bite of the tsetse fly transmits sleeping sickness. This is a dangerous disease for humans, but it is even more deadly to domestic animals. Wild animals are immune.

2. The Uganda Railroad. When imperial powers wanted something, human life counted little. The British decided, in 1896, to build a railroad from Mombasa to Lake Victoria. It was a difficult job, but by 1901, a train made the trip. Even then it was using temporary track part of the way. The terrain was so difficult, it was called the Lunatic Line. Africans refused to work on the construction crews, so the British brought in labor from India, a total of 30,000 people. The cost in human lives was huge. In one place a pair of man-eating lions stopped construction. They would attack at night and drag workers screaming into the dark. The lions killed 28 workers before being tracked down and killed. A total of 2,500 workers died and 6,500 were injured during construction of the railroad.

Many of the Indian workers decided to stay in East Africa. They started shops and became prosperous business owners. The railroad became a major trade route.

3. "Chinese" Gordon at Khartoum. The British developed an interest in the Sudan almost by accident. They controlled Egypt, and Sudan was upstream. In 1884, a Muslim leader called the Mahdi declared a holy war in the Sudan. The British selected Charles "Chinese" Gordon to handle the situation. Gordon was a soldier who had seen action in the Crimea, China, and Africa. He had led Chinese troops in China, hence the name Chinese Gordon. He was a dashing leader, always in the front ranks in a fight. Sometimes he led with just a cane in his hand, no weapon. Even the English considered him a little eccentric. He was sent to Khartoum, capital of the Sudan, with orders to observe the situation, evacuate the city, or form a government. The government gave him these three conflicting orders at different times.

Gordon arrived at Khartoum in February 1884, and decided he would stay and fight the Mahdi using the Egyptian troops there. The Mahdi's forces surrounded Khartoum. The British government dithered. Gordon led the defense fearlessly. He lived in the governor's palace and kept it brightly lighted even as the enemy artillery shells fell on the city. The siege ran for months. Gordon's hair turned white, and the people had to eat horses and rats, but no relief came. Back home, at the personal urging of Queen Victoria, the British government decided to send a relief force. The force set off, steaming up the Nile. The Mahdi's troops entered Khartoum on January 26, 1885. Gordon was speared to death in the governor's palace. Three days later the relief force arrived.

4. The Ashanti: Writing as a Charm. In the 1880's the Ashantis had a powerful kingdom in West Africa, where Ghana is today. The Ashanti were not literate, but they had great respect for writing. They considered that written words were a charm, and they eagerly bought writings from Muslims.

5. The Ashanti Stool. The stool was the symbol of leadership among the Ashanti. Each official had a stool. The most powerful and elaborate stool of all was the Golden Stool, used by the king. In fact, the stool was more important than the ruler. It was the king's job to safeguard the stool. It must never touch the ground, and no one ever sat on it. If an official lost office, the stool would be taken away. Even the king could be "destooled" if he proved unworthy. The stool remained an important symbol to the Ashanti even as they fought the Europeans. When they feared they were being conquered, they hid the Golden Stool so it would not be captured. It was found again in 1920 by accident. As a result, it was desecrated. But the Ashanti still keep part of the stool and use it for special ceremonies. At other times it is still kept in a secret hiding place.

6. Ethiopia and Italy. The Italians thought they had made Ethiopia a protectorate. They had a treaty saying that the Ethiopians *must* communicate with other powers through the king of Italy. The Ethiopians, on the other hand, had a treaty saying that they *might* communicate through the king of Italy. Why the difference? The treaty had been written in two languages, Italian and Amharic, the language of Ethiopia. The Amharic version was the only one signed by Menelek II, emperor of Ethiopia. He had followed a rule we should all use: Only sign what you have read. He couldn't read Italian. This left the Italians with no valid claim to Ethiopia.

7. The Great Trek. The Great Trek is an important event in Boer history. In 1836, thousands of Boers went on a great migration across the Orange River to found the Orange Free State and Transvaal. They saw it as fleeing British tyranny. What was the tyranny they were fleeing? British law was freeing the slaves, and in two more years the blacks would be given rights to move freely, own land, and even to work at their own choice. The Boers believed in slavery and strict control of blacks, so they made the trek to maintain a society of white supremacy.

8. Blood River. The Boers have a history of fighting against overwhelming odds. One of the most dramatic examples is Blood River. In the year 1838, a group of 500 Boers put their wagons in a *laager,* a sort of circle and fort, and held out against 15,000 Zulus, killing about 3,000 of them. No Boers were killed. The nearby river ran red with the blood of slain Zulus. Now it is called Blood River. The Afrikaners take this as a sign that God has chosen them to rule over blacks. Each year the Afrikaners, who are descended from the Boers, commemorate the event. There is a monument on the spot.

9. Boer War Concentration Camps. During the Boer War the British found themselves fighting a guerrilla war. Small bands of Boers moved about making hit-and-run raids, supported by the Boer farmers in the area. The British hit upon a simple, if brutal, solution. They removed the farmers, thus destroying the support network the Boers needed. The farmers, mostly women and children, were put in camps to concentrate the population. These were the first concentration camps. There were 117,000 in the camps. About 30,000 died.

10. The Boer War and Boy Scouts. The Boer War led to the creation of the Boy Scouts. During the war, an officer named Robert Stephenson Smyth Baden-Powell became a hero by leading the British defense of Mafeking. The Boers were running circles around the British Army because Dutch settlers knew how to camp and live off the land. Baden-Powell wrote a book called *Aids to Scouting* (1899) to help the British learn to live better outdoors. Soon it was being used by the British Army and groups of boys back home. Later Baden-Powell wrote a book called *Scouting for Boys* (1907). Soon after that, he resigned from the army and devoted the rest of his life to the Boy Scouts.

11. The British Empire. In 1900, the British could observe proudly that the sun never set on the British Empire. The empire stretched around the world, including huge areas like Canada and India. It also included tiny places located at critical points on the sea like Gibraltar, Suez, and Singapore. But wherever the sun was shining on earth, it was shining on some piece of land controlled by Britain. The 41 million people in the mother country controlled an empire totaling 400 million people. The British went out to the empire as settlers in some cases: Australia, New Zealand, Rhodesia, and Canada. In others, like Burma, they went as rulers or soldiers. Wherever they went they took the British way of life. They dressed in proper formal suits and long dresses.

They built proper British houses in Kenya and Bengal. They played active sports: polo, cricket, and tennis. All this vigorous activity in tropical climates was radically different from local custom.

One satirical Englishman observed in a song that only mad dogs and Englishmen went out in the midday sun. As the sun set on the Britons' particular bit of empire, they drank a toast: "The Queen." Everybody understood they meant Queen Victoria, a tiny woman not five feet tall, who ruled the largest empire on earth.

D. LATIN AMERICA

1. Santa Anna. During the years 1821 to 1857, Santa Anna was the most prominent leader in Mexico. He headed 11 of the 50 governments formed during that period. He was the commander of the Mexican force of 6,000 that wiped out the rebellious Texans in the Alamo. Two months later, he was captured in the battle at San Jacinto and forced to recognize the independence of Texas. After being sent to Washington in handcuffs, he was released and returned in disgrace to Mexico. Less than two years later, Santa Anna fought the French in a conflict called "the Pastry War." In that war his foot was blown off by a cannon, and he became a hero. After the war, he took over the Mexican government and buried his foot with full military honors. He was in and out of office several times after that. He was leader of Mexico during the Mexican War, when the United States defeated Mexico and took half its territory.

2. Mexico and Abraham Lincoln. Abraham Lincoln is one American who is liked in Mexico, because as a congressman Lincoln opposed the Mexican War. The Mexicans also admire Henry David Thoreau for the same reason. Thoreau went to jail rather than pay taxes to support the war.

3. The Panama Canal. The Spanish-American War showed the American Navy it had a need for a canal through Central America. First there was the battleship *Oregon,* located in Bremerton, Washington, and needed in Cuba. It had to steam all the way around South America to take part in the Battle of Santiago Bay. There was also the matter of Commodore Dewey, who had easily taken Manila Bay in the Philippines. He needed reinforcements, but the U.S. fleet was concentrated around Cuba. If there had been a Central American canal it would have been easy to send battleships like the *Iowa, Indiana,* or *Oregon* to the Philippines. Instead, the navy had to send two monitors it had in California. The monitor design was of Civil War vintage. After these experiences, the U.S. Navy really wanted a canal.

4. Porfirio Díaz. Díaz was dictator of Mexico from 1876 to 1911. He was corrupt, and tended to buy off trouble-makers. He bought the army's cooperation by giving generals good-paying jobs in government. He even bought off bandits. He made them part of his police for the Rurales. This made them no more honest, perhaps, but at least they were no longer outlaws.

CHAPTER XVIII
World War I

— Overview —

World War I was the great catastrophe of the Europeans. It destroyed millions of lives and a way of life. In some ways we are still working out its results. These days we like to speak of abstract causes for the war, like imperialism, militarism, and alliances rather than individuals' actions. But are individuals helpless before ideas, or do they shape them?

The fighting was a horror, especially the trench warfare. Even air war was a deadly business, not a romantic adventure. Russia had a revolution and was taken over by the Communists, and Arab nationalism came alive. The diplomats at the peace conference had to try to heal a shattered world.

Your students could write a paper on "Was World War I Inevitable?" "Did the Kaiser Start the War?" or "Was World War I Started by Ideas or by Individuals?" Students could write papers comparing the situation in 1914 with the situation today: Are we headed toward World War III? You could grade such papers on their supporting facts and reasoning rather than any specific list of causes. Students could write papers comparing and contrasting the February and October revolutions in Russia. Students could write "letters home" from a World War I trench.

A. THE CAUSES

1. Militarism and Sea Power. A history book once helped start a war. Its title was *The Influence of Sea Power Upon History,* and it was written by an American naval officer named Alfred T. Mahan. It seems that this book played a major role in setting off the big naval arms race that helped start World War I.

In his 1890 book, Mahan spelled out a theory of history. He argued that history showed that the great powers of world history had always been great naval powers. He analyzed a series of wars and sea battles to prove his point. The main focus of his book was the 17th and 18th centuries, but he also argued that the Romans had won the Punic Wars with sea power.

Mahan's book was read and admired by Americans and Europeans. His ideas became the inspiration for the great burst of American naval building before the Spanish-American War. The British, who were both a great power and a great sea power, read the book and were pleased and flattered. They entertained Mahan lavishly when he visited Britain. Wilhelm II, kaiser of Germany, also read the book and was impressed by it. It influenced him to begin serious work on a German navy. This in turn led to a naval arms race between Germany and Britain, which became a part of the tensions leading to World War I.

2. The *Dreadnought*. Sometimes a new invention changes the world. The battleship *Dreadnought,* launched by the British in 1906, changed the world's navies and may have helped to start World War I. The navies of the world had been experimenting with the design of steam-powered ships of iron and steel since the American Civil War. By 1906, modern navies had fleets of battleships bristling with a variety of guns. The U.S.S. *Oregon* is one early example. It displaced 11,700 tons, had armor 18 inches thick, and reached a speed of 15 nautical miles per hour. It had four 13-inch guns, eight 8-inch guns, and a variety of smaller guns plus torpedo tubes. In its day (1898) it was a marvel.

The *Dreadnought* was far better than that. It displaced 21,845 tons, nearly twice the weight of the *Oregon.* Its speed was 21 knots, about 50 percent faster than the *Oregon,* and it carried ten 12-inch guns that could shoot farther than any on the U.S. ship. The *Dreadnought* had the capacity to sink an older enemy battleship before the enemy guns were within range, and it could outrun any ship. Suddenly all the navies of the world were obsolete, including the British. If an enemy of the British built one copy of the *Dreadnought,* the older British ships would be helpless before it. The solution was obvious; build more *Dreadnought*s.

The result was a frantic naval arms race. The British tried to maintain a navy equal to the combined strength of the second and third naval powers in the world. The Germans tried to build a navy competitive with Britain. This competition led to a feeling of rivalry between the two nations that contributed to World War I.

3. The Schlieffen Plan. The German general staff had spent considerable time studying the problem of fighting a two-front war. By 1906, they had a plan for fighting a war against both Russia and France called the Schlieffen Plan, after General von Schlieffen, Chief of Staff.

The plan was modeled from Hannibal's victory over the Romans at Cannae in the Punic Wars. In that ancient battle, Hannibal had surrounded the Romans and wiped them out. Schlieffen planned to do the same to the French. The plan assumed that the Russians would be very slow to mobilize. The Germans would place a small force on their eastern front and concentrate on the French first. Most of the western front would be lightly manned, but the extreme right flank would be crammed with troops. This powerful right flank would sweep through Belgium, march along the French coast, and then swing inland to surround Paris and the French Army. This plan became the set way of thinking of German officers and politicans. There is a story that Schlieffen's dying words were "Keep the right flank strong."

Later critics have noted problems with the plan. Belgium was a neutral country. Moving troops through would violate that nation's neutrality, and this could have serious diplomatic consequences. In the actual war, the Belgians refused to allow the Germans passage for the troops. The Germans invaded anyway, but were delayed by Belgian resistance. The invasion of Belgium stirred such emotion in England that Britain declared war. The "Rape of Belgium" hurt the Germans in American public opinion too. The public relations damage was made worse by a German diplomat who remarked that the treaty of neutrality with Belgium was "only a scrap of paper."

4. Wilhelm II. Wilhelm II, kaiser of Germany, was a key decision-maker as World War I started. When he was born, his left arm was crippled, and it never recovered. It seems clear that Wilhelm spent the rest of his life compensating for this inadequacy. It is very clear that it influenced his style of dress, but less clear how far it influenced his politics. Wilhelm was related to many of the other crowned heads of Europe. Queen Victoria of Britain was his grandmother, and Tsar Nicholas II of Russia was his cousin. Wilhelm was always a little jealous of Nicholas, but during the crisis in 1914, they exchanged telegrams in a frantic effort to avoid war. Wilhelm liked to make warlike speeches and adopt threatening positions, so it was easy for Allied propaganda during the war to blame him for starting World War I. He said things like, "We can hold up the sky on top of German bayonets," and he was the first to compare the Germans to Huns. When the war went badly and Germany tried to surrender, Wilhelm was forced to abdicate. President Woodrow Wilson refused to deal with Germany while it was a monarchy. Wilhelm crossed the border into Holland on November 10, 1918, one day before the Armistice.

B. The Western Front

1. French Taxicabs and the Battle of the Marne. As the Germans lauched their first attack in 1914, the French fell back. But just as the situation seemed hopeless, the Germans left a gap in their line and the chance for the French to strike a counterblow. How could this be done? One answer was found in the taxis of Paris. The army took over 500 taxis and put 5 soldiers in each. The French generals figured they could move 60,000 troops to the front in a matter of hours. The French general in charge observed, "Well, here at least is something unusual." It also was something effective. The French and British stopped the Germans at the Battle of the Marne.

2. Hazards of Air Combat. The airplane was only 11 years old when World War I began. The Wright brothers had flown the first powered plane in 1903; the war started in 1914. Planes were very primitive, and the military had limited ideas about their use.

In the U.S. Army the early pilots were part of the Signal Corps. Planes were seen as another version of the observation balloon. Since the American Civil War, armies had used balloons to get up high and observe the distant enemy. The balloons were tethered, and a telegraph wire ran from the balloon to the ground, allowing the balloon crew to report to the commander below. Telegraph operators were, of course, in the Signal Corps. In 1914, airplane pilots and observers were to perform the same mission, but they could fly around more freely. Many of the early aircraft were called scouts. The pilots would write down their observations and drop them to the waiting commander.

Air combat began in a pretty haphazard way. At first pilots from the two sides simply waved when they met, but soon they started to fight. The first efforts are almost comic. They threw bricks at each other or tried to tangle cables around the enemy's propeller. Some tried to shoot with rifles or pistols. Things turned serious when they started using machine guns.

Some early planes had a gunner in back who fired toward the rear. One experiment featured a pusher propeller on the back of the plane with machine guns firing forward. Others mounted the machine gun on the upper wing. (Most World War I aircraft were biplanes.) This system had one drawback. To fire the gun, the pilot had to stand up and control the plane with his feet and knees while firing the gun, a tricky process. The best way to aim the guns was simply to have them point straight ahead. If the guns were mounted in front of the pilot, he could simply point his plane at the enemy and reach up and pull the trigger. This system, too, had a flaw. The propeller was turning in front of the guns, and when a shot hit the wooden blade, the pilot had shot himself down!

A creative Allied pilot came up with the idea of putting a metal plate on the prop to protect it. Then the bullets would bounce off and do no harm. Some shots, however, might bounce straight back at the pilot. Nevertheless, this system gave the Allies a great advantage for a time.

When the Germans captured a plane equipped with these propeller plates, they improved on it. A Dutch designer named Fokker developed an interrupter gear, which allowed the propeller to stop the guns from firing when it was in front of them. Soon both sides were using the Fokker system.

Much has been made of the romance of World War I air combat, and few realize the risks. The planes were flimsy structures with cloth-covered wooden frames braced by wires. Even in peacetime they were unreliable and unpleasant to fly. The pilot flew with his face out in the wind and so was forced to wear helmet and goggles. It's true the early planes did less than 100 miles per hour, but even 90 miles per hour is a stiff wind. If there was a problem, the pilot often didn't have a parachute. Commanders discouraged parachutes because they thought the bailout devices reduced fighting spirit. The planes were literally deafening. Pilots who survived years of flying lost their hearing because of the engine noise. This was not much of a problem in World War I because the average combat pilot only lived two weeks.

3. The Red Baron. There really was a Red Baron. Manfred von Richthofen was the son of a noble Prussian family. He first served in the cavalry, then requested transfer to planes. Eventually he became an "ace" and commander of his own squadron. An ace was a pilot who had five or more confirmed victories.

The Red Baron was a major story in German newspapers, perhaps because the war news was otherwise so grim. Von Richthofen enjoyed the fame. He even painted his personal aircraft, a Fokker triplane, a bright red and flew out in front of his formations when going to fight. After each kill he had a silver cup made engraved with the date. He ran up a total of 80 victories.

It's not entirely clear how the Red Baron died. One story says he was shot down by ground fire. Another says that a Canadian named Roy Brown shot him down. Brown was flying a Sopwith Camel.

4. German Casualties. The casualty rate in World War I was often very high. As an example, in the German Army, the 16th Bavarian Reserve Infantry Regiment saw fierce action against the British. The Regiment started with 3,500 soldiers, and in four days it was reduced to 600. Among the survivors was an Austrian volunteer named Adolf Hitler.

5. Films. Many historical films about World War I contain a clip showing British troops going over the top, out of the trench to attack. One soldier on the right just gets his head aboveground, then slides back into the trench to move no more. For a few seconds the troops advance through barbed wire. Two more soldiers slowly collapse onto the ground. This is the real thing, trench warfare.

Alas, the reality was a little different. Kevin Brownlow, who wrote a history of silent filmmaking called *The War, the West, and the Wilderness,* reports that this film clip was shot at a training ground in England. He first points out that the camera angle is such that in real fighting the photographer would have been exposed to fire. Then he goes on to tell how the photographer in question liked to stretch the truth. Finally he quotes a witness who later talked to one of the soldiers who had "died" in the trenches and was wondering how the film turned out.

6. "Lafayette, We Are Here." On the Fourth of July, 1917, the American Army in France held a ceremony to raise Allied morale. One battalion of the 16th Infantry marched in a parade through the streets of Paris. At the tomb of General Lafayette, a U.S. quartermaster colonel made the statement often attributed to General Pershing: "Lafayette, we are here." While the Americans were indeed in France, it would be months before they were trained to go into the trenches, even in a quiet sector. They lacked weapons, and many soldiers had not even heard of some of the weapons used in this war.

7. Trench Foot. World War I soldiers faced many forms of danger: machine-gun fire, artillery, and poison gas, to name a few. The soldiers were in danger even when they were simply standing around waiting for something to happen. The problem was the trenches themselves. Often trenches were full of mud; some trenches were 5 feet deep where the water table was 18 inches. They were ditches full of water. The soldiers would stand for days with their feet in cold water or mud with little chance to move around. They wore tight leggings around their calves, and never took off their boots. As a result, the circulation to their feet was poor. After weeks of this, their feet would begin to rot. When the troops pulled off their boots after being rotated to the rear of the lines, they would find their toes were falling off. Surgeons cut off the infected parts.

Preventive treatment was very simple. Keep circulation in the feet. Troops were told to take boots off once a day and masssage the feet. They were also made to stamp their feet up and down as they stood in the trenches. These simple measures helped them beat one of the sneakiest enemies, trench foot.

8. Trench Coats. World War I had a significant impact on the design of uniforms. No longer could armies parade in uniforms of red, blue, or white. They had to wear dull colors that blended well with mud. They also needed a special design of clothes. The trench coat was a style designed for combat. The coat was to serve as a raincoat, so it was made of water-repellent material. There was a double layer over the shoulders and back. The right shoulder had an extra layer in front to pad it where the soldier held his rifle. The coat had belts and rings for hanging grenades and other equipment. There were epaulets on the shoulders where the emblems of rank could be displayed. There was a slit up the back held together by a button. If the soldier rode a horse, he unbuttoned the slit. These days those features are simply style, but in World War I they served practical purposes.

9. Trench Conditions. The trenches of the western front were horrors even in restful times. They were full of mud and infested with rats. One young lieutenant was awakened while sleeping in a dugout by a sound from a corner. He switched on his flashlight to reveal a large rat dragging something. In a moment he could make out that it was a human hand. Such was a restful night in World War I.

10. The Tank. The tank was invented during World War I, but it would not reach its full potential until later. It was developed in spite of the ignorance and hostility of tradition-bound generals. Only after some demonstrations on the battlefield did it gain their support.

The idea for the tank occurred to Lieutenent Colonel Ernest Swinton. He noticed that the only motorized vehicle that could reliably travel through the rough country and mud of the western front was an American-made caterpillar tractor propelled by moving treads. It occurred to him that these tractors could be covered with armor and become fighting machines. He wrote a paper about the idea and sent it to the British government. Eventually the paper reached Winston Churchill, who was in charge of the British Navy. Churchill liked the idea of a "land battleship" and began the process of development. For a time the tank was a navy project, but it was soon transferred to another department.

While building the tractor and armor protection, the workers in the plant were told they were working on water carriers for the Mesopotamian campaign. They were soon calling them "tanks," as in water tanks. The name was later made official.

The first tanks were very unpleasant machines and not very reliable. They had treads all the way around the hull. (Notice the navy word *hull,* reflecting the early naval involvement.) The treads enabled the tank to climb obstacles 4½ feet tall and cross a trench 11½ feet wide. The tank moved at a speed of 3.7 miles per hour. A crew of eight was crammed into it. They could not sit upright, and after half an hour of operation the temperature rose to 100°F. It was so noisy the crew couldn't hear themselves talk, so they communicated by code banged out with a hammer. After a drive, the crew would be sick from the fumes.

The first tank attack took place on September 15, 1916. There were 49 tanks available, but only 36 were in running condition when the attack started. Most of these broke down pretty quickly, but the few that did break through German lines caused panic. The generals were impressed. They ordered more and started to study how to use them more effectively. At the Battle of Cambrai on November 20, 1917, the Allies started with 476 tanks massed together followed by infantry. By the end of the first day, only 100 tanks were still operating, but they had opened a major gap in the German lines. A new era in warfare was beginning.

C. The Russian Revolution

1. February Revolution. The Russians call it the February Revolution, but for the rest of us it is the March Revolution. The explanation is simple. The Russian calendar in use in 1917 was 13 days behind the calendar used in Europe and America. Using either day, the Russian February 23, 1917, or Europe's March 8, the calendars agreed it was Women's Day, a workers' holiday observed by socialist parties. They planned a quiet observance with meetings and speeches, but no strikes. Contrary to plans, the women workers went on strike, poured out of the factories, and soon turned to marching in the streets, rioting for bread. These protests grew and were joined by military units on February 27, or March 12. The soldiers simply announced, "We will not shoot." In the next few days, the officers quietly left and the soldiers joined the revolutionaries. This revolution was not led by the men who would later run the Bolshevik Revolution. They were all far away. Lenin was in Switzerland. Stalin was in Siberia, and Trotsky was in New York. Historians of all viewpoints agreee that this February or March Revolution happened more or less by accident. It had no famous leaders. The people were simply hungry and desperate.

2. Lenin Returns to Russia. After the February (March) Revolution, the Bolsheviks settled down to cooperate with the new provisional government. They saw this as the early stages of a middle-class revolution. Any good Marxist knows that history moves in stages. The middle-class revolution would establish democracy and capitalism. Later would come a workers' revolution that would produce socialism and eventually communism. So the Bolsheviks were pleased to see this new stage of history start. They knew their day would come later, probably years later. All this changed when Lenin arrived.

Lenin had been in exile since 1908, and was living in Switzerland when the revolution broke out. He needed to get to Russia, but how? The German General Staff agreed to transport him to Russia. For the Germans this was an investment. They thought that Lenin and the other revolutionaries they helped would probably cause all kinds of political turmoil in Russia. This would help the Germans in their war on the eastern front. They provided a train known to history as the "sealed train" for Lenin and other revolutionaries in Switzerland to ride to Russia. They were very careful that none of these radicals got off the train in Germany.

The Bolsheviks were delighted to have Lenin back. They met him at Finland station in Petrograd on April 16, 1917. The greeting committee gave a little speech and presented him with a bouquet of flowers. Lenin did not like flowers. He rode in an armored car to a meetng of the assembled Bolsheviks. That very night Lenin gave them a two-hour speech telling them that the time was now. They should plan to take over this revolution and make it a revolution of the workers, a socialist revolution. The Bolsheviks were startled by the idea, but Lenin devoted his energy to it. The result was the October (November) Revolution.

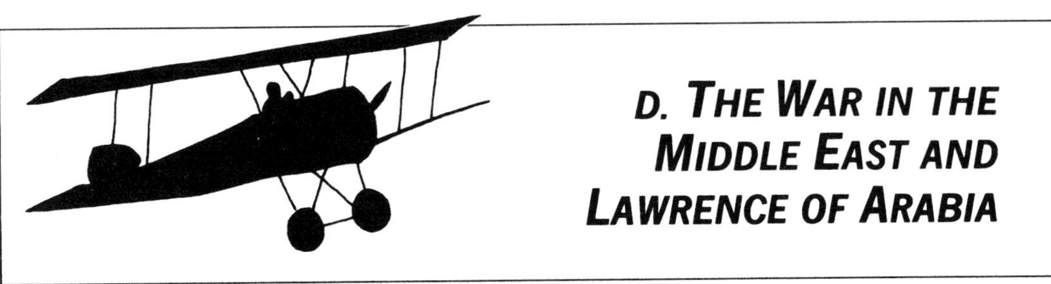

D. The War in the Middle East and Lawrence of Arabia

1. Lawrence of Arabia. Lawrence of Arabia was one of the most colorful personalities of World War I. He dressed like an Arab, spoke Arabic, and lived among Arabs, but he was an Oxford-educated British army officer. His mission was to stir up the Arabs against the Turks. If the Turks were busy fighting Arabs, they would be less able to help out the Central Powers. Lawrence helped plan and lead an Arab uprising that killed 35,000 Turks and captured or wounded another 35,000. The uprising was fought guerrilla style. The Arabs made hit-and-run raids on the railroad running from Baghdad to Medina. The Turks had to commit thousands of troops to protecting the railway. Lawrence didn't want the railroad destroyed. He wanted it just barely running and to keep all those Turkish soldiers busy guarding it.

The British talked of self-rule for the Arabs after the war, in payment for the Arab military help, but somehow it didn't happen. Lawrence, who may have begun to think he was an Arab, was deeply disappointed. After the war he was famous but tried to live a quiet life, using other names. He died in 1935 in a motorcycle accident while using the name T. E. Shaw.

E. The Peace Conference

1. Clemenceau. When the American president, Woodrow Wilson, announced his Fourteen Points, some Allies were not favorably impressed. The French prime minister, Clemenceau, is reported to have said, "God almighty only had ten."

2. Lloyd George. The British prime minister at the Versailles Conference, Lloyd George, had campaigned for election on the slogans "Hang the Kaiser" and "Make the Germans Pay!" and "Squeeze the Germans Until the Pips Squeak." He may have moderated his views later to support the Fourteen Points, but there was always pressure from home to live up to his campaign promises.

CHAPTER XIX

Europe After World War I

— Overview —

This was the great age of dictators in Europe. In Russia the Communists were taking over, and Stalin became their leader. Mussolini became dictator of Italy and set a pattern for future right-wing dictators. A few years later, Hitler took over Germany. The Fascist forces were on the march through other European countries.

Students can do comparison-contrast papers on any two of the major dictators: Stalin, Hitler, Mussolini. They can also compare and contrast fascism, nazism, and communism. Artistic students can make bulletin boards about "Communism," "Fascism," or "Nazism." The imaginative student can write "I Saw a Soviet Purge Trial," "Correspondent's Report from Ethiopia," or "Letter from a Spanish Citizen."

A. RUSSIA

1. Allied Intervention in the Russian Civil War. The American tourist returning from the former Soviet Union will sometimes bring back reports of a museum commemorating an American invasion of Russia. Could it be that the Americans once sent soldiers to fight the Communists in Russia?

Here, in brief, is what happened. When the Bolsheviks took over Russia, they quickly negotiated a peace with Germany. The World War I Allies were horrified. They didn't care for the Bolsheviks and badly wanted the war in the east to continue. So for these and other reasons they landed troops in Russia. As a result they became entangled in the Russian civil war.

The Americans were trying to achieve two goals. President Wilson wanted to help out some Czechoslovakian soldiers, about 40,000, who were trying to join the Allied armies and protect supplies the Allies had sent to Russia from falling into Bolshevik hands. These goals were not identical with those of other Allies. The French and some British leaders, like Winston Churchill, wanted to wipe out the "Reds," the Bolsheviks. The Japanese were clearly looking for a chance to take over a good-sized slice of eastern Russia. These differences in goals helped muddle the conduct of the operation.

The Americans landed troops at Archangel in European Russia. The U.S. 339th Infantry Regiment served there under a British commander and saw some very nasty fighting in the winter of 1918–19. The total Allied force including Americans, Canadians, French, and a few White Russians was about 1,700. They battled Red Army forces, who were driving out invaders, as they saw it. An estimated 3,000 Bolsheviks were in the battle. By the time the Americans pulled out in the summer of 1919, 150 American soldiers had been killed.

About 7,500 Americans landed in Vladivostok in August of 1918. They joined the Japanese, who had around 70,000 troops in Russia. The Americans spent their time doing nothing, not an easy task when their ally Japan was vigorously fighting Bolsheviks for control of the area. But the Americans had not fired a shot when they pulled out and were entirely gone from Vladivostok by April of 1920. The Japanese stayed a while longer.

Clearly the American role in the Allied intervention was small and did not constitute an effort to drive out the Bolsheviks. If the United States had wanted to do that, it could have sent more troops. Americans tend to think of the intervention as a minor incident in the context of World War I. It was obviously a much more important part of Russian history, and Russians remember it as they saw it in the context of their civil war.

2. **The Red Army.** The Red Army organized by Leon Trotsky is the model all later Communist forces have imitated. Trotsky was facing a variety of White Army forces and he needed to build an army from scratch. He turned to his old enemies and used officers from the tsarist armies to lead his Red Army forces. But since these officers were not politically reliable, Trotsky also put a political commissar in each unit to supervise the military commander. He also made sure that the enlisted personnel received a heavy dose of political indoctrination. They studied both rifle shooting and revolutionary theory. Trotsky used the army training to sell the Revolution to the ordinary soldiers. The Whites in the Russian Civil War were confused and divided about what they were fighting for, but every Red Army soldier was fighting for the workers, the peasants, and the Revolution. The Soviet armed forces maintain a strong

tradition of political training, although the details of organization have changed. Later Communist forces in China and Vietnam, for example, always emphasized political training. In contrast, the U.S. Army gives strictly military training and leaves politics to the civilians.

3. The Soviet Union. It was under Lenin that Russia became the Union of Soviet Socialist Republics. The name told a lot about the country. It was a union of republics, 15 in all. This was Lenin's way of compromising with the nationalist movements in the civil war. Each big nationality got a republic. Republics ran local affairs, so the nationalities were somewhat free of Russian domination. The republics were socialist because, in the jargon of communism, they were in the socialist stage of history. They had been through the workers' revolution, which destroyed capitalism, and were now building socialism so they could eventually reach communism. The word *soviet* told how they were governed. In Russian, *soviet* means "council." During both the 1905 and the 1917 revolutions, the revolutionaries formed soviets, or councils. Each village or town had a soviet, and the national legislature was the Supreme Soviet. Layers between also had their soviets.

So what once was Russia became the Soviet Union, or U.S.S.R. for short. In the Cyrillic Alphabet, that is C.C.C.P., or what we would call S.S.S.R. "Union of Soviet Socialist Republics" was, after all, our translation of their Russian-language name, so our initials for it are also a translation.

4. Stalin in Lenin's Testament. Lenin wrote a "testament" in 1922, discussing the question of who should follow him as Soviet leader. He reviewed all the top leaders of the time and endorsed no one candidate. He later added a codicil in which he said, "Stalin is too rude," and he proposed to remove Stalin from the position of Communist party secretary. But before Lenin could act, he had a stroke. He died a few months later. After Lenin's death, Stalin used his position as party secretary—where he had, in Lenin's words, "enormous power"—to take over the control of the party and the government.

5. Trotsky. After Lenin's death, Trotsky looked like a prime candidate to be the next leader of the Soviet Union. He had been Lenin's second in the 1917 revolution. He had organized the Red Guards that fought in the October Revolution and the Red Army in the civil war. He had also negotiated the Treaty of Brest-Litovsk ending Russian participation in World War I. His revolutionary record went back to 1905, when he had led workers during that revolution.

But Stalin tricked Trotsky and overpowered him. Trotsky was dealing with a crisis in the country when Lenin died. Stalin telegraphed him to keep working on the problem and not return to Moscow for Lenin's funeral. Trotsky's failure to return offended some key Bolsheviks. Stalin then used his office of party secretary to pack the party leadership with his suporters. Soon Trotsky was driven into exile, finally settling in Mexico. In Stalin's Soviet Union, being a Trotsky supporter became a crime.

Trotsky supported himself by writing books. His history of the Russian Revolution is a valuable source of insider information. He also carried on some radical politics. He was killed in 1940 by a man who had become a trusted friend. One day when they were alone, the killer pulled out a folding pick used by mountain climbers to make a hold on glacier ice. He attacked Trotsky with it and killed him. The Mexican police took the assassin into custody. He seemed to be mentally unstable. There was a strong presumption that he was an agent of Stalin.

6. The Purges. During the purges of the 1930's in the Soviet Union, an honest mistake could result in imprisonment. Nickolai Polikarpov and Dimitri Gregorovich were aircraft designers who each produced unsatisfactory aircraft. They were both tried for "conspiring to sabotage the aircraft industry." Then, once inside the prison camps, they were allowed to lead an aircraft design bureau made up of prisoners who were also engineers and designers. They produced the I-5, an excellent fighter plane for its time, and were both then given their freedom.

B. THE DEPRESSION

1. Keynesian Economics. The Great Depression of the 1930's was worldwide. All the industrial countries found that businesses were going broke, people were unemployed, and the economy just didn't work. The British government responded as many other governments did by cutting back on spending and trying to get enough taxes coming in. This was exactly the wrong approach, according to one British economist, John Maynard Keynes. While most economists were saying that a depression was a part of the business cycle and had to be endured, Keynes said depressions could be cured. He argued that the key was to get businesses producing again. To do this, government should spend money on projects to give the unemployed money. These people would in turn buy things they needed, like clothes and food. These purchases would result in orders for factories. The factories would hire more people. They would in turn buy more products, and an upward spiral would pull the country out of the depression.

The one disadvantage to the idea was the fact that it required the government to run into debt. But, Keynes argued, this could be made up when the economy was booming. As prices rose, causing inflation, the government should raise taxes and cut spending, thus stabilizing prices. If this approach, called a "fiscal policy," was used correctly, Keynes argued, both depression and inflation could be controlled.

The British government was unimpressed. Some Americans, however, were quite interested, and Keynes even had a short meeting with President Franklin D. Roosevelt. The New Deal tried some policies based on Keynes's ideas, but the Roosevelt administration was too hesitant about the debt to go as far as needed. Later, in World War II, massive government spending would indeed produce jobs for all.

Keynes changed the face of economics. Before, economists had treated depressions as inevitable natural disasters, like floods. After Keynes, not everybody agreed that his ideas were right, but they all agreed that governments could manage the economy. They argued over how this should be done.

C. ITALY

1. Mussolini. Mussolini was raised to be a leftist revolutionary. His father was a blacksmith and an active socialist. The senior Mussolini named his son Benito after the Mexican revolutionary Benito Juárez.

2. The March on Rome. The Fascist march on Rome in 1922 was not exactly a march. Mostly the Fascists simply got on trains and rode into Rome. They didn't bother to buy tickets. Mussolini would claim that 100,000 "marched," but more careful counts place the number around 15,000. In any case, the existing government gave in and asked Mussolini to form a new government. So, a day after the march, Mussolini boarded a special train made up of a locomotive and one sleeping car and headed for Rome.

3. Fascist Harassment. The Fascists were often violent towards those who opposed them. In one case in 1922, the Fascists took an opponent and painted his face green, white, and red, the colors of the Italian flag. Then they forced him to run through the streets yelling, "Long live fascism!" After that they made him drink quarts of castor oil. This was one of their milder techniques of harassment.

4. Mussolini at Work. People who admired the Fascist dictatorship reported that Mussolini made the trains run on time. Admirers could pass by and see the lights burning brightly in the dictator's office even late at night. But they didn't know that Mussolini left the lights on when he went to his apartment to entertain his girlfriend.

5. Mussolini and the Ethiopian War. During the Ethiopian war, Mussolini made a big show of being the war's military leader. He always wore a uniform, and every day he pored over maps with his top general. He had a big map covered with arrows and flags. One day an aide accidentally knocked over some of the flags. He put them back in a confused mix of positions. Mussolini never noticed. This whole farce was, of course, played out in Rome, nowhere near the actual conflict.

D. GERMANY

1. The German Military. The treaty of Versailles limited the German military, but the Germans soon figured out ways to cheat. The treaty said the German Army could be a maximum of only 100,000 soldiers. The Germans observed this limit, but each of the 100,000 was very carefully trained, so in a short time each could lead 1,000 others. The army was not permitted to have tanks, but during the 1920's they secretly arranged to conduct maneuvers in the Soviet Union using automobiles as tank substitutes. This enabled them to study tank warfare.

The Germans were not supposed to build warplanes. Instead, they built commercial airliners, some designed to be converted to bombers. Racing planes could become fighters. While not permitted to train air force pilots, the Germans encouraged young people to build model airplanes and join glider clubs. Glider pilots could quickly learn to fly airplanes.

The treaty also limited the size of surface ships the Germans could build. In this case they simply lied. They built ships that they said were under the limit when the ships were actually over by more than 50 percent.

Hitler even set up labor groups that went through military drill with shovels. Soon he simply declared that Germany had a right to be armed and ignored the treaty.

2. Inflation in Germany. Inflation in Germany after World War I was very serious. The mark was 4.2 to the dollar in 1918, and by the end of 1922, it took 7,000 marks to equal a dollar. Inflation at this level tends to turn the world upside down. Thrift becomes foolishness and foolishness, thrift. There is a story of two brothers. Both inherited a share of their father's fortune. One was a prudent fellow who saved his money and made careful, conservative investments. The other was an alcoholic. He bought a wine cellar and promptly drank it dry, keeping only the empty bottles. When inflation hit, the thrifty brother found that his investments were worthless, not even enough to buy a haircut. The alcoholic, however, was the owner of wine bottles worth a fortune for resale to bottlers.

3. Inflation in Germany: Losing Value. Postwar inflation in Germany caused prices to change at a startling rate. The story is told of a young man who took the train from his house to the university. He carried with him enough money to pay for his year's schooling. When he got off the train after an overnight trip, he found that prices had gone up so much, all his money would only buy him a streetcar ride to the school.

4. Inflation in Germany: A Cup of Coffee. Inflation in Germany was so bad that people tried to spend their money fast, before it lost value. Restaurants did not print menus because prices would become out-of-date too fast. Instead, they wrote prices on a blackboard and could erase and change them easily. A customer could buy a cup of coffee at one price, drink it, and find when the check came, that the price had doubled.

5. Hitler in Prison. Not only was Hitler's sentence for leading the Beer Hall Putsch short, his time in prison was also made very comfortable. Photographs show that his cell was pleasantly decorated, much like a dormitory room. He had excellent food and a steady flow of visitors. He had the services of a secretary, Rudolph Hess, who was also a prisoner. It was here that Hitler began to write *Mein Kampf.*

6. Reichstag Fire. Hitler used the Reichstag fire to wipe out the German Communist party. According to one biographer of Hitler, this was no accident. The Nazis themselves set the fire and arranged for a Communist to take the blame. They had considered faking a Communist attack on Hitler, but instead decided to set the Reichstag building on fire. A tunnel linked the office of Gestapo leader Goering with the building across the street. A group of S.A. men led by Karl Ernst, leader of the Berlin S.A., went through the tunnel on the night of February 27, 1933, and set a number of delayed-action chemicals in the building. They then returned through the tunnel. As they were leaving, a young Dutch Communist named van der Lubbe climbed into the Reichstag building and began setting fires. He was a pyromaniac. By the time the fire department arrived, the building was doomed.

The next day, Hitler issued a decree suspending the individual liberties guaranteed under the Weimar Constitution. The move was called a "defensive measure against Communist acts of violence."

7. Night of the Long Knives. Adolf Hitler was willing to do anything to get power. By June of 1934, he was chancellor, but had not yet reached absolute power. President Hindenburg was an obstacle, but he was very old and would die soon. The army was a problem. Hitler had to have army support to get complete control, and the army was suspicious of the S.A.—the Brown Shirts, or Storm Troopers. The army thought the S.A. was scum. This was because the S.A. *was* scum. It was a collection of thugs who had beat up Hitler's political opponents. Its leader, Ernst Röhm, sexually abused boys. He had ambitions to merge the S.A. and army, then become the leader of this new force. The army hated this idea.

Apparently Hitler made a deal with the army. Hitler would reduce the S.A.'s power and the army would accept Hitler as dictator. On June 30, 1934, Hitler acted. Röhm was arrested and shot. Death squads drove through the streets of German cities arresting and executing S.A. leaders. One victim, Willi Schmidt, was a newspaper music critic. He happened to have the same name as an S.A. leader. The total killed is hard to establish. Hitler admitted 58 deaths by execution, plus some others. A later study said 401 were killed. This whole purge was called the Night of the Long Knives, or the Blood Purge.

From Hitler's point of view it succeeded. Hindenburg died in August, and the army took an oath of loyalty to Adolf Hitler.

8. **The Rhineland.** The remilitarization of the Rhineland was a golden opportunity for the Allies to stop Hitler. They failed. When the Germans sent troops into the Rhineland in defiance of the Versailles Treaty, the German generals were very shaky. They did not feel their army was ready to fight. They only sent in three battalions, about 3,000 soldiers. If there had been any resistance, they were ready to pull back at once.

The Allies believed that the Germans had sent in 35,000 troops. The French government wanted to act, but the French generals were even more timid than the Germans. All they did was send 13 divisions to reinforce the Maginot Line. A force of that size in the Rhineland would have destroyed the Germans. The French government did try to get support from Britain, but the British attitude was that this wasn't worth a military effort. Hitler was only strolling in his own backyard.

If Hitler had been stopped at the Rhineland, he could well have been forced to resign in disgrace. Instead, he won his gamble and came to believe he knew more than his generals.

9. **The Spanish Civil War.** The civil war in Spain was a bitter struggle between the right-wing Nationalists and the leftist Loyalists. The Catholic Church took the side of the right wing. The leftists were so anticlerical they tore down crosses and burned them. Soon outside forces joined the struggle. Hitler and Mussolini both sent volunteers to help General Franco and his Nationalists. This was a wonderful chance to battle-test the new tanks and aircraft. The Soviet Union sent aid to the leftists, who included Communists. The people of Spain had a role to play, too. They were the victims.

The Nazis did an experiment in terror bombing on the Basque town of Guernica, leveling it with bombs. Pablo Picasso, who was a leftist, took this destruction as the inspiration for his painting "Guernica." It is a large black-and-white painting full of distorted abstract images, very unsettling to look at. A legend says a Fascist soldier walked into Picasso's studio and saw it. "Did you do this?" he asked.

"No," Picasso replied. "You did."

When General Franco won in 1939, he became dictator of Spain. As long as Franco ruled Spain, Picasso refused to live there.

10. The 1936 Olympics: Jesse Owens and Hitler. The 1936 Olympics were scheduled in Berlin. There was some concern about holding the Olympics in a Nazy country. The Nazis were very anti-Semitic and clearly racists. They looked forward to a victory by their Aryan athletes representing the master race. Under pressure, the Nazis agreed to let Jews and blacks compete in the Berlin Olympics and to stop their persecution of Jews temporarily. Hitler was willing to make a few adjustments to show off the master race.

Jesse Owens, one of ten blacks on the American team, made a serious dent in the master race theory. He won four gold medals and set a world record and three Olympic records. First he won the 100-meter dash. The next event was the long jump, called the broad jump then, and Owens had a problem. In the qualifying round he kept stepping ahead of the takeoff board and scratching. He had lost two efforts when a German athlete, Luz Long, suggested that he simply mark a takeoff point a foot behind the board and jump from there. Owens tried it and qualified easily. Then in the final, Owens set an Olympic record, beating his closest competitor, Luz Long. The two athletes became friends. Owens went on to win the 200-meter dash and to run the first leg for the winning 400-meter relay team. Somehow Hitler was never available to congratulate Owens.

11. Boxing. The 1930's were a time of crisis. In the middle of the diplomatic events came a boxing event that did serious damage to Hitler's master race theories. Hitler believed that blacks were racially inferior to whites. He was, therefore, quite pleased when German heavyweight Max Schmeling beat "Brown Bomber" Joe Louis. Hitler had personally congratulated Schmeling and watched a film of the fight. A second Louis-Schmeling fight was scheduled for June 22, 1938. Now Louis was the heavyweight champion, so the stakes were bigger—in several ways. The press on both sides of the Atlantic made the fight a symbolic battle between an Aryan of the "master race" and a black American. Louis knocked Schmeling out in the first round. After a celebration, the American newspapers once again focused on the crisis in Europe.

12. *The Sound of Music.* Those of us who have seen *The Sound of Music* either as a play or film have seen what happened to one family as the Nazis took over Austria. The story is based on the experience of the von Trapps, a famous family singing group. While the von Trapp family was anti-Nazi and insisted they were Austrians, not Germans, they had a friend who collaborated and became an official in the new government. The von Trapps were forced to perform in a festival concert for the new rulers, but fled the event before it was over. This set off a search by Nazi authorities. In the final scene the von Trapps were hiking out of Austria to escape life under the Nazis.

CHAPTER XX

Asia, the Middle East, Africa, and Latin America After World War I

— Overview —

The whole world was changing during the years between the world wars. In India, Gandhi was beginning to use civil disobedience against the British. China was changing, pushed by Nationalists, Communists, and the Japanese. Japan became a more hostile and aggressive power. In the Middle East a number of people were moving toward freedom. Atatürk was modernizing Turkey, and Persia (Iran) was also changing. Colonialism continued in Africa, and Ethiopia fought for its freedom. In Latin America, there were some radical political developments.

Your students could write papers comparing Atatürk's changes with those in Persia. They could also compare the problem of self-rule and modernization in China with that in India. They could compare Pancho Villa with Augusto Sandino. They could also compare the legal ideals of women's rights in China with the actual practice.

A. India

1. Gandhi. Mohandas Gandhi led a campaign of civil disobedience against the British. One of his most famous acts of disobedience was his Salt March in 1930. The British had a law taxing salt and making it illegal for anyone to produce salt. Gandhi felt this was an unjust law, because it taxed the poor. Gandhi led a group of 79 people on a walk of roughly 240 miles to the seashore. While there, he collected natural salt found along the shore, violating the British law. A few weeks later, he was arrested and put into prison. The British now had a serious problem because other Indians were also going to the sea and making salt in support of Gandhi. They too had to be arrested and imprisoned, all 100,000 of them. Soon the British government reached an agreement with Gandhi. He would stop civil disobedience, and they would change the salt law and release all people convicted under it. After World War II, Ghandi would use civil disobedience to win inndependence for India.

B. China

1. Women's Rights. In the early 20th century, Chinese women in the cities began to push for change. By 1902, anti-foot-binding societies existed in the cities. They even had the approval of the Empress Dowager. About the same time, wealthy families began to send their girls to school. In 1924, the Nationalist Party under Sun Yat-sen issued a manifesto recognizing the principle of equality between the sexes and had two women on its Central Executive Committee.

2. The Soong Sisters. Charlie Soong had three daughters. He had made his way from China to the United States and back to play an active role in Chinese revolutionary politics. His daughters would each in her own way be a power in shaping the future of China.

The eldest daughter, Soong Ai-ling, married H. H. Kung, a very wealthy man. They met at a family dinner in the Soong household. Kung was a descendant of Confucius and the most powerful banker in Nationalist China. He also founded a series of Chinese colleges patterned after the American model. At least one expert says that the real guiding force behind all this was Ai-ling. She may have been the most powerful person in her family and perhaps in all China.

The second daughter, Soong Ching-ling, was a romantic revolutionary. She defied her family and eloped with Sun Yat-sen, head of the Nationalist movement, in spite of the fact that Sun was already married and was roughly her father's age. The family was shocked and treated Ching-ling as an outcast. She devoted the rest of her life to Sun, working with him to encourage the revolution. When he died, Ching-ling carried on alone. At one point she had to flee to Moscow and later to Berlin. She returned to China when Sun's remains were entombed in a massive mausoleum. Ching-ling was opposed to the Nationalists as led by Chiang Kai-shek and issued statements spelling this out. At one time, the Nationalists muttered threats to cut off her head. She told them if they were real revolutionaries, they would do it. When the Communists took over China, Ching-ling was awarded the Stalin Peace Prize, and in the 1950's, she became vice-chairman of the People's Republic. In her later years, she retired from politics and lived in the old Soong home.

Soong Mei-ling got an American education at Wellesley College and returned to China. There she married Chiang Kai-shek, leader of the Nationalists after Sun Yat-sen died. The marriage was arranged by Soong Ai-ling, although Chiang was previously married. As Madam Chiang Kai-shek, Mei-ling became a major force in Chinese-American relations. She spoke English with a Southern accent and had a knack for charming visiting American politicians. She acted as official commander of the Flying Tigers. She made trips to America and wrote extensively, selling the idea of U.S. aid to Nationalist China during World War II. For many years she was listed as one of the ten most admired women in polls taken in the United States. After the defeat of the Nationalists, she moved to Formosa and, after her husband's death, to the United States.

3. The Price of a Girl. The peasants of China were among the poorest people on the planet. They paid rents, taxes, and high interest rates on loans. If a peasant failed to meet payments, his family could be seized and sold into slavery. In a poor crop year, the selling price for a teenage girl was less than 110 pounds of grain.

4. Warlords. In the early years after the Nationalists' revolt, China was ruled by a group of warlords. About the only thing they had in common was the fact that each had an army of some sort and a territory that he ruled. Feng Yu-hsiang was called "the Christian General." He had baptized his whole army with a hose. He disciplined his troops not to commit the atrocities most armies committed. He even inspected them for clean fingernails. Wu Pei-fu, the warlord of Honan, liked trees and flowers. He planted them along the railroads he controlled. Once in a battle, an opposing warlord was chasing him and in the process had his army cut down the trees. To foreigners these armies might seem comic, but they kept China divided until the Nationalists could force unity.

5. Founding of the Chinese Communist Party. The First Congress of the Communist Party of China was made up of 13 delegates. One of these was Mao Zedong. None of the delegates was a worker or peasant. There were, however, 2 representatives of the Comintern, one Dutch and one Russian. The meeting took place in Shanghai at the Boai Girls' School on Joyful Undertaking Street in July 1921.

Someone spotted a possible spy lurking nearby, so they moved the meeting to a pleasure boat where the delegates fished, debated, and founded the Chinese Communist Party.

6. The Xian Incident. The Chinese did not unite to fight the Japanese invasion until December 1936. Up to that time the Nationalists under Generalissimo Chiang Kai-shek concentrated on fighting against the Communists. On December 7, 1936, Chiang Kai-shek went to Xian province, and there he was caught in a mutiny.

On December 12, the rebels, elements of the local army, struck. They had to shoot their way into the house where the Generalissimo was staying. He escaped by climbing the garden wall barefoot in his nightshirt without his false teeth, and hid in a cave. When the rebels found him, they began to negotiate a new policy. His captors wanted him to stop fighting the Communists and fight the Japanese instead. The Chinese Communist party supported this idea and was eager to join in fighting the Japanese. The Communists also wanted Chiang released. After much hard bargaining and several messages from Madame Chiang at the capitol, Chiang was released, flew back to Nanking, and followed the policy of fighting Japan. The leaders of the uprising meekly surrendered to him, and he locked them up.

C. JAPAN

1. The Japanese Navy. From the viewpoint of the Japanese Navy, the Americans created the need for Japan's naval building program by first weakening the Japanese Navy and then expanding the U.S. Navy, thus threatening Japan. During the 1920's and 1930's, the Japanese Navy was very defense-oriented. The Japanese tried to design their ships so they could operate most effectively in home waters. Since 1918,

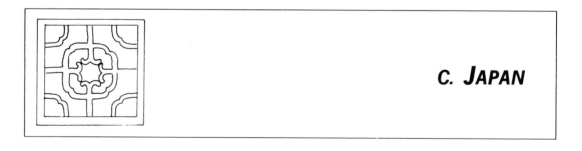

Japan had rated the United States as its most likely enemy, with the Soviet Union second. Therefore, the Washington Naval Conference of 1921 created a problem for the Japanese Navy. Japan argued that a ratio of seven Japanese battleships to ten United States battleships was ideal. Neither side would have enough of an advantage to attack the other successfully. The Conference settled on three Japanese to five United States ships, and that made the Japanese feel threatened, because under that ratio, Americans were strong enough to attack successfully. The Japanese viewpoint was again ignored in the London Naval Conference of 1930. This led the Japanese to give notice in 1934 that they were withdrawing from the earlier treaties. One of the events pressuring them to do this was an American naval building program that brought the U.S. fleet up to the strength permitted in the treaty. The Japanese felt very threatened by this and tried to compensate by building better-quality ships. They started construction on the largest battleships ever built, the *Yamato* and *Musashi,* monsters that carried 18-inch guns while U.S. battleships carried 16-inch guns. This was all in response to what the Japanese saw as the American threat.

2. The Manchurian Incident. The Japanese government did not want to attack the Chinese in Manchuria, but army officers made the attack nonetheless. The army had its own policy, and it deeply resented the interference of civilian politicians.

The foreign minister heard reports of a plan for action in Manchuria. He protested to the minister of war, who was a general in the army. He also protested to the emperor. The emperor told the general to restrain the army. The general wrote a letter to the commander of the army in the area telling him not to attack Manchuria. Then he gave the letter to an officer who was known to support the idea of military action. This officer in turn carried the letter by the slowest route possible, riding a train through Korea when he could have used a plane. When he arrived at Mukden, he went to a geisha house rather than delivering the letter to military headquarters. That night while he was still in the geisha house, the "Manchurian Incident" started. The army quickly overran Manchuria, and the Japanese public was pleased. The government now had to accept the conquest of Manchuria.

3. The *Panay* Incident. The first bomb hit at 1:38 P.M. Japanese planes were attacking the U.S. Navy's *Panay* as it steamed on China's Yangtze River on December 12, 1937. The incident had several odd elements. What were the Japanese and the Americans doing in China? Was the bombing an accident? How did the two governments react? How do we happen to have film of the event?

The U.S. Navy operated a squadron of eight river gunboats that patrolled the Yangtze, protecting American life and property. It says a lot about the weakness of the Chinese government that such a group of armed ships from a foreign country patrolled Chinese waters. The Japanese had noted this weakness and were invading China in what they called "the China Incident." It was actually the first stage of World War II in Asia. At the time of the attack on the *Panay,* the Japanese were pushing a siege of Nanking. The films of the attack clearly show Japanese markings on the planes. There is little chance the bombing was in error, The *Panay* displayed an American flag and had an American flag 23 by 32 feet painted on its deck. The weather was bright and clear.

In spite of a spirited defense, the ship was sunk and survivors had to scramble ashore. One sailor manned his gun in only a shirt and life vest—no pants. All this was recorded by two Italians, Luigi Borgini and Sando Sandri, who were aboard. They were newsreel photographers and managed to shoot film of the planes and the defenders. Shortly after the event, these films were shown in movie theaters.

The two governments were remarkably calm throughout the crisis. The United States delivered a note of protest. The Japanese made a complete apology for their pilots' mistake and paid an indemnity of over $2 million.

D. The Middle East

1. Afghanistan Gets Independence. The people of Afghanistan fought a guerrilla war against the British. This led to the treaty of Rawalpindi in 1919. The treaty gave Afghanistan independence and confirmed its border with Pakistan. The British also gave the Afghans ten airplanes for their air force.

2. The British in Egypt. Even after Egypt was technically free in 1922, the British continued to treat the country like a colony. The following incident was told to an American writer by Anwar Sadat. Sadat grew up just a few miles away from the village of Denshway. Near this village British soldiers were hunting pigeons when they accidentally set fire to a silo. As the local farmers fought the fire, a soldier shot at them. The farmers attacked and killed him. The British promptly arrested and tried a number of farmers. Even before the trial was over, they were building gallows. A local man named Zahran, who was the first hanged, became a local hero because of the brave way he died. His story became a ballad sung throughout Egypt. He served as a symbol of resistance to British oppression.

3. Atatürk and the Fez. For Turks in the early 20th century, the fez was the symbol of being Muslim. In the Turkish language the word for putting on a hat also was understood as giving up Islam. In spite of this, Atatürk believed a person could wear a hat and still be a Muslim. Atatürk insisted that the hat was part of modern dress and that Turks should wear hats, rather than the fez.

4. Atatürk and the Alphabet. Atatürk changed Turkish writing from the Arabic to the Roman alphabet. He personally traveled around Turkey attending classes in the new alphabet.

5. Atatürk and Women's Rights. Atatürk's reforms included women's rights. Historically, Turkish women had been independent. There had been Turkish queens equal to kings. But under the influence of Persia and the Byzantines, the Turks had adopted the harem, veils for women, and the attitude that women were objects. Now Atatürk set about changing things. Women became part of the army. In 1921, they were admitted to Istanbul University. When the Turks adopted the Swiss Civil Code as their law system, women's status changed. Polygamy became illegal, and women had more equal rights about divorce and inheritance. Women first voted in Turkish local elections in 1930 and in national elections in 1934.

6. Persian Oil. The first oil discovered in the Middle East was in Persia. A private company had drilled several dry holes, and headquarters had actually sent a telegram to stop drilling when the crew hit oil on May 16, 1908. The company was supported by the British government, which needed a reliable supply of oil because the British Navy was converting to oil. Earlier steamships burned coal, but in 1912, the British built the first oil-fueled battleship. In 1914, the British government bought the Anglo-Persian Oil Company. By 1919, the British had plans to make Persia a protectorate, but the Persian government refused to ratify the agreement.

7. Persia and the Shah. In 1921, there was an uprising, and when the dust settled, the man in charge was Reza Khan, an army officer. Khan began an extensive program of modernization. He became shah of Iran in 1925 and took the name Reza Shah Pahlavi. He built the trans-Iranian railroad. He sent Persian students out to Europe to learn things that would help Persia, but cautioned them not to become a bad copy of Europeans. In 1936, he encouraged Iranian women not to wear the veil. He also forced nomadic tribes to settle down, and had constant trouble with religious authorities. Reza Shah was a great admirer of Atatürk, who was doing similar things in Turkey and having similar problems with religious leaders.

The shah visited Turkey in 1934, and took a tour by train with Atatürk. The shah was sleeping, but Atatürk was still up late at night when a crowd of admirers gathered to greet Atatürk at a station. They were led by a mufti, a religious leader. Atatürk was furious that they would be led by such a person and gave them a tongue-lashing. When the shah woke up the next morning and heard about it, he was deeply impressed.

E. AFRICA

1. The British in Kenya. The British in Kenya enjoyed a pleasant life. They had all the comforts of home plus cheap native labor. They could drink, dance, and party endlessly. They had cricket, polo, tennis, and horse racing. They could even go fox hunting, but they had to use a jackal or an antelope as the fox. They could play golf, but in some courses the roughs were really rough—they featured lions.

2. The Ethiopian Air Force. During the 1930's, Ethiopia was working at building an image as a power in Africa. This included building an air force. At first the French served as aviation advisors, but the Ethiopians did not like the idea of Europeans leading their air force. The "Black Eagle" saved them from that dilemma. His name was Hubert Fauntleroy Julian, and he came from New York City. He was a tall, athletic African-American who spoke fluent French and flew planes with a dramatic flair. *Dashing* and *flamboyant* are words too mild for the Black Eagle. He became the future emperor's personal favorite until Julian's downfall. The Black Eagle had trained two Ethiopian cadets to fly. The future emperor wanted to see them actually fly, so on October 31, 1930, he came to the airport. The Ethiopian Air Force at the time had only three planes. The Ethiopian pilots took off in two German-built Junkers monoplanes. All was going well, and the future emperor was pleased, until Julian decided to take off in the British-made Gypsy Moth that was the rest of the Ethiopian Air Force.

This was a violation of strict orders not to fly this plane. It was the emperor's personal plane and wasn't to be flown until the coronation a few days later. When Julian took off, the future emperor was furious. To make matters worse, Julian put the Gypsy Moth into a dive and when he pulled on the stick to pull out, nothing happened. The dive continued and the plane crashed into a tree. Julian was unhurt, but in deep trouble. The next day, the Black Eagle was shipped home in disgrace. He was lucky to escape with his life.

In 1935, when Mussolini attacked Ethiopia, Julian again volunteered to serve. He was allowed nowhere near the Ethiopian Air Force, which was now made up of four planes. Instead, he was put in command of an army unit. He led the men with his usual dash, riding a handsome white horse past the press corps. He was a heroic figure, a friend of the emperor once more and good for morale. The Italians started a rumor that Julian was in their pay. Although it was never substantiated, and Julian denied it, the damage was done. He left Ethiopia again. A few months later, Ethiopia was conquered by Italy.

F. LATIN AMERICA

1. The Mexican Revolution. The Mexican Revolution was a confused affair, a series of oppressive presidents opposed by a variety of revolutionaries. Two of the more prominent revolutionaries were Pancho Villa and Emiliano Zapata. Once the two met in Mexico City. They had control of the capitol, and the presidential chair, a cushioned armchair painted gold, was in the room. Villa urged Zapata to sit in it. Zapata refused, saying that it would be better to burn it, because everyone who had sat in it had become an enemy of the people.

2. Pancho Villa. During the Mexican Revolution, Pancho Villa found a creative way to raise money. He signed a contract with the Mutual Film Corporation, giving the company exclusive rights to film his battles. Mutual paid him $25,000. Villa delayed his Ojinaga attack until the cameras were ready. He cooperated with the photographers and gave them transportation and an escort. They got their own boxcar when Villa's army moved by rail. Villa loved to be photographed and spent hours riding before the cameras.

3. Nicaragua. In the year 1912, a skinny teenager watched as government soldiers dragged the body of a dead rebel through the streets. The place was the Nicaraguan village called Niquinohomo and the teenager was Augusto César Sandino. The anger felt by Sandino on that day would have consequences for years to come. U.S. Marines had helped capture the rebel in question. The Marines occupied Nicaragua from 1912 to 1925 and returned in 1926 to stay until 1933. Sandino began to fight the Marines in 1926, and for the next seven years he led a fight by Nicaragua against the foreign occupation. He developed a guerrilla style of warfare and was quite successful. The Marines never caught him, and his movement was still strong in 1933 when the Marines left. They left behind a government friendly to the United States led by Anastasio Somoza García. Sandino had been fighting to drive out the Marines, so he gave up his rebellion and surrendered to Somoza. They even posed for a picture with their arms around each other's shoulders. Shortly after that, in 1934, Somoza's forces killed Sandino. But his memory remained. The Somoza family ruled Nicaragua until 1979, when they were overthrown by a rebellion. The rebellion was led by the Sandinista Front of National Liberation, more commonly called Sandinistas, after Sandino.

CHAPTER XXI

World War II in Europe and North Africa

— Overview —

This chapter is mainly a military view of the war, but it does include material on Swiss neutrality and events inside Germany, notably the Holocaust and the plot against Hitler. Some unexpected people show up fighting the war, like the Finns, Russian women, and African-Americans. There is some material on technology on land, on sea, and in the air.

You might want to send out your students to interview veterans. (They should be careful about believing all they hear. I met a teacher in Chicago once who said his students had interviewed five veterans, each of whom was the first man across the bridge at Remagen.) Students could compare land warfare in World War II with World War I.

There are lots of topics for bulletin boards: for example, "World War II Aircraft," "Leaders of World War II," or "The Soldiers of World War II." Students can probably find old souvenirs in closets and attics. They include helmets, uniforms, and bayonets, and they make excellent bases for reports.

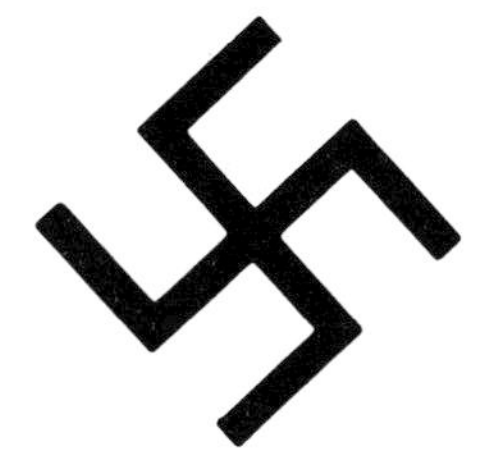

A. SMALL COUNTRIES

1. Finland's Winter War. For 105 days during the winter of 1939–40, the Soviet Union tried to conquer Finland. World War II was already under way in western Europe, so Stalin decided to conquer his smaller neighbor. Finland was small, but not weak. The Finns fought bravely and effectively. The Soviet Army was weakened by many problems, the most noticeable being the fact that in each unit all decisions had to be approved by a political officer. Soviet equipment broke down in the cold and snow, and the Finns swooped down on the Soviets on skis. The Finns made the Soviet Army look so bad that Hitler thought of it as weak, encouraging his decision to invade the Soviet Union. Eventually the superior numbers of the Soviet forces prevailed over the Finns. The negotiated peace gave the Soviet Union 22,000 square miles of land, just enough to bury their estimated one million dead. By the time the Germans invaded the U.S.S.R. in 1941, the Soviet Army was reorganized, using the lessons it had learned during the Winter War.

2. Switzerland and Neutrality. The Swiss knew just what to do when World War II started. They called up their army and elected a general. In peace, the Swiss Army has no generals. In World War II, General Heenri Guisan led Switzerland. His mission was to avoid fighting a war and to uphold the rights of Switzerland as a neutral country. It was not an easy task.

The Swiss have a long tradition of neutrality, but they also have political opinions. Many Swiss speak German; others speak French. The German-speaking Swiss were very anti-German, because they could turn on their radios and listen to Hitler's speeches. They disliked the combination of German nationalism and racism in what they heard. The Germans were constantly pressing the Swiss to tone down criticism of Hitler in Swiss newspapers.

One asset the Swiss had was the ability to fight. The Swiss Army consisted of all able-bodied Swiss males, 435,000 men. They had their weapons and uniforms at home and were ready to fight within hours after Germany invaded Poland. They also had anti-aircraft guns and planes, including 50 German-made Messerschmitt Me 109's. General Guison made it clear to all concerned that the Swiss would fight if invaded by either side. He also let it be known that he had charges in place to blow up mountain passes and railroad tunnels if attacked. The army would also shoot down planes violating Swiss airspace. Swiss planes shot down 15 planes during the war, and anit-aircraft guns downed another 9.

Also, the Swiss were useful to both sides as long as they were neutral. They sold precision equipment, like watches, to both sides. They acted as diplomatic go-betweens on issues like treatment of prisoners of war. Switzerland was a great meeting place for spies from all sides. The Swiss helped bring Jews out of Germany, and the International Red Cross had its headquarters in Switzerland.

The Swiss managed to survive the war by using a combination of tact, diplomatic skill, and toughness. As an example, take the case of the Me 110 that landed in Switzerland in April 1944. It carried the latest in top-secret German radar. The Swiss refused to return the plane. The Germans wanted to destroy the radar and might have bombed the airport, but the Swiss hid the radar in a secret bomb shelter in the Alps. Finally they negotiated a compromise. The Swiss would destroy the plane and radar while German diplomats watched. In return, the Germans had to give the Swiss 12 new Me 109 fighters for the Swiss Air Force. Later, when American bombing damaged Switzerland, the Swiss demanded and got damage payments. They were truly neutrals. Neither side could take advantage of them.

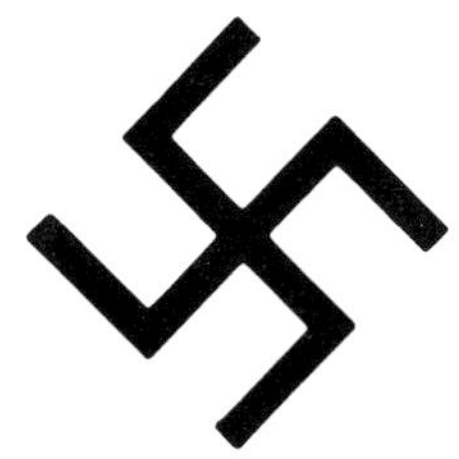

B. North Africa

1. Conditions. The climate in North Africa was hostile. It was so dry that every drop of water had to be hauled in. There was nothing green. The land was rocks and sand. The sun blazed down and raised temperatures to over 130°F. On this land the Italians, Germans, British, and Americans had to survive and fight. The Germans once made a film for their civilians showing eggs frying on the armor of a tank as it sat in the desert sun. What the film did not show was that General Rommel was inside the tank with a blowtorch. North Africa was hot, but not quite that hot.

2. Rommel's Goggles. General Rommel commanded the German forces in North Africa and became famous as Desert Fox, commander of the *Afrika Korps*. His trademark was a pair of goggles tied to his uniform cap. This is how he got them.

The war in North Africa was a war of movement. The British Eighth Army and the *Afrika Korps* chased each other back and forth as the advantage shifted. Each side captured and used the other's equipment. They particularly liked capturing food from the other side, because it relieved the monotony of their own rations. Once the *Afrika Korps* captured Mechili, a little fort, and with it some British generals and their command trucks. For the rest of the war in North Africa Rommel used one of these captured British trucks as his command post vehicle. As he inspected these trucks, he saw some goggles, picked them up, and remarked, "Booty—permissible, I take it, even for a general." Then he tied them on over his cap.

The remark about booty was a joke. The goggles were made in Canada of cheap plastic stapled to canvas and tied on with shoestrings.

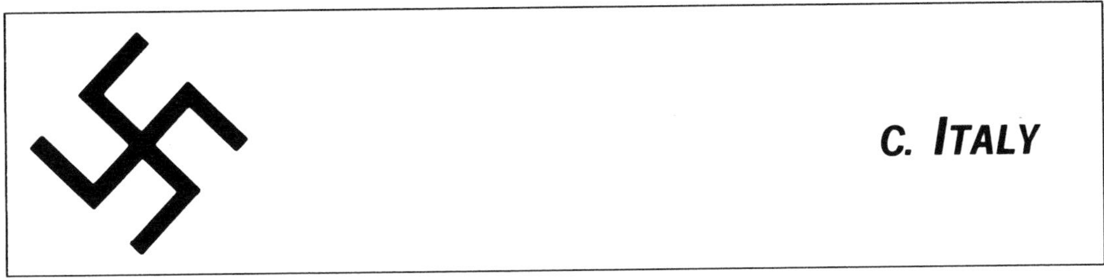

C. Italy

1. The Man Who Never Was. When planning Operation Husky, the invasion of Sicily, British intelligence decided to plant false documents to mislead the Germans about where the Allies intended to attack. They decided that a British officer killed in an air crash would be a believable way to deliver the letters. They obtained the body of man who died of pneumonia; because of this, the body would have fluid in its lungs, just as a person who drowned might have. Then they gave the corpse an identity, Major Willam Martin, Royal Marines. He carried some top-secret letters about the invasion. He also carried some love letters from his fiancée, theater ticket stubs, and the bill for his engagement ring. All these were added to make the body believably real. A British submarine carried Major Martin to a spot near the coast of Spain and set him afloat. The Spanish authorities recovered the body and read the letters. They passed on the information to the Germans. Even Hitler was fooled. The Germans deployed their forces to meet two invasions mentioned in the captured letters, one on Sardinia, another on Greece. This resulted in a much-reduced defense of Sicily, thanks to the services of Major William Martin, the man who never was.

2. The End of Mussolini. By July of 1943, the Italians were sick of Mussolini and his war. On July 25, 1943, King Victor Emmanuel held a short meeting with Mussolini and dismissed him. As Mussolini left the building, he was arrested. The official announcement came out about 11:00 P.M., but in spite of the late hour, the people rushed out into the streets cheering.

The Germans continued the war in Italy even after the Italian government changed to the Allied side. The Germans managed to make a daring raid and free Mussolini, although being made a puppet of Hitler wasn't exactly being free. Mussolini had to listen to a long speech from Hitler, then go back and lead the defense of northern Italy.

By April of 1945, the Allies were closing in, and Mussolini tried to escape to Switzerland. Instead, he was caught by Italian partisans. They took him to a quiet country road and shot him. The next day they loaded his body onto a truck, drove to Milan, and hung the corpse upside down for Italians to spit on.

D. GERMANY

1. Hitler's Jet Planes. The Germans were the first to use rocket-propelled and jet aircraft in combat. They started work on jets in 1938, and if Hitler had not slowed this development, jets and rockets could have drastically changed the war. The Messerschmitt Me 163 was in action in May of 1944. It was a small, rocket-powered plane with a rudder but no tail. It blasted into the air, then dived onto Allied bombers and glided to a landing. Landings were often dangerous. The Me 163 exploded a lot. The first combat jet was the Messserschmitt Me 262, a twin-engine swept-wing plane that began development in 1938. When Hitler heard of it in November 1943, after its first flight, he ordered it to be produced as a bomber. There was also a ground attack version and a night fighter. Designing and producing all these variants slowed production and kept material from being used to produce the most deadly version of the plane, the fighter-interceptor. About 100 of these flew against Allied bombers, and Allied fighters were not fast enough to catch them.

2. Hitler's Guided Missiles. During World War II, the Germans developed very advanced guided missiles. Fortunately, Hitler was not willing to give these high priority, so they never reached full potential. The V-1, "vengeance weapon-one" to the Germans, was called the "buzz bomb" by the Allies. It was a cruise missile, a small jet airplane with a built-in explosive charge of about 2,000 pounds. The pulse jet engine powering it is now obsolete. It operated by opening shutters on the front, scooping in air, and shutting the front, then igniting kerosene in the combustion chamber to produce jet thrust. The rapid-fire series of explosions produced the buzz that was the missile's trademark. The V-1 was shot off a launching rail and guided along a straight line. At a predetermined distance, it shut off its engine and dived into its target. The V-1 was slow enough that it could be intercepted and shot down by Allied fighter aircraft.

The V-2 was actually a short-range (under 200 miles) ballistic missile. It was a rocket powered by a mixture of liquid fuel and liquid oxygen. When working right, it was fired up as high as 60 or 70 miles and then dropped in on its targets at supersonic speed. It carried a warhead weighing one ton, and its speed made it unstoppable. When working wrong, it was even more spectacular. The liquid oxygen had to be very cold to stay liquid, and the fuel was very flammable. As a result, the V-2 was a dangerous weapon to handle. Early German films show some truly spectacular explosions.

The V-2 was the grandfather of the ICBM's used by Americans and others today. During the war, the Americans captured many V-2's and sent them to the United States for research use. After the war, more than 200 German rocket scientists came to the United States to continue their work. Wernher von Braun, for example, worked at the U.S. Army's Redstone Arsenal for years. Most of the German scientists fled to America to escape the Soviets. The Soviets did, however, capture Peenemünde, the German missile design and testing site, including some German scientists. Thus, the German guided missile program was used by both sides in the Cold War.

3. The "Final Solution" to the "Jewish Problem." The Nazis decided that the final solution to the Jewish "problem" was to exterminate the Jews. Hitler had called for "annihilation of the Jewish race" in 1939. By 1941, there were orders out for carrying it through. There is no record of when or where the decision to do this was made.

There were 11 million Jews in Europe. The Nazis operated some camps where they simply shot Jews. These were Riga, Vilna, Minsk, Kaunas, and Lvov. The more efficient camps were Treblinka, Bergen-Belsen, Sobibor, Chelmno, and the largest, at Auschwitz. Auschwitz had the capacity to kill 6,000 people a day. The people sent to these camps were too old, too young, or too sick to be used for slave labor. They would be taken to buildings marked "baths." The people took off their clothes and went inside. The doors were sealed, and crystals of poison gas, hydrogen cyanide or zyklon B would be released. The guards said they could tell the victims were dead when the screaming stopped. Then the bodies were taken out, by other prisoners. Corpses were checked, and any gold in their teeth was pulled out. Then the bodies were cremated in huge gas ovens. Other camps were less efficient. Nazi guards simply had Jews dig mass graves, then shot the grave-diggers so they fell into the open pit.

Such simple killing may have been less horrible than some other things. Nazi doctors conducted medical experiments. Some prisoners were kept outside in freezing weather as water was poured over them. Doctors took temperature readings as they froze to death. Some medical schools selected living prisoners to be killed for their collection of skeletons. Some brutality was less scientific. Some tattooed prisoners were killed so their skins could be made into lamp shades.

The Nazis kept careful records of the deaths. Each prisoner had a serial number tattooed on his or her arm and a file in the camp records. Six million Jews were killed in these camps. This was the ultimate expression of Hitler's hatred of the Jews.

4. Gypsies. Hitler's racist ideas did not focus on Jews alone. The Gypsies were also victims. Nazis referred to the "Gypsy menace." As the war went on, Gypsies were imprisoned in Auschwitz, Ravensbruck, Bergen-Belsen, and Birkenau. They were gassed in large numbers and made the subjects of experiments exposing them to poison gas and deadly diseases. Over one million Gypsies were killed during the war. After the war, the West German government refused to accept responsibility for the Gypsy deaths.

5. The Plot to Kill Hitler. As the war began to go badly for Germany, some army officers began to think seriously of getting rid of Hitler. They thought that if Hitler was gone, they could fight the war more skillfully and perhaps negotiate a peace. If these two goals seem somewhat conflicting, it may be because different groups in the plot had different hopes for what would happen after Hitler's removal. They made several attempts before they nearly succeeded. On July 20, 1944, they came within a few feet of killing Hitler.

Lieutenant Werner von Haeften, a staff officer, carried a bomb in his briefcase as he attended a meeting with Hitler at "The Wolf's Lair," Rostenburg in East Prussia. Von Haeften succeeeded in getting the bomb past the sentries and into the conference room. It was a small, hot room only 30 by 15 feet with 10 windows open to catch any breezes. There was an oak table 18 by 5 feet in the center of the room. Von Haeften arrived a little late; the conference had started. Hitler was seated at the table. Von Haeften put the briefcase down near Hitler, started the time fuse on the bomb, and slipped out. As the conference continued, Colonel Brandt leaned over the table to see a map better and bumped into the briefcase. He picked it up and shifted it out of his way. This moved the bomb so Hitler was protected by the heavy oak table.

At 12:42 the bomb went off. The plotters, seeing the explosion, assumed that Hitler had been killed. In fact, he was not badly hurt. His right arm was temporarily paralyzed. His eardrums were punctured. He was burned and blackened with smoke and his hair singed. He recovered quickly enough to publicly escort Mussolini to his train that afternoon.

Meanwhile, the plotters were wasting time. They had carefully laid plans for taking over after Hitler's death, but some of them doubted the dictator was dead. They argued and did nothing.

Hitler had no doubts or hesitation. He ordered that all the plotters be tracked down and killed. He sent Himmler to Berlin to put down any political takeover. Hitler was furious. The plotters would die.

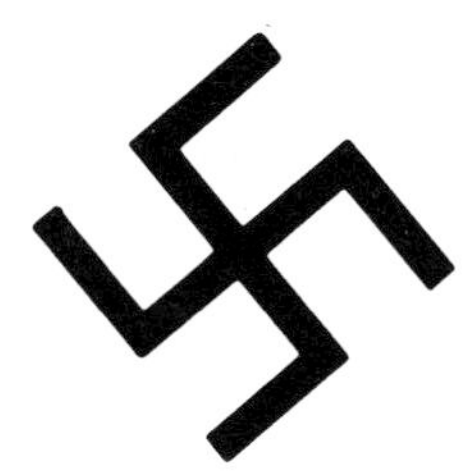

E. The Atlantic

1. Baby Flattops. Control of the Atlantic sea lanes was vital to Allied victory in World War II. Supplies had to cross the Atlantic in spite of Axis air attacks and submarines. One of the creative ideas used to protect convoys crossing the Atlantic was the "baby flattop," or escort carrier. This was a relatively small aircraft carrier designed to escort convoys. Planes from the carrier could protect the convoy from bomber attack and serve to seek out and destroy submarines. One of these baby flattops, the *Guadalcanal,* had a most unusual adventure. Most submarines were destroyed by bombs or depth charges. A few were sunk by gunfire. The crew of the *Guadalcanal,* however, actually boarded and captured a submarine. The *Guadalcanal's* crew had very high morale based on faith in their ship. They called her the "Can Do" because they thought she could do anything. Their captain, Daniel V. Gallery, was a man of wit and imagination. Somehow he had the idea it might be possible to capture a submarine. The "Can Do" routinely had a roster of men for a boarding party, just in case.

On June 4, 1944, a Sunday, they made contact with a submarine. The *Guadalcanal* and destroyers with her began a depth-charge attack. About 12 minutes later the submarine surfaced, and its crew hurriedly abandoned ship. The Germans later said they were just sitting down to Sunday dinner when the depth charges went off. They were so surprised that some of them panicked and reported the ship was sinking. The captain believed them, brought his boat to the surface, and abandoned ship.

Aboard the *Guadalcanal,* Gallery watched all this and saw his chance. He ordered, "Away all boarding parties," just like in the old days of sailing ships. The boarders found the submarine relatively undamaged, her motors still running. They had only to turn off the motors and shut off a number of valves and the ship was theirs. The German crew was taken prisoner. The captured U-515 submarine was renamed the "Can Do Junior," sometimes shortened to "Junior," and taken in tow. She was a gold mine of information, charts, orders, and code books. These all helped the Allies more effectively combat German U-boat attacks. The U-515 was towed to Bermuda. After the war, she was taken to Chicago and is on display there in the Museum of Science and Industry.

2. Listening Devices. The Battle of the Atlantic was a war between convoys and submarines, a replay of World War I, but the equipment on both sides had improved. Just how good was detection gear on United States destroyers? The following example gives some idea. The *Batfish,* an American submarine, did some practice maneuvers off Newport, Rhode Island. The boat was in telephone contact with destroyers above. The *Batfish* crew understood that the destroyers could hear machinery running, a pump working, or even a dropped wrench. They soon found that the listeners above could hear a lot more. As they started the exercise, the destroyer above phoned the boat that somebody was using the head. *Head* is the navy word for "rest room." A quick trip to the head did indeed confirm the report.

3. **Sonar.** One of the deadliest submarine-locating devices in World War II was sonar. In this system, a surface ship sent out a pulse of sound. When the sound hit an object, it echoed back to a receiver on the ship. The operator then saw a blip on a screen. Using this device, the Allies could locate a submarine even if it was sitting underwater in absolute silence. Devices like this helped the Allies destroy German U-boats and move needed supplies to Britain.

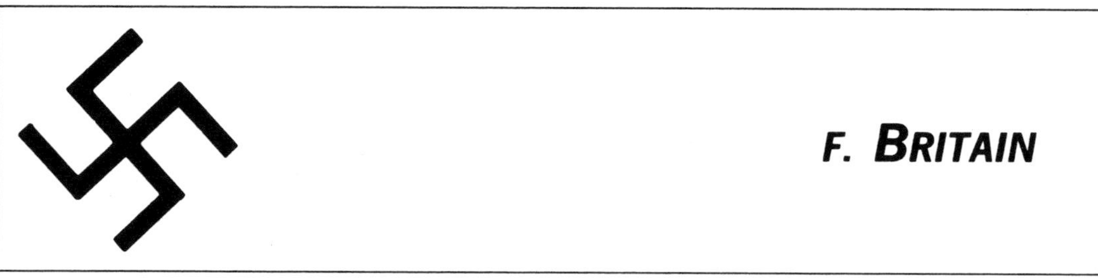

F. BRITAIN

1. **Douglas Bader, Fighter Pilot.** Douglas Bader served as a group captain in the RAF during the Battle of Britain, scoring 22½ German aircraft destroyed. This was a remarkable record in itself, but Bader added another dimension. He had lost both his legs in an accident. The RAF had discharged him for medical reasons in 1931, but he returned in 1939. He flew over Dunkirk and in the Battle of Britain. He was shot down over France in August 1941. He was a difficult prisoner of war, escaping three times. The enemy recaptured him each time, so he was not free until April 1945. Bader retired from the RAF in 1946 but continued to be active in aviation. He also wrote a series of books about his adventures.

2. **Business as Usual.** British newspapers ran two photographs during the Battle of Britain. The first picture showed a German bomber with its tail shot off diving toward a tobacco store on the corner of Victoria Station in London. The plane was about 200 feet above the shop. The second picture showed the ruins of the store. The shop owner was standing in front of the ruins with a table made of sawhorses and boards. The storekeeper was grinning. He had some cigarettes on the table and a sign written in pencil saying, "Business as usual." Such was the spirit of the British people during the Battle of Britain.

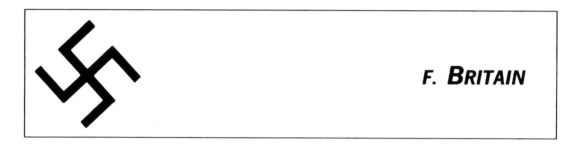

3. Spying and Double Agents. One of the great assets British intelligence enjoyed during World War II was control of the German spy network in Britain. Early in the war the British began to take over German agents. As time went on, they found they controlled most German spies in Britain. The information the Germans received from their spies was fed to them by British intelligence. Some of it was true, a device to build up the reputation of the spy. Carefully designed false information was fed to the Germans as well. The fake data informed the Germans that the British were very well prepared for gas warfare. This discouraged the Germans from using gas. After the war, German documents confirmed that the Nazis had been deceived. The British code name for the operation was appropriate. They called it the Double-Cross System.

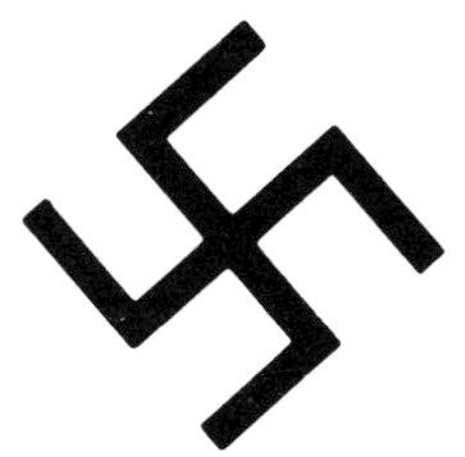

G. Eastern Front

1. Nazi Liberators. The Ukrainians, although they were part of the Russian Republic and the Soviet Union, were always nationalistic. They made it clear that they were not Russians. When the German forces invaded the Soviet Union, the Ukrainians at first welcomed them as liberators.

2. The Soviet Union's Women Pilots. Women flew for the United States, but only in the Soviet Union did women pilot combat aircraft. Three air regiments were made up entirely of women: the 586th Fighter Regiment, the 587th Bomber Regiment, and the 588th Bomber Regiment. The women of the 588th flew PO-2 biplanes as night bombers and were called the Night Witches. One woman fighter pilot, Lilya Litvyals, shot down 12 planes. She was known as the White Rose of Stalingrad.

3. Stalingrad. The eastern front was the most deadly place for a German soldier. There is a case to be made that the Soviets won the war for the Allies. Stalingrad was the first great Soviet victory. The battle started on November 19, 1942, in a blizzard. The Soviets launched two attacks in a giant pincer movement, surrounding the German Sixth Army commanded by General von Paulus. Within three days, the Soviets had closed the pincers. Hitler ordered von Paulus to form a defense and hold on. Supplies would be flown in. But the Soviets controlled the air, and Hitler did not have enough transport planes. The Germans then launched an attack to break into Stalingrad. They were threatened by another Soviet pincer. The Sixth Army might have been able to fight its way out, but Hitler refused to let them leave Stalingrad. He promoted von Paulus to field marshal because no German field marshal had ever surrendered, and ordered the Sixth Army to fight to the last man. The Soviets twice offered von Paulus a chance to surrender, but he refused. The last survivors held out until February 2, 1943. Von Paulus was taken alive. Hitler was furious. It was 24°F below zero in Stalingrad. Roughly 2 out of 3 Germans froze or starved to death or were killed. Out of the 300,000 soldiers the German Army lost at Stalingrad, only 91,000 were lost as prisoners. Among these were 24 generals.

It was a massive defeat—a whole field army gone. It was a turning point in the war. Now the Soviets would be on the offensive. They would advance all the way to Berlin.

4. German Generals' Opinion. After the war, military experts interviewed German generals. One of the first questions was "What went wrong on the eastern front?"

The reply was "Way too many Russians and one too many Germans—Hitler." In other words, Hitler by his constant interference with his generals helped lose the war on the eastern front.

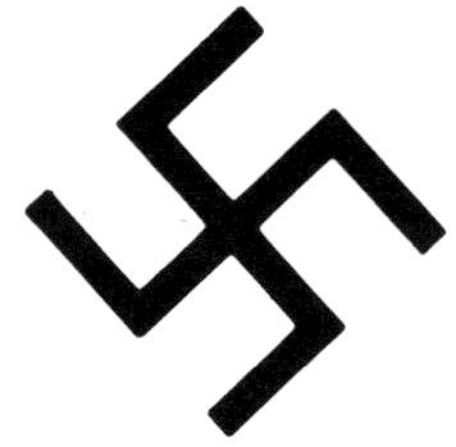

H. The Western Front

1. D-Day Deception. The Allies worked very hard at keeping the date and location of the big European invasion secret. They even created an imaginary army to deceive the Germans. They set up a group of decoy bases in southern England and made them look as realistic as possible. Pilots of German planes flying overhead would see tanks parked in large numbers. What they couldn't see was that the tanks were made of rubber and inflated like balloons. The German pilots could see the tracks of many trucks, but didn't know these tracks were made by just a few trucks operated by drivers who had the job of leaving lots of tracks. German radio operators could listen in on the radio transmissions of this phony army. The transmissions were the work of a group of radio men assigned to send carefully written messages. The Germans even learned that the commander of this invasion army was General George Patton and that its intended goal was Calais.

The deception was a success. The Germans were completely surprised by the Normandy invasion. Rommel, who commanded the beach defenses, was home on leave. The Germans also were slow in reacting to the Normandy invasion because Hitler remained convinced that it was just a diversion, that the real invasion would come at Calais.

2. Hedgerows. After the Allied landing in Normandy, most things went well, but the land itself created a problem. The farmers of Normandy surrounded their fields with hedges. These very strong walls of green presented a real problem. American tanks couldn't push through them. The solution came from the beaches. The Germans had put sharp steel bars along the coast. The bars were designed to rip the bottom out of boats that passed over them. Now the Allies tore up the bars and welded them to the front of the tanks. The sharpened bars were very effective in cutting holes in the hedges of Normandy.

3. The Gooney Bird. It had several names: Skytrain, Skytrooper, and Gooney Bird. The British called it Dakota. The Russians called it Li-2 and claimed they invented it. General Eisenhower said it was one of the four items most important in winning the war. What it lacked in glamour, it made up by being tough. It was the military version of the DC-3 airliner.

The design had been developed in the 1930's and already had a reputation for rugged reliability before the war. During the war this military DC-3 became a legend. More than a thousand DC-3's dropped 20,000 paratroopers and tons of supplies and equipment as part of the Normandy invasion. DC-3's also towed gliders full of troops. Some were converted to flying ambulances. DC-3's carried passengers and all kinds of freight, including jeeps. If somebody needed something fast, the DC-3 flew it in over the Sahara, Alaska, or the Himalayas.

Officially the place had a 28-passenger capacity; in the field it flew whatever was needed. Once in China, a DC-3 evacuated 68 passengers, one of them General Jimmy Doolittle. There was no time to waste as the Japanese Army closed in. In 1941, a Japanese attack destroyed the wing of a China National Airways DC-3. A DC-2 wing was flown to the airport strapped outside a DC-3. The replacement wing was a few feet shorter than the original, but the repaired plane flew.

By the end of the war, the Douglas Aircraft Corporation had produced over 10,000 of these sturdy, reliable, twin-engined transports. After the war, these veterans of military service were eagerly bought by commercial airlines. Some of them stayed in service for decades and were flying passengers and freight 50 years after the first DC-3 had rolled out.

4. The Bridge at Remagen. As the Allied forces advanced on Germany, the last natural barrier was the Rhine River. The German Army fell back and efficiently blew up the bridges. Crossing the Rhine would require a major effort—except at Remagen. There on March 7, 1945, the U.S. First Army found the railroad bridge still standing as they approached the town. The troops moved quickly to take Remagen. Now they could see Germans on the other side preparing to blow up the bridge. Sure enough, a little before 4:00 P.M., there was an explosion, but the bridge remained standing. An infantry platoon crossed the bridge. They found it was all set to be blown. Detonator wires ran to a 500-pound charge. The men quickly cut the wires. Troops were rushed across to defend the bridge, and engineers went to work strengthening it so it could support tanks. After that, tanks and men poured across. German resistance during all this was relatively weak. Engineers built a pontoon bridge over the Rhine to speed the river crossing. A few days later the bridge at Remagen collapsed. By that time, Allied troops had crossed the Rhine in force.

5. The Battle of the Bulge. It was Hitler's idea, and like many of his ideas, it was a bit out of touch with reality. It was supposed to win World War II for Germany, but it didn't quite make it. The idea was based on two facts. In December 1944, the Allied armies were spread pretty thin in the Ardennes. They had hit the beach at Normandy on June 6, and advanced briskly. Now they were getting careless. Also, the sky in December was full of snow and clouds. That meant the Allies couldn't use close air support as they usually did. So the Germans gathered their forces and tried to punch through Allied lines and win the war. The Germans had 25 divisions, 10 of them armored. They started the attack at 5:30 A.M. on December 16, 1944. This began the Battle of the Bulge, so called because the German pressure would produce a bulge in the Allied lines in Belgium. A bulge is not a breakthrough, however.

The Allied response was faster than the Germans had expected. Several Allied units that were hit early resisted stubbornly in spite of the cold, snow, and massive attacks. The Allies pulled soldiers out of kitchens, offices, and other noncombat jobs to fight. Eisenhower, Supreme Allied Commander, quickly organized reinforcements. The town of Bastogne in Belgium was the key. It was defended by the American 101st Airborne Division. The Germans surrounded Bastogne and offered General McAuliffe, commanding the 101st, a chance to surrender. McAuliffe's reply, according to legend, was "Nuts!" That was on December 22. Four days later General Patton's Third Army broke through to Bastogne. Soon the weather cleared, and Allied planes returned to the skies. By January 28, the Allies were back at the line where it had all started.

The Allies had lost roughly 8,500 killed, with 46,000 wounded and 21,000 missing. The Germans had over 12,000 killed, 57,000 wounded, and 50,000 captured. Those were the last of the German reserves. Their loss seriously weakened the defense of Germany. Hitler's idea had backfired.

6. African-American Troops. African-Americans fought in the Battle of the Bulge. The U.S. Army was segregated in World War II. Blacks and whites served in different units, and usually blacks served in noncombat roles like driving trucks in the Transportation Corps. But in the Battle of the Bulge there was a shortage of infantry, and Eisenhower offered "Negro soldiers," as the Army official history calls them, a chance to volunteer. Over 4,500 responded. They were grouped in special companies in some cases, and in others they served in special platoons attached to white companies. A company is roughly 200 soldiers. These volunteers fought very well. Their excellent record helped lead to the integration of the U.S. Army in the 1950's.

CHAPTER XXII

World War II in Asia and the Pacific

— Overview —

The war in Asia and the Pacific was fought by some colorful leaders. Relations among allies were not always smooth, and there was interservice rivalry even among American forces. The Japanese had their own disagreements and a brilliant leader in Yamamoto. At first the war went badly for the Allies, but Midway was a turning point, and Guadalcanal began the Allied offensive actions. As the war went badly for them, the Japanese tried some desperate measures, like kamikazes. Finally atomic bomb attacks brought the Japanese decision to surrender.

Your students could write papers on "Should the Atomic Bomb Have Been Dropped on Japan?" on "The Role of Luck in World War II," or on "The Individual in History: The Case of ________." The blank could be filled by any of the following names: Yamamoto, Chiang Kai-shek, Stilwell, MacArthur, Boyington, John Gay.

The artistic student could make a bulletin board about "Pearl Harbor," "Leaders of the Pacific War," or "The Atomic Bomb." Imaginative students could write letters home from Guadalcanal from an American (or Japanese) Marine.

A. CHINA

1. The Flying Tigers. December 1941 was a dark time for the Allies. The Japanese bombed Pearl Harbor, sank the *Prince of Wales* and the *Repulse,* and were advancing throughout Asia and the Pacific. One bright spot came on December 23, 1941, when a Japanese air raid on Rangoon was intercepted by the Flying Tigers, who shot down ten planes. The Flying Tigers were officially the American Volunteer Group in the Chinese Air Force. The Chinese government had hired an American officer, Claire Chennault, to recruit and train American pilots. The Chinese had bought 100 planes that were considered obsolete, P-40B's. With these the American pilots would fight against the Zero and other first-line Japanese aircraft. The Americans decorated each P-40 with a shark's mouth and a cartoon of a tiger flying through a *V* for "victory." Chennault, who was an expert on fighter planes, especially Japanese planes, taught the pilots how to use their P-40's to best advantage. As a result, the Flying Tigers became one of the most effective fighter units in aviation history. They shot down a total of 297 Japanese planes while losing only 4 pilots in air combat. The Chinese government paid $500 for each plane shot down, so the standard for a confirmed victory was very strict.

The Flying Tigers served in the skies over Burma and China until July 4, 1942, when their contracts expired. A few remained to serve in the U.S. Air Corps in China with Chennault, but many of them returned to the United States. Later they would fight again in American service.

There is a very old (1942) and very bad John Wayne film called *The Flying Tigers.* It was based on a story written by two Tiger veterans. There is also a Flying Tiger airline, started after the war by some ex-Tigers. Nearly every model shop has a kit of a P-40 with shark's mouth and Chinese markings, the plane flown by the Flying Tigers.

2. Vinegar Joe. Officially China was one of the "Big Five" powers in World War II: the United States, Great Britain, the Soviet Union, France, and China. In fact, the last two were included for propaganda purposes. France was occupied during most of the war, and China was a poor country that needed aid just to survive. To help the Chinese be more effective, the Americans sent them "Vinegar Joe" Stilwell. In some ways the choice made sense. Stilwell had served in China before the war and knew the situation well. But his temperament was a problem. He was a very outspoken soldier. That was why he was called Vinegar Joe.

The most vivid example of Stilwell's character came during the Burma campaign. The Japanese swept Burma with ease. The British and Chinese forces fled before them, discouraged and disorganized. Stilwell refused to be airlifted out. Instead he chose to walk out leading a mixed group of soldiers and European missionaries. The other commanders were telling the press about strategic withdrawals and getting the troops into defensive positions. When Stilwell hiked out of the jungle he bluntly told the press, "We took a hell of a licking."

Stilwell called Chiang Kai-shek, leader of China, "Peanut," at least once in his diary. He distrusted the British in India because he thought they were mainly trying to protect their hold on the colonies. He was an infantry officer and feuded with the Army Air Corps commander in China, Claire Chennault. The only group Stilwell was impressed by was the Communists. They were at least honest and efficient, in his opinion.

Stilwell irritated everyone, especially Chiang, who hated him. But he also did his job. He trained Chinese soldiers and found them capable if properly led. Leadership was so poor that Stilwell actually went to the front and kicked one commander to get him to attack.

Stilwell got the Burma Road reopened. It was named the Stilwell Road in his honor. Eventually the political pressure became too great, and the U.S. government recalled the controversial officer.

3. Chiang Kai-shek and the Communists. During World War II, Chiang Kai-shek was often accused of not fighting the Japanese very hard and saving his troops to fight the Communists. He is quoted as saying, "The Japanese are a disease of the skin. The Communists are a disease of the heart."

4. Inflation in China. During World War II, China had a terrible inflation rate. In 1940, prices rose 124 percent; in 1941, they rose by 173 percent, and 1942 saw 235 percent price increases. Currency exchange rates were rigged. The official rate was one American dollar for 20 Chinese dollars. The unofficial rate, reflecting real prices, was one American dollar for 3,250 Chinese dollars. There was a joke in China that building a privy in China cost 10,000 American dollars; that is, if it cost 60 U.S. dollars in real terms, at the unofficial rate, it would be $9,750 at the official rate.

B. THE PACIFIC

1. Pearl Harbor Warning. On Sunday, December 7, 1941, the Opana radar station was operated from 4:00 to 7:00 A.M., as was the usual procedure. The radar should have been shut down at 7:00, but the truck to take the operators to breakfast was late, so they kept the radar on. A few minutes later they spotted a huge number of blips on the screen—a large number of planes were coming toward Hawaii from the north. They called the duty officer and reported. He thought it was probably a flight of B-17 bombers due in that day. He told them not to worry about it. The blips had been the Japanese attacking flight headed for Pearl Harbor. They had been spotted roughly 40 minutes before they made their attack, and nothing was done.

2. Battleships. World War II was not a good war for battleships. At Pearl Harbor, stationary American battleships took terrible punishment from aircraft carriers they never saw. But naval tradition said that a battleship at sea able to move and defend itself was another matter. On December 10, 1941, the battleship navy got another shock. The British had sent the Battleship *Prince of Wales* and the battle cruiser *Repulse* to aid in the defense of Singapore. The two ships had steamed out of Singapore to intercept a Japanese invasion fleet, but instead, the Japanese found them. Japanese torpedo bombers flying off air bases in French Indochina attacked them. The *Repulse* was gone 20 minutes after the first torpedo hit. The *Prince of Wales* went under 20 minutes later. In less than an hour, two of the most powerful surface ships had been lost.

3. Malaya and Singapore. There is an old saying that if you believe each nation's history, the armies on both sides of any battle were outnumbered. Certainly in December of 1941, it seemed the Japanese were everywhere at once in overwhelming force. One of their most spectacular successes was their attack on Malaya. They stormed down the Malay Peninsula and took Singapore. Singapore was supposed to be an impregnable city, but the defenses were pointed out to sea. The Japanese came through the jungles on the land side. Allied news reports made a big thing of Japanese troops' special training for jungle warfare.

Since the war, the Japanese staff officer who planned the invasion has published his memoirs, *Singapore: The Japanese Version.* The author, Masanobu Tsuji, says that the British actually outnumbered the Japanese forces two to one, but the British officers were incompetent and their troops not very loyal. Tsuji's troops were pulled out of fighting in China and sent to Malaya. The only special jungle training was a pamphlet the troops were given to read on the boat. Tsuji reprints the pamphlet in full as an appendix. It is a very short, simple little booklet.

Tsuji also says that the invasion was planned on short notice. He took one quick flight over the area and began developing plans. In Allied news reports, the attack was treated as if it were the product of years of planning. Now who are we supposed to believe?

4. Yamamoto. Admiral Isoroku Yamamoto was a Harvard graduate. He was a teetotaler and liked to play poker. He knew Americans well enough that he opposed the war, predicting that if war came, the Japanese would have six months of victories and then the Americans would recover. He was so opposed to war that he was in danger from assassins who killed known supporters of peace. To save him from this danger, some friends arranged for him to be reassigned from the Naval Ministry to Commander of the Fleet.

Yamamoto was a pilot and fully understood that aircraft would dominate the seas. He wanted to wipe out American carriers at Pearl Harbor, but none was in port on December 7, so the Pearl Harbor raid failed in its most important goal. Later, at Midway, the surviving American carriers inflicted a crushing defeat on the Imperial Japanese Navy.

Yamamoto died a warrior's death in a plane flying in a combat zone. He was flying to Bougainville to inspect troops when his plane, a Betty bomber, was shot down by American P-38 fighters. The Americans had read a coded message saying when Yamamoto would arrive.

5. A Witness to Midway. Ensign John Gay was the sole survivor of Torpedo Squadron 8. The squadron flew in to attack the Japaanese fleet approaching Midway, and all of the Devastator torpedo bombers were shot down. Gay found himself floating in the middle of the Japanese fleet. His first worry was being captured. He tried to hide behind his floating seat cushion so he would not be seen and picked up. He was floating among the Japanese ships as American dive bombers attacked and destroyed four Japanese aircraft carriers. Later, after the Japanese fleet moved on, he inflated his life raft and was picked up by a navy rescue plane. He was flown to Pearl Harbor, where he was hospitalized. While there, he was visited by admirals who wanted to talk to an American eyewitness to the Battle of Midway.

6. Code-Breaking at Midway. As the Japanese were planning their big attack on Midway Island in 1942, American naval intelligence was listening in. The Americans had cracked the Japanese code and knew something was planned for an attack on "AF." The question then became, what was "AF"? The intelligence people believed it was Midway but needed to confirm this suspicion. They arranged for Midway to report in the clear that its water distillation equipment had broken down. The Japanese soon reported that "AF" was having trouble with its water supply. Now the report could go to Admiral Nimitz that Midway was the target of a major Japanese attack. This information let Nimitz make the plan that would lead to the crushing American victory at Midway.

7. Guadalcanal Surprise. The first Allied offensive action in the Pacific was the landing on the island of Guadalcanal. It was a complete surprise. The U.S. Marines waded ashore without opposition and found Japanese mess halls with food still on the tables. The meal had been interrupted by the invasion. Saburo Sakai, Japanese fighter pilot, remembers that he had to look up Guadalcanal on his maps. He had never heard of it before. Within a few days, the whole world would know about Guadalcanal. The Japanese continued to hold part of the island, and their effort to retake the rest produced some of the most savage fighting in the war. Both sides had fleets fighting to bring in supplies and troops. So many ships were sunk in the sea battles near this little island that the nearby waters were called Iron Bottom Sound.

8. Guadalcanal Marines. The fighting on Guadalcanal was fierce. Tradition says that a sign was put up on the island. It read, "When you die and go to heaven, Saint Peter you can tell, 'Another Marine reporting, sir. I've served my time in Hell.' "

9. Carrier War. World War II in the Pacific was very much a war of aircraft carriers. Finding the enemy was a tricky task. Once this was done, the attacker launched planes. The pilots had to locate the target, often a fleet moving about 20 miles per hour. Then they had to make their attack and return to their own carriers, not easy in the best of times. In the Battle of the Coral Sea during May of 1942, six Japanese planes tried to land on the U.S. Navy's *Yorktown*. Earlier in their mission they had lost nine aircraft when they met fighter planes from the *Fletcher*. The Japanese planes that found their way back to their own carriers also had a hard time. Eleven were lost trying to make night landings.

10. *Baa Baa Black Sheep*. While the TV series and the movie may confuse a few facts, there really was a Gregory "Pappy" Boyington and a Black Sheep squadron. Gregory Boyington was one of the original Flying Tigers. He had been flying as a Marine pilot when the recruiter came around for the American Volunteer Group, as the Tigers were officially known. The Chinese government was hiring these pilots and the pay was impressive. Boyington had debts, and he figured he could get rich shooting down Japanese planes and collecting the $500-a-plane bonus.

Boyington was a good fighter pilot, but never easy to get along with. He admitted he was an alcoholic. He had disliked his Marine superiors. Eventually he quarreled with the commander of the Flying Tigers, left China, and returned to the United States. There he rejoined the Marines and found himself stuck in a desk job. He cut his way through the red tape and organized a fighter squadron that flew Corsairs in the South Pacific. By now he was the oldest surviving pilot in the Marines, so the younger pilots called him "Pappy." The Japanese called the big blue Corsairs with their gull wings "whistling death." With Greg Boyington at the controls, they lived up to the name. He shot down 28 Japanese planes. This earned him the Congressional Medal of Honor, the highest U.S. medal for bravery. Boyington didn't even know he'd been awarded the medal, because he had been shot down and taken prisoner by the Japanese. He wasn't released until the war was over.

After the war, Boyington wrote his memoirs, called *Baa Baa Black Sheep.* The TV series based on them did show real Corsairs. There are a few surviving from the war. The Japanese planes in the TV series were modified American trainers. The most glaring departure from reality in the series was the group of nurses so close to the airfield. In the South Pacific, American women were very rare.

11. MacArthur. General Douglas MacArthur was a towering figure in the Pacific war. He was an old hand in the area. His father had fought in the Philippines, and MacArthur had served several years in Asian countries. When war broke out in 1941, he was in the Philippines and commanded their defense. The Japanese took the Philippines. MacArthur left after issuing his famous statement, "I shall return." He refused to go by submarine because it looked like sneaking out. Instead, he left on a PT boat, a small, speedy motorboat. MacArthur set up headquarters in Australia and became the U.S. Army commander in the area. He devoted a lot of effort to returning to the Philippines. This made him a pain in the side of the U.S. Navy. The Navy argued that the Philippines didn't matter much. The main objective should be to defeat Japan, and that could be done without taking the Philippines. MacArthur insisted and did return as promised. The news photographers got their pictures of the general wading ashore, and he was quoted, "I have returned."

The U.S. Marines had a rivalry with the Army and with MacArthur in particular. They like to tell the following story. Early in the Philippine campaign MacArthur inspected some Marines. They were just out of combat and the men were dirty, but their rifles were clean. Clean rifles are a point of pride to Marines. MacArthur chewed out the Marines for being sloppy. The story reached the Marine brass, as top officers were called, and they resented it. The next time MacArthur inspected Marines, they were wearing clean uniforms especially flown in at the order of an admiral. As he marched down the line of Marines, he noticed a sign at the end. It read, "With the help of God and a few Marines MacArthur liberated the Philippines." The general exploded into a temper tantrum that has had the Marines chuckling ever since.

12. Japanese Balloon Bombers. In late 1944 and early 1945, the Japanese launched 9,300 balloons designed to carry bombs to the United States. At the time these weapons were being launched, the Americans were bombing Japan heavily, so the Japanese wanted revenge. The balloons were launched from Japan and rose into the upper atmosphere. Wind currents carried them to the coast of the United States in a matter of days. The balloons were rigged with a device to drop ballast as they lost altitude. They rose higher in the sunlight and dipped down at night. After a certain number of days drifting, they released their bombs. The balloons carried explosive bombs and incendiary bombs to start fires in forests. The only casualties occurred near Bly, Oregon, when six people on a church outing were killed on May 5, 1945. They apparently clustered around the bomb and pulled on it. The Japanese launched a total of 9,300 balloons, but only a fraction of them reached land. Balloon bombs fell on several states, Canada, and Mexico, but did relatively little damage.

Balloon bombs landed in the following states: Washington, 20; California, 19; Oregon, 33; Idaho, 7; Nevada, 6; Montana, 26; Texas, 2; Iowa, 3; Wyoming, 9; Utah, 5; Arizona, 2; North Dakota, 2; South Dakota, 8; Nebraska, 5; Kansas, 1. Canada was hit by 78 bombs and Mexico by 2.

13. Kamikazes. As the war began to go badly, the Japanese military decided their best hope was to use kamikazes, suicide planes. They may have seen it as a temporary measure until they could come up with something more effective. It became their last weapon. The pilots were volunteers, typically teenage schoolboys. At first they were the poorer pilots. Japan saved its good pilots to defend the home islands.

How did the Japanese military get volunteers? The Japanese attitude toward suicide is different from the Western viewpoint. Suicide for the Japanese is much more acceptable and in some cases a duty. A disgraced officer was expected to commit suicide. Japanese soldiers were expected to die rather than surrender, and on many Pacific islands they did. Japanese soldiers were taught that death was light as a feather and that dying for the emperor was glorious. The volunteers were typically serious, patriotic young men. Whatever their private feelings, they put up a brave front as they were sent off with bombs mounted on their planes. They would try to pick out important ships and crash plane, pilot, and bombs into them.

For the American Navy, facing the kamikazes was a horror. The only way to stop them was to kill them before they killed you. They came out by the hundreds. In one 36-hour period in April 1945, there were 355 kamikaze attacks at Okinawa. April through June saw a total of 1,465 kamikaze attacks. Kamikazes sank 21 ships and damaged 66. It was Japan's last desperate attempt to stop the advancing Allies, and it failed.

14. The Atomic Bomb. The atomic bomb and the more powerful hydrogen bomb are based on nuclear physics now known by scientists anywhere in the world. This means the bombs can be made by anyone able to get the materials. Here in simplified form is the recipe for an atomic bomb, a fission bomb.

A fission bomb gets its energy from the fission, or splitting, of the nucleus of an atom. That is why it is called an atomic bomb. The bomb dropped on Hiroshima used a uranium isotope called U-235 as its basic material. When enough U-235 is packed together, a chain reaction of fission occurs. Atoms are split, and tremendous radiation, heat, and blast are released. The amount needed to create this chain reaction is called critical mass. Critical mass for U-235 is about 110 pounds (50 kg). The trick is to build a bomb that does not reach critical mass until it's on target.

The Hiroshima bomb, code-named Little Boy, had two pieces of U-235, both smaller than critical mass. One piece was shaped like a doughnut and was called the target. The other piece was shaped to plug the hole in the doughnut and was held in what was called a gun. The mechanism was designed so the gun fired and shot the smaller piece into the hole in the target. At that point a critical mass of U-235 existed, and atoms were split, causing a massive explosion.

There is a second way to build a fission bomb. In this version, plutonium is the fissionable material. Plutonium is made from uranium, and has a critical mass of 35.2 pounds (16 kg). Notice that this is much less than the critical mass for U-235. Plutonium is a less stable material than U-235, so the bomb design is more complex. In this case a number of pieces of plutonium are placed around the edge of a ball-shaped case. Then they are all shot together into the middle to form a critical mass. This type of bomb was used on Nagasaki. It was code-named Fat Man because of its shape.

All this is more complicated than it sounds. Making safety devices so the bombs do not go off by accident is a complication, and so is getting the mechanism to work exactly right. The materials involved are very dangerous and require complicated scientific equipment to produce them. So while the ideas behind atomic bombs are now widely known, it is very expensive and dangerous to make the bombs.

15. The Effects of an Atomic Bomb. An atomic bomb produces four effects when it is detonated. They are radiation, heat, explosion, and fallout.

Radiation is the direct result of the splitting of atoms in the explosion. Thousands of neutrons are released. The effect is like an X-ray, but thousands of times more powerful. You may have noticed if you have had a dental X-ray that your body was covered with a heavy lead-filled apron. The X-ray operator probably stepped out of the room. This is because exposure to too much radiation can cause leukemia. People who were exposed to radiation from an atomic bomb found that their hair fell out, they bled for no apparent reason, and they were weak. For weeks after the Hiroshima attack, people died of radiation sickness.

One of the most dramatic features of a nuclear explosion is a searing flash and then a ball of fire. Some people close to the Hiroshima bomb left only their shadows behind. They were burned to ashes, but their shadows were burned into a nearby wall. Others had the pattern of their clothes burned into their skins.

The explosion, or blast effect, is much like conventional explosions, but much bigger. The Hiroshima bomb was equal to 20,000 tons of TNT. The blast effect digs a hole in the ground and knocks down buildings. In the case of the explosion, as with radiation and heat, the effect is less severe farther from the center of the explosion. Also, shielding by a hill or sturdy building reduces the injury. While Hiroshima lost 66,000 lives, Nagasaki, which had hills that sheltered some people, lost 39,000.

Fallout is a lingering effect. When the explosion occurs, there is some radioactive waste. This is carried up into the atmosphere with the fireball and mixed with other material sucked up in the rising air currents. Later this radioactive material falls—with rain, for example—and brings with it a milder dose of radiation. The most radioactive fallout tends to hit areas just downwind from the target area, but milder doses travel hundreds of miles. There it can find its way into food and water supplies and cause health problems. It was concern about fallout from nuclear tests that led to the nuclear test ban treaty.

CHAPTER XXIII

The Cold War in Europe

— Overview —

World War II left us facing a new challenge—the Cold War, with the Soviet Union facing the United states in a state of near constant tension. This chapter provides a collection of examples designed to give an idea of what Soviet life was like from the 1950's to 1990. It also has material about the NATO nations and the nuclear weapons problem. With the end of the Cold War and the breakup of the Soviet Union, perhaps all this will become simply history, not a daily concern.

Your students could write papers comparing and contrasting Stalin and Khrushchev as Soviet leaders. They could also compare and contrast the Soviet economy in the 1950's with that of Western Europe at the same time. They could compare and contrast Europe after World War I with Europe after World War II. The creative student could write a paper on "My Trip to the Soviet Union in 1955."

A. THE SOVIET UNION

1. In the United Nations. During the conferences working out arrangements for the United Nations organization, the Soviet Union argued that each of its fifteen republics should be given a membership. Naturally, the Americans resisted this and pointed out that it would be like giving the United States forty-eight memberships, one for each state (Alaska and Hawaii were not yet states). The result was a compromise. The Soviet Union would get three memberships, one for the Soviet Union and also one each for the Byelorussian Soviet Socialist Republic and the Ukrainian Soviet Socialist Republic.

2. Tito. After the end of World War II, Soviet troops occupied Eastern Europe. This was as agreed in conferences during the war. But it soon became clear that the Soviets were not holding the free and democratic elections specified in those agreements. Instead, they were installing Communists in the governments and making the nations satellites, puppets of the Soviet Union. It looked as if Eastern Europe was one solid Communist bloc. But in 1948, the bloc split. Yugoslavia was expelled from the Cominform, the organization of all Communists. Why had this happened? Who was Tito of Yugoslavia that he could defy Stalin?

His real name was Josip Broz, but history knows him as Tito. He was a devoted Communist. During World War I, he had been a prisoner of war in Russia and witnessed the Bolshevik revolution. After the war he became a revolutionary, and later a political prisoner. Then he became a Soviet-trained Communist agent. In World War II, he led the resistance to the Nazis in Yugoslavia. His partisan force managed to survive, although surrounded by German forces. He even managed to set up a government for Yugoslavia. It is worth noticing that Tito was a self-made man who had put himself in power. The other Eastern European rulers owed their power to the Soviet military, but Tito had even felt free to protest to Stalin about how the Soviet Army had acted as it helped liberate Yugoslavia.

While Tito was a Communist and agreed in general with Stalin's policies, he also had his own ideas. This led to arguments with Stalin and eventually to Yugoslavia's expulsion from the Cominform. Tito then revised some of his foreign policies. He had been encouraging a Communist rebellion in Greece. He soon closed down that support. He accepted aid from the British and Americans and became one of the first leaders to be nonaligned, refusing to take sides in the Cold War.

Stalin was furious at this independence. He said, "I will shake my little finger and there will be no Tito." But when Stalin died in 1953, Tito was still ruling an independent Yugoslavia. He had shown Stalin and the West that all Communists were not alike.

3. Borrowed Technology. The Soviet Union tended to lag behind the West in several areas of technology. In cases like this, the party that is behind can often catch up quickly by copying. The U.S.S.R. clearly did this with jet aircraft. The British government sent the Soviets an advanced Rolls-Royce jet engine. The Soviets copied it without a license and mounted it in an airframe developed using captured German research about swept wings. They also added a few touches of their own and produced a plane called the MiG-15. It was a top-quality jet fighter in the early 1950's.

4. Stalin's Statue. When the Soviets took over Eastern Europe after World War II, they shut off a lot of freedoms. One they could not stop was the telling of stories like this:

The village was being told by the local Communist authorities that they had to put up a statue of Stalin. Most of the villagers were against it except for one old man. When they asked him why he favored the statue, he said, "Look at it this way. It will give us shade in summer, shelter from the wind in the winter, and a chance for the birds to express our opinion of Stalin."

5. Khrushchev and Stalin. In 1956, Khrushchev made his secret speech revealing a number of errors and atrocities by Stalin. After the speech, Khrushchev accepted written questions. He read one of them: "Considering how horrible Stalin was, somebody should have spoken out and opposed him. Where were you, Comrade, at that time?"

This question infuriated Khrushchev. He turned red and called out, "Who sent this question? Where is this person?"

The assembled delegates were frozen in terror. In those days, such impertinence could lead to death. The group was silent. No one stepped forward.

Khrushchev continued, "Comrades, let me tell you, wherever he is, that's where I was during Stalin's crimes."

6. Khrushchev at the United Nations. In 1960, Khrushchev paid a visit to the United Nations. This session had also attracted a number of other leaders, including Fidel Castro of Cuba. Castro had very pointedly moved into a hotel in Harlem. This was his way of showing solidarity with "oppressed" African-Americans. Khrushchev visited him there.

Khrushchev gave two speeches at the United Nations, but the most famous incident happened while he was listening to a speech. While a Western delegate was speaking, Khrushchev became angry and began shouting. He then took off his shoe and pounded it on his desk. Later the Soviet Union was fined $10,000 for this breach of proper diplomatic procedure.

7. Place Names. The Russians have always changed place names to reflect politics. When Peter the Great started his new capital on the Baltic, he called it St. Petersburg after his patron saint. During World War I, St. Petersburg sounded too German, so the town was renamed Petrograd. After the Communists took over, the city was renamed Leningrad.

During Stalin's rule, every town had at least a Stalin Street. Lesser political figures had other streets or buildings named after them. It got so the citizens of the Soviet Union could read the political news in their street signs. When a street changed its name, that meant the person it had been named for had been ousted.

Khrushchev in his 1956 secret speech condemned this naming and renaming practice. He saw it as a part of the cult of the individual that had grown up under Stalin. In the process called de-Stalinization, the Soviets changed the names of many cities. The most noticeable change turned the city of Stalingrad into Volgograd, after the Volga River on which it is located.

8. Khrushchev and Farming. Khrushchev talked of "goulash socialism," meaning, he said, that the socialists and capitalists should compete to see who could make better goulash. But to make better goulash you first must grow the food, and Soviet agriculture was a weak point. Khrushchev set out to change this. He tried to reorganize the Soviet farms and introduce new crops. He became particularly interested in corn.

In his study of corn, he met Roswell Garst of Coon Rapids, Iowa, who was a major producer of seed corn. In 1958, Khrushchev made a trip to Iowa to see U.S. farming methods firsthand. He was a guest at the Garst farm. While walking around on a tour of the farm, the journalists following him got too close. Khrushchev grabbed a handful of silage and threw it at the reporters.

He returned home full of enthusiasm and started the virgin lands project. Soviet farmers plowed some land never farmed before and planted corn. Unfortunately, the climate in the virgin lands was too dry for corn, so the experiment failed.

9. Historical Research. From the time of Stalin into the 1980's the authorities of the Soviet Union manipulated history. A Polish history researcher told the following story. He was visiting the U.S.S.R. and happily researching early Russian diplomacy in the area of Constantinople. He was reading about plots to poison troublesome individuals and other colorful details. As he was researching, the Turkish ambassador came to Moscow to talk about cultural exchanges. Suddenly the retired KGB colonel who supervised the archives took away the material the Pole had been researching. The Pole protested and was told that if he wrote an article about Russian plots against Turks, even centuries ago, it might damage relations. The material was no longer available. A few days later, the Turkish ambassador broke off the talks and returned home. There would be no friendly exchanges. Suddenly the historical material became available again.

10. History Tests. For years, the authorities in the Soviet Union managed history. Depending on the political trends, a person could be a hero or a villain, or simply not exist, in the official histories. Schools were expected to teach this official version. Each spring at the end of the school year students would take a massive examination, standardized for the entire Soviet Union. Their scores on these examinations would determine who would go to the university and generally what future training each student would get.

When Gorbachev started his *glasnost,* or "openness," policy, things changed. Suddenly history was being rewritten, and politicans who had been unmentionable, like Trotsky, were back in the history of the Soviet Union. Developments came very quickly and were mostly reported in the newspapers. School textbooks lagged so far behind that teachers had to rely on newspaper clippings to keep history classes up-to-date. Things were changing so rapidly that it was hard to tell what the "correct" history was. As a result, in the spring of 1988, all history examinations in the Soviet Union were canceled. Somehow the students made the sacrifice.

11. Soviet Consumer Goods. The Soviet Union has often sacrificed production of consumer goods in favor of more basic products like steel. As a result, the Soviet consumer spends a lot of time standing in line to get clothing, groceries, and other items. There is the story of the Soviet citizen who made a trip to the United States. He completed his official mission and then visited some American stores. When he returned home, he was asked if America had more consumer goods. "Yes," he said. "It is true that American stores have more goods on display than our stores, but the Americans cannot afford to buy these things."

How did he know this, he was asked. "I never saw any Americans lining up to buy them."

The story does reflect an attitude found among Soviet citizens. When Lieutenant Victor Belenko flew his MiG-25 to Japan and was taken to America, he was shown some typical American stores, and he suspected that they were a special display staged just for him. He simply could not believe that consumer goods could be available in the amounts and variety he saw. This chronic shortage of consumer goods is one of the problems the former Soviet Union must overcome.

12. Soviet Maps. Starting in the 1930's and continuing until 1989, the Soviet Union falsified public maps of the country. Accurate maps were classified as secret. Soviet mapmakers moved rivers around and even changed the location of towns. The town of Logashkino near the East Siberian Sea was moved around several times. Once it even disappeared from the maps entirely. This was done out of a fear of spies. Foreigners, it was feared, would use these maps to plan attacks on the Soviet Union. This did lead to some inconvenience for travelers in the Soviet Union. However, there was one good map of Moscow available, published by the American CIA. Eventually, in the 1980's under Gorbachev's policy of *glasnost,* or "openness", the Soviet authorities decided to admit what they had been doing and produce accurate maps. They had only been keeping secrets from themselves.

13. Gorbachev: Nobel Peace Prize. In 1990, the Nobel Peace Prize was awarded to Soviet President Mikhail Gorbachev. He seemed like a reasonable choice. He had introduced *glasnost* ("openness") to the Soviet Union, including more political freedoms. His *perestroika,* "restructuring," called for adoption of some features of a market economy in the Soviet Union. He had set free the satellite states of Eastern Europe and built friendships with the West.

But change did not come easily. The dramatic reforms of *glasnost* allowed opposition leaders like Boris Yeltsin to win office and criticize Gorbachev. The Baltic republics—Latvia, Estonia, and Lithuania—tried to become independent, and other regions were restless. More traditional Soviet Communists were skeptical. The economic *perestroika* was not well defined, and meanwhile the Soviet Union was suffering from a food shortage. Political cartoonists were quick to pounce on the problems. One cartoon showed two Russians talking. The first says, "Gorbachev got the Nobel Peace Prize." The other asks, "Can we eat it?" Another cartoon showed Gorbachev talking to a Soviet citizen. Gorbachev says, "What do you think of my Nobel Peace Prize?" The citizen has taken a bite out of the medal and replies, "It needs salt."

14. Lech Walesa. Two men stood on a bulldozer arguing. One of them was the manager of the Gdansk shipyard, and the other was an electrician the manager had fired a few years before. It was a confrontation that would change Poland and start one of the two men toward becoming president of that nation.

In August of 1980, Poland was ruled by a Communist government that was supported and controlled by the threat of Soviet intervention. But communism did not fit Poland. Communists were atheists, while Poles were devoted Catholics. The Church was often a center of resistance. The Poles were a freedom-loving people who resented outside domination and considered the Soviets backward. Labor unions were becoming centers of resistance as well. On August 14, the workers in the Gdansk shipyard went on strike. The workers were milling around in the shipyard when the manager climbed up on a bulldozer to talk. Then Lech Walesa climbed over the fence and jumped up on the bulldozer. "Remember me? I worked ten years in this shipyard, but you fired me four years ago." The workers cheered. "We're now beginning a sit-in strike," Walesa shouted. A few days later, the independent trade union Solidarity was formed with Lech Walesa leading it. Solidarity became a powerful force in Poland, and Lech Walesa became a symbol of Poland's struggle for freedom.

It was a long, hard struggle against the odds, but eventually Poland's Communist party stepped down, and it was Solidarity's turn to try to solve the many problems of Poland. The 1990 presidential election was the first free and open election since 1939. Lech Walesa was the front-runner in the first balloting, but did not get a majority. In the runoff election on December 9, 1990, he won by a ratio of three to one. Both Poland and President Walesa had come a long way from the bulldozer in Gdansk.

B. NATO COUNTRIES

1. NATO. American soldiers have reported for work daily on a hill in Berlin. The hill is made of the rubble from bombed buildings. The radio reception there is good, so it permitted the Americans to listen in on the Soviets and their allies. At sea the U.S. Navy has carried out maneuvers with Canadian, Dutch, German, Portuguese, and British ships. The mixed fleet has acted as one command. Each year U.S. Air Force units have crossed the Atlantic and practiced flying off German airstrips and working with German units. These are just a few examples of the way NATO operates. The North Atlantic Treaty Organization is based on the North Atlantic Treaty signed in 1949. The heart of the treaty is Article 5: "The parties agree that an armed attack against one or more of them in Europe or North America shall be considered an attack against them all. . . ." The 16 members of NATO are committed to defend each other, so they cooperate on defense matters. There is a European Commander in Belgium, who is always an American general. The Commander of the Atlantic is an American admiral in Norfolk, Virginia. This alliance solidly commits the United States to the defense of Europe. It is America's most important alliance.

All parties understood that the presumed enemy of NATO was the Soviet Union, but this changed with the breakup of the U.S.S.R. and the dissolution of the Warsaw Pact. In July of 1990, NATO invited President Gorbachev to address the North Atlantic Council and invited other Eastern European countries to ". . . come to NATO, not just to visit, but to establish regular diplomatic liaison with NATO. This will make it possible for us to share with our thinking and deliberating in this historic period of change."

2. The Nuclear Standoff. A treaty named START represents a step away from a strategy called MAD. Start stands for Strategic Arms Reduction Treaty. MAD stood for Mutually Assured Destruction. Both the United States and the Soviet Union maintained the ability to kill millions of the other's citizens. Both sides put a lot of effort into making sure they had the capacity to nearly wipe out the other's population.

The Soviets put a massive investment into nuclear-tipped missiles in underground silos. They also had a force of bombers and some missile-carying submarines.

The Americans also invested heavily in underground missile silos, but emphasized variety. Americans used a "triad" of land-bound missiles, aircraft, and missile submarines.

Somehow while living with all this potential destruction, the world has avoided World War III. The theory of deterrence argued that war was avoided because of this potential destruction. The argument ran that each side was deterred from starting a war by the threat to its own people. While there was no world war from the 1940's to the 1990's, there was always the danger of accident, misunderstanding, or an unbalanced ruler. The world lived roughly 45 minutes away from destruction at all times. This terrifying situation was labeled "the balance of terror."

Then the Cold War began to thaw, and relations between the United States and the Soviet Union became less tense. On July 31, 1991, American President Bush and Soviet President Gorbachev signed START. This Strategic Arms Reduction Treaty took nine years to negotiate. The treaty reduced strategic arms—nuclear-armed missiles, bombers, and submarine-launched missiles—by 30 percent. START represented a significant step back from a nuclear arms race.

3. The European Community. Europe now has a flag, a plain blue field with 12 gold stars forming a circle. It symbolizes the European community, 12 countries united for economic purposes. They already have what every government needs—bureaucrats—but in this case they are called Eurocrats and are located in Brussels, Belgium. Europe even owns some railroad cars. In 1951, 6 nations started the Coal and Steel Community to try to unify their coal and steel industries. Part of that effort involved buying more railroad cars to haul coal and steel. Later, in 1967, the Coal and Steel Community became part of the European Community. The organization has grown from the original 6—Belgium, Luxembourg, Holland, France, West Germany (now Germany, including the former East Germany), and Italy—to 12, including Denmark, Greece, Ireland, Portugal, Spain, and the United Kingdom. These nations' total population in 1990 was about 345 million. The EC has been working toward a common outer tarrif, a common currency, and a common policy on agriculture. In trade conferences they have negotiated as a single organization. The European Community has grown to be a major economic power in the world.

4. Bikini. Bikini Island was the site of a series of atomic bomb tests in 1946. This was the same year that Jacques Heim, a French designer, designed a daring two-piece bathing suit. He named his suit the bikini after the island that had recently been in the news.

5. World War IV. A widely quoted statement on nuclear war is attributed to Albert Einstein: "I don't know what weapons will be used to fight World War III, but I do know what will be used in World War IV. Rocks."

6. The Berlin Wall. The city of Berlin was divided by treaty before it was divided by the Wall. As the capital of Germany, Berlin was divided into zones of occupation by the Allied powers at the close of World War II. Soon these zones became two cities: East Berlin, the Soviet zone; and West Berlin, the American,

British, and French zones. As the Cold War developed, Berlin was often the focus of crises. Yet in some ways the city stayed united. Travel between the two cities was so easy, thousands of East Berliners commuted to jobs in West Berlin. Thousands of East Germans also used West Berlin as an escape route, crossing into West Berlin and flying out to West Germany. This created a problem for the East German government, which felt it could not allow this flow of emigrants. On the night of August 13, 1961, the East German authorities moved in swiftly and built a barbed-wire barrier between the two cities. As days went on, this was strengthened into a concrete wall with a guarded death strip on the East German side.

Winston Churchill had already coined the phrase "iron curtain" to describe the division between Communist Eastern Europe and the West. The Wall was the most visible symbol of that division. Escaping East Germans crossed it by jumping out of high windows into safety nets held by West German police. They tunneled under the Wall. A hundred or more (estimates vary) died trying to cross it. It became a sort of stage setting for American politicians giving speeches against communism. John F. Kennedy proclaimed, "*Ich bin ein Berliner*" ("I am a Berliner"), and decades later Ronald Reagan challenged, "Mr. Gorbachev, tear down this wall."

Then suddenly things changed. Gorbachev began his policy of *glasnost,* "openness," and East European governments began to open up to ideas like freedom and democracy. On the night of November 9, 1989, the East German government announced that East Berliners would be free to cross into West Berlin at midnight. The event became a huge party. People danced on the Wall and shared hugs and champagne. East Berliners gaped in awe at well-stocked shops in West Berlin and were shocked by the high prices. People attacked the wall, chipping off pieces and carrying them away as souvenirs. The capitalist spirit triumphed. Soon pieces of the Wall were on sale as well as T-shirts saying "I was there—9 November 1989!" A dramatic symbol of the Cold War had ceased to exist.

7. Germany United. For 45 years Germany was divided. Then on October 3, 1990, the two Germanys were united again. Some outsiders had objected. The Soviet Union feared that NATO troops would move into the former East Germany. The Poles remembered Hitler's invasion of them in 1939 and worried about their border. People who recalled World War II wondered if there was a chance of the new Germany following a new Hitler. But a series of treaties and reassuring articles about the new Germany quieted these questions.

The biggest problem may have been internal. The Germans were now one nation, but they had had two economies for 45 years. The West German economy was one of the strongest in the world, but the East German economy was considerably weaker. As the two economies merged, Eastern firms were wiped out by Western competition and nearly 500,000 Eastern workers became unemployed. The government was estimating that it would cost $79 billion a year for five years to bring the East up to Western standards.

In the euphoria of unity, the West Germans embraced the Easterners. Later, when they realized the cost, their attitude changed. In 1991, the following joke circulated among West Germans.

"How can you tell which computer an East German has been working on?"

"By the White-Out on the screen."

8. Margaret Thatcher. Margaret Thatcher's career was a series of paradoxes. She was the first woman to become prime minister of Great Britain, and she did it as the head of the Conservative party. The Conservatives were the most tradition-bound party in Britain. They usually chose a son of the upper classes to be their leader, not the daughter of a grocer. But Thatcher had worked long and hard for the party and was elected leader in February of 1975. It was four years later in May of 1979 that the Conservatives won a majority of seats in the House of Commons. Then, as tradition requires, the queen asked Thatcher to serve as the queen's prime minister.

Many of Thatcher's policies were controversial, but her conduct of the Falkland Islands War was very popular. Thatcher became the only British prime minister in the 20th century to win three consecutive elections.

Her loss of office came because of disagreements within her own party. Some objected to Thatcher's resistance to the European Community. Others were troubled by her poll tax, which would place a heavy burden on the poor. The Conservatives began to think Thatcher would lose the next election, so the party members in Parliament met to elect a new leader. Thatcher refused to step down and even managed to win a majority of votes on the first ballot. But the rules required a 60 percent majority. Before a second ballot was taken, Thatcher agreed to withdraw her candidacy. The Conservative party then elected John Major to be their new leader. Thatcher stepped down as prime minister, and the queen called on John Major to be her new prime minister.

As Margaret Thatcher looked back over her 11 years as prime minister, she summed it up: "It's a funny old world."

CHAPTER XXIV

Struggles in Asia

— Overview —

Asia has exploded since 1945. India gained independence but in the process was split along religious lines. China rejected the Nationalists, and the Communists who took over have been in turmoil. Japan became a democracy and a Western ally. Little countries that had been too small to capture the world's notice before became the focus of nasty police actions or conflicts.

You could set up a "democracy wall" and your students could write their own "great character posters." I find my chalkboard on the side of the room is ideal for this. Your students could also write their versions of *Quotations from Chairman Mao.* (One of my students once did a book of quotations from me.) A map with each conflict marked by a red star and dates makes a dramatic bulletin board.

A. INDIA

1. Hindu-Muslim Differences. After World War II, the pressure on Britain to grant independence to India was intense, but there was a complication. British India included the whole Indian subcontinent, stretching from Afghanistan to Burma. A mix of Hindus and Muslims lived in that area. The two religions did not get along well. Mohammed Ali Jinnah, president of the Muslim League, listed the following differences in an interview. The two religions do not intermarry. They use different calendars. The Muslims believe in one God; Hindus worship idols. Muslims believe all people are equal, while Hindus believe in a caste system. Hindus worship animals; Muslims think this is nonsense. While Hindus think cows are sacred, Muslims want to eat the cow. Hindus will not eat Muslim food or even eat Hindu food if a Muslim's shadow has fallen on it. Citing these differences, Mohammed Ali Jinnah and the Muslim League argued for the partition of India into a Hindu state and a Muslim state.

B. CHINA

1. Mao Zedong on Guerrilla War. The strategy of the Chinese Communists in taking over China was guerrilla warfare. Chairman Mao spelled out the basics of this kind of warfare in his 1938 lectures later published as *Basic Tactics.* It is a very unconventional approach to war, but it has become the model for other revolutionaries.

People might be tempted to feel that they cannot resist a well-armed enemy, but Mao argues that the people have many weapons that can kill a soldier. He points out that a kitchen knife, a wooden club, an axe, a hoe, a wooden stool, or even a stone can kill a person. Also there are other more subtle ways of fighting against an army. The people can cut electric lines, destroy bridges, start rumors, spread poison, or cut off supplies.

A face-to-face battle is to be avoided at all costs. The ideal guerrilla attack is an ambush in which all of the enemy is wiped out and no guerrillas are hurt. The guiding principle is always to strike at weakness. When the enemy advances, the guerrillas should retreat. When the enemy retreats, the guerrillas should follow. When the enemy halts, the guerrillas should harass and let them have no rest.

Guerrilla operations demand that the soldiers be in small units. They must therefore be strictly disciplined and politically indoctrinated. They are to move among the people as fish move in the sea. Using these tactics Mao was able to rise to power, confirming his maxim, "Political power grows out of the barrel of a gun."

2. Inflation. In China shortly after World War II, the inflation rate reached new highs. One U.S. dollar would buy $11 million in Chinese currency.

3. Corruption. About 1945, the American Red Cross donated blood plasma to China. It was intended for wounded soldiers. The plasma was offered for sale in Shanghai drugstores for $25 a pint.

4. Literacy. The Communists have changed things in China. In 1949, when they came to power, 25 percent of China's population was literate. By 1984, more than 75 percent was literate.

5. Mao's Hundred Flowers. In the 1950's, the Chinese Communists tried an experiment in free speech. It was started by a 1956 address by Chairman Mao called the "Hundred Flowers" speech. This was a time when world communism was apperently becoming less dictatorial. Khrushchev had recently given his "Secret Speech," and the Soviet Union was de-Stalinizing.

Mao was apparently encouraged by the lack of resistance to his efforts to move Chinese farmers into communes. He seems to have felt that the Chinese were accepting Communist rule. So he proclaimed, "Let a hundred flowers blossom" and "Let a hundred schools of thought contend." Mao had once been a poet and student of Confucius, and the slogans came out of that tradition. They mean let people speak freely and argue. In the speech, Mao argued that free speech was a way of letting arts and sciences progress. He spoke of the benefits of free discussion.

This became the new policy, but the Chinese people were skeptical. At first very little was said. Then criticism of local officials was heard. When this was accepted, critics became bolder and criticized the higher officials, communism, and Mao himself. Then suddenly, it was all shut down. There was a sweeping purge. Over a million government officials were transferred and hundreds were fired. We don't know what happened to them after that, for China was a closed society again.

Outside observers were puzzled by all this. Was the Hundred Flowers speech an effort to get critics out in the open so they could be destroyed? Or had Mao misread the feelings of the people and then reacted out of shock when the criticism became too extreme? Could China have communism and free speech at the same time?

6. The Red Guard. Mao needed allies during the Great Proletarian Cultural Revolution of 1966 to 1969. He turned to the students, who formed the Red Guards. They paraded waving the Little Red Book of Chairman Mao. How could they do this and still study? The answer is they couldn't, so Mao closed all the schools. If revolutionary fervor was more important than practical knowledge, school didn't matter. The Red Guards often turned against their teachers, a horrifying development. They forced elderly teachers to run up and down stairs until exhausted. The teachers' crime had been making the students study too hard and neglecting the thoughts of Chairman Mao. People who wanted to keep a school running had to do it secretly. One group ran a school for veterinarians while operating a farm as a cover. The Red Guard also marched through the country seeking other "capitalist roaders" and struggling with them in the name of Mao.

7. Posters. During the Great Proletarian Cultural Revolution, foreigners were not able to get reliable information through regular channels. They were able to get some information from "great character posters." These were signs stuck up on walls. They often told what people were thinking. "It is better to be Red than expert." "Down with middle-class revisionists." "Death to capitalist roaders." All these stressed that being revolutionary was more important than simply doing your job well. Mao wrote his own great character poster: "Attack the headquarters." The Red Guard soon understood that this meant attack the leaders of the Communist party itself. Mao was using the Red Guards to combat Liu Shaoqi, who was a top party leader. Liu was removed from all posts and banished to a distant province, where he died in 1969. Once the Cultural Revolution was over, the "democracy walls" where the great character posters had been put up were removed.

8. The Old Man and the Mountain. During the Great Proletarian Cultural Revolution, the Chinese relied heavily on the sheer amount of human labor available coupled, of course, with the thoughts of Chairman Mao. The following story was said to be one of Mao's favorites.

Once there was an old man who lived with his sons. They lived near a mountain that shaded the house so the sun did not shine on it. The old man decided to change this, so he and his sons set out with shovels and baskets and began to dig away the mountain. People laughed at them and said the old man was crazy. But the old man explained what he was doing. "Now you laugh at us, but consider. Each day we dig on the mountain. The mountain never grows, so each time we remove dirt, the mountain is smaller. As I and my children and my children's children dig, we are removing the mountain. Eventually the mountain will be gone, and the sun will shine on our house."

9. Women in China. Chairman Mao said, "Women hold up half the sky." This is usually taken as Mao's endorsement of equal rights for women. The new marriage law enacted in 1950 was designed to protect women and children. It abolished arranged marriages, bigamy, killing babies, and buying of women. It gave women equal status in the home and the right to divorce and to inherit property. It's easier to make changes in the law than changes in the way people live. A 1983 survey found that about eight percent of Chinese couples surveyed married by free choice. The rest followed some kind of recommendation. The attitude that boys are better still survives. Since China tries to limit each family to one child, there has been a rise in the killing of female babies.

10. Ping-Pong Diplomacy. A series of Ping-Pong games in 1971 made history. After the Nationalists were driven off the mainland in 1949, the United States refused to recognize the People's Republic of China and supported the Nationalists as "China" in the United Nations. U.S. relations with the People's Republic were often hostile. In the Korean police action, Americans fought Chinese. But eventually both sides moderated their views. As is often the case, the first move by the Chinese was indirect.

The American table tennis team was competing in Japan when the Chinese invited them to visit. The Americans accepted. Suddenly many reporters became sportswriters specializing in table tennis. The year was 1971, and American reporters hadn't been allowed in China since 1949. Many reporters wanted to see China, and a few were privileged to travel with the team. The outcome of the table tennis matches was predictable. China had some of the best players in the world, and they beat the Americans with lopsided scores. But the matches were played in the spirit of "Friendship first, competition second." The Chinese would soundly defeat the Americans, then tell them, "We learn from you." All this was a signal from the Chinese government to the American government that friendly relations were possible. Within a year, President Nixon visited China. His way had been paved by Ping-Pong diplomacy.

11. Tiananmen Square. During the spring of 1989, Tiananmen Square in Beijing was the site of a remarkable series of demonstrations that were put down by a massacre.

One of the leaders of the efforts to reform and modernize China was Hu Yaobang, former general secretary of the Chinese Communist party. He died on April 15, 1989. His funeral became a political protest. Ten thousands students gathered. On April 21, a crowd of 100,000 was in Tiananmen Square in spite of official efforts to keep them out. In the following weeks the protests would grow larger, peaking at one million participants.

The student protest had a defiant spirit and was rich in symbolism. Crowds cheered as speakers who rose to address them bravely gave their full names so police informers would know who they were. Students at Beijing University broke soft-drink bottles. These were small bottles, *xioping* in Chinese. The word was pronounced like the name of the top Communist, Deng Xioping. Art students made a plaster statue and called it "Goddess of Democracy." The goddess looked very much like the Statue of Liberty. Thousands of students began a hunger strike, refusing to eat until the leaders made reforms.

Then the government brought more pressure to bear, declaring martial law on May 19. The People's Liberation Army was now in charge of enforcing order. Tension built as the army tried to find ways to remove the students. The students were worn down from fasting, and sanitation in the square was horrible. The numbers of students in the square were dwindling, but support in the city was strong. When the army tried to move troops into Beijing, crowds of people blocked the streets and turned them away. In one dramatic moment captured by a photographer, a single man stepped in front of a column of tanks. The tanks stopped. The man walked up to the lead tank and briefly talked to the soldiers inside, then moved away. For that fleeting moment an unarmed man had faced tanks for freedom.

But it did not last. On the night of June 3, the army attacked, marching into the square and firing. The massacre was carried out in the dark, so cameras could not record it, and reporters were kept away. Soon the official news agency reported that the soldiers had been attacked and were putting down riots. After that, the government offered rewards for information leading to the arrest of student leaders. Tiananmen Square was carefully scrubbed clean of bloodstains. Beijing University was closed for a year. All students spent that year in the army getting a course of military and political discipline.

C. Japan

1. MacArthur in Japan: A Joke. After Japan's defeat in World War II, the occupation was run by American General Douglas MacArthur, a man of towering ego. It is reported that if you got up early enough, you could see the general taking his morning stroll on the moat of the Imperial Palace. The Japanese government was redesigned by Americans. The new constitution set up a democratic government and made it illegal for Japan to have an army or navy. The Japanese reaction to the new constitution is reflected in the following.

First Japanese: "Have you read our new constitution?"

Second Japanese: "No. I can't read English."

This constitution is still in effect for Japan. Japan's defense is provided by American armed services.

2. Women's Status. Japanese attitudes toward women change slowly. Shortly after World War II, the following story was in circulation. Two Americans on Okinawa were discussing the changes that occupation had brought to Japan. "Now look at that," said the first. "See over there—the wife is walking in front of the husband. Before the war the wife always followed meekly behind."

His companion was curious. "Let's ask them about that." So they approached the Japanese couple and asked the husband, "Why is it that your wife is walking in front of you now?"

"Simple," he replied. "Since the war there are many land mines left on the island."

The war may not have changed attitudes much, but by 1989, there were some signs of change. Sosuke Uno was selected to be prime minster after a major bribery scandal had damaged the reputations of many Japanese political leaders. Sosuke Uno was reported to be "Mister Clean," free of any taint of bribery. But soon reports were published that from 1985 to 1986 he had paid a geisha to be his mistress. Japanese women's groups met and passed a resolution calling for a fight against commercial sex. The prime minister treated this as a strictly private matter, but there was a public policy issue involved. Japanese prostitution law made it illegal to be a prostitute, but not to be a customer. This was clearly discriminatory against women. When an American research institute noted the status of women in 1988, Japan ranked 34th among the 99 countries.

Perhaps Japanese women have become more outspoken because of the International Women's Decade 1975–1985 sponsored by the United Nations. Whatever the reason, things have begun to change.

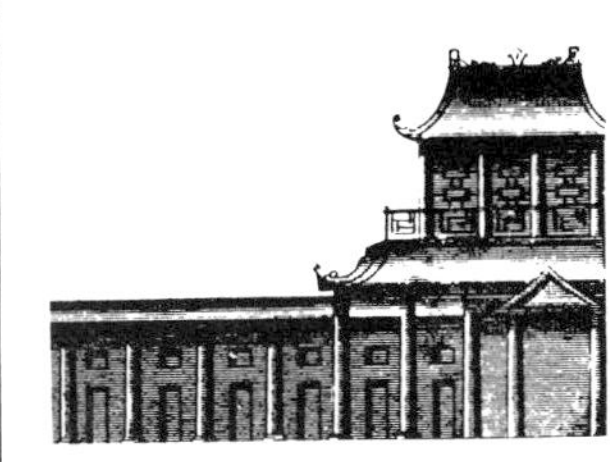

D. Korea

1. Police Action. This is the story of the veto that never happened. The United Nations Charter clearly specifies that the Security Council is the organ of the United Nations that deals with threats to international peace and security. It also provides that the five permanent members of the Security Council—the United States, the United Kingdom, France, the Soviet Union, and China—have vetoes. This means that a no vote from any one of these countries kills the resolution. So it's reasonable to expect that when the North Koreans invaded South Korea and the matter came up before the Security Council, the Soviet Union would simply veto any action against North Korea. Bu the United Nations decided in 1950 to start a police action, and the result was a three-year military conflict in Korea followed by apparently endless negotiations. Why wasn't there a veto?

The Soviet Union found itself in a minority in the United Nations during the 1950's. The U.N. had 51 original members. Only about a dozen of these were Communist—the Soviet Union and its Eastern European satellite countries. They were routinely outvoted by the United States and its allies in Western Europe and Latin America. As a result, the Soviet ambassador to the U.N. took to protesting by walking out.

As a resolution was passed, he would simply get up and stalk out, followed by the ambassadors of the other members of the Communist bloc. American reporters compared it to a mother duck leading her babies along all in a row. As luck would have it, the Soviets had walked out shortly before the Korean conflict came to the Security

Council. The resolution to support South Korea sailed through the Security Council, and the Korean police action started. Shortly after that, the Soviet ambassador returned. The Soviets did no further walkouts.

2. *M*A*S*H.* The TV series *M*A*S*H,* now in reruns, is set during the Korean War. There really were such Mobile Army Surgical Hospitals in Korea. The movie that inspired the series was based on a novel by a doctor who had served in one. While the TV series stressed a story line, it used some background facts from the Korean police action. Characters talk about General Douglas MacArthur, who commanded during the early years, and President Truman, who fired him. Some of the patients at TV's *M*A*S*H* came from units that actually served in Korea—Greeks, Turks, French, and British.

3. The Conflict Lingers. The major fighting in the Korean conflict stopped in July 1953, but the two Koreas remain divided, and there is continuing hostility. The United States has kept troops stationed in South Korea all this time. Their mission is to defend South Korea and keep a wary eye on North Korea. Sometimes it is dangerous. In 1976 two American officers, Captain Arthur Boniface and Lieutenant Mark Barrett, led a group of soldiers out to cut down a yellow poplar tree that was blocking the view of a North Korean position. The North Koreans attacked them while they worked, and the two officers were killed. A few days later, the Americans alerted bombers, aircraft carriers, and soldiers as another group of soldiers went out and cut down the tree. A U.S. Army spokesman called it "one of the most expensive tree-trimming operations in history."

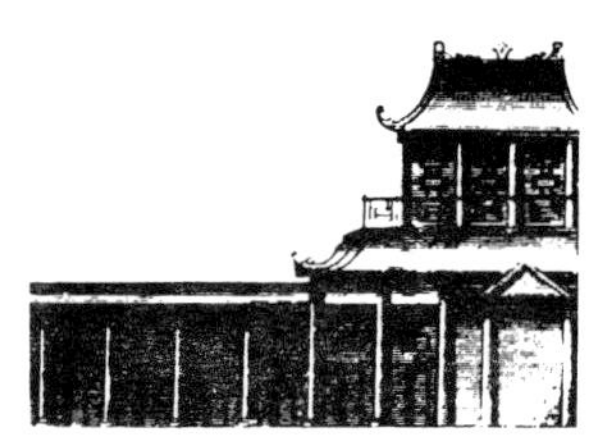

E. VIETNAM

1. Geneva, 1954. The Geneva Conference of 1954 ended the war between the French and the Viet Minh. According to the agreement, French Indochina became Laos, Cambodia, and North and South Vietnam. The two Vietnams were to be unified after an election to be held within two years. But there was still a feeling of hostility between certain parties at the conference. Zhou Enlai was there representing China. He offered his hand to John Foster Dulles, the American representative. Dulles refused to shake hands. This was a public snub and humiliation to Zhou. Later the American government (under President Eisenhower with Dulles as secretary of state) would refuse to allow the election scheduled for 1956 to be held, because they feared that the Communists would win and rule all Vietnam.

2. An Old Warrior. During the American effort to resist the Communist takeover of Vietnam, the United States relied heavily on technology. Aircraft played a major role in attempts to hold off the Vietcong and advancing North Vietnamese troops. Both ultramodern jets and sophisticated helicopters played a major role. But one of the most effective aerial weapons was nearly an antique. Its official designation was AC-47, more often called "Puff, the Magic Dragon." Some said the *A* in "AC" stood for "ancient." The aircraft in question was an attack aircraft designed to spray a wide swath of death through the jungles and rice paddies of Vietnam. AC-47's had high-speed machine guns mounted pointing out the side of the plane. With these they swept a deadly strip of fire. The planes themselves were the military version of the DC-3, a twin-engine propeller-driven plane designed in 1935. During the Second World War, DC-3's had plodded along carrying cargo and troops. In the strange conflict in Vietnam this old plowhorse became a deadly fighting machine.

3. The Bicycle in the War. The guerrillas who fought the French, and later the Americans, in Vietnam used the bicycle to move supplies. They worked out a network of trails through the jungle called the Ho Chi Minh Trail. They would take a French-made Peugeot bicycle and add bamboo poles to increase its carrying capacity. A man could walk along with 500 pounds loaded on such a machine. All they needed were narrow trails and bridges made of bamboo and planks. These brought in the necessary supplies. During the siege of Dien Bien Phu, bicycles brought in 70 tons of food and 2 tons of medical supplies every day.

In the 1960's the bicycle was used as a bomb. The Vietcong would pack the tubes of the bike with explosives and rig a detonator using the headlight batteries or a generator. The guerrilla would simply ride the bike into the city, park it, and hurry away. The first time the bike was moved, it would explode, splattering the area with fragments of bicycle frame.

Both the French and Americans tried to close off the Ho Chi Minh Trail by using air power, but the supplies kept coming and the guerrillas won the war. Harrison Salisbury of *The New York Times* visited Hanoi in North Vietnam and later told a U.S. Senate committee that without bicycles the North Vietnamese would have had to give up the war.

F. The Philippines

1. Ferdinand E. Marcos. A dictator like Ferdinand Marcos can suppress democracy and damage the economy of a country. Marcos was also a world-class thief. He fled the Philippines with a fortune after over 20 years on an official salary of $5,700 a year. Marcos declared martial law in 1972, and drafted a new constitution in 1973. These moves let him rule the country as he saw fit. The crisis that brought the end started in 1983 when Benigno Aquino, an opposition leader, was allowed to return to the Philippines from exile. As he stepped off the plane, he was shot down in a flurry of fire. Witnesses said the military bodyguard fired at Aquino, but the government arrested another suspect.

Marcos called for a presidential election in February 1986. Corazon Aquino, widow of Benigno Aquino, became the candidate of the opposition. While the government count showed Marcos winning the election, American observers reported that Aquino had actually received more votes. There was a series of protests and peaceful demonstrations. Marcos left the presidential palace in a fleet of American helicopters. Later he flew to Hawaii with crates of money, gold, and other valuables. He left behind political turmoil, economic problems, and 6,000 pairs of shoes owned by his wife Imelda. In July 1988, Marcos offered to pay $5 billion to be allowed to return to the Philippines. This was presumably only part of his fortune. The Philippine gross national product is roughly $33 billion per year.

2. "Cory" Aquino. It looked like a hopeless struggle: the petite widow in a yellow dress against the dictator of the Philippines. But "Cory" Aquino showed skill and courage. In the end she and a wave of "people power" drove out Ferdinand Marcos, longtime dictator. After her husband was assassinated in 1983, Corazon Aquino became the leader of the opposition. In the 1986 presidential election she was the opposition candidate. She had to back down some established male candidates to be nominated. The voters responded to to her with enthusiasm in an election riddled with fraud. The government declared Marcos the winner, but American observers reported that Aquino clearly got more votes. As a result of peaceful public demonstrations, Marcos fled the country. The onetime housewife was president of the Philippines, a country with a shaky economy and a stormy political situation. In 1986, the future of the Philippines was an open question, but there was no doubt Cory Aquino was the woman of the year.

CHAPTER XXV

Independence in Africa

— Overview —

The big story in Africa since 1945 has been self-rule. African peoples now rule most of Africa. Africans find themselves facing the collection of problems common to new governments and weak economies. In the south of Africa one country was still ruled by whites into the 1990's. It is a place where the phrase "master race" is still used after the rest of the world has rejected the idea.

Your students can locate an article in a newspaper or magazine about Africa and write a summary of it. They can write a paper comparing and contrasting the problems of gaining independence in a selected African country with the American Revolution. They could compare the Belgian way of resisting African independence with the British attitude. They could write a paper comparing racial discrimination in South Africa with current attitudes about race in the United States. They could write a paper on the topic "What is the U.S. interest in preserving wildlife and forests in Africa?"

A. AFRICANS PUSH FOR INDEPENDENCE

1. Veterans. World War II educated many Africans. East Africa had 200,000 veterans of the war. Roughly half had been in combat. They had fought in Ethiopia against Italians, in North Africa against Germans and Italians, or in Burma against the Japanese. They had heard Allied propaganda about a war for freedom and how bad it was for one people to rule over another. They had also learned that as soldiers they were as good as any Europeans. When they returned home, these veterans became a major source of pressure for independence.

2. Mau Mau. The Mau Mau rebellion against British colonial rule ran from 1952 to 1956 and was centered among the Kikuyu, a people in Kenya. But not all Kikuyu were Mau Mau supporters. In fact, more Africans than Europeans died fighting the Mau Mau. Fewer than 100 Europeans died fighting the Mau Mau, but roughly 2,000 Africans died. The Mau Mau casualties were over 11,000. The cost to Britain was £60 million (roughly $90 million). Although the Mau Mau were defeated militarily, they played an important role in getting independence for Kenya.

Jomo Kenyatta was tried and imprisoned in 1952 after being charged with "managing" the Mau Mau terrorist organization. Kenyatta denied the charge. He had even made a public statement against the Mau Mau. There was little evidence against him, but he was the most prominent African nationalist leader. He was in prison for 8½ years.

3. Angola and Mozambique. Before independence came to Angola and Mozambique, the strain of trying to hold onto them destroyed the Portuguese government. From 1932 until the 1970's the government of Portugal was a dictatorship. The government claimed that the two African colonies were treated as provinces of Portugal. They pointed out that Portuguese colonies did not discriminate on the basis of race; any person who could read, write, and speak Portuguese was entitled to full citizenship. Observers confirmed that Angola and Mozambique had a fairly free intermingling of the races. Observers also pointed out that, in effect, the Africans had to give up their culture to become full citizens.

While other European countries were freeing their colonies, Portugal held on to hers and fought off the independence movements that developed in the early 1960's. The Portuguese Army was successful in holding both colonies, but the struggle seemed endless. The army became disgusted with the government and formed the Armed Forces Movement. On April 25, 1974, this movement seized power in Portugal and set up a government of generals. Then they quickly negotiated independence for Angola and Mozambique effective in 1975.

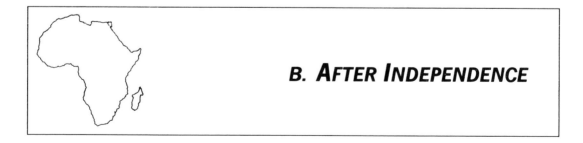

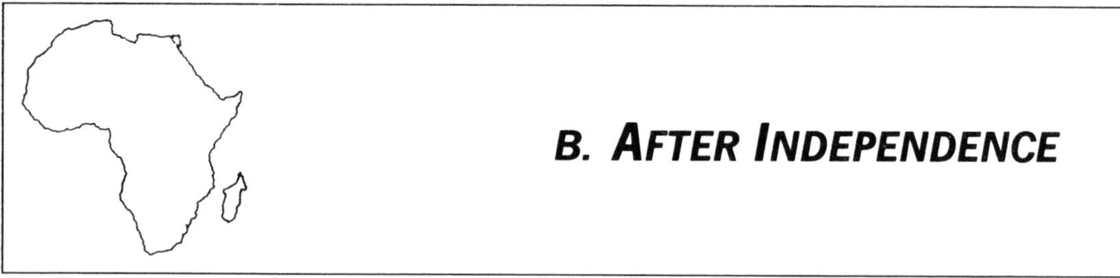

B. AFTER INDEPENDENCE

1. Education in the Belgian Congo. In 1960, the country known as the Belgian Congo became independent and African-ruled. The country soon became divided in a confusing civil war. The president and the prime minister fought for control of the central government, while in the provinces leaders tried to pull out and become independent. Generally the United States supported President Kasavubu, and the Soviets supported Prime Minister Lumumba. The Belgians supported Moise Tshombe, who tried to secede with Katanga province, an area with important copper deposits. The United Nations sent a peacekeeping force to bring some stability. After things settled down, the country changed its name to Zaire.

How can a country have so much trouble? Part of the credit goes to Belgium. It had a policy of keeping the Congolese uneducated. Belgian authorities only offered schools up to the third-grade level for people in the Congo. The Belgians hoped that if the people were poorly educated, they would not learn about the nationalism sweeping Africa. The policy failed. The Congolese demanded their independence, and Belgium quickly gave it to them. The country was pitifully unprepared. No black resident had held a position higher than postmaster before independence, and fewer than 20 Congolese held college degrees. With this inadequate preparation, an independent Congo was doomed to face major difficulties.

2. *Ujamaa,* African Socialism. After independence, many African leaders looked to African traditions to guide their countries. Among these was Julius K. Nyerere, president of the Republic of Tanganyika, which later became Tanzania. Nyerere rejected both Marxism and capitalism. He proposed that his people live according to *ujamaa,* or, as translated from the Swahili, "familyhood." Africans, he argued, would live as one large extended family. In this system everybody shared and everybody worked. Nyerere argued that all Africans were workers and all were equal. He quoted traditional Swahili sayings like "Treat your guest as a guest for two days; on the third day, give him a hoe." Nyerere's Tanu political party began its creed with "I believe in human brotherhood and the unity of Africa."

3. Culture. As African countries gained independence, they often made a point of stressing African culture and rejecting the culture of their former European rulers. In 1981, for example, Kenya adopted a policy that Shakespeare's plays should not be taught in the high schools. An official report said this was a way to get rid of "the colonial hangover in independent Kenya."

4. Kenya and Ivory. For Kenya, tourism is a major industry. The visitors come to see the fabulous African wildlife. Protecting that wildlife has become a serious problem. Poachers kill elephants for the ivory in the tusks, and prevention is very difficult. In 1989, to dramatize the problem, Kenya burned ivory worth millions of dollars confiscated from poachers. They were trying to send the world a message: Do not buy ivory, because that encourages poachers.

5. Wood Shortage. The less-developed countries of the earth are facing a serious energy shortage. They are using up their trees. In Africa, wood produces more than 70 percent of energy used. The United Nations sees this as a serious problem and devoted the January 1989 issue of UNESCO's *The Courier* to discussing the world's forests.

As the African population grows, the people are using wood faster than the trees are growing to replace it. The growth of cities makes the problem worse, because in cities people use charcoal. Charcoal is a less efficient energy source because 50 percent of the energy in wood is lost in making charcoal. This problem is costing Africans money, and African women are finding it costs them time. Women are in charge of gathering wood, and this chore is taking more and more time. In extreme cases like the African Sahel, women can spend as much as 300 days a year gathering wood. They could use dried dung as a fuel, but it is needed as a fertilizer, so burning it results in poorer crops.

6. Asians. It is important to remember that African history is not a simple matter of black and white. Of course there are Africans, and Europeans, but there are also 300,000 Asians—for example, 300,000 in Kenya and Tanzania. The Asians are mostly Muslims. Often they are businesspeople operating small shops and stores, a middle class. They can be a target for African dictators. In 1972, Idi Amin of Uganda ordered all 30,000 Asians who were not Ugandan citizens out of the country. Finding homes for 30,000 displaced Asians created a problem for the rest of the world.

7. Women's Role in Morocco. Social change comes in unexpected ways. In Morocco it may have come in the form of a petite (five foot three inches tall) young woman named Nawai El Moutawakel. When she was a girl, she liked to run, and found she could beat other children in races. She became a dedicated runner jogging through the streets of Casablanca in shorts. At the time, this was scandalous. Children would throw stones at her and hurl curses. Women in those days in Morocco did not run in shorts. They wore long tights and long sleeves and a veil, even when running in track meets. Soldiers were stationed at the meets to keep out spectators because the sight of women running was obscene.

Nawai El Moutawakel may have changed that attitude. She became African champion in the 100-meter high hurdles and ran ninth in the 1983 world championships. This led to a chance to go to the United States to run for Iowa State University in Ames, Iowa. There she got expert coaching, a chance to run in competition, and an introduction to frigid winters. In the 1984 Olympics representing Morocco, she won a gold medal in the 400-meter hurdles. Back home, Morocco went crazy. Nawai El Moutawakel was on the front pages of newspapers, and baby girls were named after her. When she went home, she was amazed to see women running on the streets and on the beach. Could it be that one small woman and a gold medal produced this change?

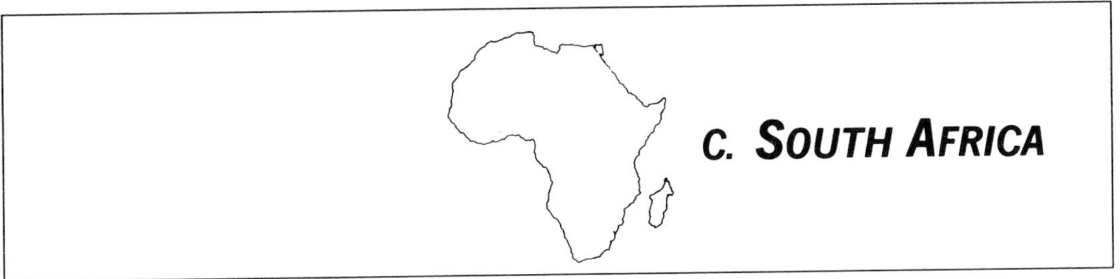

C. South Africa

1. Cape Coloured. "Cape coloured" is defined in South African law as a race made up of a mix of white, African, and Asian. South Africa is the only place where this mix is considered a race, and even there its definition is unclear. In the 1960's, a Greek immigrant took a ship to South Africa to join his father and brother. He got a tan while traveling. When he tried to land at a South African port, immigration officials rejected him as too dark. He went back aboard ship and stayed in his cabin until his tan faded. Later, at another port, he was allowed to land.

In another case, a daughter of a white farmer was declared coloured. All the rest of the family—father, mother, and other children—were white. Under South African law the girl was required to move to a residential area reserved for coloureds. The only way she could legally live with her family was to get a special permit to become a resident servant.

2. Fear of Attack. South African whites seemed to live in constant fear of black attack. In the 1960's a fashion note came out of South Africa. A designer had developed a bra with a built-in holster.

3. Heart Transplant. The white settlers of South Africa lived in a very modern way. The first heart transplant was done in South Africa by Doctor Christiaan Barnard. In one ironic case he took a heart from a coloured donor and gave it to a white patient. This was one of the few cases of approved race mixing in South Africa.

4. Nelson Mandela. The South African government wanted Nelson Mandela out of prison, but he refused to go. In 1964, he had been sentenced to life plus five years. By 1985, the government was offering him freedom. Mandela refused release from prison because of the conditions attached to the release.

Nelson Mandela was not an ordinary prisoner. He was put in jail in 1962 on minor charges. In 1964, he was convicted of treason and sabotage and given the sentence of life plus five years. Mandela had been a leader of the African National Congress, a violent black resistance organization in South Africa. He admitted he had done the sabotage. While in prison he became an even bigger problem for the government. He studied, wrote, and became a symbol of oppression. In 1976, riots broke out in Soweto Township. Young blacks who participated were arrested and sentenced to Robben Island prison. Mandela turned Robben Island prison into Mandela University, where he taught the youths his revolutionary ideas. The authorities transferred him to another prison, but pressure was building to have Mandela released. In 1985, the government offered Mandela release on conditions: renounce violence; go into exile; go to Transkei, a homeland for blacks.

The negotiations continued. The prisoner met with a series of government officials, four cabinet ministers and two state presidents. Meanwhile, the pressure on the government built. The administration under President F. W. de Klerk said that white rule of South Africa was ending. But to bring that about, the government needed to negotiate with the African National Congress, and the ANC wanted Mandela freed. On February 11, 1990, Nelson Mandela walked out of prison unconditionally. He had survived imprisonment; now he had to face the challenge of leading the African National Congress and negotiating for the freedom of all the blacks in South Africa.

CHAPTER XXVI

Turmoil in the Middle East

— Overview —

It sometimes seems as if "Middle East conflict" is one word, the way "damn Yankees" once was. Since 1945, the Arabs and Israelis have fought four wars and made seemingly thousands of raids and strikes back and forth. There have also been numerous political conflicts within countries. Iran has become a major concern, because even in such a troubled area it is especially turbulent. In such a tangle of conflicts, the Iarq-Kuwait border dispute seemed minor until it became a short but dramatic war.

Your students could collect and summarize articles on conflicts in the Middle East. They could made a bulletin board listing and locating all the conflicts in the area. They could make a bulletin board on "Leaders in the Middle East."

The imaginative student could write a paper on "A Day in a Palestinian Refugee Camp," "Letter From Iran," or "Letter Home From Desert Storm."

A. Arab-Israeli Conflict

1. The Six-Day War. The Arabs and Israelis fought a short war in June 1967. It was a lopsided Israeli victory often called the Six-Day War. On the first day of the war, June 5, 1967, the Israeli Air Force made a series of strikes on Egyptian airfields, wiping out 400 Egyptian aircraft on the ground. After that, the Israeli aircraft controlled the sky over the battlefields and made victory for land forces easy.

Why were those early strikes against the airfields so successful? The Egyptian commander, Field Marshal Abdel Omer, was flying over the Sinai. He ordered that while he was in the air all Egyptian antiaircraft guns and missiles were not to fire. His order served to insure his own safety—and the safety of attacking Israeli planes. An investigation after the war showed that Omer also let incompetents serve as officers. Many Egyptian officers ran from battle in 1967. Shortly after the war, Field Marshal Abdel Omer was forced to resign. He later committed suicide.

2. Resolution 242. Sometimes a single small word can make a very significant difference. In 1967, the United States vetoed a Security Council resolution over the word *the.* In 1967, Israel soundly defeated its Arab enemies and conquered territory that was larger than its own area. The United Nations Security Council had a difficult time wording a resolution dealing with the conflict. Eventually the Council worked out a resolution. It called for all parties to stop fighting and recognize the right of each country to exist. The Arabs had never recognized Israel as a country, so this was very important to Israel.

The resolution also called for Israel to return "the territories" conquered in the 1967 Six-Day War. This was important to the Arabs, who wanted the land back. The United States, acting as a friend of Israel, vetoed the measure. The reason was that "the territories" meant that all land conquered in 1967 would have to be returned. This would in turn leave Israel with little to bargain about in any peace talks and strip it of territory needed for defense. After further discussion, the resolution was amended. The word *the* was removed and Resolution 242 passed. Both sides then said they supported Resolution 242. But they had differing versions of how it should be applied.

3. Terrorism in the Olympics. The 1972 Olympics were held in Munich. The West Germans were eager to be genial hosts because of the haunting shadow of the 1936 Olympics. Instead, the 1972 Olympics became the Olympics of the Terrorists. On September 5, a group of eight Palestinian terrorists, members of a group called Black September, climbed the fence of the Olympic Village dressed in sweat suits and carrying weapons in sports duffle bags. They seized nine Israeli athletes, killing two others in the process. Then, while the world watched in horror, the terrorists demanded the release of 200 Palestinians being held in Israel.

The negotiations were covered live by the TV networks. Sportscasters found themselves covering a major political story. After over 20 hours, the terrorists and their hostages were flown in three helicopters to Furstenfeldbruck Airport. After midnight, the authorities stormed the helicopters. Television pictures showed flashes of guns firing in the dark. Five terrorists were killed and three arrested. One policeman and all nine hostages were killed. The next day, the Olympic stadium was filled for a memorial service. Then the Games resumed.

4. Yom Kippur War. Around 1973, the magazine *Strategy and Tactics* was working on a simulation of warfare in the Middle East. The editors reviewed the forces of each country and came up with an interesting discovery. Egypt's armed forces were well equipped and much improved since their defeat in 1967. In fact, they were capable of attacking across the Suez Canal and hitting the Israelis hard.

On October 6, 1973, this observation was confirmed. On Yom Kippur, the Jewish Day of Atonement, the Egyptians and Syrians attacked Israel. The Egyptians crossed the Suez Canal and pushed the Israelis back. For the first time, an Egyptian army was winning against the Israelis. The Israelis recovered and made their own attack, crossing the Suez. But the Arabs had another weapon—oil. The OPEC countries used oil to pressure the Americans and Europeans who had supported Israel to be more neutral. Soon both Egypt and Israel accepted a cease-fire based on a United Nations Security Council resolution.

As a result of this war, the Arabs regained their pride and self-confidence. From such a position they could talk of peace without seeming to surrender. The stage was set for the Camp David Accords.

5. Golda Meir. Golda Meir was prime minister of Israel from 1969 to 1974. She emigrated to Palestine from the United States in 1921 and was active in the Jewish struggle in Palestine. On one trip to the United States she raised $50 million for Israel from American Jews. When Israel became independent in 1948, Meir was made minister to Moscow. From 1949 to 1965, she was in every cabinet Israel had, always the only woman. She was no soft touch, believing in a strong Israel. She led Israel during the October 1973 Yom Kippur War.

6. Nuclear Bomb. Will the next Arab-Israeli war be a nuclear one? The answer could be yes. Press reports based on CIA information say the Israelis had nuclear bombs nearly ready to go in 1973. The Israelis deny they have a nuclear bomb but say that they could produce one in a short time. They also say they will not be the first to introduce nuclear weapons into the Middle East.

What about the Arabs? Iraq seems to have tried to build a bomb. Iraq bought a research reactor from France that would operate on weapons-grade uranium. Iraq bought uranium from Portugal, Niger, and perhaps Brazil. All this looked very much as if Iraq was going to use its reactor to produce nuclear material and build a bomb. But the reactor never got to operate. On June 7, 1981, Israel bombed the reactor site and stopped construction, Aparently Iraq continued to try to build a bomb. In March 1990, U.S. and British customs officials seized a shipment of capacitors en route to Iraq. Capacitors are used as triggers for nuclear bombs. Will Iraq try to find another way to build a bomb? Will Israel decide to change its policy? Will another Middle Eastern country like Iran buy or build a bomb? These are unsettling questions in an already dangerous Middle East.

B. EGYPT

1. Aswan High Dam. The Egyptians see many benefits coming from the Aswan High Dam. Lake Nasser can hold water to irrigate more cropland, up to one third more. With the water under control, some land can yield more than one crop a year. The lake also holds water, so a dry year upstream will not mean failed crops downstream. The dam also generates 10 billion kilowatt hours of electricity.

Environmentalists see a series of problems. Before the dam, floods periodically washed over Egypt's farmland and deposited a rich layer of silt, fertilizing the soil. Now Egypt needs artificial fertilizer, and the silt is filling in Lake Nasser. The same silt used to carry nutrients into the Mediterranean Sea. Now this does not happen, and fishing is worse. The Egyptians seem to feel that the benefits of the Aswan High Dam outweigh any problems. Egypt is a relatively poor country and a very dry one. Water is precious, and the dam provides it.

2. Sadat. When Nasser died in September 1970, Anwar el-Sadat became president of Egypt. The American government's estimate was that he would last eight weeks. He was surrounded by powerful cabinet ministers and had relatively little support from the people of Egypt. He slept with a pistol beside his bed, expecting a coup at any time. He also began to reform the government. He arrested a number of cabinet ministers, charging them with corruption and bribery. Later he told the Soviet Union to remove all its military advisors. Sadat, the man who wouldn't last over two months, became an efficient and effective president of Egypt.

3. **Sadat and Peace.** Anwar el-Sadat knew the price of war. He had lost a brother in the 1973 October War (Yom Kippur War). He also knew that he had to break through the wall of suspicion between Egypt and Israel. He chose to do this with the dramatic announcement that he was willing to go to Israel seeking peace. The Israelis invited him to visit, and he accepted. While there, in November 1977, he prayed in the al-Aqsa mosque and later addressed the Knesset, the Israeli parliament. Progress toward peace was slow. In September 1978, President Carter of the United States, Prime Minister Begin of Israel, and President Sadat of Egypt met in Camp David, Maryland, and negotiated the first treaty between an Arab state and Israel. Sadat was awarded the Nobel Peace Prize for his efforts. There was a price to peace, however. The other Arab states broke relations with Egypt and were very critical. Many Arabs saw this settlement as a sellout. On October 6, 1981, while reviewing a parade, Sadat was assassinated by Muslim fundamentalists.

4. **Egypt's Economy.** In the 1980's, the average Egyptian was still quite poor. While the per-capita income in the United States was over $10,000, in Egypt it was about $600. Cairo had some of the worst slums in the world. People lived in one-room apartments, sleeping on the floor, or they lived in the streets. Drinking water came from a public faucet, and the street was their toilet. Many residents of Cairo never took a bath in their entire lives.

C. Censorship in Kuwait

An American who taught in Kuwait in 1987 reported that the sheikhdom practiced active censorship of textbooks. If a history text had any reference to the Holocaust, it was blacked out. One textbook had a picture of Muhammad on the cover. The face was blacked out by the censors. This reflected the Islamic tradition that Muhammad's face is never pictured.

D. Iran

1. Independence. America and Great Britain played a major role in keeping Iran independent after World War II. During that war, Iran was a major route for sending supplies to the Soviet Union. For that reason Iran was occupied by the Soviets and the British. Tehran was the site of a major Allied conference to decide war strategy. During that conference, the shah of Iran met privately with each participant—Churchill, Roosevelt, and Stalin—to discuss the future of Iran. At the time, this was not a major Allied concern.

After the war, the Soviets kept their troops in Iran and supported revolts in the regions of Azerbaijan and Kurdistan in northern Iran. The United States took this aggression to the United Nations Security Council. The Soviets were also resisted by some British-sponsored Iranians. The British owned the Anglo-Iranian Oil Company. Soon the Soviet troops were withdrawn.

2. Coup in 1953. The American CIA helped bring the shah to power in Iran. In 1953, the Americans and British became convinced that Premier Mohammad Mosaddeq was a tool of the Communists. Iran had nationalized the British-owned oil company, and the Iranian Communists were growing more active. The Americans sent Kermit Roosevelt, grandson of Theodore Roosevelt, to overthrow Mosaddeq.

In Iran Roosevelt used the name James Lockridge. Through a series of secret meetings with political leaders, loyal military officers, the shah, and some shadowy organizers, Roosevelt planned the coup. He reports in his book, *Counter Coup: The Struggle for the Control of Iran,* that the entire operation only cost about $100,000. After this coup, the shah went on to take dictatorial powers. There is therefore some justification in the later Iranian claims that the shah was a puppet of the United States.

3. SAVAK. During the reign of the shah, SAVAK, the secret police, were feared and hated by Iranians. SAVAK arrested, imprisoned, tortured, and executed thousands who opposed the shah. The power of SAVAK even reached to the United States. When Iranian students in the United States demonstrated against the shah, they often masked themselves because they feared reprisals by SAVAK. Since the fall of the shah, the world has learned that SAVAK agents were trained in torture methods by the American CIA.

4. Military Power. Under the shah, Iran became a very impressive military power. The shah was able to get the very latest and best military equipment from the United States. Americans could watch TV footage of the shah reviewing a long line of tanks and see the American-made jet fighters flying above. Surely, as the reporters said, the shah was a pillar of strength and stability in the Middle East. But it did not last. Could it be that there is more to stability than raw military power?

5. Ayatollah Ruhollah Khomeini. He was, to most outsiders, an unlikely person to be a political leader. He was a devout Muslim teacher and spiritual leader. He opposed the shah's program of modernization because he thought it violated Muslim religious rules. He spent 15 years in exile in Turkey, Iraq, and France before he returned to lead Iran in 1979. Khomeini stayed committed to his religious principles and tried to rule Iran by traditional Islamic law as he understood it. He wanted all women to wear the traditional veil. A thief would have his or her hand cut off. At one point Khomeini even tried to ban music. He offered a reward for the death of Salman Rushdie for writing a book the Ayatollah considered blasphemous.

Khomeini was extremely hostile to the United States and labeled it the Great Satan. He supported militants when they stormed the U.S. embassy and held 52 Americans hostage for 444 days. He fought the Iraqis to a standstill when they tried to take the Shatt al-Arab waterway away from Iran. His talk of spreading his Islamic revolution made neighboring Muslim states very nervous.

Yet the Iranians respected and followed Khomeini. More than a million Iranians died fighting against Iraq. Many of them were volunteers. When Khomeini died in 1989, his funeral was attended by an estimated 2 million loyal followers. Many mourners died, and around 11,000 people were reported injured during the three-day period of grieving. Khomeini's coffin was torn apart by believers seeking a holy relic. A replacement was used. Such devotion is hard for Westerners to understand. We tended to see Khomeini as an unbalanced old man and a tyrant. Perhaps we have much to learn about other cultures.

6. Iranian Women. The Islamic revolution in Iran has had a paradoxical impact on women. In many ways the revolution moved women back to old ways. The law restricting polygamy was abolished. Women were encouraged to wear the traditional veil. In fact, they could be fired from work if they refused to wear a veil. Women were banned from being lawyers or judges. At the same time, women were part of the Revolutionary Guards. They were trained as commandos, learning to operate M-16 rifles.

E. Iraq Crisis

1. Sources of Arms. When Iraq occupied Kuwait on August 2, 1990, the Iraqi military forces were rated fourth largest in the world. How does a country of 18 million people become the number 4 military power in the world? Answer: It gets a lot of outside help.

The Soviet Union provided the Iraqis with the biggest share of military equipment. The Iraqi Army was organized on the Soviet model and equipped by the U.S.S.R. The T-72 main battle tank, which was the heart of the Iraqi forces, was the Soviet Union's second-best tank. The Iraqi Air Force flew a number of Soviet MiG-29 fighter planes. The Iraqi Scud missiles that were fired at Israel and Saudi Arabia were an early Soviet type officially called SS-1, "surface-to-surface missile—1." The name Scud was the NATO code name for this Soviet missile.

The French were the second most important supplier. The best fighter plane in the Iraqi Air Force was the French-made Mirage F-1. Many of these were flown to Iran during the war and were impounded. These planes were armed with Exocet missiles, capable of inflicting serious wounds on warships. Exocets could also be launched from the patrol boats of the Iraqi Navy.

A number of other countries provided parts of the arsenal. China had sold Iraq tanks, armored personnel carriers, and a missile called Silkworm. A German company provided the expertise to build a chemical weapons plant. There were even reports that the Iraqis had American-made Stinger missiles passed on to them by sources in Afghanistan.

None of these weapons is cheap, so Iraq needed financial assistance to purchase them. They got it from a variety of sources. The United States guaranteed about $400 million in loans for food. This freed up money to buy arms. Saudi Arabia provided financial assistance while Iraq fought Iran. During the same period, Kuwait loaned the Iraqis over $6 billion.

2. Saudi Women and Desert Storm. Saudi Arabia in 1990 was a conservative Muslim country that enforced strict standards of conduct for women. The presence of American soldiers during Operation Desert Storm was unsettling for both Saudis and Americans.

Saudi women were expected to wear a veil when in public and be carefully isolated from men. They were not permitted to visit stores selling disco music and were forbidden to drive cars in the cities. These rules were enforced by a morals police who patrolled the cities. While some Saudi women got modern educations in places like the United States, others attended universities in Saudi Arabia. These schools were female-only institutions. Male instructors were not allowed in the room with women students. Instead, the instructor lectured over television and the students asked questions over phones at their desks.

The arrival of American women as soldiers produced some shocks for the Arabs. Female soldiers drove trucks, gave orders to men, and at first dressed as in America. The American military quickly insisted that women soldiers visiting Arabian cities when off duty wear the traditional veil, which the military authorities provided. While on duty, the women in the American armed forces carried on in uniforms without veils. Saudi women noticed these freedoms, and some of them acted to gain some for themselves. On November 6, 1990, 50 Saudi women staged a protest by driving cars on the streets of Riyadh. The police took them all to the police station, where they signed a pledge not to do this again. The protest was not a total break with tradition, however. The women wore veils and black cloaks while driving.

3. American Women in Desert Storm. The American news media ran a series of stories about mothers going off to war and speculated about female casualties. As the fighting started, the concern deepened. Early in the fighting, Army Specialist Melissa Rathbun-Nealy was captured. Her story became a front-page item. (Specialist Rathbun-Nealy was later returned in a prisoner exchange.) When a Scud missile hit a barracks in the rear area, two women were among those killed. While women had been involved in every American war, including the Revolution, questions still arose. Should mothers be sent into combat? Why should women be limited to so-called noncombat roles when participating troops in those activities are likely to be killed and captured, yet kept out of combat roles, which are the best ticket to promotion? What are the roles women should play in the modern military world?

4. Missile Joke. On August 2, 1990, the forces of Iraq invaded and occupied Kuwait. Soon there was a flurry of United Nations resolutions as troops from several countries moved to Saudi Arabia to "draw a line in the sand" against further Iraqi advances. The military code name for this defensive effort was Operation Desert Shield. A few months later, the coalition forces began a military action against the Iraqi forces code-named Operation Desert Storm. The first phase of Desert Storm was a massive aerial attack. This was reported in detail by television crews who broadcast pictures of both the attacking planes and the cities they attacked. But the most spectacular pictures of the bombing were taken by the bombs themselves. The U.S. Air Force was using smart bombs, which were guided to their target by the bomber pilots. The bombs broadcast images from a TV camera in the nose, and the pilots directed them so precisely that the bombs not only hit the building they were intended for, but could even hit a selected door or window. Air Force people were very pleased with this performance and told the following "knock-knock" joke:

Q: What does a smart bomb say before it goes through a door?

A: Knock! Knock!

Q: Who's there?

A: Ka.

Q: Ka who?

A: Kaboom!

5. Stealth Fighter. Among the star performers in the air war over Iraq was the F-117A "Stealth" fighter. The mission of this rather odd-looking airplane was to fly into Iraq ahead of other planes and destroy Iraqi radar. The Stealth could do this because it carried a missile designed to fly down radar beams and then blow up. The plane also had another important feature. It was nearly invisible to radar.

Every feature of the plane was designed to reduce its radar cross-section, that is, its reflection of radar. The Stealth was a relatively slow plane and hard to fly. Its nickname was the Wobbly Goblin. Speed and maneuverability were sacrificed to gain stealth. The plane's fuselage was an irregular mass of flat surfaces and odd angles, and its cockpit had triangular windows. The flat surfaces were called facets, and they were angled to reflect radar beams away from the radar station instead of back to it. The plane had no square corners to catch and reflect radar. The F-117A's triangular windows were covered with radar-absorbing material, and their shape trapped radar beams. The F-117A's body was wide to include its two jet engines well inside with their air scoops carefully shielded.

Not only was the Stealth's shape carefully arranged to minimize radar reflection, the material in the plane was a special composite that absorbed radar beams. The Stealth was painted black, with a special radar-absorbing paint that cost millions of dollars to develop. Black was also the best color for invisibility on night missions. Planes could be detected by sound, and infrared detectors detected heat. So the noise of the jet engines was muffled to a whistle and the hot exhaust was dispersed. For years this plane was so secret that the Air Force refused even to admit they had it.

6. Iraqi Defeat. When the coalition forces launched their land assault on February 24, 1991, the Iraqi forces had been softened up by the air attack, which had started January 17, 1991. Although Iraqi President Saddam Hussein had promised "the mother of all battles," the land war proved to be a quick victory, a "100-hour war." The Iraqi forces had lost their will to fight, as shown by the following incident. One coalition soldier got lost in the desert and, worse yet, his truck got stuck. An Iraqi tank approached the immobilized soldier. The Iraqis then towed the truck out of the soft spot and surrendered to its driver.

CHAPTER XXVII

New Directions in Latin America

— Overview —

It may be unfair to Latin American to depict it as a land of dictators and revolutions, but these are what make the headlines and the history books. The instability of the region has been further confused by a Cold War dimension, by the complexity of the world economy, and by the weapons trade. It is very difficult to write about the political situation in Latin America and have the information remain current. I once taped a television special for my classes. At that time it was legal to show the tape within ten days. The reporter mentioned that one country had held an election and that this would settle things there for the next four years. Before I was able to show the tape three days later, the newly elected government had been overthrown.

You may want your students to locate current articles on Latin America and write summaries of them. The artistic student could prepare a map of Latin America and shade the countries by type of government: red for democracy, blue for military dictatorship, brown for Castro-style dictatorship, and so on. Your students might want to research the current United States policy toward Latin America.

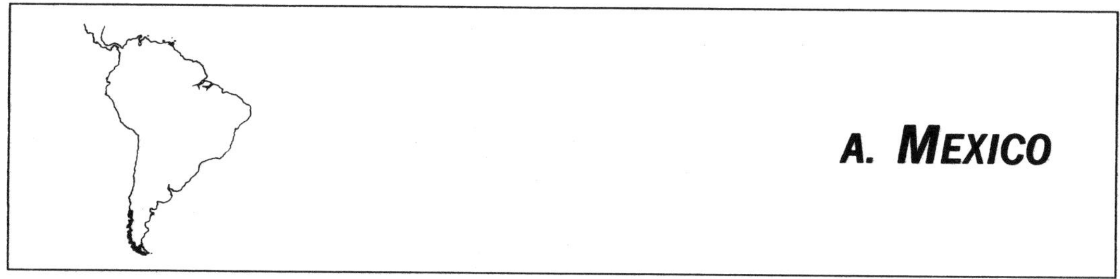

A. Mexico

1. Government. Mexico's government is led by a president, who serves a single six-year term. During this term, the president has great power, and nobody disagrees with the president. There is a joke that if the president asks, "What time is it?" the proper reply is "Whatever time you say it is, Mr. President."

Mexico has a congress, but as a practical matter it has little power. One senator said, "We're paid to applaud." At the end of the term, Mexico's president selects a leader within the PRI, the Institutional Revolutionary Party, who is then elected to the next six-year presidential term. The PRI has never lost an election since its founding.

2. Corruption. Tips, bribes, or *La Mordida,* "the bite," are a way of life for police in Mexico. The pay of police and other officials is so low they feel they have to supplement their income by taking bribes. As Alan Riding reports in his book, *Distant Neighbors: A Portrait of the Mexicans,* this can lead to rather odd police work. If a crime is reported, police units will race each other to the scene, not to arrest the offender, but to get the bribe they will be paid to release the criminal. In cases that make headlines, the police can be quite vigorous in searching for a person to charge, and they are free to use torture to obtain confessions. In one case of a violent death, Mexican police produced 21 people who confessed to the killing. This is pretty impressive, considering the death was a suicide.

3. The Poor. The poor people of Mexico are often illiterate. This creates a market for a rather unusual business. Letter-writers set up stalls on the sidewalk and offer their services to passersby.

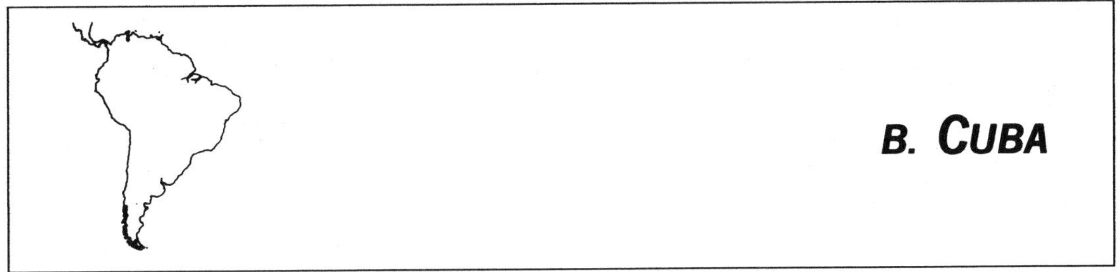

B. Cuba

1. Revolution. When Fidel Castro began his rebellion against the Batista government in Cuba, many Americans were pleased to see someone resist the dictator. American news magazines carried favorable stories about the idealistic young rebel. Photographers sent back pictures of Castro and his rebels wearing beards and fatigue uniforms as they hid in the mountains. One cartoonist showed a sketch of Castro saying to his comrades, "How many men do we have? Not counting *Life* photographers, of course."

2. The Bay of Pigs. The reasons the Bay of Pigs Invasion failed can be summarized simply. The people planning the operation didn't know much about Cuba or Latin America, and they failed to plan the details well. The CIA operative in Miami was using the cover name Frank Bender. He did not speak Spanish and knew very little about Latin America. In the CIA-run training camp in Guatemala, Cuban exiles were training for the invasion. They soon figured out that the CIA agent there was ignorant of Latin America. They made a game of asking him questions and listening to his mistaken answers.

The most critical mistakes were made in the attempt to destroy the Cuban Air Force. There was supposed to be an initial air strike, and it was designed to look as if it was the work of defectors from the Cuban Air Force. Some B-26 aircraft took off from Guatemala on April 15, 1961, made the attack in Cuba, and landed in Florida. The pilots claimed they were defecting from the Cuban Air Force. The planes were cleverly painted to resemble Cuban Air Force planes. Unfortunately they were the wrong model of B-26. The Cuban Air Force had B-26's with clear acrylic plastic noses. These planes had metal noses.

The pilots reported the raid had wiped out the Cuban Air Force planes. But when the exiled Cubans landed at the Bay of Pigs on April 17, they found this was not true. As the exiles fought on the beaches, Cuban Air Force planes sank the ship carrying the invaders' ammunition. This was a critical loss. Soon after this, the invaders were surrounded by Castro's defense forces and surrendered.

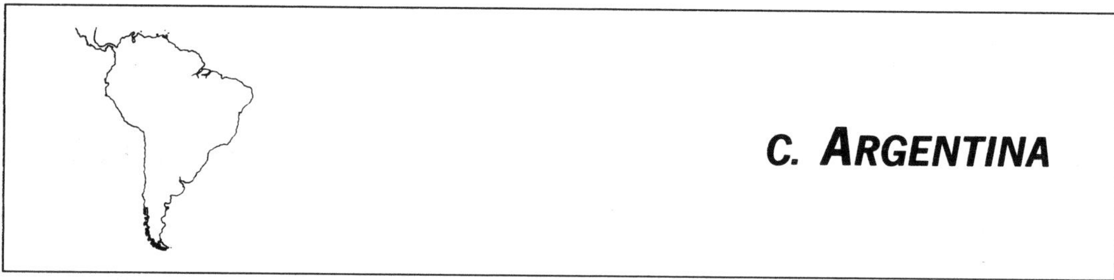

C. ARGENTINA

1. Evita Perón. The official facts tell less than half the story. Officially, Juan Perón was the president of Argentina from 1946 to 1955, then again from 1973 to 1974. But this overlooks the fact that Perón was unofficial ruler from 1943 to 1946, and it also overlooks Evita, his wife. Her name was officially María Eva Duarte de Perón. When she died, the Argentine union of food workers asked the pope to make her a saint. Her embalmed body became a political symbol sought by both friends and enemies. Even in death she was a figure to be reckoned with. Who was this woman?

Eva Perón was the illegitimate child of a poor woman who worked as a servant. Eva moved to Buenos Aires to become an actress, doing small parts in film and radio. She was, by all accounts, a poor actress, but she chose her friends well. She became mistress to Juan Perón, military strongman, in 1944, and married him in 1945. Eva became a major force shaping Juan's policies. At first, Juan Perón was simply a Fascist. He admired Mussolini and even made attacks on Jews. Later he dropped the anti-Semitism.

Eva added a new dimension to the ideology. She made Juan the benefactor of the poor, the *decamisados,* or "shirtless ones." She took over the labor department and raised wages for workers. She ran a charity and personally held office hours when she would talk to poor people. She would give a person in need a free house if the person pleaded well. Others received money or other help. Sometimes she and Juan would walk through the poor neighborhoods. He would take a census. She handed out money and gifts. She built 1,000 schools and 62 new hospitals from 1946 to 1949. No wonder the poor workers roared "Evita!" when Argentina's first lady appeared on a balcony next to her husband.

The rich and respectable scorned Eva Perón, and she hated them. Wealthy women of the Argentine upper class would not let her join their clubs. She in turn made fiery speeches against the rich.

Not that Eva Perón was opposed to living well; she dressed in diamonds and furs on even the warmest days. She was a beautiful woman and a dramatic figure wherever she went. She made a tour of Europe. Franco of Spain gave her a medal. She had an audience with the pope. The British refused her request to be a guest in Buckingham Palace, so she went to Switzerland instead.

She had secret bank accounts in Switzerland and closets full of furs and designer dresses at home. Most of this she got by skimming off the government charity money she managed. She never kept records of the money.

Argentina was a dictatorship, and anybody who offended Evita was in trouble. She always evened the score. A director who had been hard on her when they were making a film, an actress who made a slighting remark, a politician who disagreed with Juan—all had to pay. Most critics were allowed to move quietly to Uruguay.

Then Eva became ill and died in 1952, probably of leukemia. With her death, much of the fire went out of the Peronist movement. Juan Perón was overthrown in 1955. But Eva Perón's memory lingers. Her story was made into a Broadway musical, *Evita!* and in 1973 Juan Perón returned to rule Argentina. He died in 1974, and his body was embalmed and laid in state next to the carefully preserved remains of Evita.

2. Falkland Islands War. It's hard even to name this war. Most English-speaking people would call it the Falkland Islands War, but the Argentinians would call it the Struggle for the Malvinas. It seems the history of the islands is a muddle of conflicting claims. Argentina claimed to own the Malvinas by right of first discovery. The British claimed they owned the Falklands because they had ruled them for a long time. The two parties had negotiated for 17 years when, in 1982, fighting broke out.

Argentina made the first move. Argentine forces landed on the islands and overwhelmed the tiny force of Royal Marines the British had there. The Argentines said that they had invaded because of their national desire to reclaim the Malvinas. Others noticed that the president of Argentina, General Leopoldo Galtieri, was a dictator. People who opposed him disappeared, never to be seen again. Inflation in Argentina raged at a fantastic rate. A war would be a great distraction. The British decided to fight, surprising the Argentine government. The British government talked of self-determination for the 1,800 people on the islands. Cynics noted that the war boosted Prime Minister Margaret Thatcher's popularity.

The British assembled a fleet and an invasion force, which set off for the Falklands. There was fierce fighting at sea and in the air, but once British troops landed, they soon had the islands and thousands of Argentine prisoners.

The war was a study in the 20th-century arms trade. The Argentine Air Force flew American-made A-4's and French-made Mirage fighters. Their most dramatic new weapon was the French-made Exocet missile. Several of their ships were British-made. The British used their Harrier jets equipped with American-made Sidewinder AIM-9L missiles to control the skies. After the war, the French advertised the Exocet as battle-proven, and the American Marines ordered Harriers.

After all the missiles' red glare and bombs thudding on ships, the political issue was not settled. The Galtieri government was overthrown and elections held. Mrs. Thatcher's popularity soared. Negotiations continued.

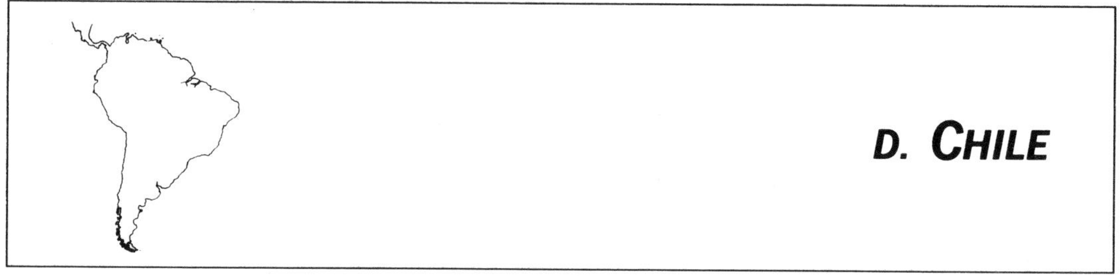

D. CHILE

1. U.S. Destabilization of Allende. Salvador Allende was a socialist and a Marxist. Therefore, American companies and the American government did not want him elected president of Chile. They made a strenuous and expensive effort to stop him.

American companies had a major interest in Chile. Copper was Chile's biggest export. American companies, Anaconda and Kennecott, owned 80 percent of Chile's copper. The telecommunications were owned by ITT. President Nixon and the CIA feared a Marxist president of Chile. According to a U.S. Senate committee, American companies contributed $700,000 to stop Allende's election in 1970. The CIA managed to place 726 articles, broadcasts, editorials, and other material in the Chilean news media. In spite of this, Allende got 36.3 percent of the vote. He was the front-runner, but because he did not get 50 percent of the vote, the election went to the Chilean congress. Again the CIA made a major effort, but the congress voted 133 to 35 in favor of Allende. He became the legally elected president of Chile. President Nixon did not send the usual telegram of congratulations. The American effort clearly failed to stop Allende. Later, in September 1973, the Chilean Army would throw him out.

2. Allende's Death. Latin American revolutions have become almost a ritual. The president (or whoever is being thrown out) receives a phone call or other warning that there will be a coup. The president is then offered a plane, and he and his family fly off to a comfortable exile in Spain or Florida. Latin American presidents usually have sizable bank accounts overseas for just such emergencies.

Salvador Allende did not follow this tradition. On September 11, 1973, he was killed after a five-hour battle. He was offered a plane about 8:00 A.M., before the coup started, but refused it. He holed up in the presidential palace and faced soldiers, Sherman tanks, and jet dive bombers. He fought back using a submachine gun given him as a gift by Fidel Castro. About 40 of his loyal guards helped him, but eventually the army battered its way in and killed Allende. During the day, he had scorned chances to surrender. Allende was not a typical Latin American president.

3. Pinochet. Augusto Pinochet became president as a result of the coup that killed Salvador Allende. Pinochet's new government killed between 20,000 and 30,000 people during its first month. Informed estimates claim the government jailed 100,000 citizens. One of the most dramatic incidents happened on July 2, 1986. Rodrigo Rojas de Negri, a 19-year-old Chilean residing in the United States, returned to his homeland for a visit. While there, he participated in an anti-Pinochet demonstration. He and Carmen Gloria Quintana were seized by soldiers, beaten, soaked with gasoline, and set afire. Only Quintana survived.

The Pinochet regime has been cited for violations of human rights. As early as 1981, the United Nations General Assembly passed a resolution against the Pinochet government.

Somehow Pinochet had the idea he was popular in Chile. In October 1988 he permitted an open vote on the question: Should Pinochet continue to be president, or should there be elections? Pinochet lost. Roughly 55 percent of the voters wanted an election.

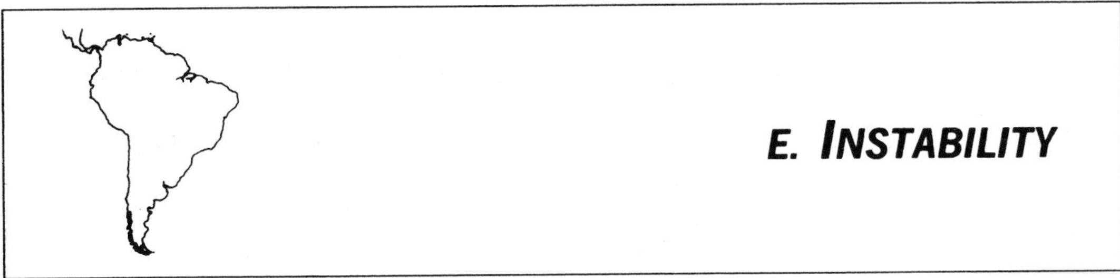

E. INSTABILITY

1. Latin American Revolutions. Henry Ford once remarked that Latin America seemed to have more revolutions per minute than some of his cars.

2. El Salvador Death Squads. In El Salvador during the 1980's, it could be fatal to be of the wrong political opinion. People who were considered too left-wing (liberal) were often killed by right-wing (conservative) death squads. One of these was Archbishop Oscar A. Romero, who was killed on March 24, 1980. He had just spoken out against the violence in his country by both right and left. He was shot while conducting a memorial service. Four American churchwomen were killed December 2, 1980, as they drove from the El Salvador International Airport. Their car was burned, and their bodies were buried in a shallow grave. After much pressure from the United States, the El Salvador government arrested members of the National Guard. There was widespread belief that the guardsmen arrested were merely tools of higher authority.

Violence also came from guerrillas on the left. The U.S. Department of State reports that in 1981, about 5,000 Salvadorans were killed for political reasons. By 1986, the number was down to 200. The population of El Salvador is roughly 5 million.

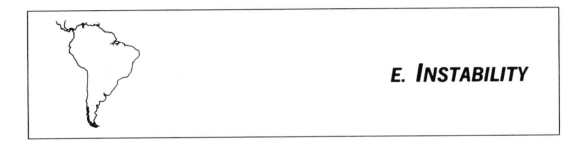

3. Venezuelan Debt. When Venezuela was enjoying prosperity from selling oil, it borrowed a little money, $32 billion from 450 foreign banks. Venezuela could easily handle this amount. It had 26 billion barrels of proven oil reserves, and in 1987, this rose to 55 billion barrels. With oil prices in 1985 at $25.89 a barrel, what could possibly go wrong? Well, for one thing, the price could drop. In early 1988, oil was selling for $13.82, about half the 1985 price. Suddenly even paying interest on the debt became a strain. Venezuela did pay full interest and some principal in 1987, but other Latin American debtor nations were less willing or able to do this. For example, in February 1987 Brazil refused even to pay any interest on its loans.

4. Haitian Poverty. Haiti is a sad example of a country with serious economic problems. For example, in 1987 when the average American earned about $12,000 a year, the average Haitian lived on $379 annually. For Americans an unemployment rate of 10 percent would be very bad news, and it rarely gets that high. Haiti has experienced 49 percent unemployment. Half of Haitian workers couldn't find work. The population of Haiti is growing faster than the gross national product. If that trend continues, the average Haitian will get poorer every year. Most of them won't read about these problems, though. More than three out of four Haitians can't read.

All of this affects people's lives. Sometimes it ends their lives. On the average, out of every 1,000 births in Haiti, 124 infants die in their first year. While the average American can expect to live past 70, the average Haitian lives to 54, about 20 years less.

5. Drug Dealing. Latin American farmers are often very poor. In the 1980's, they found some new crops that paid very well—drugs. Opium poppies and marijuana became important parts of the economy. Since these crops are illegal, nobody can reliably measure how economically important they are. The governments of some Latin American countries have been seriously corrupted by the drug trade. In Panama, President Noriega continued to rule even after a grand jury in Miami, Florida, indicted him. The indictment accused Noriega of laundering money for drug dealers and protecting drug dealers living in Panama. The indictment was handed down in February 1988, and Noriega remained president until December 20, 1989, when American armed forces intervened and took him to the United States for trial.

Index

Allies, 150, 185, 202. *See also* World War I; World War II.

ɔid You Know?

ıe ancient Romans were among the :est bridge builders in history. They loped a type of natural cement that d be used to bond stones together. also developed the cofferdam. This ·atertight enclosure in which the piers, h support the bridge, can be built. The ans also took full advantage of the cir- masonry arch. Examples of the skill e Romans in building bridges can still en. Some of the bridges they built are in use.

or Discussion

ıe text discusses the main types of es. Are there any bridges in your town ty? What types of bridges are they?

AMS

m is a structure that is placed across a block the flow of water. This is usually r one of two reasons. The most common for damming a river is to create a water ir for nearby communities. Fig. 9-15. r important reason to dam a river is to water to power the water turbines in a ectric power station.

Because a dam has a major effect on the surrounding environment, the site for the dam must be selected very carefully. Civil engineers typically spend years studying the characteristics of the land near a proposed dam site. The reservoir created by the dam may flood land that was previously inhabited or used for farming. Arrangements must be made to relocate people and structures that will be flooded. Fig. 9-16.

The construction of a dam is a major undertaking. A large dam may take ten years or longer to construct. A tremendous amount of earthworking must be done before construction on the dam can even be started. The soil must be made strong enough to hold both the dam and the weight of the water in the reservoir created by the dam. The earth must be built into an embankment to keep water from spilling around the dam. The dam itself must have a solid, strong foundation so that it will not wash away when the river swells. The dam must have strong gates to allow water to pass through the dam in controlled amounts.

A spillway must also be constructed. A **spillway** is a safety valve that allows excess water to bypass the dam. This is necessary because few dams are strong enough to withstand the force of floodwater. If the water could not bypass the dam, the dam would break.

Many underwater parts of the dam must be built on dry ground. To be able to work on dry ground, the construction workers must divert the river. This alone can be a major project if the river is a large one. A **cofferdam**, or watertight wall, 2 must be built to keep water out of the worker's way. Fig. 9-17. This temporary wall can be made of timber, concrete, soil, or sheets of steel.

As work on the dam progresses, another cofferdam is built farther out in the river, and the first cofferdam is removed. This allows the water to flow around the sides of the construction site so that the river is not obstructed. After the workers finish the last underwater portion of the dam, the cofferdam is removed entirely.

a group of students research and present a r oral report on dam collapses. Ask them to ize those points that would help in the design dams.

2. Explain that cofferdams are used for building the underwater parts of bridge abutments as well as parts of dams.

For Discussion

Tunnels are more common in regions where there are mountains and rivers. In or near your city or town, are there any tunnels that are used for traffic?

Fig. 9-11. This pedestrian bridge allows school children to cross a busy highway safely.

BRIDGES

A bridge is a structure that is built to span, or cross over, a river or a gap in the earth. A bridge provides a way for people and vehicles to cross from one side to the other. Bridges can also span other structures. A bridge on a highway might cross over railroad tracks or over another highway. Different types of bridges carry rail-
1 roads, highway traffic, pipelines, and foot traffic. Fig. 9-11. Sometimes bridges are made with movable sections that can be raised or swung out of the way so that large boats can pass by. 2
Fig. 9-12.

Bridges can be constructed in several different ways, depending on the required length of the bridge and on the weight it must support.

Fig. 9-12. This bridge can be raised to allow barges to pass through.

1. Ask a student or group of students to research and report on how bridge abutments are built under water.

2. Explain that concrete can be poured under water as long as it does not mix with the water. Concrete sets under water as well as in the air.

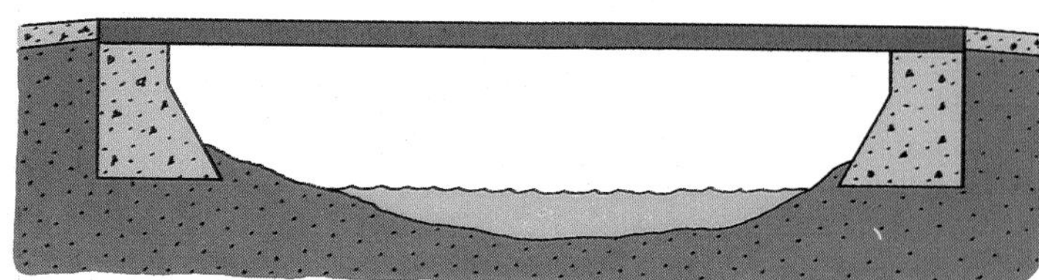

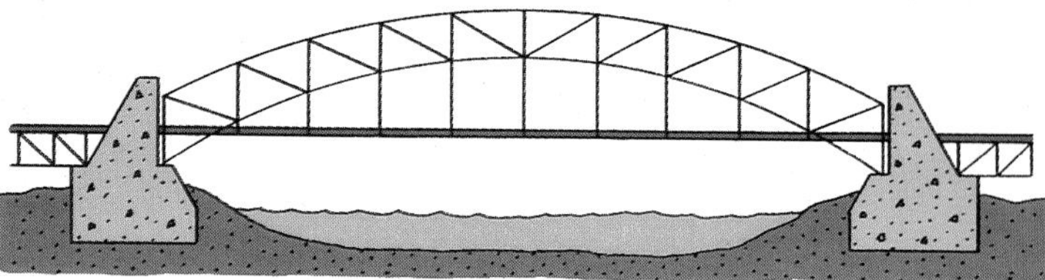

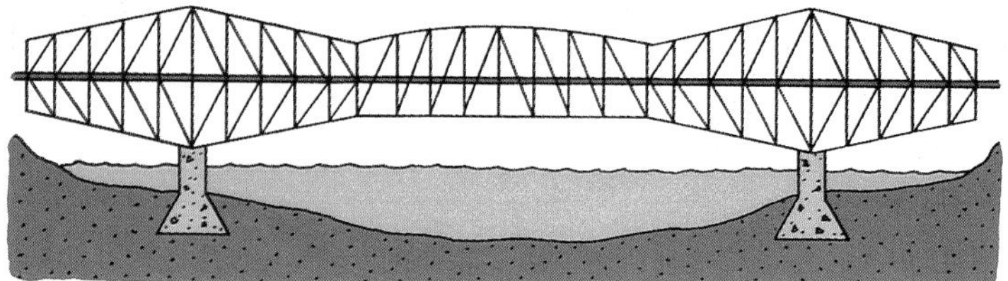

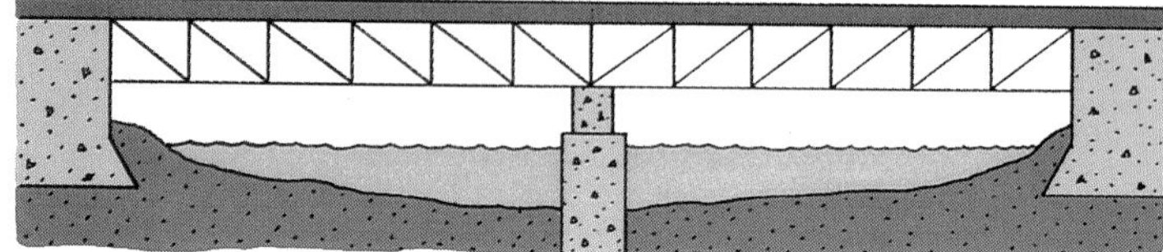

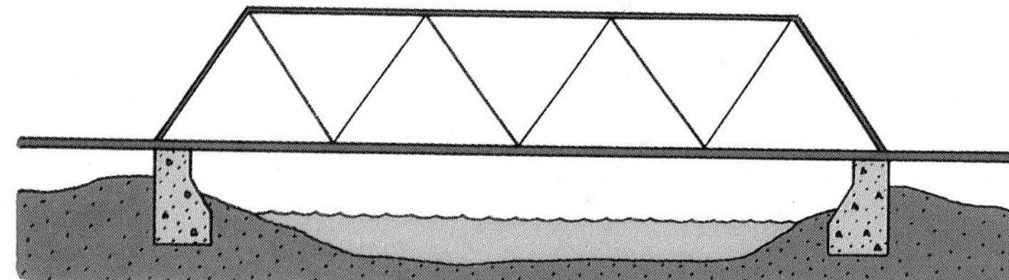

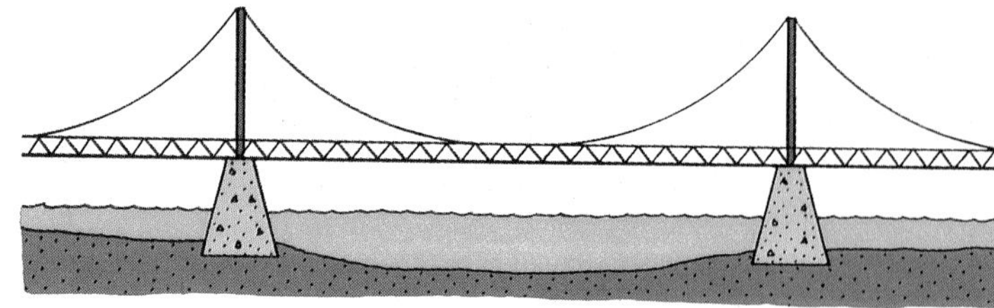

Fig. 9-13. Different kinds of bridges: slab, arch, truss (two types), cantilever, and suspension. 1

1. Discuss how a truss bridge differs from a cantilever bridge. Explain how a cantilever bridge is supported.

Fig. 9-13. Most bridges are anchored on each end by supports called abutments. The simplest type of bridge, the **slab bridge**, consists of a concrete slab supported by abutments. Some of the longer slab bridges are also supported by a pier, or beam, in the middle. This type of bridge is usually made of steel or steel-reinforced concrete and is used mostly for light loads and short spans.

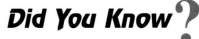

Did You Know?

1 Computers are used to solve many design problems. This is especially true in the construction industry. For example, in designing suspension bridges, engineers have been able to calculate the shape of the suspension cables under changing loads.

2 An **arch bridge** is one in which an arch is used to carry the weight of the bridge. Arch bridges are made of concrete or steel and are usually constructed over deep ravines. **Truss bridges** are supported by steel or wooden trusses, or beams that are put together to form triangular shapes. Triangles are used because the triangle is a particularly strong structural shape. Trusses are also used in combination with other bridges to give them additional support. One type of bridge that commonly uses trusses is a cantilever bridge. A **cantilever bridge** is used for fairly long spans. It has two beams, or cantilevers, that extend from the ends of the bridge. They are joined in the middle by a connecting section called a *suspended span*. The whole structure usually receives additional support from steel trusses.

1. Ask each student to suggest an example of the use of the computer in the construction industry.
2. Explain why an arch is an effective means of carrying the weight of a long, heavy structure such as a bridge.

The very longest cross suspension bridges. **Susp** suspended from cables n steel wires wound togetl example of a suspension Gate Bridge in San Fran

Fig. 9-14. The Golden Gat is an example of a suspe

3. Explain to the class forces on the different

 1

Fig. 9-15. The Hoover Dam, also known as Boulder Dam, is a dam on the Colorado River. The lake formed behind the dam is Lake Mead.

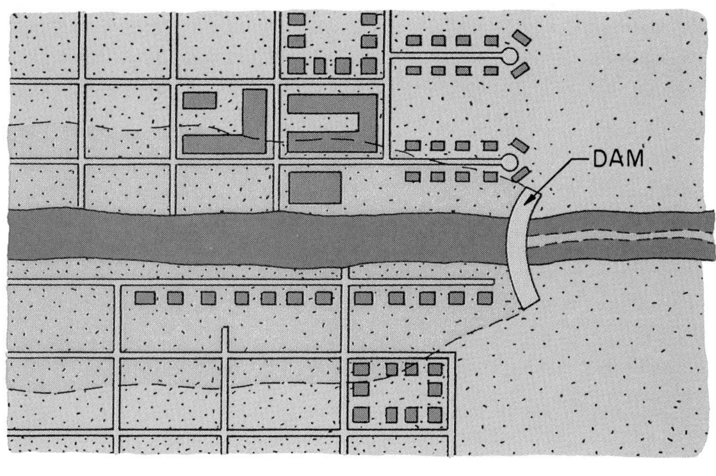

RIVER BEFORE DAM

RIVER AFTER DAM

Fig. 9-16. The area shaded light 2
blue in this illustration represents land that will be submerged after the dam is built. People who live in this area must make arrangements to move.

1. A great deal of soil mechanics and geology as well as engineering is involved in planning and building a dam. Ask a group of students to study and report on these.

2. Discuss the social impact that the building of a dam can have on inhabitants of the area. Consider, for example, the effect on a school district that would be split.

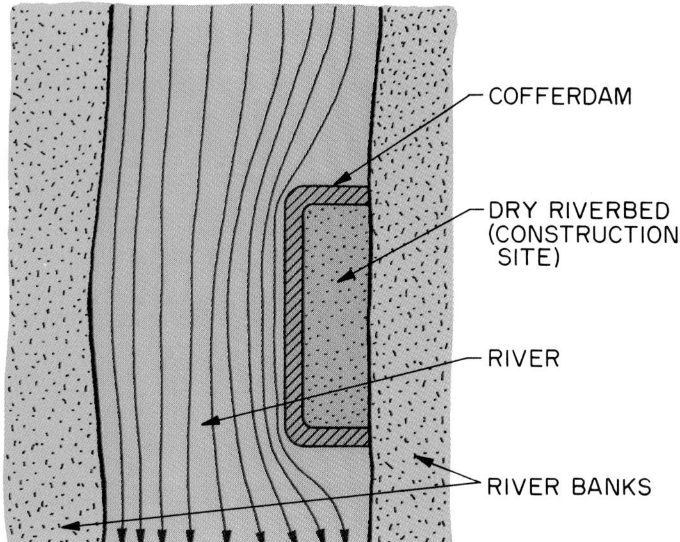

Fig. 9-17. A cofferdam diverts the river so that workers can build the underwater parts of a dam.

Did You Know?

The designers of some dams have considered the needs of migratory fish, such as salmon. For example, adult salmon will try to swim upstream to their spawning grounds. Young salmon will try to swim downstream, away from the spawning grounds. A dam will prevent this. To allow the fish to swim past the dam, fish passes have been built at some dams. These sometimes take the form of fish ladders. A fish ladder consists of a series of small pools. The fish move from one pool to the next. Such conservation measures have been introduced in Canada, the northwest United States, and Scotland.

For Discussion

Are there any dams in or near your community? Are the dams used to create a
water reservoir or to power hydroelectric 1
turbines? Are the dams used for both?

1. Have a student look up and explain to the class what causes quicksand. This will help the class gain a better understanding of the effect that the water behind the dam can have on areas just below the dam.

Construction Facts

TENN-TOM HEAVY CONSTRUCTION

In late 1986, Alabama and Mississippi celebrated the opening of a 234-mile (375-km) waterway. This mammoth waterway connects northeastern Mississippi to the gulf coast of Alabama. It connected the Tennessee and Tombigbee rivers to open up a whole new commercial waterway in the southeastern
1 United States. Its name, appropriately enough, is the Tennessee-Tombigbee Waterway, or Tenn-Tom.

Tenn-Tom is the largest marine construction project ever attempted in the United States. This massive earthmoving job was begun in 1972. Three hundred million cubic yards of earth were moved to prepare the waterway.

To meet the construction schedule, Tenn-Tom constructors spent $43 million on specially designed equipment and put their workers on a three-shift-per-day schedule. One interesting piece of heavy equipment used on the job was a specially-built excavator-loader. Powered by a pair of large bulldozers, the machine could fill a 50-ton dump truck in less than one minute.

One problem with this massive excavation was what to do with the excavated earth. Thirty-eight different disposal sites, located in deep valleys, were the solution. The excavated soil was spread over 5,000 acres (2000 hectares) of land.

1. Discuss the advantages and disadvantages of water transportation for freight. Are projects such as the Tenn-Tom always cost beneficial? For what reason is the federal government usually involved?

CHAPTER 9

REVIEW

Chapter Summary

Many different types of construction projects are designed and built. These include residential buildings, commercial buildings, and industrial buildings. Highway construction is a general term for the construction of a road or street. The construction of an airport is a combination of road construction and highway construction. Tunnels are constructed as underground passageways. They require special construction techniques. Bridges can be constructed in several different ways. There are several types of bridges: slab, arch, truss, cantilever, and suspension. A dam is a structure placed across a river to block the flow of water. A cofferdam enables the builders of the dam to work on dry ground.

Test Your Knowledge 1

1. What are the three basic types of buildings?
2. Give two examples of special construction needs that an industrial plant might have.
3. From what two types of concrete can pavement for highways be made?
4. Name four examples of road construction that must be done to build an airport.
5. Who is responsible for planning and designing most large airports?
6. What technique is used to remove hard rock from a tunnel site?
7. What type of bridge is most commonly used for short spans and light loads?
8. What type of bridge is used to span the longest crossings?
9. What is the purpose of a spillway?
10. What is a cofferdam?

1. The answers to the Test Your Knowledge questions are in the Teacher's Manual at the front of this Teacher's Annotated Edition.

REVIEW

Activities

1. Keep a log of construction projects you see being built. Make notes about what you see happening that interests you. Report your findings to your class.
2. On a sheet of paper, make four columns. Label each column with one of the four major types of construction projects. Plan a trip around your town or city to find and look at the various structures that have been built. In the appropriate column, write a short description of the type of structure. See how many of each type you can find.
3. Select an interesting structure such as one of the following:
   - Gateway Arch
   - Washington Monument
   - Crystal Palace
   - Golden Gate Bridge
   - Great Wall of China
   - Egyptian Pyramids
   - Machu Picchu

   Do library research on your selected structure. Write a one-page report on how it was built. Write also about the human needs that prompted the building of the structure. Report your findings to your class.

CHAPTER 10

THE DECISION TO BUILD

Terms to Know

alterations
bond
feasibility study
interest
letter of commitment
mortgage note
power of eminent domain
private project
public project
renovation
zoning laws

Objectives

When you have finished reading this chapter, you should be able to do the following: 1

- Identify two construction-related alternatives to building a new structure.
- Describe the difference between private and public building projects.
- Describe the process of selecting and acquiring a building site.
- List three sources of funds for construction projects.

1. Resources:
- Chapter 10 Lesson Plan in the Teacher's Manual in this Teacher's Annotated Edition and in the Teacher's Resource Guide.
- Chapter 10 Study Guide in the Student Workbook.
- Chapter 10 Visual Master in the Teacher's Resource Guide.

Every construction project begins with a decision. Someone decides that an existing structure is inadequate. Once that decision is made, many other decisions are necessary. Is a new structure needed, or can an old structure be modified to meet the need? The answer to this question determines what kind of construction work will be necessary. For example, sometimes the structure can be modified to meet the owner's needs. Other structures may present problems that are not easily solved. In these cases, the best solution may be to build a new structure.

MODIFYING AN EXISTING STRUCTURE

Modifying an existing structure can sometimes save the owner a lot of money. Even adding a room onto a house is usually much less expensive than building a new house. Many people
1 therefore decide to modify an existing structure rather than build a new one. Fig. 10-1.

Before modification can begin, the owner must decide what should be modified and the extent of the modification. Some modifications are minor, such as knocking out a wall to combine two rooms, or installing a skylight. Others are major, such as adding a room onto a house. Modifications also include additions such as patios. Fig. 10-2.

The type of modification needed depends on the present condition of the structure. Some owners need to make design alterations to meet their changing space requirements or to increase the attractiveness of the structure. Other owners may want to update part or all of a structure to provide more modern comforts and conveniences.

Alterations

Alterations are changes in the structural form of a building or other structure. These changes are usually made to make the structure more attractive or useful. If the owner of a building decides that the building is no longer adequate for its purpose, he or she may choose to *remodel*, or change, the existing building. A family may decide to add another bedroom to make room for a growing number of family members. The owners

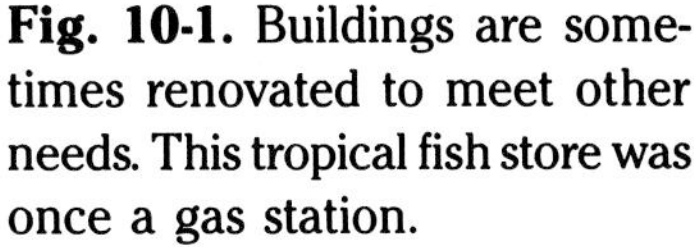

Fig. 10-1. Buildings are sometimes renovated to meet other needs. This tropical fish store was once a gas station.

1. Discuss the following with students. Suppose that a certain building is becoming inadequate. How would you go about determining its adequacy or inadequacy? How would you project future uses for that building? What options would be available when deciding how to handle building modifications? What factors would influence a final decision?

Fig. 10-2. Here a patio and family room addition are being added to an existing home.

of office buildings, supermarkets, and stores frequently remodel their buildings to make them more attractive. Factories are often remodeled to make room for new equipment and machinery.

A major remodeling project may be quite
1 expensive, but it usually costs less than building a new structure. Some contractors specialize in remodeling. These companies do not build new structures. They are experts at remodeling buildings. Most remodeling contractors can examine a proposed remodeling project and give you an idea of how much it will cost to complete the project.

Renovation

Sometimes people who own older buildings find that the buildings no longer meet their needs. However, many of these buildings have attractive characteristics that cannot easily be duplicated. For example, an old house may have a beautiful oak staircase or 10-foot ceilings. The owner of such a building may choose to renovate it.

Renovation is the process of restoring the original charm or style of the building, while at the same time adding modern conveniences such as air conditioning. Fig. 10-3. Often the plumbing and wiring systems also need to be replaced. Because of the nature of the problems that must be fixed, renovation may be a major project. Sometimes renovation even costs as much as new construction. However, the owner is able to keep the attractive feature, such as an oak staircase, without having to pay a high price to have them specially built.

Many cities are now attempting to renovate whole districts that contain old buildings. Some of these cities offer the buildings to potential buyers at an extremely low cost. One condition of these sales is that the buyers renovate the buildings within a certain time period. In this way, a city can clean up its downtown areas. At the same time, it can save historical buildings in these areas—all at a very low cost to the city.

1. Modification of an existing structure can be an inexpensive alternative only if the basic use of the structure is unchanged. One example would be enlarging a commercial building. Sometimes, the basic usage changes. For example, a filling station may be converted to a restaurant. Then many expensive changes may have to be made to the existing structure to bring it up to code.

Fig. 10-3. This house is being renovated. Renovation allows its owner to have a comfortable home and, at the same time, preserve a historical building.

HEALTH & SAFETY

Older homes are sometimes renovated to correct possible hazards. There have been a number of improvements in home construction in the last twenty years. As one example, home wiring systems have been improved. New insulating materials have been developed. Often, renovation in an older home may involve the replacement of outdated and perhaps dangerous electrical wiring. It might also involve the replacement of dangerous asbestos insulations with other insulating materials.

For Discussion

You may be familiar with the processes of
alteration and renovation. Perhaps there are
houses in your neighborhood that have been 1
altered or renovated. Perhaps you have seen
the work being done. Why do you think
the changes were made to the buildings?

BUILDING A NEW STRUCTURE

If the owner decides that altering or renovat-
ing an existing structure will not solve the prob- 2
lem, he or she probably needs to build a new
structure. After the need for the new structure

1. Before modifications are started, the owner must check that zoning regulations, plot restrictions, and building codes will not be violated. Discuss how a person would check this information.

2. Discuss why remodeling contractors are often reluctant to give a firm price on a remodeling job. If you were a remodeling contractor and the owner insisted upon a firm price, how would you decide what to charge?

is established, many more questions need to be answered. For example, what type of structure is needed? Who will pay for the construction? When, where, and how will the structure be built? These and other questions are answered by the owner or owners of the project.

Some construction projects are *privately owned.* This means that they are owned by an individual person or company. For example, most houses are privately owned. Other projects are *publicly owned.* They are paid for with taxes and belong to the public. School buildings and public libraries are common examples of publicly owned projects. Fig. 10-4.

Private Projects

When a construction project belongs to an individual or to a company, it is known as a **private project**. Some private projects are planned to meet the needs of a company or business.

Individual Ownership

Individually owned projects are usually 1
smaller than public projects. Fig. 10-5. The addition of a deck to an existing house is an example of a small, individually owned project. Even 2
the construction of a new house is a relatively small project.

When you first get the idea to build, you will need to ask yourself many questions. As an example, pretend that you want to build a new home for your family. You will need to begin by asking yourself the following questions:

- Do we really need (or want) to build this house?
- Could we add another room onto our old house instead of building a new house?
- How much better will a new house meet our family needs?

If you do decide that you need or want to build a new house, then you must ask more questions and make more decisions.

Fig. 10-4. A school is one type of public project.

1. Have a group of students report on the incentives offered to owners who restore buildings that are designated as historical buildings.
2. Mention that some building codes make allowances for code variances for buildings that have been designated as historical.

Fig. 10-5. Adding a deck to a house is an example of an individually-owned project.

- Can we afford to build a new house?
- What financing is available to help us pay for building a house?
- Can we sell our old house for a fair price?

The answers to these questions are critical. No matter how much you may want, or even need, a new house, you must approach such a project practically. If you can give satisfactory answers to these first six questions, then you can go on to define the details.

- What type of design do we want our new house to have?
- Should we build in town, near schools and shopping center, or in the country?
- What land is available, and at what price?

Corporate Ownership

Many commercial buildings are owned by corporations. Since these buildings are owned by the corporation, they are constructed as private projects. Common examples of private projects are office buildings, hospitals, warehouses, stores, and factories. Fig. 10-6.

In the case of a corporation, the decision to con- 1
struct a new building is made by the board of directors. The board of directors must study the proposed construction from every point of view. Is the building necessary? If so, what type of building would best suit the needs of the corporation? Where is the best place to build the building? Does the corporation need to buy more land or can the building be built on property the company already owns? How will the corporation pay for the building? The company could waste a lot of money by making a wrong decision about any one of these questions. The answers must therefore be carefully thought out before a company can decide to build.

1. Many buildings are constructed as rental or leasing property. Discuss why a corporation might decide to build a new office building to be rented or leased when there were several complexes in the city that are mostly empty. List the reasons on the chalkboard. Be sure to include location as one of the reasons.

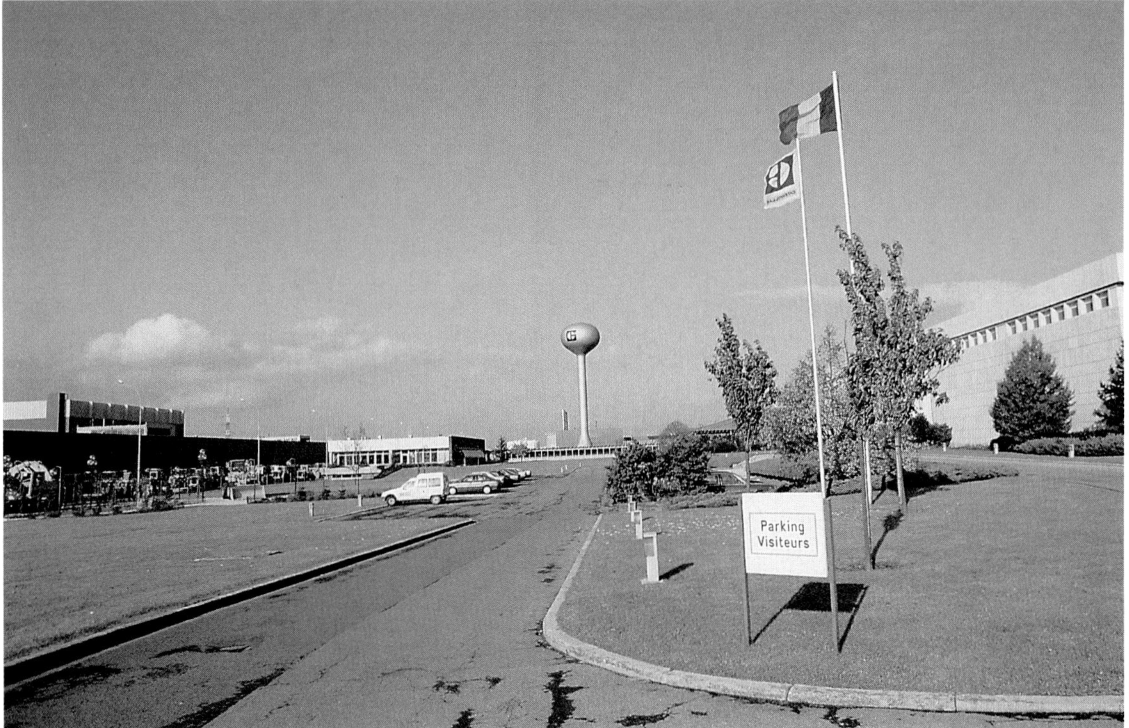

Fig. 10-6. This factory building was built to meet a company's need for manufacturing space.

Public Projects

Some projects are paid for with tax money.
1 These projects belong to the whole community and are known as **public projects**. Public projects are planned to meet the needs of the community. Fig. 10-7. Some of the projects are rather small. A new sidewalk in a city park and minor road repairs are examples of relatively small public projects. These projects may cost only a few thousand dollars. A new interstate highway is considered a large project. A new airport is also a large project. These projects may cost millions of dollars each.

1. Select a public project that has been proposed for your area. Have the students bring news articles about the proposal as it progresses. Ask them to share these with the class during the school year. If approval has not been obtained before school closes, you may want to continue following the progress next year.

Some public projects take a long time to get started because there are so many people involved in the initial, or first, decision-making process. Sometimes it is necessary to pass around a petition and get signatures from taxpayers who show their support for a project. Fig. 10-8. In some cases, people have the opportunity to vote for or against a project. Sometimes a public hearing is called so the proposed project may be discussed publicly. Fig. 10-9.

Fig. 10-7. This highway and the bridge in the background were built to meet the public's need for better transportation facilities. 1

Fig. 10-8. Sometimes taxpayers sign a petition to show their support for a proposed public project.

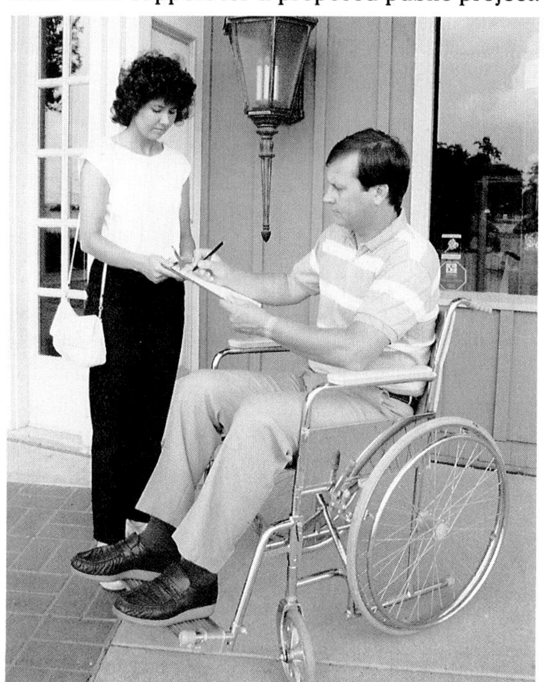

Fig. 10-9. A public hearing allows people to speak for or against a proposed project.

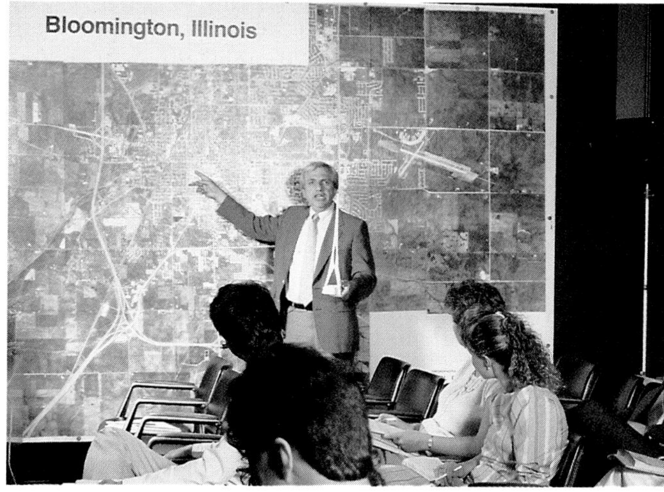

1. Point out to the class that the first group of questions listed in deciding whether or not to build a new construction project deals with needs and alternatives to building. The second group deals with financial matters. Emphasize that the planning process should begin only after these have been answered.

Did You Know?

The sites of many cities have been inhabited for hundreds of years. Often, when the foundations are being dug for a new building, workers unearth items from another time. When this happens, construction may be halted so that the site can be studied by archeologists. These are scientists who study the way humans lived a long time ago. They do this by studying their tools and weapons. Construction may be delayed to allow archeologists to study a building site more closely. If the site is very important in the eyes of the archeologist, building may be halted, or even called off. In other instances, there may be an attempt to excavate a part of the site and perhaps open it to public display.

Before construction can begin on a public project, a great deal of planning must be done. Many questions must be answered. The first questions are the same as those for a private project. Is there a need for the project? How will the project benefit the community? How will the project be financed?

After the initial decision has been made to
1 build a project, a **feasibility study** is done to gather information about the proposed project. Good information is important because it helps people make good decisions. A feasibility study helps the decision-makers decide if it is feasible, or practical, to build the project. It includes information on the cost of the project and financing options as well as the availability of land and essential materials.

1. Explain that feasibility studies are done for public construction projects. Obtain a feasibility study and share it with the class. Then discuss the assumptions that have been made in the study. What would happen if one or more of the assumptions was incorrect? Explain to the class that this is the process that must be followed by those evaluating the study.

For Discussion

The book discusses projects that are privately owned and publicly owned, can you identify some publicly owned buildings in your town or city? What are they used for?

BUILDING SITES

As you learned in Chapter 6, the location of a construction project is called a *site*. The site is an important part of any construction project. The type of foundation used for a building, for example, depends on the type of soil and, to some extent, the slope of the land. The owner must either choose a site that is appropriate for the proposed structure or design a structure that is appropriate for the site. Because choosing a site is a critical part of a construction project, gathering information about the site is part of the feasibility study. Many potential sites are studied to find the one that is best suited to the project.

Selecting the Site

Much of the success of the building project depends on making a wise site choice. Individual owners are responsible for choosing their own building sites. In private industry, managers and the board of directors must approve the site. For public projects, government officials make the site decision. Fig. 10-10.

Zoning Laws

When selecting a suitable site, the owner, directors, or officials must consider the local zon-

Fig. 10-10. Aerial photos such as this one can help owners or government officials select the best site for a new project.

ing laws. Cities are divided into residential, business, and industrial zones. The site for the pro-
1 ject must be in the proper zone. **Zoning laws** tell what kinds of structures can be built in each zone. Fig. 10-11. Residential zones are areas reserved for homes. Factories and warehouses are located in industrial zones. Industrial areas are set apart because the noise, smoke, and traffic of industries can be unpleasant in a residential area. Fig. 10-12. Commercial zones are usually located near residential zones. This allows people to get to stores and offices easily.

Did You Know?

Zoning laws were introduced in some German and Swedish cities about 1880. These laws applied to land that was being built on just outside the city. Most of the zoning laws at this time were concerned with regulating the height of buildings. In the United States, most zoning laws are concerned with regulating the use of land for a certain purpose. Thus, some locations
are zoned "commercial," or suitable only 2
for businesses. Other locations are zoned "residential," or suitable only for houses and apartments.

Other Considerations

Some of the other factors that must be considered are the location, cost, and characteristics of the site. Fig. 10-13. Land that is in the city, close to schools and shopping centers, is generally more expensive than property in the

1. Obtain a local zoning map and go over it with the class. Discuss the various zone classifications.

2. Using a zoning map, point out industrial parks, commercial areas, and residential areas. Are commercial areas concentrated near main streets? Why? Explain the reasons for strip zoning.

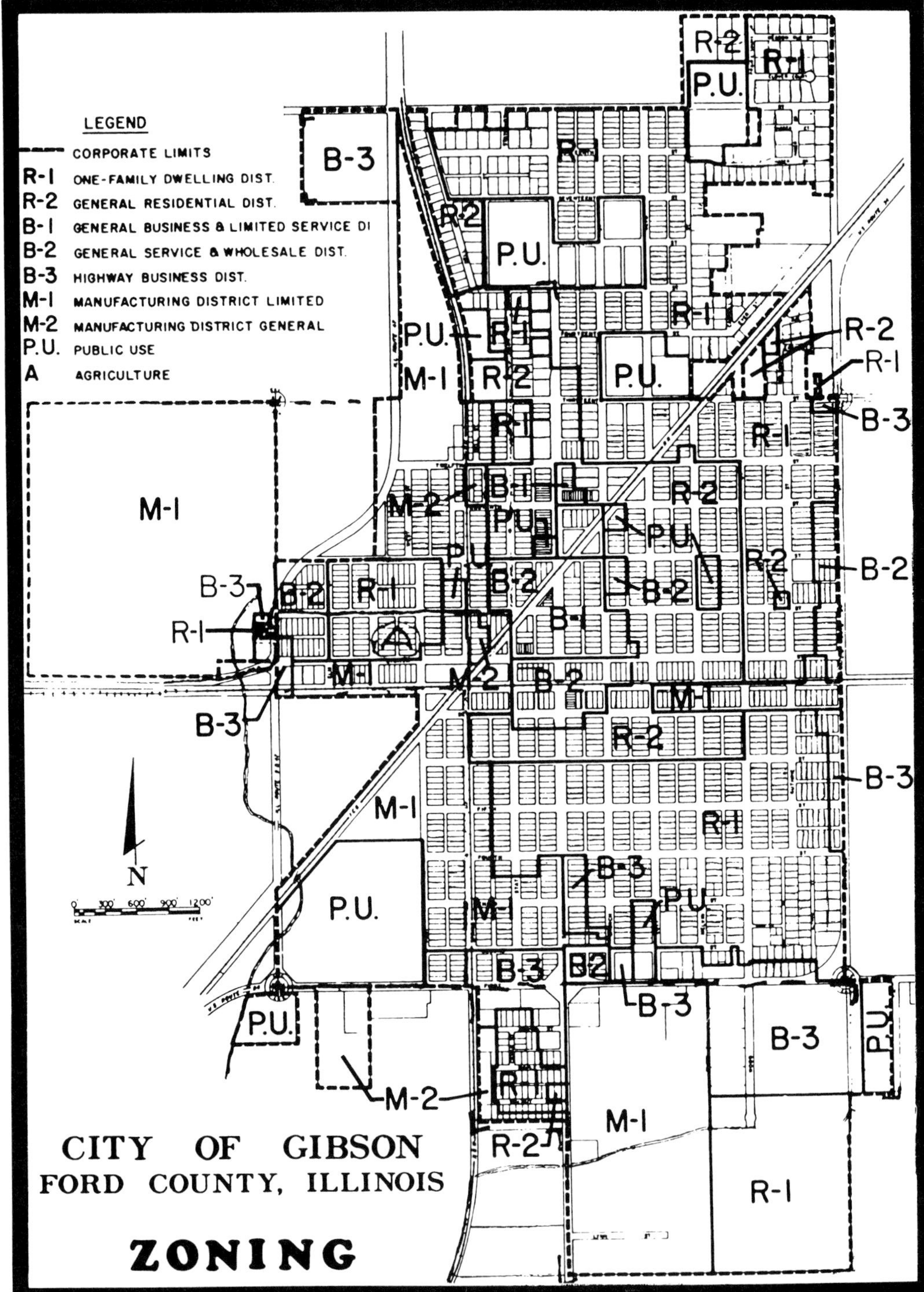

1

Fig. 10-11. The zoning map indicates the various zones in a city.

1. Point out that a zoning plan for most cities is a compromise between the ideal and what is practical. Is there any way that the zoning for a piece of property can be changed? Ask a student or group of students to report to the class on the procedure required locally.

Fig. 10-12. This area is zoned *industrial* to protect residential property owners from noise, smoke, and traffic.

Fig. 10-13. In selecting a site for
construction, many factors must
be considered. Among these fac-
1 tors are location, cost, physical
characteristics, site considerations, utilities, zoning, and
accessibility.

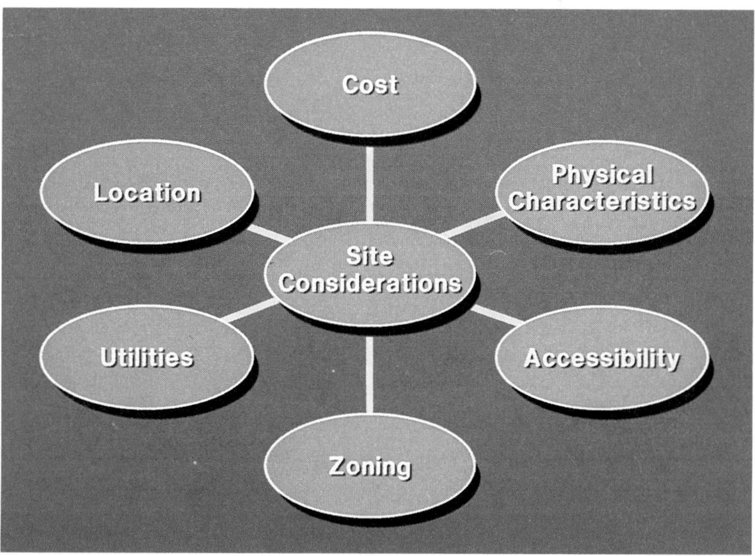

1. Divide the class into several groups and present them with this problem. You are going to build a fast-food restaurant in your city. Decide on its general location. Then look for appropriate building sites. Narrow the field to two sites. Analyze each site, using the criteria mentioned in the text and any others you feel are important. Rank and explain your choices.

country. Accessibility is an important factor, especially for residential and commercial buildings. Is the land easy to get to? Are the roads paved? Fig. 10-14. Utilities can be a critical issue if the property is too far out in the country for city water and sewers.

All the physical characteristics of the site, such as hills, trees, and soil conditions, must be considered. Is the land suited to the type of structure to be built? How much earthworking must be done to achieve the level, stable conditions
1 necessary for building a structure? All of these things need to be evaluated carefully to be sure that the most desirable site is selected.

Did You Know?

A wetland is land that contains much soil moisture. Swamps, bogs, and marshes are wetlands. In the past, wetlands often were drained. The land could then be used for farming or for building sites. Wetlands, however, provide a refuge for certain birds. They also allow a variety of interesting plants to grow. Today, there is an effort to preserve wetlands. A building site that is partially wetland is often carefully evaluated. Often, in the interests of conservation, construction may be limited to that part of the site that is not judged to be wetland.

Fig. 10-14. A paved road helps make a site easily accessible.

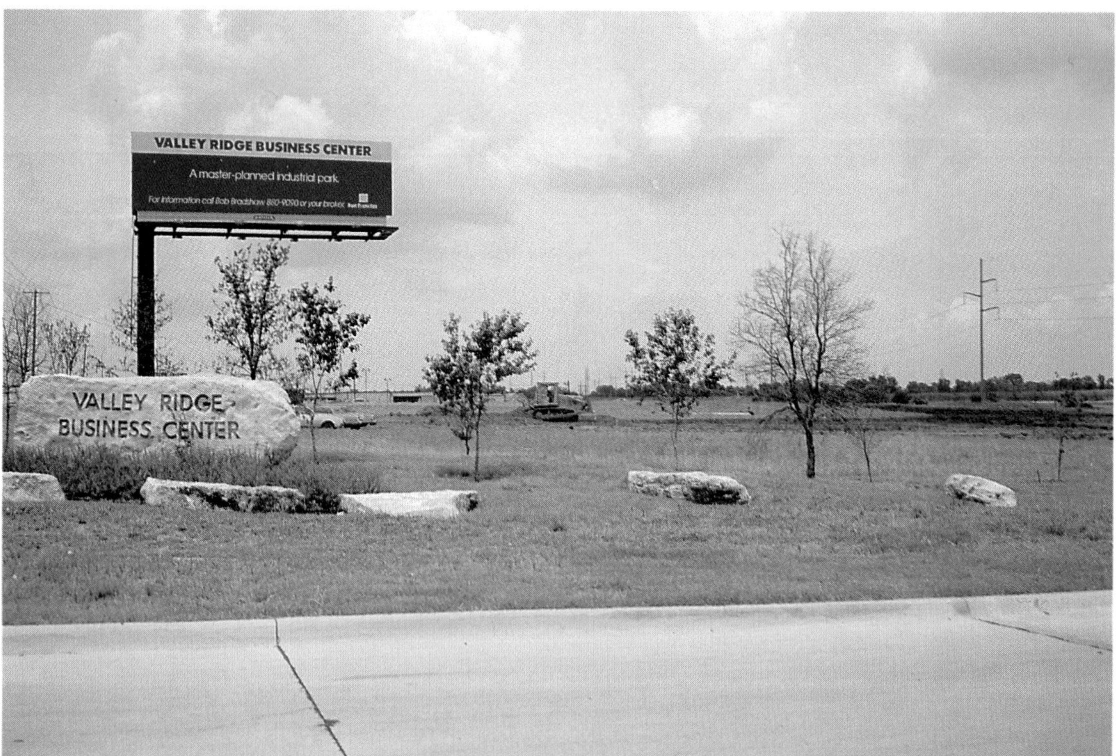

1. Ask each student to respond to the following questions in writing. You are considering having a new home built. How would you go about selecting a site? What considerations would you use for making your decision? Ask each student to list these considerations in a checklist. The considerations should be listed in the order of their importance to them.

Acquiring the Site

Once the site is selected, steps must be taken to acquire (get) the property. Sometimes this is an easy procedure that takes only a few days. Generally, however, acquiring the site is an involved process that takes a long time to complete.

Individually Owned Projects

Property for private projects is usually acquired by negotiation. *Negotiation* is the process of working out an agreement between the buyer and the seller. Imagine that you have a bicycle for sale and someone wants to buy it. The two of you will have to negotiate a final sale price with which you will both be happy. Then the sale can take place.

Negotiations for land are usually handled by a real estate agent. A real estate agent is someone who specializes in helping people find and purchase suitable property. The real estate agent helps the buyer and seller come to an agreement. Fig. 10-15.

Once the terms of the sale are agreed upon,
the sale must be made legal. When the buyer 1
and seller agree, they sign a contract. A contract is an agreement in writing that states the
terms of the sale. The written agreement ensures
that both the buyer and the seller know exactly
what is being sold and for what price. Then the
money changes hands and the land sale is
recorded in the county records. At this point, 2
the ownership of the site is legally changed.

Corporate-owned and Public Projects

The procedures for buying property for public projects and for large commercial projects are similar to those for buying individually-owned property. One difference is that the terms of the contract are usually much more complex.

Fig. 10-15. A real estate agent handles the negotiations between seller and buyer.

1. Obtain a copy of a real estate contract. Emphasize that any contract should be completely understood before it is signed. Point out that it is wise to ask questions.

2. Inform the class that property has not really been transferred until the deed has been recorded in the appropriate office in the county where it is located.

Another major difference is that an attorney is usually contacted instead of or in addition to a real estate agent. By using an attorney, the buyers make sure that all of the complicated terms of the contract are legal.

Sometimes several *tracts*, or pieces, of land are needed for a public project. Fig. 10-16. Some of the land may be owned by someone who does not want to sell. However, through the **power of eminent domain**, the government has the right to buy the property for public purposes even though the owner does not want to sell.
1 The government *condemns*, or takes, the
property in the interest of the general public. Fig. 10-16. The owner is given a fair price for the land, so he or she is not cheated, only inconvenienced.

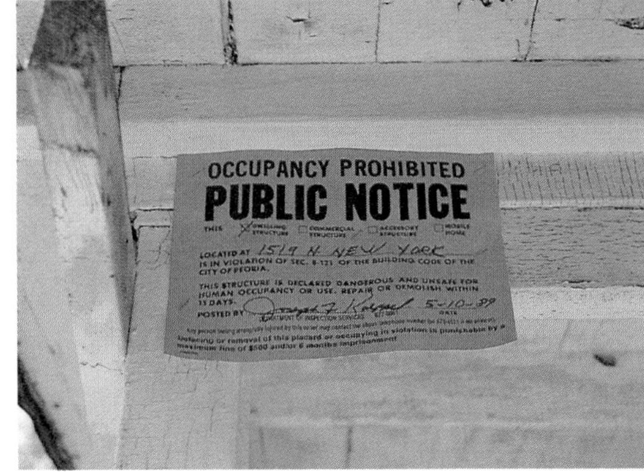

Fig. 10-16. This notice states that the property has been condemned. The building will be demolished.

For Discussion

The book discusses the need for carefully selecting a building site. All building sites are not level. In your town or city, can you point out ways in which a building has been designed for a building site that is not level?

FINANCING

After the plans for a building project have been completed, the method of financing the project must be determined. If the project is privately owned, the money is usually borrowed. For a public project, the money comes from taxes or bonds.

Mortgages

Very few people have enough cash to pay for an entire building project. The money must be borrowed from a lending institution such as a bank or a savings and loan association. First, a loan application must be submitted. Fig. 10-17. The bank checks the income and the credit rating of the person or group applying for the loan. 2
The bank needs to know whether the applicant has the ability to pay back the loan.

Letter of Commitment

Once the loan is approved, the lending institution prepares a **letter of commitment**. This states the terms and conditions that they require for payment of the loan. This letter of commitment states the loan's interest rate and the number of payments in which the borrower must pay back the loan.

The letter of commitment is important both to the lender and to the applicant. It states the specifics of the loan so that the applicant is not surprised at the last moment. The applicant knows in advance whether he or she can make the payments comfortably. For the lender, the

1. Ask a student or group of students to report to the class about condemnation proceedings.

2. Emphasize the importance of a good credit rating. Discuss with the students how a credit rating is established. Discuss those actions that can damage it.

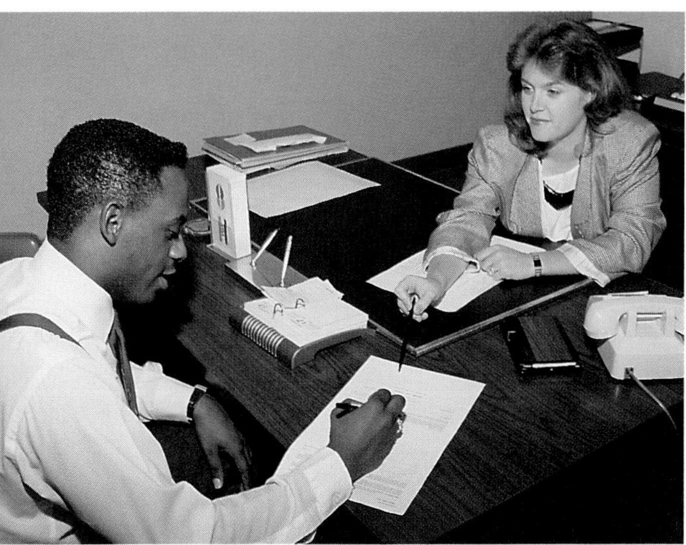

Fig. 10-17. The information on the loan application helps the lending institution decide whether to loan money to the applicant.

letter of commitment is a guarantee that the applicant is serious about wanting a loan and is willing to risk a penalty if he or she backs out at the last minute.

Mortgage Note

The next document that is signed is called
1 a **mortgage note**. The mortgage note is actually two documents. The *note* is a document in which the lender agrees to finance a project under certain conditions and at a specified interest rate. The *mortgage* pledges the property as security for the loan. In other words, if the borrower does not make the monthly payments, the property becomes the property of the lending institution that holds the mortgage.

Interest

All lending institutions charge interest on the money they lend. **Interest** is the price the borrower pays for using the lending institution's money. The rate of interest is usually expressed as a percentage of the total amount of the loan. For example, suppose that a person borrowed $100 for one year at a yearly interest rate of 10 percent. At the end of the loan period the borrower would owe the lender the $100 plus 10 percent ($10), or a total of $110. Interest makes lending worth the lender's risk and effort to make the loan. The lender decides what the interest rate will be.

Because of interest, a *mortgagor*, or borrower, actually pays much more for the property than the original selling price. However, without a mortgage, many people would never be able to own property and have a home. Most mortgage loans are made for a period between ten and thirty years. Thirty years may seem like a long time to be paying for a house, but the longer the time period is, the lower the monthly payments are. Many people prefer to stretch their house payments over many years. However, the faster the loan is repaid, the less the total cost of the property will be.

Did You Know?

It is important that mortgages be recorded. Unless there is a record of a mortgage, it would be possible for the person who has taken out the mortgage (the mortgagor) to take out another mortgage with another person. Thus, the mortgagor would be borrowing twice using the same property. By law, on the continent of Europe, mortgages have had to be recorded since the eighteenth century. In North America, their recording has been required since the nineteenth century.

1. Illustrate the total amount paid (principal and interest) on loans of various interest rates for various time periods. Contrast the difference in monthly payments between a 15-year, a 20-year, and a 30-year mortgage. Ask the students to draw some conclusions from this information. Ask them to write a one-page paper on what they have discovered.

Bonds

Bonds are usually used to help finance com-
1 mercial and public projects. A **bond** is a type
of note by which various amounts of money are borrowed from many different people or institutions at once. Fig. 10-18. The purpose of selling bonds is to obtain money for construction. For example, school districts sometimes sell bonds to finance a new school. Bonds are a common way of financing public projects such as schools, highways, and water treatment plants.

Bonds can be sold to individuals or to lending institutions. The seller pays interest on the bond over a certain number of years, called its *lifetime*. The lifetime of a bond may be 5, 10, or 20 years. In addition, the seller promises to repurchase the bonds for their face value. The *face value* is the stated amount of the bond. For example, a $1,000 bond has a face value of $1,000.

Appropriations

Public projects may also be financed with money collected as taxes. Federal, state, and local
governments *appropriate*, or set aside, tax
money for particular construction projects. The 2
appropriation money is usually placed in a special account at a bank. This money is used to pay for the site and for all the construction costs. Fig. 10-19.

For Discussion

In the area surrounding your school, there may be several types of buildings—residential, industrial, and commercial. Are there any public projects that may have been financed with bonds or with money collected as taxes?

Fig. 10-18. People buy bonds as an investment. The bonds are redeemable with interest on a specified date.

Fig. 10-19. Tax money was used to pay for the construction of this space shuttle launch site.

1. Discuss how the financial rating of a governmental unit affects the interest rate on any bonds they may issue. Point out that corporations and governmental units have credit ratings.

2. Have any commemorative or memorial structures been built in your city recently? How were they paid for? Who is responsible for their maintenance? What is the annual maintenance cost?

Construction Facts

CHUNNEL UNDER THE CHANNEL CONNECTS ENGLAND AND FRANCE

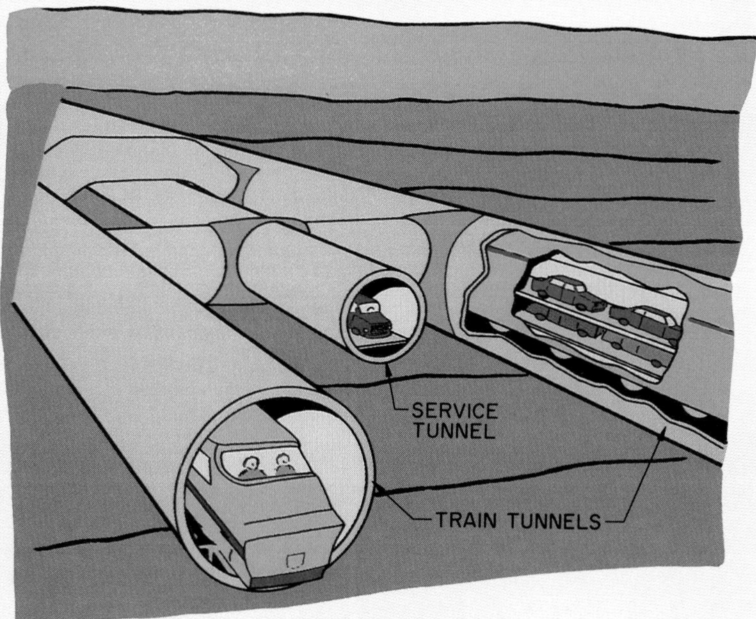

1 For over 200 years, engineers have dreamed of a tunnel beneath the English Channel that would connect England and France. Now it looks as if the "Chunnel" may one day be a reality. In 1987 work began on what is the largest civil engineering project in the history of Western Europe.

The Chunnel consists of three parallel tunnels. Two of the tunnels will be for double-deck railroad trains carrying passengers, automobiles, trucks, and buses. The trains will travel at speeds up to 100 mph. The smaller middle tunnel will be used for service and ventilation.

The tunnels will be about 300 feet below the surface and thirty-one miles long. Twenty-three of those miles will be under the water.

Both England and France are working on the Chunnel, which requires about 1000 workers.

The Chunnel is scheduled for completion in 1993. A second tunnel involving drive-through auto tunnels has been proposed for the year 2000.

1. Point out that the idea of a cross-channel tunnel was first proposed in 1753. In the 1870s, shafts were begun, but were abandoned. It is the present state of construction technology that makes the Chunnel possible. Also, traffic between England and the continent has increased to a point that it seems that the Chunnel will be profitable.

CHAPTER 10 REVIEW

Chapter Summary

Modifying an existing structure can sometimes save money. Modifications will depend on the condition of the structure. Alterations are changes in the structural form of a building. Renovation is the process of restoring the original style of a building, while adding modern conveniences. Some construction projects are privately owned. Others are publicly owned. A feasibility study gathers information about a proposed building project.

The location of a construction project is called a site. Zoning laws tell what kinds of structures can be built on each site. Acquiring the site can sometimes be an involved process. Negotiation is the process of working out an agreement between the buyer and the seller. A contract is a written agreement that states the terms of the sale. The power of eminent domain allows the government to buy property for public purposes even though the owner does not want to sell.

A letter of commitment states the terms and conditions a lending institution requires for payment of a loan. A note is a document in which the lender agrees to finance a project under certain conditions and at a specified lending rate. A mortgage pledges the property as security for a loan. Interest is the price the borrower pays for using the lending institution's money. A bond is a type of note by which various amounts of money are borrowed from many different people and institutions at once.

Test Your Knowledge 1

1. What are the two main types of modifications that can be made to a structure?
2. What are the two main types of project ownership?
3. What is the purpose of a feasibility study?
4. What is the name of the laws that control the locations at which different kinds of structures can be built?
5. Name three factors that must be considered before a site is purchased.
6. What document is a written agreement stating the terms of a sale?
7. What is the power of eminent domain?
8. How is money usually obtained to finance privately-owned projects?
9. In what two ways can a public construction project be financed?
10. What is a bond?

1. The answers to the Test Your Knowledge questions are in the Teacher's Manual at the front of this Teacher's Annotated Edition.

REVIEW

Activities

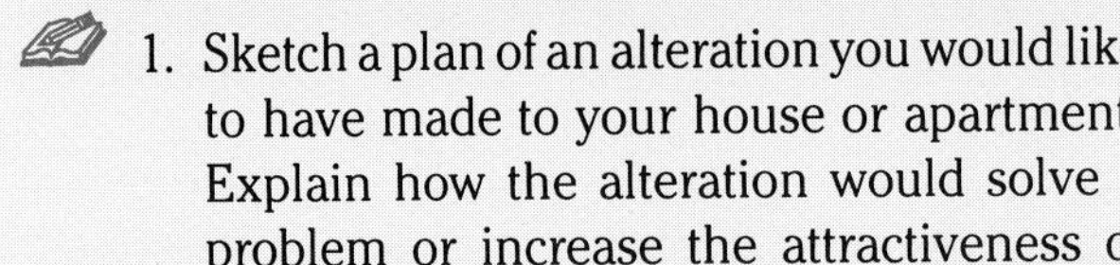

1. Sketch a plan of an alteration you would like to have made to your house or apartment. Explain how the alteration would solve a problem or increase the attractiveness of your home.
2. Do research on careers in real estate. Write a one-page report on the types of real estate personnel and their responsibilities.
3. Obtain a loan application from a bank or other lending institution in your community. Read the application carefully. Describe how the information asked for on the application can help the lending institution decide whether to loan money to an applicant.

CHAPTER 11

DESIGNING AND ENGINEERING THE PROJECT

Terms to Know

architectural drawings
Construction Specification Institute (CSI)
consultant
dead load
designing
detail drawing
drawings
electrical plans
elevations
engineering
floor plan
infrastructure
live load
mechanical plans
preliminary designs
presentation model
scale models
section drawing
site plan
specifications
specification writers
structural drawing
structural engineering
study model

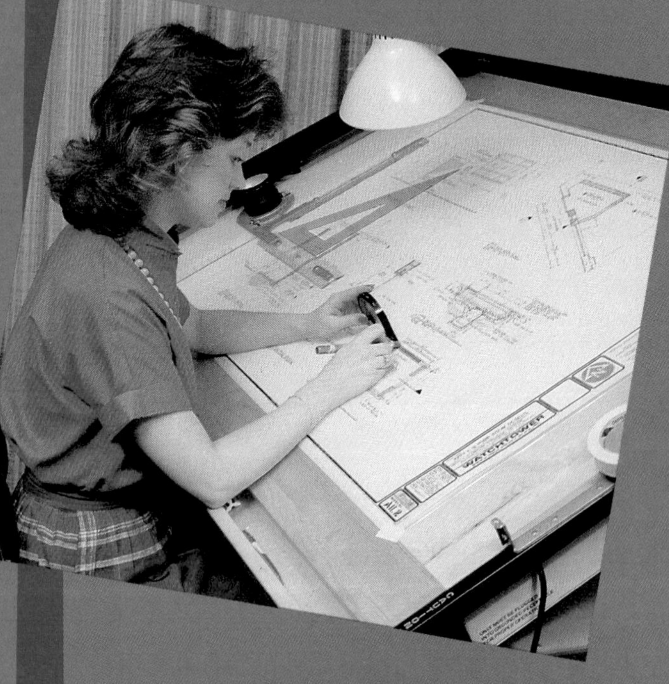

Objectives

When you have finished reading this chapter, you should be able to do the following: 1

- Explain the difference between designing and engineering.
- Name two important aspects of design.
- Define live and dead loads and give an example of each.
- Describe the three general categories of engineering.
- Describe the various drawings used in the final design.
- Explain who provides architectural and engineering services.

1. Resources:
- Chapter 11 Lesson Plan in the Teacher's Manual in this Teacher's Annotated Edition and in the Teacher's Resource Guide.
- Chapter 11 Study Guide in the Student Workbook.
- Chapter 11 Visual Master in the Teacher's Resource Guide.

Every construction project starts with a plan. The plan identifies all the details of the project. It is developed by many different people, such as architects, engineers, drafters, and specification writers.

Creating a design, or designing, is the first step in a construction project. The design of a project is closely related to two other essential steps: project management and building.

The project plan is developed by designing and engineering. **Designing** is the process of deciding what a structure will look like and how it will function. **Engineering** is the process of figuring out how the structure will be built and what structural materials will be used. Fig. 11-1.

DESIGNING

Designing a project is a challenge. A design can be entirely new. A design can also result from several ideas combined to meet the needs of a specific project. Everything about the project must be designed: its shape, style, size, and layout.

If a construction project is not well designed, thousands of dollars can be lost. If problems are found in the design after the project has been built, any needed changes may be very costly. Expensive mistakes can be avoided if the design is carefully planned and prepared.

The two most important aspects of design are
function and appearance. A good design must 1
have a balance between the two. A design that looks nice but does not do what it is supposed to do is not a good design. A design that meets the needs of the owner but does not look good is not a good design, either.

Fig. 11-1. The plans for almost all structures are developed through designing and engineering. This structure is designed to be attractive and functional. It is engineered to house spectators and players safely during sporting events.

1. Explain that the job of a good designer is to guide the owner in a series of decisions that will result in an attractive and functional design. He or she must point out the consequences of certain design decisions and their cost. Many people like everything they see. Some of these things will be incompatible either visually or functionally.

Designing a Functional Structure

The first step in designing a functional structure is to gather information about its proposed use. For example, assume that a new school is being designed. The designer must find out how many classrooms will be needed and what size the classrooms should be. The designer also needs to know how many students are expected to attend the school. The number of students affects the size of the walkways as well as the size of the auditorium and the lunchroom. Another thing the designer should know is the approximate age of the students. Very young students may require modified drinking fountains and low classroom cabinets, among other things.
1 Fig. 11-2.

The designer must also be aware of more general design characteristics. These include ease of maintenance, traffic flow, and energy efficiency. These characteristics are common to almost all structures. The design to meet such needs differs according to the type of structure. A good functional design meets the owner's needs, is easy to maintain, has a smooth traffic flow, and is as energy efficient as possible.

Designing an Attractive Structure

The *appearance* of the structure is the way it looks. Appearance is important because it gives an overall impression of the building. The
appearance of a structure affects the way peo- 2
ple feel about it. It should reflect the activities that take place within the building. For example, a school should not look like a factory. A shopping center that looks like a hospital may not attract many customers. Designers are careful to consider the effect of appearance on the people that use the building.

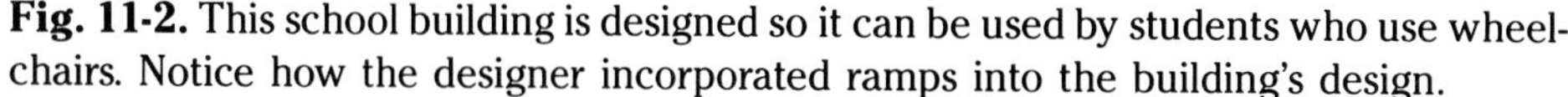
Fig. 11-2. This school building is designed so it can be used by students who use wheelchairs. Notice how the designer incorporated ramps into the building's design.

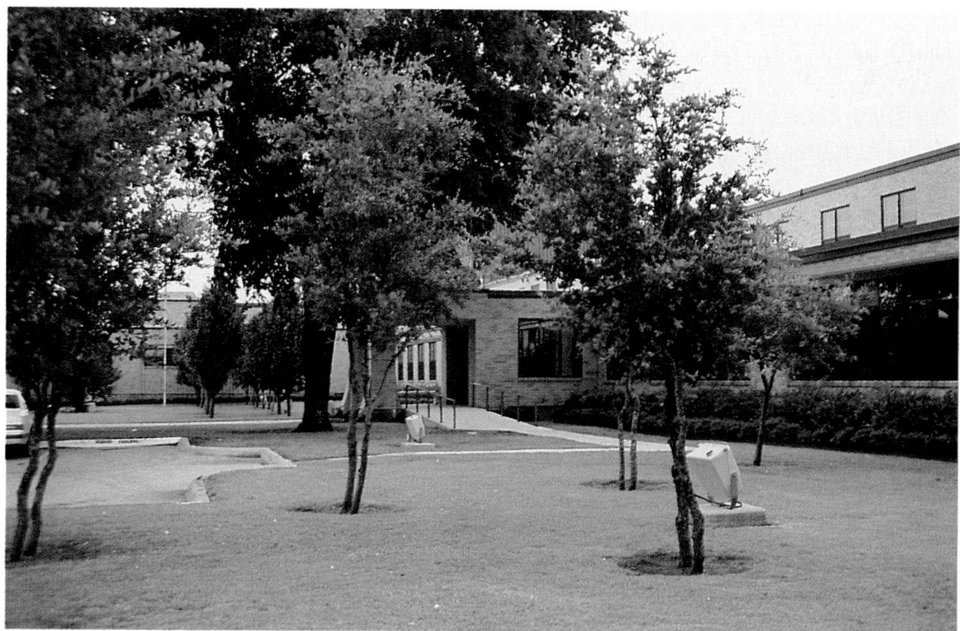

1. Explain how the fire and safety standards of building codes enter into the functional design of a building.

2. Discuss how the appearance of a building affects how you feel about the building. Ask for examples of buildings that make the student feel good and others that do not.

1 The structure must also fit into its surroundings. Fig. 11-3. For example, buildings located in the downtown area of a city usually look different than buildings located in the country. A country home would look as out-of-place in the city as a city home would in the country. Sometimes a structure can fit into its environment even though it is quite different from its surroundings. Examples are the Gateway Arch in St. Louis and the Statue of Liberty in New York. Both are monuments with unique designs, but each fits into its surroundings. Fig. 11-4.

Fig. 11-3. This house was designed to fit into its environment. (*Frank Lloyd Wright, Fallingwater*)

Fig. 11-4. Some structures fit into their environments even though they are different from their surroundings.

1. Use the split-level house as an example of a building that must fit into its environment. For what types of lots are such houses especially designed?

Did You Know?

In designing a building, an architect must consider many different things. One of the things that the architect must consider is scale. In the case of a building, scale is the proportion between one part of a building and its other parts. Proper scale in a building is important if the building is to be attractive.

The temples of ancient Greece have a pleasing scale. Among the many pleasing features of those temples are the columns. In building these temples, the Greek builders employed the base of the column as a building module. A module is a unit of measurement. All of the measurements in the temple were based on this module. This helped ensure a proper sense of scale for the building.

Making Preliminary Designs

The design process begins with the identification of the project. The need for the proposed structure is established. Next, information is gathered and evaluated to see if it is possible and practical to build the proposed structure.

An architect and an engineer are hired to help design the project. They must know the owner's requirements. They must ask some important questions to be able to design the proper building. These questions include:

- For what will the structure be used?
- What type of structure is best suited to the owner's requirements?
- How much will the structure cost?
- What zoning and title restrictions apply?

The opportunity for future expansion and the availability of utilities are also considered at this time.

Once the owner decides that the project is possible and practical, the designer begins his or her work. The designer begins by making **preliminary designs**, or first sketches of what 1
the structure might look like. During this process, many sketches are made. Fig. 11-5. All of the sketches are saved for evaluation at a later time. Not all of these preliminary ideas will be usable. However, some of the ideas shown in the sketches may provide solutions to problems that occur later in the designing process.

The designer seldom comes up with the final design right away. The preliminary designs are usually *refined*, or improved. The best ideas are then selected. Better drawings are made, showing these ideas. Ideas from several different designs may be combined into one new design. The designer then studies and compares the attractiveness, function, and efficiency of each refined design.

Finally, the designer selects his or her best ideas and presents them to the owner. The owner chooses one design to be developed into the final design and makes the decision to go ahead with the project. The plans can now be started.

For Discussion

Suppose that you are preparing the first design sketches for a children's treehouse. What design characteristics would you need to consider?

1. Discuss why the designer resorts to sketching rather than producing more formal drawings for preliminary designs. Discuss this technique of coming up with many ideas, refining the best of them, and then combining several into a design that might be acceptable. The designer may have several different designs or several variations of the same design to present to the owner.

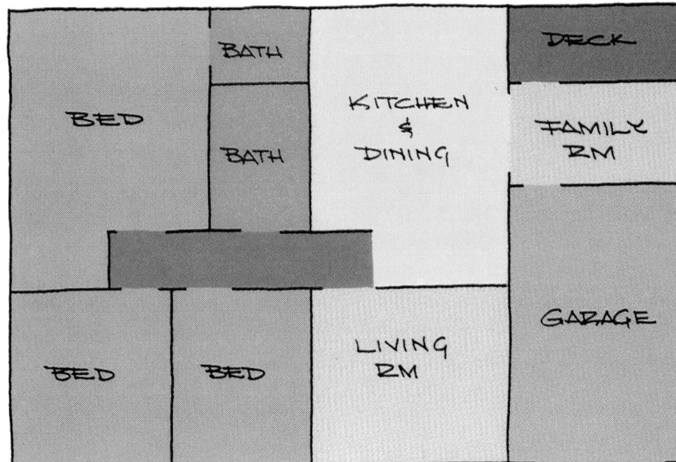

Fig. 11-5. These sketches show some of the designer's preliminary design ideas for a house.

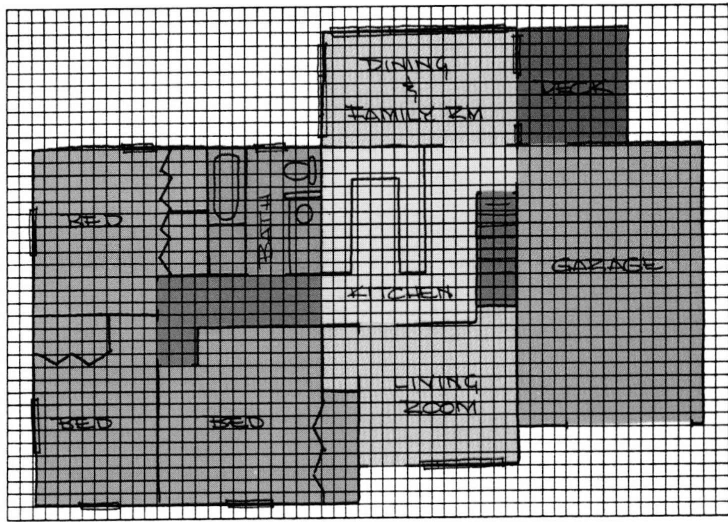

ENGINEERING

The design determines the layout and appear-
1 ance of the structure. However, other factors must be determined before a structure can be built. Engineers must calculate the sizes and types of materials needed to build the structure properly. They must find the answers to questions such as these:

- What size foundation is needed?
- How much reinforcement is needed in the concrete?
- What size pipes and wires are needed?
- How much air conditioning is needed?

The solutions to these problems can be found by the engineering process.

Engineering a structure means figuring out how it will be put together and how it will work. Fig. 11-6. To know which materials should be used in a structure, engineers must predict how the materials will act under certain conditions.

1. Explain that architects are able to provide much of the engineering portion of a building design. For example, they must do some preliminary calculations in order to keep the design from being impossible to engineer. However, most architects enjoy the work of layout and visual design much more. Thus, they leave the engineering portions for others.

Fig. 11-6. Before construction of this bridge could begin, engineers had to predict its behavior under high, unfavorable winds.

Their predictions are based on known mathematical and scientific principles.

To engineer the size of a building's foundation, it is necessary to know the type of soil on which the building will be built. The engineer must also know how much weight the soil can carry. The weight of the proposed structure must
1 also be known. Engineers can tell how much a structure will weigh. They can do this by calculating the weights of all the materials to be used. The size of the foundation can be determined from these figures.

1. Point out that, in addition to the weight of materials in the structure, the weight of anything placed in the building must be included when loads are calculated on the footings.

Did You Know?

Many engineering advances have contributed to the development of the modern high-rise building. One of these advances was the use of steel in building construction. Another advance was the ability to sink deeper foundations. This was done by using concrete that extended down to the bedrock. These advances, along with a number of other important advances, allowed architects to design taller buildings.

Structural Engineering

Structural engineering is the process of selecting appropriate materials from which to build a structure. For example, structural engineers use formulas and scientific principles to determine the stress that will be placed on the finished structure. They can then decide which materials to use in a structure and what size each type of material has to be. The foundation and the framework of the walls and roof are the most important structural parts. The structural engineers must be sure that these parts can safely carry the load they are expected to support.

Loads

To engineer a structure, engineers must know how to figure loads. The *load* is the amount of weight the structure will have to support and the forces it will have to withstand. There are
two types of loads: dead loads and live loads. 2
The **dead load** of a structure is the combined weight of all its materials. A dead load is constant; it is always there. Concrete, lumber, carpet, and even paint contribute to the dead load.

2. After discussing live and dead loads, hand out a list of items and forces that can be part of or present in a building. Have the students identify each as a live or dead load.

Fig. 11-7. Everything you see in this picture is part of the dead load of the structure.

Fig. 11-7. A **live load** is a variable, or changeable load. It is one that is there only some of the
time. People and furniture are part of the live
load in a building. Snow on the roof and wind
pushing against the side of the building are also 1
considered part of the live load. Fig. 11-8.

Safety

After the engineers have done all of the necessary calculations, they study the figures to be
sure the building will be safe. When they are
satisfied, the engineers add a safety factor into
their calculations. A safety factor is extra strength 2
that is built into a structure to provide a wide
margin of safety. For example, an elevator
designed to hold ten people will hold one or
two more before it will fail. It has a safety factor
to help prevent accidents.

Fig. 11-8. Snow is part of the live load of a building.

1. Emphasize that not all loads will be in the same direction or from the same sources. Computers have simplified many of the needed calculations.

2. Find out how much is added to engineering calculations to provide a safety factor. Discuss why this amount has been decided upon. Why not make the building even stronger?

Mechanical and Electrical Engineering

The mechanical and electrical setups of a structure are commonly referred to as its **infrastructure**. Fig. 11-9. For many small projects, the general designer plans the placement and installation of the infrastructure. He or she also specifies the type and size of wires, pipes, and other materials needed to meet safety standards and building codes. Most large projects require the services of mechanical and electrical engineers. These specialists design the complicated mechanical and electrical systems for hotels, large office complexes, and similar structures.

Mechanical Engineering

The mechanical devices in a building are
1 usually classified by system. The plumbing system provides drinking water and carries away wastewater. Every part of this system has to be engineered. The sizes of all the pipes, the hot water heater, and the drinking fountains have to be chosen to fill the needs of the structure. The drain pipes and other parts of the wastewater system also have to be engineered.

Another mechanical system is the HVAC system. *HVAC* stands for *h*eating, *v*entilating, and *a*ir *c*onditioning. The air conditioner, furnace, and ducts must be the correct size.

Electrical Engineering

The installation of electrical wires and devices in a structure must also be carefully engineered. Wire has to be large enough to allow electrical current to flow through safely without overheating the wire. There must be enough electrical circuits to provide power to all motors and lights. Fig. 11-10. By calculating the amount of electrical power needed in the proposed building, 2
engineers can determine correct sizes.

Systems Costs

The best-engineered design is one that does the job efficiently at the least possible cost. It would not make sense to put an expensive, 500-horsepower engine into a small passenger car. It could be done, but the result would not be very efficient. To do so could be an example of *over-engineering*. A 60-horsepower engine

Fig. 11-9. The mechanical and electrical systems are part of a building's infrastructure. Each system is engineered to fill the needs of the structure it will serve.

1. The sizing and bending of plumbing pipes and ventilating ducts affects the capacity of the pipe or duct to carry a fluid. Explain that standards have been developed as guidelines for the engineer.

2. Explain that the National Electrical Code is the only part of the building code that is accepted nationwide. This is an advantage to electrical engineers who design electrical systems for buildings.

Fig. 11-10. Electrical systems are engineered to provide the right amount of power for a specific facility. The lighting in a theatre must be specially designed.

could provide enough power for the car and would cost a reasonable amount. Using a 60-horsepower engine is an example of *engineering efficiency.*

Engineering efficiency must also be considered by structural engineers. The engineers want the structure to be safe but not overly expensive. As all the calculations are being made, the engineer looks over all the parts of the design again. He or she checks to be sure that the materials specified are practical and are used as efficiently as possible. Checking the efficiency of materials is often called *value engineering.*

For Discussion

In this section, *dead load* and *live load* have been discussed. The *live load* is described as being variable, or changeable. Examples of live loads include people and furniture. Name some other examples of dead loads and live loads.

THE FINAL DESIGN

After all the calculations have been made, the design becomes final. This final design is used to prepare a set of drawings to be used by the builder to construct the project. Several kinds of drawings are needed to show all the construction information. The **drawings** show the plans 1
for a structure in graphic form. For a large construction project, such as a power plant, there may be more than a hundred drawings in the set. Each of the different types of drawings shows special information that is needed for the project. Symbols are used on the drawings to represent the methods of construction and materials to be used. Fig. 11-11. A set of specifications is also prepared. The **specifications** tell the contractor exactly what materials to use and how to use them. The drawings and specifications give all the information necessary to build the structure exactly as it was designed and engineered. Sometimes a model is also built so that people may see how the finished structure will look.

1. Obtain a set of plans for a simple building like a garage. Using these plans, explain the basics of blueprint reading. Once the students can find information from the simple plans, provide them with a set of plans for a house. Use these to illustrate the various types of drawings and the information to be found on each.

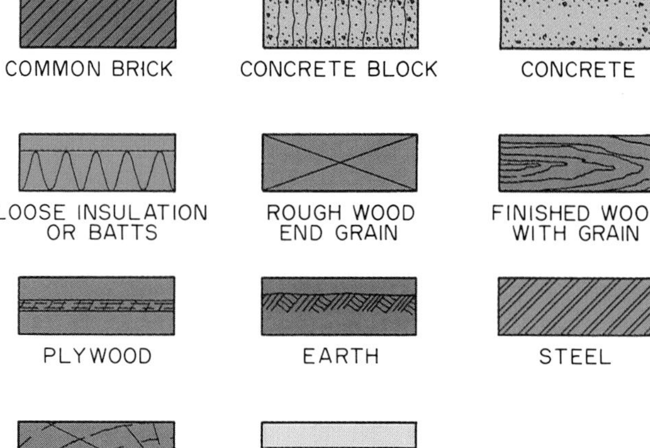

Fig. 11-11. Symbols are used on construction drawings to show different kinds of materials that will be used.

Architectural Drawings

Architectural drawings are those that show the layout of a building. It is impractical to make the drawings the size of the actual struc-
1 ture. Thus, engineers make them *to scale*. This
means that actual measurements are converted to smaller measurements that will fit on the drawing sheet. Everything is still in the right proportion, just smaller. For example, one common architectural scale is the quarter-inch scale, in which each ¼ inch represents 1 foot.

Many different kinds of architectural drawings are needed to make every aspect of construction clear. Some of the most common kinds of architectural drawings are floor plans, site plans, elevations, section drawings, and detail drawings.

Floor Plan

The **floor plan** shows the layout of all the rooms on one floor of a building. Fig. 11-12. It also shows the locations of all the walls and other built-in items. A separate floor plan is made for each floor in a building.

1. Develop an exercise in which the students draw lines to various scales that represent given distances. Demonstrate the use of the architect's scale.

Site Plan

The **site plan** shows what the site should look like when the job is finished. Fig. 11-13. The location of the building, new roads and parking lots, and even trees are shown. The finished contour of the earth is also shown.

Elevations

Elevations are drawings that show the outside of the structure. An elevation drawing is made for each side of the structure. The complete set of elevation drawings for a house shows a front, a rear, and two side views. Fig. 11-14. These drawings contain information about the
placement of joists, siding, and roofing materials 2
that will be used for the structure.

In addition to exterior elevations, the plans usually include interior elevations. Interior elevations are often needed for the kitchen. The heights of kitchen counters, cabinets, and shelves are shown on an interior elevation.

2. Discuss what happens to a part of an elevation that is at an angle other than 90 degrees with the projection plane. Explain how an auxiliary view can show that part of the elevation in true size and shape.

1

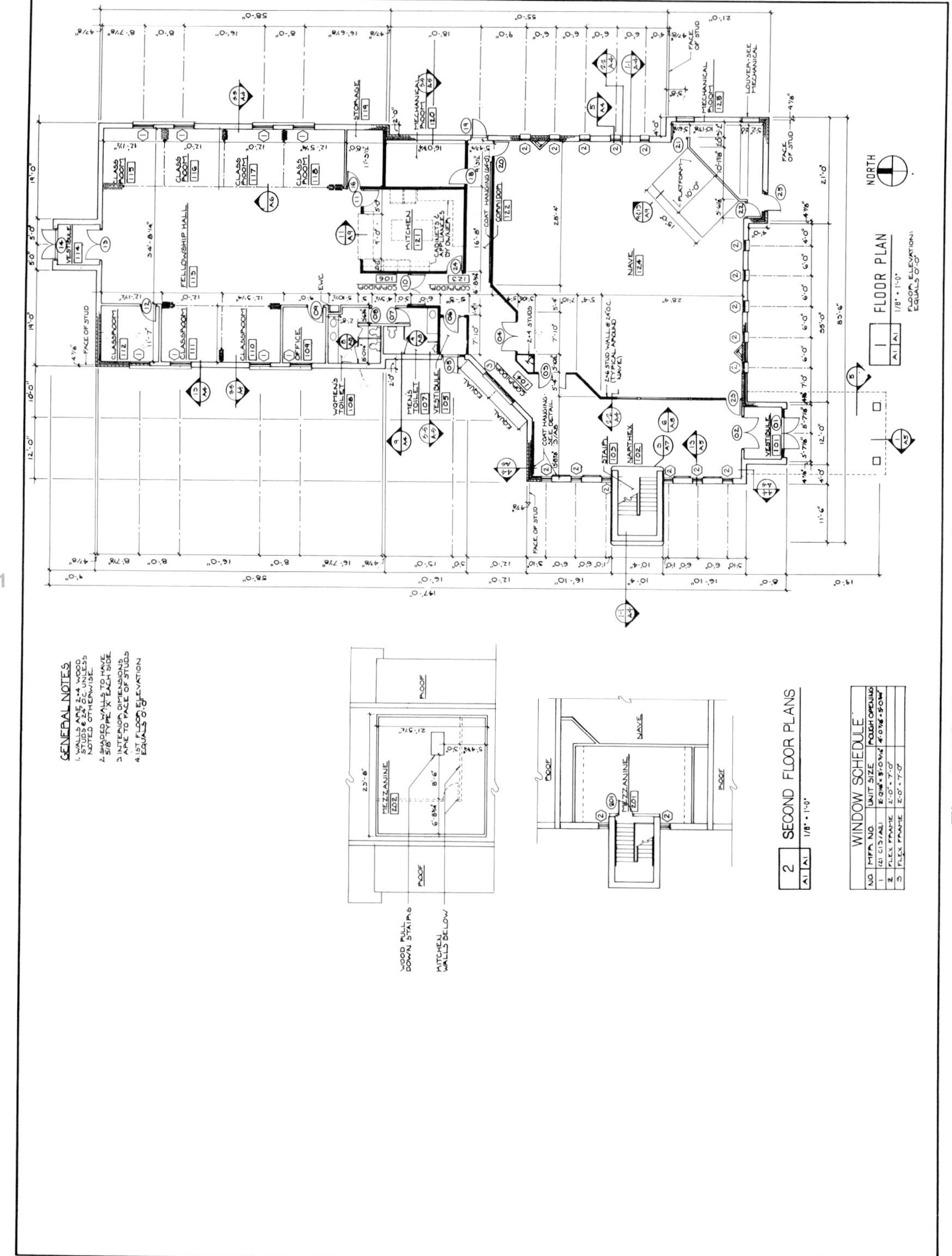

Fig. 11-12. An example of a floor plan.

1. Explain how the floor plan is arrived at by passing an imaginary cutting plane through the walls parallel with the floor. If possible, use an illustration to demonstrate this concept.

1

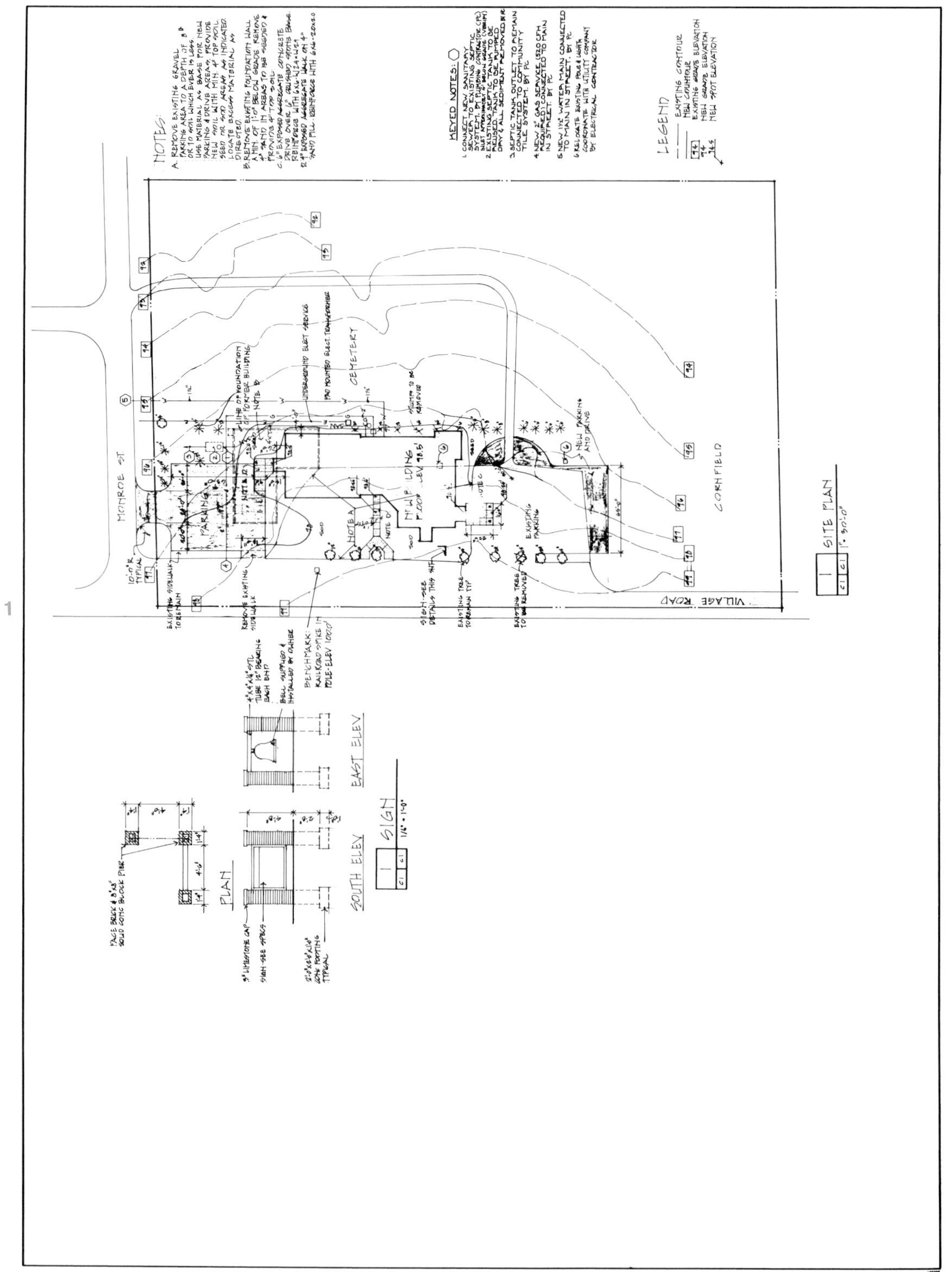

Fig. 11-13. The site plan is sometimes called a plot plan.

1. Discuss the information that is being combined in the site plan. Explain why this information is important to the contractor before and during construction.

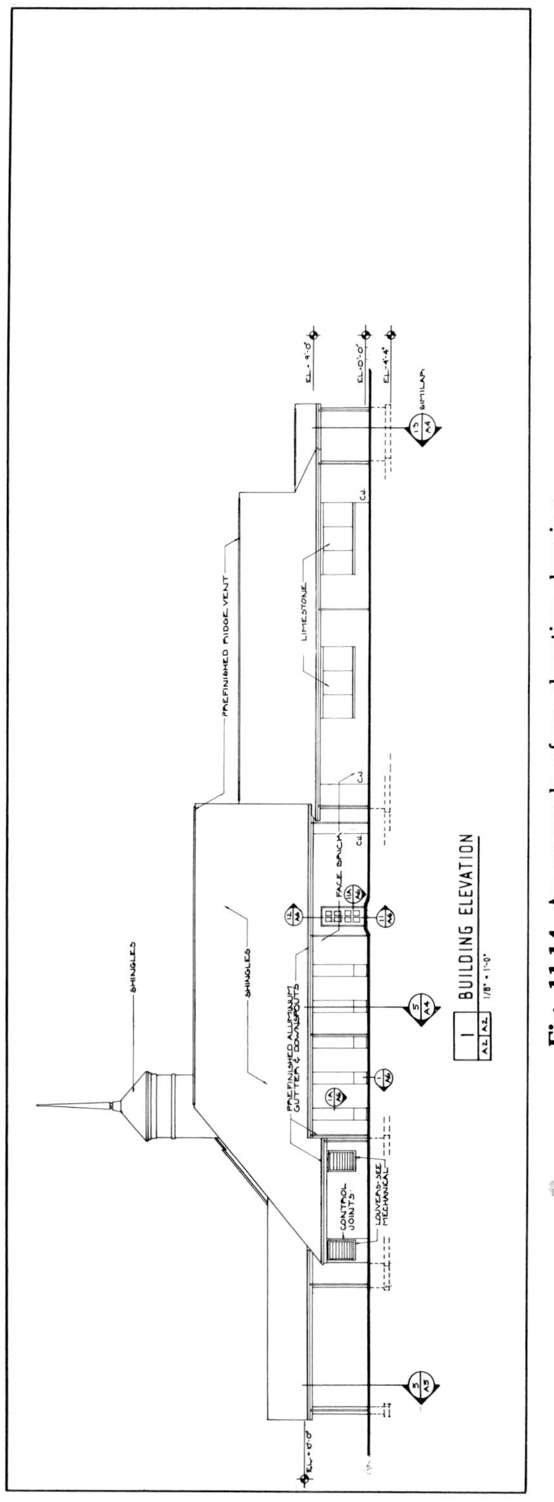

1

Fig. 11-14. An example of an elevation drawing.

1. If possible, provide the class with other examples of elevation drawings. Point out the information they are meant to convey.

Section Drawings

1 A **section drawing** is one that shows a section, or slice, of the structure. In this drawing, a part of the building is shown as if it were cut in two and separated. This allows the viewer to see the inside of the structure. Fig. 11-15. If most of the walls will have the same construction, a typical wall section is drawn to show their interior detail. If the walls will have different constructions, a section view is drawn of each kind of wall.

Detail Drawings

A **detail drawing** is one that shows a particular part of the structure. It shows how things
fit together. Detail drawings normally are drawn 2
to a larger scale than other drawings. This makes them easy to read and eliminates confusion about each particular point in the structure. Fig. 11-16.

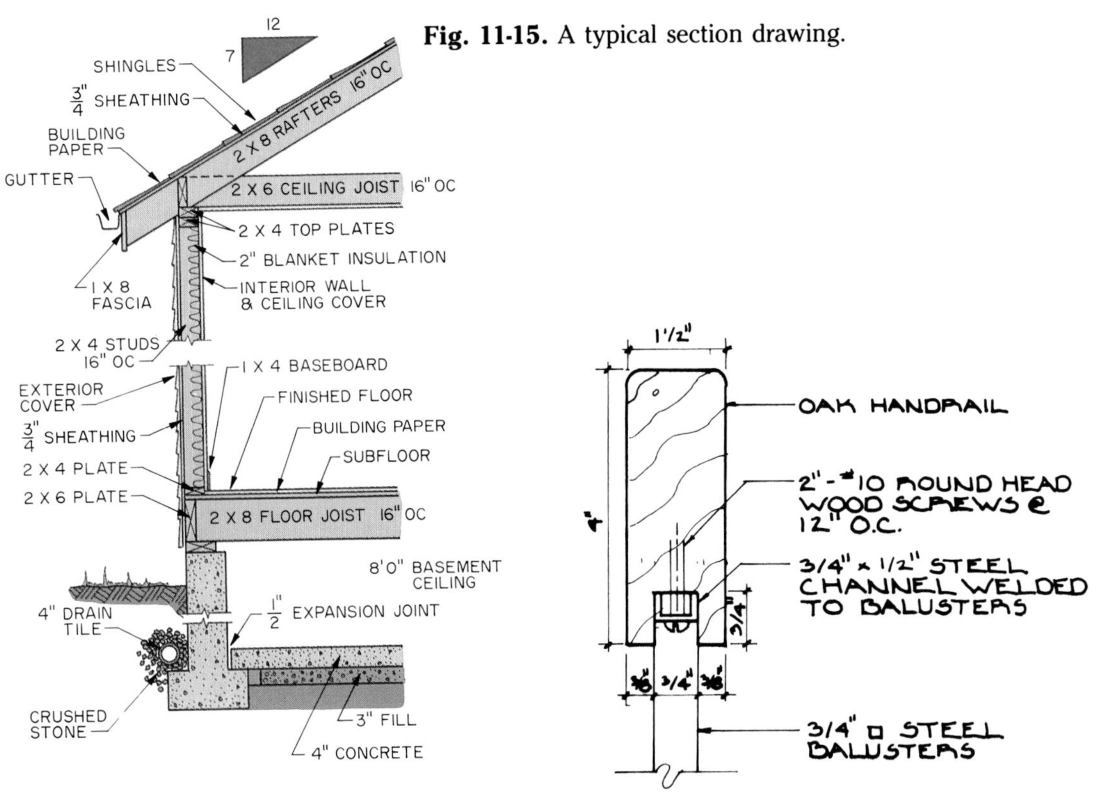

Fig. 11-15. A typical section drawing.

Fig. 11-16. An example of an architectural detail drawing. This is a detail drawing of an oak handrail on a staircase.

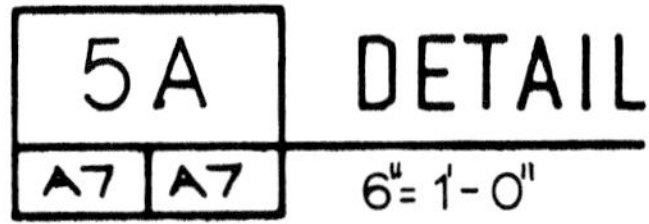

1. Show how to identify the location of any section taken. Explain how to read the reference numbers in the balloons shown on the section lines.

2. Show how to identify the location of any detail drawings. Explain how to read the reference numbers in the balloons that accompany the circle that identifies where the detail is taken from.

Did You Know?

Architectural drawings were made nearly four thousand years ago by the Babylonians. The Babylonians were a people who lived in what is now Iraq. For example, a stone engraving of the plan of a fortress has been found. Archeologists think that this stone engraving was made about 2000 B.C. The ancient Romans also produced architectural drawings. In about 27 B.C., the Roman architect Vitruvius wrote what might be the first book on engineering drawings.

Structural Drawings

A **structural drawing** gives information 1
about the location and sizes of the structural materials. The size and type of foundations, the location of steel columns and beams, and the placement of roof trusses are found on the structural plan. Fig. 11-17 (page 254). Structural plans are prepared by a structural engineer.

Mechanical and Electrical Plans

The mechanical and electrical plans show how to construct the various systems in a structure. 2
Mechanical plans are prepared for the plumbing and piping systems. Fig. 11-18. Mechanical

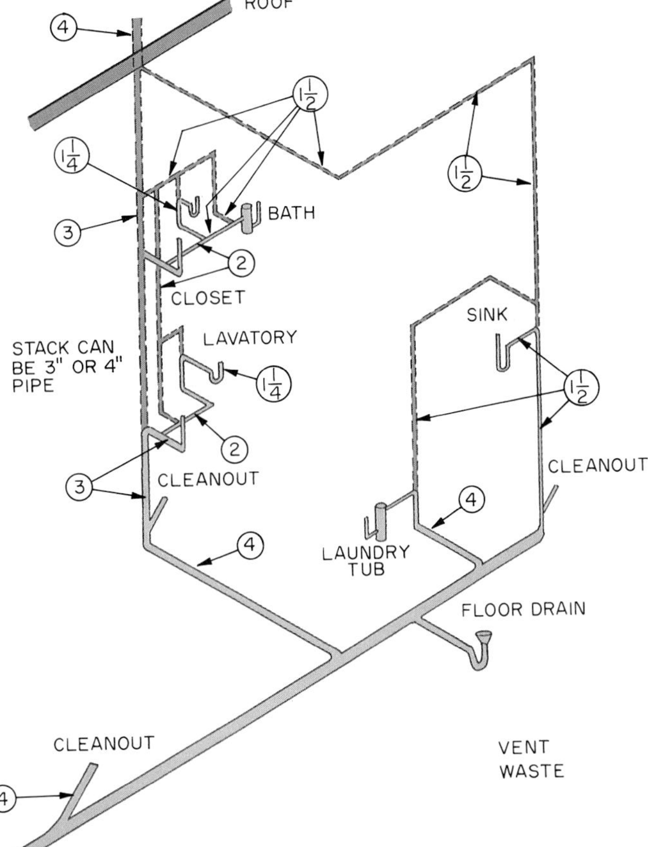

Fig. 11-18. This plumbing diagram is part of the mechanical plans of a structure.

1. Show how structural and sectional drawings frequently require detail drawings.
2. Emphasize that not all details are given in electrical and mechanical plans.

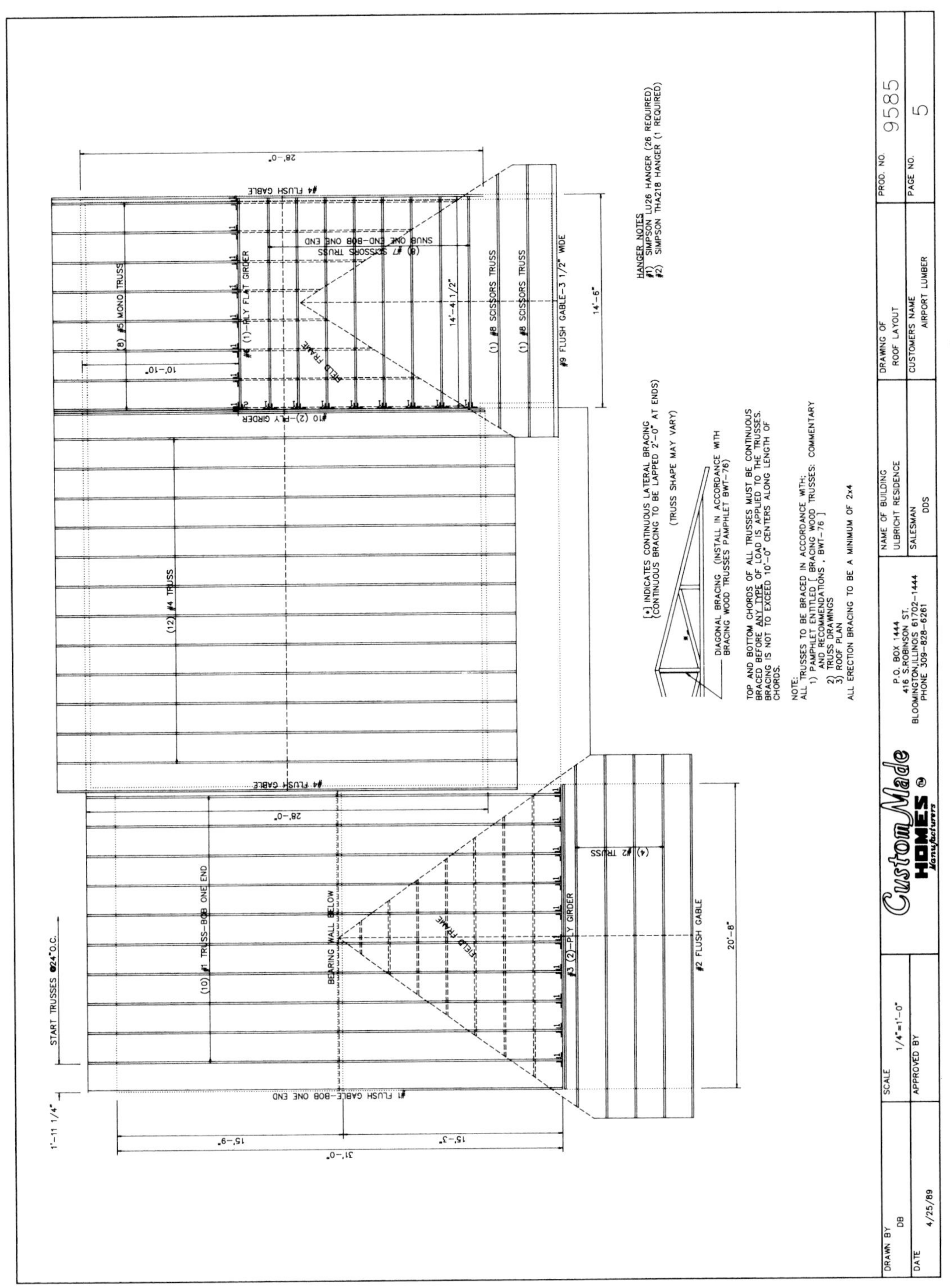

Fig. 11-17. A structural plan shows how the parts of the frame fit together.

1

1. Review the kinds of information found on structural drawings.

drawings are also made to show the construction and placement of the HVAC system. The **electrical plans** show the location of all the light fixtures, switches, and other electrical devices. Fig. 11-19.

Specifications

Drawings alone cannot tell the contractor everything he or she needs to know about a project. For example, it would be difficult to try to describe all the types and colors of finishing materials such as paint, ceramic flooring, and wallpaper. Therefore, written specifications are developed. These describe details that cannot
1 be shown easily on a drawing.

In addition to describing materials, the specifications explain the procedure that should be used to perform each task. Especially difficult or unusual procedures are described in detail. Construction standards are also included to make sure the finished project will conform to federal, state, and local requirements.

Writing the Specifications

The specifications for a major construction project can be so extensive that they are bound in two or three volumes. To make sure that all the information can be found easily, the specification writer must keep it in a logical order. Most specifications for large construction projects follow the format presented by the **Construction Specification Institute (CSI)**. The CSI guide- 2
lines are presented in outline form. Fig. 11-20. Every type of construction job is classified in one of 16 categories. The categories are meant to follow the actual order of construction as far as possible. They also keep all the information about a subject in one place. For example, all the instructions for plumbing installation would be found together in one part of the specifications.

Writing the specifications for a large project is an involved and difficult procedure. The specifications must meet the requirements of the owner, the architect, and the engineer. They must also comply with the rules and regulations set forth by city, county, state, and

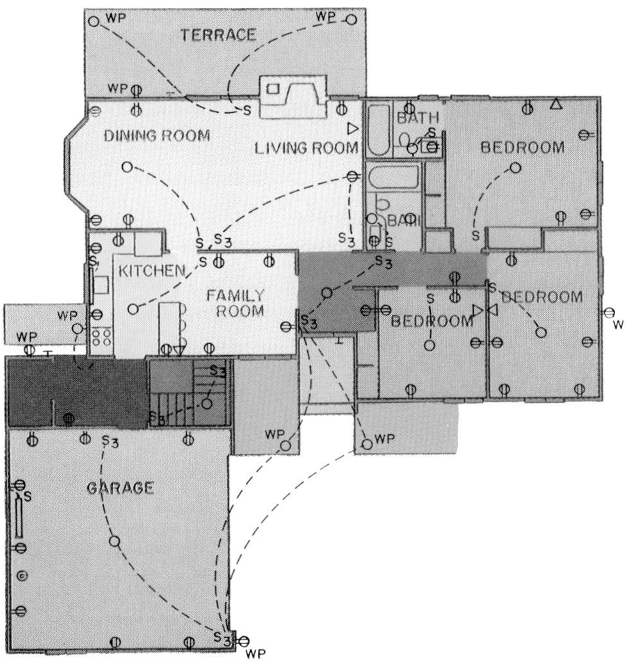

Fig. 11-19. An example of an electrical plan.

1. Provide a set of specifications for a plan. Show how they complement the plan. Emphasize that it would be impossible to place the specification information on the plans without making them confusing.

2. Discuss how the organization of specifications using the CSI format would affect the work of a person who had to estimate the HVAC for a construction job.

2.02 Chalkboards and Tackboards

.1 Types

a) Where chalkboard (CB) units are indicated, they shall be Claridge 4′ high factory-built units, Series 4, with continuous chalk trough, flat type on lower edge of chalkboard. Provide individual units as indicated.

b) Where "full height" units are indicated, they shall consist of 6′ high, 4′ wide units with color-matched "H" trim at all interior vertical joints. Perimeter trim shall have same appearance as Series 4 factory-built units except without continuous chalk trough on lower edge. Provide two (2) 2′-0″ pieces of magnetic chalk trough at each teaching area.

.2 Chalkboard Construction: Shall be Claridge porcelain enamel steel with the following characteristics:

— 24 gauge "Vitracite" face.
— 3/8″ particleboard or "Duracore".
— .005″ aluminum sheet panel backing.
— Total thickness of 1/2″.
— Warranted for the life of the building.
— Provide chalk trough for each unit.
— Provide map rail for each unit.
— Chalkboard color shall be as selected by Architect from not less than six (6) standard colors.

Fig. 11-20. The CSI format for specifications is used for most large construction projects. This set of specifications is for a new school building. Notice the detailed specifications for the chalkboard.

federal governments. While meeting all of the above requirements, the specifications must remain within the owner's budget.

A great deal of knowledge and experience is needed to put the specifications together. Most large construction companies have specialized
1 employees called **specification writers** to do this work. Specification writers must have a good understanding of construction practices and an up-to-date knowledge of materials. They must also be familiar with the current costs of materials and with the regulations that apply in their area.

Using the Specifications

Specifications are important in every phase of the project. They are sent to several contractors before a contractor is chosen for the job. The contractors use the specifications to estimate the cost of materials and labor. They use that information to bid on the contract. During construction, the chosen contractor must follow all the guidelines set forth in the specifications. If the drawings and the specifications disagree, the contractor
follows the specifications. When the project has 2
been completed, inspectors check the structure against the specifications. The specifications help them make sure that the work was done correctly and that the proper materials were used.

Models

Scale models are sometimes made to help visualize how the final design will look. These models have proportions that the finished building will have. However, they are built on a much smaller scale. There are two basic types: presentation models and study models.

1. List on the chalkboard the skills that a specification writer would need. What types of classes in junior and senior high school would help one prepare for this job?

2. Discuss the process a contractor must follow if he or she desires to substitute materials or equipment for those listed in the specifications.

Presentation Models

A model that is made to show people how the finished design will look is called a **presentation model**. Fig. 11-21. Some people have difficulty imagining the finished appearance of the building by just looking at the plans. A three-dimensional model helps them understand the structure. Models of many commercial projects are put on public display. Perhaps you have seen a presentation model of a bank, church, or other structure.

Study Models

Sometimes a **study model** of a design is made
1 so that the design can be tested. For example, a scale model of a bridge can be loaded with weights and observed. A scale model of a building can be tested in a wind tunnel to see how it might act in a hurricane.

Today most study models are made by computer simulation. All the mathematical information about a structure is entered into a computer. 2
The model appears on the screen. Fig. 11-22. The engineer or architect can change the parts of the model or turn it around. Then a simulation program is run that *simulates*, or imitates, what would happen to the structure under certain conditions. The information can then be printed out. It can then be studied to find weaknesses and ways to improve the building.

Fig. 11-21. A presentation model helps people visualize the final design.

1. Show the class several pictorial drawings that have been made to show owners what a proposed building will look like. Why might such drawings be a less expensive alternative to a scale model?

2. Discuss why each student today should have a certain level of computer literacy. Ask the students whether they have had the opportunity to learn as much about computers as they would like.

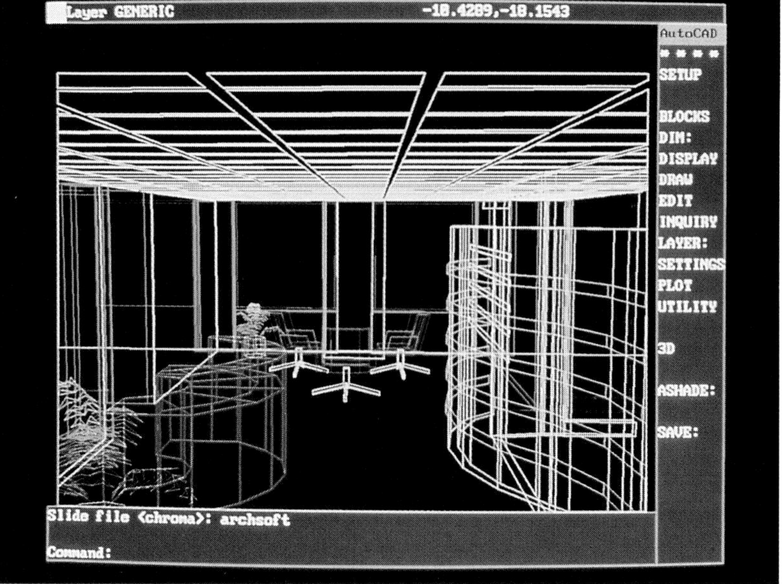

Fig. 11-22. A computerized
study model can be tested
using a simulation program. In
this study model the size of the
1 roof and wall beams can be
changed.

HEALTH & SAFETY

Some bridges have collapsed during heavy storms. To help prevent such disasters, engineers have various techniques available. One of these involves the use of a wind tunnel. In a wind tunnel, fans are used to create a stream of air. The force and direction of this stream of air can be controlled. This controlled stream of air can then be directed on a scale model.

For example, a scale model of a bridge might be placed in the wind tunnel. Then the stream of air might be adjusted to simulate the force of a hurricane. This will allow engineers to closely observe the effects of high winds on the scale model. By studying the results, engineers can plan improvements that will help make the bridge safer.

For Discussion

This section discusses the various plans needed in the building of a modern house. Clearly, houses built today are different from those built one hundred and fifty years ago. What would be missing from the plans of a house one hundred and fifty years ago that would be present in the plans for a house today?

1. How has the computer simplified the development of complicated engineering structures? Ask students if they think that we have reached the point where computers will be used for such purposes. Ask them if they can think of any possible new uses.

ARCHITECTURAL AND ENGINEERING SERVICES

The architect and engineer often work together to design a project. They agree to work for the owner for a fee. The amount of the fee depends upon the size of the project. A company that does designing and engineering is known as an A/E (architectural and engineering) firm.

Just as a medical doctor must have a license to practice medicine, architects and engineers
1 must have a license to practice their professions. The license means that the person is legally qualified to design and engineer a structure. In fact, he or she must sign the drawings and stamp his or her official seal over the signature. Fig. 11-23. This shows that the person is legally responsible for the designing and engineering work on the drawing.

Fig. 11-23. The architect's or engineer's seal and signature on a set of drawings means that he or she is responsible for the design.

1. Discuss the process architects and engineers must go through in order to obtain a license.

Architects

The main job of the architect is to design and create plans for structures. Architects design houses, churches, office buildings, and shopping centers. Fig. 11-24. They also design community projects such as auditoriums and sports arenas.

The architect is the supervising designer in
most building projects. During project construc- 2
tion, the architect checks that the contractor is following specifications. The architect approves samples of the materials to be used on the project. He or she must also approve substitute materials or changes in construction methods. The architect works for the owner and with the contractor to make sure that construction is done according to the plans.

Fig. 11-24. An architect designed the layout and appearance of this shopping mall.

2. Explain that the architect may hire persons with the necessary skills to act as the architect's representative on the job. This provides another check to ensure that the construction is done as specified.

1

Fig. 11-25. Each of these construction projects — the water tower and the bridge — was designed and engineered by an engineer.

1. Point out that large construction projects require the cooperation of several people. These include the project manager, the building officials, the architectural representative, and the owner. Emphasize that all of these people, plus all of the workers and subcontractors, must cooperate to finish the job correctly and on time.

Engineers

Engineers help design and engineer all types of structures. However, they are usually the supervising designers of heavy construction projects such as bridges, roads, and utility systems. Fig. 11-25. The engineer's duties and responsibilities are similar to those of the architect. The engineer makes sure that the specifications are being followed and that the construction is done correctly. He or she also
1 inspects the project materials and workmanship.

Did You Know?

The earliest engineers were military engineers. They were responsible for the design and construction of many of the surviving fortifications of the ancient world. In Asia, one example of the work of military engineers is the Great Wall of China, which extends 1,500 miles.

In Europe, examples of the work of Roman military engineers can still be seen. Among them is Hadrian's Wall, which extended for 73 miles. It was intended to protect the northern frontier of Roman Britain. The term civil engineer was not used until the eighteenth century. It was used to indicate that the civil engineer was concerned with the building of public works.

Consultants

A **consultant** is an expert in a specific area. 2
He or she may be called upon to give advice on a certain part of the design of the construction project. The consultant works as a subcontractor for part of the designing and engineering work.

It is common practice for an architect to hire consultants for special parts of the design work. For example, an architect may be designing a new concert hall. The design of the hall will have an effect on the sound the audience will hear when music is played. The architect may call in a consulting engineer who specializes in *acoustics*, or sound. The consultant provides advice about the overall design as it applies to the acoustics. Structural, foundation, and mechanical engineers often serve as consultants. Another commonly used consultant is an interior designer. He or she works with the architect to design the appearance of the interior of the building. Fig. 11-26.

For Discussion

It is mentioned that an interior designer might work with the architect. How would an architect and an interior designer work together to design the interior of a building?

1. Review the responsibilities of the various types of engineers mentioned in this chapter. Point out that the education of each of these will be different to meet different job requirements.

2. Discuss how the use of consultants can improve the design of a building. Might this practice enable a smaller architectural firm to compete? When might it be economical for even a large firm to hire an expert?

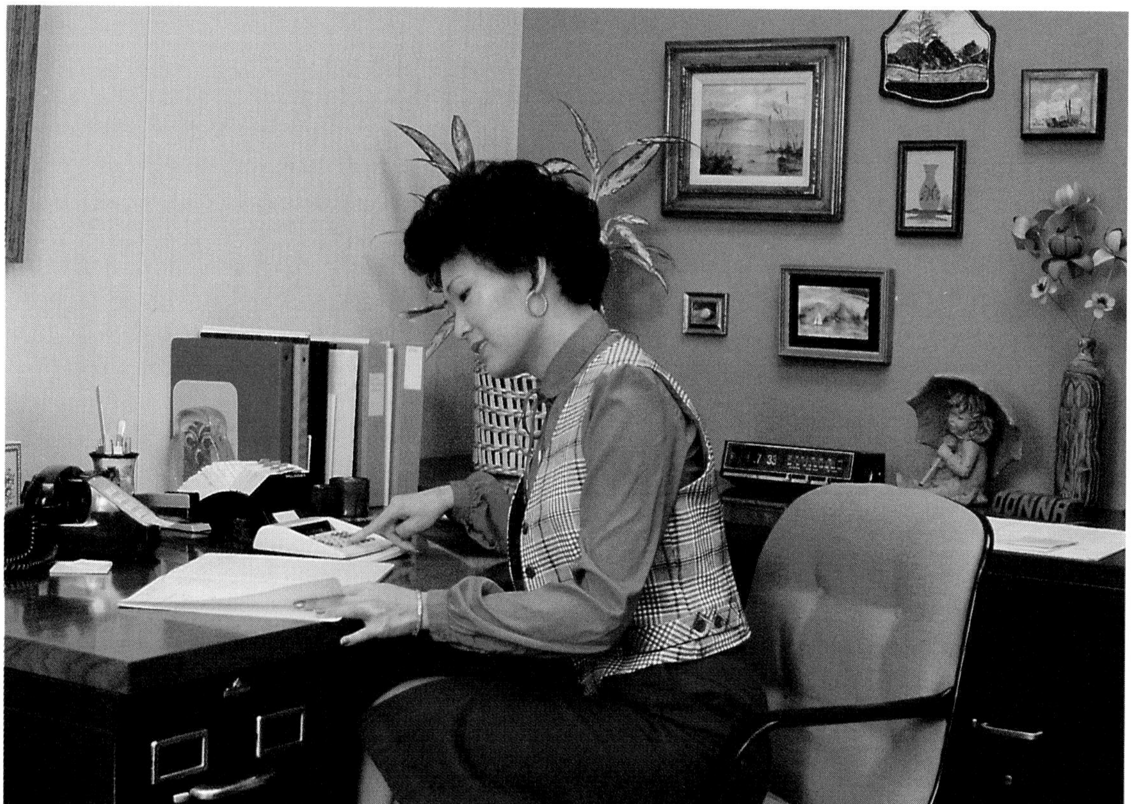

1 **Fig. 11-26.** An interior designer helped the architect design this office.

1. Point out that many buildings built for use as offices are rented with the interior space unfinished. The renter may hire an interior designer to do the office layout and coordinate decorations and furniture.

Construction Facts

JOHN ROEBLING AND THE BROOKLYN BRIDGE

In the late 1860s, the people of New York decided that a bridge was needed to connect
1 Brooklyn and Manhattan. They called upon an engineer who was considered the leading bridge designer of that time: John Roebling. Mr. Roebling suggested a new design for the bridge. He had developed a new cable-weaving technique that would enable him to design a strong, safe bridge that could hang from wire cables.

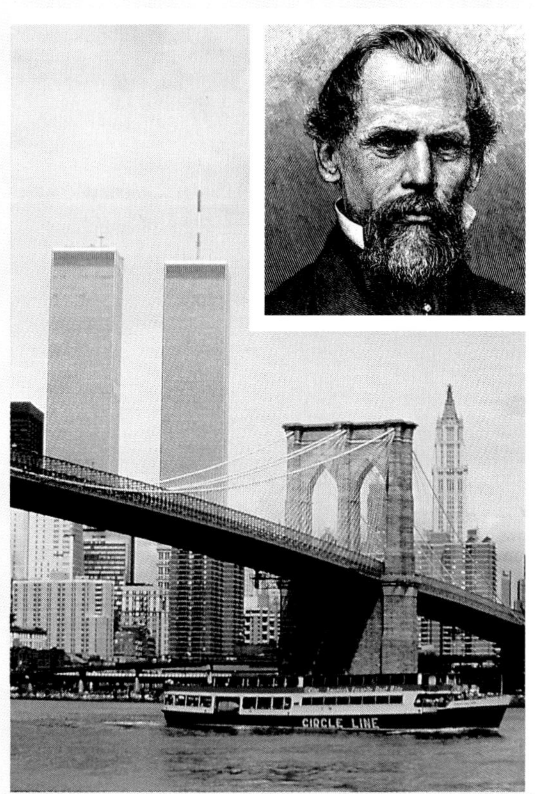

According to his design, four fifteen-inch-thick cables would hold up the bridge. Each cable would be made up of 19 strands of wire designed by Roebling. Each strand would be made up of 278 separate wires. Each wire would be continuous—there would be no wire ends to break apart.

The people approved. They put John Roebling in charge of building the new bridge. Unfortunately, John Roebling died before the construction could begin. His son, also a civil engineer, took charge of the project. Washington Roebling began the construction in January, 1870, and completed the project according to his father's design in 1883.

John Roebling designed and engineered the bridge carefully. His design far exceeded the safety limits needed for traffic of the 1800s. As a matter of fact, the safety factor he used is adequate for today's heavy traffic flow. The Brooklyn Bridge is still considered a mighty engineering feat. The enormous weight of the
massive road is still supported effortlessly by 2
the weblike structures of wire.

1. Ask a student or group of students to do further research and report on the design and construction of the Brooklyn Bridge.

2. Discuss the great feat of engineering that was accomplished in designing the Brooklyn Bridge. Compare the way mathematical problems were solved then with the way in which they are solved today.

CHAPTER 11

REVIEW

Chapter Summary

Every construction project requires a project plan. A project plan requires designing and engineering. A structure must be functional and attractive. In designing a project, preliminary designs are made. Engineers figure out how the structure will be built. They select the appropriate materials. Engineers also figure the loads and determine whether the building will be safe. The mechanical and electrical setups of a building are referred to as its infrastructure. The design of the infrastructure is the work of mechanical engineers and electrical engineers. The drawings for a building show the plans for a structure in graphic form.

The specifications tell the contractor what materials to use. Architectural drawings show the layout of the building. Architectural drawings include floor plans, site plans, elevations, section drawings, and detail drawings. Structural drawings give information about the location and sizes of structural materials. Mechanical and electrical plans show how to construct the various systems in a structure. Specifications for a construction project must be accurately written. Models are sometimes used to help visualize how the final design will look. Architects and engineers often work together in designing a project.

Test Your Knowledge [1]

1. What is the difference between designing and engineering?
2. What are two major factors that need to be taken into consideration in the design process?
3. What is the difference between a live and dead load? Give two examples of each.
4. Why do engineers include a safety factor in their calculations?
5. Name five types of architectural drawings.
6. What are specifications? What purpose do they serve?
7. What two types of models are used for construction purposes?
8. How can a computer simulation be used to test a proposed design for a structure?
9. What kinds of projects do architects usually design and engineer?
10. What kinds of projects do engineers usually design and engineer?
11. Why are consultants used to help design some projects?

1. The answers to the Test Your Knowledge questions are in the Teacher's Manual at the front of this Teacher's Annotated Edition.

REVIEW

Activities

 1. Sketch a floor plan of your house or apartment. Analyze the layout. How functional do you think it is? Write a description of your opinion.

 2. Look around your community. Identify by name or address two structures that you think are well designed and one that you think is poorly designed. Give reasons for your opinions.

 3. Choose any room in a building. Make a list of all the things you see. Tell whether each item contributes to the live load or dead load of the building.

 4. Obtain a set of plans for a construction project. Study the drawings and see if you can find examples of the different types of drawings.

 5. Make a scale presentation model of your house or apartment.

CHAPTER 12

CONSTRUCTION PROCESSES

Terms to Know

armored cable
batter boards
bearing-wall structure
conduit
excavating
finishing stage
floating
footing
forms
foundation
foundation wall
frame structure
laying out
load-bearing ability
molding
nonmetallic sheathed cable
roof truss
roughing in
screeding
service drop
service panel
sheathing
shoring
site
slump test
superstructure
troweling

Objectives

When you have completed reading this chapter, you should be able to do the following: 1

- Explain the process of preparing a construction site.
- Describe three major types of structural work.
- Explain the difference between a frame structure and a bearing-wall structure.
- Describe three basic types of utility systems.
- Describe five major types of finish work.

1. Resources:
- Chapter 12 Lesson Plan in the Teacher's Manual in this Teacher's Annotated Edition and in the Teacher's Resource Guide.
- Chapter 12 Study Guide in the Student Workbook.
- Chapter 12 Visual Master in the Teacher's Resource Guide.

Construction processes are all the procedures that are used to build a construction project. Most construction projects are very complex. They require a great many processes before they are ready to be used. For a building, the construction processes include activities ranging from the initial preparation of the site to the installation of the wallpaper. Most of these
1 processes are carried out by workers who specialize in just a few processes. These specialized workers are able to work quickly and efficiently.

In reading this chapter you will learn about many of the major processes required to complete a structure. As you read about these processes, you will see their complexity. This will help you understand why construction workers must specialize in one or only a few processes.

PREPARING THE SITE

The land on which a project will be constructed is called the **site**. Fig. 12-1. The plans for a project give the details about how the site should look when the project is complete. These plans also tell the workers what needs to be done to the site before the building is started. Plans were discussed in Chapter 11.

Three major steps are involved in preparing a site for construction. First, the land is surveyed
to establish its boundaries. Then the site is 2
cleared. The last step is to lay out the boundaries of the building.

Fig. 12-1. A site is the land on which a construction project is built.

1. Discuss the specialization of labor. Why can the specialist do the job better and faster than one who does that job only once in a while? How does specialization reduce the amount of tools and equipment needed?

2. Have a student or group of students research and report on the history of surveying. Make the class aware that George Washington spent his early years as a land surveyor.

Surveying the Site

The first step in preparing the site is to identify the boundaries of the property. Surveyors measure the property to establish property lines. They use a transit and a measuring tape called a *chain* to measure very accurately. Fig. 12-2.
1 The slightest mistake in measurement can cause the property lines to be wrong. After measuring the land, the surveyors set stakes at each corner of the property.

Clearing the Site

Once the property boundaries have been defined, the next step is to remove anything that is in the way of the new construction. Trees,
dirt, and old buildings are a few of the things 2
that may need to be removed. Bulldozers are usually used to push trees, excess dirt, and other unwanted materials out of the way.

Demolition, or wrecking, is used to clear buildings from a site. There are various ways of demolishing old structures. One common demolition method is to use a crane with a wrecking ball. Other demolition methods include using bulldozers or explosives to break up a structure. Fig. 12-3.

Fig. 12-2. This surveyor is using a transit to establish the boundaries of a site.

Did You Know?

Explosives can be used to demolish tall buildings. Some demolition companies specialize in this type of site preparation for construction. The explosives are precisely placed. Also, the amount of the explosive varies from one location to the next in the building that is to be demolished. Used in these ways, the explosives can be used to demolish a building without damaging nearby buildings. This method of demolition is sometimes used to remove fairly tall office buildings.

Laying Out the Site

Laying out the site is the process of identifying the location of the proposed structure on the property. The corners and edges of the building to be constructed are marked with stakes and string. Proposed parking lots and roadways are also marked at this time.

To lay out a site, construction workers use the boundary stakes left by the surveyors as points of reference. They measure from these stakes to the corners and edges of a proposed building.

1. Demonstrate how a transit is set up. Show how it is used to lay out angles, line up stakes, measure elevations, and plumb corners. Show the class how 90° angles can be laid out by using the 6-8-10 method (Pythagorean theorem).

2. Emphasize that, with the trend toward protecting the environment, a greater attempt is being made to disturb fewer trees and other natural features on a building site. Not too long ago, all trees were usually removed from a building site.

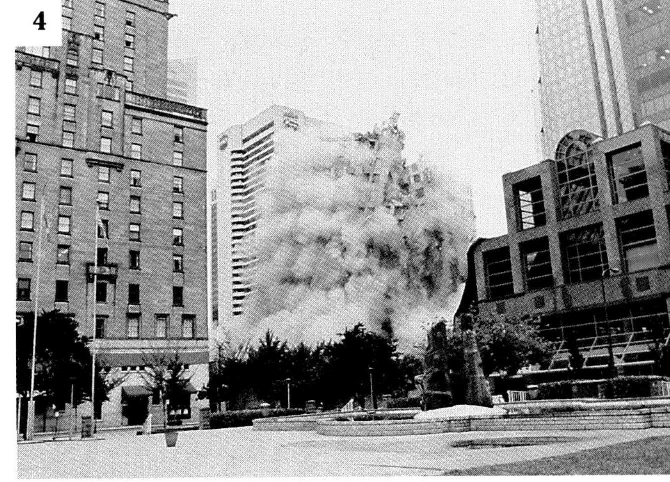

1 **Fig. 12-3.** Explosive demolition is a fast way to demolish an old structure. This series of photos shows the stages in a building's collapse.

1. Ask a student or group of students to research and report on the problems presented by the disposal of used building materials that result from demolition. What are some of those materials that might present a threat to the environment?

The boundaries of the building are usually
1 marked by **batter boards**. A batter board is a board held horizontally by stakes driven into the ground. String is used to connect the batter board with another at the opposite end of a wall. The batter boards are placed outside the building's boundaries so that the attached strings cross over the corners of the building. Fig. 12-4. This ensures that workers will know where the boundaries are even after excavation begins and the boundary stakes are removed.

The building layout is important because it shows the shape and size of the planned structure. Like the surveyors, construction workers must measure very accurately. If there are any mistakes in measuring at this point, the whole structure will be built in the wrong place or to the wrong size.

Excavating and Earthworking

The next step in constructing a building is to condition the earth. **Excavating**, or digging, can begin as soon as the site has been laid out. In addition to excavating, other earthworking—such as leveling, grading, and soil stabilization—may be needed. Soil may also need to be removed from or added to the site so that the proper elevation is achieved.

Excavating

One of the main reasons for excavation is to provide a place for the foundation, or base, of the structure. The foundation is an important part of the structure because it supports the structure's entire weight. The foundation must be strong and rigid enough to hold up all the building materials used in the structure. It must also support the weight of the furnishings and the people who will use the finished structure.

The type of excavation depends on the project and its location. Sometimes the hole must be dug straight down. For example, the foundation for a new skyscraper being built between two existing buildings would need a deep, narrow hole. Fig. 12-5. The walls of the excavation must be dug carefully so that the sides do not
cave in. This kind of excavation is called *trim-* 2
ming and shaping.

Another kind of excavation must be done to make trenches for pipelines. This type of excavation is called *trenching*. Fig. 12-6. Water, sewer, or natural-gas pipelines are placed in the trenches. Then the earth that was dug from the trench is replaced.

Leveling and Grading

Leveling and grading are processes that change land elevation and slope. They do this by filling in low spots and shaving off high spots.

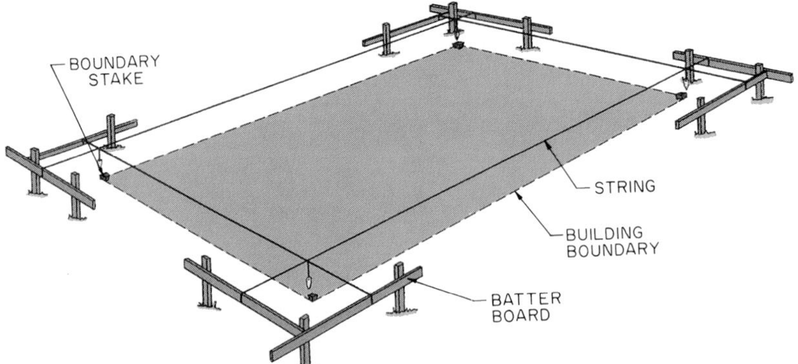

Fig. 12-4. Batter boards and string can be used to lay out a building's location.

1. Explain how batter boards are installed. Emphasize that they are used during excavation, placement of footings, and placement of the foundations. Also mention the consequences of batter boards being disturbed during use.

2. Ask a student or group of students to research and report on underpinning, shoring, and other methods of supporting an excavation very close to adjoining buildings or property lines.

Fig. 12-5. Excavating in a confined area is a difficult job. It must be done carefully so that the surrounding structures will not be damaged. This building will be demolished. Then excavation will begin for the foundation of a new six-story office building.

This is especially important in building roads 1
and parking lots. Fig. 12-7. The proper elevation and slope are indicated by the surveyor. Workers follow the surveyor's guidelines to level and grade the site.

Stabilizing the Soil

Before a structure can be erected on a site, the soil must be firm and stable. The soil must not move or shift beneath the foundation. The first step in soil stabilization is to determine the **load-bearing ability** of the soil. This is the amount of weight that soil can safely support without shifting. The load-bearing ability of the soil is measured by a geologist or soil engineer.

If the soil is too weak to support the proposed
structure, it must be stabilized. One of several 2
methods may be used. One method of stabilizing

Fig. 12-6. This trenching machine is being used to dig a trench for an underground drainage pipe.

1. Review the types of equipment used for leveling and grading. Explain how grade stakes are installed and used as guides for the leveling and grading equipment.

2. The load-bearing quality of soil is expressed in tons (2000 pounds) per square foot. Have a group of students report on ways in which the bearing qualities of soil can be enhanced. The vibra-floatation method is one interesting technique.

Fig. 12-7. This scraper is being used to level the earth for a road project.

soil involves pounding it with heavy rams or rolling it with heavy rollers. These methods make the soil more compact. It can then bear heavier loads than would otherwise be possible.

When soil must be stabilized around a hole
1 or trench, sheathing and shoring are used. The banks or walls of soil are covered with sheets of steel called **sheathing**. The sheathing is usually held in place by long strips of metal driven into the earth. This method of holding sheathing in place is called **shoring**. Shoring can also be used without sheathing to stabilize
2 soil and reduce the chance of cave-ins. Fig. 12-8.

Soil can also be made firm by adding certain chemicals to it. Loose soil can be filled with a chemical solution that reacts with the soil to make it harder. The hardened soil can then provide a solid base for construction work.

For Discussion

The text discusses the various ways in which a site is cleared. Is there any construction taking place near your school? What was done to clear the construction site?

1. What methods are used to protect workers from cave-ins while they install piping in trenches?

2. The angle of repose of soil is the angle at which it will stand without collapsing into the excavation. This angle changes with different types of soil. When possible, the sides of a hole should be excavated with this angle.

Fig. 12-8. This metal shoring prevents the soil from caving in.

BUILDING THE FOUNDATION

When the site work has been completed, work on the structure begins. The structure is made of two basic parts: the foundation and the superstructure. The **foundation** is the part of the structure that is beneath the first floor. It includes the footing and the foundation wálls. The rest of the building, beginning with the first floor, is called the **superstructure**. You should note that some foundations extend above the ground. Therefore, the generalization that everything below ground level is the foundation and everything above is the superstructure is incorrect. You will learn more about superstructures later in this chapter.

The **footing** is the part of the structure that
1 distributes the structure's weight. It is usually
made of reinforced concrete. The footing must
be placed beneath the *frost line*. It must be deep
enough so that the soil around it will not freeze
2 in winter. Soil above the frost line expands as
it freezes. Therefore, footings placed above the
frost line are unstable.

1. Explain why the footing is usually made wider than the thickness of the foundation. This is called a spread footing. At times the total soil area beneath the building will be needed for support of the building. Then, a mat footing is used.

The wall that is built directly on the footing is called the **foundation wall**. It transmits the weight of the superstructure to the footing. Fig. 12-9. The foundation walls for most structures are made of steel-reinforced concrete.

Preparing for the Foundation

Before the concrete can be poured for a foundation, two major preparatory steps must be completed. First, forms must be assembled to contain the concrete. **Forms** are the molds that

Fig. 12-9. The foundation wall transmits the weight of the superstructure to the footing, which distributes the weight to the stable soil around it.

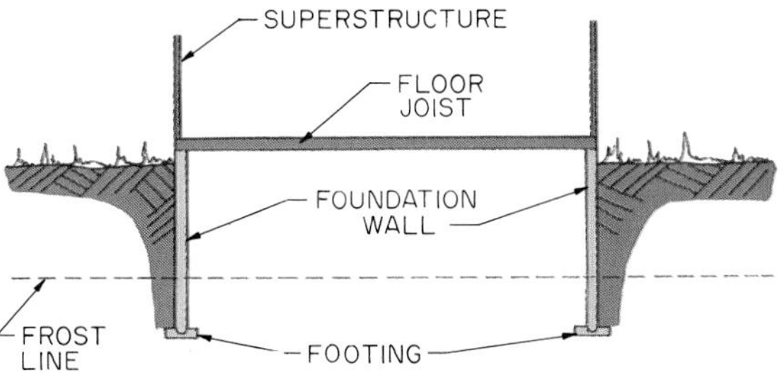

2. In areas where footings do not need to be deep, some buildings are constructed with monolithic slabs. These are a combination of footing and floor in one piece.

contain the concrete until it hardens. They are made in the shape that the finished concrete should have. Fig. 12-10. Forms can be either custom-built or patented. *Custom-built forms* are
1 wooden forms made by carpenters on the site. This kind of form is used only once. *Patented forms* are made in a factory by a company that then patents the design. These reusable forms are bolted together in sections. After the concrete has set, the forms are disassembled and stored for the next job.

When the concrete forms have been securely fastened in place, steel reinforcement is prepared and put into the forms. The reinforcement is a very important part of the foundation. It provides extra strength to keep the concrete from breaking under the weight of the structure. Fig. 12-11.

Fig. 12-10. Concrete assumes the shape of the form into which it is placed.

The size and placement of the steel reinforcement are calculated to give maximum strength.
Depending on the shape and thickness of the 2
footing, either wire mesh or reinforcing bars are used. There may be several different layers of reinforcing in a slab of concrete. All the reinforcing is connected to make a rigid framework that will stay in place.

Pouring the Concrete

Once the forms and reinforcement are in place, the concrete can be poured. The concrete is usually delivered to the site in cement trucks. These trucks thoroughly mix the concrete as they are driven to the job site. Concrete from these trucks is sometimes called *ready-mix*. This is because the concrete is already mixed and ready to pour into the forms.

Before the concrete is poured into the forms, two types of samples are taken for testing. A

Fig. 12-11. Steel reinforcement gives the concrete extra strength.

1. Acquaint the class with the terms used for various parts of a concrete form. Show how the parts go together. Suggest that a student group make a model of a set of footing or foundation forms.

2. Steel reinforcement for most foundations is placed after the outside portion of the forms has been placed, but before the inside forms are placed. This allows room for the workers to install the reinforcement.

slump test is made to check the workability
1 of the concrete. Fig. 12-12. Another kind of sample is taken in special test cylinders. This sample is later tested in a laboratory to determine the finished strength of the concrete.

The concrete is poured in the forms using one of several methods. It can be poured directly from the truck by means of a chute. It can also be pumped into the forms using a concrete pump and hose. Another common way to pour concrete is to use a bucket on a crane. The bucket is filled with concrete. The crane lifts and positions the bucket over the form. Then the bucket is emptied and the concrete flows into the form.

As the concrete is poured into the form, special care is taken to make sure all parts of the form are filled. A mechanical vibrator is used to help remove air pockets and to make sure that the concrete fills the form thoroughly. Next the concrete is screeded. **Screeding** is the process of moving a straight board back and forth across the top of the form. This removes any excess concrete and levels the top of the concrete.

Concrete slabs such as floors and sidewalks must be smooth and level. For these surfaces additional finishing steps are required. After the concrete is screeded, the surface is floated. **Floating** is the process of moving coarse aggregate down into the concrete, leaving only fine aggregate and sand on top. This is accomplished by moving a wooden or magnesium *float* back and forth over the surface. Then, after the concrete has begun to set, a steel trowel is used to smooth the surface. This final smoothing is called **troweling**. Fig. 12-13.

Fig. 12-12. This worker is doing a slump test on concrete. Basically, this test involves placing the concrete in the mold shown here. The mold is then removed and the slump of the concrete is measured. This is the distance from the top of the mold to the top of the concrete sample.

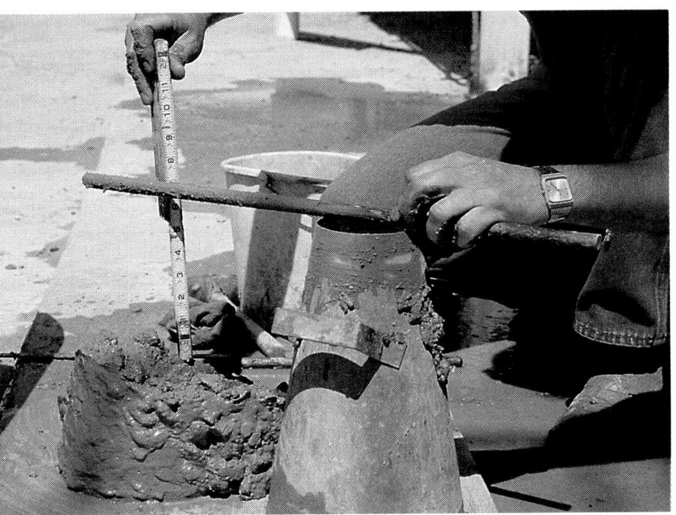

Fig. 12-13. A power trowel is used to finish concrete.

1. Demonstrate how a slump test is taken. Explain the purpose for taking it. Emphasize the importance of having concrete that is workable and yet does not have too much water to weaken the concrete. Also explain how the test cylinders are cured and broken in order to test the ultimate strength of concrete that is in place.

After the surface of the concrete has been finished, the concrete is allowed to cure. A chemical reaction takes place between the cement and
1 the water to give concrete its strength and hardness. For proper curing, however, the concrete must not dry too fast. To keep the moisture in, the concrete is covered with plastic or sprayed with a liquid sealer. Fig. 12-14. After the concrete is sufficiently cured, the forms can be removed.

For Discussion

You have probably seen large concrete trucks on a construction job. These trucks carry the concrete in a large drum that turns on the back of the truck. What are the obvious advantages of having concrete delivered to a construction site in that way? Can you suggest some ways in which preparing and pouring concrete would have been different in the days before such trucks?

HEALTH & SAFETY

For reasons of health and safety, many new construction materials have been introduced. In past years, lead-based paint was widely used in interior decoration. The health hazards of lead are now widely realized. Now, water-based paints are in wide use. In the past, plumbing systems were constructed using pipe that contained a high percentage of lead. Today, pipes of other materials, including types of plastics, are in general use.

BUILDING THE SUPERSTRUCTURE

The superstructure is built on the finished foundation. The superstructure includes all of 2
the structural parts above the foundation of a

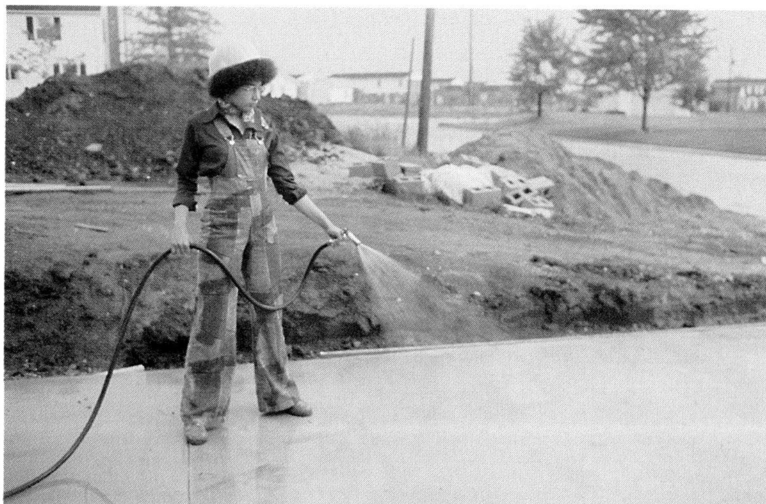

Fig. 12-14. Spraying a liquid sealer onto new concrete seals in the moisture so that the concrete does not dry too fast.

1. Explain the curing process. Emphasize that it takes an extended period of time for concrete to gain the desired strength. Moisture must be present continuously for curing to take place. Curing takes from seven to twenty-eight days.

2. Divide the class into several groups. Ask each group to research and build models of various types of superstructure systems. Ask each group to explain the materials and methods used in their type of construction.

building. It also includes the roofing materials, windows and doors, and all of the finishing materials that are used.

The three main structural parts of a building are the floors, walls, and roof structure. The floors divide the building into levels. The walls divide it into rooms. The roof structure provides support for the cover over the building.

Floors are made of wood or steel frames or of solid concrete. In a house, the ground floor may be made of concrete or of a wood frame covered with wood. The second floor usually consists of a wood-covered wood frame. In a commercial building, the ground floor is usually a concrete slab. Other floors have steel or concrete frames. These floor frames are then covered with a concrete surface.

The type of walls used for a building depends on the type of structural support the building has. You will learn more about structural support later in this chapter. In general, walls can be made of wood, reinforced concrete, steel, or masonry.

Most buildings have a framed roof. The frame spans the distance from wall to wall. Roof trusses
are frequently used because they are both strong 1
and lightweight. Fig. 12-15. A **roof truss** is a preassembled frame of wood or steel that is designed to support a roof. Roof trusses are lighter than other types of roof supports, but they are just as strong.

Structural Support

Structures are commonly classified according to how the weight of the structure is supported. There are basically two types of structures. A **bearing-wall structure** is one in which heavy
walls support the weight of the building. This 2
type of structure has no frame. The outside walls are usually *bearing walls*; that is, they are weight-supporting walls. In addition, some of the inner walls are bearing walls. Bearing walls are usually made of concrete blocks or of solid concrete. Fig. 12-16. This type of construction is most often used for low buildings of one or two stories.

A **frame structure** is one in which a frame supports the weight of the building. The frame of a frame structure is made up of many connected frame members that are covered by sheathing. The frame members carry the weight of the structure and its contents. The framing can be made of wood, steel, or reinforced concrete.

Fig. 12-15. Roof trusses are lightweight, yet strong enough to bear the weight of roofing materials.

1. Have a group of students study roof trusses. Encourage them to make models of roof trusses. Have them test the strength of each model. Testing can be done by hanging known amounts of weight on each model until failure results.

2. Discuss the difference between a bearing wall structure and a frame structure. Why are bearing wall structures not used for high-rise buildings? Were they ever used for such buildings?

Fig. 12-16. Concrete is often used for bearing walls.

Wood framing is used for many houses and other small structures. Carpenters build and erect the wood frame at the site. Fig. 12-17. Large commercial structures, such as office buildings, have frames of steel. Fig. 12-18. The steel for these 1
frames is prepared in a fabricating shop. Ironworkers assemble and erect the steel on the site according to the building plan. The steel parts are bolted, riveted, or welded to make a rigid frame.

Other large structures are supported by frames of steel-reinforced concrete. The concrete can either be poured at the site or preformed elsewhere. Preformed concrete frames are assembled at the site in much the same way that steel frames are assembled. Fig. 12-19.

Fig. 12-17. Parts of a typical wood-frame wall.

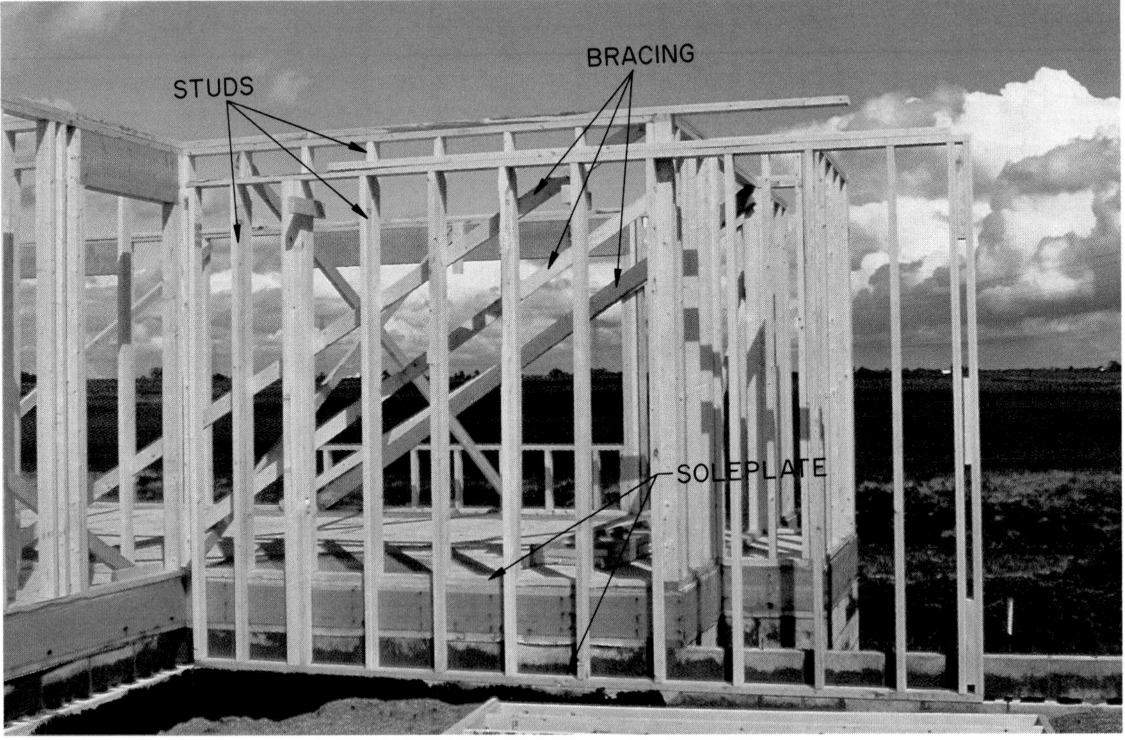

1. Explain to the class the differences among columns, girders, beams, spandrels, and braces in a frame superstructure. A model would be helpful to illustrate the differences.

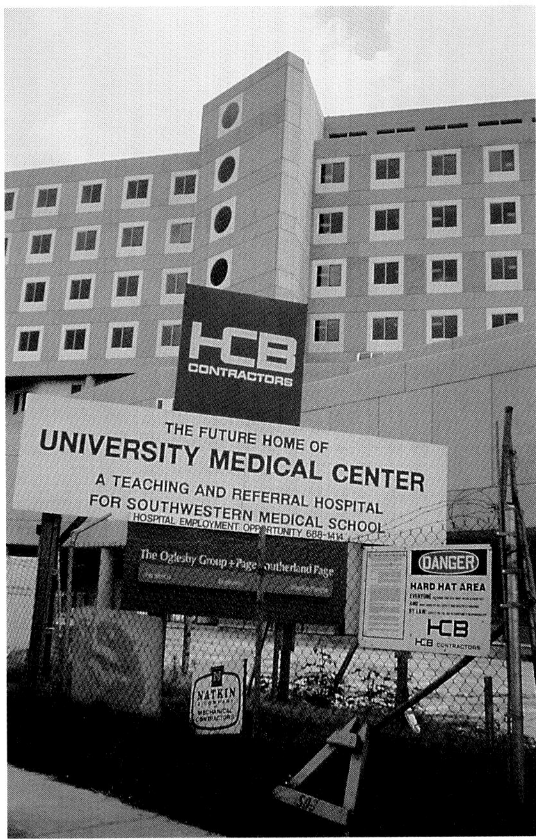

Fig. 12-18. This hospital is a steel-frame structure.

Enclosing the Structure

Before any further work can be done to the 1
inside of the building, it must be enclosed to protect it from the weather. Exterior walls must be finished. Windows and doors must be installed, and the roofing must be completed. The appropriate materials for enclosing the structure are usually chosen by the architect.

Exterior Walls

Exterior walls perform many functions in a structure. They protect the inside from the weather and provide privacy for the occupants. They can also be decorative, providing a pleasing view from the outside.

Fig. 12-19. Preformed, steel-reinforced concrete framing members are assembled at the construction site.

1. Ask students to research and compare the fire resistance of several types of superstructure construction.

Fig. 12-20. The sheathing on this house will help protect it from the weather.

The first step in completing the exterior walls is to apply the sheathing. **Sheathing** is a layer
1 of material that is placed between the framing and the finished exterior to provide additional insulation. Fig. 12-20. Sheathing usually consists of sheets of plywood, fiberboard, or plastic foam panels that have been nailed or screwed to the framework.

After the sheathing has been installed, the exterior walls are completed using various materials. Fig. 12-21. The following list describes a few of the most common possibilities.

- *Panels* are large sheets of exterior finishing material made of wood, vinyl, aluminum, steel, or marble. They are nailed, bolted, or glued to the framework of buildings.
- *Siding* consists of long, narrow strips of wood, aluminum, steel, or vinyl. It is applied over sheathing and is nailed to the studs of a wood frame. Siding is usually used on residential structures.
- *Masonry* is one of the most practical coverings for exterior walls. Masonry walls include brick, concrete block, and stone. These walls require little maintenance and are fireproof.

Windows and Doors

Wall openings are enclosed with windows and
doors. Windows provide light and ventilation. 2
Doors provide a method of entry and exit from the building. The windows and doors are held in place by frames of wood, aluminum, or steel. They are fastened according to the building plans.

1. Sheathing can also act to brace and strengthen the frame of the building. Explain that if the sheathing used is not strong enough to do this, diagonal bracing must be installed on the framework.

2. Have the class find out what curtain walls are. Ask each student to write a brief description of their function. Emphasize that they are not meant to provide strength to the frame.

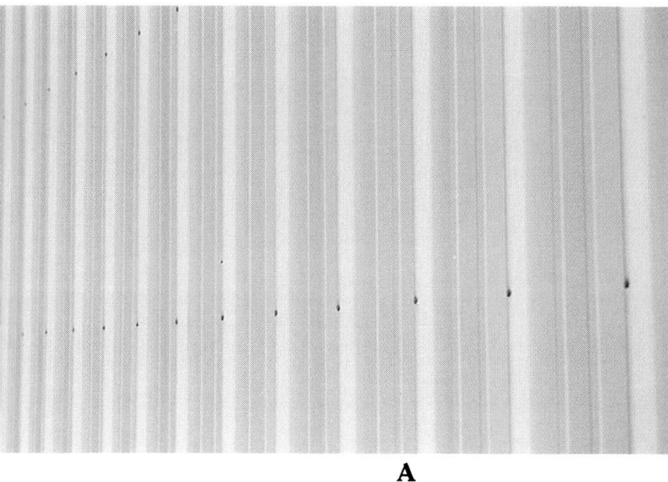

A

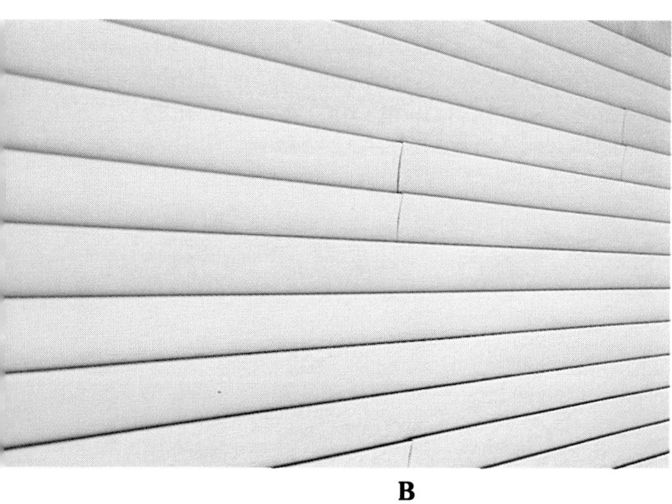

B

C

Fig. 12-21. Types of exterior walls: (a) panels; (b) siding; (c) masonry.

Roofing

Several kinds of roofing materials are available to cover the roof framing and sheathing. 1
Each is adapted to a certain kind of roof. The
following are a few of the most common roofing 2
materials.

Shingles are thin, flat pieces of asbestos, wood, asphalt, or fiberglass. Shingles are applied over a layer of roofing felt, which covers the sheathing. Fig. 12-22. The shingles are overlapped to keep water out. They are suitable for use only on sloping roofs. When properly applied, they are attractive, waterproof, and long lasting.

Built-up roofing is made by alternating several layers of roofing felt and hot bitumen. Bitumen is liquid asphalt or coal tar pitch. When the bitumen cools, it forms a waterproof seal. After several layers of felt and bitumen have been built

Fig. 12-22. Shingles are used on many sloping roofs.

1. Collect as many different kinds of roofing materials as possible. Show them to the class. Discuss where each would be used, their advantages, disadvantages, methods of application, and relative costs.

2. Discuss the advantage of having a roof material that is one continuous piece. What disadvantages are apparent? If the material is only fastened around the edges, how is the rest of it held in place?

up, a layer of gravel is put on top. The gravel reflects the sun and helps protect the roof from severe weather. Built-up roofing is used mainly on flat roofs. Fig. 12-23.

Sheet metal roofs may be found on industrial,
1 commercial, and farm buildings. Fig. 12-24. They are made of metal sheets that can be attached directly to a metal or wooden frame. No sheathing is needed between the frame and the metal sheets. The metals most commonly used are copper, corrugated steel, and aluminum. Sheet metal is used only for sloping roofs.

Membrane roofing is a relatively new kind of roofing that can be used on flat roofs. Thin rubber or plastic sheets are stretched over the roof to form a continuous membrane. The edges of the membrane are fastened to the structure with an adhesive. Fig. 12-25. The membrane stretches and gives with the slightest movement of the roof. The plastic or rubber is resistant to heavy rain, the damaging ultraviolet rays of sunlight, and heat. The sheets are made at a factory to the correct size and shape. Then the roof is folded and shipped to the site. There it is unfolded and fitted over the roof.

Fig. 12-24. Sheet metal is a practical type of roofing that is long lasting and requires little maintenance.

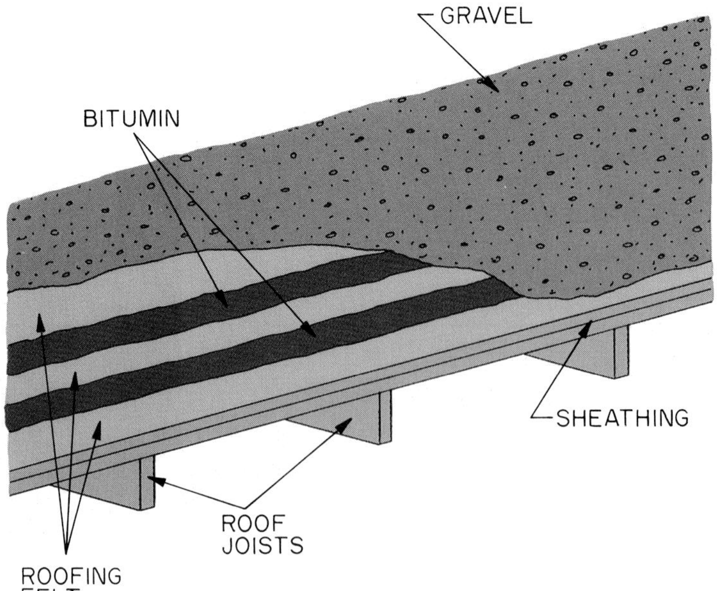

Fig. 12-23. A built-up roof is used on flat roofs.

1. Explain how vent stacks, chimneys, and adjoining walls are flashed to keep these areas weatherproof.

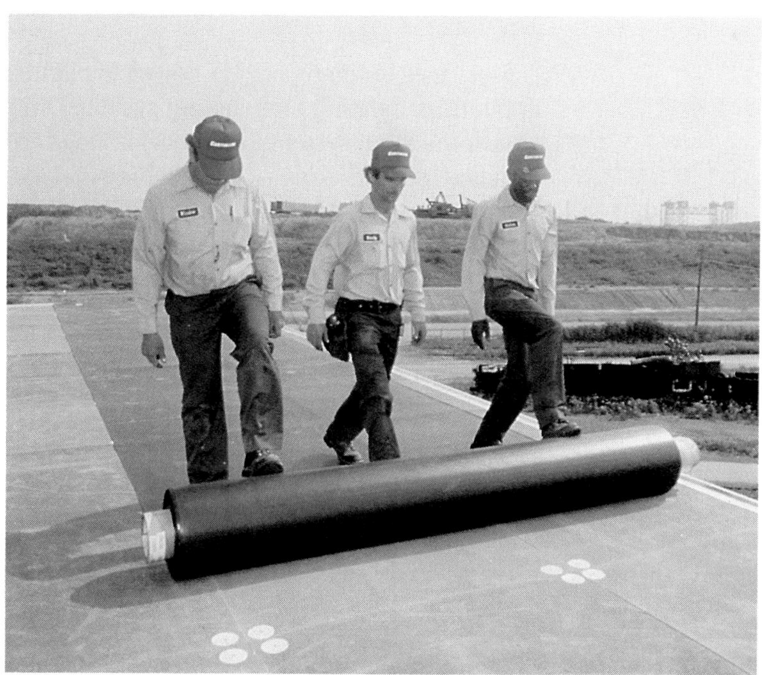

Fig. 12-25. Some flat-roofed buildings have a membrane roof. The membrane stretches from one side of the roof to the other to form a waterproof seal.

For Discussion

As mentioned, the frame structure supports the weight of the building. Wood frames, steel frames, and steel-reinforced concrete frames are discussed. The type of frame used will depend on the type of building. Is there any construction around your school? If there is, what type of frames are being built?

INSTALLING UTILITIES

After the frame of the building has been enclosed, the utilities are installed. The three basic types of utilities are plumbing systems; electrical systems; and heating, ventilating, and air conditioning (HVAC) systems. Utility installation is a two-stage process. The first stage, **roughing in**, is the installation of the basic pipes 1
and wiring that must be placed within the walls, floor, and roof. This must be done before the 2
interior walls are covered. Fig. 12-26.

Later, after the walls have been covered, the installation of the utilities is finished. The **finishing stage** of utility installation readies the utilities for use. Faucets and other plumbing fixtures are installed. Light switches and fixtures, wall receptacles, and plates for telephone and cable television connectors are also installed at this time.

1. Explain that the roughed-in utilities must be inspected by the appropriate building inspector before they are covered. If inspections are not made and the utilities are covered, the contractor may have to uncover them at his or her expense.

2. Discuss how the contractor can provide electricity to power the equipment needed for construction. What factors should be considered? At what point in construction can the change be made to the permanent electrical system?

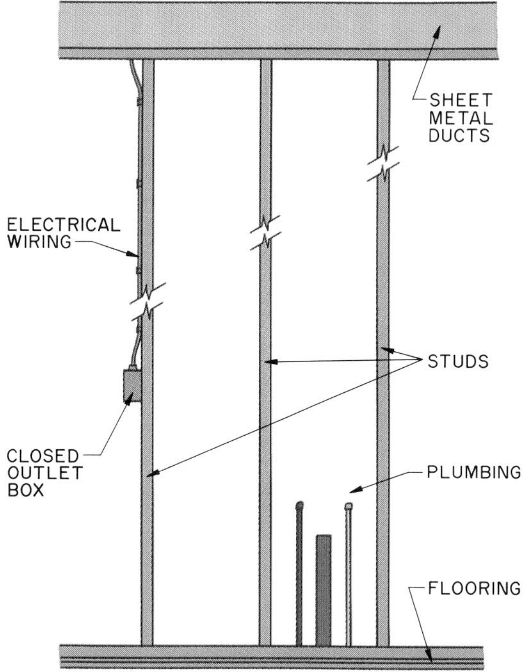

Fig. 12-26. Utilities must be roughed in before interior walls can be finished.

Electrical Systems

Electrical utilities provide power for lights, appliances, heating and cooling systems, and communication systems. Electrical utilities are installed by electricians. At the roughing-in stage, the electrician marks the locations of all the switches, junction boxes, and fixtures. He or she drills holes so that the wires can be pulled through walls and floors. Then the electrical boxes and wires are installed. Fig. 12-27. The wires are pulled into the boxes and left there to be connected at a later time. At this point, roughing in is complete. An electrical inspector checks to make sure that the wiring is acceptable and has been installed according to building codes.

Circuitry

Electrical power enters a building through a
service drop. The **service drop** is the wiring
that connects a building to the electric company's 1
overhead or underground wires. Fig. 12-28. A
meter located near the service drop measures
the amount of power used. Near the meter, but
inside the building, a service panel is installed.
The **service panel** is a box that contains cir- 2
cuit breakers for each individual, or *branch* circuit. It also contains a *main* circuit breaker. This
controls all of the individual circuits collectively.

Each branch circuit provides electricity to the outlets, lights, and switches of one or more rooms. Each circuit is protected from an overload of electricity by the circuit breaker in the service panel. If too many appliances on a circuit are used at one time, the circuit breaker opens the circuit. This prevents the wire in the circuits from overheating and starting a fire.

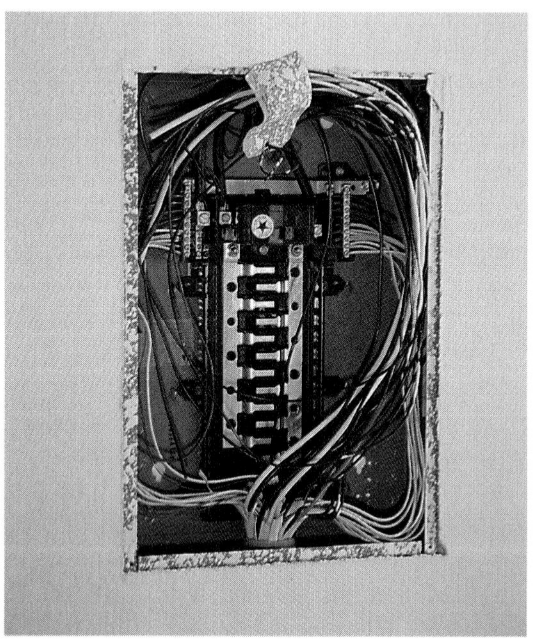

Fig. 12-27. Electrical roughing-in includes installing junction boxes and wires.

1. Explain the differences among ampacity, voltage, and wattage. Show how the ampacity of the service drop is determined by the size of the wire used.
2. Trace the flow of electricity through the service drop, meter, service panel, circuit breaker, and branch circuit to the individual switch, outlet, or appliance.

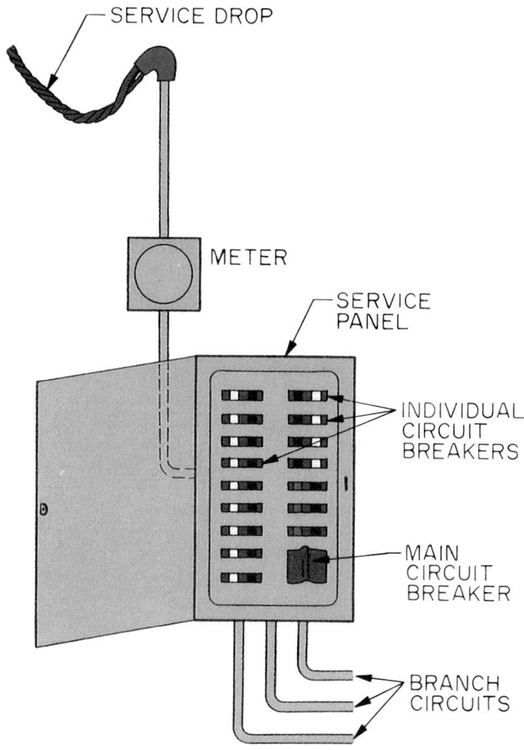

Fig. 12-28. Typical electrical wiring for residential service.

Types of Wiring

There are three basic types of electrical wir-
1 ing. Fig. 12-29. The type of wire used depends on local building codes, on the proposed use of the wire, and on the type of building being constructed. **Conduit** is a pipe through which individual wires can be pulled. It is used in concrete walls and floors to allow easy access to the wires for maintenance and repair. **Nonmetallic sheathed cable** is made of several wires wrapped together inside a plastic coating of insulation. It is very flexible and easy to install. **Armored cable** is made of several wires inside a flexible metal casing. It is used in dry environments where sturdy, yet flexible, wiring is needed.

1. Obtain samples of the basic types of wiring and various materials, such as boxes, outlets, switches, and circuit breakers. Show these to the class and explain how they fit into the system.

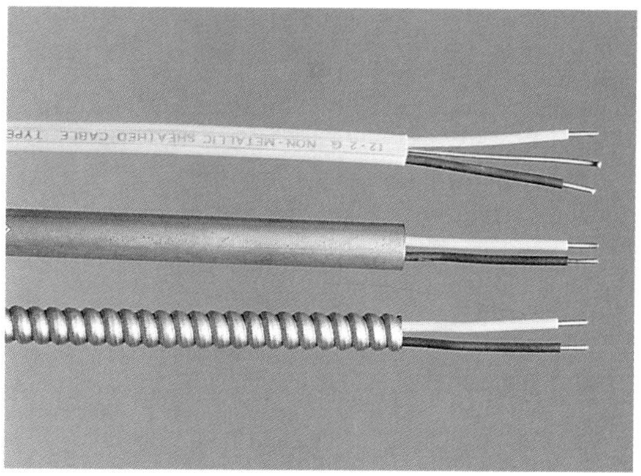

Fig. 12-29. Types of wiring from top to bottom: nonmetallic sheathed cable; conduit with individual wires; armored cable.

Plumbing Systems

Plumbing systems provide buildings with water and drainage. The plumbing system in a frame structure is installed within the wall, floor, and ceiling frames. In structures that are built on concrete slabs, some piping must be installed before the concrete can be poured. Fig.
12-30. Plumbing pipes are usually made of cop- 2
per, galvanized iron, or plastic.

Fig. 12-30. In buildings that have a slab foundation, some plumbing must be done before the concrete can be poured.

2. Discuss water hammer in a plumbing supply system. Explain that liquids are noncompressible. Therefore, air must be introduced somewhere in the system to act as a cushion to avoid this annoying problem.

Supply plumbing is the part of the plumbing system that supplies fresh water for drinking and washing. A service tap provides a supply of water from the city water main. A building supply line runs from the service tap to the water meter. Beyond the water meter, branch lines run to each location in the building where water is needed. Fig. 12-31. Because supply plumbing operates under pressure, the whole system must be leakproof. Valves are used to control the flow of the water.

Drainage plumbing is the part of the plumbing system that carries wastewater away from the structure. This part of the system is made up of drain and vent pipes. Fig. 12-32. Sometimes this part of the system is known as *DWV* (drainage, waste, and vent) plumbing. Copper, cast iron, and plastic pipes are used for drain-
1 age plumbing.

Did You Know?

Plumbing is not a recent invention. It was used in 2000 B.C. at the royal palace at Minos, in ancient Crete. Crete is an island in the Mediterranean. The royal palace had a system for bringing water into the palace. There also was a system for removing waste water. There also was a water-flushing toilet. Though it was simple, this plumbing system was effective. In its basic design, it was similar to modern plumbing systems.

Fig. 12-31. A typical residential water supply system.

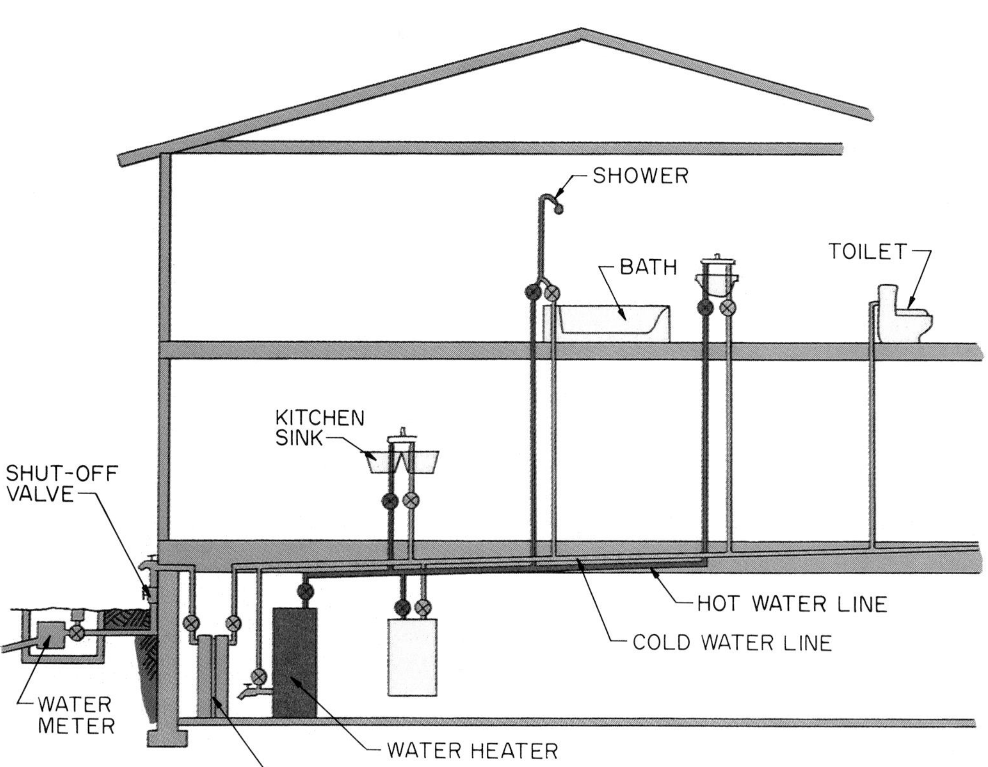

1. Explain why the supply and drainage portions of a plumbing system should not be interconnected. Show how backwater siphonage can occur. Explain the danger it causes and how it can be avoided. Point out that faucets are set with their spouts above the fill level of sinks and tubs. Mention that air gaps are left on all other connections to avoid backwater siphonage.

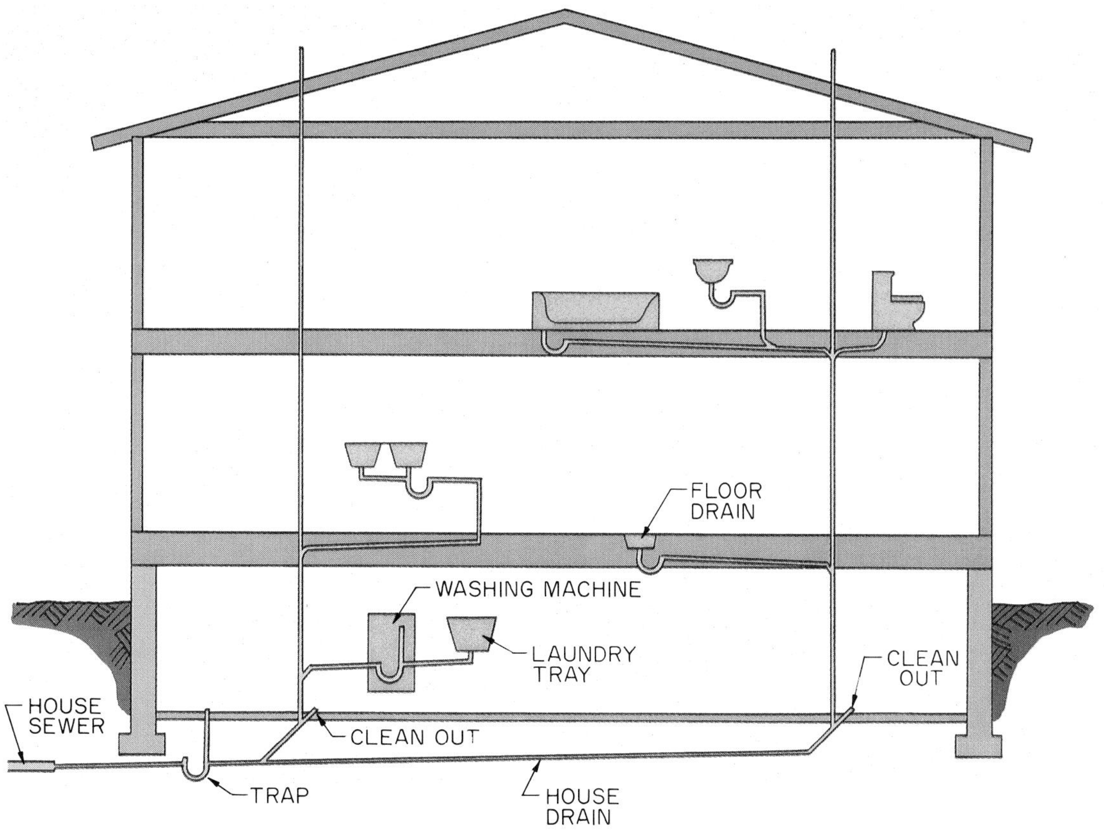

Fig. 12-32. A typical drainage system for a house.

Other Piping Systems

Pipes other than those used in supply and drainage plumbing are simply called *piping*. These pipes are used to carry natural gas, com-
1 pressed air, steam, and water for fire protection. Most piping systems are installed by specialists called *pipefitters*. Pipes for these systems are available in a variety of materials and sizes. The type of pipe that is used depends on the purpose of the system.

HVAC Systems

The HVAC system controls the environment inside a building. This system consists of an air-handling unit, an air conditioner and furnace, and ducts. Installing this system is a very com- 2
plex job. All of the parts have to work together properly. The installer needs to be familiar with the electrical, piping, and mechanical parts of the HVAC system.

The *air-handling unit (AHU)* is made up of a fan and a motor enclosed in a large, sheet-metal box. The AHU is the part of a HVAC system that moves the air through the building. As the air moves through the building, the *air conditioner and furnace* condition the air by changing its temperature. *Ducts* are the large pipes or tubes that carry the air to and from the air conditioner and furnace. *Supply ducts* carry air from the air conditioner and furnace to the

1. Have a student or group of students research and report on fire protection systems, their design and function.

2. Discuss the loss of heat from a building and natural air convection. Show how this influences the placement of supply outlets and return air ducts.

rooms of the building. *Return-air ducts* carry the room air back to the air conditioner and furnace to be conditioned again. *Dampers* are valves that control the flow of air. *Thermostats* are automatic switches that measure temperature. They turn the system on or off to maintain a preset temperature range. Fig. 12-33.

For Discussion

Most stores and office buildings are now air conditioned. What effect has the use of air conditioning in buildings had on their general design?

Fig. 12-33. The thermostat measures the surrounding air temperature. It then switches the furnace or air conditioner on and off to maintain a preset temperature range.

FINISH WORK

After the utilities have been installed, the building is ready to be finished. Finish work completes the structure according to the building plans. It includes covering walls and ceilings, applying paint and wall covering, installing trim and hardware, paving and landscaping, and general cleanup. These final touches make the structure attractive and give the building a distinctive look.

Covering Interior Walls and Ceilings

Several materials may be used to cover interior walls and ceilings. The most common wall covering is drywall. Others include wood paneling and many different kinds of tile. Ceilings are usually covered with ceiling tiles or drywall.

Drywall is a general term used for plasterboard or wallboard. If both the ceiling and the walls 1
are to be covered with drywall, first the ceiling is covered and then the walls. Drywall is fastened directly to ceiling joists and wall *studs*, or framing members. Next, the joints and nail holes are filled with drywall joint compound. The surface is then painted or covered with wallpaper.

Manufactured *wood paneling* often is used for interior walls. The panels are attached to the walls with nails or with an adhesive. Panels can be applied over drywall or nailed to furring strips attached to the studs. Drywall provides more uniform support for the panels than do furring strips.

Tiles are another common interior finish. Most wall tiles are made of ceramic. However, tiles can also be made of glass, steel, or plastic. Because they are easy to clean and maintain, tiles are used in restaurants, bathrooms, kitchens, and other places where cleanliness is important. Fig. 12-34. Wall tiles are applied

1. Discuss the advantages of drywall.

Fig. 12-34. Ceramic tile is used for walls that need to be cleaned often, such as walls in fast-food restaurants.

with adhesive to a special drywall backing. The
1 tile joints are filled with *grout*, or cement, after
the tile is in place.

Ceiling tiles are made of fiberboard or fiberglass. Some ceiling tiles are glued or stapled in place. Others are held in a suspended ceiling system. In a suspended ceiling system, metal strips are hung from the ceiling. The tiles are held in place by the metal strips. Fig. 12-35.

Painting and Wall Covering

Paint and wall covering are decorative finishes that are applied to interior walls. Both protect wall surfaces so that they last longer. They also make the walls easier to clean and maintain.

Fig. 12-35. A suspended ceiling system consists of tiles held by metal strips that are suspended from the ceiling.

1. Until recent times, plaster was the most popular interior wall covering. What materials can be used as a plaster base? In what layers is plaster applied? What plaster finishes are available? What makes plaster so versatile?

Paint is a surface treatment that adds color to interior and exterior walls. It can be applied by brushing, rolling, or spraying. The kind of equipment used is determined by the size of the surface to be covered. Large surfaces are either rolled or sprayed. Fig. 12-36.

Wallpaper is an alternative to painting interior walls. Actually, most wallpaper is no longer made of paper. It is made of a thin layer of decorated vinyl. Wallpaper comes in many attractive colors and patterns. It is purchased by the roll and is cut to size by the installer. The pieces are applied to the wall with adhesive.

Did You Know?

In Europe wallpaper was developed in the late 1400s. The earliest European wallpapers were stencilled or painted by hand. The first wallpapers were meant to be decorative. They also were meant to resemble cloth wall hangings and wood paneling. It was only later that other wallpaper designs were introduced.

Installing Floor Covering

A floor covering is installed on the floors of most buildings. Floor coverings add to the beauty 1
of the building. In addition, some types of floor covering provide cushioning against a hard concrete or wood floor. Floor tiles, sheet goods, and carpet are among the most common floor coverings. Fig. 12-37.

- *Floor tiles* are individual pieces of carpet, vinyl, or stone, usually 12 inches square. Adhesive is used to apply them to the floor.
- *Sheet goods* are large vinyl rolls, or sheets, of floor covering, usually 12 feet wide. The sheets are rolled out and cut to fit the room. Sheet goods usually are applied with adhesive.
- *Carpet* is a popular floor covering made of nylon, polyester, wool, or other fibers. Carpet comes in rolls that are 12 feet wide. The carpet is installed over a plastic or rubber-foam pad that acts as a cushion.

Installing Trim and Hardware

The last step in finishing the interior of a struc- 2
ture is installing the trim and hardware. Trim is installed around windows and doors. Special

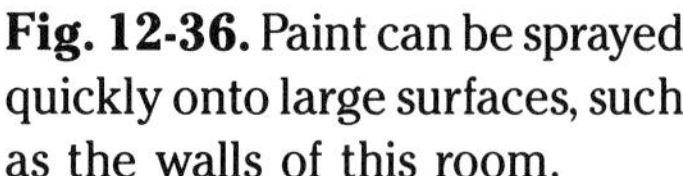

Fig. 12-36. Paint can be sprayed quickly onto large surfaces, such as the walls of this room.

1. Collect samples of the various types of floor coverings. Label these samples and pass them around the class as you talk about the various ones. How do the various types compare in cost, durability, and ease of installation? What standards should be used to judge quality?

2. Show the class various types of moldings used for trim. Demonstrate how mitered and coped joints are made. Tell where each is used. Make several jigs. Have each student make a mitered and coped joint on molding.

trim called **molding** is used to cover joints where floors, walls, and ceilings meet. Fig. 12-38. This phase of building also includes installing cabi- 1
nets, shelving, and other accessories. The hardware installed includes towel bars, soap holders, doorknobs, and shelf brackets.

At this point the second stage of the utility work must be done. Lights, fans, and other electrical fixtures are installed. Sinks, tubs, and faucets also are installed at this time. HVAC vents are put in place, and telephones are installed.

Finishing the Outside

After the structure has been completed, the outside work must be done to finish the site. There are four major kinds of outside finishing tasks: completing structural details, paving, land- 2
scaping, and cleaning up. Structural details

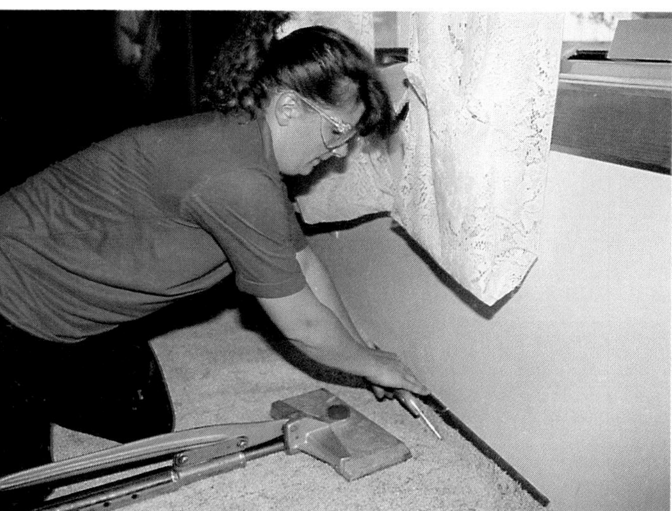

Fig. 12-37. Floor tiles, sheet goods, and carpet are three common floor coverings.

1. Describe the installation of doors. Emphasize that many doors are now prehung. Demonstrate how to cut a hinge gain with a chisel. Describe how this is done with a router. Also describe how door hardware is installed.

Fig. 12-38. Molding and trim are used to cover joints at the floor and ceiling and around doors and windows.

2. Have a student or group of students research and report on landscaping procedures in your area. How does your climate affect the landscaping used?

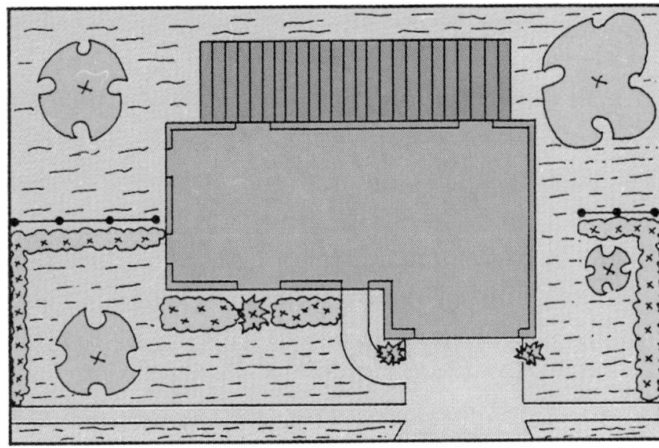

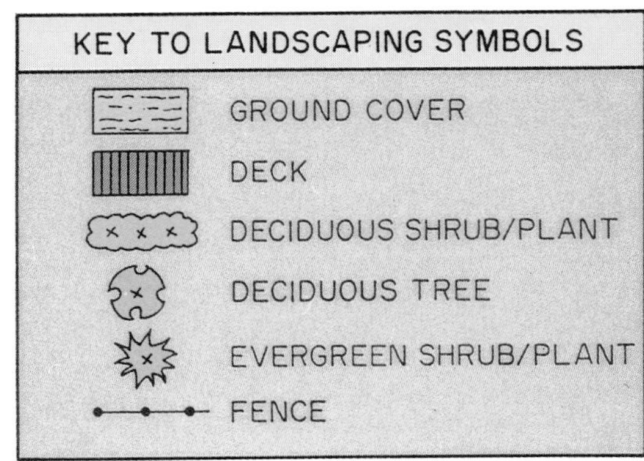

Fig. 12-39. The landscaping plan shows workers what to plant and where to plant it.

include tasks that must be done to finish the structure. The windows must be *caulked*, or sealed with a special compound. The exterior walls of most structures must be painted. (Stone and brick structures usually are exceptions.) Trim must be added, and porches and decks must be finished.

All of the paving is done at this time. Areas to be used for driveways, parking lots, and walkways need to be paved with asphalt or concrete.

Fig. 12-40. Flower beds are an attractive highlight in any landscape plan.

First the earth is leveled and compacted. Then the pavement is laid in place and finished. Final paving work includes painting stripes for parking spaces.

Landscaping is done according to a landscaping plan, which shows how the finished site 1
should look. It shows what is to be planted and where. Fig. 12-39. Trees, bushes, grass, and ground cover are planted in topsoil treated with lime and fertilizer to ensure better plant growth. Lawns are either seeded or sodded. Flower beds
are planted to add beauty and color to the land- 2
scaping. Fig. 12-40.

The final step is to give the site a general cleaning. Any leftover debris is hauled away. The contractor makes a general tour of inspection and removes any tools and equipment that may still be at the site.

For Discussion

Landscaping is an important step in finishing a construction project. In some cities, awards are given for beautiful landscaping. Is the land around your school landscaped? Can you suggest any improvements in the landscaping?

1. Have a student or group of students develop a landscape plan for a building site. Encourage them to produce a pictorial drawing of what the finished job will look like.

2. Show before and after photos illustrating how landscaping adds to the external beauty of a building. Talk about the need to understand that shrubs and trees will mature, changing the look of the landscaping.

Construction Facts

STOP LANDSLIDES—USE SAWDUST!

Portions of Highway 55 near Boise, Idaho, are on a steep slope on the side of a mountain range. Landslides in this area are frequent and severe. They have been a recurring problem since 1946. Before this problem was solved, the roadbed in one 3½-mile (5.6-km) section kept slipping down the mountainside in eight different places.

In this particularly bad slide zone, engineers have used an unusual material to stop the slides: sawdust. Sawdust fill was used to stabilize the soil under the roadbed. Replacing the heavy existing soil with lightweight sawdust relieved some of the pressure on the water-saturated, unstable soil on the downhill side of the roadbed.

More than 33,000 cubic yards (25,000 cubic metres) of sawdust were dumped on the site. The sawdust was spread, mixed, and compacted. Then the regular rock roadbed, a seal coat of asphalt, and 1¼ inches (32 mm) of asphaltic concrete pavement were laid.

The decision to use sawdust was based on its success in other places. Also, the sawdust
was available from a lumber mill 2½ miles
(4 km) away. The lightweight material has
done a good job of stabilizing the road. At 1
the same time, the sawdust has been put to
good use.

1. Different materials find different uses in construction. Encourage the students to bring in samples of building materials that you have studied. Emphasize that these should be different from any you already have in the classroom. Ask them to turn in a written description of the material, telling what it is called, where and how it is used, and the manufacturer's name. Give each sample a code. Start a file with the written descriptions arranged according to the same code.

CHAPTER 12

REVIEW

Chapter Summary

Construction processes are the processes used to build a construction project. The land on which the project will be constructed is called the site. The site must be surveyed and cleared. Laying out the site is the process of identifying the location of the proposed structure on the property. The excavation provides a place for the structure's foundation. The site must be leveled and graded. The soil must be stabilized to support the structure.

The foundation is that part of the structure that is below the first floor. The superstructure is the rest of the building. The footing is the part of the structure that distributes the structure's weight. The wall that is built directly on the footing is called the foundation wall. Forms are the molds that contain the concrete until it hardens. A slump test is made to test the workability of concrete. Screeding removes excess concrete and levels the top of the concrete. Floating is the process of moving coarse aggregate down into the concrete. The final smoothing is called troweling.

The three main structural parts of a building are the floors, walls, and roof structure. In bearing-wall structures, the walls support the weight of the building. In frame structures, the frame supports the weight of the building. The utilities are installed after the frame of the building has been enclosed. The service drop is wiring that connects a building to the electric company's wires.

There are three basic types of electrical wiring: conduit, nonmetallic sheathed cable, and armored cable. Plumbing systems supply buildings with water and drainage. The HVAC system controls the environment inside a building. Finish work completes the structure. Several materials may be used to cover interior walls and ceilings. The last step in finishing the structure is installing the trim and hardware.

Test Your Knowledge 1

1. What three steps are involved in preparing a site?
2. What are the markers called that identify a building's boundaries even after excavation has begun?
3. What name is given to a long, narrow excavation that is meant to hold pipelines?
4. Name three general methods of soil stabilization.
5. What are the two basic parts of a structure?
6. What three processes are used to smooth the surface of concrete?
7. In a bearing-wall structure, what supports the weight of the building?
8. What are the three main structural parts of a building?
9. What is a roof truss?
10. Name two types of roofing that can be used on flat roofs.

1. The answers to the Test Your Knowledge questions are in the Teacher's Manual at the front of this Teacher's Annotated Edition.

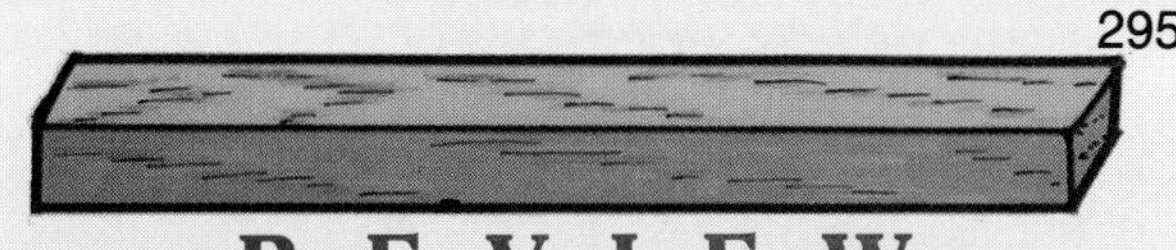

REVIEW

11. What are the three main types of utility systems?
12. What are the three basic types of electrical wiring?
13. What is the name of the utility system that controls the temperature inside a building?
14. Name three common types of floor covering.
15. What four things must be done to finish the area outside of a structure?

Activities

1. Find and observe a new building under construction. Report to your class on the type of structure it is.

2. Check the utilities in your house or apartment. Find out what utilities are available, where the meters are located, and who supplies each utility.

3. Choose a construction site in your area. Pretend that you are a contractor in charge of that building site. Plan what type of structure you will build. Put your plans on paper, showing what types of walls, flooring, roofing, and so on, you will use. Be ready to explain your decisions.

CHAPTER 13

THE COMPLETED PROJECT

Terms to Know

certificate of occupancy
claim
final inspection
final payment
lien
maintenance
notice of completion
punch list
release of claims
release of liens
repair
warranty

Objectives

When you have finished reading this chapter, you should be able to do the following: 1

- Describe the final inspection process.
- Explain what a punch list is, who makes it, and what is done with it.
- List the steps to transfer ownership of a construction project.
- Explain how releases protect the owner.
- Explain the difference between maintenance and repair and give one example of each.

1. Resources:
- Chapter 13 Lesson Plan in the Teacher's Manual in this Teacher's Annotated Edition and in the Teacher's Resource Guide.
- Chapter 13 Study Guide in the Student Workbook.
- Chapter 13 Visual Master in the Teacher's Resource Guide.

After a project has been completed, it is turned over to the owner. The owner makes the final payment to the contractor and takes responsibility for the structure. However, before the contract is considered officially fulfilled, several steps must be taken. This chapter will help you understand how a contract is concluded.

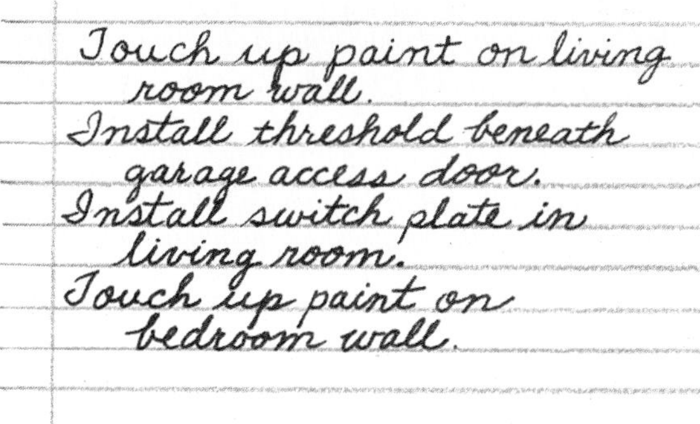

Touch up paint on living room wall.
Install threshold beneath garage access door.
Install switch plate in living room.
Touch up paint on bedroom wall.

Fig. 13-1. A punch list is made by the final inspection team to let the contractor know what corrections need to be made.

FINAL INSPECTION

Several inspections are made of a project while it is being constructed. The **final inspection**
1 is made after a construction project has been
completed. In this section, you will learn about the final inspection of a typical building. Every construction project must have a final inspection.

The building must be inspected to make sure that the job was done properly and according to the terms of the contract. The final inspection is made by several people working together as a team. The owner, the architect or engineer, and the contractor each has a representative on the team. The inspectors begin at the bottom of the building and work their way to the top. They look at everything. They inspect every room. They check to see that all mechanical and
2 electrical equipment is working properly. They
also make sure that everything has been installed safely. If, for example, electrical wiring was installed improperly, someone could be injured. The owner would be held responsible.

The Punch List

During the inspection, the inspectors list things they see that need to be corrected. This list is called a **punch list**. Fig. 13-1. Big problems, such as a crack in a ceiling, are on the list. However, the list also includes even the slightest defect, such as a missing screw or a mark on a wall. Fig. 13-2. When the inspection is complete, the punch list is given to the contractor. The contractor is then responsible for making the necessary corrections.

Fig. 13-2. Even very minor defects such as this missing screw are listed on the punch list.

1. Point out that, when the final inspection is being made, the contractor still has a considerable amount of money coming from the owner. At this point, this gives the owner leverage to get work corrected that appears to be substandard.

2. Discuss why it might be a good idea to withhold a portion of the amount due to any subcontractor until the building has had a satisfactory final inspection.

HEALTH & SAFETY

Many of the inspection procedures on a new building are concerned with health and safety. Building inspectors are especially interested in making sure that the building will be safe for people to live and work in. They are concerned with the strength of materials. They also check that the correct construction techniques have been properly used. The laws regarding building inspection have become more strict in recent years. A hundred years ago, newly constructed buildings were not subject to the same careful inspection.

Corrections

Usually the inspectors give the contractor a *deadline*, or date by which the corrections must be completed. The contractor must evaluate the punch list and plan how each item will be corrected. The contractor must also determine who is at fault. If the contractor is at fault, company workers will make the corrections. If a subcontractor is at fault, that company must be notified that corrections are necessary.

After the corrections have been done, another inspection is made. This time, the inspectors check the corrected items closely. They also take another look around the structure. If the corrections are satisfactory and they do not find any new defects, the job is officially finished. However, if the corrections are not satisfactory or if new defects are found, the process is repeated. When everyone is finally satisfied that all of the contract requirements have been met, the owner formally accepts the building.

1. Have an official from the local building department visit the class. Ask him or her to describe the work that is done when an inspection takes place. Have him or her describe what would be checked before a certificate of occupancy would be issued. When

Certificate of Occupancy

If people are going to occupy the building, it must be approved by the city or county in which
it was built. The building inspection department 1
makes its own final inspection of the building. This is the same agency that issued the building permit that allowed construction to begin.

For a building to be approved for use, a **certificate of occupancy** must be issued by the building inspection department. This certificate shows that the building has passed the building inspector's check of the structure. It means that the building has been built according to federal, state, and local building codes. It means that the building is safe for people to use.

For Discussion

Assume that you are one of the inspectors making the final inspection on a building. What would you check in the building to make sure that the building was without defects? Describe the method you would use to make sure that you had carefully checked the entire building.

TRANSFERRING OWNERSHIP

After the inspections, punch list corrections, and final inspection have been made, the job is considered complete. The owner then files a formal **notice of completion**. This legal document lets everyone know that the job is finished.

inviting guests, it is a good idea to provide them with a topic outline of what you would like covered. You might also give them a list of questions that they can answer in their presentation.

Before the owner files the notice, however, he or she must receive certain documents from the contractor.

Releases

Before the property owner accepts ownership of the building from the contractor, the owner must get legal releases from the contractor. The two most common releases are the release of claims and the release of liens. These releases protect the owner from future claims for money and from liens on the building.

Release of Claims

A **claim** is a legal demand for money. A contractor may file a claim against the owner if the contractor runs into a problem that was not shown on the plans. For example, suppose that the contractor discovered poor soil on the site. The soil was not shown on the plans. It costs extra money to remove the poor soil and bring in better soil. The contractor did not expect to have to upgrade the soil. Thus, he or she did not include the cost of upgrading the soil in the contract price. Fig. 13-3.

To get a reasonable payment for the work, the contractor may file a claim for extra money from the owner. If the claim is not settled by the time the work is done, the claim is said to be outstanding. Both parties work toward an agreement so the claim can be settled. When an agreement cannot be reached, the claim must be settled in court.

Before the owner accepts the building, therefore, the contractor must provide the owner with a release of claims. A **release of claims** is a legal document in which the contractor gives up the right to file any claim against the owner. The contractor must check to be sure all claims have been satisfied before he or she signs the release of claims. If there are any unsettled
1 claims, they are automatically cancelled when the contractor signs the release.

1. Show the class the part of a standard construction contract that deals with claims for unforeseen conditions. Emphasize that a body of law has been developed that helps define the rights and responsibilities of the contractor and the owner.

Fig. 13-3. In situations where unexpected problems are encountered, the contractor may have to file a claim.

Release of Liens

Any worker or supplier that has not been paid for materials or services can get a lien against the owner's property. A **lien** is similar to a claim, 2
except that the owner's property becomes security for the amount due the worker. If the amount

2. Explain that lien laws have changed in recent years. It is important to know how they apply in your state. For example, in some states a lien has to be filed before any material is delivered or work is done.

is not paid, the person who holds the lien can have the property sold. He or she can then take the amount due from the amount received from the sale. Thus, it is to the owner's advantage to make sure that the contractor has paid all the bills.

A **release of liens** is a formal, written state-
1 ment that everyone has been properly paid by
the contractor. The release provides assurance that no liens for unpaid bills can be put on the owner's property. When the contractor is satisfied that all the people involved in the project have been paid, then he or she can sign a release of liens. The owner then knows that the property is not in danger of being sold to pay a debt.

Warranties

A **warranty** is a guarantee or promise that a job has been done well or that the materials have no defects. When a project is finished, the contractor gives the owner certain warranties. The *contractor's warranty* is a promise that there are no defects in the work. The contractor promises to fix any flaws in workmanship within a certain time. This time is usually within one year of the issue date of the warranty. For example, if a door will not close properly, the contractor will fix it at no cost to the owner. The contractor wants to protect the reputation of the company. The warranty helps protect the construction company's good name.

The *supplier's warranty* is a guarantee that there are no defects in the materials supplied. Defects that might be found will be fixed by the supplier at no cost to the owner. Supplier's warranties cover items such as furnaces, air conditioners, and water heaters. Fig. 13-4.

When the construction is finished, the contractor gives the new owner a copy of the warranties. The contractor also makes sure that the
owner receives the operating and service 2
manuals for the equipment that has been installed.

Final Payment

As the owner receives the releases, warranties, and other items, he or she makes the **final payment**. This is the last step in transferring ownership. The owner pays the construction

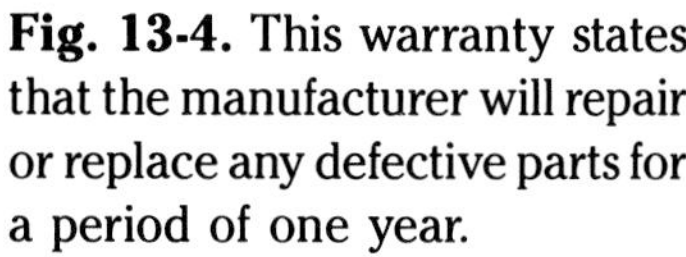

Fig. 13-4. This warranty states that the manufacturer will repair or replace any defective parts for a period of one year.

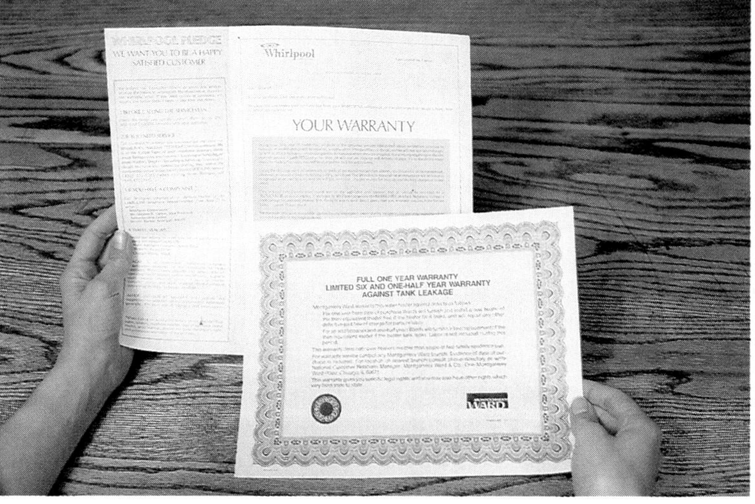

1. Show the class a copy of a completed release of liens statement from your state. What would happen if a contractor signed this without having all bills paid?

2. Ask a student or group of students to report on the Home Owner's Warranty program that was developed by the National Association of Home Builders. Who pays the cost and how is it operated?

1 company all the money due according to the contract. Now the deal is closed and the owner can move in. The building has become the
2 owner's responsibility.

Did You Know?

The lien is not a new idea. The principle of the lien was present in the law of the ancient Romans. The early English courts also recognized the right of a creditor to keep possession of a debtor's goods until a debt was paid.

For Discussion

From reading the text, you can see that warranties are important in building construction. In the past fifty years, buildings have become more complicated. Building contractors now install complex equipment in some buildings. One example of such equipment is a heating and ventilating system. Discuss the items that might need to be covered in such a product warranty.

MAINTENANCE AND REPAIR

The owner is responsible for the completed project, including all maintenance of the building and grounds. Most repairs are made initially by the suppliers and contractor under the construction warranties. However, after the term of the warranty is up, the owner is responsible for repairs.

Maintenance

Maintenance is taking care of an object or structure so that it continues to function the way it was intended. When you clean your room you are maintaining it. You put everything in its place. Then, the next time you look for your books, you will be able to find them. The maintenance your family does on your home includes keeping it clean and attractive inside and out. Fig. 13-5.

Some maintenance work needs to be done only occasionally, when the need arises. For example, when a light bulb burns out, you replace it. When the furnace filter gets dirty, you clean or replace it. Fig. 13-6.

Fig. 13-5. This homeowner is maintaining his house by checking the fit of screens and storm windows.

1. Explain that the final payment will usually amount to at least ten percent of the total cost of the project. Until final payment has been made, the contractor may have more money in the project than he or she has been paid.

2. Give the class several problems in which they will have to calculate profit and percent of profit.

Fig. 13-6. Changing a furnace filter is an example of maintenance that needs to be done at certain intervals.

Other maintenance needs to be done on a regular basis. This type of maintenance is called
1 *preventive maintenance* because it is done to prevent a problem from occurring. For example, a wood-frame house must be painted every three or four years to keep the wood from rotting and to maintain a neat appearance. The blower motor on a furnace or air conditioner must be oiled periodically to prevent the motor from failing.

Repair

Repair is the process of restoring an object or structure to its original appearance or working order. There are several reasons why repairs might need to be done. Many materials naturally *deteriorate* (wear out). They can also be damaged by extreme weather conditions and air pollution. Roofing materials, for example, wear out in time and must be replaced with new materials. Replacing broken or worn equipment is another kind of repair. For example, a dishwasher may wear out and need to be replaced.

Repairs may be minor and inexpensive. Repairs may also be major and require expensive, specialized help. For example, patching a hole in a wall is a minor repair. However, fixing an air conditioner or replacing a roof is considered a
major repair. Fig. 13-7. In many cases, proper 2
maintenance will help reduce the need for both minor and major repairs.

For Discussion

Maintenance is important in keeping a building in good shape. In the last twenty years, several materials have been introduced that reduce the need for building maintenance. Can you identify some of these new materials? What effects have the use of these new materials had on building maintenance practices?

Fig. 13-7. A special crew of workers is needed to repair this roof.

1. Discuss how the neglect of preventive maintenance can lead to the need for repairs. Ask for examples from the class. Which is usually the most costly?

2. Have the class develop a maintenance schedule for the storage building discussed in Chapter 14. Discuss each maintenance item. Decide upon the time interval in which it should be done.

Construction Facts

THE ENERGY HOME

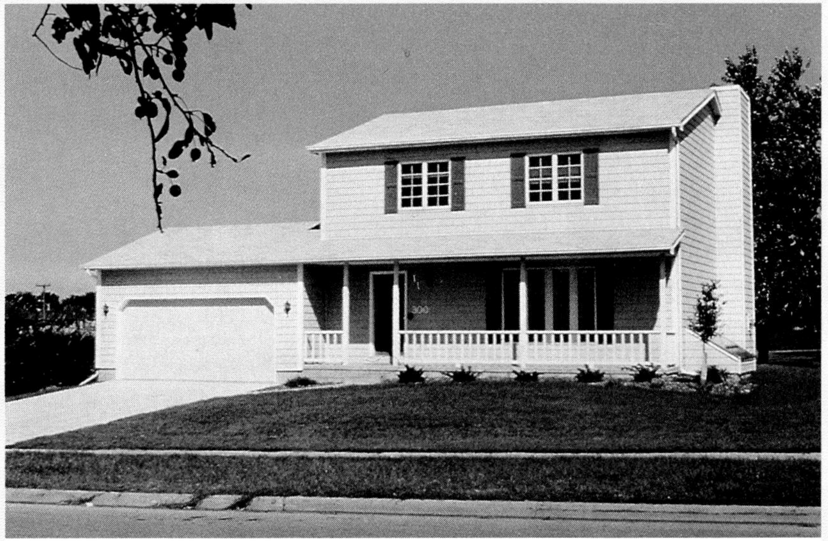

A house built in central Illinois is a show-
1 case for many new developments in construction technology. Called the Energy Home, this 1,700 square foot (157 square metre), two-story house is a single family dwelling. It incorporates a number of unusual construction techniques. In time, however, some of the new ideas may become more common in the construction industry. For example, the foundation is made of plastic foam blocks. These plastic blocks were filled with concrete and reinforced with steel bars. The blocks were then covered with a waterproof coating.

The beams of the house are rectangular wooden trusses, rather than wooden beams. Such trusses were used because they could be easily made in the size and shape needed. It took only two days to enclose the Energy Home using the pre-cut trusses.

Heat is provided by a water heater/air handler system. This works in the same way as a traditional furnace. It is, however, more efficient. Air conditioning is provided by a gas-fired water chiller. This will reduce air conditioning costs. Natural gas is piped through semi-rigid stainless steel piping.

The windows were designed to reduce heating and air conditioning costs. The house also has been built along an east-west axis.

1. What criteria will be used for judging the completeness and adequacy of a construction project? Discuss the written and implied standards that are used to judge whether a good job has been done.

CHAPTER 13

REVIEW

Chapter Summary

Several inspections are made while a project is being constructed. After the project has been completed, the final inspection is made. During this inspection, a punch list is drawn up. This lists defects found during the inspection. These defects must be corrected by the contractor before a certain deadline. The owner accepts the building only when all of the contract requirements have been met. For a building to be approved for use, a certificate of occupancy must be issued. After the job is considered to be complete, the owner files a formal notice of completion. Before accepting ownership from the contractor, the owner must obtain legal releases. The two most common releases are the release of claims and the release of liens. A claim is a legal demand for money. In filing a release of claims, the contractor gives up any right to file any claim against the owner.

A lien is similar to a claim. In a lien, the owner's property is security for the amount owed the workers. A release of claims acknowledges that everyone has been properly paid by the contractor. A warranty is a guarantee that the job has been done well and is free of defects. A suppliers' warranty is a guarantee that there were no defects in the materials as supplied. The owner makes the final payment when he or she receives the release, warranties, and other needed items. Maintenance and repair are essential if the house is to be kept in good condition.

Test Your Knowledge [1]

1. When is the final inspection of a construction project made?
2. Who makes the final inspection?
3. What is a punch list?
4. Who is responsible for seeing that all the needed corrections are made?
5. Who issues a certificate of occupancy?
6. Name two types of releases that an owner should get from a contractor before accepting ownership of the building.
7. What is a warranty?
8. Name two kinds of warranties.
9. What is the last step in transferring ownership from the contractor to the owner?
10. What is the difference between maintenance and repair?

1. The answers to the Test Your Knowledge questions are in the Teacher's Manual at the front of this Teacher's Annotated Edition.

REVIEW

Activities

1. Visit a public building such as a library or courthouse. Find the certificate of occupancy posted on a wall somewhere in the building. You may need to ask to see it. Make a list of the conditions stated on it (maximum occupancy, etc.).
2. Look around your house or apartment. Do the following:
   a. Make a list of things that need to be done as the need arises.
   b. Make a list of things that need preventive maintenance.

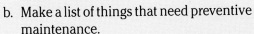

CHAPTER 14

STUDENT ENTERPRISE

Terms to Know

on contract
speculation
unit cost

Objectives

When you have finished reading this chapter, you should be able to do the following: 1

- Participate in the formation of a class company.
- Participate in estimating and planning a construction project.
- Participate in building a structure as a member of a class construction company.

1. Resources:
- Chapter 14 Lesson Plan in the Teacher's Manual in this Teacher's Annotated Edition and in the Teacher's Resource Guide.
- Chapter 14 Study Guide in the Student Workbook.
- Chapter 14 Visual Master in the Teacher's Resource Guide.

You have studied construction and learned about tools, materials, and processes. You have learned how construction companies are organized and how they conduct business. You have also learned that much is involved in building any construction project. Now it is time for you to put into practice some of what you have learned. This chapter is designed to give you the opportunity to do some of the things you have read about. Most of the information in this chapter should be familiar.

Before you make any decisions about an enterprise project, you should read this chapter completely. Then you will know the facts needed to make wise decisions.

FORMING A CONSTRUCTION COMPANY

The development of your construction com-
1 pany will require the talents and abilities of every person in your class. To make sure that every student can take an active role in the company, you should form a corporation. You may wish to review the information about corporations in Chapter 7 before you begin to organize your company. Every student in your class should be a member of the board of directors. As such, each student will have full voting privileges and can participate in company decisions.

Company Organization

Successful companies are well organized. Each employee knows what he or she is supposed to do. Some people are managers. Others work with records and other paperwork. Still others do the physical work. Each worker is important. Each person must do his or her job well if the company is to be a success. Your board of directors will be responsible for organizing all of these activities.

You (the board of directors) should first elect the company managers. Fig. 14-1. You will need a project manager, a finance manager, a construction superintendent, a marketing director, and a personnel director. You will also need a manager for each part of the construction project. For example, there should be a manager

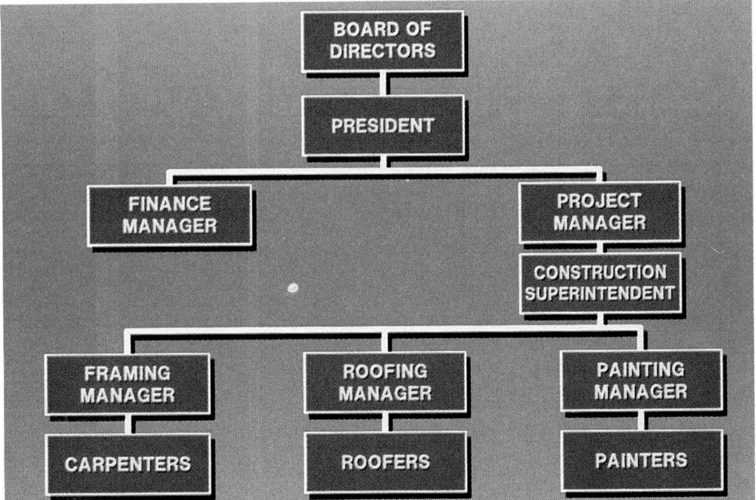

Fig. 14-1. A sample construction corporation organization chart.

1. To be successful, a student enterprise must be organized so that each student feels that he or she is an important part of the program. As the program develops, be sensitive to the feelings of the various students. Be sure to find an important part for each one to play. By now you may have identified the strengths and weaknesses of each student. Capitalize on this knowledge.

for framing, one for roofing, and one for painting. The construction superintendent will coordinate the activities of the individual managers.

The marketing director will coordinate the advertising campaign and the sale of your project. He or she should be familiar with advertising techniques. The marketing director can also assume the responsibilities of finance manager. You can choose another student to handle your company's finances.

The personnel director will be responsible for hiring all the other students in the class. The personnel director should assign the jobs according to each student's desires and qualifications. The board of directors should approve each job assignment. Every student should be given a meaningful job. This will allow each student to see the dignity in honest labor. If there are too many jobs for the number of students available, some students may volunteer to do more than one job.

The personnel director must be sure that no one student is overburdened with responsibilities. This might prevent them from developing productive work habits. If there are too many students for the number of jobs available, the personnel director should consult the board of directors. The board of directors may vote
1 on the best way to involve all the students in the company.

Company Organization and Leadership

The organization of a company provides opportunities to develop leadership skills. For example, the person in charge of a painting crew would need to direct those on the crew. Construction is a team effort. In any team effort, organization is important. Proper leadership helps organize a construction project.

One way to develop leadership skills is by joining a club. In your school, there probably are many clubs. Each club brings together people with an interest in one activity. For example, there are stamp clubs and speech clubs. There also are technology and vocational education clubs. There are two national organizations of such clubs. These two organizations are the Technology Student Association (TSA) and the Vocational Industrial Clubs of America (VICA). Each seeks to develop an understanding of technology.

The development of leadership skills will help you throughout life. Such skills will be valuable to you in any career you choose. The development of leadership skills will help you:

- To improve consumer understanding.
- To make good use of your leisure time.
- To recognize high standards of achievement.

Taking part in the activities of a club can help you develop leadership skills. Participation in club activities will help you learn:

- To prepare for effective citizenship.
- To be an officer in the organization.
- To prepare for effective participation in our democratic society.
- To conduct a meeting according to the rules of parliamentary procedure.

Taking part in group activities will also help you develop your social skills. These are the skills that help you get along with others. In any career you choose, it will be important for you to be able:

- To speak clearly.
- To write clearly and express your ideas precisely.
- To complete a job with or without direction.

The development of leadership skills is important. While in school, you should try to develop these skills as fully as possible. The organization of a construction company provides you with a good opportunity.

Project Financing

There are two ways your company can approach a construction project. You can build

1. It will be the instructor's job to get the organization of the corporation started. Have the class develop articles of incorporation under your leadership. Pass out sample articles of incorporation, but use them only as a starting point. Modify them according to the wishes of the class. Select a name for the corporation by allowing the students to think about it first. Then list suggested names. Finally, vote on the name to be used. Be aware that there may be some political maneuvering behind the scenes. That, however, is also part of the learning process.

it on speculation or on contract. **Speculation** means that you build the project and then find
1 someone to buy it. To build a project **on contract** means that you have a buyer before you start. You and the buyer, or owner, sign a contract. You build the project the way the owner wants it built.

If you can find an owner, or buyer, for the project your company intends to build, the owner will pay for the materials. However, if you build your project on speculation, your company will need money to buy materials for the project. Because your company is a corporation, you can sell shares of stock. The money raised from the sale of stock can be used to buy materials. Of course, the stockholders will expect a share of the profits after the project is sold. Another convenient way for your corporation to finance the project is to borrow the money. Perhaps your school will make the loan. Keep in mind, however, that the loan will have to be repaid after the project is sold.

For Discussion

Building a house on speculation is different from building a house on contract. The person who builds a house on contract already has a buyer. The person who builds a house on speculation does not have a buyer. Building a house on speculation is more risky than building a house on contract. The person who is considering building a house on speculation should consider several things before beginning the project. What are some of the things that he or she should consider?

THE CONSTRUCTION PROJECT

The construction project your company will build is a utility shed. Plans and specifications are provided here for a relatively low-cost, easy-to-build shed. The shed can be used to store firewood, garden equipment, bicycles, or almost anything. Fig. 14-2.

Fig. 14-2. This utility shed is an excellent project for your construction company to build.

1. Although the utility shed illustrated in the book is a good one, the marketing director may find a market for some other design. If this happens, and the board of directors chooses to build to the market, new plans will need to be developed, new material lists made, and a new cost estimate produced. Several new positions may have to be created. Make the class aware that all of this will take time.

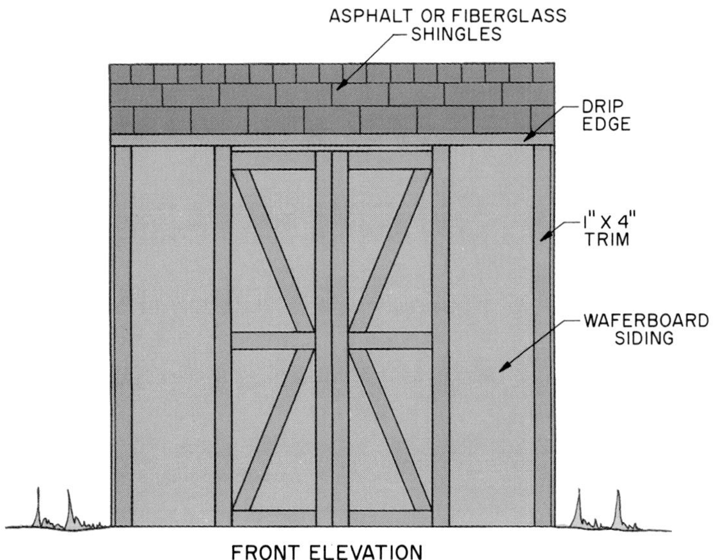

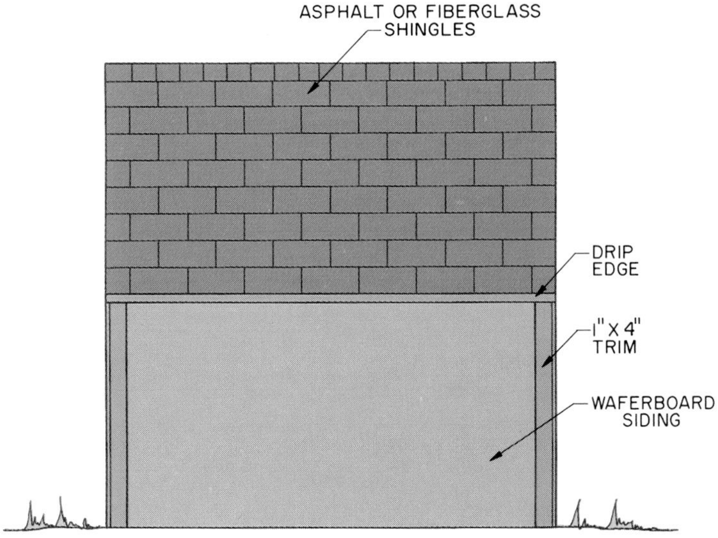

ASPHALT OR FIBERGLASS SHINGLES
DRIP EDGE
1" X 4" TRIM
WAFERBOARD SIDING

FRONT ELEVATION

ASPHALT OR FIBERGLASS SHINGLES
DRIP EDGE
1" X 4" TRIM
WAFERBOARD SIDING

REAR ELEVATION

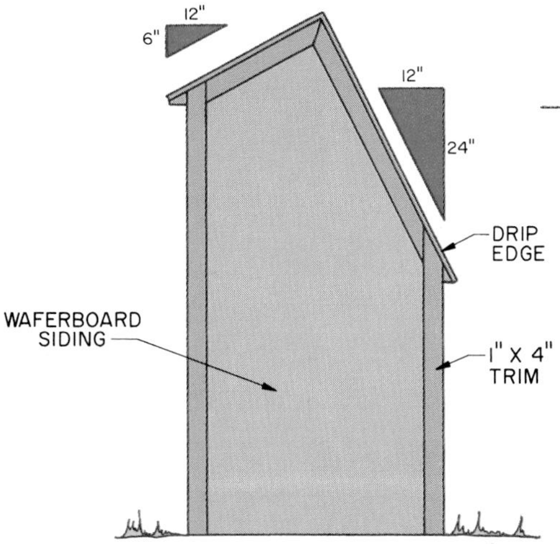

12"
6"
12"
24"
DRIP EDGE
WAFERBOARD SIDING
1" X 4" TRIM

SIDE ELEVATION

Fig. 14-3. Elevations for the utility shed: front elevation, rear elevation, and side elevation.

1. Before beginning the project, the marketing director should survey the market for the style of utility shed proposed. A marketing strategy should then be planned. The marketing director should work closely with the finance manager and report frequently to the board of directors. The results of the marketing survey will have an important bearing on how the project will be financed.

Plans and Specifications

Figure 14-3 shows the elevation views of the shed. General specifications are given in Fig. 14-4. Figures 14-5 through 14-13 show various details of the shed's construction. Study the plans and specifications carefully. Try to understand all of the parts and how they fit together.

Project Specifications

Size: 4′ × 8′ × approximately 8′ tall. 4′ door opening.
Framing: 2″ × 4″ pine or fir, 12d or 16d common nails.
Siding, flooring, and roof sheathing: 7/16″ waferboard, 6d common nails.
Trim: 1″ × 4″ pine or fir, 8d finishing nails.
Roofing: 15 lb. felt, aluminum drip edge, asphalt or fiberglass shingles, 1″ galvanized roofing nails.
Paint: exterior grade, flat, any color.

Fig. 14-4. Specifications for the utility shed.

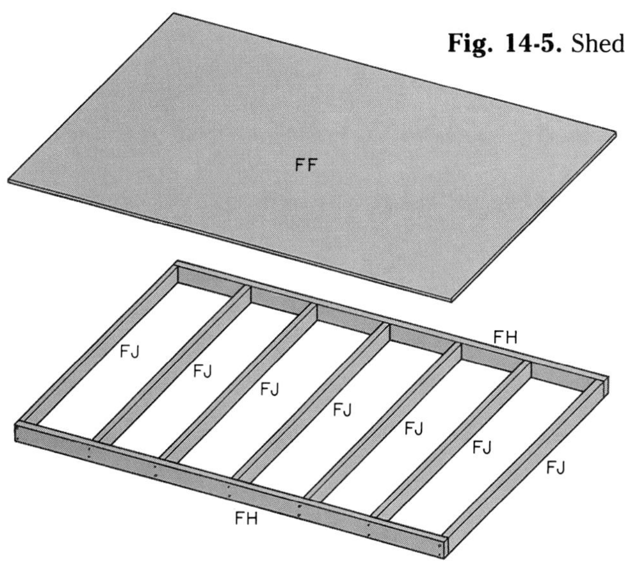

Fig. 14-5. Shed floor framing plan.

CODE	PART	SIZE
FH	HEADER	2″ × 4″ × 93½″
FJ	JOIST	2″ × 4″ × 45″
FF	FLOOR	7/16″ × 4′ × 8′

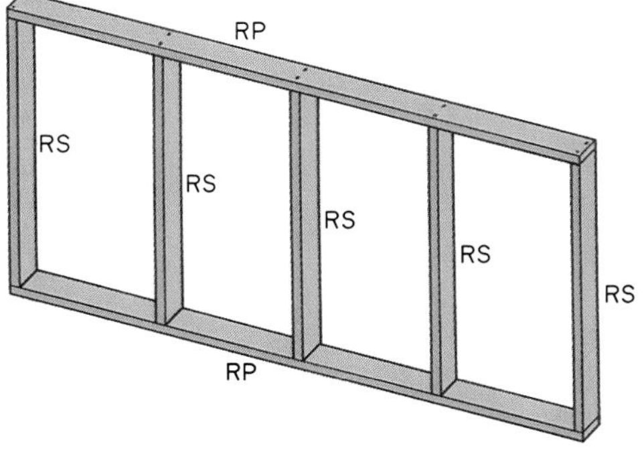

Fig. 14-6. Shed rear wall framing plan.

CODE	PART	SIZE
RP	PLATE	2″ × 4″ × 93½″
RS	STUD	2″ × 4″ × 41″

1

1. Some students will have had more experience than others in working with the tools and materials used in construction. Assist the personnel director in setting up the work groups. Suggest that each group have a student with some experience, a student with a little experience, and students who have not had any experience.

CODE	PART	SIZE
SP	PLATE	2″ × 4″ × 41″
SS	STUD	2″ × 4″ × 41″

Fig. 14-7. Shed side wall framing plan.

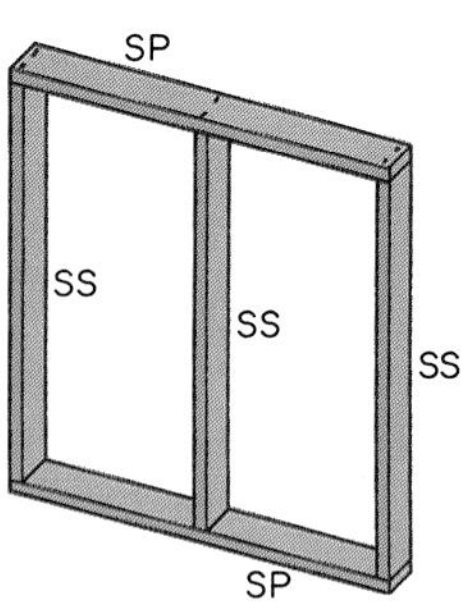

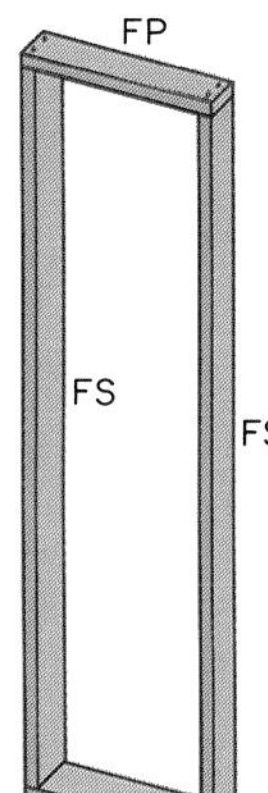

CODE	PART	SIZE
FP	PLATE	2″ × 4″ × 21″
FS	STUD	2″ × 4″ × 74″

Fig. 14-8. Shed front wall framing plan.

Fig. 14-9. Shed door frame detail.

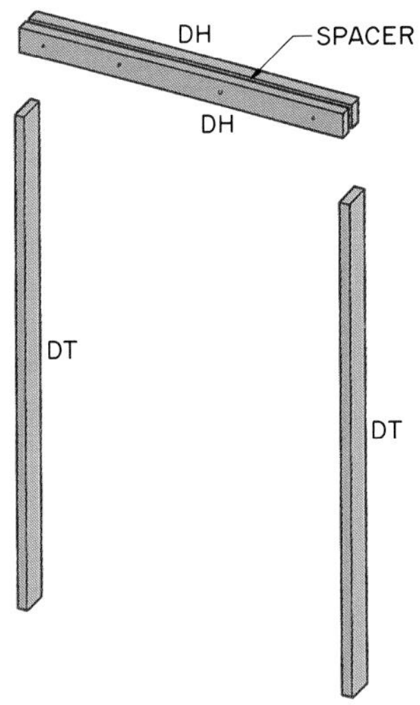

1

CODE	PART	SIZE
DT	TRIMMER	2″ × 4″ × 73½″
DH	HEADER	2″ × 4″ × 51½″

Fig. 14-10. Shed assembly detail.

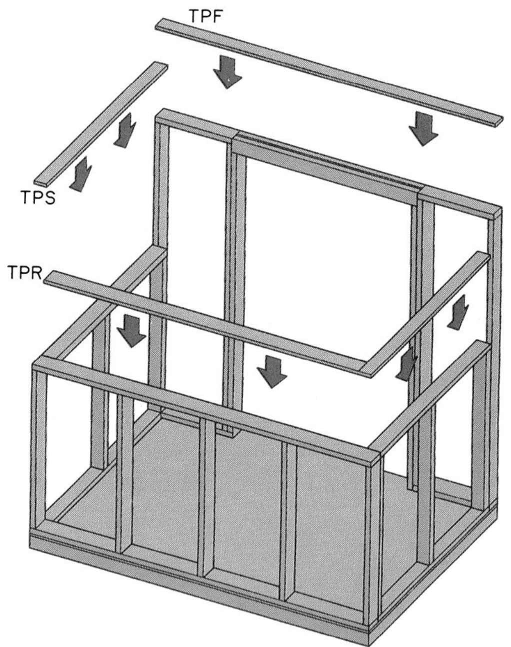

CODE	PART	SIZE
TPF	TOP PLATE	1″ × 4″ × 93½″
TPR	TOP PLATE	1″ × 4″ × 86½″
TPS	TOP PLATE	1″ × 4″ × 44½″

1. It will be the instructor's job to give the proper guidance without making it appear that the instructor is forcing the class to do things his or her way. Look for serious pitfalls that might jeopardize the project. Do not try to eliminate all problems. Much can be learned by the group if they must solve some problems.

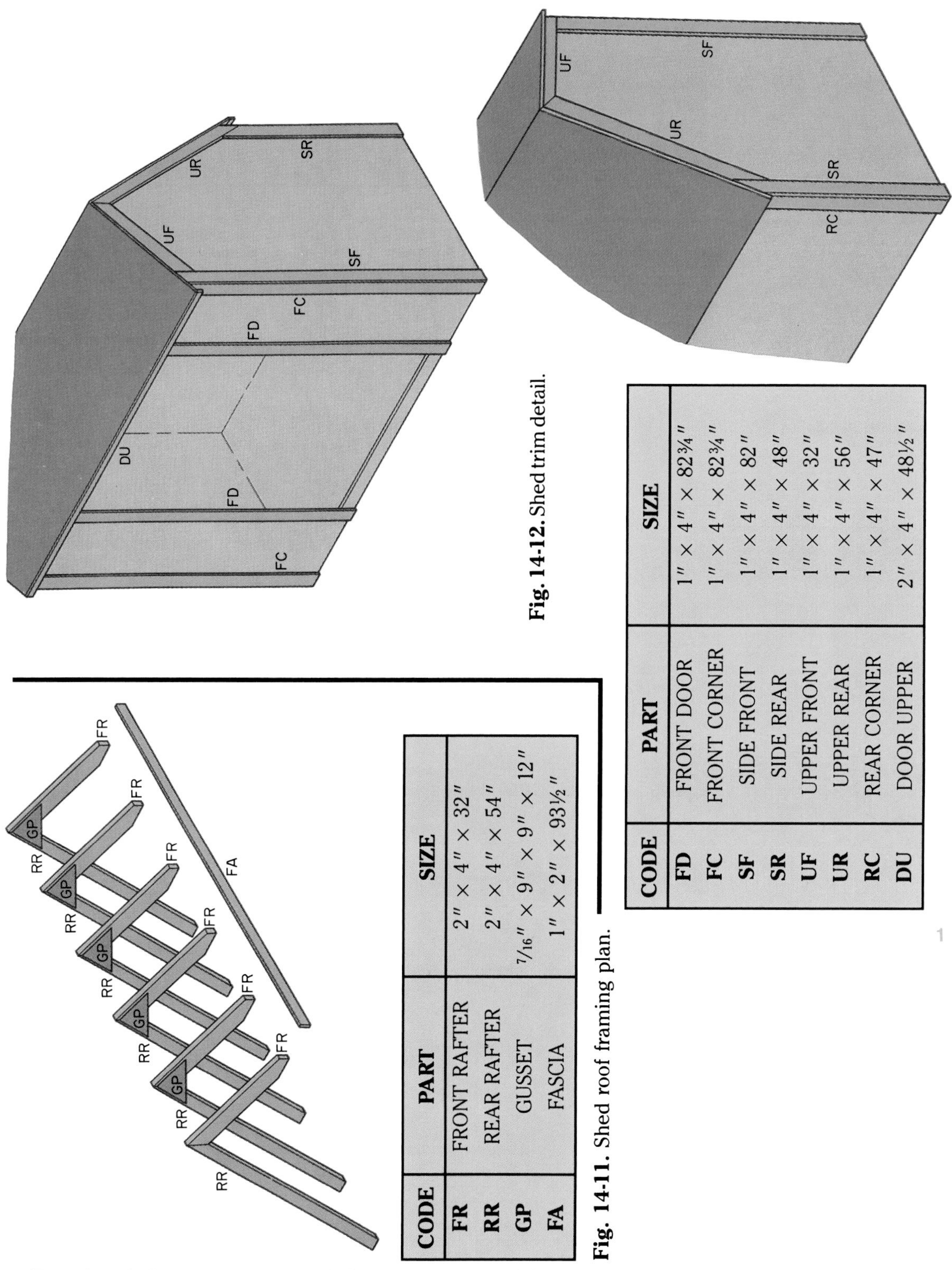

CODE	PART	SIZE
FR	FRONT RAFTER	2″ × 4″ × 32″
RR	REAR RAFTER	2″ × 4″ × 54″
GP	GUSSET	7/16″ × 9″ × 9″ × 12″
FA	FASCIA	1″ × 2″ × 93½″

Fig. 14-11. Shed roof framing plan.

CODE	PART	SIZE
FD	FRONT DOOR	1″ × 4″ × 82¾″
FC	FRONT CORNER	1″ × 4″ × 82¾″
SF	SIDE FRONT	1″ × 4″ × 82″
SR	SIDE REAR	1″ × 4″ × 48″
UF	UPPER FRONT	1″ × 4″ × 32″
UR	UPPER REAR	1″ × 4″ × 56″
RC	REAR CORNER	1″ × 4″ × 47″
DU	DOOR UPPER	2″ × 4″ × 48½″

Fig. 14-12. Shed trim detail.

1

1. Even though the project may be sold in advance, money will be needed for purchasing materials. If at all possible, stock should be sold in the corporation. This is a valuable learning experience for the class. It will help them understand corporate finance. You might even help students set up a stock market at which, once a week, stock could be bought and sold during the life of the corporation. The value of the stock could be graphed.

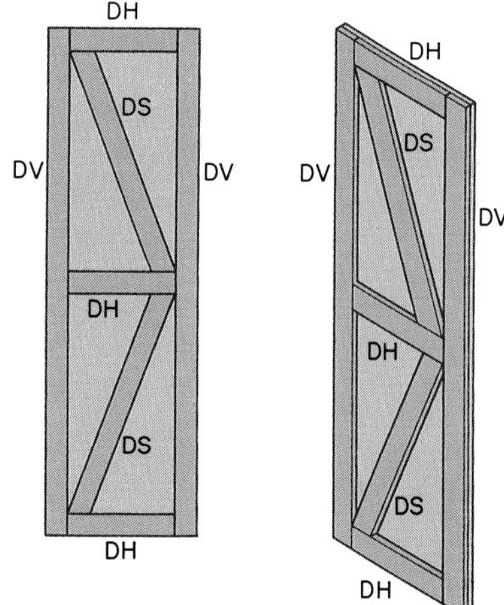

CODE	PART	SIZE
DD	DOOR	7/16″ × 24″ × 79″
DV	VERTICAL TRIM	1″ × 4″ × 79″
DH	HORIZ. TRIM	1″ × 4″ × 17″
DS	SLANTED TRIM	1″ × 4″ × 40″

Fig. 14-13. Shed door detail.

Estimating Materials

Before you begin building, you will need to order materials. To buy the materials, you must know how much of each is needed. Therefore you will need to estimate the quantities of
1 the materials. Then you will need to determine their cost.

Your finance manager will be responsible for making a list similar to the one shown in Fig. 14-14. This list will help to determine the material quantities. Then study the plans and count how many of each type of material is needed. To make the estimate easier, round off all lengths to the next whole foot. Write your figures in the *quantity* column.

After the quantities have been determined, calculate the costs. You will need to know the unit cost for each material. **Unit cost** is the cost of the material per selling unit. When you find the cost of an item, write it in the *unit cost*

Fig. 14-14. Sample material takeoff and cost estimating form.

Material	Used for	Unit	Quantity	Unit cost	Extension
2″ × 4″	framing	LF			
1″ × 4″	trim, top plates	LF			
Waferboard	floor, siding, roof sheathing, doors	sheet			
Roofing Materials					
15-lb. felt	underlayment	SF			
drip edge	drip edge	LF			
shingles	roof	square			
Miscellaneous					
Nails					
16d common	framing	lb			
6d common	sheathing	lb			
8d finish	trim	lb			
1″ galvanized roofing	shingles	lb			
Hardware					
Hinges	doors	pair			
Hasp	doors	each			
Paint	siding	gal			
	trim	qt			

1. Remind the finance manager that solid lumber can be purchased only in two-foot increments. Also, lumber species and grades will have to be decided upon. They are not specified in the specifications.

column. Construction materials are commonly sold in units such as linear foot (LF), square foot (SF), pound (lb), or square. In addition, some materials are sold individually. These materials are designated by the word *each* in the *unit* column. Once you know the unit cost, multiply it by the quantity. Write that amount in the *extension* column. Finally, add the dollar amounts in the *extension* column to get a total cost estimate for the project.

Planning and Scheduling the Work

To work efficiently, your company must have a work plan. This plan should include a list of the work to be done, who is to do the work, and when it is to be done. The whole project should be divided into small, manageable jobs. For example, the jobs may be floor framing, wall framing, roofing, and so on. Your project manager and construction superintendent should see that the work plan is made.

After you have identified the small jobs, you should decide on the order of work. Then you can begin to make job assignments. Obviously, not everyone can work on the same task at the same time. Therefore a schedule is needed. This is the job of your project manager. He or she should decide how much time each task should
1 take, then make a large bar chart similar to the one in Fig. 14-15. Put the chart on a wall where everyone can see it.

The use of such a bar chart will encourage the construction team members to develop dependable work habits. It will also encourage them to be on time for their job assignments. Such a chart also will help build a spirit of teamwork.

Did You Know?

The first shelters constructed by humans probably were small, simple windbreaks. These may have been constructed from whatever materials were available. Reeds and branches from trees and shrubbery may have been used. These might have been fixed together by crudely interweaving them.

By stabilizing the windbreak and adding a roof to it, the windbreak became a crude lean-to. If the lean-to was enclosed, a simple shed was created. Each of these improvements resulted in a structure that offered more protection against the weather. As the shelter was completely enclosed, it also offered some slight protection against wild animals.

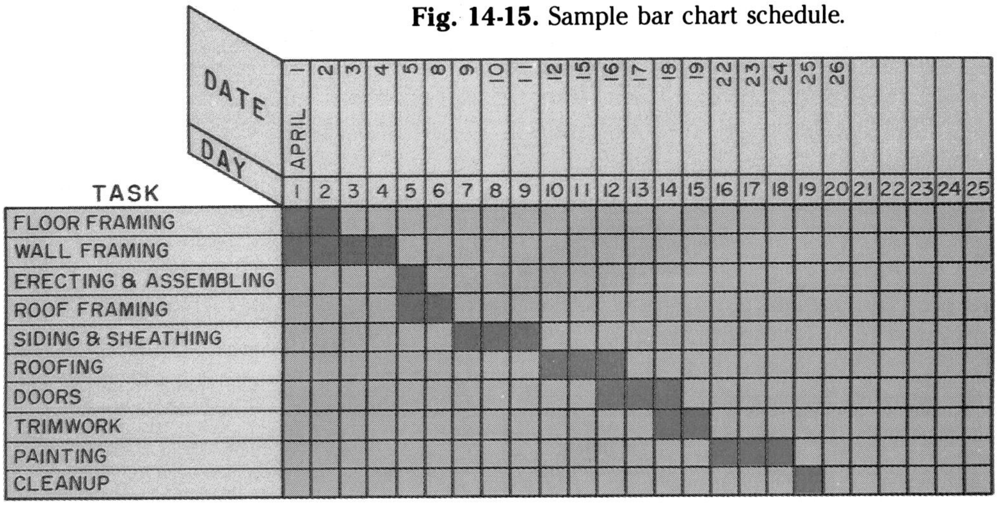

Fig. 14-15. Sample bar chart schedule.

DATE	APRIL 1	2	3	4	5	8	9	10	11	12	15	16	17	18	19	22	23	24	25	26					
TASK / DAY	1	2	3	4	5	6	7	8	9	10	11	12	13	14	15	16	17	18	19	20	21	22	23	24	25
FLOOR FRAMING																									
WALL FRAMING																									
ERECTING & ASSEMBLING																									
ROOF FRAMING																									
SIDING & SHEATHING																									
ROOFING																									
DOORS																									
TRIMWORK																									
PAINTING																									
CLEANUP																									

1. Remind the project manager and construction superintendent that time may be needed by the instructor at the beginning of each class. A clean-up period will be needed at the end of each class.

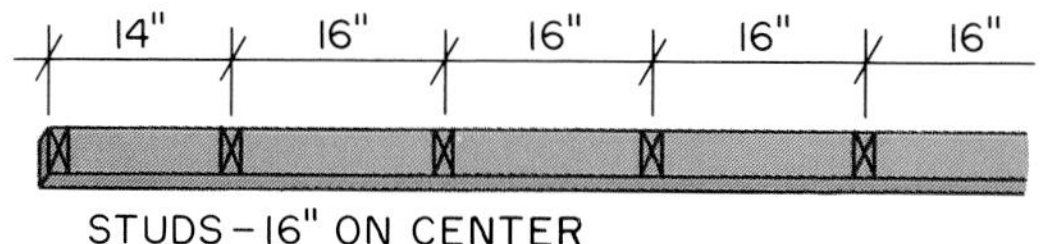

Fig. 14-16. Floor header layout.

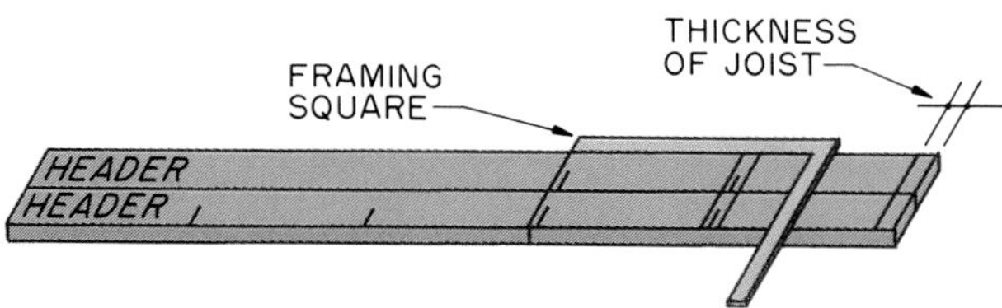

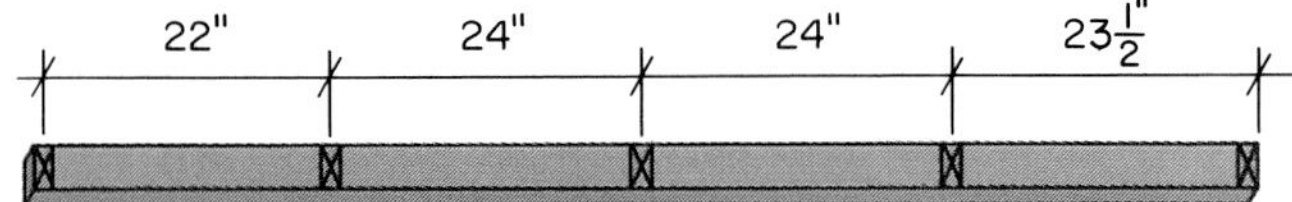

Fig. 14-17. Rear wall plate layout.

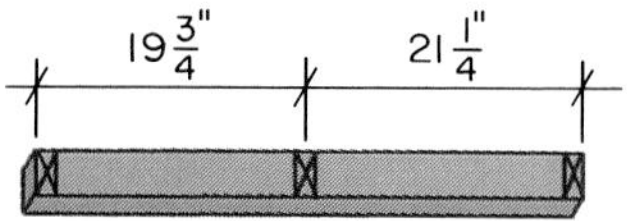

Fig. 14-18. Side wall plate layout.

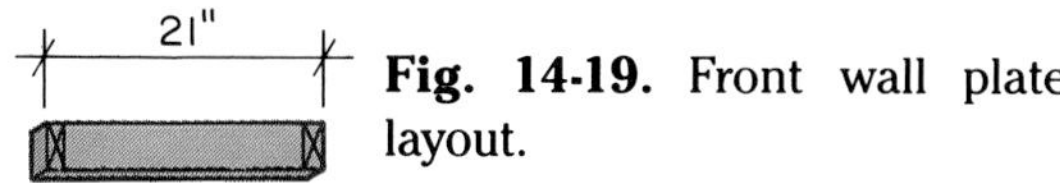

Fig. 14-19. Front wall plate layout.

Building the Structure

Your project manager and construction
1 superintendent are in charge of the project. You
will need to follow their directions. Figures 14-16
through 14-39 show various construction details
2 you will need to know. Also, you will need to
refer back to Figs. 14-5 through 14-13.

Floor Framing

Cut the required lumber to the correct sizes. Mark the code letters on each piece as you cut them. Lay out the headers as shown in Fig. 14-16. Nail the headers to the joists using 16d common nails. Then nail the floor to the floor frame using 6d common nails spaced about 6 inches apart.

Wall Framing

Cut the required lumber to the correct sizes. Be sure also to cut the door trimmer studs and the door header parts at this time. Mark each piece with the correct code letters as you cut it. Lay out the top and bottom plates as shown in Figs. 14-17, 14-18, and 14-19. Nail the plates to the studs using 16d common nails.

Erecting and Assembling

Start by erecting the rear wall. Set it in place and align it flush with the edge of the floor. Fig. 14-20. Then nail it in place using 16d nails. Erect the side walls next using the same procedure. Then erect the front walls, again using the same procedure.

1. Before construction actually begins, the construction superintendent and the various managers should recommend, and the board of directors should decide upon, the tolerances that will be acceptable at each stage of construction.

2. The instructor should review the safe use of the various tools. Demonstrate such methods as how to assemble a wall frame, how to check for accuracy, and how to square a panel.

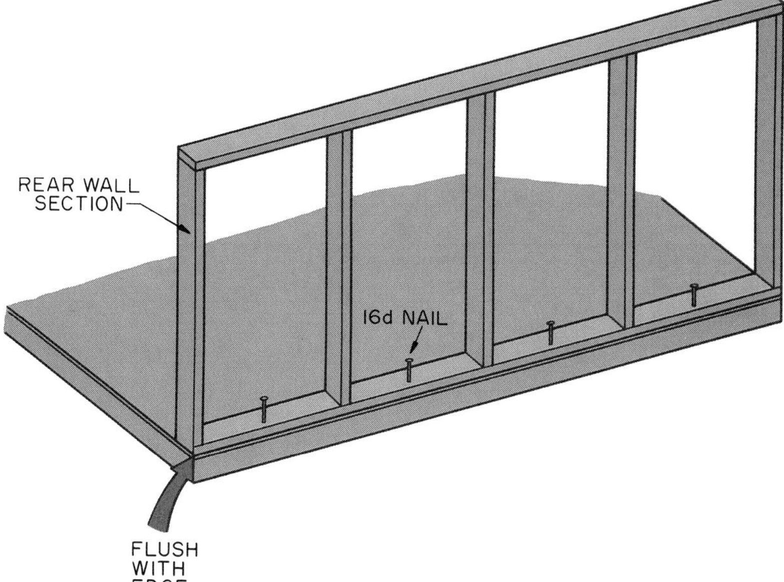

Fig. 14-20. Erecting the rear wall. Nail the wall to the floor so the nails extend into the header. Be sure to anchor the wall securely to the header.

1 After the walls have been fastened to the floor, they should be nailed together. Start at a rear corner. *Make sure the wall frames are square before you nail anything*. Nail the two walls together starting at the bottom and working up. Fig. 14-21. Repeat this procedure for all four corners.

Next, nail the door trimmer studs in place. Nail the door headers together with the waferboard spacer between them. Then nail the header in place on top of the trimmers. Fig. 14-22.

Finally, nail the double top plates in place. Be careful to align the walls as you nail the plates. Use 16d nails.

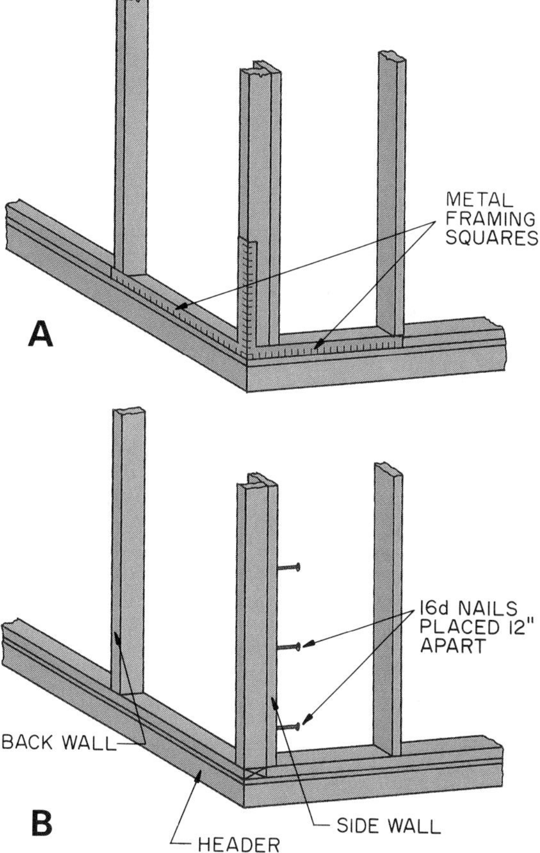

Fig. 14-21. Use a framing square to make sure the walls are square as shown in (a). Then nail the walls together as shown in (b).

1. Because all phases of construction will not be taking place at the same time, the instructor must plan activities for those students who cannot be working on the job. To avoid disciplinary problems, these activities should require active effort. Activity examples include working with materials other than those involved in the project, making structural models, and conducting experiments with project materials and structural designs. Before the project construction begins, have each student define an activity and present a written plan to the instructor.

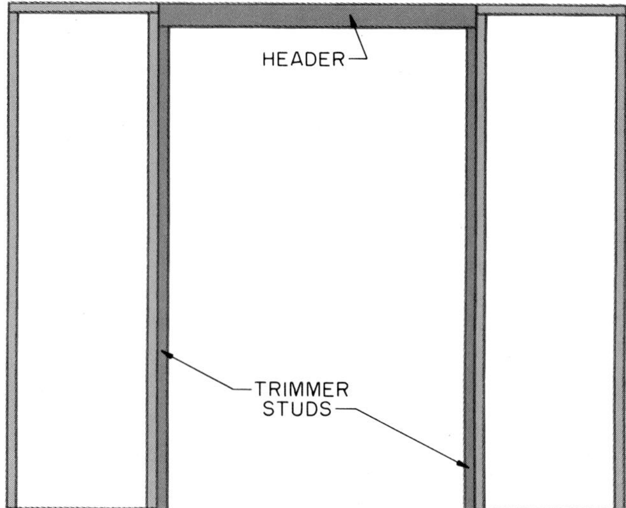

Fig. 14-22. Door frame assembly.

Roof Framing

Cut the required lumber to the correct sizes and angles. Figs. 14-23 and 14-24. Mark each piece with the correct code letters. Assemble the rafters and gusset plates using glue and 6d common nails. Use a framing square to align the parts while you assemble them. Fig. 14-25. Note that the
1 end rafters need gusset plates on one side only.

Next, nail the rafters in place. The two end rafters should be flush with the end walls and the others should be 24 inches on center. Use 16d nails. Then nail the fascia board in place using 8d finishing nails. Fig. 14-26.

Siding and Sheathing

You will need three full sheets of waferboard. You will need one for the rear wall and one for
2 each side wall. Use 6d nails spaced about 6 inches apart to attach all siding and sheathing. Begin by cutting the rear siding to size and nailing it in place.

Next, temporarily nail a sheet of waferboard to an end (side) wall. Use four nails and drive them only partly in. Mark the back side at the rafter line. Fig. 14-27. Then take the panel down and cut it to shape. Reinstall the siding and nail it in place permanently. Mark and cut the other end wall and nail it in place.

Measure both sides of the front wall and cut the siding to fit. Nail it in place on both sides. Note that no siding should be placed above the doorway.

Cut the roof sheathing to size. Nail the pieces in place. Fig. 14-28. Be sure that everything is aligned properly before you nail the parts permanently.

Trim

Cut the required lumber to the correct sizes. Note that the angles are the same ones used for the roof rafters. Refer to the elevation drawings in Fig. 14-3 for proper placement of the trim. Nail all the trim pieces in place using 8d finishing nails. Be careful not to damage the trim lumber. Refer again to Fig. 14-12.

1. Demonstrate and discuss how a jig may be made to assist in the assembly of the rafters and gusset plates. Emphasize that this is one of the advantages of modular construction. This project is a type of modular construction.

2. Explain that, before any siding is marked, each wall should be checked for squareness and braced diagonally on the inside. The bracing should be left in place until the siding has been nailed permanently into place.

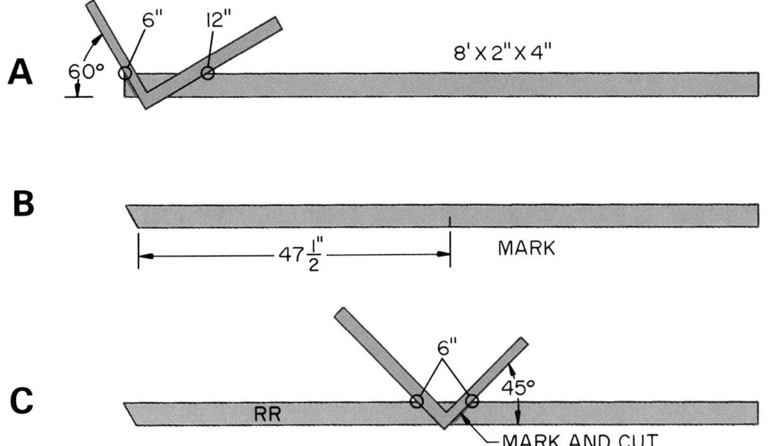

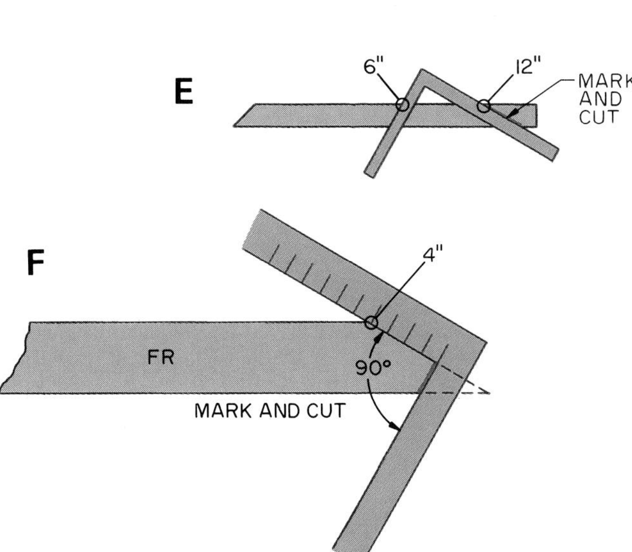

Fig. 14-23. Rafter layout. One 8-foot 2 × 4 will yield one RR and one FR.

(a) At one end of the 2 × 4, use a framing square to mark a 60-degree angle; then cut.

(b) Measure 47½″ from the base of the angle and mark that place on the wood.

(c) Use a framing square to mark a 45-degree angle, starting at the mark you made in step (*b*); then cut. This cut completes piece RR.

(d) Using the remaining portion of the 2 × 4, measure 22¼″ from the top of the angled end and mark that place on the wood.

(e) Use a framing square to mark a 60-degree angle starting at the mark you made in step (*d*); then cut.

(f) Measure down 4″ along the cut you made
in step (*e*). Using the framing square, mark 1
and cut a 90-degree angle. This cut completes
piece FR.

1. As construction progresses, check each step for accuracy, alignment, and squareness. Some reworking may be necessary. It may be demoralizing, however, to have to make extensive changes after the project has been assembled.

6"
9"
12"

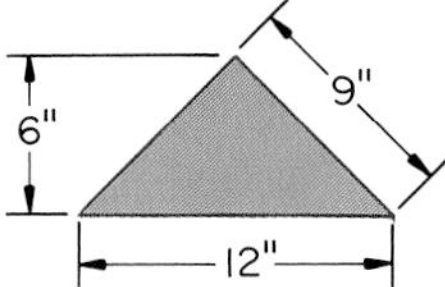

Fig. 14-24. Gusset layout.

$\frac{7}{16}$" X 6" X 96" WAFERBOARD
GP GP GP GP GP GP GP GP
USE THIS PIECE
FOR DOOR HEADER

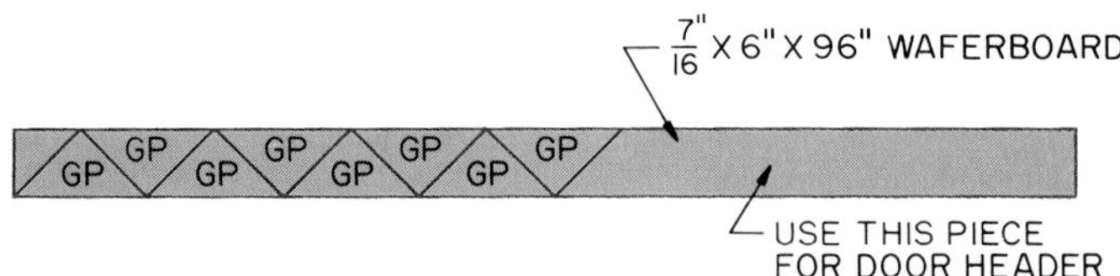

Fig. 14-25. Rafter assembly.

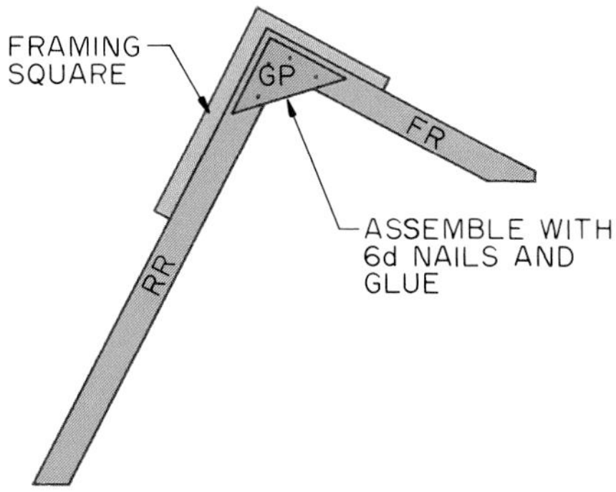

FRAMING
SQUARE
GP
FR
RR
ASSEMBLE WITH
6d NAILS AND
GLUE

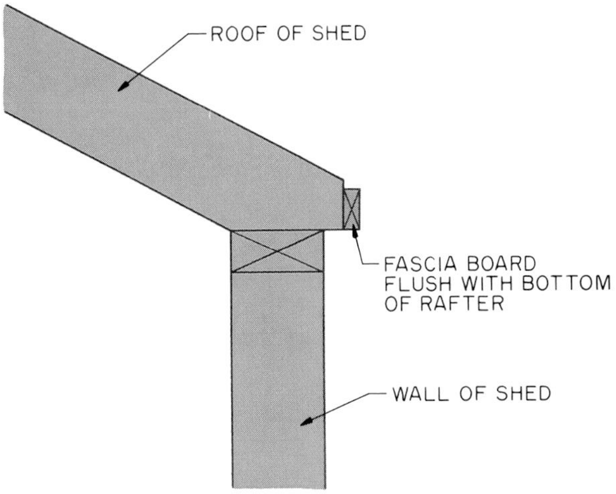

ROOF OF SHED
FASCIA BOARD
FLUSH WITH BOTTOM
OF RAFTER
WALL OF SHED

Fig. 14-26. Fascia board assembly.

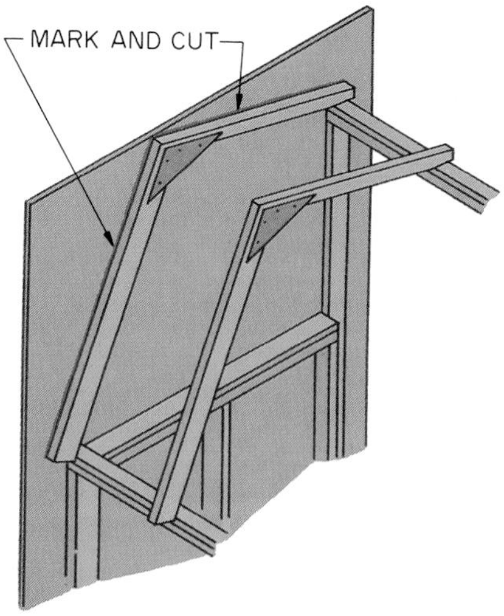

MARK AND CUT

Fig. 14-27. Marking end wall siding.

1

1. Explain that lack of accuracy can affect the quality of the finished product. As examples, you might discuss a power hand saw base plate that is not square, a cut that does not follow the squared line, or a joint that is not pulled up tight. Explain that each of these can affect the accuracy of the component and the finished project.

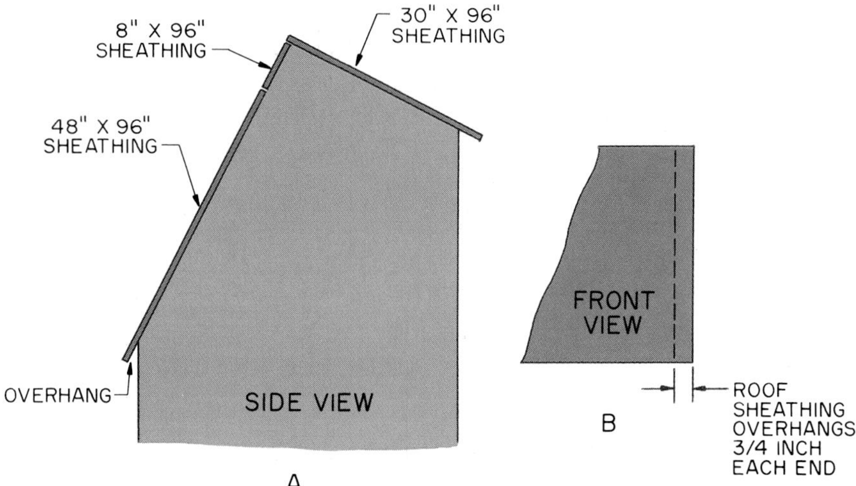

Fig. 14-28. Roof sheathing details.

Did You Know?

Most roofs today are covered with shingles. However, a variety of other roofing materials are available. These include clay roofing tiles, copper, and wood shingles. Throughout history, humans have chosen roofing materials from what was available to them. You may have seen pictures of cottages with thatched roofs. The thatched roof was used in rural areas of England, Scotland, and Ireland.

The thatched roof was used because it could be cheaply made from a material that was readily at hand—long grasses. These might be flax or rye. Today, the thatched roof is not common. It is, however, still found in parts of Ireland and Scotland. The thatch is applied as follows. The straw is laid in bundles on a sloped roof. The straw is then held down with ropes.

Roofing

Measure and cut the drip edge to length for the 1
front and rear eaves. Nail the drip edge to the roof using roofing nails. Then staple the 15-pound felt in place. Fig. 14-29. Start at the bottom and work toward the top. Overlap each layer by about 2 inches. Overlap the pieces at the top.

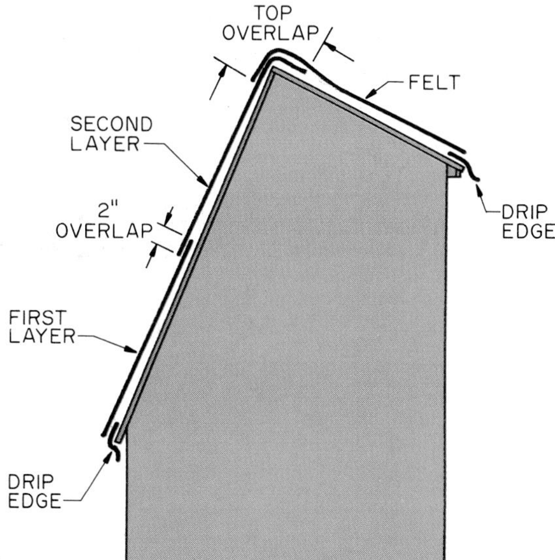

Fig. 14-29. Drip edge and felt detail.

1. Point out why the drip edge is placed on the front and rear of the shed before the felt is installed. Explain also why it is placed on the ends after the felt has been installed. A demonstration should be given showing how the drip edge is cut and installed at corners and joints, how shingles are installed, and how the ridge cap is cut and installed.

Measure, cut, and bend the drip edge on the rake, or side, ends of the roof. This drip edge is nailed down *over* the felt. Fig. 14-30.

Next, install the shingles. For the starter course, turn the shingles so the tabs are toward the top. Start with a two and one-half tab shingle by cutting off half a tab. Nail this course as shown in Fig. 14-31. The purpose of the starter course is to strengthen the edge of the roof. Then place and nail the first course directly on top of the starter

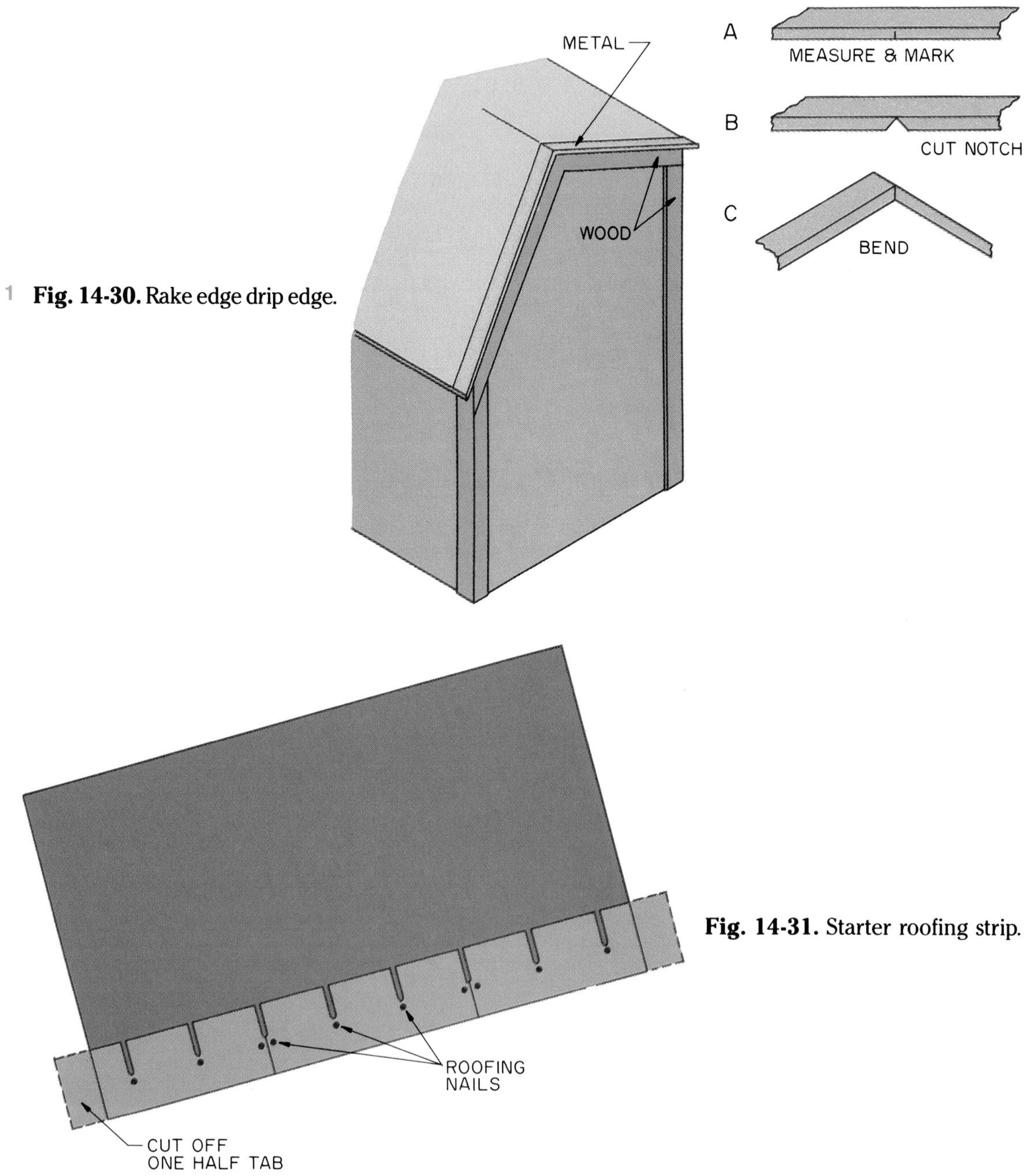

1 **Fig. 14-30.** Rake edge drip edge.

Fig. 14-31. Starter roofing strip.

1. Remember that the place where the project will be assembled will be dependent upon whether there is nearby an opening of adequate size to move the completed project from the building.

course as shown in Fig. 14-32. Be sure that the tabs are facing toward the bottom. Place and nail the succeeding courses as shown in Fig. 14-33.

For the ridge, cut the shingles as shown in Fig. 14-34. Starting at one end of the ridge, nail the first shingle as shown in Fig. 14-35. Place and nail the other ridge shingles as shown in Fig. 14-36. The last shingle will need to be cut short and nailed carefully in place. Fig. 14-37.

1 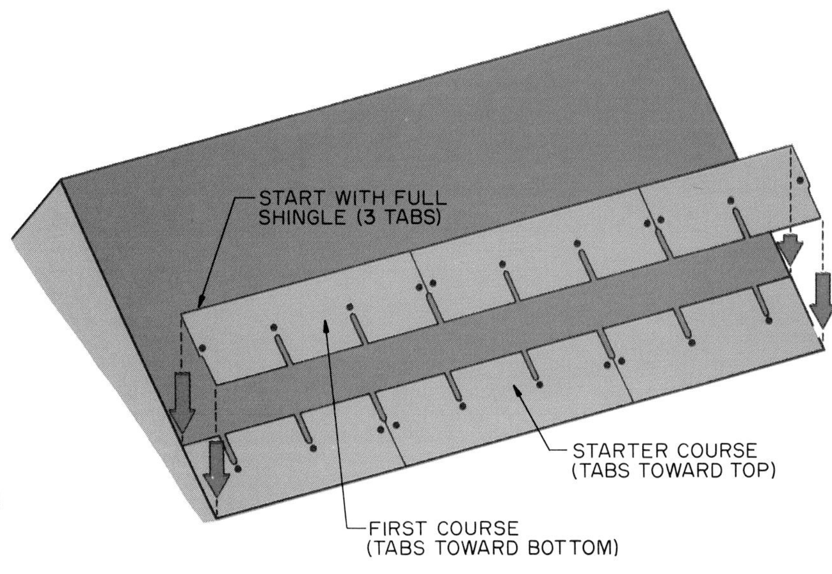

Fig. 14-32. The first course of shingles should be placed over the starter course.

Fig. 14-33. Succeeding courses of shingles. Note that the measurement increases 2
by 5 inches for each course and that each starting shingle is ½-tab shorter than the preceding one.

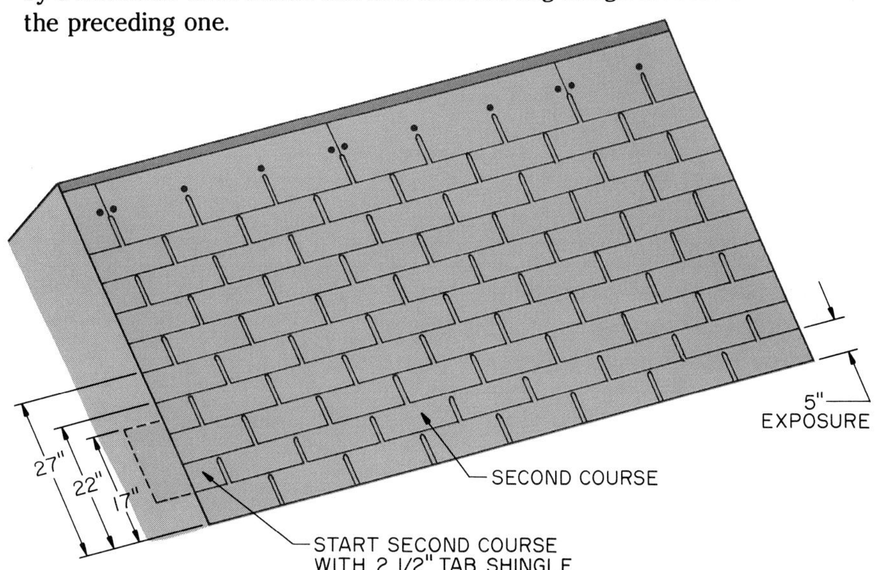

1. Check all joints for accuracy. If angles must be cut, have the students cut the angles on pieces that are extra long until the desired fit is obtained. Then the other end of the piece can be cut to length.

2. Even though the whole class will not be involved in every phase of construction, the instructor should be sure to point out important construction items to everyone as construction progresses.

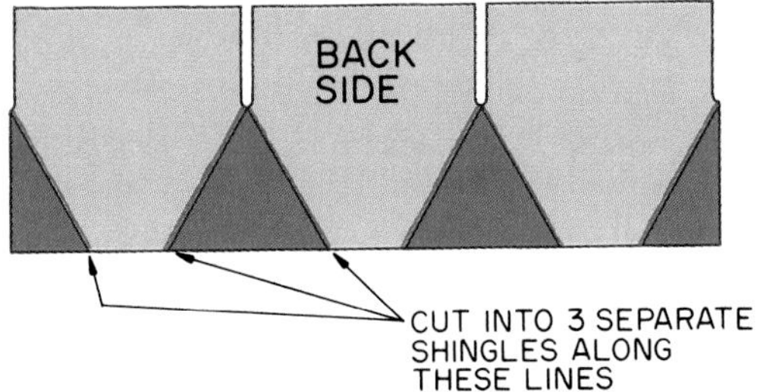

Fig. 14-34. Cutting ridge shingles.

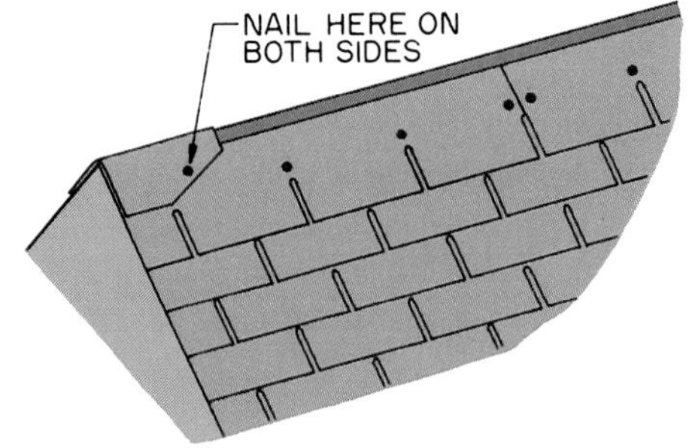

Fig. 14-35. Applying the first ridge shingle.

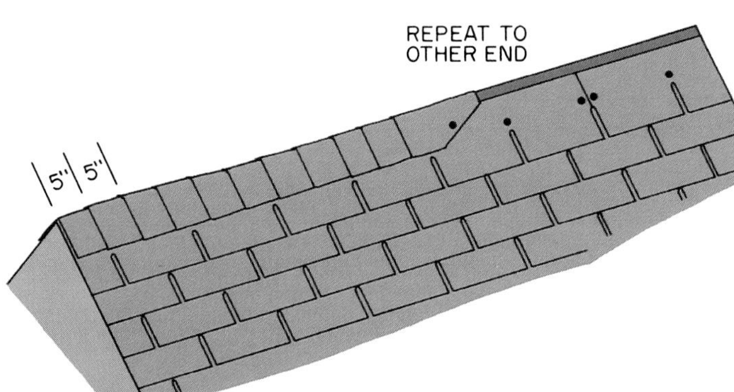

Fig. 14-36. Applying ridge shingles.

Did You Know?

In ancient times, doors were flexible. They were, for example, made of hanging hides or cloths. The use of rigid materials—such as wood—for doors was a later development. Stone doors were used by both the Greeks and the Romans. These doors opened on pivots placed at the top and bottom. However, the most common rigid door was the wooden door. Generally, these were quite simple. In design, many of them were quite similar to modern wooden doors.

In the middle ages, the most common type of wooden door was made of vertical boards. These boards were braced on the back with diagonal or horizontal braces.

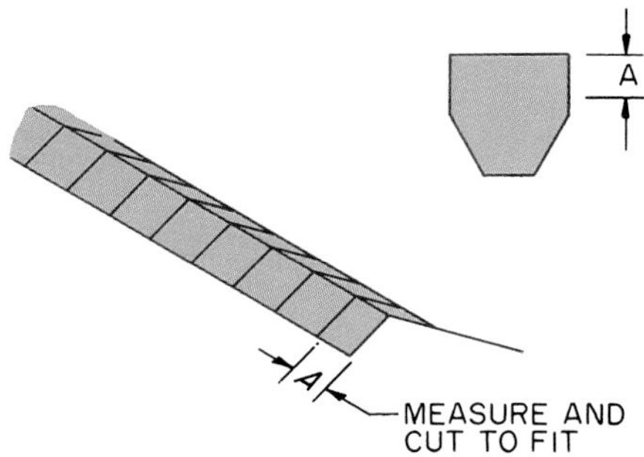

Fig. 14-37. Applying the last ridge shingle.

Doors

The doors require one full sheet of waferboard. 1
Cut the sheet in half lengthwise. Then measure and cut each piece to the correct length. Next
cut the door trim pieces. Attach the trim pieces 2
to the waferboard using glue and 8d finishing

1. Point out that the glue used for attaching the door trim to the door panels should be a waterproof variety.
2. Proper installation of the doors is very important because their operation will be crucial to the owner's satisfaction. Discuss this with the class.

nails. Fig. 14-38. *Clinch*, or bend over, the nails on the back side.

Fasten the hinges to the doors. Then lift one door into place. Mark the hinge hole locations on the front door trim (FD). Be sure to leave a space of $1/8$ inch between the door and the side of the building. Leave a ¼-inch space between the door and the top of the door frame. Fig. 14-39. Do the same for the other door. Then install the hasp and loop.

Painting

1 Put a first coat of paint on all bare exterior wood surfaces. Allow the paint to dry thoroughly. Then apply a second coat to the siding and doors. Let that coat dry. Finally, paint the trim pieces with a contrasting color. Be careful not to get trim paint on the siding.

Did You Know?

The first paints were used primarily for decoration. You may have heard of the cave paintings at Lascaux, France. These paintings on rock were made about 17,000 years ago. They are decorations on the cave walls. They show some of the animals familiar to early humans. In the 1500s in Europe, paint began to be used to protect and preserve objects.

Paint then was made by hand. It was expensive. It was only in the 1800s that paint became widely available—and cheaper. In the twentieth century, manufacturing increased. Many of the items manufactured needed painting. This led to growth in the paint industry. Today, a wide variety of paints is available. There are paints for many uses.

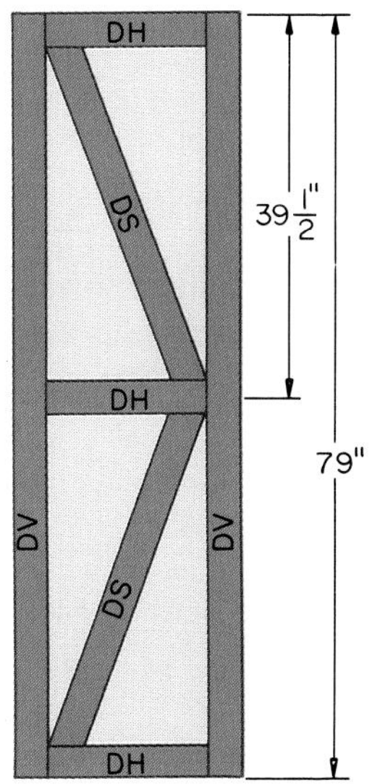

Fig. 14-38. Door layout.

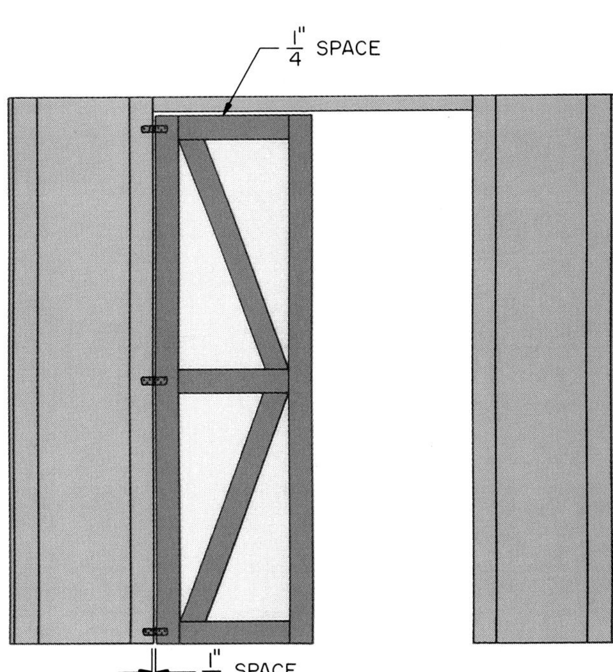

Fig. 14-39. Door installation detail.

1. If the project is sold before it is started, the owner will select the paint colors. If it is to be sold upon completion, colors will have to be selected. Suggest that the painting manager and the project manager survey possible color combinations that are popular for utility buildings and report their findings to the board of directors. The group can then decide upon a color scheme that will make the building most salable.

For Discussion

As you can see, building any structure requires a number of different construction steps. Many of these basic steps have not changed in the last one hundred years. Only the tools needed may have changed. One other thing that may have changed is the time schedule. Many buildings today are built to meet a tight deadline. Discuss the effects of these changes on the need for careful organization of the steps in building construction.

DETERMINING A PROFIT OR LOSS

After the project has been completed, your company must sell the project if it has not already been sold. The project must also be delivered to the new owner. Then your company will need to account for the money it spent and received.

Marketing

If you built the shed on contract, it was sold before you started. If, however, you built the shed on speculation, you must find a buyer. The first task is to decide on a fair price for your project. Then you will need to let people know that you have a shed for sale. Possible ways to advertise are as follows:

- Post notices on school bulletin boards.
- Ask a local radio station to broadcast the availability of your product.
- Advertise in a local newspaper by having the paper publish a news story about your class.
- Another possibility is to try to sell your product by *word of mouth*.

Financial Accounting

The last step in your construction enterprise 1
is to prepare a financial accounting. This will be your profit and loss statement. It will show in detail all the money the company received and spent. Figure 14-40 shows a sample profit and loss statement. If you sold shares of stock, any profit you make should be divided among the stockholders. If you borrowed the money for your project, you will need to pay back the amount you borrowed plus interest. Any amount that remains after the loan is repaid should be divided among the stockholders.

Fig. 14-40. Sample profit and loss statement.

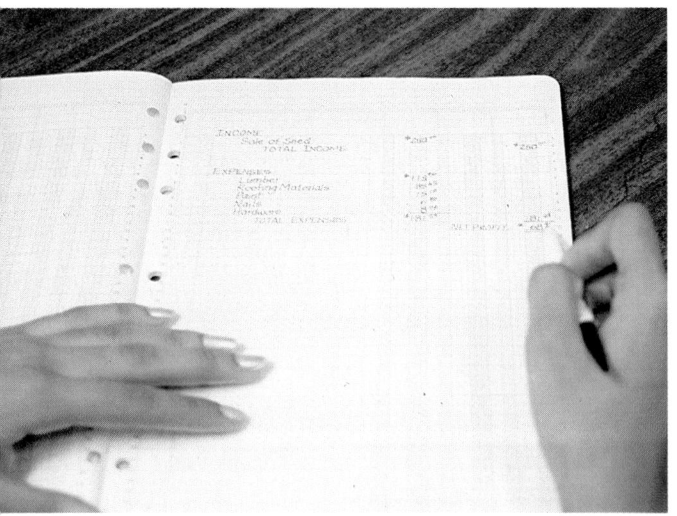

For Discussion

The text suggests several methods for marketing your product. Analyze these various methods. Which of them, in your opinion, would be most effective in your community?

1. Review the profit and loss statement with the board of directors. Teach the class how to read a profit and loss statement. Discuss how changes could be made in future operations to increase the profit without lowering the quality. Allow the board of directors to decide upon a fair dividend to be paid on shares of stock. If any money remains after the stock has been liquidated, let the board of directors decide what is to be done with it.

Construction Facts

A HOUSE IN THE WOODS

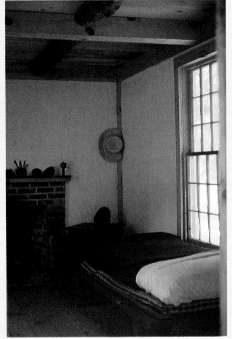

"Near the end of March, 1845, I borrowed an axe and went down to the woods by Walden Pond, nearest to where I intended to build my house, and began to cut down some tall arrowy white pines . . . for timber."

This begins Henry David Thoreau's account of how he built his own house. One of our great writers, Thoreau was an independent thinker who liked solitude. His goal was to live simply and economically.

Here is what he says about his work:

"I hewed the main timbers six inches square, most of the studs on two sides only, and the rafters and floor timbers on one side, leaving the rest of the bark on, so that they were much stronger than sawed ones."

"At length in the beginning of May . . . I set up the frame of my house . . . I began to occupy my house on the 4th of July.

"I have thus a tight shingled and plastered house, ten feet wide by fifteen long, with a garret and a closet, a large window on each side, one door, and a brick fireplace." 1

Thoreau was to live in the house year-round for two years and two months. When asked about the value of his experience for the young people of his time, Thoreau said: "I mean that they [students] should not *play* at life, or *study* it merely, while the community supports them at this expensive game, but earnestly *live* it from beginning to end."

1. The construction materials for Thoreau's small house are set down fairly clearly in his book, *Walden*. Ask a student or group of students to prepare a list of these construction materials. Then ask them to prepare a cost estimate for constructing a cabin identical to Thoreau's in your community. Exclude the cost of the land.

CHAPTER 14 REVIEW

Chapter Summary

The development of your construction company will require the talents of every person in the class. In your company, you will need a project manager, a finance manager, a construction superintendent, a marketing director, and a personnel director. You will also need a manager for each major part of the project. You can build the project on speculation or on contract. In either case, you will need to make a careful estimate of the materials you will need. You also will need to develop a work plan.

The actual building of the shed is divided into several work areas. These are floor framing, wall framing, erecting and assembling, roof framing, siding and sheathing, work on trim, roofing, and doors, and painting. After completing the project, you will need to market it. You will then need to determine your profit or loss. You will do this by preparing a financial accounting.

1 Test Your Knowledge

1. Which corporation official is responsible for hiring employees?
2. What does it mean to build a project on speculation?
3. What is meant by unit cost?
4. Identify one way to develop leadership skills in school.
5. What is the purpose of a bar chart in scheduling work?

Activities

1. The organization of any project requires leadership. Using resources in your library, research the lives of two great leaders. Then, compare the lives and achievements of these leaders. Look especially for qualities that they shared. Using this comparison, identify those personal qualities that helped each of these individuals develop leadership.
2. After completing the student enterprise, identify those qualities essential for teamwork. Think about your role in the work team. Think about how your job related to the jobs of others on your team. Then write a one-page essay on the qualities that you think are essential for teamwork on a group project.
3. In your work on this student enterprise, you may have set some personal goals for yourself. For example, you may have set for yourself a goal of accomplishing so much work in a single class session. Proper management can help you reach personal goals on the job. List some ways in which proper management can assist you in reaching personal goals.

1. The answers to the Test Your Knowledge questions are in the Teacher's Manual at the front of this Teacher's Annotated Edition.

REVIEW

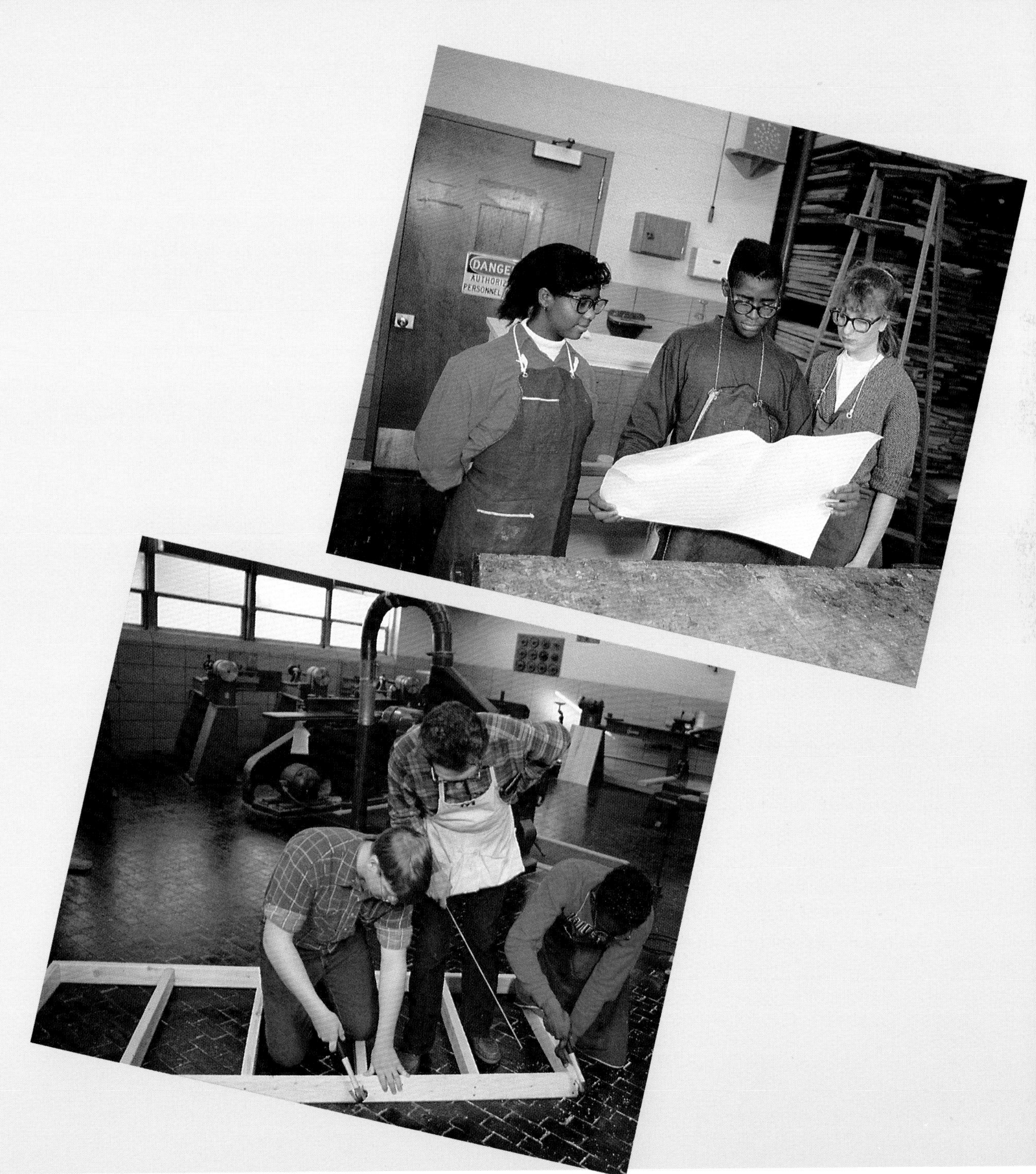

ACTIVITIES

Activity 1: Building and Testing a Model Bridge

Objective

After completing this activity, you will become familiar with the basic design features of today's basic bridge structures. The bridge models produced can also be used to test the strength of each support system. You also will become familiar with the basic principles of materials testing.

Materials Needed

For this activity, you will be working with a teammate. The materials list below assumes that there are ten teams of two students each.

- 120 1/8″ × 1/4″ × 36″ strips of balsa wood (12 per team)
- 10 1/16″ × 3″ × 36″ strips of balsa wood (1 per group)
- 10 containers of glue (1 per group)
- 10 spools of thread (1 per group)
- 100 1″ wire brads (10 per group)

Steps of Procedure

1. Cut all balsa wood strips into 12″ lengths.
2. With your teammate, decide on the type of bridge you intend to construct. You may get your ideas from local bridge construction in your area. You might also research bridge design in your school library. Figure A shows the basic types of bridges.
3. After you have chosen a bridge, you should research that type of bridge. You should research its historical development. You also should attempt to find out the location of a similar bridge.
4. After you have identified the type of bridge you plan to build, you should make a working drawing of the bridge. With your teammate, you should construct a model of the bridge you have chosen. Each model should have an overall size of 12″ × 3″ × 6″.
5. After you have completed the construction of your bridge, share your research information with the other teams.
6. To test the strength of your bridge, place two tables about one foot apart. Span the bridge between them.
7. Place a cardboard box beneath the bridge to protect the floor.
8. To test the strength of the bridge, place gym weights on the bridge—one at a time. Place the lightest weights first. Gradually add more weight. Record the amount of weight each bridge can hold before it collapses.
9. What type of bridge was able to hold the most weight? Why do you think some bridge designs are stronger than others.

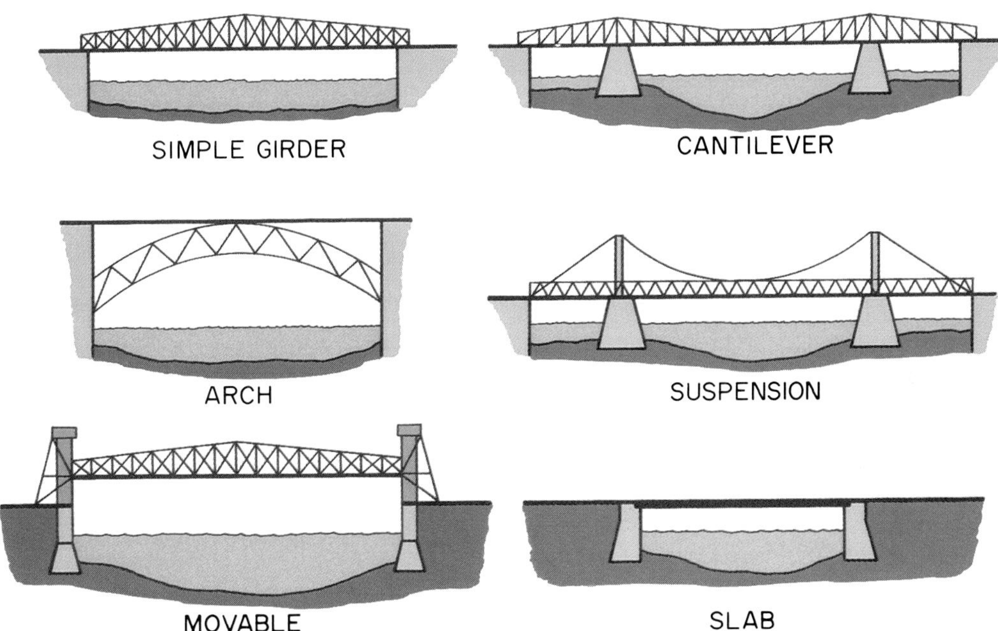

Fig. A. The main types of bridges.

Activity 2: Building a Model Lock-and-Dam System

Objective

After completing this activity, you will be familiar with a basic lock-and-dam system. This is the type of system used in canal and river transportation, irrigation, and flood control. You also will have a basic knowledge of the plumbing skills used while working with plastic water pipe.

Materials Needed

- 3′ × 1′ × 1′ watertight container. (This may be made of sheet metal.)
- 4 3/8″ NPT/female adapters
- 3 3/8″ compression Ts
- 3 3/8″ compression water valves
- 5′ 3/8″ plastic water line pipe
- 2 3/8″ 90° elbows
- 1 garden hose
- 2-1′ × 1′ × 1″ pieces of cork board. (These pieces may also be the height and width of the water container.)
- 1-2″ × 4″ × 6″ wood block. (This is needed for the barge.)

- 1 permanent colored marker
- 1 tube clear silicone caulking
- 1 small container of PVC glue
- 1 hacksaw

Steps of Procedure
Constructing the Lock and Dam

1. Divide the water tank into three equal sections across the bottom of the tank. Mark with the permanent marker. Fig. A.
2. Cut a 2″ strip from the 1′ × 1′ cork board. Place the strips over one of the dividing lines. Fig. 1.
3. Cut the 10″ × 12″ cork board (from Step 2) into two 10″ × 6″ pieces. Place these two halves on top of the 2″ strip to form Gate 1. Fig. A.
4. Cut the remaining 1′ × 1′ cork board in half. Place the two halves on the second dividing line to form Gate 2. Both Gate 1 and Gate 2 should fit snugly to prevent leakage. Fig. A.
5. Drill a ⅜″ hole in the bottom of each compartment.
6. Drill a ⅜″ hole in the end of the tank nearest to Gate 2. Drill the hole 2″ up from the bottom.
7. Place silicone on the threads of each adapter. Fasten each of the four adapters in the four ⅜″ holes just drilled. The silicone should act as a gasket to seal these fittings. Fig. B.
8. Cut a 1′ section of ⅜″ plastic water line. Attach it to the end adapter using PVC glue. This stem will help simulate the continuous flow of water moving downriver.
9. Using the compression valves, Ts, elbows, PVC glue, and ⅜″ water line, connect the water flow control system as shown in Fig. B.

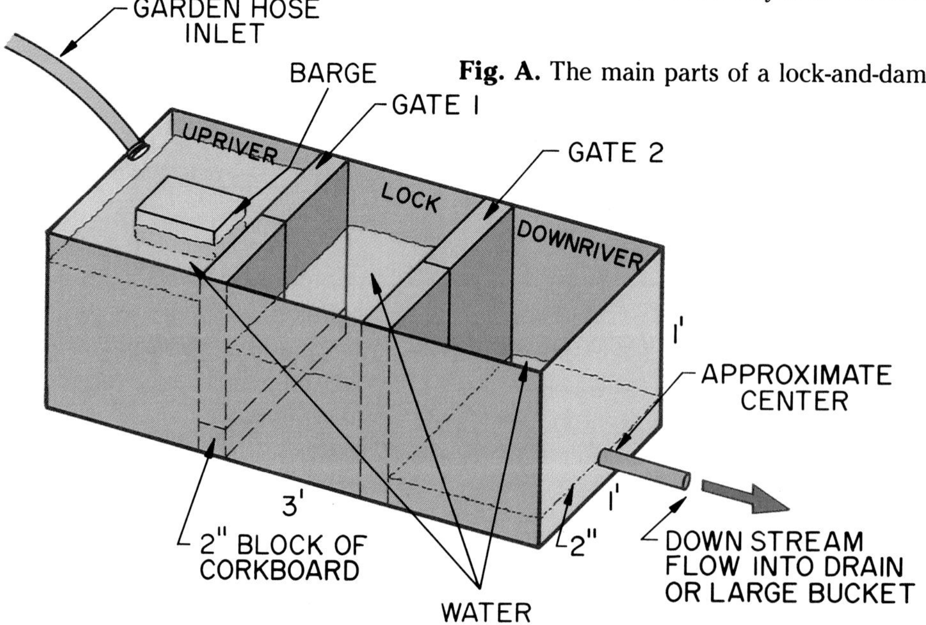

Fig. A. The main parts of a lock-and-dam system.

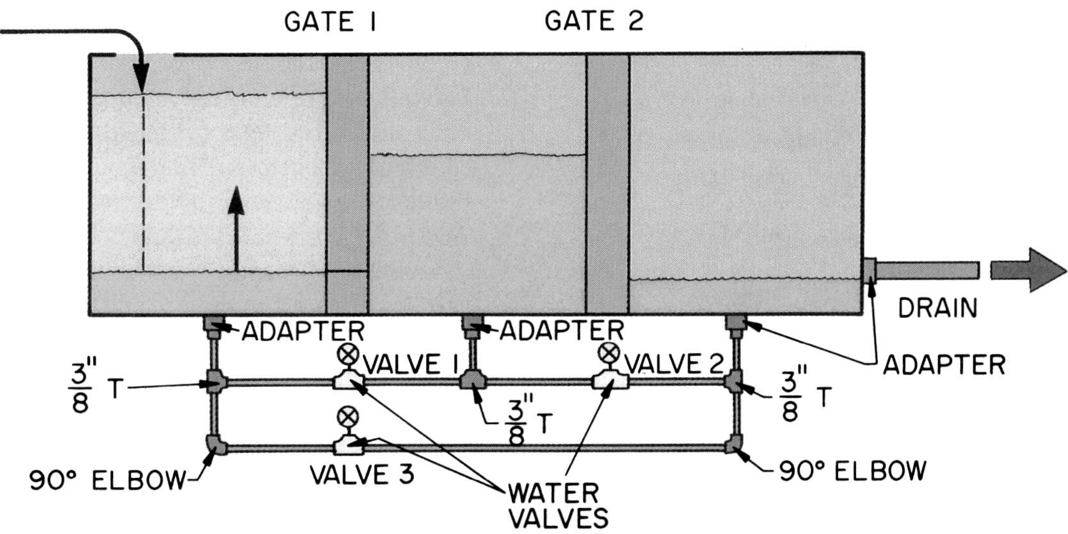

Fig. B. A side view of the water flow control system in a lock-and-dam system.

Steps of Procedure

Operating the Lock and Dam

1. Refer to Fig. B. Close all valves.
2. Run a garden hose to the "up-river" compartment. Turn on the water. Adjust it to a medium rate of flow.
3. Place the barge in the "up-river" compartment.
4. Open Valve 1 all the way. The lock will begin to fill.
5. As the first two compartments fill with water, you will need to open Valve 3. You will need to do this to keep a flood from occurring.
6. Once the first two compartments have balanced water levels, you may open Gate 1 and drive the barge into the lock.
7. Close Gate 1. Close Valves 1 and 3. Open Valve 2. The lock and down-river compartments should now be in balance.
8. Open Gate 2. Drive the barge downriver to allow the barge to pass out of the lock.

Activity 3: Building a Concrete-Block Wall

Objective

After completing this activity, you will have become familiar with the process of laying block. You also will have learned how to mix mortar and build a wall that is straight and level.

Materials Needed (Refer to Fig. A on the following page.)

- 9 concrete or cinder blocks
- 1-10-lb. sack of cement

- 5′ of string
- 1 gallon bucket of water
- 20 lbs. of sand
- 1-3′ × 3′ × ½″ sheet of plywood
- 2 trowels
- 1-36″ level
- 1 chalk line
- 1 strike-off tool

Steps of Procedure

1. Find a fairly level surface in your lab area. A smooth concrete floor is best.
2. Clean the edges and surfaces of all the concrete or cinder blocks.
3. Mix the cement on the 3′ × 3′ piece of plywood. This will serve as a mortar board. Using the trowel, mix five parts (scoops) of sand with three parts of cement. Mix the sand and cement on the mortar board. Work the mixture until it has an even gray color.
4. Add water to the mixture. Add only a small amount at first. Mix the water with the sand cement mixture. Continue to add water and mix the mortar until the mortar can be scraped to the middle of the mortar board and still hold its shape. The mortar should not be runny. It should hold its shape when scooped up with a trowel. When dropped on the mortar board, it should flatten slightly.

Fig. A. Masonry tools and materials. The items shown here will be needed to build the wall described in this activity.

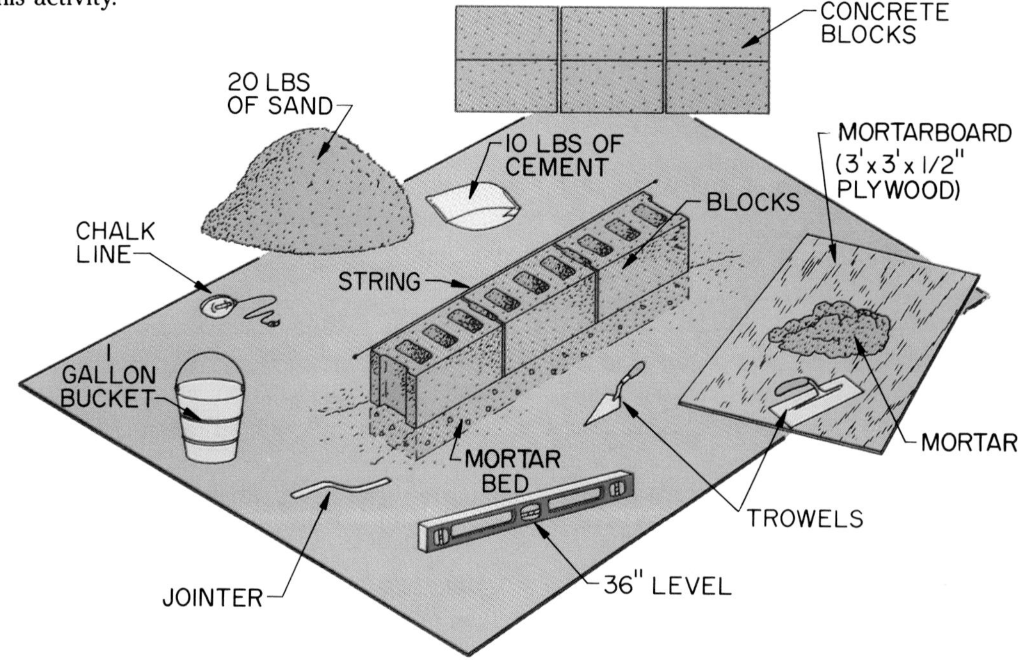

5. Strike a chalk line about 4′ long on the floor where you plan to construct your wall.
6. Using your trowel, set a continuous bed, or layer, of cement along the edge of the chalk line. This bed should be approximately 2″ wide and 1″ high.
7. Set a second bed parallel to the first at a distance equal to the width of the block.
8. Lay three beds of mortar across the parallels to rest the first block on.
9. Set the first block in position. Tap it down into the mortar with the handle of the trowel. The mortar should be about 3/8″ thick. Strike away any excess mortar from the edge of the block. Mix this mortar back into the cement.
10. Lay three more beds of mortar for the second block. Set the second block and tap it into position. Using a level, check that the tops of the blocks are level. Check that the mortar has a uniform thickness.
11. Check that the wall is straight. Do this by holding the string at the ends and corners of the tops of the two blocks. To align the blocks with the string, tap them in or out.
12. Continue this process with the third block. You will then have completed the bottom level of your wall.
13. Add the two remaining levels to the wall.
14. Ask your instructor to check your work before it completely dries.
15. Disassemble the wall and clean all of the blocks.
16. Rinse all tools in clean water. Do not wash your tools in a sink or it will become clogged.

Activity 4: Constructing a Model Shed

Objective

After completing this activity, you will know how to construct a simple model to represent the shape and size of a fully constructed shed.

Materials Needed

- 1-12″ × 18″ × 1/8″ sheet of foam board (available in local art supply stores)
- 1 sharp, pointed model knife
- 1-12″ metal straightedge to guide the cutting knife
- cutting board about 12″ × 12″
- 1-12″ scale
- drawing board and T-square

Steps of Procedure

1. The shed for which you will construct a model is described in full detail in Chapter 14. Figures A, B, and C provide you with the basic dimensions of the shed. The shed is 94″ long and 48″ wide. Figure A shows the construction of the shed walls.
2. The pitch of the roof is critical to the overall appearance of the shed. Place the foam board on the drawing board and measure 3″ (1/16″ equals 1″). Therefore, 3″ is composed of 48 1/16″ units. Use the triangle to extend a light pencil line vertically from the 3″ mark.
3. Next, measure up from the bottom a distance of 3″ to represent the shortest height of the shed (48″). On the left side measure up a distance of 5 1/8″ to represent the tallest side of the shed (82″).

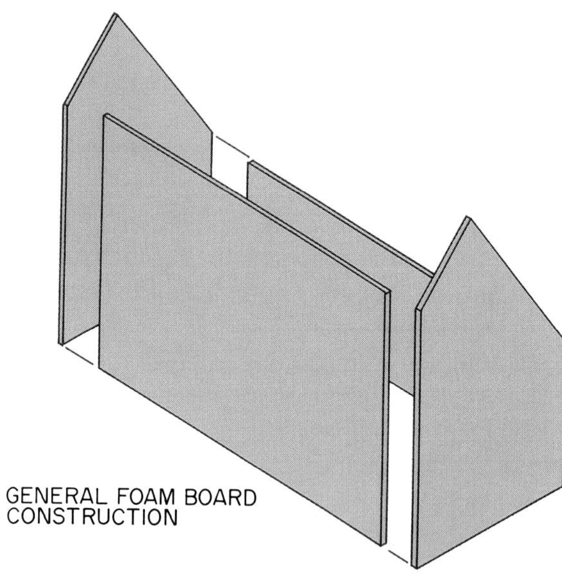

Fig. A. The construction of the shed walls.

4. Refer to Fig. B to calculate the pitch of the roof. The slope from the left has a 6″ rise for each 12″ of movement to the right. This has been calculated to have an angle of 36½°. The angle from the right is steeper, with a rise of 24″ for each 12″ of movement to the left. This has been calculated to have an angle of 62½°. You can construct the pitch for each side or use a protractor to create the angles. You will need to trace these two pieces on the foam board.
5. The front and rear of the shed are fairly easy pieces to make. The front of the shed has an overall measurement of 82″ × 94″. The rear of the shed measures 48″ × 94″. Fig. C. Converted to the scale used in constructing the sides, this means the front will measure 5⅛″ high × 5⅞″ long. The rear will measure 3″ high × 5⅞″ long.
6. After marking these four pieces on the foam board, cut them out. Put the foam board on your cutting board. Place a metal straightedge along each line. Carefully insert the cutting knife into the foam board. Keep the knife straight up and down while slowly pulling it along the pencil line. Take care not to cut across the line into another section of the shed. **NOTE:** Hold the straightedge firmly and keep your fingers back from the blade.
7. When you have cut out all four pieces, hold them together. Check that they have the general shape of the shed. Measure the distance across the front of the shed. Let the ends of the shed be the outside pieces. Fit the front between these two ends.
8. You will discover the shed is actually 6⅛″ in length, rather than 5⅞″. The reason for this difference is the thickness of the foam board. To obtain an accurate representation of the shed, you will need to cut ¼″ from the length of the front and rear sections.
9. Begin construction by applying a small amount of hot glue along one edge of the front shed section. Place the tallest portion of an end section against the glue. Hold it in place until the glue hardens. Be certain to hold the section straight up and down.
10. Next, place glue along the other end of the front section. Attach the other end in the same manner. Since the glue hardens very quickly, do not put the glue on both ends at the same time.
11. Repeat the process for the rear section.

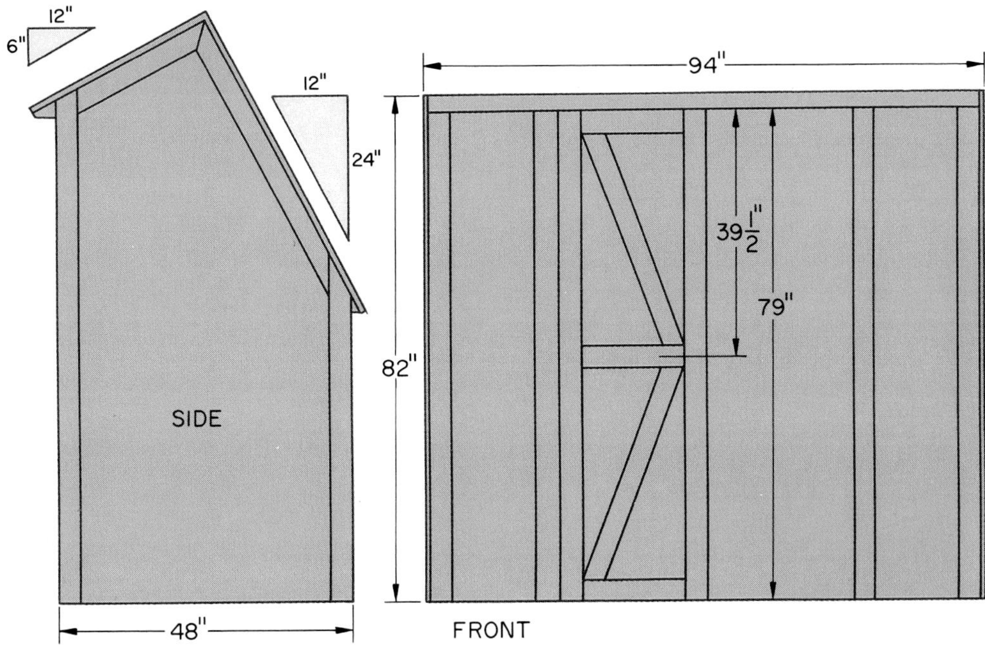

Fig. B. Panel dimensions and roof pitch.

12. Measure the distance of the longest slope of the shed roof. The distance should be 3⅛″ (50″) in length from the peak to the rear wall of the shed. This roof will also have an overhang of ⅛″ (2″) in the rear and on both sides. Cut a piece of foam board 3¼″ (52″) × 6⅛″ (98″).
13. Glue the rear roof section into place.
14. Measure the distance from the top end of the rear roof section to the front edge of the shed. Once again, allow ⅛″ (2″) of overhang along the front and on both ends. The piece of foam board should measure 2″ (32″) × 6⅛″ (98″). Glue this section in place so the front section of the roof overlaps the leading edge of the rear roof section.
15. Your model can be further refined by painting the trim on or by cutting the doors.

Fig. C. The rear panel.

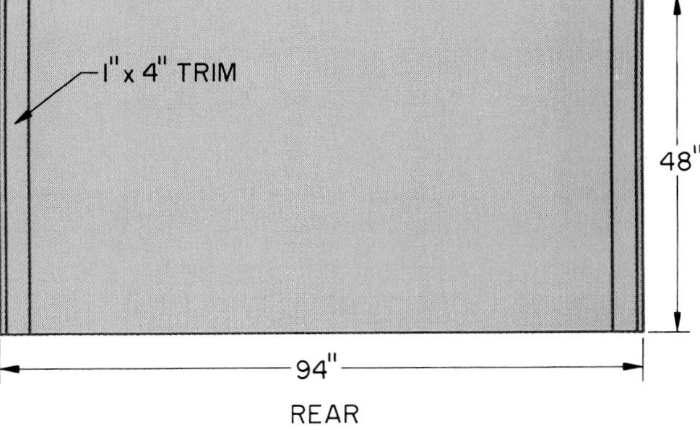

SECTION

CAREERS

CHAPTER 15

PREPARING FOR CONSTRUCTION CAREERS

Terms to Know

ability
apprentice
aptitude
bachelor's degree
career
community college
Dictionary of Occupational Titles (DOT)
general education
job
Occupational Outlook Handbook
on-the-job training
technical institute

Objectives

When you have finished reading this chapter, you should be able to do the following:

- Know where to find information relating to construction careers.
- Identify careers related to construction.
- Know the different sources of training for construction-related careers.

1. Resources:
- Chapter 15 Lesson Plan in the Teacher's Manual in this Teacher's Annotated Edition and in the Teacher's Resource Guide.
- Chapter 15 Study Guide in the Student Workbook.
- Chapter 15 Visual Master in the Teacher's Resource Guide.

One of the most important decisions you will ever have to make is the decision regarding the career you want to pursue. *Career* is not simply another word for *job.* A **job** is a paid position at a specific place or setting. A **career** is a sequence of related jobs that a person holds throughout his or her working life. Fig. 15-1. Your choice of career may affect every aspect of your future. Your relationships, your lifestyle, and even
1 your health depend to a great extent on your choice of a career.

The field of construction provides many different career opportunities for people with different interests. As you study construction technology, you may find an area of construction that interests you.

DETERMINING YOUR CAREER INTERESTS

Choosing a career and planning how you will prepare yourself for it can be confusing. There are so many exciting possibilities from which to choose! Do not be disappointed if you cannot decide on a career path in just a few weeks. Also, do not feel that you must make a career decision now. Rather, you should start exploring career options now. While you explore, you should be getting a basic education. A basic education is necessary for almost any career you choose. Fig. 15-2.

Fig. 15-1. A career is a sequence of related jobs. A carpenter, for example, might work his way up from laborer to construction superintendent over a period of many years.

Fig. 15-2. Almost every career now requires a high-school diploma. Many careers even require a minimum of a college degree.

1. Have each student prepare a career profile of a famous person. Ask the student to describe in writing the jobs and careers that the person has had during his or her lifetime. Were all of the jobs interrelated in a single career or did the person make one or more career changes? Ask them what led the person they profiled to make the particular career choice that they made. How old were they when they decided upon the career? Who influenced them in their decision? Had their past education prepared them for the career that they entered?

The years you spend in school can be some of the most exciting years of your life. Every week you learn new ideas and face new challenges. Many of these ideas and challenges are designed to provide you with the basic skills you will need after your school years are finished. You may not find all of the skills and information you receive interesting or of use to you right now. However, do not underestimate the value of this knowledge. As you grow older, you may be surprised at how well a good education can serve you.

Learning to Make Choices

The best way to go about making a career
1 choice is to learn about all the possibilities. You will want to make a wise choice. Your choice of career, after all, will affect you for many years to come. Wise choices are choices that are made on the basis of *knowledge*.

At one time, most of the decisions in your life were made for you. The clothes you wore and the food you ate were chosen by your parents. You were not given any choices. Then, as you grew older, your parents began to ask your opinion about clothes, food, and other necessities. You began to choose food and clothing you knew that you liked. You based your choices on past experience.

Later in life, you started to make decisions without having first experienced the choices. When selecting courses in school, for example, you probably selected some that you were not familiar with. In these cases, you could not rely on experience to help you make your decisions. Instead, your decisions were probably based on information you received from others. You may also have found information in the course guide. In other words, you based your decisions on research.

Choosing a career also requires research. Few
people are able to make career decisions based 2
on experience in the career. In most cases, people must make career decisions long before they actually work in the career. Because of this, it is most important that you gather information now so that when the time comes to make a career choice, you will be prepared. Fig. 15-3.

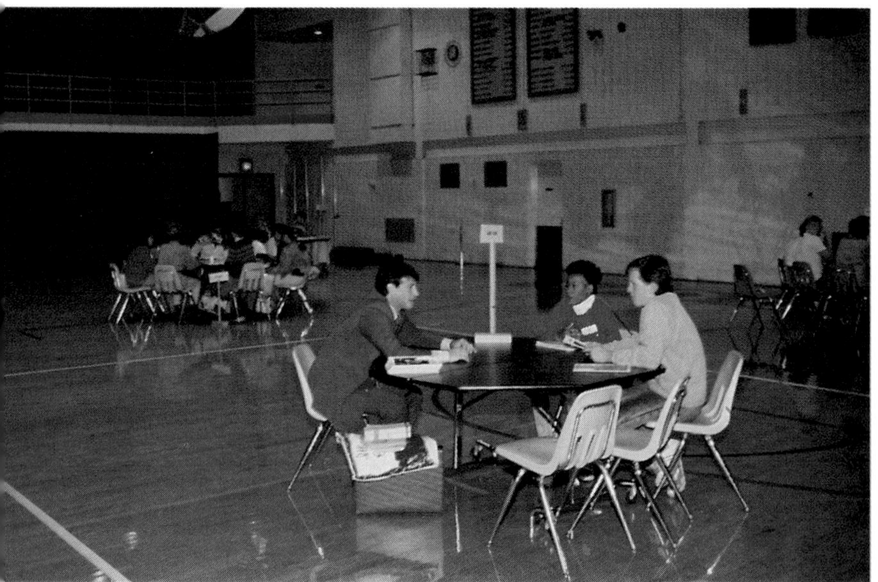

Fig. 15-3. Many schools hold a Career Day once a year to help students become familiar with career opportunities.

1. The instructor should make the point that regardless of how well a person likes his or her career, there are times when the person may wish that a different career path had been chosen.

2. Invite a person who is involved in career counseling in your school system to visit the class. Ask this person to describe to the class how students can be tested to ascertain their interests, aptitudes, and abilities.

Knowing Yourself

Before you can start making career decisions, you need to learn as much as you can about yourself. You have interests, abilities, aptitudes, and values that will play important roles in your future career. In fact, how successful you become in a career and how much you enjoy the career depend largely on these personal characteristics. By learning about yourself, you can better focus on careers that will be best suited to you.

Identifying Your Interests

Your interests are all those things you most like to do. Think about your hobbies and your favorite subjects in school. Activities that you enjoy may be a good basis for a career. Do you like to work with your hands? Do you enjoy solving puzzles? Do you like to be outdoors? Fig.
15-4. The answers to these questions and others 1
like them reflect your interests.

Once you know your interests, you can begin to think about how they relate to career possibilities. For example, if you like working with your hands, you may enjoy a career as an assembler. If you also like being outdoors, you may consider a career as a carpenter.

Identifying Your Aptitudes and Abilities

Interests should be an important factor in choosing a career. However, you cannot base a career choice on interest alone. To be successful in a chosen career, you must have the aptitudes and abilities to do the work well. Aptitudes and abilities are very closely related. An **aptitude** is a natural talent for learning a skill. Fig. 15-5. An **ability** is something you have already learned how to do—a skill you have mastered. Fig. 15-6. For example, if you do well in your algebra class, you probably have the ability to solve mathematical equations. This may also indicate that you have an aptitude for math-related studies. You may find that you have a natural talent for learning math-related subjects.

Ability is often a good indication of aptitude. If you are good at building model airplanes, you probably have an aptitude for working with your hands. If you enjoy experimenting with radio kits, you may have an aptitude for electronics. Make a list of your abilities and aptitudes to refer to when you select a career.

Fig. 15-4. This student likes to work with her hands. What type of career might she be interested in?

1. Have each student prepare a written list of their interests both in and outside of school. Ask them also to list their interests as they remember them two years ago. Ask them to list their interests in the order of their importance. They should then compare the two lists to see how their interests may have changed. They also should look for new interests that have been acquired. Explain that adolescents are expected to change their interests. It is a normal part of maturation. There may be some keys, however, in interests that have remained or even grown in importance.

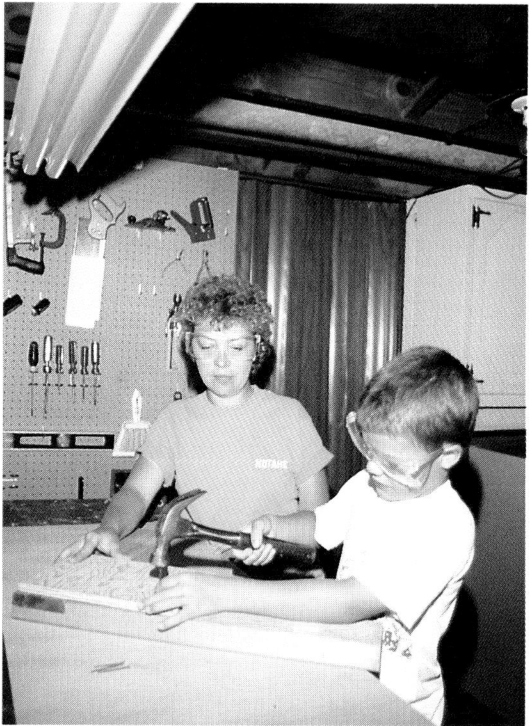

Fig. 15-5. An aptitude is a natural talent for learning a skill. This young man has an aptitude for carpentry.

Fig. 15-6. Ann has already perfected the skill of painting. She has the ability to paint a wall.

Identifying Your Values

Your **values** are your beliefs and ideas about
1 things that you think are important. Your values may include security, honesty, family relationships, money, or any combination of these or other values. Fig. 15-7. Take a close look at your values before you choose a career. Suppose you value family relationships. You probably would not be happy in a career in which you were required to work a lot of overtime, even if you were interested in that career. Such a career would disrupt your family life. In this case, you would want to look for a career that would allow you to spend time with your family. When your career is compatible with your values, it can be both rewarding and fulfilling.

For Discussion

As mentioned in the text, your choice of a career will depend on your interests, aptitudes, abilities, and values. Discuss the importance of each of these in coming to a decision about a career.

1. Discuss values. Discuss what they are, how they are developed, and where they are obtained. List some sources of values on the board. Emphasize that the values of each student are being shaped by his or her surroundings and the activities that he or she chooses to undertake. Values also are shaped by parents and companions. Illustrate how very different values may lead two people to the same career. Point out also that the different values will affect how they perform in that career.

Fig. 15-7. Tom values people and enjoys spending time with them. What type of career might he find rewarding?

EXPLORING CAREER POSSIBILITIES

To decide which careers interest you, you must first find out what careers are available. Chapter 16 describes some of the careers that are available in the construction field. Although many careers are described in these chapters, many more exist. How can you find out about all the possibilities?

Talking to People

One way to get career information is to talk
1 to people. Parents, relatives, and friends may be able to tell you about their careers. They may also be able to tell you about other types of careers at their places of employment. A school counselor can tell you about many different kinds of careers. He or she may be able to direct you to other sources of career information. Many of these sources contain firsthand information about the duties and requirements of selected careers. Fig. 15-8.

1. Invite a person who teaches construction-related subjects at a nearby technical school, community college, college, or university to visit the class. Ask them to talk about the career opportunities available in the construction industry. Have the class prepare for the visit by listing questions they would like to ask.

Understanding Dependability

In any job you take, you must be willing to demonstrate dependability. Dependability involves several things. It means, for example, that you will be attentive to the job. It also means that you will carry out a work task thoroughly. Dependability also requires that you be punctual, or on time for work.

You should also understand that good health is important in effective job performance. You should make every effort to avoid foods and practices that can harm your health. As part of being health-conscious, you also should be aware of the advantages of regular exercise. Good health, combined with good grooming, will help make you a more effective employee.

Fig. 15-8. Some companies send representatives to local schools to talk about career opportunities. Ask your guidance counselor about any representatives that are scheduled to appear at your school.

Did You Know?

In medieval times, crafts and skills were sometimes handed down from one generation to the next within one family. For example, a father who was a carpenter might teach carpentry skills to his children. Thus, the same crafts and skills might be practiced in a single family for generations. In fact, family members might become associated with the practice of a certain craft or skill. This might lead others to give them a family name that described their craft. Many family names still used today were given in this way. Examples are Sawyer (one who saws) and Smith (one who works with metals).

Using the Library

Another source of career information is your library. Most libraries have the publications of the U.S. Department of Labor. Two that will be of interest to you are the *Occupational Outlook Handbook* and the *Dictionary of Occupational Titles (DOT)*.

The **Occupational Outlook Handbook** 1
contains information about 200 careers. This handbook refers to careers as *occupations*. The careers, or occupations, are listed in the table of contents under general classifications. Some of the classifications under which construction-related careers may be found are:

- Construction occupations.
- Engineers, surveyors, and architects. 2
- Technologists and technicians.

When you find a listing that interests you, turn to the correct page and read the entry. The hand-

1. Assign a short written assignment in which the student will be required to obtain information from the *Occupational Outlook Handbook*. Structure the assignment to require information from several categories within this reference.

2. Discuss the future demand for workers in construction-related occupations as shown by the *Occupational Outlook Handbook*. How does this demand compare to the demand for workers in manufacturing occupations?

book provides information about the duties and responsibilities of each career. It also provides information on the following:

- Working conditions, hours, and earnings.
- Training and education needed.
- The *outlook*, or future, of the career.
- Where to find more information about the career.

This information is updated every two years. The "Index to Occupations" at the back of the handbook lists careers by title. Just after this index is a cross-referenced index to the *Dictionary of Occupational Titles*. The **Dictionary of**
1 **Occupational Titles (DOT)** describes over
20,000 jobs relating to many different careers. In the *DOT* you can look for construction-related jobs in the index under the name of each job.

Most libraries have other books that describe various careers. Fig. 15-9. You may want to look in the card catalog under "Careers" for books about specific careers. For information on a career you think might be interesting, look in the card catalog under that particular career name.

Magazines, too, can be a source of career information. To find magazine articles about careers, use the *Readers' Guide to Periodical Literature*. In it you will find articles listed alphabetically by subject. It also tells you the magazine in which you can find the article.

Participating in Student Shop Enterprises

You can get a general idea of what some construction careers might be like by participating 2
in your laboratory or shop activities. Fig. 15-10. Use this opportunity to learn as much as you can about the duties and responsibilities related to your construction enterprise. Keep in mind, however, that your shop experience cannot show you all the aspects of any career. If you decide that you are interested, look for further information about a career in construction.

Taking a Part-time Job

When you reach the minimum employment age, you may want to take a part-time job in a field that interests you. Fig. 15-11. This is an excellent way to become familiar with the requirements and responsibilities of a job. Keep in mind that jobs in many construction occupations

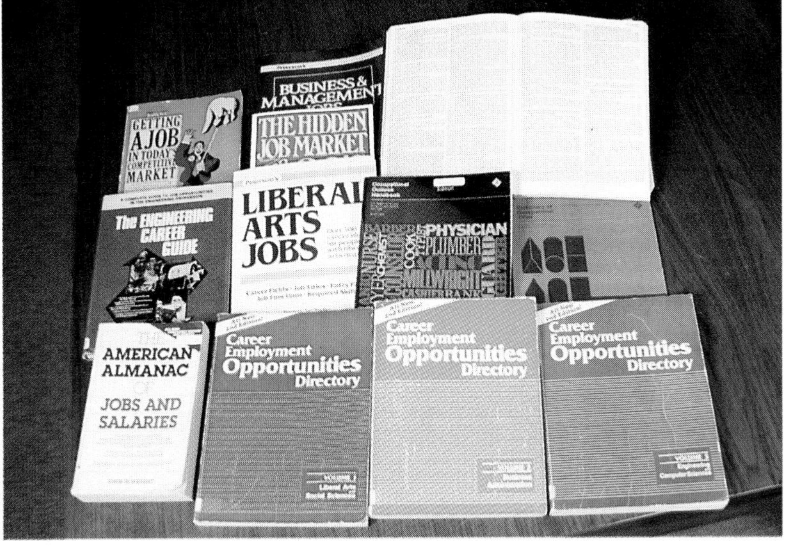

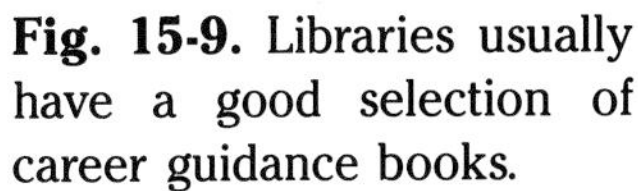
Fig. 15-9. Libraries usually have a good selection of career guidance books.

1. Prepare a short written assignment in which the student will be required to obtain information from the *Dictionary of Occupational Titles*. Part of the assignment can be specific and another part open-ended.

2. Discuss the need for staying in school. Relate this to the job opportunities that are lost by those who do not have a high school diploma.

Fig. 15-10. Your technology education laboratory is a good place to explore your interest in a particular career area.

1 **Fig. 15-11.** This student wanted to find out more about a career in construction. He took a part-time job after school as a laborer for a construction company.

1. Some nations utilize a tracking system of education. In this system, each student is tested. In their early teens, he or she is placed in a college-bound or vocational career track. Describe this process with your class. Discuss the pros and cons of such an educational strategy.

require training that you do not yet have. However, you can learn much from simply watching people who are working in jobs you find interesting.

You might not actually do the work you find interesting. However, you would be in a good position to learn more about it. By talking with the other employees, you would be able to learn about advancement opportunities. You might also learn about the advantages and disadvantages of a certain career.

For Discussion

This section of the text discussed several ways in which you might explore careers. As you can see, some of the methods involved library research. Others required personal interviews. Others were related to shop activities or part-time jobs. Discuss the advantages and disadvantages of each of these methods.

GETTING THE RIGHT EDUCATION

Once you have chosen a career in which you are interested, you will need to plan your edu-
1 cation for that career. It is wise to plan your career and education in advance. Planning for a career does not mean that you will be "stuck" in a particular career path. If, in preparing for a career, you find that the career does not suit you, you can always change. In fact, the planning you do now will probably help you no matter what career you eventually decide to pursue.

Everyone needs a good education to be able to work well in construction or any other type of career. At one time, graduation from high school was not necessary to get a job in construction. Today, there are very few construction jobs that do not require at least a high school diploma. Employers like to hire workers who are willing to complete whatever they start.

General Preparations

General education is made up of the basic
courses, such as reading, writing, mathematics, 2
science, and history, that are required in school. General education is the foundation for further learning. You would have difficulty learning specific career-related skills without first getting a good background in general education. Fig. 15-12.

Fig. 15-12. Construction workers must be able to read notes and dimensions on a set of plans in order to build a structure.

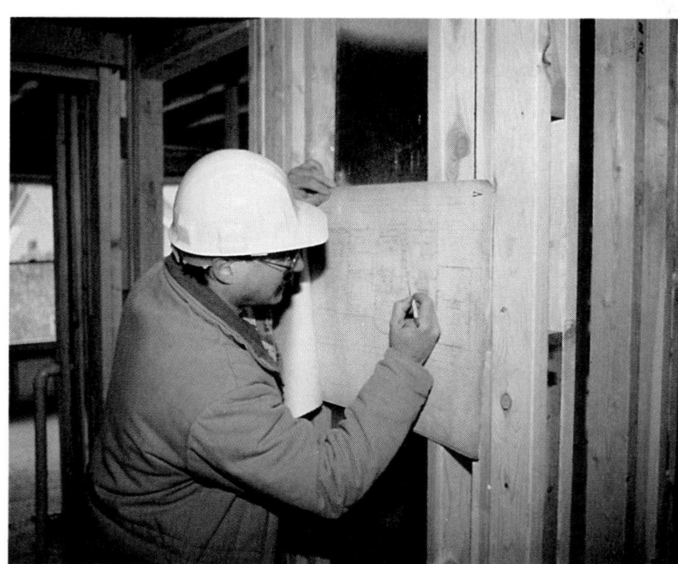

1. Assign each student to select a construction-related career that interests them. Ask them to find three post-secondary schools that offer it as a major. Find out the general entrance requirements for each school and the specific requirements for each program.

2. Have a student or group of students study curricula from several post-secondary schools with construction-related programs. Ask them to identify the general education classes that are a required part of each curriculum.

In preparing for a career, you must consider the education you will need in addition to your general education. For example, suppose you are interested in a career that requires many years of college. You may wish to find out now which colleges offer the type of degree you will need in your chosen career. What are the entrance requirements of these colleges? Are your grades good enough to qualify you for acceptance? Good grades now will increase your chances of being accepted into the college of your choice. Also, the good study habits you create now will influence your success throughout your education.

If you are interested in a career that requires apprenticeship or other on-the-job training, you may wish to become familiar with the types of opportunities available in your area. Keep up with developments and new programs that may be offered by private companies. When the time comes to enter such a program, you will be well informed. This will help you make an intelligent decision about which opportunity to take.

Educational Options

The type of education you will need will depend on the career in which you are
1 interested. For example, the training needed to be a carpenter is obviously different from that needed to design machines and equipment. To meet these various needs, many kinds of education and training programs are available.

On-the-Job Training

Some industries train workers on the job. **On-the-job training** is training that a person receives after he or she has been hired. A company may hire a person who has a solid basic education and a good attitude and who is willing to work hard. This person is called a *trainee.* He or she is trained by an experienced worker. The employer may also offer company training sessions to provide trainees with knowledge and skills required on a job. Fig. 15-13. Training may last for a few weeks or for two years or more, depending on the job. As trainees become more skilled and experienced, they advance in their career path. This is an excellent way to earn money while learning the skills necessary for a career.

1. Are there any vocational building construction classes in your school system? If so, find out what is necessary to enter one. Inquire about the placement of program graduates, beginning pay scales, and opportunities for advancement.

Apprenticeship

One way to begin a career in most of the skilled crafts is through apprentice training. Fig. 15-14.

Fig. 15-13. Employers sometimes offer workshops to help trainees learn the skills they need.

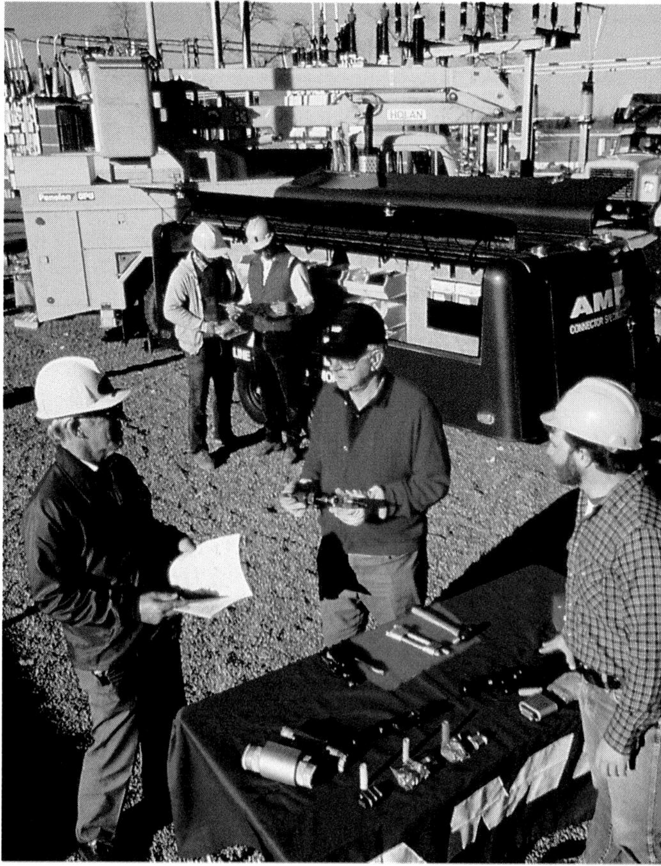

Fig. 15-14. The construction industry trains many of its workers through apprenticeships.

Fig. 15-15. Apprentices spend a lot of time learning from skilled workers, both in the classroom and on the job.

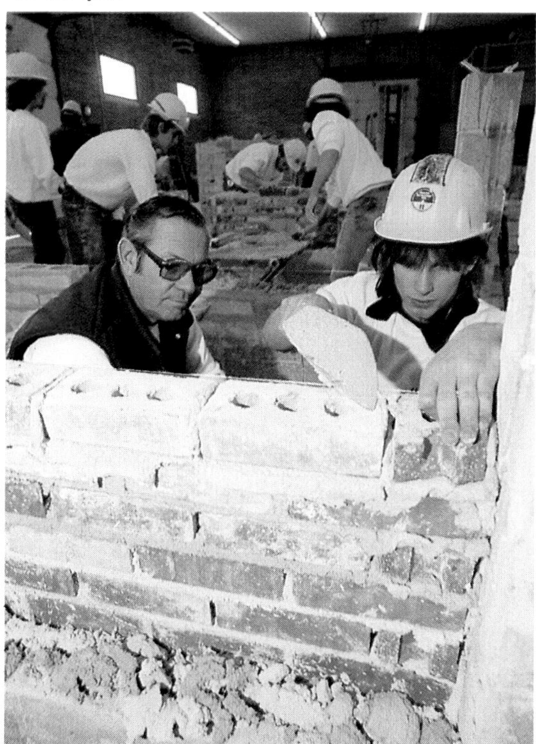

1. Ask each student to select an apprenticeship program in which they might be interested. Ask them to find out the following: minimum age for entry, length of apprenticeship, entrance requirements, class time per week, pay schedule, and number of openings.

Plumbers and electricians are examples of people skilled in crafts related to construction. An 1
apprentice learns from a skilled worker while on the job. The apprentice also receives classroom instruction. He or she signs an agreement to work and learn for a period of two to five years. Fig. 15-15.

Did You Know?

The practice of training workers through an apprenticeship was known in ancient Egypt. This system of worker training was also used in the Middle Ages in Europe. At that time, the skilled members of those practicing a single craft, such as woodworking, organized into a guild. The experienced craftsmen in the guild were known as master craftsmen. These master craftsmen took on apprentices.

These apprentices were then to learn the skills of the master craftsmen. This period of on-the-job training usually lasted seven years. At the end of that time, the apprentice was expected to demonstrate a skill. The apprentice did this by producing an item that exhibited the skills associated with the craft. This piece was called the masterpiece. This is the origin of a word that is still used.

Technical Institutes and Community Colleges

Some construction-related careers may require only two years of schooling beyond high school. 2
One source of training is a **technical institute**. A technical institute is a school that offers technical training for specific careers. In two-year technical programs, only technical courses are offered. These programs usually include hands-

2. Ask the students to look over catalogs from a technical institute and a community college. How do the types of curricula and classes offered differ? How are they the same?

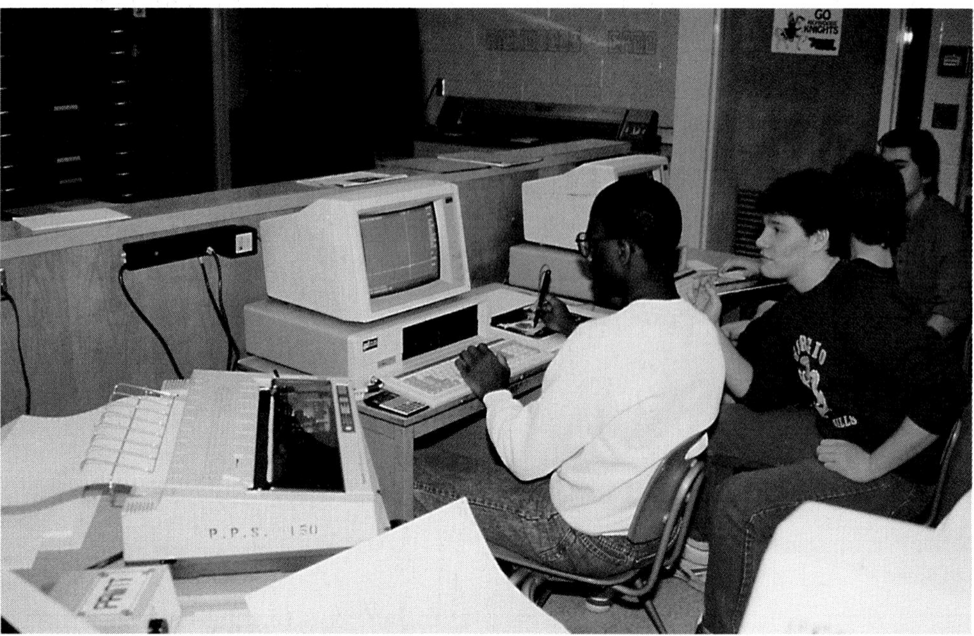

Fig. 15-16. Community colleges often offer applied technology courses. This class is learning computer-aided design techniques.

Fig. 15-17. This college student is studying for a degree in engineering.

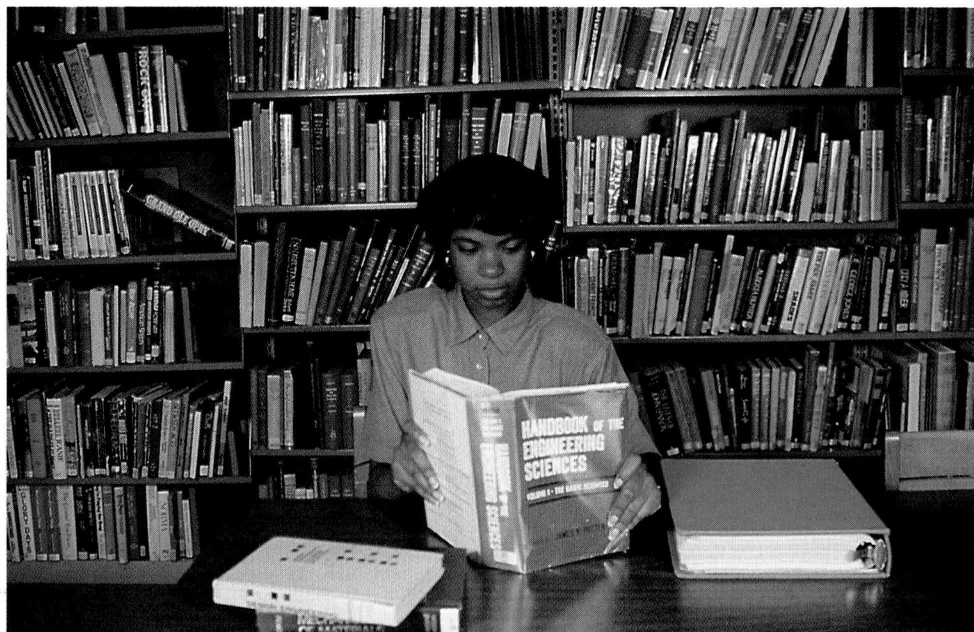

1

1. Ask each student to find out the minimum age in your state at which a person can be employed in a construction-related job. Are special permits required for workers under eighteen years of age? Are there restrictions on what an underage person can do? How can a person obtain experience without being formally employed?

on training to prepare students to obtain a job immediately after they complete the program. Taking courses of this type can help you determine which careers you might like to pursue.

Another source of technical education is a community college. A **community college** is a local, two-year school that is usually supported in part by the state and/or local government. Many community colleges offer courses in accounting, finance, management theory, marketing, industrial supervision, and labor relations. They also offer some technical courses. Figs. 15-16 and 15-17.

Engineers and architects must have at least a **bachelor's degree**. This is a degree awarded for completion of work at a four-year college. They must also have a special state license to practice their profession. Fig. 15-18. Some positions require a higher degree, such as a master's degree or a doctorate. These degrees are awarded for more advanced work beyond that done for a bachelor's degree. Masters and doctorate programs do not usually include any general edu- 1
cation at all. Instead, they concentrate on specialized education.

Fig. 15-18. Architects must have at least a bachelor's degree and a state license to practice their profession.

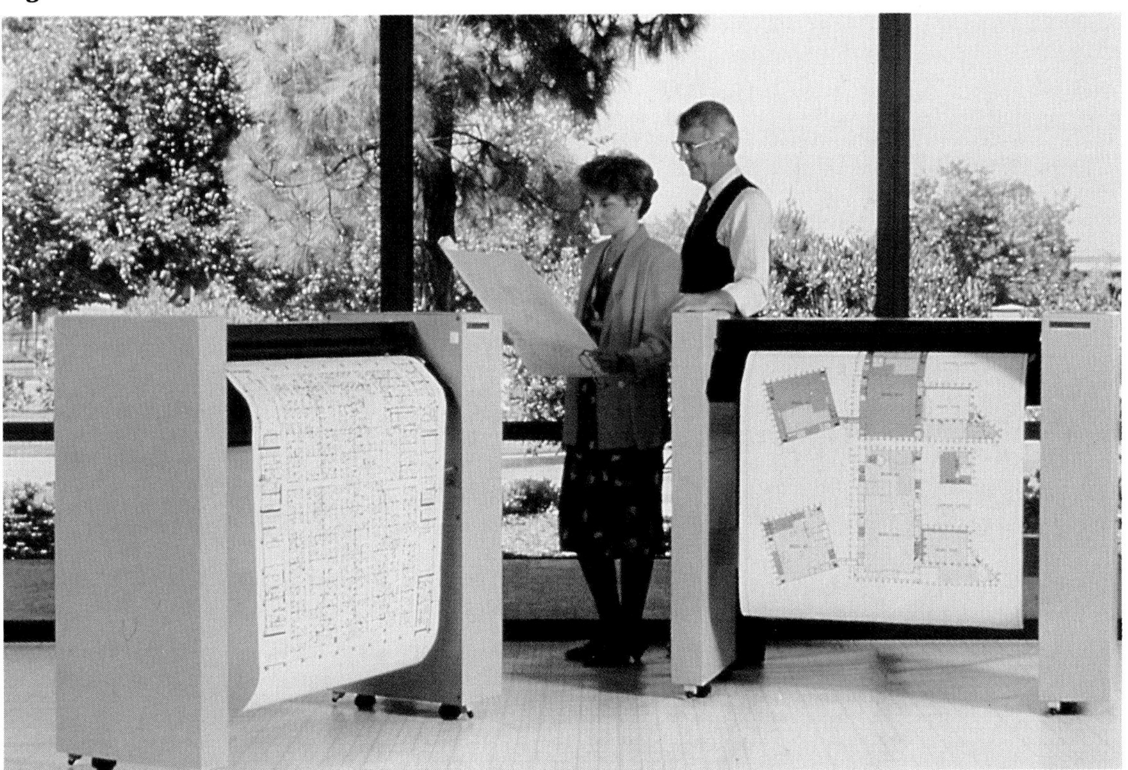

1. Discuss how an employee's educational level affects his or her chances for advancement. What factors besides education would an employer consider when choosing a person for advancement?

Did You Know?

You may have identified a career. However, you may wonder how you will be able to pay for the education or training you will need. For advice, you should consult your school guidance counselor. Many organizations offer scholarships, loans, and work-study programs. Individual states provide financial aid programs. Also, student loans are available through banks and other private lenders. You should be able to identify the various types of financial institutions. A *commercial bank* offers the widest variety of loans. Loans are also available from a *savings and loan institution*. Savings and loan institutions, however, often specialize in making loans for home mortgages.

The Federal government also provides several kinds of financial assistance to students. Financial help may make the difference in helping you to pursue the career of your choice.

For Discussion

In this section, various methods of obtaining training have been discussed. Among these are technical colleges and community colleges. Are there any technical institutes or community colleges in your town? If there are, do they offer courses that would help you prepare for a career in which you might be interested? 1

1. Have each student write a one-page report on how the study of this chapter and the research that they have done has affected or changed their attitude toward making a career choice. Has it increased the options available? Has it changed their attitudes toward post-secondary education?

Construction Facts

LIKE FATHER, LIKE DAUGHTER?

Stacey Linsworth is a student at Brindall Junior High School. She does well in most of her school courses, but she is more interested in her father's custom carpentry business.

Recently, Stacey's father asked her if she had thought about what career she wanted to pursue. Stacey told her father that she had always just assumed she would follow in his footsteps and become a carpenter. Stacey's father told her, though, that she should investigate other careers, too.

Stacey decided that she could at least look into a few different types of careers. Her father told her she should think about a career that related to her interests and abilities. Stacey visited her guidance counselor at school and glanced through some of the books the counselor suggested. She discovered many options that she had not even thought about. She decided to begin by doing research on architects and interior designers. She discovered that to work as an architect she would need a five-year college degree as well as a state license.

To become an interior designer, she would have to attend a professional school for three years or earn a bachelor's degree.

1 When Stacey told her father about her research, he complimented her on her work. He explained to Stacey that the more she learns about possible careers, the better prepared she will be to make a career decision.

Stacey is not yet ready to make a career decision. She is still interested in her father's carpentry business. However, she is becoming more interested in architecture and design. Now Stacey reads everything she can find about these subjects. She is also beginning to take an interest in her grades. After all, she may go to college, and good grades can help her. Right now, she is happy knowing that her preparations will help her when she does choose a career.

1. Ask students to check the local newspaper for construction-related jobs that do not specify or appear to require experience. Call one or two and ask if they give on-the-job training. If they do, find out the minimum educational requirements and the pay scale. Do employers pay as much to a trainee as they do to one who is already experienced? Why?

CHAPTER 15 REVIEW

Chapter Summary

A career is a sequence of related jobs that a person holds throughout his or her working life. Career choices need to be carefully made. In making a career choice, you should consider your interests, abilities, aptitudes, and values. An interest relates to something that you like to do. An aptitude is a natural talent for learning a skill. An ability is a skill you have mastered. Values are beliefs and ideas about things that you think are important. There are several methods of exploring career possibilities. These include personal interviews, using library resources, student shop enterprises, and taking a part-time job. In preparing for a career, you need to plan your education. You will need to plan your general classroom education. You might also consider on-the-job training and apprenticeship courses. Technical colleges and community colleges also offer programs of technical education.

Test Your Knowledge 1

1. Explain the difference between a *job* and a *career.*
2. What are four things you should know about yourself before you choose a career?
3. Why should you consider your values when you make a career choice?
4. What is the difference between an ability and an aptitude?
5. List four ways in which you can get information about careers.
6. Name two publications of the U.S. Department of Labor that can help you learn about career choices.
7. If you wanted to look up information in a magazine about a career, what reference source would you use to locate an article about that career?
8. How can taking a part-time job in a field that interests you help you learn about that field?
9. Name at least four options that will advance your education beyond high school.
10. What is the title given a person who is being trained on the job by an experienced worker?

1. The answers to the Test Your Knowledge questions are in the Teacher's Manual at the front of this Teacher's Annotated Edition.

REVIEW

Activities

1. Look up a construction-related occupation of your choice in the *Occupational Outlook Handbook*. Give the class a brief summary of the information you found.

2. In the library, find a source of career information that is not mentioned in this chapter. Describe the source to the class and the kind of information you found in it.

3. You should have some understanding of personal loans. Your ability to obtain a loan is based on your credit worthiness. Your credit worthiness reflects your ability to repay a loan. Several factors influence your credit worthiness. These include your job, your income, and your past record of repaying your debts. Obtain a blank loan application from a bank. Identify those questions on the loan application that directly relate to the applicant's credit worthiness.

4. Good money management is essential in any career. Once you get a job, the first thing you may want to do is to open a checking account. There are two general types of checking accounts. In one, the checking account holder is charged a certain amount for every check that he or she writes. In the other, the person is charged a flat fee, regardless of the number of checks that he or she writes. Obtain from a bank the basic information on their checking accounts. Evaluate this information. Then prepare a short written report on the advantages and disadvantages of each type of checking account.

CHAPTER 16

CAREERS IN CONSTRUCTION

Terms to Know

architect
bricklayer
building trades and crafts
carpenters
construction managers
electricians
engineer
estimator
ironworkers
laborers
office personnel
operating engineers
pipefitters
plumbers
surveyors
technicians

Objectives

When you have finished reading this chapter, you should be able to do the following: 1

- Name some common construction-related trades and crafts.
- Identify some construction-related professions.
- Find more information about specific construction-related careers.

1. Resources:
- Chapter 16 Lesson Plan in the Teacher's Manual in this Teacher's Annotated Edition and in the Teacher's Resource Guide.
- Chapter 16 Study Guide in the Student Workbook.
- Chapter 16 Visual Master in the Teacher's Resource Guide.

Many people in different occupations work together as a team to create the communities in which we live. Construction projects create many career opportunities all over the United States. As a matter of fact, almost five million men and women are now employed in the construction industry. The figure is still grow-
1 ing. Men and women with a wide range of skills are needed to work in construction. Fig. 16-1.

The development of a building project does not happen overnight. Project development is a big undertaking that requires the skills and talents of many people working together on a team. The team members have the same goal: to complete the building project. Each person does his or her part to achieve this goal.

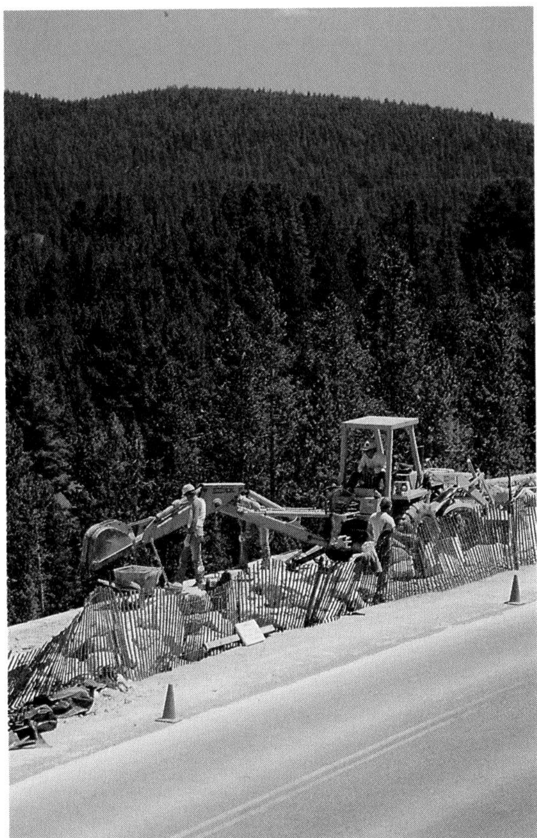

Fig. 16-1. The many people who work at a construction site do many different types of work.

Workers involved in a construction project range from highly trained people with college degrees to unskilled laborers. Fig. 16-2. Each person plays an important part in the construction process. Construction careers may be classified into three main categories:

- Trades and crafts.
- Construction-related professions.
- Design and engineering professions.

Within each of these categories lies a wide vari- 2
ety of career choices.

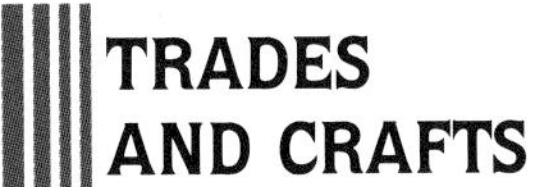

TRADES AND CRAFTS

The people who do the physical work of construction are very important. Without their skills and knowledge, a project could not be built. These people work in careers known as the **building trades and crafts**. They are responsible for doing the on-site work needed to complete the project. Most tradespeople learn their trade through a formal apprenticeship program and on-the-job experience. Fig. 16-3. Many tradespeople start as laborers and work their way up to skilled positions. Some vocational and technical schools also offer courses in some building trades, such as carpentry and electricity.

1. Discuss how automation will affect the construction industry. Ask students if they think that robots could do much of the work done on a construction site? Discuss the difference between automation and mechanization.

2. With students, discuss those factors that will affect the growth of the construction industry. Will the nation reach a point where very little more new construction is needed? Why?

Fig. 16-2. The careers available in the construction industry include a wide range of opportunities. Architects, estimators, laborers, and many other people are needed to complete a project.

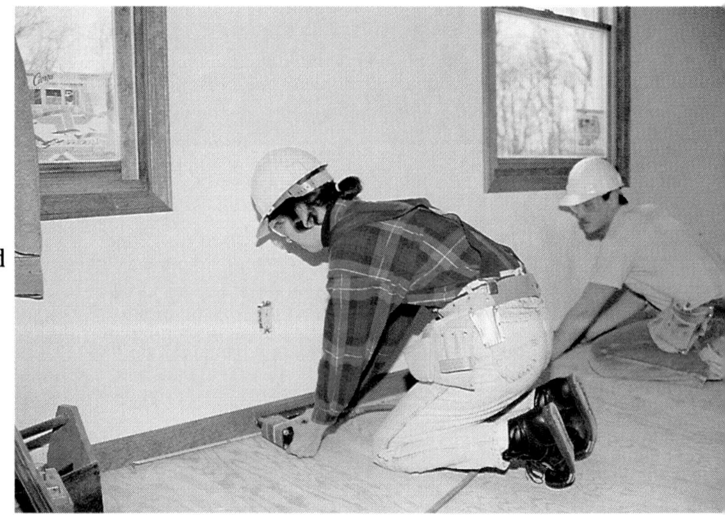

1 **Fig. 16-3.** Tradespeople learn the skills they need in apprenticeship classes.

1. Point out that as new construction declines, remodeling and renovation increase. This helps take care of some of the unemployment in the construction industry.

Although each type of trade or craft involves different skills and knowledge, most require the same types of qualifications. Tradespeople must be in good physical condition. Their work usually
1 involves lifting heavy objects. Most trades require some knowledge of general math. Nearly all tradespeople must have a good sense of balance. They must be able to work well with their hands.

Workers from many different trades and crafts work together at a construction site. Each trade specializes in a single aspect of the construction work. A few of the most common trades are listed in the paragraphs that follow.

Did You Know?

The introduction of new building materials has changed the role of the carpenter in building construction. In earlier times, buildings in many parts of the world were built entirely, or mostly, of wood. On such buildings, the carpenter was the principal worker. Now, however, the use of materials other than wood has changed the work role of the carpenter. Today, the carpenter works as one member of a team. Formerly, the carpenter might have been responsible for most of the work on a job. Now, he or she shares the job responsibility with others.

Carpenters

Carpenters are tradespeople who work with wood and wood products. Fig. 16-4. They build
the framework for houses and other structures. 2
They also install doors and windows and do any other carpentry that is required. In most homes, carpenters install the kitchen cabinets, wood paneling, and flooring. In heavy construction, carpenters build wooden bridges, piers, and temporary supports for tunnels and bridges. During the construction process, carpenters also build scaffolding to support workers and the wooden forms into which concrete is poured.

The duties of a carpenter vary. They depend on the construction company, the type of construction project, and the preference and skills of the carpenter. Some carpenters do general construction carpentry. Others specialize in one type of carpentry, such as installing cabinets or building bridges and bridge supports.

Fig. 16-4. Carpenters work with wood and wood products.

1. Discuss the part that unions play in the building trades and crafts area. How are they engaged in education? How are work rules defined? What are jurisdictional disputes and how are they settled?

2. Familiarize the students with the *Dictionary of Occupational Titles*. Ask them to list as many areas as possible in which carpenters can specialize. Ask them to identify the basic skills every carpenter would need.

Bricklayers

A **bricklayer** is a tradesperson who works with masonry. Bricklayers use bricks or concrete blocks and mortar to build walls, fireplaces, floors, partitions, and other structural elements. Fig. 16-5. One special kind of bricklayer is a *refractory bricklayer.* Refractory bricklayers
1 install and repair firebrick linings and refractory tile in industrial furnaces and other high-temperature industrial areas.

Fig. 16-5. This bricklayer's skill will determine the appearance of the finished wall.

Electricians

Electricians assemble, install, and maintain electrical wiring and fixtures. Fig. 16-6. They install wiring in new structures and rewire older structures. An electrician's work includes measuring and cutting lengths of conduit, wire, and cable. Electricians need to be good in math. They must enjoy problem-solving, because each electrical circuit must be calculated accurately. Electricity is dangerous. It is important for electricians to follow safety rules.

Plumbers and Pipefitters

Plumbing and pipefitting are so closely related that they are sometimes considered a single trade. **Plumbers** install, maintain, and repair the plumbing systems that carry fresh water to buildings and wastewater away from buildings. They also build drainage pipes and gas systems in commercial and industrial buildings and in homes.

Pipefitters build and repair pressurized pipes to carry compressed air and steam in HVAC sys-
2 tems and for special applications in factories. They also build special pipe systems for transportation and for power plants. Fig. 16-7.

1. What kind of entry-level job might prepare one to learn bricklaying? Point out that some masonry companies are specialized, while others do all types of masonry work.

2. In some areas, the people who install the pressurized systems for air conditioning and for heat pumps are classified as pipefitters. Discuss the level of experience needed to install and service such systems.

Fig. 16-6. This electrician is installing a switch.

1

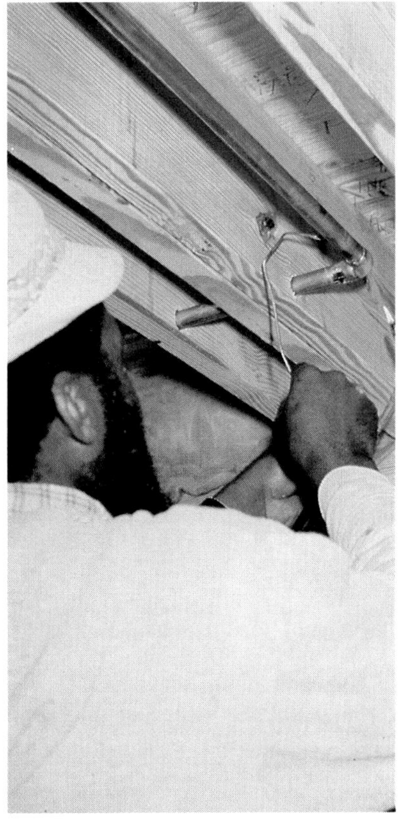

Fig. 16-7. Plumbers and pipefitters install and maintain piping systems.

2

1. Are the economy and the level of construction activity at the same level in all areas of the country? Discuss how this affects the life of some construction workers. How might their families be affected?

2. Discuss the seasonal nature of some types of construction occupations. On the chalkboard, list jobs that would be dependent upon the weather. How do these workers manage financially when they are out of work?

Ironworkers

The tradespeople who build steel-framed structures are called **ironworkers**. Fig. 16-8.
1 Ironworkers frequently work high in the air while they weld or bolt the structural steel framework for skyscrapers and bridges. Ironworkers also build and install steel stairs, lampposts, iron fences, ladders, and metal cabinets in industrial and commercial buildings. In addition, ironworkers often weld or bolt prefabricated panels of aluminum or other metal to the sides of buildings.

On the construction site, ironworkers assemble the cranes and derricks that are used to move heavy equipment and materials into place. For example, structural steel, large buckets of wet concrete, and sometimes even equipment must be moved by cranes. Ironworkers are also responsible for positioning reinforcing bars in concrete forms before the concrete is poured.

Operating Engineers

The people who run construction equipment are known as **operating engineers**. Driving construction equipment may sound easy. However, much knowledge, coordination, and skill are needed. Fig. 16-9. For example, crane operators must place large, heavy materials and equipment accurately on the upper stories of tall buildings. Operating engineers also operate bulldozers, excavators, and other kinds of equipment. These workers may go to special training sessions periodically. The sessions are usually sponsored by the equipment manufacturers. The manufacturers teach the operating
engineers how to operate and maintain their 2
machines.

Fig. 16-8. Ironworkers sometimes work high in the air to build the structural framework for a building.

1. Emphasize that although ironworkers may work high in the air, most construction workers will be expected to work at some height. An extreme fear of heights will be a definite handicap to someone who wants to be a construction worker.

2. Have the class list the equipment that would be run by operating engineers. Will an operating engineer be able to operate all of the equipment? Why might an operator specialize?

Fig. 16-9. Operating engineers need to know how to run large pieces of equipment safely. This crane operator must consider the wind and many other factors to be able to place this precast support accurately.

Laborers

Laborers do the supportive physical work at the construction site. Although laborers are not considered tradespeople, they are mentioned here because many laborers go on to become tradespeople. The job requires just what its title implies: hard work. Laborers work as assistants to tradespeople. Fig. 16-10. They dig, shovel, clean up, and do other jobs. They also operate motorized lifts and other equipment.

Most beginning jobs for laborers do not require training. Laborers do need to be in excellent physical condition because of the strenuous nature of the job. Laborers do a lot of standing, walking, and climbing. They must also be able to lift heavy objects. Some employers require laborers to have at least a general knowledge
of construction methods and materials. A high 1
school education is helpful but not necessary.

Fig. 16-10. This laborer is assisting a bricklayer by bringing mortar.

1. Have each student find out as much as possible about a construction laborer's job responsibilities. Ask each student to write a one-page report on the advantages and disadvantages of being a construction laborer.

For Discussion

This section of the text has presented information on several different jobs in construction. As you can see, each job is different. To some degree, there have been specialized jobs in construction for centuries. For example, in medieval times, there were guilds. These guilds were organizations of workers skilled in a particular craft. What are the advantages of job specialization in construction?

CONSTRUCTION-RELATED PROFESSIONS

Construction-related professions are those construction-related careers that require specialized, formal education beyond high school. Most of the managerial and supervisory positions fall into this category. Other construction-related professions include support personnel such as estimators, surveyors, and technicians.

Construction Managers

For the work on a project to get done, someone needs to plan how to get it done. On large projects, **construction managers** organize all the necessary materials and people. They assign the work to the workers. Managers must control and check on the work that is being done to see that the workers are doing their jobs properly. Managers also determine whether the
1 work is being done according to specifications. Without managers to give orders and to oversee the job, little would be accomplished. Some jobs might have to be done over because they were done improperly or in the wrong order.

Project Managers

The project manager is responsible for the construction project from start to finish. Fig. 16-11. A project manager usually works in the home office. He or she may be responsible for more than one project at a time.

Fig. 16-11. The project manager manages the project. He or she is responsible for checking all aspects of the job.

1. Explain the need for someone who can look at the job as a whole. Most people involved in the construction of a building are involved in some phase or in only a portion of the building. It is the job of the construction manager to combine the money, material, equipment, and personal resources in the proper proportions and at the proper time to satisfactorily complete the project in the time allowed.

The project manager plans, organizes, and controls a construction project. He or she must be able to manage and lead people, make decisions, and keep track of several projects at once. Most project managers have college degrees. Project managers are required by many companies
1 to have engineering skills and on-the-job construction experience.

Construction Superintendent

The manager that is directly in charge of one particular project is called the construction superintendent. He or she works under the direction of a project manager. The construction superintendent has basically the same duties as the project manager, but on a smaller scale. The construction superintendent usually has a field office at the site. Fig. 16-12.

The construction superintendent's job starts before the construction begins. He or she develops schedules and decides when each construction task should be started and finished. Then the superintendent hires the workers and checks on materials and equipment. Once the construction begins, the construction superintendent supervises the workers, keeps the job on schedule, and tries to stay within the budget.

Construction superintendents are usually promoted from a construction-related trade or craft. Many have college degrees in construction technology. Construction superintendents need to be able to make good decisions under pressure because deadlines need to be met constantly. Management and leadership skills are
2 also essential.

Other Construction-related Professions

Construction-related professions cover a wide range of careers in addition to managerial positions. Estimators, surveyors, and technicians are examples of professionals that contribute to a construction project. Office personnel such as secretaries and receptionists also contribute to the overall project.

Fig. 16-12. The construction superintendent is responsible for everything that happens on the site.

1. Ask students to list the skills a project manager needs. Compare these skills with the skills taught in college courses needed to obtain a construction management degree. Does the course list suggest skills that the students had forgotten?

2. Discuss how important it would be for the construction superintendent to communicate in writing. Where does one begin to learn to develop management and leadership skills? Mention school club participation as one way a student can develop these skills.

Estimators

The **estimator** for a project carefully calculates what the job will cost. The contractor depends heavily on the skills of the estimator. The success or failure of a project depends on the estimator's ability. If the estimator's figures are too high, the contractor may not get the job. If the estimator's figures are too low, the contractor cannot make a profit on the project. Without profits, a contractor cannot stay in business. Therefore, a good estimator plays a very important part in the construction industry.

The estimator bases his or her estimate on the cost of materials, labor, equipment, overhead, and the amount of profit that the contractor wants to make. To do this, the estimator must be able to read construction prints and understand specifications. He or she must, of course, have good math skills. Construction experience 1
is also helpful.

Surveyors

Surveyors measure and record the physical features of the construction site. They survey the property and establish its official boundaries. Fig. 16-13. They also lay out, or measure and mark, the construction project. Surveying is an important part of construction and must be done very precisely. If the surveyor makes a mistake, the whole project could be built in the wrong place or to the wrong specifications.

Fig. 16-13. The surveyor determines the precise boundaries of the site.

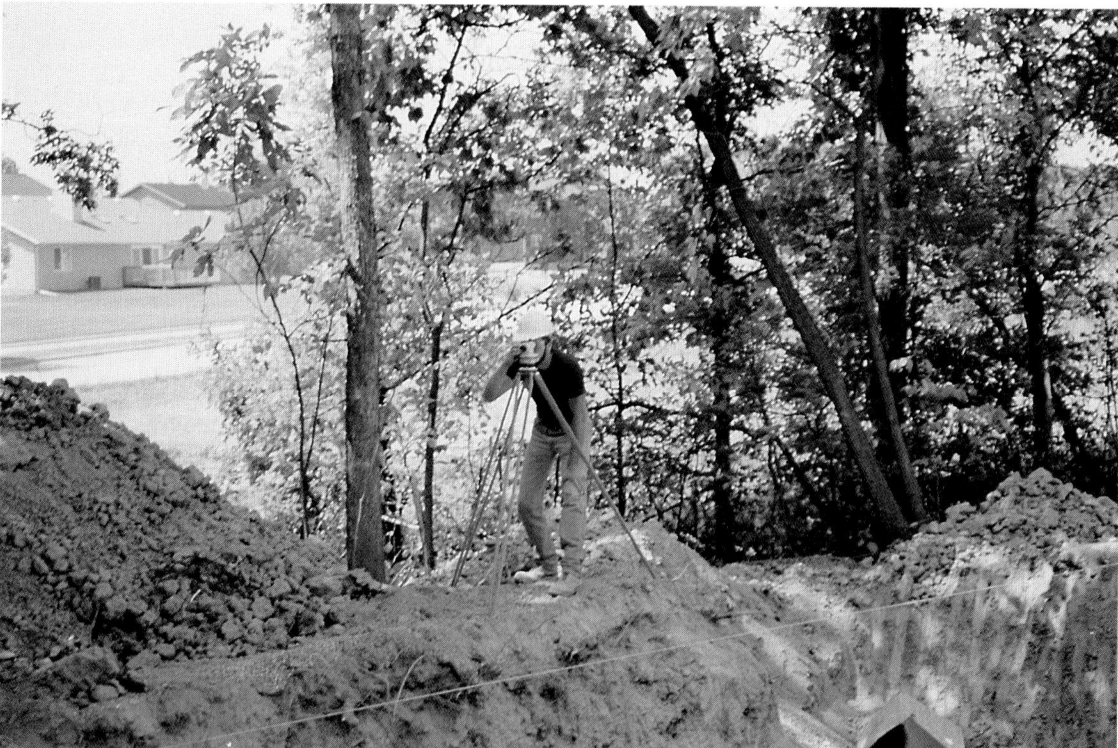

1. Use the discussion of an estimator's job to lead into a discussion of responsibility. Do all construction-related jobs carry the same level of responsibility? Is there a correlation between responsibility and wages? Is there any job without responsibility? Discuss how a worker's attitude toward responsibility can affect such items as continued employment, pay level, and possibility for advancement.

Technicians

Technicians are construction personnel who work neither in the home office nor at the site. They work in laboratories, testing soil samples and concrete and asphalt materials being used on the project. Fig. 16-14. These workers test the sample that is taken from each batch of concrete that is poured. Technicians work for individual testing laboratories. They are usually trained by
1 the laboratory for which they work.

Office Personnel

Office personnel is a general term for all of the clerical and secretarial employees of a company, together with their managers and supervisors. An *office manager* runs the business office of a construction company and oversees the work of the office personnel. He or she is responsible for contracts and other legal requirements for each project. *Secretaries, clerks*, and *receptionists* perform tasks such as typing, filing, and answering the telephone. Fig. 16-15. Office personnel keep detailed records and provide the information needed by the contractor to keep construction operations running 2
smoothly.

Fig. 16-14. Engineers need to know about the soil conditions on a site before they can design a proper foundation. Here a technician performs a soil test using a machine that brings up soil samples.

1. Have a student or group of students study and report on the work of various technicians in the construction industry. How do they help us to be more confident about the safety of our buildings?

2. Ask students to discuss how the computer has changed the job responsibilities of office personnel. Ask them how educational requirements for office workers have changed. Discuss ways that office operation might change in the next ten years.

Fig. 16-15. The office personnel help keep the company running smoothly.

For Discussion

As you have read, any construction project requires people working behind the scenes. These jobs range from the technical to the routine. If the members of this support team are to work together, they must have certain qualities. Discuss the qualities that the members of the support team should have if they are to provide the greatest help to the construction team.

DESIGN AND ENGINEERING PROFESSIONS

Architects and engineers often work together to design and engineer each element of a project. For example, a shopping center building is designed by an architect. An engineer designs the utility system, drainage plan, and structural system for the shopping center. The architect is concerned with making the overall design. The engineer is concerned with the structural features that the design requires.

Architects

Architects create new building designs. They 1
plan details such as the efficient use of space for homes, office buildings, shopping centers, and community projects. Fig. 16-16. Architects

1. Discuss the need for the ability to visualize, to use one's imagination to see what something will look like before a line has been drawn. This ability will be possessed in varying degrees by different people. The architect must have a good ability for this. Ask students to identify workers in other construction-related occupations who would need this ability.

are responsible for the beauty and usefulness of a structure. They must mold the owner's ideas into a workable, problem-free design. As the construction progresses, the contractor may call upon the architect to solve design problems as they arise.

Architects must have a college degree in architecture. Creativity and the ability to make decisions and share ideas are also very important characteristics for an architect. He or she must be able to get along well with people and must be able to express ideas clearly.

Engineers

Engineers are responsible for the structural
1 design of a project. Fig. 16-17. They work with architects to be sure that the architectural design is structurally sound. The engineer's responsibilities include making sure that the structure is safe, that the utility systems are designed properly, and that site drainage is adequate. In other words, the engineer is responsible for all of the details that make a structure sound, safe, and convenient.

Many different kinds of engineers may work together on a large construction project. *Civil engineers* are responsible for correct land elevation and structural layout. *Structural engineers* oversee the placement of structural materials and calculate the load that will be supported by each structural element. *Electrical engineers* oversee the installation of electrical wiring. *Mechanical engineers* assist with the plumbing and piping layouts.

In heavy construction, engineers plan and design bridges, dams, highways, tunnels, and other structures. The amount of stress that each of these structures will receive is a critical factor. For example, a dam must be able to withstand the pressure of the huge wall of water it will hold back. A bridge must withstand the weight of heavy traffic as well as the forces of wind and water. The engineer calculates the stress that each structure must withstand. He or she then designs the structure accordingly.

Fig. 16-16. Architects plan the use of space in a building.

1. Ask each student to suppose that he or she is in charge of the planning of a construction project. Explain that it is up to them to assign various parts of the job to their staff. What parts would they assign to architects? What parts would they assign to engineers? What type of engineer would they assign to each part?

Fig. 16-17. This engineer designed part of this project. Now the engineer is checking the construction.

Did You Know?

The civil engineer is concerned with the building of dams, bridges, and highways. He or she is also involved in the construction of buildings. The first school of civil engineering was founded in Paris in 1747. This school was the National School of Bridges and Highways. Here, students were instructed in the basic principles of engineering. This school was the first suc-
1 cessful attempt to set up a specialized program of instruction for civil engineers.

1. Refer students to Chapter 11 for more information on the various types of engineers, their responsibilities, and their skills.

For Discussion

On any construction project, there must be close cooperation between the architect and the engineer. As mentioned, the job of the architect and the job of the engineer are similar. Each job requires special technical knowledge. Good math skills also are essential. Though the jobs of an engineer and an architect are similar, can you think of any special skills that an architect might need?

YOUR CAREER INTERESTS

If you are interested in a career in the construction industry, perhaps you should find out more about those careers that interest you most. One good way to find out about a career is to look it up in a career handbook such as the
1 *Occupational Outlook Handbook* or the *Dictionary of Occupational Titles*. These career guides can tell you what each career involves and what kind of education or training is needed. They can also tell you what the average pay is and whether the need for workers in that field is growing or declining.

Another way to find out about construction-
2 related careers is to visit a building site. Then you can see for yourself what the different jobs involve. You may be able to talk to some of the workers during their breaks to find out more about construction.

If you decide you are interested in one of the construction trades, you may consider taking a part-time job as a laborer. This will enable you to experience construction work firsthand. Remember, you will not be able to start out at the top with high pay. You will probably have to start at the minimum wage and work your way up. If you find that you would rather do a different kind of work, you can. If you decide to stay in a construction-related career, you will have a head start in gaining the necessary knowledge and experience.

THE ENTREPRENEUR AND CONSTRUCTION TECHNOLOGY

A person who starts a business is usually an **entrepreneur**. This term may be unfamiliar to you. However, you certainly know some entrepreneurs. An entrepreneur is anyone who organizes and manages a business. This person also assumes the risks of the business. This means that the entrepreneur is responsible for paying the business expenses. All responsibility for the success of the business rests with the entrepreneur. A person who is self-employed, or in business for himself or herself, is an entrepreneur.

All entrepreneurs face four similar problems. These problems are:

- Identifying a need.
- Finding a product to satisfy the need.
- Financing the business.
- Selling the product.

Perhaps you will decide that you would like to be in business for yourself. Being in business for yourself is not always easy. If you are to be successful, you must be able to deal with each of the four problems listed above.

The spirit of entrepreneurship has been important in construction. Several massive construction projects were guided by the energy and vision of a single individual. For example, the Eiffel Tower and the Suez Canal were among the most remarkable construction projects of the time. Each of these projects was considered risky. Many said they could not be built. Yet, each of these projects was guided to its successful completion by the energy and vision of a single person. That person was an entrepreneur. An entrepreneur is a person who assumes the risks of a business in the hope of making a profit from it. In the case of the Eiffel Tower, the entrepreneur was Gustave Eiffel. In the case of the Suez Canal, it was Ferdinand de Lesseps.

The late nineteenth century saw a rapid growth in entrepreneurship. That growth has continued into our own time. Entrepreneurs today are responsible for much of the growth in the construction industry. Many construction businesses are owned by entrepreneurs, people who invest their money and effort into their

1. For more information on use of the *Occupational Outlook Handbook* and the *Dictionary of Occupational Titles*, refer students to the portion of Chapter 15 that covers that subject.

2. Caution the class about entering construction sites without permission. Visitors should always ask permission to enter, conduct themselves responsibly, and keep out of the way of the workers.

own business. A successful entrepreneur is also a leader. He or she is able to inspire and lead a construction team. The practice of effective leadership is essential to entrepreneurship. To be an effective leader, the entrepreneur must also understand teamwork.

In our time, the entrepreneur has attracted the attention of investors known as venture capitalists. These are people who provide capital (money) for someone to use in a business. Generally, venture capitalists invest in new technologies. Of course, these new technologies also attract investment from other individuals. In fact, one of the foremost construction projects of our time, the Chunnel, is being financed in part through the sale of shares of stock to individual investors.

Not everyone is suited for self-employment. Some people are more comfortable and happy working for others. In examining career choices,
1 though, you will want to consider all aspects of construction technology.

Understanding Yourself

In any job you take, you should have a good understanding of your own abilities. Not every aspect of a job may be appealing to you. For example, some parts of the job may be more attractive than others. To be effective, though, you should give equal attention to all aspects of your job.

You should also recognize the importance of learning to accept criticism. If the criticism is deserved, you should be willing to put it to good use. You might, for example, use it to improve your job performance.

Human relationships will be important in your career. You will probably be working with other people. Your success on the job will depend heavily on your ability to get along with the other members of your work team. To get along with others, you will need to exercise self-control and cooperation.

DEVELOPING LEADERSHIP

We live in a democratic society. In our society, everyone is urged to develop their skills to the fullest. By doing this, they will be able to participate as more active members of society. In developing your skills, you also can develop some of the qualities of leadership.

All of us have known leaders. You may have noticed that all leaders have certain characteristics. For example, good leaders are good communicators. They are also able to concentrate their attention on a single project. They are determined. They are able to instill confidence in others. Of course, these qualities are more apparent in some people than in others. However, all of us can develop leadership skills. One way of developing such skills is by joining student clubs. Club membership provides an opportunity to practice effective communication. It also offers you practice in teamwork and the other skills needed to work within a group. Throughout your life, you will be given many opportunities for leadership. Now is the time to develop the skills you will need.

1. Ask each student to write a short paper describing what they find most interesting in the construction industry. Ask them also to discuss that part of the construction industry they find the least interesting. Ask them how this class on construction technology has changed their attitudes toward construction. Do they look at a construction project in the same way they did before they took the class?

Construction Facts

CHANG CONSTRUCTION COMPANY

Thoun Chang is a student with a very special dream. He wants to own and operate a construction company. Ever since he was a child, Thoun has been fascinated by the construction of large buildings and by the people who build them. Although he is only in junior high, Thoun knows how he will prepare for his career. Even now, he is beginning his preparations by taking an industrial arts course at his school.

Thoun has talked to his guidance counselor at school, to his parents, and to a neighbor who is a field engineer for a local construction company. From them, he has gained various insights and viewpoints about the construction industry. His neighbor advised him to take business courses in school. He might even want to go to college and major in business. He will need plenty of knowledge and business experience to operate a large company successfully.

At the same time, he will need to know every phase of the construction work. He plans to gain this experience slowly, while still in school. As soon as he can, he will get a part-time job as a laborer in a construction company. He knows he can learn a lot just from being at a construction site. He would like to spend his summers doing various types of construction jobs.

As Thoun prepares for his chosen career, he encourages his friends to "start looking" now to find a career they might enjoy. He thinks that having a purpose makes school more interesting. Thoun knows that he has a long way to go before he accomplishes his
goal. However, he is satisfied that he is doing 1
all he can to prepare himself to be the owner of Chang Construction Company.

1. Ask each student to select a career in the construction industry in which they are particularly interested. Ask each student to write a plan of activity for the future. Ask them to tell how each element of their plan could help them to reach their goal of entering a specific career.

CHAPTER 16

REVIEW

Chapter Summary

Construction projects employ people in a variety of trades and occupations. Workers in the building trades and crafts are responsible for doing the on-site work needed to complete the project. These workers include carpenters, bricklayers, electricians, plumbers, pipefitters, ironworkers, operating engineers, and laborers. Workers in construction-related professions often work as managers or supervisors. Other workers are support personnel, such as estimators, surveyors, and technicians. Planning on a construction project is done by construction managers.

The project manager is responsible for the construction project from start to finish. The manager directly in charge of one particular project is called a construction superintendent. Construction-related professions include estimators, surveyors, technicians, and office personnel. Architects create new building designs. Engineers are responsible for the structural design of a project. If you are interested in a career in construction, you should find out more about that career by checking the *Occupational Outlook Handbook* or the *Dictionary of Occupational Titles*. These books will be at your library.

Test Your Knowledge 1

1. What are the three main categories of construction careers?
2. In what two ways do most tradespeople get their training?
3. Name at least four careers that are considered construction trades.
4. What is the name given to workers who assist tradespeople?
5. What is a construction-related profession?
6. Name two differences between a project manager and a construction superintendent.
7. What professional is responsible for the usefulness of the space in a building?
8. What professional is responsible for structural soundness?
9. Name four different types of engineers that might be involved in a large construction project.
10. Name at least two ways to find out more about a construction-related career.

1. The answers to the Test Your Knowledge questions are in the Teacher's Manual at the front of this Teacher's Annotated Edition.

REVIEW

Activities

1. Look up a construction-related career of your choice in the *Occupational Outlook Handbook*. Give the class a brief summary of the information you find.
2. Visit a building site near your home. Make a list of all the different types of careers that are represented at the site.
3. At times, there is more construction than at other times. The rise and fall of residential construction follows the economy very closely. On the other hand, because of the amount of lead time needed for large construction projects, commercial and heavy construction may be quite plentiful during economic downturns. This factor also helps minimize employment in the construction industry. Prepare a short written report on the present level of construction activity in your community.
4. You may not be happy in the job you choose. If this is the case, you may want to find a new job. Generally, it is important that you obtain a new job before leaving your old job. This will help you avoid anxiety. You will want to leave your job in good standing. You will want to work hard and attentively through your last work day. It will also be important for you to obtain a good recommendation from your employer. Assume that you are unhappy in your present job. Research procedures for leaving a job. Then prepare a short written report outlining your plan for getting another job in the same field. Your report should include information on ways of identifying possible new employers, securing an interview, and presenting your job qualifications. You also should include information on giving your employer notice that you intend to leave the job. You should arrange for his or her recommendation.
5. Find out how many construction permits were issued in your community last year. Find out also how many construction permits were issued the year before that. Figure out the percentage of increase or decrease in construction activity in your community. 

ACTIVITIES

Activity 1: Measuring Height Using an Inclinometer

Objective

An inclinometer is an instrument used to measure height. After completing this activity, you will know how to use an inclinometer to measure the height of a tree, building, power pole, and other objects.

Materials Needed

- 10 sheets of grid paper (10 squares per inch)
- 1 small bench level
- 1-6″ protractor
- 1 squared block of wood 1½″ × 7″ × 5″
- 1 nut for a ¼″ carriage bolt
- 1¼″ carriage bolt, wing nut, and washer
- 3-50″ sections of ¾″ metal conduit
- 1-10″ circle of ⅝″ or ¾″ plywood
- 3-3½″ × ¼″ carriage bolts with washers and wing nuts
- 3- ½″ metal screws
- 1-60″ length of lightweight chain

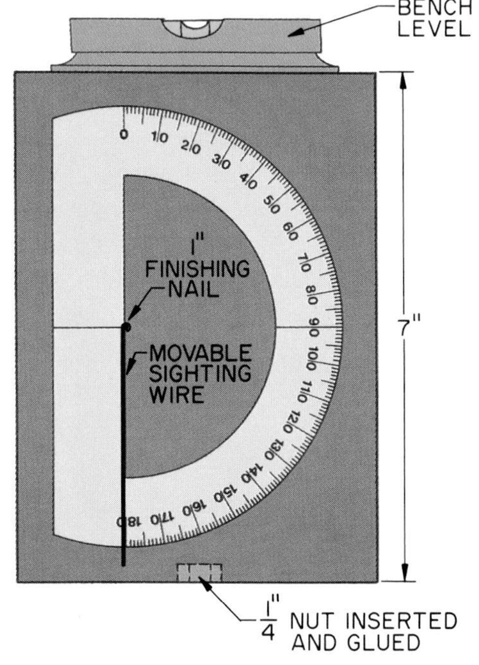

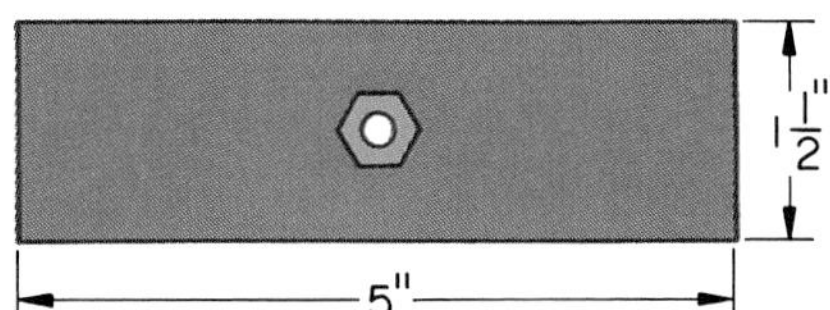

Fig. A. Constructing the inclinometer.

Steps of Procedure

1. Figure A illustrates the general construction of the inclinometer. The bench level will be used to level the inclinometer from front to back and side to side. It is important to position the protractor on the side of the board so that the 90° line is exactly parallel with the bench level. The accuracy of your inclinometer begins with this placement. A hot-glue gun can be used to attach the protractor to the board.
2. Use a small, sharp knife to carefully cut a hexagon-shaped hole in the bottom of the board. This hole should be ¼″ deep. Place a small amount of hot glue on the flat sides of the nut and insert it into the hole. Be careful not to get glue inside the nut, where the threads are located. This nut will be used to attach the inclinometer to a photographic tripod or a stand you can construct.
3. The final step in constructing the inclinometer is to add a sighting pointer. This is accomplished by first placing a small, 1″ finishing

nail at the intersection of the 0°, 90°, and 180° points of the attached protractor. Allow about ½″ of the nail to extend from the board.

4. Select a small, straight wire 5″ in length. Use a pair of small needlenose pliers to form a loop at one end. Place this loop around the nail. Tighten it so it swings freely but does not fall off. Use a wire cutter to shorten the wire so it extends about ¼″ past the protractor's outer edge. Be careful not to bend this wire. It is your pointer to obtain accurate degree readings on the protractor.
5. If you do not have a photographic tripod, you will need to construct a tripod stand. This stand will have several uses in other activities you may develop. Figures B and C show the general construction of this stand.
6. Flatten three 50″ pieces of ¾″ metal conduit on one end. Drill as shown with a ¼″ metal drill. The square ends can be rounded on a grinder. Fig. C.
7. Prepare the wooden attachment board from a round piece of ⅝″ to ¾″ plywood 10″ in diameter. Cut the wings and notches in the plywood disc using a coping saw.
8. Drill each projection for a 3½″ × ¼″ carriage bolt, washer, and wing nut. It is recommended that you attach a stabilizing chain about halfway down the conduit to join all three legs. Fig. C. A ½″ metal screw can be used for this purpose. Drill a ¼″ hole in the center of the attachment board for attaching the inclinometer.

Fig. B. Constructing the wooden attachment board.

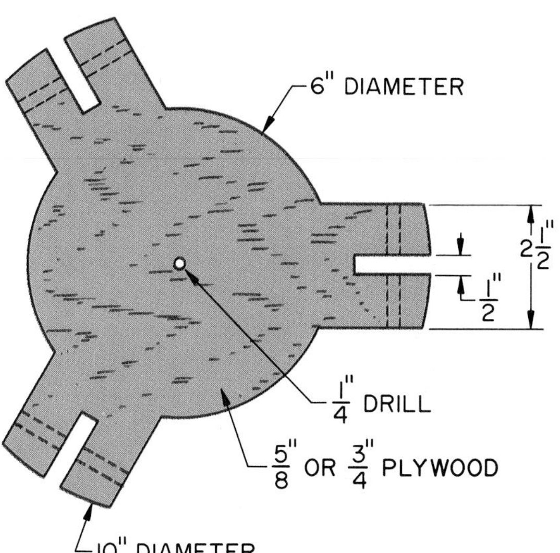

Fig. C. Constructing the tripod.

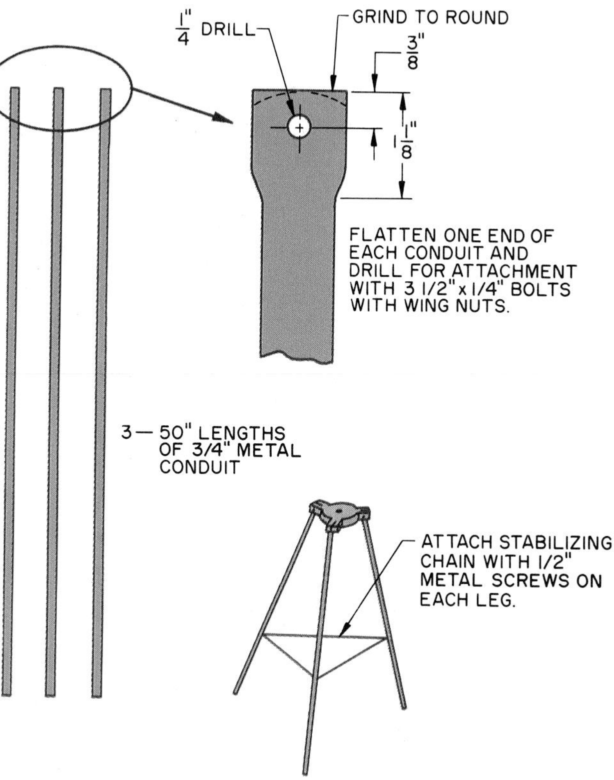

9. Mount the inclinometer on a tripod stand. Select a tree and move far enough away so you can easily see both the base and top of the tree. Position the inclinometer with the 90° edge of the protractor pointing at the tree. Carefully adjust the legs to bring the inclinometer into level from front to back and from side to side.
10. Next, use a tape measure to determine the exact distance from the base of the tree to the inclinometer. For final graphing of the data it is best if the selected distance is 25′, 50′, 75′, or 100′. Also measure the distance from the ground to the 90° line on the protractor. This may be useful depending on how your teacher wants you to analyze your data. Fig. D.
11. You are now ready to make your first measurement. This is best done with a partner. Use your finger or a pencil point to carefully raise the sighting wire until it is pointing at the base of the tree. Sight along the wire. Have your partner record the degree reading. If you are on level ground, the degree reading will be slightly more than 90°. If you are uphill from the tree, it will be considerably more than 90°. If you are downhill from the tree it will be less than 90°.
12. Make your final reading by raising the sighting wire to point at the top of the tree. Fig. D. Again, have your partner record the degree of angle. Repeat each measurement two or three times to confirm your readings.

Fig. D. Measuring the height of a tree.

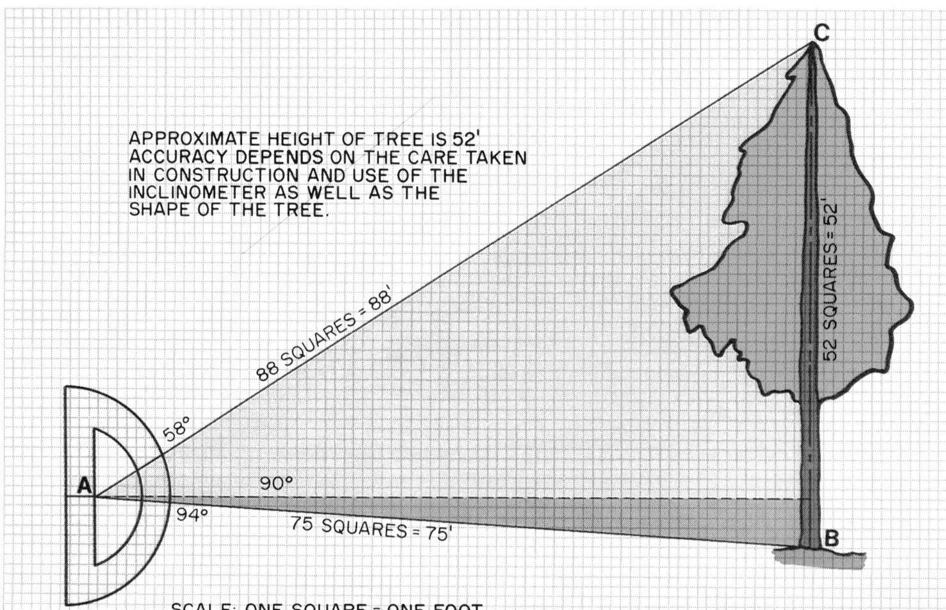

13. The data you have collected can now be graphed to show the height of the tree. The data collected for Tree "A" follows:

DATA FOR TREE "A"

DISTANCE FROM TREE BASE	75′
DEGREE READING OF TREE BASE	94°
DEGREE READING OF TREE TOP	58°

Locate a point on the grid paper near the left-hand side as shown in Figure D. This will be Point A. Place the protractor on the point as indicated and mark the 58° and 94° positions. Use a straightedge and pencil to join and extend lines through Points A and B and Points A and C.

14. Place a piece of grid paper along line AB. Count over 75 squares from Point A. Since there are 10 squares in each inch this is a distance of 7½″. Each square represents one foot. Now use a straightedge and pencil to extend a line from Point B to intersect with line AC. This intersect point becomes Point C.

15. Now count the number of squares between Point B and C. Depending on the accuracy of your construction, the count should be near 52 squares. Thus, the tree is approximately 52′ in height.

16. Refer to Fig. E. Tree "B" was measured in a similar manner. Note that the 90° line points to a position about 18.5 squares or 18.5′ up the tree. It is assumed this measurement was taken while standing uphill from the tree. Also note how a strip of grid paper is placed along lines AB and AC to determine the distance.

Fig. E. Graphing the results.

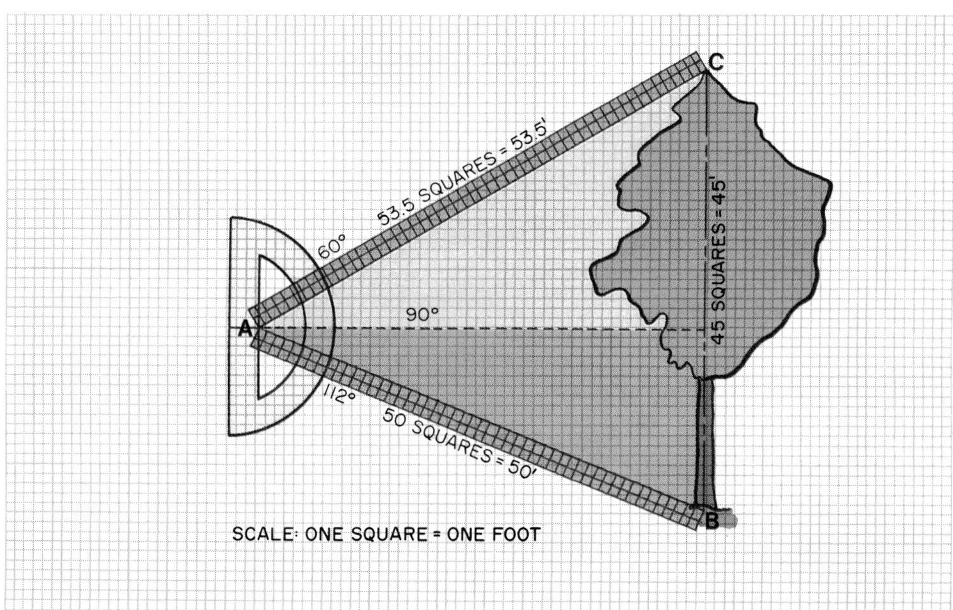

Activity 2: Conducting a Soil Compaction Test

Objective

After completing this activity, you will know how to construct and use a simple device to measure soil compaction. This is an important test prior to beginning a construction project.

Materials Needed

- 2 blocks of wood 1½″ × 4″ × 9″
- 1-1″ × 4″ × 10′ length of lumber
- 3 weights, 5 lbs each
- 1-8″ × 12″ piece of ½″ plywood
- 1-12″ ruler
- 1 watch with a second hand

Steps of Procedure

1. Each student will construct a simple, four-sided box frame from 1″ × 4″ × 10′ lumber. Construct the frame shown in Fig. A. This frame should have an inside dimension exactly 4″ wide × 9″ long × 4″ deep. The surface area of the frame is 36 square inches. The box has a cubic volume of 144 cubic inches.
2. The 1½″ × 4″ × 9″ solid blocks of wood may be cut from a piece of 2″ × 6″ stock lumber. These blocks of wood should fit loosely inside the frame constructed above. Be certain they do not bind when slid down in the frame. These blocks will serve as pistons when the soil sample is compacted.
3. Weigh the blocks and record their weight.
4. Each student or team of students should bring soil samples to test. The size of the sample should be large enough to fill the wood frame level full. A wide variety of samples will prompt comparison and discussion of the characteristics of the different samples.

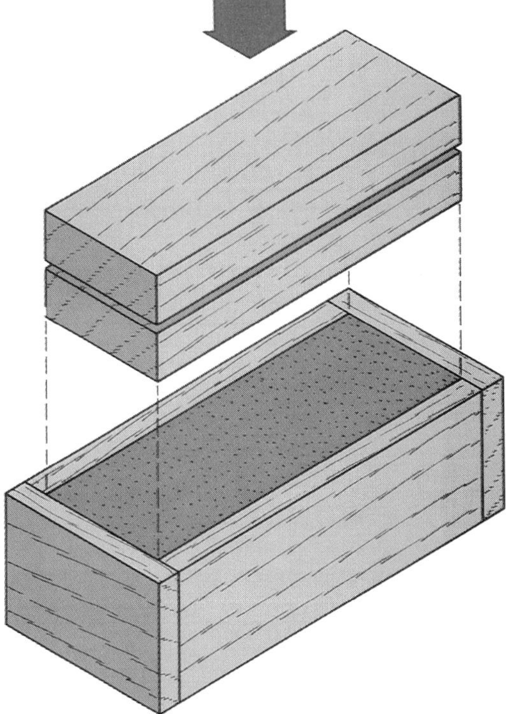

Fig. A. The construction of the box frame.

5. Place the wooden frame on the 8″ × 12″ piece of ½″ plywood. Pour the soil sample into the frame. Using a metal straightedge, scrape away the excess soil to make it exactly level with the top of the frame. Be careful not to compact the soil while doing this.
6. Now place the two 1½″ × 4″ × 9″ blocks of wood on top of the soil sample so one block is exactly on top of the other. Immediately measure and record the exact height

the blocks extend above the upper edge of the wooden frame. Place a 5-lb weight on top of the wood blocks.

7. At one-minute intervals, measure and record the height the two blocks extend above the wood frame. Continue this measurement until the wooden piston stops moving or until you have made at least 15 measurements. Fig. B.
8. The amount of load present on each square inch of the soil's surface is easily calculated. The block has a surface area of 36 square inches. Divide 5 lbs by 36. The result is the pressure on each square inch of surface. You will discover this is 0.1388 lbs per square inch. Divide the combined weight of the two blocks of wood by 36 and add the resulting answer to 0.1388 lbs to obtain the total weight on each square inch. Assume the blocks have a combined weight of 1.2 lbs. This would add 0.0333 lbs per square inch, giving a total of 0.1721 lbs per square inch.
9. Use the data you have collected to create a simple line graph showing the rate (speed) and amount (distance) of compaction for the soil sample. Fig. C.

Application

The degree of soil compactibility is very important when constructing a shed, house, building, or other large structures. It may be necessary to check the compactibility characteristics to a depth of several feet. Soil compactibility differences help to explain much of the damage or lack of damage in the various areas of San Francisco during the 1989 earthquake.

Fig. B. Recording the settlement values.

INCHES	MINUTES
3.75	1
2.25	2
1.25	3
0.75	4
0.65	5
0.50	6
0.50	7
0.50	8
0.50	9
0.50	10

Fig. C. Plotting the settlement values.

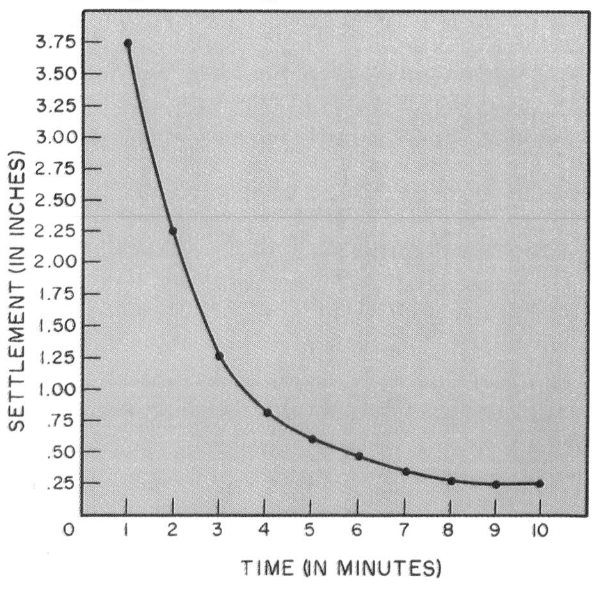

Activity 3: Measuring Distance with a Plane Table

Objective

After completing this activity, you will know how to use a simple plane table to create maps similar to those developed by early mapmakers. You also will have developed practice in the use of the metric system of measurement.

Materials Needed

- paper
- 2-6″ protractors, each 152 mm wide
- 1 small bench level
- 1 squared block of wood 38 mm × 178 mm × 127 mm
- 1 nut for 1/4″ carriage bolt
- 2 sewing needles at least 35 mm long
- 1 piece of wood 5 mm × 8 mm × 83 mm
- metric scale 300 mm in length
- metric stick or metric tape measure

Steps of Procedure

1. This activity is a metric activity. It will help you gain practice in the use of the metric system of measurement. Though the United States has used the customary system of measurement, most other countries use the metric system of measurement (also called the International System of Units).

   In the customary system, measurements of length are made in feet, inches, or parts of an inch. In the metric system, measurements of length are made in kilometers, meters, and centimeters. The way in which these units relate to one another is given in Table A. Table B lists some metric equivalents of customary units.
2. Your teacher may provide materials not listed above to complete this construction.
3. The construction of the plane table is similar to the construction of the inclinometer described in Activity 1, Section V. It will be necessary to use a tripod to support the plane table. If you do not have access to a camera tripod, you can construct a tripod identical to the one described in Activity 1, Section V.
4. Figure A illustrates the general construction of the plane table. Attach a 152-mm plastic or metal protractor on one side of the 127-mm × 178-mm wooden block. A hot glue gun can be used to make this attachment. Place the straight side of the protractor exactly parallel to the long edge of the wooden block.
5. Place the 1/4″ nut in the center of the lower surface of the 127-mm × 178-mm block. Use a small, sharp knife to cut a hexagonal hole 6 mm deep in the bottom of the board.

Table A. Metric Units of Linear Measure

Property	Unit name	Symbol	Relationship of units
LINEAR MEASURE	millimeter	mm	1 mm = 0.001 m
	centimeter	cm	1 cm = 10 mm
	decimeter	dm	1 dm = 10 cm or 100 mm
	meter	m	1 m = 100 cm or 1000 mm
	kilometer	km	1 km = 1000 m

Table B. Metric Equivalents of Some Customary Measures of Length

Customary Measure	Metric Equivalent
1 inch	2.54 mm
1 foot	0.304 m
1 yard	0.914 m
1 mile	1.60 km

Then place a small amount of hot glue on the flat sides of the nut and insert it into the hole. Be careful not to get glue on the inside area where the threads are located. This nut will be used to attach the plane table to the tripod.

6. Construct the pointer as shown in Fig. A. After shaping the pointer, make a hole 5 mm from the square end of the pointer exactly in the middle of its 8 mm width.

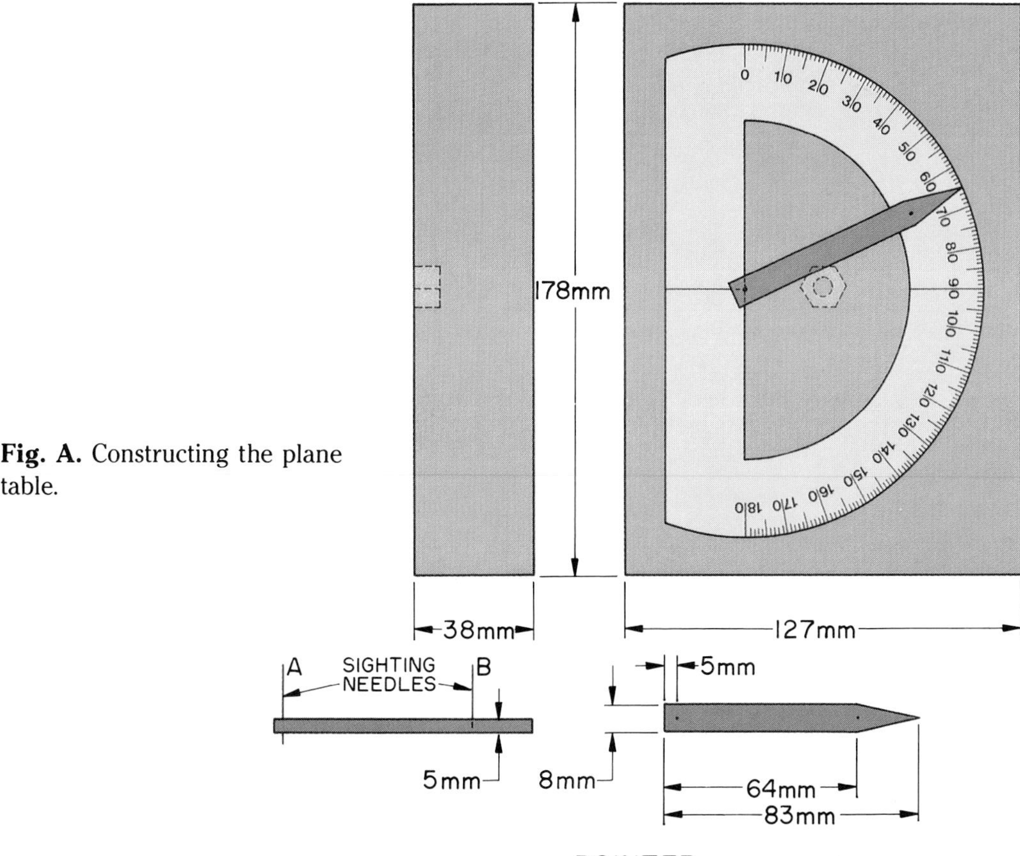

Fig. A. Constructing the plane table.

7. Place the second needle 64 mm from the first needle's location and exactly in the middle of the 8-mm width about two-thirds of the way through the pointer. When sighting along the pointer, the two needles should align with each other and the pointed end of the wooden sighting bar. The needles should be exactly straight up-and-down.
8. You are now ready to collect mapping data. To complete this activity, it is best to work in teams of two. Select an area along a straight section of sidewalk or fence. Use a metric stick or metric tape measure to locate two points exactly 15 m apart. Mark these two points with a piece of chalk or short wooden sticks. As you face the area you are to measure, let the point you marked on the left represent Point A and the other Point B.
9. Place the tripod over Point A so the middle of the protractor is exactly over that point. The long edge of the plane table should be parallel to the area you are to measure. To test this, move your pointer to the 180° mark. The pointer should be pointing exactly at Point B. If it is not, keep turning the table until it does.
10. Use the bench level to level the plane table from left to right and front to back.
11. Once you have positioned the plane table, you are ready to begin collecting data. It is possible to take several sightings of various objects before moving to Point B, providing you can also see the same objects from Point B. You may want to check this before beginning the readings. Also, it is best to sight on objects that are no more than 15 m to 25 m from your table.
12. Now select the first object to sight from Point A. Record a brief description of the object and assign it No. 1. Sight along the wooden pointer. Move the pointer until sighting needle "B" is in perfect line with the stationary sighting needle "A." Record the degree reading at the end of the wooden pointer on your chart under "Readings for Point A."
13. Repeat this process for other objects you would like to sight from Point A. Number these objects No. 2, No. 3, etc.
14. Move your plane table to Point B. Once again, level and align it for sightings to the objects you viewed from Point A. This time, check your alignment with Point A by placing the wooden pointer on 0° and turning the table until the wood pointer is pointing exactly at Point A. Now move the pointer to point at each object viewed from Point A. Record the readings on your chart. Once you have completed this series of readings, you are ready to place your data on the paper. **NOTE:** Do not use your plane table to measure Point A and your partner's table to measure Point B. Being hand constructed, they will have minor differences and produce greater error in the data. Use the same instrument at both points.
15. Use a straightedge to draw a line 100 mm long across the bottom edge of your paper. The left end of the line will represent Point A. The right end, a distance of 15 m away, will represent Point B. Now use the protractor at Point A to project the first degree reading as shown in Fig. B. Use a straightedge to extend a line from Point A through the mark. Now repeat this process at Point B with the reading to the same object. Use

the straightedge to extend the line until the two lines intersect at Point C.

16. Use the metric scale to measure the distance to the object. One centimeter will represent a distance of one meter. Each millimeter will represent one decimeter. Use the 300-mm scale to measure the distance along line AC and BC. Write both the degree readings and the number of meters, decimeters, and centimeters from one point to the other. See Fig. B.
17. Are you ready to test the accuracy of your instrument? If so, go back to Point A with your partner and the meter stick or metric tape measure. Measure the exact number of meters and parts of a meter from Point A to the object you have just recorded on your paper. Then go to Point B and also measure the distance. These measurements should not vary more than a few centimeters from what you plotted on the paper. **NOTE:** This will be true only if the land is flat and you have carefully constructed and used your plane table. You are sighting in a straight line. In hilly country you may have to walk down 100 meters and up 100 meters to get an object only 35 meters from your plane table.

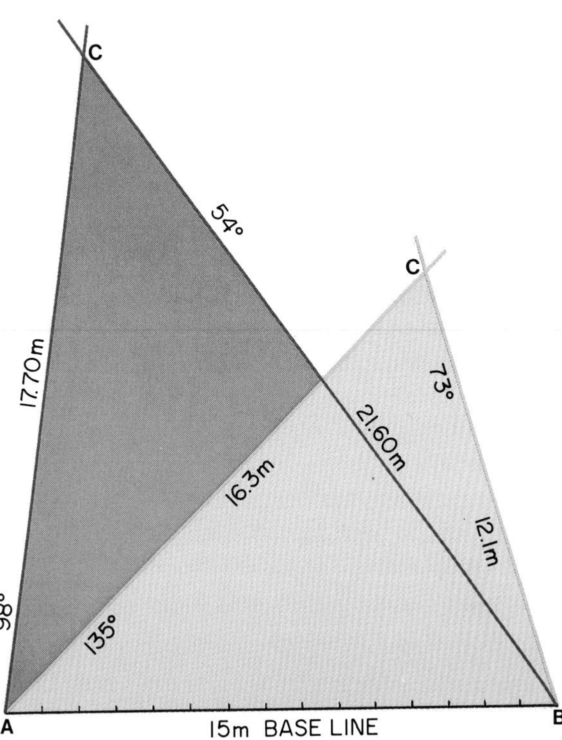

Fig. B. Graphing the data.

GLOSSARY

A list of words in construction technology, with their meanings

ability. Something you have already learned how to do—a skill you have mastered.

accident. An unexpected happening that results in injury, loss, or damage.

adhesives. Materials that hold, or bond, other materials together.

admixtures. Anything added to a batch of concrete other than cement, water, and aggregate.

aggregate. The sand and rocks used in concrete.

alterations. Changes in the structural form of a building or other structure. These changes are usually made to make the structure more attractive or useful.

apprentice. One who learns from a skilled worker while on the job. The apprentice also receives classroom instruction.

aptitude. A natural talent for learning a skill.

arch bridge. This type of bridge uses an arch to carry the weight of the bridge. Arch bridges are made of concrete or steel and are usually constructed over deep ravines.

architects. People who create new building designs. They plan details such as the efficient use of space for homes, office buildings, shopping centers, and community projects.

architectural drawings. Drawings that show the layout of a building. Some of the most common kinds of architectural drawings are floor plans, site plans, elevations, section drawings, and detail drawings.

arc welding machines. A machine used to weld materials such as steel beams at construction sites. An arc welding machine, or arc welder, uses an electric arc to melt portions of the metal beams and thus weld them together. A gasoline engine powers the machine. The engine turns an electrical generator, which provides the electric arc.

armored cable. Cable made of several wires inside a flexible metal casing. It is used in dry environments where sturdy, yet flexible, wiring is needed.

asphalt. A petroleum product made from crude oil.

bachelor's degree. This is a degree awarded for completion of work at a four-year college.

backhoe. A type of excavator that is used for general digging. It is usually mounted on either a crawler or a truck frame. A dipper bucket is attached to a boom that is operated by hydraulic cylinders. The bucket is designed to dig toward the machine.

backsaw. A handsaw with a very thin blade reinforced with a heavy metal back. This keeps the thin saw blade from bending. The backsaw is used to make very straight cuts, such as those on trim and molding.

bar chart. A chart that is easy to read and interpret. For example, months may be listed across the top of the chart. All the major jobs are listed down the side of the chart. A bar is then used to show the starting and completion dates for each job.

batter boards. Boards held horizontally by stakes driven into the ground to mark the boundaries of a building. String is used to connect a batter board with another at the opposite end of a wall. The batter boards are placed outside the building's boundaries so that the attached strings cross over the corners of the building.

bearing-wall structure. In this type of structure, heavy walls support the weight of the building. This type of structure has no frame.

bids. A company quotes a price for which it will do a particular job. Construction companies obtain most of their work through the competitive bidding process.

blind riveter. A tool used by sheet metal workers to fasten pieces of sheet metal together. With a blind riveter the worker can do the entire riveting operation from one side of the sheet metal.

board lumber. Lumber that measures less than 1½ inches thick and 4 or more inches wide.

bond. A bond provides protection for the owner in the event the contractor does not follow the terms of the contract. To get a bond, a construction company must have a good reputation and financial dependability. The contractor pays a fee to the bonding company. In return for the fee, the bonding company issues the bond.

boom. The long arm of the crane that directs the cable.

bricklayer. A tradesperson who works with masonry. Bricklayers use bricks or concrete blocks and mortar to build walls, fireplaces, floors, partitions, and other structural elements.

brick trowel. Masons use brick trowels to place and trim mortar between bricks or concrete blocks. Brick trowels are usually made of steel and have handles of wood or sturdy, high-impact plastic.

building trades and crafts. The skills practiced by people who are responsible for doing the on-site work needed to complete the project.

built environment. Structures such as buildings, bridges, and highways as well as other parts of the environment that people have shaped or altered.

bulldozer. A tractor equipped with a front-mounted pushing blade. The bulldozer is one of the most basic and versatile pieces of construction equipment. One of its primary parts is the blade, which is attached to the frame of the machine. It is designed for clearing land of bushes and trees.

bull float. A tool used by cement finishers to smooth the surface of wet concrete. The face of the float, the part that touches the cement, is made of softwood.

cantilever bridge. This type of bridge is used for fairly long spans. It has two beams, or cantilevers, that extend from the ends of the bridge. They are joined in the middle by a connecting section called a suspended span. The whole structure usually receives additional support from steel trusses.

career. A sequence of related jobs that a person holds throughout his or her working life.

carpenters. Tradespeople who work with wood and wood products.

certificate of occupancy. A certificate issued by the building inspection department which approves a building for use. This certificate shows that the building has passed the building inspector's check of the structure.

chalk line. A chalk line, or chalk box, is used to mark a straight line. A chalk line consists of a line (string) that is contained in a housing filled with chalk. The chalk coats the line as the line is drawn out of the housing.

claim. A legal demand for money.

claw hammer. A common type of hammer. The face, or pounding surface, of the claw hammer is used to drive nails. Opposite the face is a V-shaped notch called a claw. The claw is used to remove nails from boards.

cofferdam. A watertight wall, built to keep water out of the worker's way. This temporary wall can be made of timber, concrete, soil, or sheets of steel.

cold chisel. Cold chisels are made of solid steel. They can be used to cut sheet metal, round objects such as chain links, bars, bolts, and various other types and shapes of metal. A cold chisel is driven by hammer blows to its flat end.

commerce. The buying and selling of goods that require transportation from one place to another.

commercial buildings. Structures designed to accommodate businesses. Commercial buildings include buildings such as stores, office complexes, and many types of community service buildings.

community college. A local, two-year school that is usually supported in part by the state and/or local government.

compactor. A compactor, or roller, is used to compact the soil of a roadway just before the road is paved. Types of compactors include steel drum rollers, tamping-foot rollers, grid or mesh rollers, and rubber-tired rollers.

com-ply. Com-ply, or composit-ply, is made of several plies of veneer strips laminated to a core of particle board.

compressive strength. A term which means something, such as a concrete driveway, can carry a lot of weight per square inch (psi).

computer-aided design (CAD). The use of computers for designing and engineering construction projects speeds up the work. CAD also provides great accuracy in design calculations.

concrete. A mixture of sand, rocks, and a binder. Concrete is one of the most common construction materials.

concrete pump. Moves concrete from the concrete mixer to the concrete form efficiently. The pump is usually mounted on a truck. It has a boom, or long arm, that can be pointed in any direction. The boom holds and directs a hose through which the concrete is pumped.

conduit. A pipe through which individual wires can be pulled. It is used in concrete walls and floors to allow easy access to the wires for maintenance and repair.

construction. The building of structures, to provide us with shelter and with places to work. Construction is also the process by which we build roads, highways, bridges, and tunnels to use in transporting people and products from place to place.

construction laser. A versatile instrument that can be used as a level or as an alignment tool. It flashes a narrow, accurate beam of light that workers can use as a baseline for additional measurements.

construction managers. People who organize all the necessary materials and people and assign the work to the workers. Managers must control and check on the work that is being done to see that it is done properly and according to specifications.

construction process. Everything that happens from the decision to build a structure to the owner's acceptance of the completed structure.

Construction Specification Institute (CSI). CSI guidelines are presented in outline form. Every type of construction job is classified in one of 16 categories. The categories follow the actual order of construction as far as possible. They also keep all the information about a subject in one place. Most specifications for large construction projects follow the format presented by the CSI.

construction superintendent. The person who controls all activity at the construction site. He or she must be aware of any problems and make corrections when they are needed. At the same time, he or she must keep a close watch on the materials that are bought and how much they cost. The cost of materials is checked through an accounting system.

construction technology. The use of tools, materials, and processes to build structures such as buildings, highways, and dams. Construction technology also relates to the knowledge we have gained about how to build structures to meet our needs.

consultant. An expert in a specific area who may be called upon to give advice on a certain part of the design of the construction project. The consultant works as a subcontractor for part of the designing and engineering work.

contact cement. An adhesive that is applied to the surfaces of materials and then allowed to dry before the materials are combined. When the materials are finally combined, the contact cement instantly forms a permanent bond.

contract. A written agreement between two or more parties. The responsibilities and rights of each party are stated in the contract. The contract contains information about the amount of work to be done, the price to be paid, and the method of payment. All parties sign the contracts. The contract is a legal document.

conveyor. Used in construction to speed the movement of materials. Roofers, for example, use conveyors to carry heavy bundles of shingles and other materials from the ground to the roof of a building.

cost-plus contract. In this type of contract, the owner agrees to pay all the costs of construction, including materials and labor. In addition, the owner agrees to pay the contractor an extra amount to cover the contractor's overhead and profit. There are two types of cost-plus contracts. One is cost plus a fixed fee. The other is cost plus a percentage of the cost.

cranes. Machines that lift large and heavy loads. They can also move loads horizontally by carrying them along a radius. Cranes are classified according to the weight they can lift safely.

crawler crane. A crane mounted on metal treads so that it can move over rough terrain at a construction site.

critical path method (CPM) chart. A chart, or diagram, made of circles and lines. Each line and circle has a meaning. This kind of schedule is useful because it shows the critical parts of the job clearly.

crosscut saw. A saw used to cut across the grain of the wood. Its teeth are shaped and sharpened in such a way that it actually cuts two lines very close together and removes the sawdust between them.

dam. A structure that is built across a river to block the flow of water. This is usually done for one of two reasons: to create a water reservoir for nearby communities or to collect water to power the water turbines in a hydroelectric power station.

dead load. The combined weight of all the materials in a structure. A dead load is constant; it is always there.

designing. The process of deciding what a structure will look like and how it will function.

detail drawing. A drawing that shows a particular part of the structure. It shows how things fit together. Detail drawings normally are drawn to a larger scale than other drawings.

Dictionary of Occupational Titles (DOT). A U.S. Government publication that describes over 20,000 jobs relating to many different careers.

digital rules. Measurement tools used to measure relatively long distances, such as those in highway construction projects.

dimension lumber. Lumber that measures between 2 and 5 inches thick.

drawings. Drawings show the plans for a structure in graphic form. Each of the different types of drawings shows special information that is needed for the project. Symbols are used on the drawings to represent the methods of construction and materials to be used.

ecology. The study of the way plants and animals exist together. It also studies the relationship of plants and animals to their environment.

electrical plans. These plans show the location of all the light fixtures, switches, and other electrical devices.

electricians. Workers who assemble, install, and maintain electrical wiring and fixtures.

elevations. Drawings that show the outside of the structure. An elevation drawing is made for each side of the structure.

engineering. The process of figuring out how the structure will be built and what structural materials will be used.

engineers. People who are responsible for the structural design of a project.

environment. Our surroundings, most often thought of as trees, lakes, and mountains. However, structures such as buildings, bridges, and highways are part of the environment, too.

environmental impact study. A study meant to bring to light the effect of a construction project on the environment.

equipment. A term that refers to large, complex tools and machines. Each type of equipment is designed to do a certain job. Most of the equipment that is used in construction falls into one of the following categories: surveying equipment, pumps, conveyors, and welding machines.

estimator. The person who calculates what the job will cost.

excavating. Excavating, or digging, to condition the earth for construction. This step can begin as soon as the site has been laid out.

excavator. A machine that is used for digging. It scoops up earth from one place and deposits it in another. Excavators are among the most common types of construction equipment because almost every construction job requires some excavation.

feasibility study. Research done to gather information about a proposed project. A feasibility study helps the decision-makers decide if it is feasible, or practical, to build the project. It includes information on the cost of the project and financing options as well as the availability of land and essential materials.

fiberboard. Building material made from vegetable fibers, such as corn or sugarcane stalks. It is not very strong, but it has good insulating properties. Therefore, it is used as insulation sheathing beneath the exterior siding of buildings.

final inspection. An inspection made after a construction project has been completed. The building is inspected to make sure that the job was done properly and according to the terms of the contract.

final payment. This is the last step in transferring ownership. The owner pays the construction company all the money due according to the contract.

financing. The term used to describe the process of obtaining the money used to pay for a project.

finishing stage. After the walls have been covered, the installation of the utilities is finished. This finishing stage readies the utilities for use by people.

first aid. The immediate care given to a person who has been injured.

floating. The process of moving coarse aggregate down into the concrete, leaving only fine aggregate and sand on top. This is accomplished by moving a wooden or magnesium float back and forth over the surface.

flooring. Floor covering used in buildings.

floor plan. This type of plan shows the layout of all the rooms on one floor of a building. It also shows the locations of all the walls and other built-in items. A separate floor plan is made for each floor in a building.

folding rules. Common measurement tools used to measure boards, pipe, wire, and other construction materials.

footing. The part of the structure that distributes the structure's weight. It is usually made of reinforced concrete.

forms. The molds that contain the concrete until it hardens. They are made in the shape that the finished concrete should have.

foundation. The part of the structure that is beneath the first floor. It includes the footing and the foundation walls.

foundation wall. The wall that is built directly on the footing. It transmits the weight of the superstructure to the footing.

frame structure. A frame which supports the weight of the building. A frame structure is made up of many connected frame members that are covered by sheathing. The frame members carry the weight of the structure and its contents. The framing can be made of wood, steel, or reinforced concrete.

framing square. A tool made of a single piece of steel and marked with standard or metric units. It is used to measure 90-degree angles at the corners of framework and joints. It can also be used to measure cutting angles on dimension lumber.

front-end loaders. Machines with large scoops used for shoveling. These machines are used to scoop up and deposit dirt or other materials. Loaders are often used to load trucks. Because a loader is mounted on a truck frame or a crawler, it can move small amounts of earth over short distances. Loaders have many other uses as well.

general contractor. The general contractor is the contractor in charge of the construction work.

general education. The basic courses, such as reading, writing, mathematics, science, and history, that are required in school. General education is the foundation for further learning.

geotextiles. Also called engineering fabrics. Geotextile material is like a large piece of plastic cloth. This fabric can be spread on the ground as an underlayment, or bottom layer, for roadbeds or slopes along a highway. It is used to keep soil in place and to prevent erosion.

grader. An earthworking machine that is used to grade, or level, the ground. It is used to prepare roadways and parking lots for paving.

hacksaw. A saw that is used to cut metal. Various types of hacksaw blades enable this saw to cut many different kinds of metal.

hand tools. Tools that use power supplied by a person.

hardboard. Hardboard is made up of very small, threadlike fibers of wood that are pressed together. Because the fibers are so small, when they are pressed together they form a very smooth and hard material. The fibers are held together by lignin, a natural adhesive found in the fibers.

hardwood. Wood that comes from deciduous trees. These trees shed their leaves each season.

heavy equipment. Large and powerful machines designed to do jobs that might be impossible to do by hand, such as lifting and moving earth or other heavy materials. Heavy equipment includes machines such as cranes, excavators, bulldozers, and loaders, as well as equipment that is used in highway construction.

highway construction. A general term used for the construction of any road or street. The basic steps of highway construction are preparing the soil, preparing the roadbed, and striping the finished road.

incentive contract. This type of contract is designed to reward or penalize the contractor, depending on when the job is completed. If the job is finished before the agreed-upon date, the contractor is rewarded with an amount of money that is specified in the contract. If the job is not done by the specified date, the contractor is penalized a certain amount of money.

industrial buildings. Structures which house the complex machinery that is used to manufacture goods. Industrial buildings are generally low buildings of only one or two stories.

infrastructure. The mechanical and electrical setups of a structure.

insulation. Material used to keep heat from penetrating a building in summer and cold from penetrating in winter. Insulation is usually made from spun glass, foamed plastics, or certain vegetable and mineral fibers.

interest. The price the borrower pays for using a lending institution's money.

ironworkers. The tradespeople who build steel-framed structures.

job. A paid position at a specific place or setting.

laborers. The workers who do the supportive physical work at the construction site.

labor unions. Worker-controlled organizations that are formed to present the demands of the workers to the management of construction and other types of companies.

laminated beams. Long, thin strips of wood that have been glued together. If the beam is to be curved, the wood strips are bent around a form and clamped until the glue dries. This process is repeated until the desired shape and thickness are reached. The resulting beam is strong and durable.

laminated joists. Laminated joists are lighter than dimension-lumber joists, but just as strong. They do not warp or shrink as easily as dimension lumber. They are made of three parts: two flanges and a web. The flanges are at right angles to the web, forming a cross-section that looks like the capital letter *I*. Each part is made of several plies of wood.

laser-powered welder. A welding machine used in special situations. A concentrated laser beam can heat metal to temperatures over 10,000 degrees Fahrenheit (5,540 °C). This makes the laser an ideal heat source for welding hard-to-melt metals, such as heat-resistant types of steel.

laying out. The process of identifying the location of the proposed structure on the building site. The corners and edges of the building to be constructed are marked with stakes and string. Proposed parking lots and roadways are also marked at this time.

letter of commitment. This document states the terms and conditions that are required for payment of a loan. The letter of commitment states the loan's interest rate and the number of payments in which the borrower must pay back the loan.

level. A long, straight tool that contains one or more vials of liquid. It is used to make sure that something is exactly horizontal (level), or vertical (plumb).

lien. This is similar to a claim, except that the owner's property becomes security for the amount due the worker.

live load. A variable, or changeable load. It is one that is there only some of the time.

load-bearing ability. This is the amount of weight that soil can safely support without shifting.

lump-sum contract. A contract in which a lump sum (fixed price) is paid for the work to be done. The fixed price is agreed upon before the work begins. The sum may be paid in several payments. The final payment is made when the work is completed satisfactorily.

maintenance. Taking care of an object or structure so that it continues to function in the way it was intended.

masonry. The process of using mortar to join bricks, blocks, or other units of construction. These materials are used mainly for exterior walls on houses and buildings.

masonry cement. A commercially prepared mixture of portland cement and hydrated lime.

mass structures. Structures that use solid material, such as concrete, for the building's walls.

materials. The substances from which products are made.

mechanical plans. Mechanical plans are prepared for the plumbing and piping systems.

mesh. A kind of reinforcing for concrete. Made from steel wire, mesh looks like a wire fence.

micro-lam. Made of pieces of veneer that have been laminated in a parallel direction. Thin, dried veneer is coated with waterproof adhesive and bonded under heat and pressure. Micro-lam is up to 30 percent stronger than comparable lumber. In addition, it uses 35 percent more of each tree than does regular lumber. The micro-lam process virtually eliminates warping, twisting, and shrinking.

miter gage. An attachment for the table saw. The miter gage can be adjusted to guide wood through the saw at an angle of up to 30 degrees.

modular construction. In this method of construction, a building is designed to be constructed with modules.

module. A standard unit that has been chosen by a manufacturer. Modules allow the material supplier to stock pieces in standard sizes. When the building is to be constructed, the contractor orders all the parts, which have already been cut to size in the factory. The builder needs only to assemble the pieces. Little or no cutting is needed at the site.

molding. Special trim used to cover joints where floors, walls, and ceilings meet.

mortgage note. The mortgage note is actually two documents: the note, in which the lender agrees to finance a project under certain conditions and at a specified interest rate; and the mortgage, which pledges the property as security for the loan.

mortar. A combination of masonry cement, sand, and water.

nailers. Sometimes called "nail guns" because they "shoot" nails. Most nailers are pneumatically powered.

nail set. A tool used to drive finishing nails below the surface of wooden trim and molding.

negotiate. To discuss the terms of a contract. When all parties agree on the terms, the contract is signed.

nominal size. The size of lumber when it is cut from the log.

nonferrous metals. Metals that do not contain iron.

nonmetallic sheathed cable. Cable made of several wires wrapped together inside a plastic coating of insulation. It is very flexible and easy to install.

notice of completion. This legal document lets everyone know that the job is finished.

Occupational Health and Safety Administration (OSHA). OSHA sets standards that regulate safety at construction sites.

Occupational Outlook Handbook. This handbook published by the U.S. Government contains information about 200 careers. It refers to careers as occupations.

office personnel. A general term for all of the clerical and secretarial employees of a company, together with their managers and supervisors.

on contract. To build on contract means that you have a buyer before you start. You and the buyer, or owner, sign a contract. You build the project the way the owner wants it built.

on-the-job training. Training that a person receives after he or she has been hired.

operating engineers. The people who run construction equipment.

oriented-strand board. A product made from small, crooked trees that otherwise would be unprofitable to harvest. About 60 percent of the product is made from pine. Hemlock and poplar make up the remaining 40 percent. All three woods are mixed together to make panels. Oriented-strand board can be used almost anywhere that plywood can be used.

overhead. The cost of doing business. Costs for electricity, water, telephone service, office salaries, and postage are examples of overhead costs. Other overhead costs include the costs of advertising, insurance, and office rent.

paneling. The term used to describe hardboard or plywood panels that have been prefinished. Paneling is used as a decorative finish on interior walls. It is available in a wide variety of colors, patterns, and wood grains.

particleboard. A material made of small wood chips that have been pressed and glued together. Particleboard is commonly used in houses as an underlayment between the subfloor and the floor.

pavers. Machines used in the construction of highways, parking lots, and airports. These machines place, spread, and finish concrete or asphalt paving material. Paving can be done very quickly using these machines.

payment bond. This type of bond guarantees that the contractor will pay his or her employees, subcontractors, and suppliers. This kind of bond is important because if someone is not paid, he or she can file a legal claim against the owner. If the contractor fails to pay a subcontractor, for example, the bonding company makes the payment. Thus, the owner is protected.

performance bond. This type of bond guarantees that the contractor will build the project according to the agreement. If the contractor is unable to finish the job, the bonding company is responsible for seeing that the rest of the work is done. This kind of bond guarantees that the owner will not have to pay additional money to another contractor to have the job completed.

Phillips screwdriver. A screwdriver with a tip shaped like an X. It is used to turn Phillips-head screws. Because it grips the screw better, there is less chance of slipping. This reduces the chances of damaging the screwdriver, the screw, and the object being worked on.

pipefitters. Workers who build and repair pressurized pipes to carry compressed air and steam in HVAC systems and for special applications in factories. They also build special pipe systems for transportation and for power plants.

pipe wrenches. Tools used to turn objects that are round, such as pipes. The most commonly used pipe wrench is the Stilson wrench.

plumbers. People who install, maintain, and repair the plumbing systems that carry fresh water to buildings and wastewater away from buildings. They also build drainage pipes and gas systems in commercial and industrial buildings and in homes.

plywood. One of the most commonly used wood composites. Plywood gets its name from its construction. It is made of several thin plies, or veneers, of wood that have been glued together. Each veneer is glued so that its grain is at right angles to the grain of the previous veneer. The cross-layered grains make plywood very stable and strong.

pneumatic hammers. Tools that strike with great force. Pneumatic hammers, or jackhammers, are used to break up concrete or asphalt paving.

portable circular saw. A portable power tool used to cut materials that are difficult to cut with stationary tools.

portland cement. The binder for concrete. Portland cement is a mixture of clay and limestone that has been roasted in a special oven called a kiln.

powder-actuated stud driver. A tool powered by a 22-caliber cartridge that contains gunpowder. A special nail or fastener is put into the barrel, and the tool is loaded with a cartridge. The gun is pressed against the parts to be fastened, and the trigger is pulled. The powder-actuated stud driver can drive ½-inch- to 3-inch-long pins into wood, steel, or concrete.

power drills. Tools used for drilling holes in wood, metal, and concrete. The size of a drill is determined by the chuck size and the power of the motor.

power miter saw. A circular saw mounted over a small table. The saw pivots to enable the worker to cut various angles in wood. A power miter saw is used to cut precise angles in wooden molding and trim.

power of eminent domain. The right of the government to buy property for public purposes even though the owner does not want to sell. The government condemns, or takes, the property in the interest of the general public. The owner is given a fair price for the land.

power screwdriver. Used to install and remove screws. It is similar to an electric drill. However, instead of a twist drill bit, a power screwdriver has a special screwdriver bit. The screwdriver bit fits into the head of the screw just like a screwdriver.

prefabricated units. Components of structures and even whole structures which are built in factories and shipped to the building site. They include the trim, plumbing, insulation, doors, and even molded-plastic bathrooms. The units are assembled at the construction site. This method is a quick and efficient way to construct a building.

preliminary designs. First sketches of what a structure might look like. During this process, many sketches are made and saved for evaluation at a later time.

presentation model. A model that is made to show people how the finished design will look.

private project. A construction project which belongs to an individual or to a company. Some private projects are planned to meet the needs of a company or business.

project accounting. An accounting of the progress made at the job site. To keep track of the progress, the contractor must keep accurate records of what has been done.

project control. The process of giving directions and making sure the job is done properly and on time.

project manager. The person appointed to coordinate the money, workers, equipment, and materials for the job. He or she develops a schedule and plans for the storage of goods at the job site.

pry bars. A tool used by carpenters to pry the boards used to form concrete away from the concrete after it has set. Pry bars come in many different styles.

public projects. Projects which belong to the whole community and which are planned to meet the needs of the community. These projects often are paid for with tax money.

punch list. A list of things that need to be corrected.

radial arm saw. A power tool that consists of a motor-driven saw blade that is hung on an arm over a table. This type of saw is used mostly for crosscutting and for cutting angles. A radial arm saw is usually considered a stationary power tool. It is set up at one place on a construction site. The lumber is then brought there to be cut.

reinforcing bars. Called **re-bars** for short, these are steel bars that run through the inside of the concrete. Most reinforcing bars have ridges on them that help the concrete grip the bar.

release of claims. A legal document in which the contractor gives up the right to file any claim against the owner. The contractor must check to be sure all claims have been satisfied before he or she signs the release of claims.

release of liens. A formal, written statement that everyone has been properly paid by the contractor. The release provides assurance that no liens for unpaid bills can be put on the owner's property.

renovation. The process of restoring the original charm or style of a building, while at the same time adding modern conveniences.

repair. The process of restoring an object or structure to its original appearance or working order.

residential buildings. Buildings in which people reside, or live. The two basic kinds of residential buildings are single-family units and multiple-family units.

ripsaw. A saw with chisel-like teeth designed for ripping, or cutting with the grain of the wood.

roof truss. A preassembled frame of wood or steel that is designed to support a roof. Roof trusses are lighter than other types of roof supports, but they are just as strong.

rotary hammer. A rotary hammer operates with both rotating and reciprocating action. It is used to drill holes in concrete.

roughing in. The installation of the basic pipes and wiring that must be placed within the walls, floor, and roof. This must be done before the interior walls are covered.

saber saw. This saw has a small knife-shaped blade that reciprocates (moves up and down) to cut curves. Plumbers and carpenters use saber saws to cut holes in floors and roofs for pipes.

safety factor. An extra measure of strength added to the design of a structure.

safety rules. Regulations aimed at preventing accidents and injuries in the workplace.

scale models. These models are made to help visualize how the final design will look. They have proportions that the finished building will have. However, they are built on a much smaller scale. There are two basic types: presentation models and study models.

scheduling. Estimating the amount of time it will take to do each part of the job. The schedule identifies who will do what job and in what order.

scraper. A machine that is used for loading, hauling, and dumping soil over medium to long distances.

screeding. The process of moving a straight board back and forth across the top of a form. This removes any excess concrete and levels the top of the concrete.

section drawing. A drawing that shows a section, or slice, of the structure. In this drawing, a part of the building is shown as if it were cut in two and separated. This allows the viewer to see the inside of the structure.

service drop. The service drop is the wiring that connects a building to the electric company's overhead or underground wires. A meter located near the service drop measures the amount of power used.

service panel. A box that contains circuit breakers for each individual, or branch circuit. It also contains a main circuit breaker. This controls all of the individual circuits collectively.

sheathing. Sheets of steel used to cover banks or walls of soil when the soil must be stabilized around a hole or trench.

shoring. Long strips of metal driven into the earth to hold sheathing. Shoring can also be used without sheathing to stabilize soil and reduce the chance of cave-ins.

site. The land on which a project will be constructed.

site plan. This type of plan shows what the site should look like when the job is finished. The locations of the building, new roads and parking lots, and even trees are shown. The finished contour of the earth is also shown.

slab bridge. This simple type of bridge consists of a concrete slab supported by abutments. Some of the longer slab bridges are also supported by a pier, or beam, in the middle. This type of bridge is usually made of steel or steel-reinforced concrete and is used mostly for light loads and short spans.

sledgehammers. Heavy hammers that are used to drive stakes into the ground and to break up concrete and stone.

slump test. A sample taken for testing to check the workability of the concrete.

softwood. Wood that comes from coniferous (evergreen) trees. Pine, fir, and spruce are some common softwoods that are used in construction.

specifications. These documents tell the contractor exactly what materials to use and how to use them.

specification writers. Construction company employees with the knowledge and experience needed to put specifications together. They must have a good understanding of construction practices and an up-to-date knowledge of materials. They must also be familiar with building regulations and the current costs of materials.

speculation. To build on speculation means that you build the project and then find someone to buy it.

spillway. A safety valve that allows excess water to bypass the dam. Few dams are strong enough to withstand the force of floodwater. If the water could not bypass the dam, the dam would break.

spiral ratchet screwdriver. A screwdriver that relies on a pushing force rather than a twisting force. The tips for a spiral ratchet screwdriver are interchangeable, so it can be used for Phillips-head or standard slotted screws.

standard screwdriver. A screwdriver with a flat tip designed to fit a standard slotted screw.

standard stock. Standard shapes and sizes of structural steel, such as horizontal steel beams and vertical steel columns.

staplers. This tool works like a nailer, but is loaded with U-shaped staples instead of nails. Some are pneumatic, and others use electricity. Roofers use staplers to fasten roof shingles to decking. Carpenters use them to staple insulation into place.

structural drawing. This type of drawing gives information about the location and sizes of the structural materials.

structural engineering. The process of selecting appropriate materials from which to build a structure.

structural steel. Steel that is used to support any part of a structure.

study model. This model of a design is made so that the design can be tested.

superstructure. The part of a building, above the foundation, beginning with the first floor.

surveyors. Workers who measure and record the physical features of the construction site. They survey the property and establish its official boundaries. They also lay out, or measure and mark, the construction project.

surveyor's level. A tool used to find an unknown elevation from a known one.

suspension bridges. The very longest crossings are spanned by suspension bridges. They are suspended from cables made of thousands of steel wires wound together.

table saw. The table saw consists of a blade mounted on an electric motor beneath a table-like surface. The blade sticks up through a slot in the table. The table saw is used for cutting large sheets of wood, plywood, and other wood products and for ripping lumber.

tape measures. Commonly used measurement tools especially useful for measuring long or curved surfaces.

technical institute. A technical institute is a school that offers technical training for specific careers.

technicians. Construction personnel who work in laboratories, testing soil samples and concrete and asphalt materials being used on the project.

technology. The use of technical methods to obtain practical results.

tool. An instrument of technology used to make a job easier.

tower crane. A tower crane, or climbing crane, has a built-in jack that raises the crane from floor to floor as the building is constructed.

A tower crane is used in the construction of tall buildings. It is usually positioned in the elevator shaft. When its job is done, another crane is used to remove the tower crane from the building.

transfer of ownership. A formal notice of completion, which legally establishes that the job is done.

transit. A tool that measures horizontal and vertical angles. Surveyors use it to measure relative land elevation.

trencher. A special kind of excavator that is used to dig trenches, or long, narrow ditches, for pipelines and cables. This machine is made of a series of small buckets attached to a wheel or chain. As the wheel or chain rotates, each bucket digs a small amount of earth. The operator controls the depth and length of the trench.

troweling. The final smoothing of concrete. After the concrete has begun to set, a steel trowel is used to smooth the surface.

truck crane. A crane mounted on a truck frame so that it can be driven to the site.

truss bridges. Truss bridges are supported by steel or wooden trusses, or beams that are joined to form triangular shapes. Triangular shapes are used because the triangle is a particularly strong structural shape. Trusses are also used in combination with other bridges to give them additional support.

twist drill bit. A drill with spiral grooves. A ½-inch drill will hold a bit with a diameter up to ½-inch. Some drills have reversible motors so that they can turn forward or backward. Some are even battery powered for use in places where there is no electrical service.

unit cost. The cost of the material per selling unit.

unit-price contract. In this type of contract, the contractor gives the owner a price that he or she will charge for each unit of work.

vapor barrier. A vapor barrier is placed between the inside wall of the building and the insulation to prevent water from condensing. The vapor barrier can be made of plastic, foil, or asphalt. It should always be placed on the interior side of the insulation.

waferboard. A material made of large wood chips that are pressed and glued together and then cured with heat. Waferboard is not quite as strong as plywood, but it can be used instead of plywood in many applications.

warranty. A guarantee or promise that a job has been done well or that the materials have no defects. It is usually written.

water pumps. Used to pump water out of holes in the ground so that work can be done. These pumps are usually powered by small gasoline engines. Because they do not require electricity, they are considered very portable.

wood chisels. Tools with a wedge-shaped blade, used to trim wood. They are used to pare or clear away excess material from wood joints and to remove wood to make gains (recessed areas) for hinges.

wood composites. Products that are made from a mixture of wood and other materials. Most wood composites are produced in large sheets, usually 4 feet wide and 8 feet long.

zoning laws. Cities are divided into residential, business, and industrial zones. The site for a project must be in the proper zone. Zoning laws tell what kinds of structures can be built in each zone.

SECTION ACTIVITIES

Section I: Introduction

Section II: Materials, Tools, and Processes

Section III: The Construction Company

Section IV: The Construction Project

Section V: Careers

PHOTO CREDITS

Abbey Floors, Ann Garvin, 291
Acker Drill Co., Inc., Scranton, PA, 369
Alaska Division of Tourism, 24, 35
AMP Incorporated, 350
Armstrong World Industries, Inc., 98
Arnold & Brown, 38, 51, 59, 63, 86, 285, 297
Austin Commercial, Inc./Ann Garvin, 155, 184
Autodesk Inc., 19, 147, 258

Sandar Balantini/San Francisco Convention & Visitors Bureau, 211
Roger B. Bean, 5, 16, 27, 29, 31, 37, 39, 45, 53, 56, 58, 62, 82, 87, 156, 165, 183, 184, 222, 223, 225, 232, 246, 260, 277, 278, 279, 280, 281, 282, 288, 291, 300, 302, 344, 370
Bethlehem Steel/Bell Atlantic, 279
The Bettman Archive, 8, 41, 42, 263
Black & Decker, 8, 76, 116, 117, 118, 119

Canfor Limited, 91
Cardinal Industries, 140, 141
Caterpillar Inc., 126, 127, 128, 129, 130, 173, 271, 272
The Ceco Corporation, Oakbrook Terrace, IL, 274
Centimark Corporation, 123, 283
CertainTeed Corporation, 94
The Chicago Convention & Visitors Bureau, 18
CILCO, 25, 67
Coherent General, Inc., 124
Colonial Pipeline Co., 360
Combustion Engineering Inc., 43
Harold Corsini, Western Pennsylvania Conservancy, 241
Coventry Creative Graphics, 172, 181, 186, 256
CSA, 62, 162, 229, 307
Custom Cabinets, Carney & Sons, Ann Garvin, 86

Danforth Floor Covering, Roger B. Bean, 291
Howard Davis, 84, 88, 89, 90, 95, 96, 100, 101, 102, 103, 110, 111, 112, 113, 114, 115, 116, 125, 182, 187, 208, 210, 213, 214, 235, 243, 248, 252, 253, 255, 259, 270, 273, 282, 284, 285, 286, 287, 292, 309, 310, 311, 312, 313, 315, 316, 317, 318, 319, 320, 321, 322, 323, 324, 325; Activities
Design Associates, Inc., 231, 237, 292
Diamond-Star Motors Corp./James Gaffney, 166

Dow Corning Corporation, 22
Duo-Fast, Beach & Barnes, 120
Duo-Fast Corporation, 104
Du Pont, 105
Dykon, Inc., 269

Emerson Electric Co., 41
English Heritage, 14

David Falconer, David R. Frazier Photolibrary Inc., 340
Randy Feucht Construction, Inc., Ann Garvin, 92, 275
L.B. Foster Company, 273
Fox & Jacobs, Ann Garvin, 285
Dr. Ed Francis, Dept. of Industrial Technology, Illinois State University, 303
Franklin Street Bridge, Roger B. Bean, 209
David R. Frazier Photolibrary Inc., 2, 21, 351, 359, 366
French Government Tourist Office, 16, 241

Jim Gaffney, 90
Ann Garvin, 2, 14, 23, 28, 30, 36, 38, 39, 44, 46, 47, 55, 77, 80, 92, 93, 95, 97, 100, 109, 122, 145, 162, 164, 179, 183, 198, 202, 203, 204, 209, 220, 221, 229, 230, 233, 240, 245, 259, 267, 271, 284, 295, 301, 343, 344, 348, 355, 357, 362, 365
Georgia Port Authority, 227
Greater Peoria Airport Authority, 205
Jeff Greenberg, Ridgewood Newspapers, 49
Betty Groskin/Jeff Greenberg, 152

Bob Harr, Hedrich-Blessing/Pentair, 143
Noah Herman Sons, House of the 1990s, Roger B. Bean, 170, 265
Rick Herrig, Congra, Inc., 346
Hewlett Packard, 142, 156, 353, 371
Peter Honig/Jeff Greenberg Collection, 2

Idaho Transportation Department, 293
Illinois Department of Transportation, 26, 180
Illinois Laborers and Contractors Training Program, 166
Imperial Irrigation District, Imperial, CA, 24
Ingersoll-Rand Company, 119
ITW Ramset/Red Head, 120

Chip Jamison, Pennwalt Corp., 206
Jefferson National Expansion/National Park Service, 33
Mike Jenkins, McDonald's, 289
Chris Jones, Ashland Oil Inc., 50

Kerr-McGee Corp., 203
Kruse Brothers Bldg., Inc., Roger B. Bean, 83, 96

Lab Safety Supply, Inc., 58, 60
Lake Cities Concrete, Ann Garvin, 80, 81, 275
Laser Alignment Inc., 12, 122, 139
Stef Leinwohl Photo, 57, 302
Larry Levine, 207
The Lietz Company, 121
Lindal Cedar Homes Inc., 78, 245
Michael J. London/Lone Star Industries, 178
Louisburg Construction Ltd., 131

Manhattan Construction Co./Ann Garvin, 161
The Manitowoc Company, 40, 52, 126, 200, 239, 244, 365
Manual High School, Roger B. Bean, 306, 329, 348
Master Builders, Inc., 178
McCormick Properties, Inc./Archie Johnson, 201
Robert McElwee, 158, 189, 289, 299, 360
Micro-Lam® L.U.L., 138
Herman Miller, Inc., 338
Mississippi Department of Economic Development, 215
MMFG Company, Bristol, Virginia, 137
Mason Morfit/Lone Star Industries, 135
Morton High School, Roger B. Bean, 305, 345

NASA, 134
NASA/Paul Field, 144
NASA, Kennedy Space Center, FL, 234
National Oak Flooring, 98
University of Nevada/Manis Collection, 213
New York Dept. of Economic Development, 17, 263
North Wind Picture Archives, 13, 26, 65

Paluska & Weinstein Plumbing, Roger B. Bean, 351
Peoria Public Library, 347, 352
Judith Peterson, 61, 341

Brent Phelps, 108, 165, 219, 234, 361, 363, 372
Port Authority of New York, 202
Porter-Cable Corp., 54
The Principal Financial Group, 79, 158
Liz Purcell, 19, 82, 297
P & W Builders, Roger B. Bean, 2, 154, 169, 175, 218, 252, 266, 274, 296, 339, 349, 360, 368

QA Photos Ltd., 19, 160, 199

Randolph & Associates, Architectural Services, Inc., 249, 250, 251, 252
Richwoods High School, Roger B. Bean, 352
Mark Romine, 20, 153, 238, 358

Sears Roebuck Co., 118, 119
Bob Shimer, Hedrich-Blessing/Pentair, 133
E.M. Smith & Company, Roger B. Bean, 124
R. Hamilton Smith, Master Builders, Inc., 123
Spaw-Glass General Contracting, Inc./Brent Phelps, 179
Spirit of Peoria, CILCO, 217
David S. Strickler, Strix Pix, 341
Sverdrup Corp., 257

The Tenkar Corporation, 136
Tennessee Valley Authority, 32
Tennessee Wildlife Resource Agency, 43
TJI®, 87

U.S. Sprint, 163

Valhi, 107

Wagner Spray Tech Corporation, 290
Walden Pond State Reservation, 327
Wallace Tile Company, Ann Garvin, 291
Doug Wilson/David R. Frazier Photolibrary Inc., 367
Wolf Creek/Colorado Tourism Board, 39
Woodruff High School, Roger B. Bean, 51, 171, 247, 326, 342, 375

Interior Design by Benoit Design and Nancy Norrall DESiGN

INDEX

R

S